Intimate Relationships

SECOND EDITION

Thomas N. Bradbury

University of California, Los Angeles

Benjamin R. Karney

University of California, Los Angeles

W. W. NORTON & COMPANY

NEW YORK ■ LONDON

W. W. Norton & Company has been independent since its founding in 1923, when William Warder Norton and Mary D. Herter Norton first published lectures delivered at the People's Institute, the adult education division of New York City's Cooper Union. The firm soon expanded its program beyond the Institute, publishing books by celebrated academics from America and abroad. By mid-century, the two major pillars of Norton's publishing program—trade books and college texts—were firmly established. In the 1950s, the Norton family transferred control of the company to its employees, and today—with a staff of four hundred and a comparable number of trade, college, and professional titles published each year—W. W. Norton & Company stands as the largest and oldest publishing house owned wholly by its employees.

Editor: Sheri Snavely
Development and copyeditor: Betsy Dilernia
Project editor: Melissa Atkin
Editorial assistant: Shira Averbuch
Production manager: Ashley Horna
Design director: Rubina Yeh
Book designer: Lissi Sigillo
Permissions manager: Megan Jackson
Photo editors: Evan Luberger and Trish Marx
Emedia editor: Patrick Shriner
Ancillary editor: Callinda Taylor
Marketing manager: Lauren Winkler
Illustrations by Penumbra Design, Inc.
Composition by Achorn International, Inc.
Manufacturing by Marquis Book Printing

Library of Congress Cataloging-in-Publication Data

Bradbury, Thomas N.
    Intimate relationships / Thomas N. Bradbury, University of California, Los Angeles, Benjamin R. Karney, University of California, Los Angeles. — Second edition.
        pages cm
    Includes bibliographical references and index.
    ISBN 978-0-393-92023-9 (pbk.)
    1. Interpersonal relations.   I. Karney, Benjamin R.   II. Title.
    HM1106.B733 2014
    302—dc23

                                                            2013020027

W. W. Norton & Company, Inc., 500 Fifth Avenue, New York, N.Y. 10110
        www.wwnorton.com
W. W. Norton & Company Ltd., Castle House, 75/76 Wells Street, London W1T 3QT
1 2 3 4 5 6 7 8 9 0

*The scientific study of intimate relationships
would not exist without the visionary work of*

*John Bowlby
Urie Bronfenbrenner
Reuben Hill
Neil Jacobson
Harold Kelley*

With gratitude, we dedicate this book to them.

about the authors

THOMAS N. BRADBURY earned his BA in psychobiology from Hamilton College, his MA in general psychology from Wake Forest University, and his PhD in clinical psychology from the University of Illinois. A professor of psychology at the University of California, Los Angeles since 1990, Bradbury specializes in using observational and longitudinal methods to examine how newlywed marriages develop and change. The recipient of the American Psychology Association's Distinguished Early Career Award, Bradbury has edited two books: *The Psychology of Marriage* (with Frank Fincham) and *The Developmental Course of Marital Dysfunction*. Each year he teaches a large undergraduate class and small honors seminars on intimate relationships, and in 2000 he was awarded the Distinguished Teaching Award from the UCLA Department of Psychology. Tom lives in Los Angeles with Cindy, his wife of 25 years, their two children, Timothy and Nicholas, and two very large and affectionate Bernese mountain dogs.

BENJAMIN R. KARNEY earned his BA in psychology from Harvard University and his MA and PhD in social psychology from the University of California, Los Angeles. Before joining the faculty in the Department of Psychology at UCLA in 2007, Karney was a professor at the University of Florida, where he received numerous awards for his teaching, including the Teacher of the Year Award in 2003. At UCLA, he offers graduate and undergraduate classes on intimate relationships, and received the Distinguished Teaching Award from the UCLA Department of Psychology in 2011. Honored for Early Career Achievement by the International Association for Relationship Research, Karney has directed research funded by the National Institutes of Health, the Administration on Children and Families, and the Department of Defense. He has published extensively on the various ways that intimate partners interpret the events of their relationships, and the effects of stress on lower-income and military marriages. Ben lives north of Los Angeles, is the proud parent of two children, Daniella and Gabriel, and owns far too many books.

Together, Bradbury and Karney founded and co-direct the Relationship Institute at UCLA, a center dedicated to disseminating the results of relationship science to the public. In the more than 20 years they have been collaborating, their work has twice received the National Council on Family Relations Reuben Hill Research and Theory Award for outstanding contributions to family science.

brief contents

If you are reading this book, chances are good that we have something in common. Maybe you've wondered how two people who began the day as strangers can fall deeply in love, and why two other similar people may not. Perhaps you have wondered, as we have, how two completely committed partners can declare their undying love for each other, but then grow unhappy and distant. Maybe you've felt frustrated or confused with your own relationship but mystified about how to strengthen it or move it forward. Or perhaps you have been so overjoyed that you wanted to know every possible way to make your relationship last forever.

We think constantly about questions like these, and we are lucky to be in a profession where we can try to answer them. The scientific study of human intimacy and relationships has grown rapidly over the past several decades, with scholars in various fields, including psychology, family studies, sociology, communications, social work, economics, and anthropology, all wondering: How do intimate relationships work? What makes them succeed or fail? How can we make them better? We wrote this book to give you the most up-to-date answers to these and many other relevant questions. In doing so, we highlight research studies and ideas that are particularly insightful, and then pull them together in ways that reveal important truths about human intimacy.

We love to read books that make us smarter about compelling subjects, and we kept this goal—making you smarter about intimate relationships—in the forefront of our minds as we wrote these chapters. Simply presenting research studies and interesting examples is a great way to accomplish this goal, but more than anything else, we wrote this book to help you become more critical, analytical, and thoughtful, when it comes to topics like attraction, love, closeness, and effective communication. Our goal is not simply to present you with this information but to show you how to critique it, evaluate it, and apply it to your life.

If you are a curious person who likes an occasional challenge or puzzle, then this is a book that will draw you in, keep you captivated, and help you see why we and so many others are fascinated by intimate relationships. If you have ideas for improving the next edition, please let us know.

Thomas Bradbury, bradbury@psych.ucla.edu
Benjamin Karney, karney@psych.ucla.edu

Scope, Purpose, and Approach

Welcome to the second edition of *Intimate Relationships*. Before the first edition was published, we had each been teaching classes and seminars on human intimacy and relationships for several years. Even then, we could not believe our good fortune at having such rich material and such enthusiastic audiences, and we were eager to showcase all the remarkable theories and new discoveries in this rapidly changing field. The books available at the time brought us reasonably close to this goal, but we wanted something different for our students: a fresh and up-to-date introduction to all the key facets of intimate relationships, combining surprising insights from research with critical analysis of influential theories and studies. Conversations with colleagues confirmed the need for a lively but tightly organized text that would sharpen and deepen students' grasp of human intimacy. Equally apparent was the need for an ancillary package that would give instructors tools they could use to be more effective and efficient in the classroom.

We wrote the book to address these needs, but our agenda was even broader. We wanted to give our undergraduates a book they could not wait to read. We wanted to cover topics that other books had only glossed over, topics like gender and sexual orientation, the biological basis of intimacy, stressful circumstances, cultural influences on relationships, couples therapy, and the role of intimacy across the lifespan. We wanted to produce video clips featuring students and leading scholars discussing their ideas about intimate relationships, so that instructors could teach and spark discussions in new ways. We wanted to show our colleagues that the study of intimate relationships is now a well-established topic of profound importance in the social sciences, as well as a topic long overdue for a scholarly text with an ancillary package coordinated by active researchers. Above all, we set out to capture the excitement we felt after reading a well-crafted journal article, hearing a great talk or lecture, interviewing couples in our research studies and after our workshops, or watching a good movie or reading a good novel: Intimate relationships are fascinating! Look at the diverse forms they take; how much they've changed over the years and how much they remain the same. That excitement naturally led to inquiries: How do they work? Why are relationships so hard sometimes? What are the principles that guide them? How can we use what we know to make improvements?

In the first edition of our textbook, we drew on hundreds of research reports and dozens of scholarly books to answer these questions. In the years since that edition was published, the science of intimate relationships has continued to grow and mature. With this fully updated and revised second edition, we have kept our eyes on the cutting edge, building on the accumulated wisdom of researchers, while describing the most exciting new developments. We have done something else as well. Feedback from more than a thousand of our own students, along with comments from expert reviews by our colleagues in the field, have allowed us to build upon the strengths of the first edition, while listening and responding to the occasional constructive criticism. Some users of the first edition noted that, in our enthusiasm, we occasionally used several words when one or two might have been sufficient. Those readers will be pleased to find the second edition more streamlined and focused.

Our excitement for the field—and for teaching this class—has only grown. We hope students will sense our enthusiasm on every page, and we hope you will find this book and the supporting resources essential to your success in teaching this material.

Organization of the Book

One of our greatest challenges in developing this book was to impose an intuitive but incisive organizational structure on the wealth of available material. After considering several alternatives, we settled on 13 chapters that we believe mirror the distinctions people naturally make when discussing and investigating intimate relationships. Although we believe there are some advantages to presenting the material to students in the sequence we chose (particularly starting with Chapters 1, 2, and 3), we wrote the chapters so they can be taught in any order. While giving instructors flexibility in how they move through the various topics, we've also included cross-references between chapters to give students a sense of continuity, as well as opportunities to see familiar ideas extended to new areas.

From foundations to elements and processes to changes in intimate relationships, we believe that these 13 chapters provide students with an introduction to this complex and fascinating subject that is at once broad and deep, classic and contemporary, rigorous and relevant. Arguably, though, the most important part of this book is not in the chapters, but in the roughly 2,000 published works we cite in the reference section. These publications span an incredible array of topics and academic disciplines, and a disproportionate number were published in just the last 10 years—clear evidence that rapid advances are continuing to be made in our understanding of intimate relationships. This work is the driving force behind our desire to provide our students and yours with a timely new perspective on this vital field.

Special Features

Although the topics covered in the chapters are diverse and varied, they are unified by a clear design and consistent format. The first page of each chapter presents students with a Chapter Outline listing the major section headings that organize the material. Every chapter starts with an opening vignette taken from movies, television shows, books, and real life, each one designed to draw students in and highlight a different side of intimate relationships. Here are some examples:

- The relationships of Albert Einstein, the smartest man in the world (Chapter 1)
- Insight from comedians on the truth about men and women (Chapter 4)
- The enduring business of matchmaking (Chapter 5)
- Intimacy and aggression in the marriage of Joe DiMaggio and Marilyn Monroe (Chapter 8)
- The experience of a bisexual college student coming out to her Indian parents in the 1980s (Chapter 9)
- Intimate relationships in the wake of 9/11 (Chapter 11)

Each vignette prompts a series of specific questions that encourage students to read more deeply, while familiarizing them with asking critical questions and thinking about the evidence they need to answer them. The key questions that will be addressed later in the chapter are also presented here.

The chapters are populated with graphs that illustrate important concepts and research findings, tables that summarize or sample widely used measurement tools, and case studies. The text is also enriched with many kinds of other materials—poems, songs, cartoons, photographs, and actual dialogue from couples—to show how so many of the ideas connect with everyday experiences. Every main section within each chapter is anchored by a list of Main Points that provide quick and effective reviews of all the key ideas.

At least once in each chapter, we shine a Spotlight on an idea from the text and then develop it in a new or controversial direction. Our students enjoy these spotlights and in fact have suggested a few. In each case, we identify a provocative, well-defined question or problem, explain its significance, and give students a focused briefing on that issue. Here are some examples:

- The surprising complexity of measuring relationship satisfaction (Chapter 2)
- Why people sometimes remain in physically abusive relationships (Chapter 3)
- Men and women looking for love online (Chapter 4)
- Changing places and gender roles (Chapter 4)
- Hooking up and its prevalence among college students (Chapter 5)

- The science and the politics of divorce (Chapter 6)
- Arranged marriages compared to those in which spouses select each other (Chapter 9)

Though the chapters are independent enough to be taught in any order, a goal of ours was to write a book with a strong narrative flow from chapter to chapter, which we saw as an improvement over the more typical topic-by-topic organization. At the end of each chapter, we reinforce this flow with Conclusions that relate back to the opening vignette and forward to the chapter that follows. For example, Chapter 7 begins with an uplifting letter a soldier wrote to his wife back home, setting us up to discuss the various ways partners create and maintain intimacy. The chapter ends by noting that, as powerful as they are for keeping two people connected, these experiences of closeness must coexist alongside partners' disagreements and differences of opinion. How do partners navigate these differences? What does relationship science have to say about the effective management of the differing agendas that are inevitable in relationships? Chapter 8, on verbal conflict and aggression, gives students some clues, and in the process builds a logical bridge between these two domains of interpersonal interaction.

New to the Second Edition

As we considered how to update and improve *Intimate Relationships* for this second edition, we solicited feedback not only from the thousands of students who have used the book in our own classes, but also from colleagues who have been teaching from the book at other universities. We received lots of praise for some of the features that we were especially excited about in the first edition: the way our chapters organize the field, our emphasis on identifying the key questions of this field and the progress we've made in answering them, our extensive ancillary package, and the book's inviting graphic design. All these features have been preserved in this second edition.

We also received a number of requests for new features and material that users of the book hoped to see in a next edition. This second edition responds to these requests in a number of ways:

- The text has been streamlined and more sharply focused throughout.
- Each chapter includes updated references, reflecting the latest developments in relationship science.
- Each main section of every chapter ends with a list of Main Points that clearly capture and summarize the key ideas.
- Throughout the new edition, we have included new examples and references to research on ethnically diverse and same-sex relationships.
- Chapter 2 features a new Spotlight box on the Actor-Partner-Interdependence Model.

- The treatment of attachment theory in Chapter 3 has been rewritten and updated.

- In addition to updating Chapter 4 on gender and sexual orientation, increased attention is paid to same-sex relationships throughout the book, including a new vignette in Chapter 9 about the experience of coming out.

- Chapter 5 on attraction and mate selection features an extended discussion of online dating and social networks.

- Chapter 12 discusses the latest results of national experiments on the effectiveness of relationship education in low-income populations.

The Ancillary Package

We know from teaching large-market courses, such as introductory psychology, social psychology, and abnormal psychology, that students benefit when instructors have excellent supplemental resources, and we were surprised that few of the existing texts on intimate relationships offered instructors much ancillary support. We received a lot of gratified responses to the extensive ancillary package that accompanied the first edition of *Intimate Relationships*, and all of those features have been updated for the second edition.

The ancillary feature that we are perhaps the most excited about is *The Norton Intimate Relationships Videos*, a collection of video clips that we created to accompany each chapter. Because the scientific study of intimate relationships is still relatively new as a discipline, many highly influential scholars are alive today and can share their insights with us. To capitalize on this fact, we worked with filmmakers David Lederman and Trisha Solyn to interview several of the most prominent relationship scholars working today. These interviews of scholars sharing their wisdom and perspectives, along with young adults and couples giving their opinions and relating their experiences, have been edited together to create fascinating and entertaining video material relevant to each chapter in the book. In several videos, we also present extended case studies. These include a young gay man discussing his experience with coming out, a young woman talking about how her early difficulties with a stepfather affected her later relationships, a young woman talking about conflict and aggression in her relationships, and a middle-aged couple talking about how chronic financial stress affected their relationship and the husband's health. At 10 minutes in length or less per clip, the individual videos can easily be shown during class.

Instructors can access the videos through the Interactive Instructor's Guide (IIG), a repository of lecture and teaching materials for instructors accessible through the Norton website. Teaching materials can be easily sorted by either the textbook chapter/headings or key phrases. The videos are accompanied by teaching tips and suggested discussion questions, which can be used either in the classroom or as homework. The IIG also offers chapter summaries, additional teaching suggestions, discussion questions, and suggested additional resources to help instructors plan their courses.

The ancillary package also includes student study resources which instructors can make available through their Learning Management System (Blackboard, Moodle, etc.). Free to instructors and students, these packaged materials (course packs) include the Intimate Relationships Videos, including additional "Thinking About Intimate Relationships" clips, with related critical-thinking questions; chapter summaries; quizzes which can be assigned or made available for self-guided study; and flashcards to help students study.

Several other instructor resources are available to enhance student learning. These include:

- PowerPoint Slides for each chapter, which include all the photographs and illustrations from the text along with lecture suggestions from instructors who have taught the course for many years.

- A Test Bank, featuring concept outlines and approximately 50 multiple-choice and 15 short-answer/essay questions per chapter, available in Word RTF and through the ExamView Assessment Suite (which can be downloaded free of charge from the Norton website by instructors using *Intimate Relationships*). The Test Bank contains a flexible pool of questions for each chapter that allows instructors to create a quiz or test that meets their individual requirements. Questions can be easily sorted by difficulty or question type, making it easy to construct tests that are meaningful and diagnostic.

Acknowledgments

Many people contributed to this book, and we are indebted to all of them for their efforts and fine work. First and foremost, we are so grateful to Sheri Snavely, our editor at W. W. Norton, for her constant enthusiasm and commitment to this book. Over the years that we have been fortunate enough to work with her, Sheri has always given us the latitude to write what we wanted to write, while at the same time pushing us to meet the highest standards and make this book the very best it could be. Sheri has brought out the best in us.

And we are not alone. In preparing the first edition and again in developing this new edition, Sheri has collected and wrangled a tremendous team of talented individuals. Sarah England deserves special mention for her role as Associate Editor when we were developing the first edition of this text. Sarah's close reading of our initial drafts of these chapters powerfully shaped the final product, and her influence over this text is still felt throughout. In revising and updating this book for the second edition, we had the great fortune to work with Betsy Dilernia, the most careful, insightful, and rigorous developmental editor and copyeditor. Betsy is the taskmaster we needed to rein in our natural exuberance, and this book is leaner and much better as a result of her excellent judgment.

Through the production process, project editor Melissa Atkin managed the flow of chapters and somehow got everyone to do their jobs while she remained unfailingly calm and pleasant. Production manager Ashley Horna kept us on schedule and ensured that the book came out on time. Proofreader Lynne Cannon Menges brought the text to a fine polish. Photo editors Evan Luberger and Trish Marx and photo researcher Jane Sanders Miller dug into the deepest recesses of the Internet to find photographs illustrating ideas we could only vaguely articulate. Media/ancillary editor Callinda Taylor helped create a support package that is second to none. Shira Averbuch provided enthusiastic, cheerful, and invaluable editorial assistance throughout the lengthy revision process. If you like the cover of this book (and we adore it), then you have the brilliant Debra Morton Hoyt, Corporate Art Director, to thank for it. Design director Rubina Yeh and book designer Lissi Sigillo designed this beautiful book you hold in your hands. And last but not least, we thank Jenni Fiederer, our capable administrative assistant, for coordinating our efforts with W. W. Norton and for helping us to keep this project moving forward.

For our first and second editions, several scholars provided excellent feedback, and their insights continue to inform the material. We gratefully acknowledge the valuable feedback we received from:

Susan D. Boon, *University of Calgary*
M. Jennifer Brougham, *Arizona State University*
Jennifer L. Butler, *Case Western Reserve University*
Rod Cate, *University of Arizona*
Melissa Curran, *Norton School of Family and Consumer Sciences*
Carolyn Cutrona, *Iowa State University*
Crystal Dehle, *University of Oregon*
Lisa M. Diamond, *University of Utah*
Brent Donellan, *Michigan State University*
William Dragon, *Cornell College*
Paul Eastwick, *University of Texas, Austin*
Eli Finkel, *Northwestern University*
Omri Gillath, *University of Kansas*
Mo Therese Hannah, *Siena College*
Meara Habashi, *University of Iowa*
Chandice Haste-Jackson, *Syracuse University*
John Holmes, *University of Waterloo*
Lauren M. Papp, *University of Wisconsin-Madison*
Nicole Shelton, *Princeton University*

We are particularly grateful to all the distinguished scholars who took the time to be filmed for our video clips: Chris Agnew, Purdue University; Art Aron, Stony Brook University; Niall Bolger, Columbia University; Andrew

Christensen, UCLA; Nancy Collins, University of California, Santa Barbara; Joanne Davila, Stony Brook University; Lisa Diamond, University of Utah; Garth Fletcher, University of Canterbury; John Holmes, University of Waterloo; John Lydon, McGill University; Neil Malamuth, UCLA; Gayla Margolin, University of Southern California; Harry Reis, University of Rochester; Rena Repetti, UCLA; Philip Shaver, University of California, Davis; Jeffry Simpson, University of Minnesota; and Gail Wyatt, UCLA. We consider ourselves extremely fortunate to have the opportunity to include these scholars in this project. Several students and acquaintances also devoted their time and insights to the video series, and we thank them for their willingness to talk about their personal lives with us. Although the final set of video clips is about 2 hours in total duration, those 2 hours were gleaned from more than 100 hours of interviews that we conducted in collaboration with David Lederman and Trisha Solyn. David and Trisha delivered a final product that far exceeded our expectations, and it is because of their devotion to the project and their sheer brilliance as filmmakers that we are able to offer students and instructors this fine series of clips.

Other aspects of the ancillary package were produced by equally industrious and talented people. Nancy Frye at Long Island University created the PowerPoint lectures and student study materials, Jennifer Gonyea at the University of Georgia authored the *Interactive Instructor's Guide*, and Katherine Regan at Vancouver Island University co-authored and revised the Test Bank.

contents

3

Theoretical Frameworks 82

4   Men and Women, Gay and Straight   131

10   Understanding Each Other   336

13   Relationships Across the Lifespan   453

HISTORICAL PERSPECTIVES   501

CONCLUSION   504

1

Why Study Intimate Relationships?

The Relationships of the Smartest Man in the World

While Albert Einstein's prodigious professional accomplishments are well known, the details of his private life were not fully appreciated until 2006, when much of his personal correspondence was released to the public. These and other documents reveal that Einstein's incomparable brilliance as a scientist stands in stark contrast to his turbulent personal relationships.

The most prominent figure in Einstein's intimate life was his first wife, Mileva Maric (FIGURE 1.1). They met in 1896 as students at the Zurich Polytechnic; Einstein was 17, Mileva nearly 21. Their shared passion for physics gradually became a shared passion for one another, but Mileva's unexpected pregnancy in 1901 would bring about a series of important events. Einstein rarely saw Mileva during the pregnancy; he preferred to spend summer in the Alps, and his job as a tutor took him away from Zurich. Einstein never told his family or friends about his daughter, Lieserl, nor did he ever see her himself; born in 1902, she probably died of scarlet fever in 1903. Although Einstein and Mileva married that year, he later wrote that he married her out of a sense of duty.

Several challenges cast a shadow upon Mileva and Albert's marriage, including the birth of boys in 1904 and 1910; Mileva's health problems; Einstein's regular travel to give talks around Europe; and his interest in other women. Estranged by 1914, Mileva eventually rejected Einstein's conditions for the continuation of their relationship:

You will obey the following points in your relations with me: (1) you will not expect any intimacy from me, nor will you reproach me in any way; (2) you will stop talking to me if I request it; (3) you will leave my bedroom or study immediately without protest if I request it. (Isaacson, 2007, p. 186)

1

FIGURE 1.1 Albert Einstein with his first wife, Mileva Maric, in 1911.

The couple separated that year and divorced in 1918. His younger son later commented, "The worst destiny is to have no destiny, and also to be the destiny of no one else" (Overbye, 2000, p. 375). His older son would remark, "Probably the only project he ever gave up on was me" (Pais, 2005, p. 453).

Contributing to the demise of Einstein's first marriage was his relationship with his first cousin, Elsa. Einstein had known Elsa since childhood, but in 1913 their relationship deepened when he visited Berlin to see Elsa, who was divorced with two daughters. Elsa eased Einstein's day-to-day concerns by managing their apartment and his finances, while Einstein provided Elsa and her daughters with security and a link to fame and fortune. Married in 1919, Einstein and Elsa established a comfortable relationship, despite his affairs with several women. Elsa died in 1936, leaving Einstein to live out his years with his sister and stepdaughter. Before he died, he wrote a letter to the son of one of his close friends who had just passed away: "What I admired most about [your father] was the fact that he was able to live so many years with one woman, not only in peace but also in constant unity, something I have lamentably failed at twice" (Isaacson, 2007, p. 540).

Consider the paradox, the inconsistency, of Einstein's intellect! Masterful as he was at revealing great mysteries of the cosmos, Einstein puzzled in vain over matters of the heart. Can we perhaps draw some conclusions about which is the more difficult puzzle?

QUESTIONS

The fact that Albert Einstein, by his own admission, failed as a husband and struggled as a father suggests that success and fulfillment in intimate relationships requires something more than a shrewd intellect. What is it about intimate relationships that makes them difficult, and demanding, and desirable, and delightful—often all at once? What are the forces that operate within and upon intimate relationships to produce these varying experiences? What does it take to have a good relationship? For that matter, what *is* a good relationship?

This brief sketch about Einstein, Mileva, and Elsa demonstrates that intimate relationships—Einstein's certainly, but yours and mine as well—are richly textured phenomena. They are complex because they involve the personalities, emotions, thoughts, passions, and goals of two individuals. When asking and answering questions about these phenomena, relationship scientists strive to serve various masters. One demands that we capture all the subtleties and nuances that make relationships special. A second impels us to impose order on these phenomena with rigorous research, to identify the principles, laws, and regularities that govern them. A third master, never far from the other two, prompts us to apply that knowledge so that social policies, educational programs, and clinical interventions are well informed and practically useful. We wrote this book to explore how the formidable tools of science can be brought to bear upon the murky and ineffable mysteries of intimate relationships.

Characteristics of an Intimate Relationship

Somewhere, as you read this today, two people are meeting one another for the very first time. Perhaps they will share an umbrella in the rain, or their hands might touch as they both reach for the last available copy of the latest best-selling novel, or maybe they will commiserate as they wait for an English professor who has failed to show up for office hours before the first quiz. They might exchange small talk as they wait together for the rain to pass, converse about their favorite books and authors, or arrange to share notes and study together later that day; ultimately, they might exchange telephone numbers so they can meet again. No longer strangers, the two people start to talk about their mutual likes and dislikes, find out whether each is already dating someone else, arrange to spend more and more time together in a widening range of activities, and share thoughts and feelings they do not express to casual acquaintances. As time passes they think of themselves as a couple, present themselves as a couple to friends, agree to date only each other, think about one another when they are apart, experience and express sexual desire for one another, create new shared experiences, and wonder, however tentatively, about a future together.

> " Like other great forces in nature—such as gravity, electricity, and the four winds—a relationship itself is invisible; its existence can be discerned only by observing its effects."
>
> —Ellen Berscheid, social psychologist (1999, p. 261)

Most of us would think of this couple as now being in an intimate relationship. But why do we think that? What specifically are these two people doing that leads us to characterize their relationship as intimate? And what changed, exactly, over the course of those several weeks that changes how we think about them and how they think of themselves? Asking these questions about this particular couple—let's call them Keith and Marina—allows us to introduce the four criteria that define an intimate relationship: The partners are interdependent, they consider each other special and unique, they influence each other across a variety of domains, and they experience some degree of mutual sexual passion.

Interdependence as the Cornerstone of Relationships

First, and most basically, you might note that Keith and Marina affect one another's behavior to a far greater degree now than when they first met. Changes in Keith's behaviors will change or constrain actions taken by Marina so that, for example, if Keith moves to another town, Marina might contemplate moving to be with him. Referred to as **interdependence**, the mutual influence that two people have over one another is the defining feature of any social relationship, intimate or otherwise.

A key aspect of interdependence is that it exists *between* two partners in a relationship. It is clear from how they think about each other and their shared activities that Keith and Marina have formed internal representations of one another and of their relationship. By this we mean that Keith and Marina have an image of each other that they can draw upon when they are apart, and that calling up this image brings with it specific thoughts and feelings about the other person. But we can easily see that having an internal representation of another person is insufficient by itself to say that a relationship exists between two people. (Were this the case, many of us could rightly claim relationships with attractive celebrities like Matthew McConaughey and Angelina Jolie.)

In addition, for two people to be in a relationship, the interdependence that connects them must have **bidirectionality**—it has to operate in both directions. Thus, for example, changes in Marina's behavior, such as her suggesting she move with Keith, will elicit a response from him. Likewise, Keith's options and behaviors might change if Marina decided to take on a part-time job. Contrast these bidirectional effects with unidirectional effects, whereby only one person's behavior is affected. For example, when you receive spam e-mails from the guy you've never met who wants you to know about get-rich schemes in Nigeria, only your behavior is affected: You are annoyed momentarily, and you hit the delete button. One-way influences such as these are hardly enough to constitute a relationship of any kind, until you respond to them and the interdependence grows stronger.

The interdependence between Keith and Marina is not isolated to a single exchange; it extends *over time*, with later interactions between partners gaining meaning from the earlier interactions. We would not say that Keith and Marina had any real relationship to speak of after that first brief meeting, because there was no continuing mutual influence between them. However, we can see how their later musings about their good fortune in finding one another take their significance from that meeting. As ethologist Robert Hinde notes:

> "Relationship" in everyday language carries the further implication that there is some degree of continuity between the successive interactions. Each interaction is affected by interactions in the past, and may affect interactions in the future. For that reason a "relationship" between two people may continue over long periods when they do not meet or communicate with each other; the accumulated effects of past interactions will ensure that, when they next meet, they do not see each other as strangers. (1979, p. 14)

Can we conclude that the interdependence between Keith and Marina's behaviors is the reason their relationship would be distinguished as intimate? Not entirely. Interdependence is a *necessary* condition for intimacy—you cannot have intimacy without it—but it is not a *sufficient* condition for intimacy. After all, many relationships possess interdependence without intimacy, at least as we propose to define it here. A guard and a prisoner are interdependent but not intimate, as are a shopkeeper and a regular customer, a patient and a nurse, a grandparent and a grandchild, a mother-in-law and a son-in-law, two friends, and so on. In all of these relationships, the two individuals have enduring and bidirectional influences over one another—yet we would not say they are intimate. What do you think has to be added to an interdependent relationship to make it an intimate relationship?

From Impersonal Relationships to Personal Relationships

Intimate relationships occur not just between two interdependent people, but between two people who treat one another as *unique* individuals rather than as interchangeable occupants of particular social roles or positions (Blumstein & Kollock, 1988). Thus, the interdependence evident in the relationships involving the guard and prisoner, the shopkeeper and the regular customer, and the patient and the nurse are driven to a considerable degree by the contexts and roles in which these people find themselves. Substituting different people into these relationships does not change them much; your relationship with your hairdresser is probably pretty similar to my relationship with my hairdresser. These relatively **impersonal relationships** tend to be formal and task-oriented.

Personal relationships are relatively informal and engage us at a deeper emotional level. Take, for example, the personal relationships involving a grandparent and a grandchild, or a mother-in-law and a son-in-law, or two friends, or our couple Keith and Marina. Here the interdependence is likely to be longer lasting and determined less by social roles and more by the uniqueness of the individuals involved, so that swapping out one grandparent and inserting another will change the very character of the relationship. The unique character of personal versus impersonal relationships is evidenced by our very different reaction to losing a grandparent than, say, to losing our favorite Starbucks barista—no matter how good the cappuccino.

From Personal Relationships to Close Relationships

Are all personal relationships intimate ones? Probably not, because the different sorts of personal relationships vary enough that we can still make meaningful distinctions among them. Even in relationships where people treat one another as unique individuals, their degree of *closeness* varies. Most of us would probably agree that a relationship between a mother-in-law and her son-in-law is not as close as a relationship between a grandparent and grandchild, which in turn is not as close as the relationship between Keith and Marina.

But what is closeness? Harold Kelley, a leading theoretician on interdependence and closeness, has argued that "the close relationship is one of strong, frequent, and diverse interdependence that lasts over a considerable period of time" (Kelley et al., 1983, p. 38). By considering the relationship between

Keith and Marina, we can see how closeness reflects an unusually high degree of interdependence. Compared to the relationship between a mother-in-law and her daughter's husband, for example, Keith and Marina probably have far more contact with one another because they see each other nearly every day. They also are likely to have stronger influences on one another; if Marina has a bad day, her mood affects Keith a lot more than anyone else in her life. Keith and Marina also are more likely to be interdependent over a greater variety of situations. So the presence of a **close relationship** qualifies interdependent and personal relationships further, where we understand closeness to be reflected by the strength, frequency, and diversity of the influences that partners have over one another.

From Close Relationships to Intimate Relationships

Is closeness the final ingredient, the element that makes a personal relationship truly intimate? Because a lot of variety still exists, even among close relationships, the answer is again no; we probably want to reserve the term *intimate relationship* for only a subset of the relationships we would designate as close. For example, how Einstein enjoyed high degrees of closeness with his classmates as well as with his two wives, Mileva and Elsa. The interdependence that marks all of these relationships was relatively strong, and the interactions tended to be frequent, wide-ranging, and enduring. Yet our closest friendships are not the same as our intimate relationships, nor are our relationships with family members. Consider your own relationships: Are there important distinctions between your closest friendships, your family relationships, and your relationship with a boyfriend or girlfriend? If so, what would you say is the basis for these differences?

The difference between a close relationship and an intimate relationship lies, we would argue, in whether the two partners experience a mutual erotic charge, or a shared—though not necessarily articulated—feeling that they have the potential to be sexually intimate. Thus, by our definition, two people who are in a close relationship are also in an intimate relationship if they both experience a lustful, sexual passion for one another and an expectation that this passion will be consummated.

Sexual interaction without the element of closeness falls outside our definition of an intimate relationship, thus excluding "one-night stands" and sexual experiences people have when hooking up. We might say these people were physically intimate, but in the absence of "strong, frequent, and diverse interdependence that lasts over a considerable period of time," we would not say they were in an intimate relationship. Moreover, defining an intimate relationship in this way does not imply that the two partners are necessarily happy in their relationship—thus Einstein's troubled marriage to Mileva was no less an intimate relationship than was his more fulfilling marriage to

Elsa. Though discontent is likely to change the nature of the interdependence between partners, it does not eliminate the interdependencies themselves. As long as there is the prospect of sexual interaction in the context of a close relationship, we will assume that even unhappy partners are experiencing an intimate relationship.

FIGURE 1.2 captures the essence of the different types of social relationships we have described. We can now synthesize the features we've discussed, to define an **intimate relationship** as a relationship characterized by strong, sustained, mutual influence over a broad range of interactions, with the possibility of sexual involvement.

We can now answer the question that we posed earlier in this section: Why do we consider Keith and Marina's relationship to be intimate? First, Keith and Marina are in a relationship because the things they do affect one another. Keith may notice that Marina is upset, and his behavior might change somehow—he might avoid her, or console her, or criticize her—and she might then respond to what he has done, prompting his response, and so on. As partners in a relationship, their thoughts, feelings, and actions are mutually intertwined; indeed, these bidirectional interdependencies are a defining feature of being in a relationship of any kind. We can go further and say that theirs is a personal relationship rather than an impersonal one because they respond to one another as unique individuals rather than as two individuals who happen to be filling particular social roles. Keith holds special significance for Marina, and vice versa. They matter to one another because they engage each other on a more emotional level than if they were merely in an impersonal relationship. The category of personal relationships is a broad one, and within it we can see that some relationships are closer than others. We would say that Keith and Marina's relationship is close because (a) their thoughts, feelings, and behaviors routinely affect one another (e.g., they see each other at least once almost every day, and they exchange a lot of text messages when apart); (b) these influences last over time and are evident in many of the things they do each day (e.g., they study together, snuggle together, eat together, and go out together with their friends);

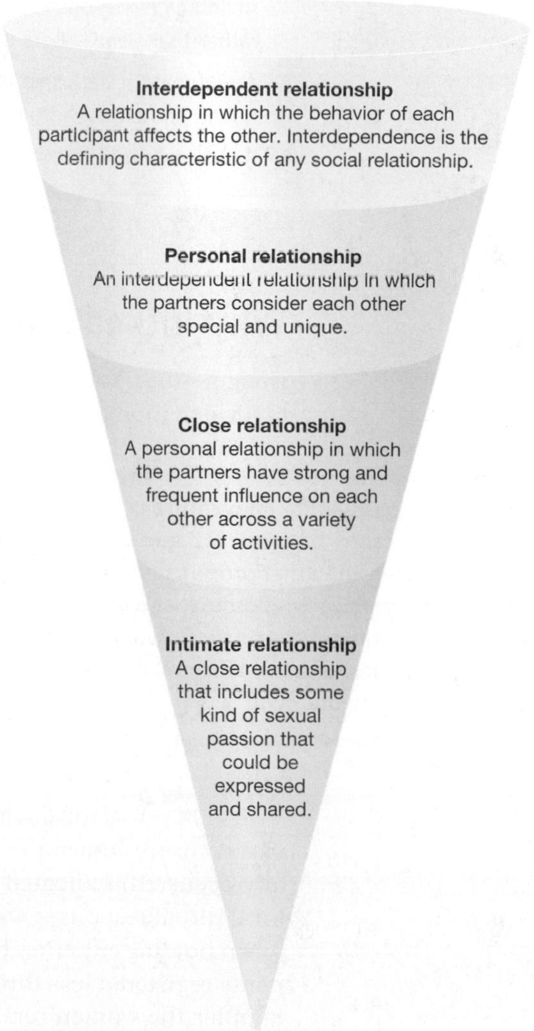

Interdependent relationship
A relationship in which the behavior of each participant affects the other. Interdependence is the defining characteristic of any social relationship.

Personal relationship
An interdependent relationship in which the partners consider each other special and unique.

Close relationship
A personal relationship in which the partners have strong and frequent influence on each other across a variety of activities.

Intimate relationship
A close relationship that includes some kind of sexual passion that could be expressed and shared.

FIGURE 1.2 Distinguishing among different types of social relationships.

and (c) their effects on one another are not trivial (e.g., Marina feels good when Keith wishes her well on a quiz; Keith feels hurt when Marina chooses to spend time with her roommates instead of him). And, finally, (d) Keith and Marina are in an intimate relationship because sexual interaction is one of the possible ways they anticipate being interdependent.

MAIN POINTS

>> Four criteria distinguish an intimate relationship from other types of social relationships.

>> An intimate relationship is interdependent; the partners' behaviors affect each other.

>> An intimate relationship is personal; the partners treat each other as special and unique, rather than as members of a generic category (e.g., classmate or neighbor).

>> An intimate relationship is close, where closeness is understood to mean strong, frequent, and diverse forms of mutual influence.

>> An intimate relationship is, or has the potential to be, sexual.

Why Intimate Relationships Are Important

Imagine this: You are lying flat on your back in an MRI scanner, looking up at a video monitor. A technician explains that when you see a red *X*, you have a 20 percent chance of receiving a small shock via an electrode attached to your ankle. When you see a blue *O*, you have a 0 percent chance of receiving a shock. The large magnet encircling your head detects minute changes in your brain activity after you see the *X* or the *O* and translates these data into images of your brain. You are shown either an *X* or an *O* under three separate conditions: while holding your intimate partner's hand, the hand of a stranger who is the same sex as your partner, or no hand at all.

> " No quality of human nature is more remarkable, both in itself and in its consequences, than that propensity we have to sympathize with others, and to receive by communication their inclinations and sentiments, however different from, or even contrary to our own."
>
> —David Hume, Scottish philosopher, *A Treatise of Human Nature* (1739–1740)

In the actual study, analysis of the brain images that were collected after a group of 16 married women were shown the dreaded *X* or the safe *O* (but before any shock actually occurred) indicated that brain regions governing emotional and behavioral threat responses were activated less when holding a partner's hand than when holding either no hand or a stranger's hand. In other words, the participants registered less threat when holding their partner's hand. Moreover, the happier the women reported being in their relationships, the less activation occurred in their threat-related brain regions (Coan, Schaefer, & Davidson, 2006) (**FIGURE 1.3**).

In another study, researchers followed a group of 188 couples dealing with one partner's congestive heart failure. Research assistants visited the couples'

(a)

(b)

(c)

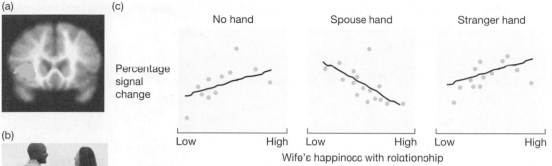

No hand   Spouse hand   Stranger hand

Percentage
signal
change

Low   High   Low   High   Low   High

Wife's happiness with relationship

FIGURE 1.3 The hand-holding study. (a) Certain brain regions, including the right anterior insula, are known to respond to threats that people perceive in their environment. (b) When women hold their husband's hand, however, these regions become less active—the "signal change" is reduced—as compared to when they hold a stranger's hand or no hand at all. (c) This benefit appears to be greatest for women in happy marriages. As shown in the middle scatter plot, women who report happier marriages show more deactivation in these regions compared to women who report less happiness: As happiness goes up, activation of these threat-related brain regions goes down.

homes, where they interviewed and gave standardized questionnaires to each partner in separate rooms. At the end of the visits, the partners were videotaped for 10 minutes talking about a topic of disagreement in their relationships. The researchers examined the videotaped conversations in detail and counted the number of times the partners said positive and negative things to one another. They combined these counts with the interview and questionnaire data the partners provided about their marriages, thus producing an index of overall relationship quality; and they used public records to determine which patients died over a span of 4 years, and when those deaths occurred. Using the composite index to distinguish between couples who were higher and lower in relationship quality, the researchers demonstrated that compared to those in unhappier relationships, patients in happier relationships were less likely to die in this 4-year period (Coyne et al., 2001) (FIGURE 1.4).

Beyond yielding groundbreaking insights about the workings of human intimacy, these two studies are noteworthy because they suggest two very different reasons for the importance of intimate relationships. First, intimate relationships are important because they are a basic feature of who we are as human beings. As the hand-holding study suggests, each of us has a nervous system that responds to and equips us not simply for social interaction, but for social interaction with an intimate partner. Biologically, we appear to be uniquely attuned to the person with whom we share an intimate bond. This human capacity for intimacy—like the capacity for language, reasoning, or social perception—contributes to our ability to regulate our emotions (and our partner's emotions) and adapt to the world in which we live. Understanding intimate relationships, this basic feature of who we are, is thus essential to understanding the human condition.

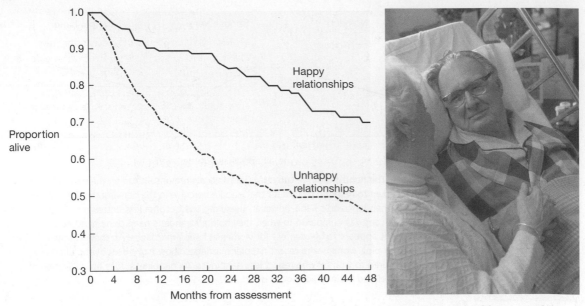

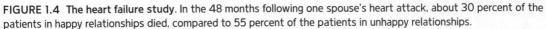

FIGURE 1.4 **The heart failure study.** In the 48 months following one spouse's heart attack, about 30 percent of the patients in happy relationships died, compared to 55 percent of the patients in unhappy relationships.

Second, intimate relationships are important because of their consequences. Although it is not a formal experiment, the congestive heart failure study suggests that how we feel about our relationship, how we think about and make sense of our relationship, and how we talk to our partner may well contribute to how long we live following a health crisis. Here we can see that intimate relationships are important for reasons beyond their very nature; they are important as one clue in other puzzles we want to solve.

Next we discuss six specific reasons why intimate relationships merit close scholarly attention. Much like the hand-holding study, the first three reasons focus on intrinsic properties of relationships. You will learn that intimate relationships are important because they determine the survival of our species, because they are a universal human experience, and because they expand our range of emotional experience. And much like the heart failure study, the second three reasons focus on extrinsic properties of relationships. Our emphasis will be on how intimate relationships affect our mental and physical health, how they influence the well-being of children, and how they form the fabric of society.

Intimate Relationships Determine the Survival of Our Species

Charles Darwin's theory of evolution, dating to 1859, reveals that who we are today as a species is a product of **natural selection** operating over a vast expanse of time. Random changes in genes from one generation to the next sometimes lead to enhanced **fitness**, or improvements in the chances that the offspring will survive and reproduce. A host of factors, including diverse forms of social relationships, determine whether a specific gene or set of genes improves fitness. "Social interactions and relationships surrounding mating, kinship, reciprocal alliances, coalitions, and hierarchies are especially critical, because all appear to have strong consequences for successful survival and reproduction" (Buss & Kenrick, 1998, p. 994; see Reis, Collins, & Berscheid, 2000). Intimate relationships in particular are implicated in the mechanisms of evolution, and fitness is affected directly or indirectly by the ways human mates attract and select each other, their willingness and tendency to procreate, the attachments they form, and their provision of support and nurturing for one another and their offspring.

> Marvel not then at the love which all men have of their offspring; for that universal love and interest is for the sake of immortality."
>
> —Diotima, speaking to Socrates, in Plato's *The Symposium*, circa 350 BCE; translation by Benjamin Jowett (1892, p. 578)

The importance of these aspects of intimacy in perpetuating our species is reflected in a wide range of biological systems. Sexual desire and interaction, as magical as they may feel, are the result of an intricate cascade of neurochemical events linking erotic stimuli, both physical and psychological, to spinal reflexes that excite the limbic system and sensory cortex, which in turn prompt the hypothalamus and the pituitary gland to produce hormones that alter the sensitivity and functioning of our sexual organs. Romantic love appears to be no less biologically based. MRI scans taken while participants gaze at their beloved partner reveal brain activation in regions that are known to be stimulated when we receive a potent award (such as money or an intravenous injection of cocaine). Such responses can impel us to pursue these rewards, just as we might pursue closeness with our mate (FIGURE 1.5). Deactivation is apparent in brain regions known to be involved in sadness and depression, negative emotions, and critical social judgments (Bartels & Zeki, 2000, 2004). Sexual desire and romantic love appear to be biologically distinct systems, joined in part by a neuropeptide called oxytocin that is released during intimate physical contact—such as during massages and sexual intercourse (Carmichael et al., 1987; Carter, 1998; Diamond, 2003). Oxytocin has been studied primarily in prairie voles, one of the 3 percent of mammalian species that are monogamous. An injection of oxytocin results in the formation of a lifelong relationship between two voles, even when sex does not occur; and chemically blocking oxytocin during sex inhibits the development of a relationship. Oxytocin may be a key ingredient in the neurobiological system that promotes feelings of calmness, sociability, and trust (Kosfeld, Heinrichs, Zak, Fischbacher, & Fehr, 2005; Uvänas-Moberg, Arn, & Magnusson, 2005), partly by reducing activity in fear-related brain structures like the amygdala and hypothalamus. Recall from the hand-holding study that activation in brain regions responsive to threats in the environment—including the hypothalamus—is reduced by the physical presence of an intimate partner and by the quality of the bond with that partner. The key

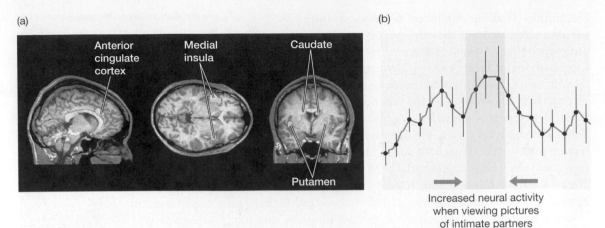

FIGURE 1.5 That special someone. (a) This MRI scan shows the brain activity (from the side, top, and front) of an individual who is viewing a picture of his or her intimate partner, after adjusting for how this individual's brain responds to a picture of his or her close friend. Viewing the partner increases activity in the anterior cingulate cortex, the medial insula, the caudate, and the putamen, brain regions known to implement a range of functions including positive emotions, empathy, reward, and emotion regulation. (b) This figure shows that presentation of the picture (indicated as the period between the two arrows) elicits an increase in anterior cingulate activity. The finding that brain activation differs in response to pictures of partners and close friends supports the distinction between relationships that are intimate and those that are merely close.

point here is that biological systems within our body respond in systematic ways to what is happening in our intimate relationships. Because we can see this correspondence, we know that intimate relationships are fundamental to who we are and to how we have evolved.

Intimate Relationships Are a Universal Human Experience

Recognizing that a capacity for intimacy comes as "standard equipment" for human beings allows us to infer another important reason for seeking to understand intimate relationships: They are a universal human experience. Couples in all societies form lasting relationships, often for the purpose of breeding. Across nearly 100 industrial and agricultural countries, for example, more than 90 percent of all men and women have experienced some form of marriage by their late 40s (Fischer, 1989). Known more generally as **pairbonds**, these unions may take different forms (e.g., legally sanctioned marriage; **cohabitation**, or living together without being married) but at their core, these unions typically involve two individuals who have some degree of emotional and practical investment in one another.

Pairbonding is often motivated by love and mutual attraction. These factors emerge as the most desirable features in a potential mate across men and women living in 37 countries on six continents and five islands (Buss et al., 1990) and are cited as the most common reasons why people have

FIGURE 1.6 Tales and myths attesting to the universality of love. Left: According to a Japanese legend, Komagawa and Asagao fall in love, but Asagao's parents have arranged for her to marry someone else. Asagao's tears blind her; despondent, she wanders the countryside singing a poem that Komagawa had written for her. When they reunite years later, "Asagao could hold up her fair head to the dew and sunshine of her lover's sheltering arms" (Davis, 1932, p. 249). Right: "Love's Passing," painted by Evelyn De Morgan in 1883, shows two young lovers seated by the River of Life. The man is captivated by the angel's piping, but the woman seems distracted by the footsteps of Old Age and Death behind her (Smith, 2002, p. 155).

sex (Meston & Buss, 2007). Anthropologists William Jankowiak and Edward Fischer (1992) identified romantic love conclusively in the vast majority of the 166 hunting, foraging, and agricultural societies they studied, leading them to conclude that "romantic love constitutes a human universal, or at the least a near-universal" (p. 154) (FIGURE 1.6).

A review of this literature and a detailed analysis of recorded stories and myths from all regions of the world—including Japanese legends of supernatural sweethearts, for example, and legends from the Heiltsuk Nation in Canada in which lovers promise to continue their relationship after death—led two English professors to conclude that "a clear preponderance of evidence derived from systematic studies of ethnography, neuroscience, folk tales, and even ethology converges to support romantic love's universality" (Gottschall & Nordlund, 2006, p. 463). The need to belong appears to be a fundamental source of motivation for human behavior (Baumeister & Leary, 1995), and people the world over commonly meet this need in intimate relationships marked by stable bonds, frequent contact, and mutual concern (Tafarodi et al., 2012; Wong & Goodwin, 2009).

Having a hardwired capacity for intimacy does not necessarily imply that this capacity is the same for all people within a culture, or for all cultures at a specific time, or for all people across historical time (Hatfield & Rapson, 1993). Thus, we might say that intimate relationships are best understood as the product of the universal capacity for intimacy *and* the prevailing cultural and historical settings in which the relationships occur. Through shared evolutionary pressures and common biology, virtually all humans have a capacity for intimate relationships, but other factors can modify how we experience and express that capacity. Within a culture, experiences in intimate relationships differ depending on whether a person is male or female, gay or straight, young or old, rich or poor. In the United States, for example, the popular media currently focuses a great deal on how men and women have different experiences in their relationships because of the different contributions they make to running a household, on how gay people lack equality in society because they cannot marry, and on how poor people are struggling more to keep their marriages and families intact during difficult economic times. We can assume that the basic capacity for intimacy is similar across these and other situations; but at the same time, this does not mean that all interpersonal bonds are identical or that all experiences within relationships are uniform. Let's take a closer look at some of the ways historical and cultural factors operate on and alter the core experience of intimacy.

> "Everywhere is love and love-making, weddings and babies from generation to generation keeping the Family of Man alive and continuing."
>
> —Carl Sandburg, American poet; from prologue to *The Family of Man* (1955)

To begin, we know that the experience of love differs across cultures. A comparison of the most popular love songs played on the radio in the United States or in China between 1987 and 1993 indicates that songs in the two places express a similar intensity of desire and longing. However, song lyrics in China refer to love as more enduring or more deeply embedded in nature; as more likely to include suffering, sadness, and pain; and as more likely to result in disappointment or regret (Rothbaum & Tsang, 1998). Cross-cultural studies of intimate feelings show further differences. For example, young adults interviewed in North America and China identify the same basic emotions and categorize positive emotions and negative emotions that same way—except in the case of love. North American students view love as intensely positive and equated with personal happiness, but Chinese students view love as negatively tinged with unrequited feelings, infatuation, and sorrow (Shaver, Wu, & Schwartz, 1991). These differences may exist because Western cultures like the United States tend to prioritize personal goals over duties to the larger group, whereas the opposite is the case among Eastern cultures like China (e.g., Triandis, 1996). Indeed, the Buddhist concept of *yuan*—that the outcome of a relationship is predestined and that little can be done to change its course—is often invoked in Asian cultures to explain these different experiences (e.g., Chang & Chan, 2007). With more constraints, less choice, less control, and more connection to surrounding circumstances, love and intimacy may well be more difficult in Eastern than Western cultures.

Between and within cultures, people initiate intimate relationships in different ways. The distinction between individualistic societies like the United States and interdependent or collectivist societies (e.g., China and India) is also manifest in cultural practices involved in mate selection. For example, in individualistic societies, the family is a support system for the individual, who leaves home, falls in love, eventually introduces the mate to the family, and pursues a romantic relationship with that person to fulfill his or her personal needs. By contrast, individuals are the support systems for families in interdependent societies. Families collaborate to find partners for their offspring, not to promote the couple's happiness but to enhance the family's stability or social standing. Romance, sexuality, and individual autonomy are not part of the script, and indeed the prospective mate is likely to meet his or her in-laws before meeting the partner (Hortaçsu, 1999).

With increased globalization, and the spread of Western values, many couples in collectivist societies now routinely select their own mate. In these societies, which do you think is more satisfying—a marriage in which the partners select one another, or a marriage in which the families choose the mate? Formal experiments that would answer this question cannot be conducted, of course, but at least two large cross-sectional studies converge on a common conclusion. In their survey of 586 women married between 1933 and 1987 in the Chinese province of Sichuan, Xiaohe and Whyte (1990) showed that women having a choice in who they married were reliably more satisfied in their relationship than those whose partner was chosen for them. Interviews conducted in 1991 with more than 10,000 Chinese couples, ranging in age from 22 to 57, similarly showed that "love" marriages were more satisfying than those arranged by the family, which were no different in happiness from those marriages arranged by friends (Jin & Xu, 2006). While we cannot know whether these findings arise due to one's perceptions of having chosen a mate (perhaps motivating people to work harder to maintain the relationship), or to the quality of the choice itself (perhaps allowing people to work less to maintain the relationship), at this point arranged marriages do not appear to be superior, at least in terms of relationship satisfaction.

What about other dimensions of comparison? Does the extended family suffer when couples initiate their own relationships? The husband's family, which would typically benefit from arranged marriages (e.g., the wife's family often pays a dowry to the husband's family; and in India, the bride moves in with her in-laws after the wedding), does indeed seem to lose out in these more modern arrangements. For example, a study conducted in Turkey shows that a shift toward couple-initiated marriages brings with it an increase in the time couples spend with the wife's family, and a decrease in the time the couple spends with the husband's family, compared to those in arranged marriages (Hortaçsu, 1999).

As other nations are adopting Westernized values and practices in intimate relationships, Westernized values and practices themselves are undergoing dramatic change (FIGURE 1.7). Marriage has been the prototypical intimate relationship for the past few hundred years. But marriage is shifting from being an institution in which social obligations have paramount importance to being a form of intimate companionship in which the emotional bonds between partners are most essential. The responsibilities of marriage were once institutionalized by religious and legal codes and closely regulated by

FIGURE 1.7 Historical and cultural shifts in intimate relationships. Because intimate relationships are a universal experience, we can expect that the people in these photographs are having relatively similar psychological experiences. At the same time, experiences of intimate relationships can be different across cultures and across historical eras. Even today, in Western cultures, people's experiences in straight relationships are likely to differ from those in same-sex relationships.

social norms and sanctions. But these effects have weakened over the past century, which has witnessed a corresponding increase in the value placed on marriage as a relationship in which partners seek happiness and emotional fulfillment. First articulated by sociologists Ernest Burgess and Harvey Locke in the middle of the last century (Burgess & Locke, 1945), this shift is viewed by historians of the family and family sociologists as being rooted in other large-scale demographic changes occurring over this period: Industrialization and the growth of cities decreased the degree to which families depended on children to sustain the family unit; increased geographic mobility reduced the degree to which parents and families could monitor and influence their children; and growing power and increasing opportunities for women gave them greater economic independence and more control over their personal decisions (e.g., Amato, Booth, Johnson, & Rogers, 2007; Coontz, 2005; Mintz & Kellogg, 1988).

Marriage is thus becoming a relationship with greater potential to make individuals happy (e.g., people can more readily leave bad marriages now than in earlier times), yet achieving this new freedom has come at the cost of making marriage more fragile (Coontz, 2005).

Although this shift in Western approaches to intimacy represented new ways of relating within marriage, another shift represents new ways of relating without marriage. Cohabitation has increased dramatically in the past two decades, for example, so that in 2007 there were over 6 million unrelated adults of the opposite sex living together—up from 1.6 million adults 20 years earlier (U.S. Census Bureau, 2007). The number of cohabiting relationships that proceed to marriage within 3 years has dropped from 60 percent to 33 percent over approximately the same period (Smock & Gupta, 2002). Child-birth patterns are also changing since marriage is no longer viewed as a pre-requisite for becoming a parent; 1 child in 6 was born to unmarried parents in 1982, and the corresponding figure today is about 1 in 3 (U.S. National Center for Health Statistics, 2003). The upshot of these changes is that marriage is no longer the "default option" it once was for adults making choices about their intimate relationships. Although marriage remains highly valued and desirable, "it has been transformed from a familial and community institution to an individualized, choice-based achievement" (Cherlin, 2004).

In sum, intimate relationships have a central and recognizable core of emotional and sexual interdependence that is easily understood. But at the same time, these core elements vary based on different cultural settings and historical periods. Intimacy merits our attention because it is a universal human experience, but we should not assume that this experience will generalize across time and place. To gain a deeper understanding of how intimacy is both universal and variable, you might consider interviewing an older family member or a fellow student from a culture unlike your own. As **BOX** 1.1 illustrates, in doing so you are likely to hear elements that are both familiar and unfamiliar to your own ideas of love and intimacy.

Intimate Relationships Expand Our Range of Emotional Experience

Love is not synonymous with intimacy, and love is not a defining characteristic of an intimate relationship, because love is not necessarily experienced in all cases. Conversely, love occurs in many kinds of relationships (e.g., parent-child, close friendships) that we would not characterize as intimate. Even so, love clearly is a valued commodity in our intimate relationships, and it is often cited as the object of our intimate quests. Due to the diverse, enduring, and sexually charged behavioral interdependencies or connections that partners form, intimate relationships are fundamentally emotional. Indeed, we often seek these emotional experiences when forming relationships, they affect us when we are in the midst of a relationship, and we reflect upon them after a relationship ends. Defining the concept of love is challenging, but over the years a picture of its essential attributes has emerged (**TABLE 1.1**).

As you might know from your own relationships, the experience of love can vary a great deal in different relationships depending on the relative presence or absence of these attributes. They can combine to produce different types of love, and the lack of consensus among classification systems for love indicates that they have been devised for different purposes, with different assumptions, and using different sources of data (see Berscheid, 2006, for

Talking About Love in Different Cultures

In most cultures, people talk about love. But how they do so, and how often, varies a great deal.

Mirgun Dev and Durga Kumari live in a tiny Nepalese village 100 miles southwest of Katmandu. Their love letters, along with others collected by anthropologist Laura Ahearn (2001, 2003), express sentiments that are surprisingly easy to understand by Western standards—despite being expressed in a cultural context markedly different from our own:

> One thing that I hope you will promise is that you will love me truly and that when you think about the future you will continue to want to do so and won't break up with me in the middle of our relationship. Okay?. . . Later on in the middle of our relationship you are not to do anything [i.e., break up]—understand? . . . I want you to love me without causing me suffering, okay?. . . Finally, if you love me, send a "reply" to this letter, okay?

This letter was sent not by e-mail, but by a younger relative who is sworn to secrecy. While arranged marriages are gradually giving way to marriages based on love in this Nepalese village, men and women are still not allowed to spend time alone together during courtship. Moreover, by answering a man's letter, a woman is essentially agreeing to marry him. She must do so based on very little contact, and she is often shamed and disgraced if she does not marry her correspondent. Can you imagine the pressure this practice places on the early development of an intimate relationship? How would you react under similar pressure? It is no wonder that Durga Kumari sought specific assurances of Mirgun Dev's love.

In contrast, this interview from the television show *60 Minutes* presents a very different attitude toward talking about love—in Finnish (Tiffin, 1993; cited in Wilkins & Gareis, 2006):

Morley Safer, moderator of *60 Minutes*: *Do people tell each other that they love each other?*

Terri Schultz, an American journalist living in Finland: *No! Oh my God no! No. Not even, I mean, even lovers, I think.*

Jan Knutas, a male journalist from Finland: *Well I'd say, you could say it once in a lifetime. If you say you have been married for 20 years, perhaps your spouse is on her death-bed. You could comfort her with saying "I love you," but umm . . .*

Safer: (laughs)

Knutas: *It's not funny.*

Arja Koriseva, a well-known female Finnish singer: *It's easier to me to say, like, to my boyfriend that "I love you." It's, we have heard it on, on TV, on movies. It's easier . . .*

Safer: (laughs)

Koriseva: *. . . to me to say "I love you" than "mina rakastan sinua." It doesn't sound very nice if I say "I love you" in Finnish.*

Safer: *You look slightly embarrassed when you say it in Finnish.*

Koriseva: (laughs) *Yeah, but we don't use "I love you" so much as you do. You love almost, almost everybody. When a Finnish guy or man says "I love you," he really means it.*

Neither of these anecdotes conclusively shows how these cultures feel about love as a whole, but they do illustrate different norms and expectations for expressing intimate feelings. How does this work for you? Why?

a recent discussion). Perhaps the most robust of these classifications contrasts **passionate love**, marked more by infatuation, intense preoccupation with the partner, strong sexual longing, throes of ecstasy, and feelings of exhilaration that come from being reunited with the partner, with **companionate love**, in which these potent feelings diminish but are enriched by warm feelings of attachment, an authentic and enduring bond, a sense of mutual commitment, the profound knowledge that you are caring for another person who is in turn caring for you, feeling proud of a mate's accomplishments, and the satisfaction that comes from sharing goals and perspectives (see Hatfield & Rapson, 1993).

Love, whatever form it takes, pulls us into intimate relationships. And when it dwindles or changes, it often motivates us to improve our relationship or seek another partner. Throughout this book we explore diverse influences on the feelings that intimate partners have for one another, but for now the key point is that intimate relationships are a crucible in which a broad range of powerful emotions such as these are felt and exchanged, further justifying their analysis.

Unfortunately, as the existentialist philosopher Jean-Paul Sartre succinctly stated in his play *No Exit* (1944), "Hell is other people." One of life's cruel ironies is that the very interdependencies that position us to revel in feelings of passion and companionship also leave us vulnerable to the pain and suffering relationships can sometimes cause. Few of us will escape any of the various unpleasant experiences that can occur in relationships. We may go from simply feeling unappreciated or ignored to dealing with jealousy and heartache to suffering through sexual rejection, verbal abuse, or infidelity. Despite the high emotional and financial costs associated with ending a marriage, divorce is common; current estimates indicate that about half of all first marriages will end (Bramlett & Mosher, 2002). Other more extreme experiences in intimate relationships are far from rare. For example, according to a 2000 survey by the U.S. Department of Justice, 4.8 million women and 2.9 million men are physically assaulted or raped by their intimate partners each year (Tjaden & Thoennes, 2000). Indeed, in the time it takes for you to complete this book, newspapers in every major city in the country are virtually certain to carry stories about how one partner has killed another, and perhaps their children, as a result of relationship difficulties.

Intimate relationships bring out the very best and the very worst in us, enabling us to soar to great heights and forcing us to plunge to great depths. The breadth and intensity of emotional experiences that typify intimate relationships thus provide another *intrinsic* reason for studying them. Any one of us has experienced firsthand the power of love or hate. It is important to realize, though, that these positive and negative experiences affect not only our emotions but our physical health and longevity, the well-being of any children we raise, and the fabric of our community. Next we take up these *extrinsic* reasons for studying intimate relationships.

Intimate Relationships Affect Our Mental and Physical Health

Are intimate relationships good for us? The short answer appears to be yes, because our **subjective well-being**—or how happy we are generally in life—is linked with various aspects of our intimate relationships. Married people

TABLE 1.1 Seven Essential Attributes of Love

1. **Desire:** Wanting to be united with the partner, physically and emotionally.

   The only thing I can compare it to is like a hunger, like being starved and really needing something. Sexually, definitely, but being around him just made me feel good, deep down. I'm not saying it was logical, but it was real, and it was deep.

2. **Idealization:** Believing the partner is unique and special.

   In 7th grade my buddies and I used to crack each other up over that line where Romeo says, "But ho! What light through yonder window breaks? It is the east, and Juliet is the sun." I could never quite believe that could actually happen, but right after I got to college, after being with Carla, I couldn't get over this feeling that she was like my Juliet. . . . I even recited this line to her!

3. **Joy:** Experiencing very strong, positive emotions.

   We were lifeguarding at the same pool every day over summer break, and we had been checking each other out, and we had this bet that whoever blew their whistle the most times had to take the other person out to dinner. He lost, on purpose I think, but then we had this amazing dinner at the beach. It was pretty intense. We both cried, we were so happy to finally be together. We stayed up all night talking, and I just felt like I was totally buzzed and energized.

4. **Preoccupation:** Thinking a lot about the partner and having little control over when these thoughts occur.

   The night before my big exam at the police academy, and I could not stop thinking about Travis. It was like this big handsome sexy perfect man had fallen into the middle of my life, and if I could not be with him then my brain was going to do all it could to get me the next best thing.

5. **Proximity:** Taking steps to maintain or restore physical closeness or emotional contact with the partner.

   I know it sounds strange, but my boyfriend is back home in Japan and so I use one of his T-shirts as a pillowcase. I never want to forget him, or his voice, or what he smells like. I like knowing that I am hugging some small part of him every night when I go to bed.

6. **Prioritizing:** Giving the relationship more importance than other interests and responsibilities.

   After Karen and I got together, I got a lot more serious about trying to get ahead in my job. Other things, like my friends, kind of took a back seat. I mean, we never talked about it, but I wanted her to know she could depend on me—I kind of wanted to prove to her I could put money in the bank.

7. **Caring:** Experiencing and expressing feelings of empathy and compassion for the partner.

   I think I really knew that I was in love with Janie when we went to the hospital to see her sister after her car accident. It was bad, and Janie was totally freaked out by the tubes and monitors, and all I could think of was to make Janie feel comfortable and safe, and to let her know everything would be OK. To reassure her. We were in a serious relationship and all, but for me that took it to a whole new level.

Sources: Adapted from Berscheid, 1998; Fehr, 1988; Harris, 1995; Hatfield, 1988; Sternberg & Grajek, 1984; Tennov, 1979; and others.

report greater happiness than do either people who are unmarried and living together or people who are divorced, separated, or widowed (Diener, Suh, Lucas, & Smith, 1999; Stack & Eshleman, 1998), indicating that **relationship status** relates to subjective well-being. Among people who have not married, those who cohabit tend to be happier than those who live alone. Although these differences are consistent across many cultures (Diener, Gohm, Suh, & Oishi, 2000), they may be relatively small, partly because single people can create social networks that contribute to their happiness and partly because couples differ widely in their degree of **relationship quality** or how good or bad they judge their relationship to be. While the average married person is happier than the average cohabiting person, for example, a married person in an unhappy relationship may well experience less subjective well-being than an unmarried person in a good relationship or even in an average relationship (e.g., Proulx, Helms, & Buehler, 2007). In fact, satisfaction with one's intimate relationship tells us more about someone's overall subjective well-being than does his or her satisfaction with any other domain in life, including work, finances, friendships, community, and health (Glenn & Weaver, 1981; Headey, Veenhoven, & Wearing, 1991; Heller, Watson, & Ilies, 2004) (FIGURE 1.8). **Relationship transitions**, or the movement into and out of partnerships, are another way that intimate relationships are linked with subjective well-being. As people approach marriage, for example, their subjective well-being increases (e.g., Stutzer & Frey, 2006). As they approach divorce, subjective well-being decreases, and it remains relatively low for several years after the divorce (Lucas, 2005). Further evidence for the importance of intimate relationships comes from studies showing that relationship difficulties increase substance abuse (Overbeek et al., 2006), diagnosable depression (Whisman & Bruce, 1999), and suicide (Stander, Hilton, Kennedy, & Robbins, 2004).

Go back and carefully reread the previous paragraph. You may realize that we cannot conclude with certainty that relationship status, relationship quality, or relationship transitions truly *caused* changes in well-being. After all, researchers typically cannot randomly assign people to a particular relationship status, or to a relationship that is high or low in quality, or to a particular relationship transition, and then see what makes people most and least happy. One reason we cannot draw this conclusion is that people

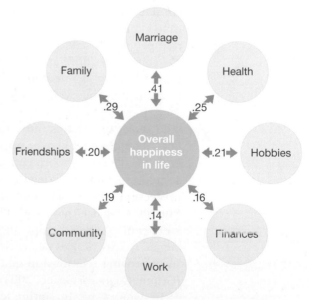

FIGURE 1.8 **Intimate relationships and personal happiness.** Overall happiness with life corresponds more closely to happiness in marriage than to satisfaction with any other domain. The numbers shown in this figure can range from 0 to 1, with higher numbers indicating stronger correspondence.

with specific characteristics may be more likely to enter into certain types of relationships or undergo particular transitions—raising the possibility that these characteristics, rather than the relationships themselves, cause their well-being. This is known as a **selection effect**, when groups of people differ—married and unmarried people, for example—not because of something special about the groups they are in, but because of the people who choose to enter those groups. For example, say that happier people are more likely to marry than to cohabit. They would be happier when married, but that happiness is not because of marriage itself but because the people who make their way into marriage are happier than those who do not marry. Evidence supports this kind of selection effect: Studies show that people who are happier are more likely to marry than to stay single, and people who are less happy before marriage are also more likely to divorce (e.g., Marks & Fleming, 1999; Stutzer & Frey, 2006).

Does this finding invalidate the argument that intimate relationships are good for us? Not entirely. As it turns out, other studies do suggest that intimate relationships may well yield mental health benefits beyond the operation of selection effects. The studies that do this first minimize the possibility that selection effects are working—usually by measuring those effects and adjusting for them statistically—and only then do they make their comparisons. For example, sociologists Allan Horwitz, Helen White, and Sandra Howell-White (1996) studied a group of married people and a group of very similar people who remained single. Depression and alcohol use among married and single people decreased over a period of 7 years—but for married people, these factors declined more quickly. S. L. Brown (2000) followed the same procedure and demonstrated that people who cohabit experience higher levels of depression and lower levels of relationship quality, compared to similar people who marry instead. These and other studies support the idea that something about relationships themselves, and not just the people who select themselves into different versions of them, really produces benefits. These are known as **protection effects**: Something about the experience itself produces protective benefits or advantages. Here, it seems that something about marriage probably does give individuals some measure of protection that is not otherwise available to single or cohabiting individuals. Further evidence that good relationships benefit mental health comes from studies of couples therapy, in which unhappy couples *can* be randomly assigned to experiences designed to improve relationships. When it is effective in improving relationship quality, couples therapy also reduces depression (Gupta, Coyne, & Beach, 2003).

In what ways do intimate relationships confer protective advantages and promote happiness? Earlier we mentioned that when we examine relationships according to their status and quality, and the transitions into and out of partnerships, we see evidence that relationships matter and have an effect on well-being. But what are some of those advantages, exactly? How do we get from the relationship to subjective well-being? What is the substance of the links? The best available evidence suggests that people who are in good relationships have more money, more sex, and better health and that they are thus happier with their lives.

Relationships are likely to affect financial well-being. People who remain married throughout their life accumulate more wealth than those who never marry, cohabit, or divorce (e.g., Hirschl, Altobelli, & Rank, 2003; Lerman, 2002; Wilmoth & Koso, 2002). At the same time, people take a large financial hit when they divorce or dissolve a cohabiting relationship. Women are particularly vulnerable: Their household income drops 58 percent when they divorce and 33 percent when they end a cohabitation (Avellar & Smock, 2005). Compared to married women, their physical health deteriorates, and medical issues become another source of financial strain (Wickrama et al., 2006).

Intimate relationships, through the sexual experiences they provide, are also connected with individuals' overall sense of happiness. You may have heard this old joke: "What do married and single people have in common?" "Each thinks the other is having more sex." It turns out that only the single people are correct, as **TABLE 1.2** shows. Compared to people who are married or living in a sexual relationship lasting 1 month or more, noncohabiting people have sex less frequently. For example, more than 70 percent of noncohabitors

TABLE 1.2 Frequency of Sex for Men and Women Based on Relationship Status

	Not at all	A few times per year	A few times per month	2 or 3 times a week	4 or more times a week
Men					
Noncohabiting	23%	25%	26%	19%	7%
Cohabiting	0	8	36	40	16
Married	1	13	43	36	7
Women					
Noncohabiting	32	23	24	15	5
Cohabiting	1	8	35	42	14
Married	3	12	47	32	7

Source: These data come from interviews conducted with a representative sample of 3,432 English-speaking men and women between the ages of 18 and 59, as part of the National Health and Social Life Survey (Michael, Gagnon, Laumann, & Kolata, 1994, Table 8).

"I can't believe this is happening to me."

FIGURE 1.9 Intimate relationships and physical health. Intimate relationships are important because they affect our health and well-being. We can expect that this man's recovery will be slowed by the woman's selfish response to his illness.

have sex a few times per month or less, but 85 percent of the cohabiting and married couples have sex a few times per month or more (Michael, Gagnon, Laumann, & Kolata, 1994). The authors of this study later note: "Happiness with partnered sex is linked to happiness with life. We cannot say which comes first—general happiness or a good sex life—but the correlations are clear and striking. And happiness is clearly linked to having just one partner—which may not be too surprising since that is the situation that society smiles upon" (p. 130).

Intimate relationships are likely to affect physical health, as we saw in the study showing that people who were in better relationships lived longer following a heart attack than did those in relatively poor relationships (see Figure 1.6). Other examples are plentiful. People experiencing unresolved conflicts in their intimate relationships are more vulnerable to catching a common cold after being exposed to an experimentally administered virus (Cohen et al., 1998). Recovery from breast cancer is markedly slower among women in distressed relationships (Yang & Schuler, 2009). Cardiovascular, endocrine, and immune functioning all are affected by observed levels of conflict and hostility in intimate relationships (Kiecolt-Glaser et al., 1993, 1996). In fact, small, experimentally created blisters on the skin heal more slowly among people who are in hostile intimate relationships; this is because conflict reduces the amount of cytokines present at the wound site. Cytokines are chemical messengers that respond to various threats to our health, and low cytokine levels are thought to reflect the body's weakened ability to mount an immune response to the wound (Kiecolt-Glaser et al., 2005). Perhaps because of the links between intimacy and health, married people live longer lives than unmarried people do (e.g., Kaplan & Kronick, 2006), particularly when their relationships are rewarding (e.g., Gallo, Troxel, Matthews, & Kuller, 2003) (**FIGURE 1.9**).

Intimate Relationships Influence the Well-Being of Children

As infants, humans enter the world with remarkable potential but nearly absolute helplessness. To survive, and to realize this potential, infants depend on devoted caregivers to provide food, shelter, safety, stimulation, and affection (followed, eventually, by expensive orthodontics, a cell phone, and a laptop computer). Due to the infant's profound dependence and vulnerability, it is easy to see how the caregivers' intimate relationships affect the developing child in a variety of ways.

Just as relationship status, relationship quality, and relationship transitions relate to the subjective well-being of people in an intimate relationship, those factors appear to contribute to the well-being of their children. For example, the relationship status of parents is more influential than their race and their education in determining whether their children will experience severe poverty. Using nationally representative data collected from 4,800 U.S. households over a 25-year period, sociologists have demonstrated that 81 percent of children with unmarried parents experienced severe poverty, compared with 69 percent of black children and 63 percent of children whose head of household had completed fewer than 12 years of school (Rank & Hirschl, 1999). Biological children of cohabiting parents display more behavioral and emotional problems, and are less engaged in their schoolwork, compared to the biological children of married parents. These differences appear to occur partly because cohabiting parents have lower levels of subjective well-being (e.g., S. L. Brown, 2004). Combined with fewer financial resources, this probably interferes with effective parenting.

> " The child, like a sailor cast forth by the cruel waves, lies naked upon the ground, speechless, in need of every kind of vital support, as soon as nature has spilt him forth with throes from his mother's womb into the regions of light."
>
> —Lucretius, Roman poet and philosopher (99 BCE–55 BCE)

The quality of the parents' relationship is also related to their children's well-being. Children are upset, for example, by demonstrations of parental conflict. Such conflict decreases the children's feelings of emotional security and increases such behavior problems as acting out and displaying aggression with their peers (e.g., Cummings, Goeke-Morey, & Papp, 2003). Relationship conflicts can lead parents to withdraw emotionally from one another and from their parental duties, and children's behavior problems and problems at school appear to increase as a consequence (e.g., Sturge-Apple, Davies, & Cummings, 2006). Conflict between parents also appears to affect a wide range of biological systems in developing children, even reducing the quality of their sleep (El-Sheikh, Buckhalt, Mize, & Acebo, 2006), speeding up the onset of puberty (Belsky et al., 2007), and compromising their physical health (Repetti, Taylor, & Seeman, 2002; Troxel & Matthews, 2004).

Finally, the relationship transitions of caregivers affect their children. Children who are exposed to more transitions tend to display more behavioral problems (Fomby & Cherlin, 2007), for example. As families negotiate the transition to divorce, their income drops sharply and the parents become less available (resulting in less supervision at home, fewer restrictions on television watching, and lowered expectations for attending college; Hanson, McLanahan, & Thomson, 1998). Though children with divorced parents differ in several developmental domains from those without divorced parents, how well the child fares seems to be more closely related to the quality of the relationship before the divorce than the divorce itself (e.g., Cherlin et al., 1991; Sun, 2001). This point helps us to see how some relationship transitions can benefit children: Child well-being improves following divorce, for example, if the parents' marriage before the divorce was marked by high levels of tension and conflict (Amato, 2003).

The bottom line here is simple: Children rely heavily on caregivers to help them make their way in the world, and the caregivers' experiences in their intimate relationships can affect their willingness and capacity to give their children the care they need. Before fully embracing this conclusion, however, we must touch on three further questions.

First, do the effects of intimate relationships on child well-being disappear as children develop through adolescence and into adulthood? No. The family circumstances children encounter will influence the way they manage their own intimate relationships decades later. For example, people whose parents had more troubled marriages tend to complete fewer years of education, have more distant relationships with their parents, feel more tension as parents themselves, and experience more marital problems of their own. In turn, they tend to raise children who grow up and follow in their footsteps (Amato & Cheadle, 2005).

Second, do patterns like these occur merely because family members often share genes—some of which (e.g., an innate tendency to be hostile) could create a range of difficulties for anyone possessing them? Stated differently, are selection effects operating to exaggerate the effects of intimate relationships in one generation on the well-being of children in the next generation? The answer to this question turns out to be no, according to studies using the children of identical twins to examine the effects of parental divorce on their children's emotional difficulties (D'Onofrio et al., 2006) and tendencies to later divorce (D'Onofrio et al., 2007). Analyses of this kind show that parental divorce really does increase the likelihood of emotional difficulties and divorce tendencies, beyond the effects of the genes shared by parents and offspring.

> " The family is the cornerstone of our society. More than any other force it shapes the attitude, the hopes, the ambitions, and the values of the child. And when the family collapses it is the children that are usually damaged. When it happens on a massive scale, the community itself is crippled."
>
> —President Lyndon B. Johnson; Commencement Address at Howard University, June 4, 1965

This brings us to our third question: To what extent is a child's fate determined by his or her caregivers' intimate relationships? The answer is incomplete, but we know that having a divorced parent increases one's chance of divorcing by about 10 percent to 20 percent beyond the level experienced by children from intact families (e.g., see Hetherington & Kelly, 2002). This is not a trivial risk by any means, but it does suggest that most children with divorced parents can go on to have relationships that are indistinguishable from those of children who have intact parents.

Intimate Relationships Form the Fabric of Society

You probably think about your intimate relationships as private rather than public affairs directly pertaining only to you and your partner, or at most to your friends and families. After all, it is hard to see how our intimate relationships affect anyone beyond our closest social circle, and it is not immediately obvious how we would be affected by others' intimate relationships outside this circle.

To what extent are intimate relationships truly private? Consider these examples. Late at night, a couple in your apartment building have a series of loud, physical confrontations—leaving you and your neighbors feeling unsafe and taking the police away from handling other crimes. Throughout the school year, a few of your child's classmates are upset over their parents' arguments and imminent divorces; these children distract the teacher, disrupt the class, and reduce the quality of their education. A dorm mate of yours, despondent because he is unable to find a steady girlfriend, gets drunk, drives through town, and accidentally kills a pedestrian. Or, more optimistically, your happy neighbors might live longer and be less of a burden on the health care system; or they might raise children who finish their schooling rather than drop out and engage in petty crimes; or they might generate a higher income and thus pay more taxes than they would if they were divorced, thus contributing to the greater good. Added up over countless children, countless relationships, and countless transitions between relationships, effects such as these accumulate, helping us see that intimate relationships are inextricably woven into the fabric—and welfare—of our society.

Social control theory helps explain this link between intimate relationships and the broader social impact of individuals' actions (e.g., Hirschi, 1969). According to this view, social relationships organize and regulate how individuals behave, such that fewer, weaker, or poorer relationships increase the occurrence of deviant behavior. This regulatory effect occurs because relationships encourage individuals to internalize and abide by societal norms, in part because people incur personal costs and sanctions when these norms are violated. Though we think naturally of relationships during childhood as those used to teach cultural rules and practices, intimate relationships in adulthood also affect whether people follow or break laws or social conventions. Alcohol, marijuana, and other drug use, for example, is known to fluctuate with changes in relationship status (Fleming, White, & Catalano, 2010), and these changes apparently are not just due to spending less time with a deviant peer group (e.g., Maume, Ousey, & Beaver, 2005). FIGURE 1.10 shows how cocaine use drops as people enter into more committed relationships and increases when committed relationships are dissolved (Bachman, Wadsworth, O'Malley, Johnston, & Schulenberg, 1997). Divorce even reduces the likelihood that people will vote in an election—probably because divorce also increases residential mobility (Kern, 2010).

Criminal behavior provides another example of how participation in intimate relationships can affect the society in which we live. Criminologists are particularly interested in understanding the complex process by which

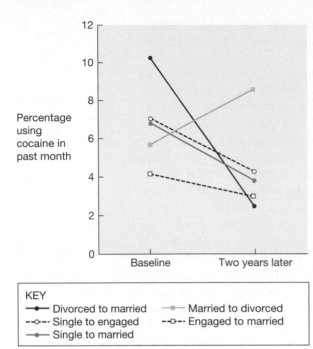

Percentage using cocaine in past month

KEY
- ●— Divorced to married
- --○-- Single to engaged
- ●— Single to married
- ■— Married to divorced
- --□-- Engaged to married

FIGURE 1.10 Intimate relationships and adherence to social norms. Data on cocaine use collected from about 33,000 men show how relationship transitions are related to deviant behaviors. Cocaine use increases only among men who transition from being married to being divorced. In contrast, cocaine use decreases as people become more committed in their relationships, particularly for divorced men who remarry. Results for women are similar but less dramatic because they tend to use less cocaine than men do.

offenders desist, or decrease the number and severity of crimes they commit. In one study of desistance, researchers observed 500 males—all of whom were sent to reform school during adolescence for repeated delinquent behavior in the 1940s—for most of their lives (Laub, Nagin, & Sampson, 1998). Why did some men reduce or stop their criminal activity when others continued? Intimate relationships turn out to figure prominently in this process, so that men who were more likely to marry, more likely to have good marriages, more likely to stay married, and more likely to have stable jobs were more likely to decrease their levels of criminal activity. Further analyses showed that it was the quality of the marriages rather than their mere presence that most influenced criminal offending, and that other plausible factors measured during childhood and adolescence (such as intelligence, personality, poverty, parental crime) could not explain these findings (Laub et al., 1998).

Ultimately, when relationships dissolve, the accumulated costs to society are high. Earlier you learned that the financial well-being of adults and children suffers when relationships dissolve. The families themselves bear some of these costs, but especially for people with lower incomes, tax-supported state and federal programs are often tapped for assistance. To our knowledge, no study has attempted to follow a representative group of divorcing or dissolving couples to assess the immediate and long-term costs of these transitions. One study conducted in Utah suggests that each divorce costs taxpayers approximately $30,000 in the form of welfare, child care, food stamps, and similar expenses (Schramm, 2006). Nearly one million divorces occurred in the United States in 2005 (Munson & Sutton, 2006), so this is a tidy sum—or as politicians like to say, a billion dollars here, a billion dollars there, and pretty soon you are talking about real money. Our key point in presenting these figures is not to assert that dissolving a relationship is uniformly bad—few of us would oppose a divorce in which either partner was physically or verbally abusive, for example. Instead, we wish to emphasize that our intimate relationships, whether they function well or poorly, are the strands and knots that comprise the very fabric of our society (as illustrated in **BOX 1.2**).

BOX 1.2 SPOTLIGHT ON . . .

Intimate Relationships and Social Conformity

Sociologist Andrea Leverentz interviewed several women at a halfway house for female ex-offenders in Illinois (2006, pp. 477–478). Among them was a woman named Linette:

Linette met her fiancé Chad when she was in a work-release program. During the interviews, they were living together in his mother's house.

She described him as "*a big help. He's always trying to understand what's going on. He's a caretaker.*"

Chad said, "*I've been into stuff myself. We both had done things . . . I'm getting too old; I woke up and realized it ain't no place to be. Now, I go to work and I come home. If I go out, we both go.*" He described Linette as "*a beautiful person, she's kind and honest. She's never told me a lie, as far as I know.*"

In talking to each of them and watching them interact with each other, they did seem to have a strong and positive relationship. Linette may have served as a direct source of social control for Chad: he did not go out, other than to work, without her. Chad was a source of emotional and financial support for Linette. To a certain extent, he also may have served as a source of direct social control, but because she was unemployed and therefore home alone during the day, she had more opportunities to go out without him (if she chose to do so). . . . They each provided a stake in conformity, as they struggled to get their lives in order, get their own apartment, and regain custody of the child they shared.

This case and the earlier study of desistance (Laub, Nagin, & Sampson, 1998) demonstrate the power of interdependence as a force in intimate relationships. They also make it clear that interdependence in high-quality relationships can encourage partners to guide one another toward socially sanctioned lifestyles.

MAIN POINTS

>> Six key reasons support the contention that intimate relationships are an important and even essential topic of study.

>> Intimate relationships reflect an evolved and therefore biological capacity to nurture others.

>> They are universal across all known cultures.

>> Intimate relationships expand our repertoire of emotional experiences in positive and negative directions.

>> They can affect the physical and emotional health of relationship partners.

>> Intimate relationships can influence the physical and emotional well-being of children.

>> They can affect society at large by discouraging crime and promoting conformity to social norms.

>> Intimate relationships are fundamental to who we are as humans and pervasive in their effects on us and those around us.

The Critical Question: Why Do Relationships Sometimes Thrive and Sometimes Falter?

When I think back to Corsica, I remember the stony mountains and the brilliant sea and the polished blues of the sky, but I also recall a creeping sensation of emptiness. Throughout our idyll there, Maureen and I were pretending to enjoy each other's company. Things had turned bad with extraordinary quickness; eighteen months was all, and nothing truly monstrous had occurred during that time. A few arguments, a few grievances that went unaddressed, a sulky mutual withdrawal, and suddenly we found that the air had been sucked out of the marriage. . . .

We had both been aware of this situation but obliquely. It was embedded in the routine of our lives, which made it, if not unnoticeable, at least easy to avoid. In Corsica, with its dazzling light and punishing heat, its salt and sand and casual nudity and freshly pressed rosé wine, we were forced by the contrast to recognize how thoroughly cold the marriage had become. I realized for the first time that I had no idea why I had gotten married.

—From John Taylor's *Falling*, in which he recounts the decline of his marriage (1999, p. 106)

Once we accept the possibility that the presence and quality of our intimate bonds are broadly influential, to the benefit and detriment of ourselves and others, we are confronted immediately with an important question: Why are intimate relationships sometimes a source of great compassion and comfort, when at other times they evoke only frustration, disappointment, and despair? This question is particularly apparent in the quote above by John Taylor, focusing on why a certain relationship can be more fulfilling at one time than at another. Did Taylor have similar doubts about why he married his wife on the day he got married? Perhaps, but it seems more likely that he, like most newlyweds, felt optimistic and confident that day. And he, like most newlyweds, no doubt wanted to maintain that optimism, knowing the pain he and his family would feel upon losing it. Indeed, he seems depressed by the change that did occur—yet it happened anyway. Taylor's experiences, like those of countless other people, help us frame an essential mystery of intimate relationships: Why do they change, despite the deepest and most fervent desires of committed individuals to maintain their initial feelings of fulfillment and hope?

Relationship quality, or people's evaluative judgments of their relationship as being relatively good or bad, is what leads people to deepen their involvement with each other, or feel more or less fulfilled, or want to end the relationship altogether (FIGURE 1.11). This book is devoted, therefore, to discussing the wide range of factors that influence judgments of relationship quality and how those judgments change over time. By studying relationship quality

FIGURE 1.11 Happy compared to what? Partners may have different perspectives on the same intimate relationship, and those perspectives may change. To truly assess the intimate relationship in this cartoon, it would be useful to ask what the woman's score was 6 months before. We would interpret her score differently, for example, if her previous score was 1 star rather than 4 stars.

in this way, we can hope to answer the critical question to most people involved in an intimate relationship: Why do relationships sometimes thrive and sometimes falter?

What do we need to know to truly answer this question? Scholars of all kinds seek answers by developing specialized techniques and research methods that allow them to test their hunches, hypotheses, and theories that pull isolated facts together into sophisticated explanations. In the next two chapters, you will learn a lot more about the most valuable methods and theories used by scholars studying intimate relationships.

MAIN POINTS

>> Relationship quality—how satisfied people are with their relationships—is the central focus of research on relationships.

>> Because variability in relationships has profound consequences for our health and well-being, relationship scientists strive to know how relationship quality varies for different people, for different relationships, and at different times in the same relationship.

>> In this book we consider various theories and research studies to address one fundamental question: Why do relationships sometimes thrive and sometimes falter?

CONCLUSION

Albert Einstein's quirks and idiosyncrasies as an intimate partner served as the starting point for this chapter, allowing us to suggest that even the world's smartest man could not solve the mysteries of human intimacy. This chapter opens up the rich and fascinating topic of human intimacy by identifying the criteria for defining an intimate relationship, and by presenting six key reasons for conducting a careful, detailed study of the subject. Some of these reasons involve inherent properties of relationships themselves. Intimacy and the formation of relationships are universal human experiences, for example, and both contribute directly to the survival of our species. Other reasons involve the consequences of relationships for our own health and happiness and for that of any children we might raise. Because vitally important aspects of our lives and communities rise and fall with the quality of our intimate bonds, explaining why some relationships thrive while others falter is the single greatest question that scholars in this field can address.

How do we generate the information we need to answer important questions about intimate relationships? Maybe Einstein has something to offer here after all. Central to Einstein's success was his use of *gedanken experiments*, or thought experiments, in which he posed seemingly absurd questions and then contemplated their implications. "What would the world look like if I could ride on a beam of light?" he asked. Though few of us can even approximate Einstein's brilliance, we all can see that understanding any set of complex phenomena involves asking well-crafted questions and striving to answer them with rigor and precision. Relationship scientists are no less bound by these challenges. In the next chapter we will see how careful assessments and sensible research designs are the only way we can gain systematic access to the nature of human intimacy.

2

Tools of Relationship Science

The Advice Peddlers

Every day, newspaper columnists, religious leaders, politicians, teachers, songwriters, family members, and counselors offer their advice on love and how to keep it alive. Falling in love may be the most natural thing in the world, but many people seem to think we need their expertise and guidance to learn how to do it right.

Books full of wisdom about intimate relationships constitute a multimillion-dollar business, with countless new books on love and intimacy published each year (FIGURE 2.1). A glance at the titles, online or in stores, reveals an unceasing concern with common issues about love: *How to Be a Great Lover; Difficult Conversations: How to Discuss What Matters Most; Cracking the Love Code; Getting the Love You Want.* Each book claims to have the answers, but questions about love never go away.

For people who dislike self-help books, therapists and counselors offer their own views. Over the past several decades, problems or disappointments in intimate relationships have been the leading reasons Americans seek counseling (Swindle, Heller, Pescosolido, & Kikuzawa, 2000; Veroff, Kulka, & Douvan, 1981). Even governments are getting involved with teaching people about their love life. In 2006, the U.S. Department of Health and Human Services allocated $750 million to fund the Healthy Marriage Initiative, a federal plan to promote relationship education programs in communities across the country. From the bookstore to the therapist's office to the classroom, helping people with their intimate relationships is big business—plenty of people are willing to offer their opinions, and plenty more are willing to pay for them.

Given the dizzying array of advice sources, it would be comforting if all these voices could reach some consensus about relationships and how they function. Unfortunately, those who write about love frequently disagree. For example, in *The Rules* (1995), a best-selling guide to finding a romantic partner, dating coaches Ellen Fein and Sherrie

33

FIGURE 2.1 Hundreds of books offer advice about intimate relationships. How do you know which advice to follow?

Schneider state that men are attracted to women who pose a challenge. They advise women to suppress every sign of reciprocating a man's interest, with rules such as "Don't Talk to a Man First" and "Rarely Return His Calls." But psychotherapist Katherine Woodward Thomas disagrees. In *Calling in "The One": 7 Weeks to Attract the Love of Your Life* (2004), she argues that the first step toward finding love is learning to love yourself. Instead of rules to follow, she presents self-affirmations and recommends that readers train themselves to be open to receiving love whenever it comes. For a person hoping to meet a life partner, these books offer quite different approaches, each one insisting that its method really works.

The cacophony of conflicting advice does not stop once partners find each other. In their best-selling book *The Unexpected Legacy of Divorce* (2000), psychologist Judith Wallerstein and her colleagues describe the lasting pain children experience after their parents' marriage ends—even into those children's adult lives. Concluding that the consequences of divorce are enduring and negative for children, the authors suggest that couples who

care about their children should strongly consider staying together. Yet when psychologist E. Mavis Hetherington and her colleagues examined the same topic 2 years later, in their own best-selling book *For Better or For Worse: Divorce Reconsidered* (2002), they reached a different conclusion. While some adult children in their study expressed pain, many did not. In fact, most participants said what really harmed them as kids was being exposed to conflict between their parents. Concluding that the consequences of divorce are complex and varied, these authors suggest that couples who are truly unhappy together may owe it to their children to end the marriage. (We will say more about this in Chapter 6.) For a husband and wife suffering at the end of their marriage, the differences between these viewpoints are stark indeed—and may have real consequences for the decisions they make.

It would be nice if we could just agree to disagree about such matters. However, if we are going to offer useful advice about better and worse ways to engage in intimate relationships, then all competing points of view cannot be equally true. To develop strategies that help people improve their relationships, we need some way of determining which statements about love and relationships are right, which are incomplete, and which are just plain wrong.

QUESTIONS

How can reasonable people decide which claims to take seriously and which ones to doubt? The ancient Greeks thought they could determine truth through careful discussion. Others measure the truth of any assertion by comparing it to a religious code. Still others decide what is true by asking themselves what "feels right." While these may be valid paths for individuals to follow, each approach can be problematic when used as a basis for advice to large groups of people, or as a foundation for social policy. After all, what feels right to one person may not feel right to another. Before advice about relationships can be taken seriously and implemented widely, we need a system for evaluating claims about how relationships work, and a way to determine which claims are true for most people and which are not.

What does that system look like? How does one begin to study phenomena as complex as intimate relationships? Biologists have their microscopes; astronomers have their telescopes. What tools have relationship researchers developed, and how are they used? How do they arrive at conclusions about intimate relationships? To the extent that even researchers often disagree, how can an interested observer tell the difference between good and bad research?

Asking and Answering Questions

Good research starts with good questions. Intimate relationships provide an especially fertile field for good research because, even after thousands of years of thinking and writing about love, so much about relationships remains puzzling. Often we need look no further than our own lives for good research questions. For example, most people have experienced losing control during a heated argument with a close friend or romantic partner and later wondered, "Why did I say that?" As we will see in Chapter 8, researchers have taken this question from the personal to the general, investigating why partners and lovers who mean well can behave badly.

Good questions also come from thoughtful, even skeptical, consideration of popular wisdom. Few areas of social life are more talked about than intimate relationships, yet much of the common wisdom is contradictory. For instance, couples considering whether to pursue a long-distance relationship may be confused by the two most common clichés about distance and relationships. Does "absence make the heart grow fonder"? Or, for an intimate relationship, does "out of sight" lead to "out of mind"? In Chapter 11 we will see how researchers have explored such contradictions by investigating when different commonly held pieces of wisdom are likely to apply.

Relationship science is essentially a set of tools for answering these questions. Social scientists wonder about what true love is, how to resolve conflicts effectively, and how to make relationships last. But they differ from all the others who write about intimate relationships in that they determine which claims about relationships are true by systematically observing and then identifying the claim that best describes what actually happens. Research on relationships is like research on chemistry, astronomy, physics, or any other science. Our primary tool for evaluating competing claims to the truth is the **scientific method**, a set of procedures for making predictions, gathering data, and comparing the validity of competing claims about the world (FIGURE 2.2). These procedures are not foolproof—as we shall see. In the long run, though, science tends to be self-correcting because the scientific method demands that we remain skeptical about all claims to the truth, especially our own. As our observations of the world around us change or grow more sophisticated, we must reject the claims that no longer match our observations and advance new claims. Thus the continuous process of

Theory:
A general
explanation for a
phenomenon

Hypothesis:
A concrete statement
about how concepts
should be associated
in the world

Analyze the
Data and
Draw Conclusions:
Should the hypothesis
be rejected?

Operationalization:
The translation of
abstract concepts
into concrete terms

Design the Study:
Correlational?
Longitudinal?
Experimental?
Archival?

Choose a
Measurement
Strategy:
Self-reports?
Observations?

▌ FIGURE 2.2 **The scientific method.**

conducting research provides a way of resolving conflicts between the conclusions reached by different people and sorting out where the truth is likely to lie.

Three Kinds of Questions

Three different kinds of questions motivate most research on intimate relationships. These questions correspond to three different kinds of research goals.

The first kind of question focuses on *description* and asks: What happens? Many of the initial questions researchers ask about intimate relationships are of this type. For example, which States in the U.S. have the highest and lowest divorce rates? How prevalent is physical violence between intimate partners? Who is more likely to initiate a breakup, a man or a woman? Addressing descriptive questions helps scientists identify the nature and scope of the problems being studied, so it is a critical first step for research.

The second kind of question focuses on *prediction* and asks: When does it happen? More specifically, predictive research asks whether knowing something about a relationship at one point in time can help us know what the relationship will be like at some future time. In other fields, scientists use predictive research to identify people likely to contract diseases, commit violent crimes, or graduate from college. For intimate relationships, many people want to predict whether couples who start out together happily will stay together happily in the future. The results of such research may help identify—before they become unhappy—couples who may need extra assistance with their relationships.

The third kind of question focuses on *explanation* and asks: Why does it happen? Predicting whether a relationship will stay happy is not the same thing as understanding why relationships deteriorate or remain satisfying. Though research focused on prediction helps identify couples who may be at risk, research focused on explanation can point out ways that relationships reach those outcomes and methods of changing or improving them. For example, individuals whose parents divorced are at substantially greater risk of divorcing themselves. The research describing this association (e.g., Gahler, Hong, & Bernhardt, 2009; Wolfinger, 2005) asked a predictive question: Does knowing that someone's parents divorced allow us to predict whether that person will also experience a divorce as an adult? If we wanted to help the children of divorce reduce their risk, however, we would have to go beyond prediction to explanation, asking: *Why* are the children of divorced parents at greater risk of getting divorced? There are several possible answers. Perhaps being exposed to the marital conflict that often precedes divorce deprives children of models of successful problem-solving behaviors. If so, then to reduce their risk they might attend classes in effective relationship communication before they get married. Or perhaps the economic and emotional hardships that can follow a divorce affect children's academic and professional achievement. If so, then programs to assist these children would have to start much earlier, and would target not only relationship skills but also academics and psychological adjustment. Addressing questions about mechanisms can help point out specific behaviors and situations leading couples to be closer to, or more distant from, each other. Thus, research aimed at explanation ideally provides the support for interventions designed to help people improve or change their relationships.

Theories and Hypotheses

Armed with a provocative and important question, researchers usually start their search for answers with some idea of what those answers might look like. Where do they come from? Figure 2.2 has an important clue. Identifying the possible answers to be evaluated requires a **theory**, or a general explanation of a phenomenon. A theory is a starting point, directing the researcher toward considering aspects of the world that might help answer the question at hand. The elements of a theory are often referred to as **variables** because scientists tend to theorize about aspects of the world that *vary* across individuals or across time. So, for example, height is a variable because different people have different heights, and age is a variable because even the same person will have different ages across time.

Even researchers who deny starting out with a guiding theory usually do have one. The variables the researcher focuses on are clues. For example, suppose we are interested in how the quality of people's intimate relationships affects their physical health. One theory might adopt a psychological perspective by suggesting that intimate relationships provide partners with crucial social and emotional support, which in turn keeps couples in good relationships happier and healthier. If this were our theory, we might conduct research the way psychologist Tracey Revenson does: by studying the specific ways couples help each other through chronic illness and examining the implications of those behaviors for managing pain (e.g., Revenson, 1994). An alternative theory might adopt a biological perspective, proposing that positive interactions with a loved one improve health through their effects on levels of stress hormones and immune functioning. This would lead us to conduct research the way clinical psychologist Janice Kiecolt-Glaser and her students do: by measuring levels of cortisol in couples before and after they have discussed difficult issues in their relationship (Robles & Kiecolt-Glaser,

2003). An initial theory thus shapes research by giving the researcher a rough idea of the kinds of variables to measure and the kinds of associations to expect. (We will review some of the most influential theories of intimate relationships in Chapter 3.)

One measure of a good theory is that it is **falsifiable**; that is, it suggests testable predictions that can be confirmed or disconfirmed through systematic observation. In other words, the best theories suggest the very kind of research that might lead the theory to be revised or even rejected altogether. The quality of being falsifiable makes a theory useful. Consider, for example, the theory that the ability to have a satisfying relationship originates in our relationships with our parents during infancy and early childhood, and that better early relationships lead to more satisfying adult relationships (e.g., Shaver, Hazan, & Bradshaw, 1988). That is a falsifiable theory. With enough time and patience, we could examine people's relationships with their parents early in life and then see whether the people with better relationships as children also had better relationships as adults. If they did, we would have confidence in our theory. If they did not, we might have less confidence, and we would be motivated to keep doing research to see where we went wrong. In fact, children with more secure relationships with their parents do grow up to have more satisfying relationships as adults (Flouri & Buchanan, 2002).

> " Insofar as a scientific statement speaks about reality, it must be falsifiable; and insofar as it is not falsifiable, it does not speak about reality."
>
> —Karl Raimund Popper, *The Logic of Scientific Discovery* (2002, p. 316)

In contrast, consider the theory that intimate relationships work out if two people are "destined" to be together (i.e., the "Hollywood romance" theory of relationship success). No conceivable observation would be able to falsify this theory. If two people stay together, the theory explains that they were indeed destined to do so; and if the same two people break up, the theory explains that they were not. Because it accounts for events only after they occur, the theory makes no predictions and suggests no research. This is not a falsifiable theory. It is useless for helping us describe, predict, or explain what happens in real relationships.

The specific predictions suggested by a theory are called **hypotheses**. While a theory provides a broad explanation that directs attention toward particular variables, a hypothesis is a concrete prediction—arising from the theory—about how different variables are likely to be associated. So, in explaining the association between relationship quality and health discussed earlier, the theory that social support makes people healthier leads to the specific prediction that couples who are better able to support each other after a serious illness should experience fewer symptoms and a higher quality of life than couples who are less able to do so (Revenson, 1994). The theory that interactions with loved ones affect stress hormones suggests the specific prediction that, compared to couples who deal with problems more effectively, partners who are more hostile during arguments should have higher levels of stress hormone in their bloodstreams afterward (Kiecolt-Glaser et al., 1996). What makes these hypotheses useful? They can be confirmed or disconfirmed through systematic observations—that is, they are falsifiable. (In fact, both of these hypotheses have been tested and confirmed.) Thus, although a program of research generally addresses a specific theory, any particular study tends to examine the evidence for specific hypotheses rather than the theory as a whole. If the research results do not confirm the specific hypothesis, then the hypothesis is rejected and our confidence in the theory is weakened.

Researchers are often quite fond of their hypotheses. If those hypotheses are not supported in a particular study, that's usually not enough to get the researcher to give up on a promising idea. This is why the scientific method values **replication**, the repetition of research that examines the same questions multiple times. A single result can be a fluke, but a result we can observe almost every time we look for it is one that we take more seriously. As research results accumulate, theories without supported hypotheses are revised or abandoned. If a specific hypothesis is confirmed, then our confidence in the theory grows. Theories suggesting hypotheses that are confirmed repeatedly are more likely to be accepted, discussed, and taught—at least until new questions and observations call for revisions of those theories.

MAIN POINTS

>> Good research starts with a good question.

>> Interesting and important questions can focus on describing a phenomenon, predicting an outcome, or explaining why an outcome comes about.

>> The starting point for answering these questions is a theory, a general idea of how a phenomenon works.

>> A researcher draws from a general theory to make specific hypotheses, or predictions about how aspects of a phenomenon are likely to be associated.

>> Scientific research addresses theories and hypotheses that are falsifiable; that is, it would be possible for systematic observations to prove them wrong.

>> Through replication, in which the same results are observed repeatedly in multiple studies, researchers gradually develop confidence in theories that accumulate consistent support and reject theories that do not.

Choosing a Measurement Strategy

One difference between theories in the social sciences (like psychology) and theories in the physical sciences (like chemistry) is that social scientists tend to theorize about variables that are intangible. Relationship research in particular addresses questions about abstract ideas like love, conflict, support, and trust. These ideas, central to thinking about intimate relationships, are known as **psychological constructs**. They are all products of human thought—as opposed to things like heat, molecules, or planets, which would exist whether humans thought about them or not. Calling love a "construct" does not mean it is imaginary. Clearly, love exists; and as a common human experience, it has real and undeniable effects on the world. But love lacks measurable physical attributes like mass or temperature, so testing predictions about love and other constructs raises some unique challenges for relationship researchers—namely, how can we measure abstract ideas?

The short answer is that we cannot, at least not directly. Instead, testing predictions about psychological constructs requires researchers to link abstract ideas to something concrete that can be observed or measured. This step of the scientific method is called **operationalization**: the translation of an abstract construct into concrete terms in order to test predictions about that construct. When psychologist Zick Rubin (1970) decided to study love, he first developed his classic Love Scale (TABLE 2.1). This instrument asks respondents to indicate their agreement with 13 statements about their feelings for their current partner by circling a number from 1 (disagree strongly) to 9 (agree strongly). The sum of those ratings is not, of course, the same thing as partners' love for each other. Rather, the ratings

TABLE 2.1 The Love Scale

Answer the following questions concerning your attitude toward your current romantic partner. Rate on a scale of 1 (indicating strong disagreement) to 9 (indicating strong agreement).

1. If my partner were feeling badly, my first duty would be to cheer him/her up. _____

2. I feel that I can confide in my partner about virtually everything. _____

3. I find it easy to ignore my partner's faults. _____

4. I would do almost anything for my partner. _____

5. I feel very possessive toward my partner. _____

6. If I could never be with my partner, I would feel miserable. _____

7. If I were lonely, my first thought would be to seek my partner out. _____

8. One of my primary concerns is my partner's welfare. _____

9. I would forgive my partner for practically anything. _____

10. I feel responsible for my partner's well-being. _____

11. When I am with my partner, I spend a good deal of time just looking at him/her. _____

12. I would greatly enjoy being confided in by my partner. _____

13. It would be hard for me to get along without my partner. _____

Source: Rubin, 1970.

are an operationalization of partners' love. That operationalization is useful only to the extent that people who are more in love with their partners in fact indicate more agreement with the items on the scale, and people less in love with their partners indicate less agreement. Indeed, research using the Love Scale has found, in studies spanning nearly 40 years, that people who score higher on the Love Scale behave in the ways you would expect people who are more in love with their partners to behave (e.g., they are more likely to end up marrying their partners and to stay married 15 years later; Hill & Peplau, 1998). By thinking about operationalization in this way, you can see that when researchers test hypotheses about psychological constructs like love, *they never actually measure the constructs themselves*. Research can only measure operationalizations of constructs.

If researchers must rely on their operationalizations to learn about constructs like love, trust, and commitment, then the quality of those operationalizations matters a great deal. Recognizing this, researchers have coined the phrase **construct validity** to describe how well an operationalization represents a particular construct. When an operationalization's construct validity is high, the specific thing a researcher is measuring (e.g., a numerical rating) is an excellent signifier of the construct being studied (e.g., feelings of love). When an operationalization is low in construct validity, the specific thing being studied is not a good representation of the construct.

Construct validity is something researchers argue about. The ways of operationalizing a given construct are limitless, and we have no clear rules about which ones are best. For example, when psychologist John Lydon and his colleagues wanted to study how the presence of an attractive alternative partner affects commitment to a current partner (a psychological construct), they had several options. To be on the safe side, they tried different operationalizations over the course of multiple studies (Lydon, Menzies-Toman, Burton, & Bell, 2008). In one study, they simply asked participants to respond to the question, "How committed are you to your relationship?" on a 5-point scale (1 = not very; 5 = very). In another study, the team took a more indirect approach by asking participants to complete a series of word fragments that had two possible answers, one relating to commitment and one not. One of the fragments, for example, was *de – – ted*, which could be completed to form *devoted* (a commitment word) or *deleted* (not a commitment word). The researchers viewed the number of times participants responded with the commitment word rather than the unrelated word as an operationalization of how much they were thinking about their current partners. Does either of these operationalizations perfectly capture the idea of commitment to a partner? Probably not. But it is noteworthy that, across both operationalizations, the results were consistent: Men were less committed after being approached by an attractive alternative, but women were more committed. In this case, the researchers recognized the limitations of each specific operationalization and strengthened their research by ensuring that the results held true no matter which operationalization they used. In other cases, some types of operationalizations are clearly more or less appropriate for different kinds of constructs. We examine the advantages and disadvantages of different approaches in the next sections.

Self-Report Measures

One straightforward way to measure people's experiences in their relationships is simply to ask them. Indeed, **self-reports** from partners—their own descriptions and evaluations of their experiences—are the most commonly used source of data in research on intimate relationships. In every case, a self-report is an operationalization of a construct; but in some cases, the operationalization is more obvious than others. The simplest kind of self-report is a direct question. For example, if a researcher asks, "Have you ever been in an intimate relationship?" an answer of yes or no represents an easy operationalization of relationship experience. Researchers also use direct questions to measure more complicated ideas. For example, when psychologists Jeffry Simpson and Steven Gangestad began studying sexual behavior, they recognized that people vary in their willingness to contemplate sex outside the context of a committed intimate relationship. This construct is known as **sociosexuality**. Because these researchers believed that sociosexuality would likely predict a range of important behaviors, they developed the Sociosexual Orientation Inventory to measure it (Simpson & Gangestad, 1991). TABLE 2.2 presents selected items from that inventory, and as you can see, there is nothing mysterious or tricky about it. To find out how comfortable people are with casual sex, the researchers came right out and asked.

Sometimes, however, researchers are interested in a construct that people may not often think about directly. In these cases, researchers typically avoid direct questions. Instead, they ask partners to report on specific information the researcher believes to indicate some construct. For example, TABLE 2.3 presents a few statements from the Marital Locus of Control Scale developed by P. C. Miller, H. M. Lefcourt, and E. E. Ware (1983). This scale was designed to measure the extent to which spouses feel they can affect events in the marriage and bring about favorable outcomes. Researchers have examined this construct because it may play an important role in the way partners resolve conflicts—specifically, partners low in feelings of control may be more willing to abandon the relationship when confronted with difficulties. Upon reading the statements in Table 2.3, you may notice that none of them directly asks: Do you feel like you have control over events in your marriage? Instead, when researchers use this type of self-report measure, partners are asked to read and indicate how much they agree or disagree with various statements that are thought to reflect the underlying idea. The sum of the ratings is taken as an operationalization of that idea—in this case, the idea that partners feel they have control over outcomes in their marriage.

The Sociosexual Orientation Inventory, the Marital Locus of Control Scale, and other survey instruments like them are known as **fixed-response scales**

TABLE 2.2 The Sociosexual Orientation Inventory

Please answer all of the following questions honestly. For the questions dealing with behavior, *write* your answers in the blank spaces provided. For the questions dealing with thoughts and attitudes, *circle* the appropriate number on the scales provided.

1. With how many different partners have you had sex (sexual intercourse) within the past year? _____

2. How many different partners do you foresee yourself having sex with during the next five years? (Please give a *specific, realistic* estimate.) _____

3. With how many different partners have you had sex on *one and only one* occasion? _____

4. How often do you fantasize about having sex with someone other than your current dating partner? (Circle one.)

> 1. never
>
> 2. once every two or three months
>
> 3. once a month
>
> 4. once every two weeks
>
> 5. once a week
>
> 6. a few times each week
>
> 7. nearly every day
>
> 8. at least once a day

5. Sex without love is OK. (Circle one.)

> I strongly disagree 1 2 3 4 5 6 7 8 9 I strongly agree

6. I can imagine myself being comfortable and enjoying "casual" sex with different partners. (Circle one.)

> I strongly disagree 1 2 3 4 5 6 7 8 9 I strongly agree

7. I would have to be closely attached to someone (both emotionally and psychologically) before I could feel comfortable and fully enjoy having sex with him or her. (Circle one.)

> I strongly disagree 1 2 3 4 5 6 7 8 9 I strongly agree

How to Score:

1. Multiply the number in Item 1 by 5 = _____

2. To ensure that Item 2 does not have disproportionate influence when constructing the composite, the maximum value of Item 2 should be limited to 30 partners foreseen in college samples. The value in Item 2 is = _____

3. Multiply the number in Item 3 by 5 = _____

4. Multiply the number in Item 4 by 4 = _____

5. Add Item 5, Item 6, and the inverse of Item 7 (i.e., 1 = 9, 2 = 8, 3 = 7, etc.) and multiply the sum by 2 = _____

6. Add together the resulting values of lines 1–5 to get your score.

Source: Adapted from Simpson & Gangestad, 1991.

TABLE 2.3 **Items from the Marital Locus of Control Scale**

Please indicate the extent to which you agree or disagree with the following statements, using a scale of 1 ("Disagree strongly") to 5 ("Agree strongly").

1. Putting effort into the relationship will practically guarantee a successful marriage.

2. Difficulties with my spouse start with chance remarks. (R)

3. When things begin to go rough in my marriage I can see that I had a part in it.

4. I can always bring about a reconciliation when my spouse and I have an argument.

5. If my marriage were a long, happy one I'd say that I must just be very lucky. (R)

6. At times, there doesn't seem to be any way out of a disagreement with my spouse. (R)

7. Couples who don't run into any marital problems at some point have simply been very lucky. (R)

8. My spouse's moods are often mysterious to me—I have little idea about what may set them off. (R)

9. There are always things I can do that will help end an argument with my spouse and leave us feeling better.

Note: The original scale consists of 35 items. An (R) indicates that scores for that item are reversed before being added into the total.
Source: Adapted from Miller, Lefcourt, & Ware, 1983.

because the researcher determines all of the specific questions and possible answers. Everyone who fills out a fixed-response scale faces the same questions and possible responses, so these scales facilitate comparisons between individuals. An alternative approach is the **open-ended question**, in which the researcher asks a question (e.g., "What do you like about your partner?") and the respondent gives any answer that comes to mind. When researchers are studying something they do not know much about, or something that has never been studied before, open-ended questions are helpful in gathering details they can then use to generate more specific hypotheses. For example, when sociologist and ethnographer Kathryn Edin wanted to study how single mothers on welfare think about marriage, she recognized early on that very little research existed to guide her. No one had asked these women about marriage before, so there was no agreement on even the right questions. To get around this problem, Edin moved herself and her family to East Camden, a poor industrial suburb of Philadelphia, and lived there for more than 2 years (Edin & Kefalas, 2005). During that time she gathered a lot of data, not through surveys or questionnaires but by recording and taking notes on many open-ended conversations with her neighbors and fellow residents. Her work is an example of **qualitative research**, an approach that relies primarily on open-ended questions and other loosely structured information. Answers to open-ended questions tend to provide a lot more information than responses to questionnaires. But as Kathryn Edin's family can attest, they also tend to be more complicated and time-consuming for the researcher to collect and analyze—which is why researchers often favor the fixed-response format.

PROS AND CONS. Whether they come from fixed-response or open-ended questions, self-reports have some advantages that explain their popularity in research on intimate relationships. On a practical level, they require little in the way of fancy equipment. More importantly, self-reports are often the only way of measuring constructs of great interest to relationship researchers. If you want to know what people are thinking and feeling, asking them to tell you is pretty much the only way to find out. Thus, when used appropriately, self-reports may have high construct validity—that is, a great deal of overlap between the operationalization and the construct.

Yet the convenience of using self-reports can lead researchers to overlook some complexities in interpreting the resulting data (**FIGURE 2.3**). Most of these complexities arise from either the questions asked or the answers people provide. Regarding the questions, one difficulty in creating self-report surveys is the specific phrasing of a question, which can affect and sometimes significantly change the way people respond (Schwarz, 1999). For example, positively phrased questions (e.g., "How likely are you to stay together with your current partner?") tend to bring to mind positive aspects of the relationship, thus leading to more positive responses. When the same questions are phrased negatively (e.g., "How likely are you to break up with your current partner?"), they tend to bring to mind negative aspects of the relationship, leading to more negative responses. This phenomenon can be a problem for researchers because couples who really feel the same way about their relationships might be classified differently, merely because they were asked questions phrased in different ways.

When fixed-response scales are used, similar problems may arise from the range of possible answers. For example, when asked to rate their relationships on a scale of 1 to 5, where 1 means "very bad" and 5 means "very good", partners in satisfying relationships may be quite willing to choose 5, the highest point on the scale. However, if the same people are asked to rate their relationships on a scale of 1 to 10, where 1 means "awful" and 10 means "perfect", far fewer partners may be willing to choose the highest possible rating. In this case the problem is

"It may surprise you to know that, contrary to your experience, you're actually very happily married."

FIGURE 2.3 Interpreting self-reports can be complex. Couples who fill out questionnaires and the people who administer those questionnaires do not always interpret the same answers in the same way.

the same: Differences in the operationalization may lead researchers to infer differences in the construct under study where none actually exist. Careful researchers must develop self-report questions that do not shape their own answers—and that can be difficult.

Self-reports can also be problematic because of the kinds of answers people provide. After agreeing to participate in research, people usually try to answer whatever questions they are asked. In practice, however, people sometimes are unable to provide meaningful answers to questions about their intimate relationships, for several reasons. First, people cannot tell you what they do not know. For example, people are not always aware of how they come across to others. When asked to describe what others think of them, they may respond with their best guess—but that guess may reflect their hopes and ideals for themselves, rather than their social standing. In this case, the self-report is a poor representation of what the researcher intends to study (i.e., construct validity is low).

A second related problem is that people cannot describe what they do not remember. Try this: Do you recall how many times you spoke on the phone last week? Probably not. When an event is mundane and occurs again and again (like talking on the phone or giving your partner a hug), memory for those events can be vague and inaccurate. Thus, self-reports about behavior, even very concrete behaviors, may be unreliable. When memory fails, people also tend to fill in the gaps with guesses, and their descriptions of what happened reflect their theories about the relationship rather than actual events. For example, one 20-year study of doctors' wives asked them to describe how their marriages changed after the first 10 years and then after the second 10 years (Karney & Coombs, 2000). When asked how their marriages had changed over time, wives reported on average that their marriages had improved over the first 10 years and then remained more stable during the second 10 years. This pattern is consistent with many people's theories about what being married to a doctor is like: The years of medical school are a time of struggle, but then life gets better. The only problem is that for these wives, the theory was incorrect. In fact, when asked how satisfied they were with their marriages at the moment, these wives on average reported marital satisfaction ratings that declined significantly across each 10-year interval (FIGURE 2.4). As this study indicates, when self-reports rely on faulty memories, the construct validity of self-reports is low.

Another problem is that people cannot provide meaningful answers if they misunderstand the questions. In studies of intimate relationships, researchers tend to ask

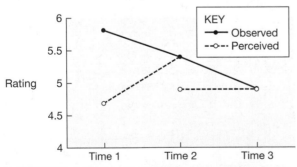

FIGURE 2.4 **Memory bias in self-reports.** When asked to describe how their marital satisfaction had changed over 20 years, wives reported improvements over the first 10 years, and stability over the next 10 years. In fact, their rates of marital satisfaction had declined over each period. When memories fail, self-reports are weak operationalizations of psychological constructs. (Source: Karney & Coombs, 2000.)

FIGURE 2.5 Simple questions are not always simple. When asked if he'd had sex with White House intern Monica Lewinsky, President Clinton answered, "I did not have sexual relations with that woman." While this sounds like a straightforward answer to a straightforward question, later disclosures led many to accuse the president of telling a straightforward lie. Published research indicates that people differ widely in their definitions of sex, and questions that seem clear to the researcher may not be as clear to the participant.

questions about things most people think a lot about—love, trust, conflict, and commitment. Yet, as we will see throughout this book, researchers may define these terms in very specific ways that are different from the way most people define them. As a result, answers may not reflect the same understanding that researchers have. A poignant example of this problem arose when President Bill Clinton was asked in 1998 whether he had had sex with Monica Lewinsky (**FIGURE 2.5**).

In a well-publicized statement the president said, "I did not have sexual relations with that woman." Later, when the graphic and highly intimate details of their activities together were made public, many—including Congress—judged that the president had been deliberately misleading and did in fact have sex with Ms. Lewinsky. Yet a survey released the next year (Sanders & Reinisch, 1999) found that most college students, when given a list of sexual activities, indicated that President Clinton's behavior (which included oral sex but not sexual intercourse with penetration) did not constitute sex as they defined it (**TABLE 2.4**). Clearly, people disagree about what it means to "have sex"—which makes the question "Have you had sex?" more complicated than it seems. To avoid misunderstandings and misinterpretations of their data, careful researchers clearly define crucial terms before asking about them, so that the meaning of the answers matches the intended meaning of the questions.

Self-reports also can be problematic because of people's reluctance to answer questions accurately when a true answer makes them look bad. The term **social desirability effect** refers to the possibility that research participants are giving answers they think will make them look good to the researchers, rather than describing what they actually know. Research on infidelity is a good example of this effect (Whisman & Snyder, 2007). Most people disapprove of extramarital affairs, and people who have extramarital affairs know this. It makes sense, then, that when married women are asked in a face-to-face interview whether they have had sex outside their marriage in the past 12 months, only a very few admit to it (1.08%). When asked the same question in a survey completed on a computer, however, the number of married women who admit to having an affair jumps considerably (6.13%). Presumably, the women who were facing an interviewer cast their reports in a positive light so they would look better to that person. In contrast, a computer

TABLE 2.4 **Would You Say You 'Had Sex' With Someone If the Most Intimate Behavior You Engaged in Was . . . ?"**

Different people can understand the same question in different ways. This table shows that people vary widely in the specific behaviors that they believe count as "having sex." If people disagree this much about the meaning of having sex, imagine the different ways that people might respond to questions about arguing, showing affection, and providing support.

Behaviors	Percentage indicating "had sex"		
	Men	Women	Overall
Deep kissing	1.4	2.9	2.0
Oral contact on your breasts/nipples	2.3	4.1	3.0
Person touches your breasts/nipples	2	4.5	3
You touch other's breasts/nipples	1.7	5.7	3.4
Oral contact on other's breasts/nipples	1.4	6.1	3.4
You touch other's genitals	11.6	17.1	13.9
Person touches your genitals	12.2	19.2	15.1
Oral contact with other's genitals	37.3	43.7	39.9
Oral contact with your genitals	37.7	43.9	40.2
Penile-anal intercourse	82.3	79.1	81.0
Penile-vaginal intercourse	99.7	99.2	99.5

Source: Sanders & Reinisch, 1999.

screen cannot pass judgment, so women who responded online may have felt freer to report on their actual experiences. Such social desirability effects are another threat to the validity of self-reports because they suggest that participants' responses to questions reflect their theories about what the researcher wants to hear, rather than the true nature of the relationship.

To avoid this problem, researchers often examine constructs indirectly. Recall the study on commitment described earlier, in which Lydon and his colleagues asked participants to complete word fragments that could be used to form words either related or unrelated to commitment (Lydon et al., 2008). As participants completed those fragments, they had no idea the researchers were really interested in how they were thinking about their relationships. If participants do not know exactly what the researcher is trying to measure, then they have no way of knowing how to shape their answers and thus are more likely to reveal their honest responses.

Given the attention directed toward understanding how people remain satisfied in their relationships, you might expect researchers to have agreed long ago on the best way to measure relationship satisfaction. Not at all. In fact, in research on marriage alone, over 30 different instruments have been used to measure how spouses feel about their relationships (Karney & Bradbury, 1995). Add the various surveys and questionnaires used for measuring satisfaction in unmarried couples, and the total number of self-report measures of relationship satisfaction is probably far higher. BOX 2.1 describes two classes of tools used to measure relationship satisfaction, and some advantages and disadvantages of each one.

Observational Measures

In addition to understanding what partners think about their intimate relationships, researchers also want to know what actually happens in a relationship. How do satisfied and unsatisfied partners behave toward each other? Which behaviors are associated with long-lasting relationships, and which ones are associated with those that end? An alternative to obtaining the partners' self-reports is obtaining the reports of observers. **Observational measures** gather data about relationship events without having to ask the people who are experiencing the events.

Although the basic idea of observational measurement seems straightforward (i.e., just go out and watch what people do), designing observational measures is—for several reasons—highly complex. The first challenge is that the researcher must decide *who* will do the observing. One option when studying couples is to ask each partner to be an observer of the other partner. In fact, early marital research took this approach, using an instrument called the Spouse Observation Checklist (Wills, Weiss, & Patterson, 1974). This eight-page measure asked each spouse to indicate which of hundreds of specific behaviors (e.g., took out the garbage, complimented me, took a walk) their partner engaged in during the previous 24 hours, and how many times each behavior occurred. Initial studies found, not surprisingly, that spouses who were more satisfied with their marriages described their partners as engaging in more positive behaviors and fewer negative ones. Researchers concluded from this finding that spouses' specific behaviors play an important role in marital satisfaction. The problem with this conclusion, however, was that no one had checked the accuracy of spouses' observations. How good are spouses at reporting on each other's behaviors? To address this question,

BOX 2.1 SPOTLIGHT ON . . .

Measuring Relationship Satisfaction

Why are there so many different tools to assess the same thing? One reason is that researchers disagree about what kind of questions are the right ones to operationalize relationship satisfaction. The earliest tools used a kitchen-sink approach, asking questions about everything that could possibly be related to satisfaction in a relationship. The Marital Adjustment Test (Locke & Wallace, 1959), one of the earliest and still widely used measures, consists of 15 questions ranging from the extent to which spouses disagree about such issues as finances and sex to whether they engage in outside interests together. Here are some examples:

- Please indicate the extent to which you and your spouse agree about . . . family finances/recreation/sex/in-laws/etc.
- When disagreements arise, they usually result in: (a) husband giving in, (b) wife giving in, (c) agreement by mutual give and take.
- Do you confide in your mate . . . (a) almost never, (b) in some things, (c) in most things, (d) in everything?

This broad approach is called an **omnibus measure**; it taps a wide range of content, reflecting the idea that satisfaction with a relationship is based on opinions about the relationship as a whole, as well as opinions about a range of specific aspects.

Omnibus measures work fine, until you want to compare those scores with scores from another tool that addresses more specific aspects of intimate relationships. For example, suppose you want to know if marital satisfaction is associated with how couples behave toward each other. You might ask couples who have already completed the Marital Adjustment Test to complete the Conflict Tactics Survey (Straus, 1979), which assesses aggressive behavior in couples. Here is how this popular instrument begins:

Below is a list of some things your spouse might have done when you had a dispute. Indicate how often in the past year your partner . . .

- discussed the issue calmly.
- sulked or refused to talk about it.
- stomped out of the room/ house, or yard.
- did or said something to spite the other.

Or maybe you would administer the Communication Patterns Questionnaire (Christensen & Sullaway, 1984),

clinical psychologists Neil Jacobson and Danny Moore (1981) simply asked each partner to report on his or her own behaviors as well as those of the partner. Upon comparing both spouses' reports of the same behaviors, these researchers found that partners agreed about which behaviors had occurred less than 50 percent of the time! In other words, spouses are not very accurate observers of each other.

These findings make sense in light of the previous discussion about problems with self-report measures. The limitations of memory and awareness affect observations of a partners' behavior, just as with self-reports. If responses to the Spouse Observation Checklist are not assessing behavior, though, what are they actually measuring? Clinical psychologist Robert Weiss (1984) suggested that partners' general feelings about the relationship frequently overwhelm their perceptions of specific aspects of the relationship—a process he called **sentiment override**. When they are asked to describe mundane events (e.g., "How many times did your partner kiss you yesterday?"), partners may think, "Well, I don't remember exactly how many times my partner kissed me yesterday, but I do feel like we have a good relationship, so it must a measure of problem-solving behavior in couples that asks:

When some problem in the relationship arises, what is the likelihood that:

- both members avoid discussing the problem?
- both members blame, accuse, and criticize each other?
- the women nags and demands while man withdraws, becomes silent, or refuses to discuss the matter further?

These three measures are all supposed to be examining different things. Do they? Many people would look at the items on all three and conclude that each is actually asking about the same ideas. This is known as the **Item-overlap problem**, and it occurs whenever questionnaires that are nominally measuring different constructs contain questions about similar topics.

To avoid this problem, some researchers (e.g., Fincham & Bradbury, 1987; Funk & Rogge, 2007) have recommended operationalizing relationship satisfaction exclusively in terms of **global measures**, or measures that ask partners only about their evaluations of their relationship as a whole. The Quality Marriage Index (Norton, 1983) is a global measure, and here it is in its entirety:

Please indicate how well the following statements describe you and your marriage (on a scale of 1 to 7).

- We have a good marriage.
- My relationship with my partner is very stable.
- Our marriage is strong.
- My relationship with my partner makes me happy.
- I really feel like part of a team with my partner.

All things considered, how happy are you in your marriage (on a scale from 1 to 10)?

Notice that all of these items are asking about spouses' general feelings about the relationship; there are no questions about communication, sex, in-laws, or anything else. By putting questions about all other aspects of the relationship on separate questionnaires, researchers can directly examine how satisfaction with the relationship as a whole may be related to the specific aspects.

have been a lot." What seems like an observational measure of behavior often boils down to another self-report measure of partners' feelings. To avoid the problem of sentiment override, most observational research today relies on observers who are completely independent of the relationship, such as trained assistants.

The second challenge in designing observational measures is deciding *what* to observe. Clearly, the question motivating the research should provide the initial direction. Researchers interested in how two strangers initially develop a relationship, for instance, will want to observe people getting to know one another. Researchers interested in how couples resolve conflicts will want to observe couples discussing an area of disagreement. Yet even after selecting a general category of experience for observation, such as communication, researchers still face an array of specific things they can choose to either attend to or ignore. For example, suppose that, like researcher Alan Sillars and his colleagues, you want to understand what it is about the way couples communicate that makes a relationship more or less likely to break up (Sillars, Roberts, Leonard, & Dun, 2000). These researchers recorded and analyzed each statement partners made when discussing areas of disagreement, to identify statements that bring couples together (e.g., "I am confident we can work something out") and those that push couples apart (e.g., "You just don't get it, do you?"). Psychologist Kurt Hahlweg and his colleagues examined partners' nonverbal behaviors, such as leaning forward (an expression of interest and engagement) and rolling the eyes (an expression of contempt; Hahlweg et al., 1984). Social psychologists Richard Slatcher and James Pennebaker ignored the surface content of partners' statements altogether. Instead, they tabulated the numbers of different types of words that appeared in couples' written messages to each other, showing that college students who used more emotion words (like "love," "excited," and "angry") in text messages to their partners were more likely to remain together (Slatcher & Pennebaker, 2006).

An exciting development in research on intimate relationships is the study of **physiological responses**, the body's involuntary reactions to experiences. For example, when psychologist Art Aron and his colleagues wanted to identify the precise area of the brain where we experience passionate love, they invited 17 young people in the early stages of a serious romantic relationship to submit to a functional magnetic resonance imaging (fMRI) scan while viewing a photograph of their partner or a photograph of a familiar but nonintimate friend (Aron et al., 2005). An area of the brain associated with reward and motivation lit up more brightly when partners gazed at their loved one than when they viewed a friend. In this study, the scanner was the observer, and the neural activity of each partner during the scan was the "behavior" being observed. In every case, deciding what to observe is a process of operationalization. In other words, the specific behaviors the researcher decides to observe should be those behaviors that best represent the construct the researcher is trying to study.

The third challenge in designing observational measures is deciding *where* to do the observing. Relationship researchers, like good anthropologists, ideally want to observe couples in their natural habitats. In most cases this means observing couples where they live, by either sending observers to visit couples' homes or sending equipment (like tape recorders or video cameras) couples can use to record themselves. Researchers who use **home-based observation** hope couples will act more naturally in their own environments, and their observed behaviors really will represent what they do when *not* being observed. The problem, however, is that home-based observation can be very intrusive, either because it requires a couple to allow a stranger into their home, or because it asks them to set up and operate recording equipment and thereby disrupt their standard routines and habits. Another disadvantage of home observations is that every couple's home has different distractions and stresses, thus complicating attempts to compare behaviors across couples.

An alternative approach is bringing couples to a controlled environment, such as a research room, and observing as they all engage in a similar task. **Laboratory-based observation** eliminates any outside factors that may alter couples' behavior while they are at home, but it also removes couples from the environment where their behaviors usually take place. How does being in an unusual setting affect the way partners interact with each other? Two studies asked couples to record themselves discussing an area of disagreement at home and then to discuss the same topic in the standardized setting of a research room (Burggraf & Sillars, 1987; Gottman, 1979). In both studies, the conversations at home were more emotional and more negative than the conversations in the research rooms. Even though couples knew they were being recorded in both settings, presumably they found it easier to forget the observers when they were at home. In a research room, the strangeness of the environment seems to dampen couples' tendency to express the darker sides of the relationship. One implication of these findings is that laboratory-based observations may lead to underestimates of the amount of negativity that goes on in couples' homes.

Perhaps the biggest challenge in designing observational measures is establishing reliability among the observers. In discussions of observational measures, **reliability** is the extent to which different observers agree that a specified behavior has or has not occurred. When the specified behavior is concrete, like an eyeblink or a touch, getting a set of observers to agree is relatively easy. Sometimes, though, researchers are interested in studying behaviors that require an observer to do some interpretation. Psychologist John Gottman (1994), for example, asked his observers to count how many times during a 10-minute conversation each partner expressed each of 10 different specific emotions (e.g., affection, fear, sadness, anger). Making fine distinctions between shades of negative emotion can be a difficult task. Imagine listening to a conversation between people you do not know. Could you always distinguish between sarcasm and a lighthearted joke? Between constructive criticism and faulting? Observers in research on relationships typically receive hours of training to learn how to make these kinds of judgments. For researchers, establishing reliability among the observers ensures that all observers are identifying the same things. When observers are reliable, researchers are more confident that what is being observed reflects what they are trying to study, rather than the observers' personal beliefs and biases.

PROS AND CONS. Why would a researcher use observational measures when the cheaper and easier self-report method is available? The primary advantage of observational measurement is that, when used appropriately, observations directly assess behaviors of great interest to relationship research. If you want to know how couples resolve conflicts, for example, watching a few hundred couples discussing their problems supplies vivid information that partners' own descriptions rarely match. If you want to know how strangers get to know one another, there are few substitutes for watching some strangers interact. In other words, well-designed observational measures have high construct validity.

A second advantage of observational measures is that they avoid some specific problems associated with self-reports of behavior. For example, observers often provide their reports during an observation or immediately afterward and so have less opportunity to rely on faulty or limited memories. Similarly, because the behaviors being observed do not reflect on the observers, their observations should not be affected by concerns about social desirability. As a result, observational measures offer a relatively objective record of what happens in relationships.

Yet gathering observed data can also work against the validity of the observations. The main problem with observational measures is the possibility of **reactivity**—sometimes the act of observing someone changes the behavior being observed. To understand the issue of reactivity, imagine walking along, singing a song you heard on the radio; then you notice someone walking next to you is listening. Maybe this stops you from singing, or maybe it makes you sing even louder. Either way, what was once a private behavior is now public, and your behavior changed. For researchers, reactivity is a big problem because they often want to study the private behavior. Since couples' behaviors change to some extent when they are being observed, what is being observed is not what the researcher wants to study, so construct validity is low.

Researchers use various techniques to minimize reactivity in observational studies. Some hide their recording equipment, hoping couples will forget about the observers and focus on each other. Gottman (1994), for example, invites couples to spend 24 hours in an apartment rigged with hidden cameras. Other researchers focus on observing behaviors that couples may not be able to control even if they want to, such as emotional or physiological responses. For example, psychologist Omri Gillath and his colleagues observe how quickly people recognize words associated with different relationship goals (e.g., "cling," "comfort," "avoid") after being shown the names of people in their lives with whom they felt either secure or insecure (Gillath et al., 2006). The researchers measure participants' reactions in milliseconds—too fast for conscious control. Still, people exposed to friends who made them feel secure were quicker to recognize words associated with good relationships, and those exposed to friends who made them feel insecure were quicker to recognize words associated with bad relationships. Even with these sorts of procedures, however, researchers never can be totally sure the behaviors they observe are representative of the behaviors couples engage in when not being observed.

Which Measurement Strategy Is Best?

After reading about the pros and cons of self-report and observational measures, you might wonder which kind is best. **TABLE 2.5** summarizes the advantages and disadvantages of both strategies. As the table shows, no approach is perfect. Even in the best of circumstances, every operationalization can be only a rough approximation of a complex psychological construct.

The best research adopts a **multiple-method approach**, operationalizing the constructs of interest in different ways, so the limitations of each measurement strategy will eventually cancel each other out, thereby letting

TABLE 2.5 Comparing Measurement Strategies

Self-Report Measures	Observational Measures
Cheap and easy to administer	Expensive and time-consuming
Appropriate for measuring perceptions	Appropriate for measuring behavior
Answers affected by how questions are phrased	Data affected by what aspects of behavior are being measured
Answers affected by respondents' memory and desirability biases	Observations may be affected by context in which behaviors occur

the effects the researcher is most focused on emerge clearly. Psychologists Dale Griffin and Kim Bartholomew took this approach when examining how people's attitudes toward their relationships are organized (Griffin & Bartholomew, 1994). Across several studies, they analyzed people's self-reports of their own attitudes, what their friends and lovers said about how the targets approached relationships, and what trained judges said about the same issues. When the results from all these different data sources converged, the researchers were that much more confident in their conclusions about how people are oriented toward relationships. (We will discuss those conclusions in the next chapter.)

MAIN POINTS

>> Relationship science addresses abstract ideas known as psychological constructs, such as love, trust, and commitment.

>> Testing predictions about constructs requires researchers to translate their ideas into concrete terms using the process of operationalization.

>> Construct validity is the degree to which a particular operationalization is a good match for what the construct researchers want to study.

>> When researchers are interested in the way partners feel or think, self-reports—simply asking people about the constructs being studied—can have high construct validity, but people cannot describe what they do not know or cannot remember, and sometimes they may distort their reports in an effort to project a positive image.

>> Observational measures, in which people other than the members of a couple report on how the partners behave, are a direct approach, but people might change their behavior when they know they are being observed.

>> To minimize the limitations of specific strategies, researchers can use a multi-method approach to operationalize the constructs of interest in different ways across different studies.

Designing the Study

After making the decision about measurement strategy, a researcher must develop a plan for organizing the study in a way that addresses important questions. Research on intimate relationships uses several study designs, each of which is appropriate for investigating different kinds of questions.

Correlational Research

Researchers conduct **correlational research** to study the naturally occurring associations among variables; it is aimed primarily at answering descriptive questions. For example, are more intelligent people more satisfied with their intimate relationships? Are people whose parents divorced at higher risk of getting divorced themselves? Are couples happier when they share similar interests? Each of these questions asks how differences in one variable may be associated with differences in another variable. When two variables are shown to be associated in some way, they are described as correlated (**FIGURE 2.6**).

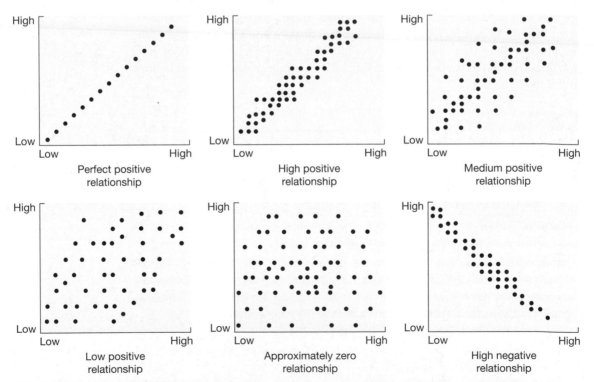

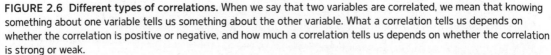

FIGURE 2.6 Different types of correlations. When we say that two variables are correlated, we mean that knowing something about one variable tells us something about the other variable. What a correlation tells us depends on whether the correlation is positive or negative, and how much a correlation tells us depends on whether the correlation is strong or weak.

A **positive correlation** indicates that when levels of one variable are high, levels of the other variable tend to be high as well; and when levels of one variable are low, levels of the other variable also tend to be low. For example, sexual satisfaction and relationship satisfaction are positively correlated because couples who are satisfied with their sex lives tend to be satisfied with their relationships, whereas couples who have complaints about their sex lives tend to feel less satisfied with their relationships (e.g., Henderson-King & Veroff, 1994).

A **negative correlation** indicates the opposite association, where high levels of one variable tend to be associated with low levels of another. For example, depression and relationship satisfaction are negatively correlated because people who are more depressed or exhibit higher levels of depressive symptoms tend to be less satisfied in their relationships, whereas people who are less depressed tend to be more satisfied (e.g., Whisman, 2001). The stronger the correlation in either direction, the more knowing where someone stands on one variable tells you about where that person stands on the other variable. A correlation of zero, therefore, means that knowing one variable tells you nothing at all about the other variable; earlobe length, for instance, has zero correlation with relationship satisfaction, since knowing how long people's earlobes are tells you nothing about how satisfied they are in their relationships.

Measuring variables and describing how they may be associated are relatively straightforward processes, and because many important questions about intimate relationships revolve around description, correlational studies account for much of the research. Virtually all studies describing gender differences in relationships are correlational—they examine how some variables may naturally differ among males and females. Studies of cultural differences in relationships are also correlational—they describe how relationships may vary across cultures, localities, or ethnicities.

PROS AND CONS. When the goal is to examine how different variables are associated in the world, no research design is more appropriate than a correlational study. Correlational research is also valuable for studying variables that cannot be manipulated or studied in other ways. Research on intimate relationships, for example, has asked how relationships are affected by a particular experience, such as a chronic illness, a previous bad relationship, or one partner's affair. Obviously, researchers cannot create or control these experiences. But one way to study them is to divide couples into those who have or have not experienced these events and then study how other aspects of the relationship vary naturally across the groups. For instance, after Hurricane Hugo devastated parts of South Carolina in 1989, psychologists Catherine Cohan and Steve Cole wanted to know how the stress of coping with the disaster affected marriages in that part of the country (Cohan & Cole, 2002). They could not change whether people experienced the event, but they could compare marriage and divorce rates in the counties that were struck by the hurricane to rates in counties that were passed over. They found that divorce rates went up shortly after the hurricane; but so did marriage rates, suggesting that the crisis prompted couples to make serious decisions about their relationships, one way or another. (We will have more to say about the effects of stress on relationships in Chapter 11.)

The drawback of this kind of research is that correlational data can support only certain kinds of conclusions. In particular, correlational data cannot be used to support statements about **causation**—the idea that one event or circumstance is the direct result of another. As important as description is, sometimes researchers want to go further and discuss whether one variable produces an effect in another. Correlational data are ill-suited for this purpose. To illustrate this point, consider a survey conducted in Oklahoma and the surrounding states of Arkansas, Kansas, and Texas (Stanley, Amato, Johnson, & Markman, 2006), where divorce rates are about 50 percent higher than in the rest of the country (Kreider & Fields, 2001). One goal of the survey was to describe how residents of those states felt about premarital education (i.e., classes on relationship skills and effective problem-solving techniques) that the state of Oklahoma was planning to offer to unmarried and engaged couples. The Oklahoma survey was a classic example of correlational research and an appropriate study design for describing attitudes toward the new policy. Among the findings were that people who had received premarital education reported being happier in their relationships and were less likely to have experienced a divorce. Put another way, taking a class on relationship skills was positively correlated with marital satisfaction and negatively correlated with risk of divorce.

By itself, this is an interesting finding—one worth examining further. However, for state officials trying to decide whether to spend taxpayer money on such programs, or for those trying to develop new state policies to improve relationships, merely describing these correlations is not enough. To justify specific efforts to improve couples' relationships, it is tempting to conclude that taking a premarital education class *causes* marriages to be more satisfying and less prone to divorce. If true, this would indeed be an important result, and it might inspire policy makers in that state to support programs for teaching communication skills to couples as a way of alleviating or preventing marital distress. The problem with this conclusion, however, is that *correlation does not imply causation*. Two variables may be associated, but that does not necessarily mean one causes the other.

Every correlation between two variables X and Y is subject to three possible interpretations:

1. *X may cause Y*. Premarital education classes may very well improve rates of marital success. It is not too hard to imagine that a class that teaches couples effective ways of resolving problems and maintaining intimacy

might help married couples stay happy and avoid divorce. However, by itself a correlation between taking a class and being happy does not rule out other equally likely interpretations, such as the following.

2. *Y may cause X.* Couples who are happier and more stable in the first place may be more likely than other couples to sign up voluntarily for premarital classes. Taking a class costs time and often money. Being willing to devote those resources to the relationship may reflect an existing commitment to the relationship that would lead to happier relationships, whether the class had an effect or not. From this perspective, taking a class would be a *result* of being happy with the relationship, rather than a *cause*. Correlational research offers researchers no way to distinguish between this possibility, the former one, or the next one.

3. *Both X and Y may be the result of some other cause.* What other variable might make both taking a premarital education class and having a good relationship more likely? One possibility involves the partners' socioeconomic status. Couples with plenty of resources and time are more likely to be able to show up together to take a class to help their relationship. Having money and time also provides space for maintaining intimacy. Stress associated with financial strains, in contrast, might make it impossible for couples to attend a class and may cause various other stresses that hurt the overall quality of the relationship. In this case, the two variables measured in the survey may have little or no causal effect on each other at all. Their significant correlation may be entirely the result of an unmeasured third variable.

It bears repeating: Correlation does not imply causation. Even the best correlational research provides no help in determining which of these three causal statements more accurately explains why taking a class and having a good relationship are correlated. Correlational research makes its important contribution to knowledge by describing how variables are associated, not how they affect each other. Yet drawing causal conclusions from correlational data is a mistake that many well-meaning people make, especially when the research results are meant to inform treatments or social policies. Teasing apart causal relationships, however, requires more complex research designs.

Thus far, our discussion of correlational research has focused on studies that collect all of their data on a single occasion. Correlational studies that are conducted only once, like many surveys and opinion polls, provide **cross-sectional data**—so named because the data describe a cross section, or a snapshot, of a single instant. But sometimes we want to know more than what a particular moment is like; we want to know what happens over time. Studies that collect measurements of the same individuals at two or more occasions are still correlational, but they provide longitudinal data.

Longitudinal Research

Longitudinal research, an important subset of correlational research, enables researchers to address two kinds of questions: description and prediction. Unlike cross-sectional studies, longitudinal studies describe not only what a phenomenon looks like at a single moment, but also how it may change over time. Describing change over time can be extremely interesting for researchers exploring intimate relationships. For example, what happens to the initially high satisfaction of couples who have just fallen in love? What happens to relationships when couples move in together, get married, or have children? Do the relationships of same-sex couples develop in the same ways as the relationships of opposite-sex couples? Describing change is a primary function of longitudinal research.

Whereas most cross-sectional research stops at description, longitudinal studies can go further to address questions of prediction. What is it about a new relationship that predicts whether the couple will eventually break up or stay together? Are couples who live together before getting married more or less likely to get divorced? Which couples do best across the transition to retirement? The most direct way to answer these sorts of questions is to initially study the behaviors of couples, and then do it again later to see what happened.

A central challenge in designing longitudinal studies is deciding on the appropriate interval between each measurement. In research to predict relationship events (e.g., having a fight, having a baby, breaking up), the interval needs to be long enough for the event being studied to occur in at least some couples. If a researcher wanted to study predictors of arguments, for example, it might make sense to evaluate a group of couples and then contact them again 2 weeks later to see which ones had arguments and which ones did not. In contrast, if a researcher wanted to study predictors of divorce, it would make no sense to examine couples over 2 weeks, because it takes years—not weeks—for a sizable number of divorces to occur in any group of marriages. Research to predict breakups in dating relationships, on the other hand, can have briefer intervals because dating relationships are more likely to end over shorter periods of time.

In research on how relationships change, the interval between measurements needs to be long enough so that some change can occur. Again, the appropriate amount of time depends on the kinds of change being studied. Satisfaction with a relationship, for example, can be fairly stable for long periods of time, especially in couples who have already been together for a while. To describe how feelings about relationships may change, researchers have conducted long-term longitudinal studies that assess couples several times over periods of 8 years (Johnson, Amoloza, & Booth, 1992), 14 years (Huston, Caughlin, Houts, Smith, & George, 2001), and 40 years (Kelly & Conley, 1987). Though studies as long as these naturally represent a huge investment by the researchers, they have the potential to capture the scope and sweep of people's lives that no other research can match. By study-ing the same couples for 40 years, for example, clinical psychologists Lowell Kelly and James Conley (1987) were able to show that spouses' personali-ties before they got married predicted whether they would still be married 40 years later. (We will discuss this finding in more detail in Chapter 6.)

In contrast, the way partners interact with each other may change daily (on Wednesday we had a fight, on Thursday we watched TV, on Friday we had a great time at the movies, etc.). To understand variability and change at this level, researchers use a **daily diary approach**. Despite the name, research using this approach rarely asks people to keep a literal journal. Instead, daily diary research simply asks people to fill out a (usually brief) questionnaire every day at about the same time. Social psychologists Anne Thompson and Niall Bolger (1999) used a design of this kind to examine how changes in the daily mood of one partner affected the other partner's feelings about the rela-tionship. They asked couples in which one partner was studying for the New York state bar exam to complete nightly surveys every day for the 35 days leading up to the exam. As you might imagine, on days when the partner who was studying felt especially crabby or anxious, the other partner was less satisfied with the relationship. However, this effect diminished as the exam got closer. In other words, although we are usually affected by our partner's negative moods, we are less affected to the extent that we can easily find an external cause for them. (We will revisit this effect in Chapter 11.)

The **experience sampling** approach goes even further. Rather than ask-ing partners to complete a single diary each day, experience sampling in-volves gathering data from people throughout the day, literally "sampling" from the totality of their daily experiences. For example, the Rochester In-teraction Record (RIR; Reis & Wheeler, 1991) asks people to fill out a very short form every time they interact with another person for more than 10 minutes, rating each interaction for how much each individual disclosed and how satisfying the interaction was. Using the RIR, researchers have learned that feeling close to someone depends less on what partners share with each other than on each partner's reaction to what the other has shared (Laurenceau, Barrett, & Pietromonaco, 1998). Unlike most longitudinal re-search, which seldom measures people more than twice, studies that use di-ary and experience sampling methods typically obtain far more measure-ments, but over a much shorter period of time. Thompson and Bolger (1999), for example, collected 35 daily measurements over the space of a month for their study of couples leading up to the bar exam; in contrast, Kelly and Con-ley (1987) collected three measurements to describe change over 40 years of marriage.

PROS AND CONS. Longitudinal studies share many of the advantages and dis-advantages of other correlational research. When researchers are interested in describing how relationships change, or predicting which relationships will last and which will end, longitudinal research is the most direct and appropriate approach. Longitudinal research also allows researchers to study processes that would be impossible or unethical to study in other ways. For example, researchers who want to understand how people cope with the end of their relationships cannot ethically cause relationships to end, but they can identify relationships that have ended and then follow both partners and measure how long it takes each one to start a new relationship. Thus, longitudinal research offers a unique window for observing how relationship processes unfold.

The challenges of longitudinal research, however, involve both expense and time. Studying a process that unfolds over 20 years, for example, takes roughly . . . 20 years. In research on how relationships change over the entire lifespan, some longitudinal studies have outlived the researchers who began them. Even a short-term longitudinal study can be a serious undertaking that requires a great deal of effort from the researchers as well as the couples who participate. The longer the study, the more likely various couples are to move

BOX 2.2 SPOTLIGHT ON . . .

The Case of the Disappearing Curve

Here is what seems like a straightforward question: On average, how do spouses' feelings about their relationship change over time? To get the answer, early marital researchers gathered large samples of married couples and compared the satisfaction of couples who were newlyweds, couples who had been married only a few years, and couples who had been married for many years. Several studies found that marital satisfaction seemed to follow a U-shaped pattern (Burr, 1970; Rollins & Cannon, 1974; Rollins & Feldman, 1970). Satisfaction was highest in the newlyweds, lowest in couples in the middle of their marriage, and then high again in couples who had been married the longest. Many researchers believed this finding was a reasonable description of how marriages may change on average. Naturally, they concluded, newlyweds are generally happy, but their happiness declines when they are raising children and have less time to enjoy each other. Later, when children are grown and have moved away, time to enjoy the pleasures of companionship return, and satisfaction with the relationship rises again.

The problem with this conclusion, however, was that none of these early studies had examined change at all. As a number of researchers were quick to observe (e.g., Spanier, Lewis, & Cole, 1975), even though couples married a long time tend to be happier than couples who have been married less time, marital satisfaction does not always increase in later marriage. These critics speculated that the least happy marriages may dissolve early, leaving only happier couples in the long-married group.

To settle the issue, the next generation of marital researchers examined how the satisfaction of particular couples develops over the course of their marriages. This kind of research took more time to conduct, of course, but when these studies were finally published, there was no evidence of the famous U-shaped curve. Vaillant and Vaillant (1993), for example, who followed a sample of 169 marriages for 40 years, found that spouses' marital satisfaction on average declined more or less linearly throughout the marriage. VanLaningham, Johnson, and Amato (2001) followed couples for merely 8 years but were able to describe how marital satisfaction changed over that time in marriages of different duration. These researchers also found that, regardless of whether they looked at early marriage, middle marriage, or late away, break up, lose contact with researchers, or simply get bored and refuse to participate anymore. The average longitudinal study of marriage, for example, loses about 30 percent of the initial sample for one of these reasons (Karney & Bradbury, 1995). This can be a problem due to the fact that the couples who drop out of a study are often the most interesting because they are experiencing the most change. When the final sample in a longitudinal study differs from the initial sample because certain kinds of couples have dropped out, the study is said to suffer from **attrition bias** (Miller & Wright, 1995). To protect the validity of their results, researchers typically go to great lengths to retain couples once they have begun participating in a longitudinal study (e.g., by keeping in touch through newsletters or offering increasing amounts of money). **BOX 2.2** describes an example of how failing to account for attrition can drastically change the conclusions researchers draw from their work.

An additional drawback to longitudinal research is that, as with all correlational research, the conclusions that can be drawn are limited. Compared to

marriage, satisfaction tended on average to decline over time. In study after longitudinal study, the results have been consistent: No U-shaped curve, no increases in later marriage, just a more-or-less steady decline (FIGURE 2.7).

The difference between the U-shaped curve, which was conventional wisdom in the field for many years, and the actual pattern of change in marital satisfaction illustrates the importance of designing studies that are appropriate to the questions being asked.

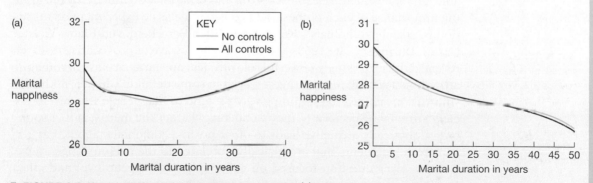

FIGURE 2.7 **How marital satisfaction changes over time.** (a) A cross-sectional analysis suggests that marital happiness is highest in early marriage, declines in the middle years, and then rises again in the later years. (b) Longitudinal data reveal the U-shaped curve to be an illusion: Marital happiness on average declines more or less linearly over time. (Source: VanLaningham, Johnson, & Amato, 2001.)

cross-sectional research, longitudinal studies do get somewhat closer to supporting causal statements, because a cause has to precede its effect. Therefore, if a longitudinal study shows that difficulty resolving problems predicts
whether a couple will break up within 2 years, the conclusion that problem-
solving skills lead to relationship stability (X causes Y) is more plausible than
the conclusion that relationship stability leads to problem-solving skills (Y
causes X). However, even when a variable precedes an outcome in time, that
variable does not necessarily *cause* the outcome. In trying to understand the
effects of problem-solving skills over time, longitudinal research alone cannot determine whether such skills themselves create more stable relationships, or whether some third variable associated with problem-solving skills
(such as relationship satisfaction) is the real cause. Although longitudinal
research is well suited for describing how relationships change and for predicting relationship outcomes, explaining those outcomes—and in particular,
drawing strong conclusions about what causes them—requires a different
kind of research design.

Experimental Research

If researchers want to understand not only *what* happens and *when* it happens, but also *why* things happen in relationships, explaining what produces
an effect in relationships requires them to go beyond passively observing how
different variables correlate. In **experimental research**, researchers take a
more active role by manipulating one element of a phenomenon to determine
its effects on the rest of the phenomenon. If changing one element while
holding the rest constant consistently leads to a particular effect, researchers
are (at last) justified in concluding that the element in question causes the
effect.

Conducting a true experiment requires four elements: a dependent variable, an independent variable, control, and random assignment. To illustrate
the importance of each of these, let's consider a classic experiment on attraction by social psychologists Karen Dion, Ellen Berscheid, and Elaine Walster
(1972). During the late 1960s and early 1970s, a wave of provocative research
revealed the surprisingly powerful role physical appearance plays in romantic
attraction. (We will discuss this research in some detail in Chapter 5.) In this
study, Dion et al. were examining why we tend to like people who are physically attractive. Specifically, they wondered whether the mere fact that someone is physically attractive leads to other positive judgments about that person, even judgments that are logically unrelated to the person's appearance.
Because their question focused on cause (physical appearance) and effect
(positive judgments), they chose to address it by conducting an experiment.

The starting point in every experiment is the **dependent variable**—the effect or outcome the researchers want to understand. In the Dion et al. (1972)
study, participants were given three photographs of people and asked to rate

their impressions of each one. For example, they were asked to guess the personality of the person in each photograph, to predict which person was most likely to be happily married, and to indicate what kind of jobs each person was more or less likely to have. These ratings were the dependent variables. They are called "dependent" because their value may depend on other aspects of the experimental situation; in this case, the physical appearance of the people in the photographs.

If the dependent variable is the possible effect, the **independent variable** is the possible cause—the aspect of the experimental situation the researcher manipulates, changing it "independently" of any other aspect to see if changes in this variable are associated with changes in the dependent variable. In the Dion et al. study (1972), the independent variable was the physical attractiveness of the people in the three photographs. How can a researcher manipulate something like physical attractiveness? Before the study began, the researchers had asked 100 college students to rate the physical attractiveness of 50 yearbook photos. In each condition of their experiment, the researchers used three photographs that had been reliably rated as highly attractive, moderately attractive, and unattractive, thereby manipulating the attractiveness of the people whom participants in the experiment would view. The researchers observed that when the person in the photograph was more attractive, participants' judgments of that person were significantly more positive; compared to the less attractive people, participants rated the more attractive people as more well adjusted, more likely to have a satisfying marriage, and more likely to have a prestigious job.

> " Research is formalized curiosity. It is poking and prying with a purpose."
>
> —Zora Neale Hurston, *Dust Tracks on a Road* (1942/ 2010, p. 143)

Could the research team now conclude that physical attractiveness causes positive judgments of people? Not yet. Perhaps there were other reasons for the differences they observed. What if the more attractive photographs were in color and the less attractive ones were in black and white? Maybe people rate targets in color photographs more positively, regardless of their physical attractiveness? What if the targets in the more attractive photographs were all male, and the targets in the less attractive photographs were all female? Maybe people generally rate men more positively than women. To support the idea that the variable they cared about (physical attractiveness) really had an effect, the researchers had to rule out all of the alternative explanations for their observations. Doing so requires researchers to **control**, or hold constant, all aspects of the experimental situation they are not manipulating.

In the Dion et al. (1972) study, the researchers were interested only in the effects of physical attractiveness. Thus, they needed to control every other way the three target photographs might vary. Using yearbook photos helped accomplish this control because they are all the same size, and each person's head fills the same amount of the frame. Further, the researchers ensured that participants saw either three males or three females, thus controlling gender in each condition of their study. Because the three pictures were alike in every way other than the attractiveness of the target, the researchers were more justified in concluding that differences in attractiveness caused the differences in how the targets were judged.

Even though researchers can control almost every aspect of an experimental situation, they cannot control the research participants. Every person who participates in a survey or an experiment brings a unique set of biases and experiences that represent a final threat to the conclusions of an experimental study. Imagine, for example, if, rather than using three different photographs, the researchers had shown different photographs to different groups of people. If the group who saw the photos of the most attractive people also made the most positive judgments, would that mean the attractiveness of the people affected the ratings? Maybe, but as an alternative, perhaps the group who saw the photos of the most attractive people was somehow more generous or more optimistic than those who saw the other photographs.

How can researchers ever hope to rule out these alternatives, when they cannot control the research participants? The solution is **random assignment**, which ensures that every research participant has an equal chance of being assigned to any condition of an experiment. Researchers think of random assignment as the great equalizer because it guarantees that participants in different experimental conditions are, on average, similar to each other before being exposed to the experimental manipulation (the independent variable). For example, suppose participants were randomly assigned to view a photograph of a very attractive, a moderately attractive, or an unattractive person. There would be no reason to expect that, *on average*, the members of any one group are different from the other two groups. Within any group, the participants vary randomly, so all of their unique prejudices and experiences cancel each other out. If the three groups still differed in their judgments of the photographs, the researchers could be reasonably certain that variations in the photographs, rather than preexisting differences in the groups, accounted for the varying judgments.

PROS AND CONS. A well-designed experiment reveals how manipulating one variable may affect a change in another variable while controlling for other possible sources of influence (TABLE 2.6). Thus, experimental research enables researchers to move beyond description and prediction to address explanatory questions about intimate relationships. What features make people more or less attractive to friends and romantic partners? Does a particular kind of therapy or program help relationships or harm them? To explain causes and effects, an experiment is the most appropriate research design.

Yet the increased control required in experimental research has its costs. By isolating the effects of specific variables, an experiment risks distorting how those variables behave in the world outside of the experiment. In the Dion et al. (1972) study, for example, research participants were asked to

TABLE 2.6 **The Elements of a True Experiment**

Element	Definition
Dependent variable	The effect or outcome the researchers want to understand.
Independent variable	The aspect of the experimental situation the researcher manipulates.
Control	Holding constant all aspects of the experimental situation that are not being manipulated.
Random assignment	The assurance that every participant has an equal chance of being assigned to any condition of an experiment.

make sweeping judgments about the people they viewed only in a photograph. Do the effects of physical attractiveness in this situation mirror the way physical attractiveness works in the real world? Maybe not. When we meet people in real life, we can withhold our judgments until we have interacted with them, or change our judgments based on our experiences with them. By itself, the fact that physical appearance affected judgments in this experiment does not mean that physical attractiveness has the same effects when we actually meet someone as when we judge photographs.

Research on couples therapy confronts this problem all the time. In controlled studies, behavioral therapies are frequently successful at teaching couples effective problem-solving skills. Consequently, experiments testing the effects of behavioral therapy for couples generally show that couples who get the therapy are happier by the end of the program than couples who do not (Jacobson, Schmaling, & Holtzworth-Munroe, 1987). But when the experiment is over, couples tend to fall back into their old habits, and their satisfaction sometimes returns to where it was before the experiment (Jacobson & Addis, 1993). In other words, what works in the experimental setting does not always work in the real world. Experimental researchers often argue about the issue of **external validity**—whether the results of an experiment apply in other situations. Naturally, researchers hope their experiments will have high external validity; that the effects they observe will apply to a wide range of people in a wide range of situations. The more factors the researcher controls and manipulates, however, the less the experimental situation resembles other situations and the more external validity is threatened.

A broader limitation of experimental research arises when a phenomenon is difficult or impossible to control, and conducting an experiment is not an option. This limitation is especially significant in research on intimate relationships, where many phenomena of great interest simply cannot be manipulated. For example, to help victims of intimate partner violence, it would be useful to know how the experience of being physically abused by a partner affects a person's behavior in future relationships. Addressing this question with an experiment, however, requires that a researcher randomly assign people to a condition in which their partner abuses them or a condition in which they are not abused. Clearly, it is unethical for researchers to manipulate the experience of abuse. Likewise, researchers cannot manipulate the experience of being male or female, being from one country or another, or being heterosexual or homosexual. Researchers would like to make causal statements about how each of these variables affects intimate relationships; but because they cannot manipulate and control these variables, they cannot conduct the experiments that would support such statements scientifically. Perhaps due to this problem, experiments make up a relatively small part of research on intimate relationships.

Archival Research

It is possible to address interesting and important questions about relationships without gathering a speck of new data. In **archival research** the researcher examines existing data that have already been gathered, usually for an unrelated purpose, by someone else. Psychologist Avshalom Caspi and his colleagues, for example, have taken great advantage of archival data to study how personality—something usually described as pretty stable across the lifespan—may change over time in married couples. One set of studies addressed whether spouses become more similar to each other over time, and if so, why this might occur (Caspi & Herbener, 1990; Caspi, Herbener, & Ozer, 1992). To examine these questions, the researchers might have conducted a longitudinal study, gathering a sample of married couples and following them for several years to see if their personalities grew more or less similar to each other. This study design would have been appropriate, but expensive and time-consuming.

Instead, these researchers drew upon three data sets that mostly were collected before any of them were born. Two of these data sets were the Berkeley Guidance Study and the Oakland Growth Study, both longitudinal projects that contacted children in the late 1920s and early 1930s and then followed them periodically for their entire lives. The third was the Kelly Longitudinal Study, a project that contacted couples who were engaged in the late 1930s and followed them for 40 years. None of these projects was designed with the goal of studying how personality changes or remains stable in marriages. Still, the data sets were rich enough that they could be used to address a variety of questions that had never occurred to the original researchers. Caspi et al. (1992), for example, were able to use these existing data sets to show that married people's personalities tend to remain relatively constant across their lives, in part because they tend to marry spouses who are similar to themselves. Due to the great expense of contacting families, researchers who collect data on families often ask more questions than needed for addressing the specific issues under study. Thus, they build into their studies the potential for later archival research.

Besides revisiting existing data sets, archival researchers generate new data from archival sources that may never have been intended for use in research. For example, high school yearbooks contain pages and pages of valuable data on people's physical appearance, at least from the shoulders up. Psychologists LeeAnne Harker and Dacher Keltner (2001) took advantage of these data to examine how women's facial expressions in their yearbook photos predicted their marital outcomes 30 years later (FIGURE 2.8). They found that the more positive the facial expressions in the yearbook photos, the more likely the women were to be married at age 27; and for those who remained married, the more satisfied they were with the marriage at age 52. These findings are powerful evidence for the role that a positive outlook can have across the lifespan, though not something yearbook committees are likely to consider at meetings.

Personal advertisements are another potential goldmine for archival researchers. To examine differences in the qualities that heterosexuals and homosexuals look for in a mate, psychologist Doug Kenrick and his colleagues analyzed the features mentioned in personal ads seeking same-sex and opposite-sex partners (Kenrick, Keefe, Bryan, Barr, & Brown, 1995). In this study, as in most archival research that draws from public documents, the features the researchers wanted to examine were not initially presented in a form they could analyze. Thus, archival researchers often need to conduct a **content analysis**, by coding their materials in such a way that they can quantify differences between

FIGURE 2.8 Reading the future in a face. College yearbooks are treasured mementos, and for psychologists they can be a source of archival data. In this study, women who had a positive expression in their yearbook photo were more likely to be happily married 30 years later. (Source: Harker & Keltner, 2001.)

units. Harker and Keltner (2001), for example, rated the degree of positivity of the expressions in their yearbook photos on a scale of 1 to 10. Kenrick et al. (1995) calculated, for each of their personal ads, the difference between the stated age of the person placing the ad and the age of that person's desired partner. In this way they revealed that, regardless of their sexual orientation, men tend to seek out partners younger than themselves; but women, regardless of their sexual orientation, are more accepting of partners their own age or older. Content analysis of archival materials is similar to coding observational data because it raises similar challenges of deciding what dimensions to code and establishing reliability among coders.

PROS AND CONS. Archival researchers are the recyclers of science. They wring new information from old data sets and find new truths, sometimes literally in other people's trash. When questions can be addressed with archival data, this approach is economical and effective. It is often more efficient than, and just as accurate as, conducting an entirely new study. To study historical trends, or to examine how variables were associated in the past, researchers often have no alternative but to conduct archival studies. As new analytical strategies and new theoretical approaches are developed, the possibility of doing archival research means that any data set may contain new insights—if not today, then in the future.

Limitations to archival research reside less in the study design than in the data themselves. Because archival researchers do not gather the data to be analyzed, they cannot control the quality of those data. If the original study was of poor quality, the archival research will be of poor quality as well. Similarly, the design of an archival study depends on the design of the original data. If the original data are cross-sectional, a reanalysis of those data years later will still be cross-sectional and will be limited to addressing the questions that cross-sectional data can answer. A final limitation of archival research, and an especially frustrating one for archival research on intimate relationships, is that the researcher can examine only the questions asked in the original study. Caspi and his colleagues wanted to understand how personality changes or remains stable across the lives of married couples (Caspi & Herbener, 1990; Caspi et al., 1992), and they could do so only because the designers of the studies they drew from had thought to include personality measures. If new theories and concerns suggest new questions that have not yet been asked in existing data sets, then the path of archival research—as economic and efficient as it may be—is nevertheless ruled out.

Which Research Design Is Best?

TABLE 2.7 compares the features of correlational, longitudinal, experimental, and archival research. We can now look at which research design is the best. As the table makes clear, the most appropriate design for any study depends on the questions being asked. If you want to know what relationships are like, correlational research is perfectly suited to describing different aspects of intimate relationships and how they are associated. Describing how relationships change, or predicting whether and when they will end, calls for longitudinal research. Understanding why relationships change and determining cause and effect require an experiment. Archival research, although rarely used for experiments, is an option for either cross-sectional or longitudinal research, depending on how the original data were collected. In every case, when the study design is tailored to the questions being asked, then the strengths of the design bolster confidence in the study conclusions.

TABLE 2.7 **Research Study Designs Compared**

	General Approach	Advantages	Disadvantages
Correlational (cross-sectional) research	Assesses several variables on a single occasion.	Can describe naturally occurring associations among variables.	Cannot support causal statements.
Longitudinal research	Assesses variables on more than one occasion.	Can describe change over time and predict outcomes.	Cannot support causal statements; attrition bias.
Experimental research	Evaluates the effects of an independent variable on a dependent variable in a controlled setting.	Can support causal statements.	Results may not generalize outside the experimental situation.
Archival research	Reanalyzes existing data originally gathered for another purpose.	Cost-effective and can provide historical perspective.	Conclusions are limited by the quality of the original data.

MAIN POINTS

» Correlational research examines the naturally occurring associations among variables; it can be either cross-sectional, measuring all variables at a single occasion, or longitudinal, collecting data from the same individuals several times.

» Examining causal effects requires experimental research, whereby participants are randomly assigned to conditions in which an independent variable is manipulated and all other variables are controlled.

» Archival research involves reexamining existing data that may have been collected for another purpose; it can address descriptive or predictive questions.

Choosing Study Participants

A provocative question, a clever operationalization, and a powerful research design do not amount to much without people who are willing to give researchers access to their personal lives. In research on human beings, the people who provide data are called the **sample** because they are a subset of a broader population that, theoretically, could have provided very similar data. Identifying exactly who provided data is another important part of evaluating whether the results of a study generalize—that is, whether a study has external validity. Unlike research in chemistry or physics (where an atom is an atom wherever you go), research on humans must cope with the fact that people who provide data may differ from people who do not provide data in ways that may skew the results.

Imagine, for example, that a researcher wants to understand the different reasons people remain in their intimate relationships. Some people might stay because they value their partner; others might stay because they share children or resources with their partner (e.g., a house and a car), and it would be too costly to leave. Which kind of reason is more important? The answer might depend largely on who is being asked. College students do not generally sign mortgage contracts or have children with their dating partners. If the sample consists entirely of college students, the researcher might conclude that satisfaction with the relationship is the only thing that keeps couples together. Among married couples, on the other hand, spouses often do share resources they would lose by ending the relationship. If the sample includes

BOX 2.3 SPOTLIGHT ON . . .

The Challenges of Studying Couples

An irony of research on intimate relationships is that most of the data are collected solely from individuals (Furman, 1984; Karney & Bradbury, 1995). Studying individuals is no easy task, but studying couples raises unique issues that more than double the complexity. Consider the challenges that researchers interested in couples must face.

■ How do you know that two people are a couple?

Married couples usually know whether or not they are married—the license, the rings, and the wedding are a dead giveaway. Expand the focus to unmarried couples, however, and the boundaries that define "couplehood" get a lot fuzzier. For example, the National Longitudinal Survey of Adolescent Health asked a large sample of high school students to list all the people with whom they had been in a romantic relationship. Because the survey included all the students in several schools, the researchers also had data from most of the people that their respondents listed, allowing them to determine how often two people agreed that they had been in a romantic relationship with each other (Kennedy, 2006). How often did they agree? Less than half the time! Not surprisingly, better data on relationships come from pairs that agreed on the status of their relationship.

■ Whose information do you trust?

You might expect that two people in a couple would agree about the concrete details of their relationship, like when they met, how long they have been together, and whether they have kids. They usually do, but not always. Sometimes partners differ in how they understand their relationship, in how they understand a particular question, or in how honest they want to be. All of these possibilities lead to the same result: The researcher has two different answers to the same question about the same relationship. Deciding which one to trust can be a problem. If the question is about a quantity (e.g., relationship duration), one option is to take the average of the two answers. Other times the researcher may decide that one partner is inherently more trustworthy (e.g., women are quicker to report a pregnancy than men are, for obvious reasons).

■ Which effects do you care about?

Suppose you want to know about how the quality of a relationship is associated with personality. If you are studying individuals, you might ask people to report on their personality and their relationship satisfaction, and then estimate the correlation between their answers.

married couples, the researcher might reach very different conclusions. In both cases, the samples must be analyzed carefully to determine whether the results are likely to apply to other groups.

Because researchers would like their studies to have high external validity, an ideal would be to collect **representative samples**—samples consisting of people who are demonstrably similar to the population to which the researchers would like to generalize. A sample consisting entirely of college students in dating couples at a particular university, for example, might be perfectly representative of other college student dating couples at that university. Most of the time, however, researchers want their results to apply more broadly so they can draw conclusions that apply to a broader range of intimate relationships. How can we decide if a given sample is representative or not? In addressing this issue, David Sears (1986) argued that the external validity of a study is threatened only by differences between the sample

Add another partner to your sample, however, and the possible associations multiply. The Actor-Partner Interdependence Model (FIGURE 2.9) points out all of the different ways that two variables may be associated with each other within a couple (Cook & Kenny, 2005). To extend the personality example, each person's personality may be associated with his or her own relationship satisfaction (the Actor effect). Each person's personality may also be associated with his or her partner's relationship satisfaction (the Partner effect). Finally, specific combinations of personality may have unique associations with relationship satisfaction, beyond the effects of each partner's individual personality (the Interaction effect). Statistical techniques have been developed to tease all of these effects apart.

By recognizing and facing the unique challenges of studying couples, researchers have developed techniques and strategies customized for this field. They help characterize relationship science as an emerging discipline.

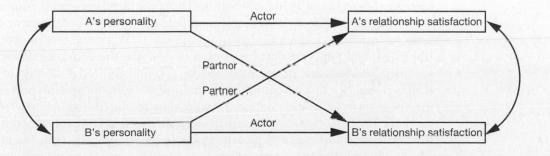

FIGURE 2.9 The Actor-Partner Interdependence Model. This diagram represents the possible associations of two variables in a couple. (Source: Adapted from Cook & Kenny, 2005.)

and the relevant population on dimensions that could conceivably affect the study results. In other words, if a researcher studies only newlywed marriages, the results may not apply to well-established marriages or same-sex couples, because it is easy to imagine potentially important ways the relationships of newlyweds may differ from relationships in the other two groups (e.g., shared resources, level of commitment, relationship duration, etc.). On the other hand, if a researcher studies only people with freckles, the results may well apply to other people as well, because no one has yet argued that having freckles affects relationship processes. (For more about the complexities of studying couples, see **BOX 2.3**.)

In research on intimate relationships, paying attention to the sample is important because most samples studied in this area have indeed differed in important ways from populations researchers might want to generalize about. One review of 280 studies published in the *Journal of Social and Personal Relationships* found that over half of all the research sampled exclusively from college students (de Jong Gierveld, 1995). Why does this field sample so many students? Not because researchers have an abiding interest in college students per se, but because they are easy to find on the campuses where much of this research takes place. Samples recruited solely because they are easy to find are called **convenience samples**. When composed of college students, convenience samples are more likely to be middle class and less likely to be married than other possible samples. Data from these samples may help us understand dating relationships among educated young people, but they may reveal little about relationships in later life or relationships among people who do not go to college. Studies that specifically address married couples have not escaped a heavy reliance on convenience samples. In fact, 75 percent of longitudinal research on marriage has addressed convenience samples that were primarily white, Protestant, and middle class (Karney & Bradbury, 1995). Again, we may know a lot about marriages in this group, but it is not clear to what extent this knowledge generalizes to marriages among other cultures, religions, or socioeconomic groups.

Samples of convenience have been a particularly thorny problem for research on same-sex intimate relationships. When research on homosexual sexuality began in the 1970s, gay men and lesbians faced enormous amounts of stigma and prejudice. Indeed, intimacy between members of the same sex was (and remains) against the law in several states. When sociologists Philip Blumstein and Pepper Schwartz wanted to describe the sexual behavior of gay men and lesbians in the early 1980s, they did not have the option of simply putting up fliers on campus, or randomly telephoning people and asking about their sexual orientation. Instead, they recruited their sample from gay bars and bath houses, where they were sure to find respondents who fit their criteria (Blumstein & Schwartz, 1983). Given the era when this research was conducted, this was a reasonable approach. Nevertheless, we might ask how well the sexual behaviors of individuals who were going to gay bars and bath houses at the time represent the habits of the entire homosexual population. More recent research on same-sex relationships has drawn instead from specific questions in the U.S. Census and on national surveys to describe the gay and lesbian population as a whole (e.g., Black et al., 2000). Although samples in research on intimate relationships have rarely been representative, this does not mean the studies are bad or the results are wrong. Rather, careful attention to the samples being studied may focus attention on questions that have yet to be asked, as well as on how much remains to be learned.

Throughout this book, we make every effort to identify and describe research that addresses the full diversity of intimate relationships across cultures and around the world. However, as just noted, this kind of truly global research is still rare. For most research, obtaining a representative sample remains an elusive goal. Until research on a broader range of couples has accumulated, careful researchers must take pains to draw conclusions appropriate only to the samples they have studied.

MAIN POINTS

>> Even when the study design is perfectly appropriate to the questions being asked, conclusions can be limited by the nature of the sample, or the subset of the population that actually provides the data.

>> Researchers try to collect data from people who represent the populations to which they would like their results to generalize, but this is hard to accomplish.

>> Most relationship science research relies on convenience samples. Even if the sample is not representative of the population, it can at least be shown to be similar to the population on dimensions that might affect the study results.

>> To the extent that a sample providing data is different from a population on those dimensions, any conclusions that apply to the sample may not apply to other groups.

Drawing Conclusions

In this chapter, we have noted that the choices researchers make at each step of the scientific method greatly shape the conclusions they can draw from their results. If we stopped right here, you might come away believing that conducting the study is the hard part and drawing conclusions is easy—just the wrap-up to a job well done. Life (at least for researchers) would be considerably simpler if that were the case. The reality, though, is that data rarely point to a single and obvious conclusion. In fact, deciding what to conclude from a given set of data can be as complicated and challenging as any other stage of the research process.

The Importance of Disconfirmation

After developing a theory and suggesting specific hypotheses that derive from the theory, researchers obviously hope their hypotheses turn out to be true.

After all, we conduct studies to develop a more accurate description of the world. Yet paradoxically, confirming hypotheses is not the goal of gathering data. Because any single study is incomplete in some way, there are not enough data in the world to ever finally confirm a hypothesis.

Instead of trying to confirm that an effect exists, scientific research is focused on disconfirming the **null hypothesis**—the hypothesis that there is no effect. Imagine, for example, that researchers want to know if taking classes about the psychology of intimate relationships affected future relationship satisfaction. By now, you might be able to suggest that the researchers conduct an experiment in which they randomly assign people to take either a relationships course or a different course, and then follow both groups over time to see how their own relationships turn out. The hypothesis, naturally, is that people who take a course on relationships will be more successful in their own relationships, but a single study cannot confirm it. Instead, the goal of the study is to reject the null hypothesis that people who take a course on relationships have the same relationship outcomes as everybody else. If even one study finds a difference between the groups, then the null hypothesis should be rejected.

In correlational research, for a different kind of example, the hypothesis is that two variables are correlated in some way. A correlational study thus tries to reject the null hypothesis that no correlation exists between two variables—that is, the correlation is zero.

In both types of studies, the results do not prove that an effect exists, but they do argue against the conclusion that *no* effect exists. The more a null hypothesis has been refuted, the more confident we can be in accepting a hypothesis as true—at least until a better hypothesis comes along.

Statistical Analysis

What exactly does it take to refute a null hypothesis? As mentioned above, a demonstrable difference between two groups can be enough to refute the null hypothesis that two groups are the same. But no two groups are ever going to be perfectly identical. There will always be some differences, however slight, even if the null hypothesis is true. So how big does an effect have to be to justify rejecting the null hypothesis? In general, an effect has to be large enough that it would be very unlikely to occur if the null hypothesis were true. Fine, you say; but how large is that, exactly? This is where statistics enter the picture. The goal of **statistical analysis** is to determine the probability of obtaining a particular result, given a particular set of conditions. Assuming a null hypothesis that there is no real effect, statistical analyses can determine the likelihood of a specific result (e.g., a difference between groups or a correlation between variables) being observed in a specific study. By convention, social scientists consider a result having a probability of less than .05 as justification to reject the null hypothesis. In other words, if my research reveals a result that would occur very rarely (less than once in every 20 cases) in a world where the null hypothesis is true, then the null hypothesis is probably false.

An example can make this even clearer. Suppose we really do want to know if taking a course on relationships improves your chances of having a satisfying relationship later in life. Suppose further that we are able to conduct a real experiment—randomly assigning 40 students to group A (whose members took a course about intimate relationships) and 40 others to group B (whose members took a course on an unrelated topic)—and then we compared the kinds of relationships the two groups were having 10 years later. Our hypothesis could be that students who take the relationships course (group A) will on average be in more satisfying relationships than the students who take the other course. What is the null hypothesis in this scenario? The null hypothesis is that the two groups will report no difference in average relationship satisfaction (i.e., taking the class on relationships had no effect). Of course, even if the class did have no effect, the average outcomes in two groups will never be *exactly* the same. Averages are not perfect, and two groups of people are never going to be the same down to the last decimal point. To reject the null hypothesis, we would want to see a substantial difference between the groups—one that would be very unlikely if there were no real effect. How big does the difference have to be before we can conclude that taking this course really does improve your intimate relationships (i.e., that there is an effect and we should reject the null hypothesis)? The difference has to be so big that, if there were actually no effect, we would expect to see it less than once every 20 times we conducted this experiment. Effects large enough to occur less than 5 percent of the time if the null hypothesis were true are called **statistically significant effects**. All of the effects described throughout this book reach that standard.

But even obtaining a statistically significant effect is not the end of the story. A probability of less than .05 means there is still a 1 in 20 chance of getting a statistically significant effect even if the null hypothesis is true. Considering that hundreds of studies are conducted and published each year, some of them are bound to be flukes—studies that just happened to obtain very unlikely results by chance. Recognition of this possibility is another reason social scientists place a high premium on replication, or obtaining the same results in multiple studies. The more a statistically significant effect can be observed repeatedly, even when different scientists look for it in different ways, the more confident we can be that the effect really exists and was not a chance occurrence.

Meta-analysis is a set of statistical techniques specifically designed to combine results across studies and reveal the overall effects observed by a body of scientific research. Meta-analysis is a powerful tool for researchers because results that are consistent across a greater number and wider variety of studies justify stronger conclusions than any single study can support. For example, as we will discuss in Chapter 4, researchers have used meta-analyses to summarize the enormous body of research on gender differences. These studies have shown that although women tend to be more empathetic and men tend to be more aggressive, these average differences are quite small (Lippa, 2005).

MAIN POINTS

>> No single study can ever have complete data, and therefore philosophers of science argue that no hypothesis can ever be finally confirmed. Instead, the goal of any one study is to refute the null hypothesis that there is no effect.

>> The null hypothesis is refuted whenever research obtains a result that would be very unlikely if the null hypothesis were true.

>> Researchers consider an effect to be statistically significant, and thus sufficient justification for rejecting the null hypothesis, when it would be observed less than 5 percent of the time in a world where the null hypothesis was true.

>> Even a statistically significant effect can be a chance result, and the strongest conclusions are drawn from results that have been replicated across many studies.

Ethical Issues

We have now discussed each stage of the scientific method, with respect to research on intimate relationships, and all scientific research proceeds along similar lines. One thing distinguishes social science research, and relationship research in particular, from other sciences: Human beings, unlike inanimate objects, can reflect on the experience of being studied, and they may have strong opinions about it. Research on relationships thus has a unique ethical dimension not found in research on other phenomena.

Imagine, for example, you have volunteered to be part of a research project on intimate relationships and now find yourself being asked to discuss a problematic issue with your partner on videotape. Or being asked to describe the strengths and weaknesses of your sex life with an interviewer. Or being asked to write down everything that irritates you about your partner, knowing your partner is in the next room answering the same question about you. How would that make you feel? Exposed? Anxious that someone you know might read your responses? Relieved at being able to share your thoughts with someone? All research on human beings requires sensitivity to the participants' feelings. But this may be especially true in studies of intimate relationships, where relationship researchers ask people to confide in strangers about issues that are—almost by definition—intensely personal and private. In studies like these, providing data to researchers places the participants in a highly vulnerable position. Researchers who study intimate relationships thus bear an especially heavy responsibility to behave ethically.

For a researcher interested in intimate relationships, what does ethical behavior entail? One guiding principle is simply to respect people who provide data. Psychologist Robert Rosenthal (1994) has argued that respect for participants carries the responsibility not to waste their time. Because every minute participants spend on research is a minute they could have spent doing something for themselves, researchers have an obligation to conduct research that meets the highest standards of scientific rigor, to ask nontrivial questions, and to utilize the data they collect to the fullest possible extent.

A second principle of ethical conduct in research is to protect participants from possible harm. In medical research, possible harm is often physical, like contracting a disease or suffering the side effects of an experimental treatment. In research on intimate relationships, possible harm is often more subtle and more psychological. For example, research on intimate relationships raises the risk that the details of participants' private lives might be made public. If a female participant discloses a sexual fantasy or an affair to a researcher, she could be greatly harmed were that information made available to friends and colleagues—or worse, to her romantic partner. To minimize this risk, researchers make every effort to maintain participants' **confidentiality**, ensuring that information is not shared or discussed with anyone not directly associated with the research. In studies where both partners provide data about each other, partners are typically urged to keep their responses private, so that answering questions about the relationship does not become a source of conflict between them. Similarly, researchers maintain the **anonymity** of their participants by identifying them with identification numbers rather than their names. That way, even if their information were to be released unintentionally, it cannot be linked to the individuals who provided it.

Another possible harm stemming from research on intimate relationships is that participants may be disturbed or upset by certain questions or research procedures. In general, current ethical standards do not allow researchers to ask potentially offensive questions or to place participants in situations they may find uncomfortable. Researchers studying survivors of sexual abuse or intimate partner violence, for example, may, in asking questions about these experiences, unintentionally lead participants to relive their trauma. One way to avoid such problems is by requiring researchers to obtain participants' informed consent before beginning the research. **Informed consent** is a written agreement signed by participants indicating they understand the research procedures and know what to expect. The consent form also guarantees participants the right to confidentiality and anonymity, as well as the right to refuse to answer any question and to withdraw from the research at any time.

By designing sensitive studies and preparing participants in advance, researchers hope participants will not be adversely affected. Even so, research on intimate relationships can still have lasting ill effects on the couples being studied. Partners are asked to consider aspects of their relationships they might not have thought about on their own. Certain questions may bring to mind issues and problems they otherwise would have overlooked or ignored. Concerned about the unintended effects of their research on the couples they study, several relationship researchers asked couples directly about those effects (Bradbury, 1994; Hughes & Surra, 2000; Rubin & Mitchell, 1976). Consistently, most participants reported that their participation did indeed affect their relationships. Most people described the effect as positive, such as increasing their awareness of the strengths of the relationship or bringing the couple closer together. However, 3–5 percent of participants described negative effects, such as recognizing unpleasant aspects of their relationships for the first time (Bradbury, 1994).

If even a few couples may be upset with what they learn as participants in research on relationships, is it ethical to conduct this research? In addressing this kind of question, Rosenthal (1994) urged that researchers consider not only the costs of conducting the research, but also the costs of failing to conduct the research. In the case of intimate relationships, research addresses questions that are fundamental to people's happiness. As we discussed in Chapter 1, relationships play a central role in emotional and physical health, and they are crucial to the continuation of the species. Forgoing the opportunity to address questions about intimate relationships could deprive future generations of the opportunity to benefit from the answers. For relationship scientists, those potential benefits motivate research in this area. Still, ethical researchers are careful to consider the feelings of even the small percentage of people likely to be upset by their research procedures. For this reason, most research on couples provides opportunities for people who have been disturbed by their participation to receive counseling if they so desire.

MAIN POINTS

>> Because research on intimate relationships addresses issues that are sensitive and private, relationship scientists have the responsibility to conduct their studies in an ethical manner.

>> One guiding principle of ethical research is to treat participants and their time respectfully, recognizing that they are partners in the research process.

>> Another principle is to protect participants from possible harm.

>> To prevent privacy violations, participants are guaranteed that the data they provide will be kept confidential and that their identities will be kept anonymous.

>> To ensure that participants are not upset or offended by research procedures, researchers obtain the informed consent of every participant before any study can begin.

>> While the guidelines for ethical research may not prevent some participants from being disturbed by things they learn as part of the study, they do ensure that the benefits of doing the research outweigh the costs.

CONCLUSION — –

Most people who read this book will not go on to careers in relationship science. But everyone will continue to be bombarded with contradictory advice about how to pursue and maintain intimate relationships: *We should confront our lovers when they disappoint us, so that minor problems do not balloon into major ones! No, we should forgive our lovers, and learn to accept disappointment! Wait, we should list and discuss each other's strengths and weaknesses! No, we should ignore each other's weaknesses!*

While it is unrealistic for researchers to conduct a study every time a new claim appears, the scientific method suggests the sorts of questions to ask when trying to distinguish between wisdom and hot air. What is the theory behind a particular claim? Is it a theory that could be tested—and, if so, has it been? What are the main constructs in the theory, and how have they been operationalized? Who was studied, and were they measured once or several times? What are the alternatives to the claim, and have they been ruled out?

As we have described it, the scientific method is simply a set of tools for evaluating competing claims about the truth. Undoubtedly, some studies of intimate relationships are better than others. This does not mean the scientific method is flawed, but rather that some researchers have used these tools more skillfully and more appropriately than others. At the same time, however, researchers hope through their studies to reveal truths about relationships that transcend their methods. In the chapters that follow, we focus on the research that succeeds in revealing those truths. This success comes from asking the most interesting questions, using the most appropriate methods, and drawing the most reasonable conclusions.

Even so, we should keep in mind the words of the late Neil Jacobson. After years of influential scientific research on marriage, Jacobson wrote:

> The intuitions of the lay public offer stiff competition to marriage researchers, since the folklore created by these intuitions extends much further in many cases than the research questions asked by scientists studying marriage. It is easy to be impatient with scientific progress in the field of marriage when it moves so slowly in comparison to the popular imagination. (Jacobson, 1990, p. 259)

Is this a critique of his field? We prefer to consider Jacobson's words a call to action—an acknowledgement that despite our considerable accomplishments, scientific techniques for capturing the full richness and complexity of intimate relationships are yet to be developed.

– –

3

Theoretical Frameworks

Great Minds Don't Think Alike

Imagine you are having some doubts about whether your partner really loves you. Should you wait and see what happens, or confront your partner with your concerns? You can't stop worrying about what to do, and it's starting to keep you awake at night.

Imagine you're also in the fortunate position of being able to turn to Sigmund Freud and B. F. Skinner for advice (FIGURE 3.1). As far as therapists go, you could do worse.

Freud (1856–1939) was the founder of **psychoanalysis**, the theory that first distinguished between the conscious and unconscious mind. Skinner (1904–1990) was the founder of **radical behaviorism**, the idea that behaviors are shaped (or "conditioned") by their consequences, and that positive consequences make behaviors more likely and negative consequences make them less likely. Neither Freud nor Skinner specialized in matters of the heart, but during their lives both of them wrote about nearly every aspect of human behavior. Certainly, both men had much to say on the topic of love. Indeed, their work provided the foundation for several of the most important theories in the field of intimate relationships.

If these two great men agreed to see you, and had neighboring offices, your experience in each place might be very different. Freud would start by asking about your earliest memories of childhood. Did you feel loved? Were your parents available when you needed them? He would want to hear about any of your recent dreams. Gradually, he would try to reveal the unhealed wounds of your earliest years and encourage you to appreciate how your current relationship insecurities might result directly from insecurities you first experienced in infancy.

Skinner might find your discussion with Freud boring and distracting. Rather than focusing on your childhood, Skinner would want to know about your current relationship. If the relationship is not rewarding, he would ask about how you and your partner allocate rewards and costs. When your partner is cool and distant, do you become even

FIGURE 3.1 Sigmund Freud and B. F. Skinner, two of the most influential psychologists of the 19th and 20th centuries. They had very different opinions about how the mind works and how people relate to one another. What do those different views say about the role of theory in shaping our understanding of intimate relationships?

more attentive? Skinner might be especially interested in hearing about recurring patterns of behavior. What happens when you try to raise difficult issues with your partner? Does your partner withdraw, or lash out at you? He might point out that you actually are reinforcing your partner's emotional distance, and that your partner is conditioning you to avoid uncomfortable topics.

Two intellectual giants, two completely different approaches to understanding intimate relationships. Why such a difference?

The difference stems from the theories that shaped each man's approach to the mind, human behavior, and—by extension—love. Freud's views about intimate relationships followed closely from his ideas about the unconscious. He proposed that mate choices in adulthood were shaped by motives developed during infancy and early childhood. Freud believed that intimate relationships have problems when partners begin to play out with each other their unresolved issues and conflicts with their parents.

Skinner's views, in contrast, followed closely from his ideas about reinforcement and conditioning. For Skinner, the forces that drive us exist primarily in the present environment, not the past. Successful relationships depend on the extent to which pleasing behaviors are rewarded and encouraged, and

displeasing behaviors are extinguished through negative reinforcement. Relationships have problems when partners unwittingly reinforce each other's displeasing behaviors.

Just as for Freud and Skinner, the same is true for anyone who studies intimate relationships (or anything else): The way we think is shaped by our theories. Sometimes our theories are explicit, well-articulated systems of thought that others may choose to adopt and follow. But whether our theories are explicit or not, they act as lenses to filter information about what we observe, emphasizing some details and minimizing others, with the goal of reaching the best understanding of the phenomenon itself. No lens is completely without flaws, however, and no theory is perfect. Theories may present a distortion, a caricature, or such a narrow window into the phenomenon that larger truths are overlooked.

QUESTIONS

For a complete understanding of any phenomenon, then, it makes sense to assess the theories used to examine and study it. What theories have influenced the way researchers have thought about intimate relationships, and why they succeed or fail? Because everyone's experiences and opinions about relationships are slightly different, on some levels there are as many theories as there are people. Among relationship scientists, however, certain theories have been described formally and specified in considerable detail. They have influenced a wide body of thinking and research, and are the theories we emphasize in this chapter.

How have the most influential theories guided the questions researchers have asked about intimate relationships? What kinds of explanations does each theory offer? Which aspects of intimate relationships do different theories emphasize, and what aspects do they minimize or ignore?

Influential Theories of Intimate Relationships

In Chapter 2 we defined a theory in terms of its function, as a general explanation of a phenomenon. We observed that theories direct efforts to answer questions about the world, providing the initial hints of where the answers might lie. A theory may be defined as an interconnected set of beliefs, knowledge, and assumptions that relate to understanding a phenomenon. This definition leaves the boundaries wide for what makes a theory. People have models, perspectives, worldviews, frameworks, schemas, scripts, and stereotypes—and in a way, all of them can be thought of as theories because they refer to ideas that guide how we explain and integrate new observations. Because they play such a large part in our lives, intimate relationships are a subject people are very likely to approach with preexisting ideas.

What makes some theories influential and some not? First, influential theories tend to be described formally; someone has articulated a set of explicit premises and explained the predictions derived from those premises. This level of specificity is one thing that distinguishes a scientific theory from the intuitions and beliefs most people have about relationships. Second, the mark of an influential theory is that it has inspired research and scholarship. All the theories in this chapter have been discussed in hundreds of studies—a testament to their power to guide inquiries into relationships. Third, influential theories make predictions that withstand multiple tests. The theories we discuss suggest predictions about how relationships work, and those predictions have been supported through multiple methods and different kinds of samples. The more findings consistent with a theory we accumulate, the more confidence we have that the theory really does describe the world accurately.

> " Science is built up of facts, as a house is built of stones; but an accumulation of facts is no more a science than a heap of stones is a house."
>
> —Henri Poincaré, French mathematician, (1854–1912)

Although we will describe the leading theories of intimate relationships, there are plenty of others scattered across the many disciplines that take an interest in intimacy. Here we provide a selective, not exhaustive, review of major theoretical approaches. Moreover, our descriptions barely scratch the surface of the rich complexity of each perspective. Each theory is far more elaborate than space allows, and every one is also constantly being revised and refined. With this in mind, we have tried to capture the flavor of these pivotal approaches, as well as offer a sense of how theories are applied and evaluated. You will find more elaboration and description of these and other theories in subsequent chapters.

The Evolutionary Perspective

Since Charles Darwin published his revolutionary book *The Origin of Species* (1859), scientists have gathered reams of evidence supporting the theory that the features that characterize different species evolved through the process of natural selection. Over the course of evolutionary history, the features that contributed to successful reproduction were passed down to subsequent generations, and those features that prevented or diminished successful reproduction gradually died out. The evolutionary perspective on intimate relationships begins by noting that human beings, like any other species, must reproduce in order to pass their genes to the next generation. Mating behaviors in humans should thus be as much the product of natural selection as mating behaviors in other species (Symons, 1979). Just as humans evolved opposable thumbs and the ability to walk upright, we evolved characteristic ways of attracting mates, selecting mates, and protecting our relationships.

This way of thinking about intimate relationships is part of the broad field of evolutionary psychology, which began in the late 1970s and early 1980s (see Buss, 1995). **Evolutionary psychology** assumes that the mind, like any other organ in the body, evolved in response to specific selection pressures that led some preferences and capacities to be associated with more successful reproduction, and other preferences and capacities to be associated with less successful reproduction. If this is true, then the features of the mind we observe in humans today exist because they were adaptive—that is, they contributed to reproductive success in our ancestral past. Identifying distinctive features of the human mind and determining why those features evolved is therefore a route toward understanding why we are the way we are. Thus, the central questions posed by evolutionary psychologists revolve around the adaptive function of human behavior. What is the purpose of the characteristic ways humans behave? How might the ways that humans conduct themselves have promoted successful reproduction in our evolutionary history?

> " Humans seek particular mates to solve specific adaptive problems that their ancestors confronted during the course of human evolution; human mate preferences and mate decisions are hypothesized to be strategic products of selection pressures operating during ancestral conditions."
>
> —Buss & Schmitt (1993, p. 205)

Fundamental Assumptions

To apply this way of thinking to intimate relationships, evolutionary psychologists draw directly from Darwin's original theory of natural selection, in which he noted that any feature of an organism can be adaptive for either of two reasons. A feature may be adaptive because it increases an organism's chances for survival; this is the basis for the idea of "survival of the fittest." A feature also may be adaptive because it directly increases an organism's chances of successfully reproducing by helping the organism compete for or attract mates. In this second way, a feature may be adaptive even if it has nothing to do with survival or even if it impedes survival. This kind of adaptation is called **sexual selection**, and examples abound in nature. Consider the male peacock's splendid plumage. Do the brilliant colors of his tail feathers help him attract food or avoid predators? No. In fact, the tail feathers may attract predators, and they certainly make it harder for the encumbered peacock to run away. So why did the characteristic pattern evolve? Sexual selection provides the answer: Large and brightly colored tail feathers help peacocks attract mates (i.e., peahens). If males with the brightest feathers are more likely to mate and reproduce than males with smaller and duller feathers, then over the course of many generations, it makes sense that males of the species would evolve the increasingly extravagant displays we see today. Similar arguments explain the elaborate antlers of the elk, the multihued beak of the toucan, and the bushy mane of the lion (**FIGURE 3.2**).

In the same way that peacocks evolved their tails and elks evolved their horns, the evolutionary perspective suggests that humans also evolved specific features to solve reproductive challenges. Some of these are physiological features, like the relative height of males and the relative curviness of females. Yet humans are also thought to have evolved **psychological mechanisms**—broadly defined as the preferences, capacities, responses, and strategies characterizing our species.

FIGURE 3.2　Look at me! In many species, males have evolved physical features and behaviors that do not appear to promote survival. How did these extravagant displays evolve? Evolutionary psychologists point out that some traits and tendencies are passed down through generations because they promote sexual selection—they increase the chances that a male will successfully attract a mate. What do you think?

Although the idea of psychological mechanisms is central to the evolutionary perspective on intimate relationships, it also causes some confusion (Simpson & Gangestad, 2001). The word "mechanism" has a deterministic sound, and some critics are concerned that thinking about psychological mechanisms implies that people are merely biological machines lacking the ability to respond to and learn from the environment. Evolutionary psychologists do not take this view; they think of psychological mechanisms as being similar to physiological organs. The heart, for example, is clearly an evolved mechanism for pumping blood; but it has evolved an acute sensitivity to environmental conditions, so it increases blood circulation when we are active or stressed and decreases it when we relax or are safe. Similarly, these researchers conceive of psychological mechanisms as being responsive to the environment; they believe humans have evolved receptivity to specific kinds of environmental cues and developed strategies designed for different contexts. The desire for sex, for example, is a psychological mechanism—and an exceptionally useful one for promoting reproduction—but for most people, this desire is highly responsive to specific cues in the environment.

Although psychological mechanisms are thought to have evolved, not all of them are likely to contribute to survival and well-being in the present day. On the contrary, anthropologists estimate that the human brain evolved to its present form about 10,000 years ago. Society has changed immeasurably since then, but, restricted by the slow and gradual pace of evolution, our brain is still more or less the brain that developed in the past. Thus, many of the behavioral tendencies and preferences we observe today may have been selected to adapt to an environment that no longer exists. One example of how the slow evolution of our brain can lead to problems is the preference for sweet flavors over bitter ones. When early humans were scrounging for food and living in caves, a preference for sweet tastes was adaptive because things that tasted sweet were likely to be more nutritious than things that tasted bitter. In today's world, however, where sugary foods are widely available, our evolved preference for sweet tastes is less adaptive and can lead to obesity and tooth decay.

Just like our food preferences, our mate preferences, our sexual behaviors, and even our emotions have also had too little time—in evolutionary terms— to have evolved much since the enormous social changes of the last several millennia. Understanding the strategies and preferences that drive human relationships today thus requires an understanding of adaptive problems faced by humans in the **environment of evolutionary adaptedness**, or the period tens of thousands of years ago during which the human species took its current form. Because this period occurred before the dawn of recorded history and is thus beyond the reach of psychological research, evolutionary psychologists must rely on the accomplishments of anthropology for their descriptions of what life was like then. Based on what they know about the selection pressures humans faced during that period, evolutionary psychologists make predictions about the psychological mechanisms that guide mating and sexual behavior in the present day.

What selection pressures might have existed in the environment of evolutionary adaptedness? To answer this question, evolutionary psychologists draw heavily on the **theory of parental investment** (Trivers, 1972). According to this extension of Darwin's original work, sexual selection pressures tend to vary based on the amount of energy and resources each sex must invest to raise surviving offspring. In humans, for example (as in most mammals), parental investment is typically high for females. A female produces a single egg during a menstrual cycle and has the capacity to reproduce for only a limited period during her lifetime. Once the egg is fertilized, gestation takes 9 months—and none of her other eggs can be fertilized while she is pregnant. Because each fertilized egg consumes her entire capacity for reproduction at the time, the adaptive problem for a female is ensuring that each child she invests in has the greatest chance of survival. The theory of parental investment predicts that, to solve this problem, females should be selective about mates and choose only high-quality partners. From this perspective, important markers of quality include a partner with lots of resources to devote toward the female and her offspring during pregnancy and childhood, who demonstrates a willingness to commit those resources, and who is big and strong to protect the female and her offspring from predators. Females who were careful about mate selection 10,000 years ago would have raised more offspring who survived. Over hundreds of generations, females would have evolved preferences for high-quality partners and therefore developed mechanisms to attract them.

In contrast to females, males have relatively low parental investment; their contribution to reproduction can be as minimal as a one-time deposit of sperm. Further, males can impregnate multiple females at the same time and remain fertile throughout their lifetimes. Though there are few restrictions on the number of offspring they can produce, males have these adaptive problems: ensuring access to the more selective females, ensuring that as many pairings as possible result in surviving offspring, and ensuring that, when they do contribute resources toward raising a child, the child is genetically related to them. An effective strategy for solving these problems would be to identify in advance which partners are likely to be fertile and then mate with as many as possible. Males who identified and mated with the largest number of fertile partners would have been more successful at producing surviving offspring. Over hundreds of generations, they would have evolved a desire for multiple partners and mechanisms for identifying which of them would likely be fertile.

In other words, the evolutionary perspective on intimate relationships suggests that, as a direct response to the different adaptive challenges each gender faced in the environment of evolutionary adaptedness, we should observe gender differences in the preferences and mating behaviors of males

FIGURE 3.3 Gender differences in mate selection preferences. Evolutionary psychologists suggest that, 10,000 years ago, a preference for taller mates was adaptive for females, for whom a taller mate meant protection and thus a greater likelihood of surviving offspring. Taller mates are less strongly associated with survival today, but in a wide range of cultures across the world, women's preference for taller mates remains.

and females today. And indeed, that is the case. Take, for example, the question of height and attractiveness. Which gender would you predict is more attracted to taller mates? If you guessed that women are more likely than men to prefer taller mates, you're right. In fact, this gender difference seems to be strongly true in Western cultures (Ellis, 1992), among tribal people in the Brazilian Amazon (Gregor, 1985), and in every other culture studied so far (**FIGURE 3.3**). Why should this be true? The evolutionary perspective suggests that a preference for taller mates was adaptive for females because a taller mate could more likely protect the female and her children from physical and sexual assaults by other males. This solved the females' adaptive problem of ensuring that each child they invest in has the greatest chance of survival. Over many generations, those females who attracted taller mates actually received protection, and their children were more likely to survive, so this preference was successfully passed down to future generations.

The evolutionary perspective can also illuminate a question about chastity. Which gender should be more interested in ensuring that their partner is a virgin? It is not hard to see that men care more about their partner's virginity than women do. Although this finding is less true now than it was half a century ago, the gender difference exists—and it exists in every culture studied (Buss, 1989). Why is it this way and not the other way around? The evolutionary perspective offers an explanation. For males, a major threat to reproductive success is the possibility that they are devoting their resources to someone else's children. Males who failed to ensure their paternity saw none of their genes passed on to subsequent generations. To avoid this genetic tragedy, males would have evolved preferences for signs that their mates are sexually faithful, and virginity is one of these signs. For females, in contrast, virginity in a mate carries few significant adaptive benefits, and so the evolutionary perspective predicts that females will care less about virginity in their mates. In contemporary cultures across the world, this prediction still seems to be accurate.

The evolutionary perspective suggests, then, that current gender differences in mate preferences and sexual behavior reflect adaptive solutions to the different reproductive challenges males and females faced over the course of evolution. As a result, females developed sensitivity to and preferences for cues indicating a partner's resources and strength (BOX 3.1). Likewise, males developed sensitivity to and preferences for cues indicating a partner's fertility and fidelity. It is crucial to note, however, that *this perspective does not suggest males and females should have developed any conscious or explicit preferences for resources or fertility per se*. Clearly, a great deal of mating and sexual behavior takes place in situations in which neither partner is the least bit interested in fertility or resources. This is perfectly consistent with the theory. The evolutionary perspective states that the preferences seen in human males and females today correspond to cues signifying fertility and resources in the environment of evolutionary adaptedness 10,000 years ago. Even if a cue like height is no longer linked to resources, and virginity is no longer linked to fertility and faithfulness, the preferences that developed over the course of human evolution persist.

How the Evolutionary Perspective Guides Research

The evolutionary perspective on intimate relationships poses some thorny problems for researchers. How does one determine whether a behavior is the product of an evolved psychological mechanism? Human mating and sexuality involve countless behaviors. Are they all the products of evolved mechanisms, or might some of them be learned during a person's lifetime or absorbed through cultural or social models? The problem is exacerbated because the definition of psychological mechanisms, including as it does the preferences, capacities, responses, and strategies characterizing the human species, is fairly broad. Most evolutionary psychologists agree that psychological mechanisms are inherited, and thus linked to biological structures of the brain, but identifying where exactly in the brain the mechanisms lie

BOX 3.1 SPOTLIGHT ON . . .

The Scent of a Man

The evolutionary perspective on intimate relationships suggests that women, as the ones with more reasons to be selective about sex partners, would have evolved sensitivity to cues that a potential partner has good genes (one of the many resources a female might look for in a mate). Those cues can be easy—or not so easy—to spot.

One sophisticated physical marker of genetic fitness is bilateral symmetry—the extent to which features appearing on both sides of the body (ears, eyes, hands, and feet) are the same size and shape (FIGURE 3.4). A number of studies confirm that, in both sexes, people who are more physically symmetric tend to demonstrate superior physical and mental health (Thornhill & Moller, 1997). Yet physical symmetry is hard to judge with the naked eye. Researchers addressing this feature use something most people do not have available—digital instruments sensitive to 0.01 millimeters. Are there any cues to genetic fitness that might be easier for selective females to monitor?

Biologist Randy Thornhill and psychologist Steven Gangestad (1999) suggested a simpler cue that might be associated with genetic fitness: the way someone smells. Lots of studies have shown that the way a partner smells is an important factor in sexual attraction and mate selection, and women report that they are more strongly affected by smells than men are (e.g., Herz & Cahill, 1997). To Thornhill and Gangestad, the idea that smell may be a good marker of genetic fitness helps explain the gender difference. Women should be more responsive to smell because they have the most interest in the genetic fitness of their partners. Further, these researchers suggested that women should be especially responsive to this marker during periods when the genetic fitness of their partners makes the most difference (i.e., when the women are ovulating).

To test these ideas, Thornhill and Gangestad rated the physical symmetry of 80 men and 82 women and then asked each of them to spend two nights sleeping in a new, white, cotton T-shirt. To control for differences in hygiene, all participants were told to shower before bed using an unscented soap provided by the researchers. After returning their shirts in sealed plastic bags, the men and women were asked to rate the scent of the T-shirts that had been worn by members of the opposite sex. As the researchers expected, the men's ratings of the female smells were unrelated to the women's physical symmetry. Similarly, the smell ratings of the nonovulating women were unrelated to the men's physical symmetry. However, women who were ovulating—that is, those women who would have the highest stake in the genetic fitness of a potential partner—rated the scent of a shirt worn by a physically symmetric man as significantly more pleasant and sexy than the scent of a shirt worn by an asymmetric man. When they were ovulating, women appeared to possess an ability to sniff out genetic fitness that women who were not ovulating lacked.

(a)　　　　　　　　　　　(b)

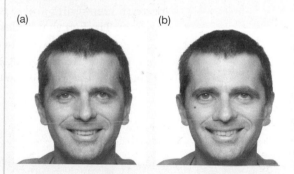

FIGURE 3.4 Bilateral symmetry and genetic fitness. Researchers asked men and women to rate the smell of T-shirts worn by men who differed in facial symmetry. Men and nonovulating women could not smell the difference. But ovulating women, for whom the genetic fitness of a potential mate could influence their reproductive potential, preferred the smell of T-shirts worn by (a) more facially symmetric men to that of (b) less facially symmetric men. (Source: Thornhill & Gangestad, 1999.)

is usually beyond the scope of this kind of research. Instead, they look for certain behaviors presumed to be the product of certain psychological mechanisms. For example, if a researcher hypothesized that males evolved a preference for younger female partners (because youth in females was associated with fertility), then the observation that most men do seem to mate with and desire younger partners would be taken as support for the existence of the mechanism (Kenrick & Keefe, 1992). The evolutionary perspective can be shown powerfully through **cross-cultural studies** in which researchers identify behaviors that characterize mating and sexuality consistently across a wide variety of countries and cultures (e.g., Buss, 1989). Evolutionary psychologists argue that if they can identify aspects of mating behavior that are common to the entire human species, then these behaviors are likely to represent evolved mechanisms.

These researchers face another problem: How does one know where to look for evidence of evolved psychological mechanisms? Obviously, they cannot return to the environment of evolutionary adaptedness 10,000 years ago and see what selection pressures were operating. Instead, evolutionary psychologists think about what that environment was probably like, what adaptive problems humans would logically have faced, and what mechanisms they may have developed to deal with those problems. One premise of the evolutionary perspective is that males and females faced very different adaptive problems relative to reproduction, so most applications of this perspective focus on identifying and explaining gender differences in mating and sexual behavior. The fact that males and females around the world demonstrate differences consistent with the presence of distinct mating strategies is taken as support for the idea that males and females evolved unique psychological mechanisms for solving their reproductive problems.

Evaluating the Evolutionary Perspective

The evolutionary perspective is best described as a collection of theories, rather than a single theory (Buss, 1995). Within a broad set of common assumptions about how human beings evolved, researchers have suggested and examined an array of more specific ideas about different kinds of selection pressures that may have affected the development of different kinds of behaviors. For understanding intimate relationships, this breadth of the evolutionary perspective is both a strength and a challenge.

The promise of the evolutionary perspective lies in its ability to address ultimate questions about how human beings attract and select mates. Why do humans behave the way they do within intimate relationships? What purposes do our behaviors, preferences, and sensitivities serve? The value of addressing these questions is particularly striking when applied to gender differences. People have been describing gender differences in human mating behaviors for thousands of years. But the evolutionary perspective moves beyond mere description and toward an understanding of the adaptive functions those differences may serve and the processes that formed them. In this way, an evolutionary perspective offers a means of linking research on relationships to research on the history and biology of our species.

Yet, despite the potential breadth of this perspective, evolutionary psychologists have thus far investigated some questions about intimate relationships far more than others. For example, proponents of the evolutionary perspective tend to focus on behaviors and gender differences that characterize most of the species, regardless of culture or historical era. In this search for absolutes, they often overlook the rich, complex variability among individuals and within each gender (Eagly & Wood, 1999)—although evolutionary thinking can be applied toward understanding this variability as well (e.g., Gangestad & Simpson, 1990). Similarly, in the search for ultimate and ancestral causes of modern behavior, evolutionary psychologists sometimes neglect to consider more immediate causes of the same behaviors. Even if all the mechanisms guiding human mating behaviors did evolve through natural selection, sometimes looking for the contemporary causes of our behavior may be more useful (e.g., if we are trying to change people's present-day behavior). Finally, evolutionary psychologists have thus far studied how men and women attract and choose mates far more than they have studied how people manage those relationships once they begin. Again, evolutionary psychology has the capacity to address the development of relationships (Buss, 1994), but so far, that territory remains mostly unmapped by this perspective.

MAIN POINTS

>> Evolutionary psychologists apply Darwin's theories of natural and sexual selection to the human mind, arguing that the preferences and tendencies characterizing humans today are those that were associated with more successful mating and reproduction thousands of years ago.

>> The evolutionary perspective draws heavily on the theory of parental investment, an elaboration of Darwin's theory proposing that the sex with the greater investment in offspring should be the one more selective about choosing mates.

>> Although people may not think consciously about successful reproduction when choosing a mate, female preferences (for older, taller, and stronger mates) and male preferences (for younger, healthier, more available mates) that may have been cues for adaptively desirable traits 10,000 years ago still remain.

>> The evolutionary perspective is well suited to address issues of why we observe specific gender differences in the world today, but the implications of this perspective for understanding variability within genders and between cultures remain to be explored.

Attachment Theory

Like the evolutionary perspective on intimate relationships, attachment theory suggests that the roots of our current intimate relationships lie in the past. While the evolutionary perspective seeks those roots in the ancestral history of the human species, attachment theory does not look back quite that far. Instead, attachment theory searches for the sources of adult experiences in the personal history of individuals. Specifically, **attachment theory** proposes that the intimate relationships we form in our adult lives are shaped largely by the nature of the bonds we form with our primary caregivers in infancy and early childhood.

The foundation of attachment theory was established in an influential three-volume series titled *Attachment and Loss*, by John Bowlby (1969, 1973, 1980). Trained in classical psychoanalysis, Bowlby was familiar with Freud's theories about the impact of early childhood on adult life. Yet his own work with children convinced Bowlby that Freud's theory, focusing on fantasies and dreams, was wrong to overlook the real experiences children were having with their primary caregivers. As Bowlby developed it, attachment theory represented a rejection of classical psychoanalytic theory. The central questions he addressed were nevertheless very similar to the ones that inspired Freud: How do experiences in early childhood shape the course of adult development? Why do some people seem to fall into the same types of relationships throughout their lives? What functions do these relationship habits serve?

Fundamental Assumptions

Like the evolutionary psychologists, Bowlby drew from anthropology in developing his approach. But he was less interested in our ancestral past than in the way our primate relatives raise their young in the present. He began by observing that, for humans as well as other primates, survival during infancy requires an ability to maintain proximity to a primary caregiver. By contrast, newborns of many other animal species, such as fish and reptiles, emerge from the egg fully capable of feeding and protecting themselves. Human infants are so immature and helpless that they need constant attention and protection. Bowlby, anticipating later developments in evolutionary psychology, suggested that the extreme dependence of human infants would have led to selection pressures favoring behaviors that create and maintain closeness between infants and an **attachment figure**—someone who provides the child with comfort and care. For an example of the behaviors Bowlby was thinking about, consider that, although human infants cannot feed or protect themselves,

> " All of us, from the cradle to the grave, are happiest when life is organized as a series of excursions, long or short, from a secure base provided by our attachment figure(s)."
>
> —John Bowlby (1979, p. 129)

no one has to teach them how to cry or smile. Even the most helpless babies engage in these behaviors shortly after being born. In Bowlby's view, human infants evolved these early capabilities as ways of attracting attention from their attachment figures and ensuring that those individuals stay around to protect and feed them. Parents, in turn, do not have to learn how to be reactive to their children's cries. Sensitivity to infant cries is also evolutionarily adaptive because parents who respond to their children are more likely (than insensitive parents) to have children who grow up to reproduce successfully.

Building on these ideas, the first premise of attachment theory is that humans have evolved, among other behavioral systems, an **attachment behavior system**—a set of behaviors and reactions that helps ensure the developing child's survival by keeping the child in close physical contact with caregivers. The caregiver's presence and protection, in turn, promote the experience of **felt security**, which makes the child feel safe and sheltered from impending threat or harm. Felt security thus frees the child to explore the nearby environment until threats arise, until the caregiver becomes unavailable or unresponsive, or until the child experiences needs that require the caregiver's attention. These threats to felt security will produce feelings of fear and anxiety, thus motivating the child to once again seek refuge with the caregiver. At this point the attachment behavior system prompts the child to evaluate whether it is possible to restore closeness, or proximity, with the caregiver. If it is possible, the system is said to be *hyperactivated*, leaving the child highly vigilant for signs of threat and abandonment, highly active in mobilizing the behaviors needed to attain proximity, and insistent in ensuring that the attachment figure remains available. Anyone who has ever spent time with infants and their parents can confirm that most infants protest loudly when separated from their mothers; this is a clear sign of the child's attempts to maintain proximity (**FIGURE 3.5**).

If the child does not have the option of restoring proximity with the caregiver, the attachment behavior system instigates *deactivating* strategies that turn off, or inhibit, the drive to restore closeness with the caregiver. The child inhibits emotional expression, tries to quell the feelings of frustration, and—in an effort to avoid further feelings of vulnerability—aims to distance himself or herself from others. A reunion with the caregiver may occur eventually, of course, at which point the infant's anxiety is reduced and the cycle begins anew.

The attachment behavior system acts as a kind of internal control system by which a child monitors three key variables: his or

FIGURE 3.5 Sound the alarm! When infants feel threatened, their cries are a signal for a caregiver to respond and restore their sense of felt security.

her own internal states, the caregiver's availability and responsiveness, and the presence of threats in the environment. This monitoring system leads to specific kinds of behavioral adjustments that in turn maximize physical proximity to the caregiver and restore the experience of felt security (Mikulincer & Shaver, 2007).

The second premise of attachment theory is that, although the presence of an attachment behavior system is common in humans, different individuals form different kinds of attachment bonds as a function of their particular interactions with caregivers during infancy and childhood. According to Bowlby (1969), infants who are exposed to responsive caregivers—those who are consistently warm and sensitive, particularly when the infant is upset and seeking comfort—come to believe that they are worthy of the love and attention of others, and that others are generally caring and dependable. Infants exposed to inconsistent or harsh caregivers—controlling, unpredictable, or overly intrusive in times of need—will come to believe the opposite: that they are unworthy of the caregiver's attention and affection, and that caregivers themselves are not dependable or trustworthy. Whether positive or negative, these accumulated experiences are assumed by attachment theory to be stored inside of us in the form of working models. **Working models** can be thought of as internal psychological structures representing the conscious and unconscious beliefs, expectations, and feelings people have about themselves, about others, and about relationships. They are presumed to influence how new experiences in our relationships are selected, interpreted, and integrated into our sense of who we are.

What does all of this work with infants have to do with intimate relationships among adults? Although much of the initial research on Bowlby's ideas focused on attachment in infancy, Bowlby himself suggested that the attachment behavior system was a central part of human functioning throughout life. Because the models of attachment developed within the relationship with the primary caregiver should affect how individuals approach each new relationship thereafter, Bowlby predicted that attachment models would be highly stable over time. Psychologists Cindy Hazan and Phil Shaver made the case for links between infant attachment and adult romantic relationships by noting that many of the features that characterize relationships between caregivers and children also characterize relationships between adults in love (Hazan & Shaver, 1987; Shaver, Hazan, & Bradshaw, 1988). Take a moment to think about the different relationships you see around you. In what kinds of relationships is it acceptable to talk "baby talk"? What kinds of relationships are characterized by a powerful urge for cuddling and other physical contact? In what kinds of relationships do partners seek each other out, gaze into each other's eyes, feel distress when separated, and express joy when reunited? In all of these behaviors and many more, Hazan and Shaver saw continuities between the way people relate to their children and the way they relate to their romantic partners. This is consistent with Bowlby's view that both types of relationships activate the same attachment behavior system.

Internal working models are the feature of attachment theory that links our early experiences with caregivers to our later experiences with romantic partners. As we mature through adolescence and into early adulthood, we transfer the focus of our attachment from a parental figure to a romantic partner (Weiss, 1986), and we ourselves become a caregiver for others in our relationships. Simultaneously, we begin to rely less on actual physical proximity to the caregiver as we become able to represent the caregiver via mental or physical images. For example, we might have our partner's picture on our cell phone to remind us of the bond we share with him or her; or, when we are apart, we might take comfort in simply thinking about our partner. Internal working models enable this process to continue from one relationship to the next, and, reciprocally, experiences in those relationships can evoke change in the working models. So, for example, being betrayed or badly deceived in a long-term relationship could make a secure person more cautious or insecure about subsequent relationships, whereas the insecure person fortunate enough to have an unconditionally supportive and understanding partner could grow to become more secure (Davila & Cobb, 2003; Ruvolo, Fabin, & Ruvolo, 2001).

Working models are assumed to be relatively stable because new information is incorporated into them based on experiences that have already occurred. Existing information tends to confirm new information. For example, a secure individual might interpret a failed relationship as due to a lack of chemistry with the partner, whereas an insecure person might explain the same event as further evidence that he or she is unlovable and unlikely to have fulfilling relationships in the future. And because internal working models are generally stable, they operate in new relationships much like they did in previous relationships—by regulating the expression and resolution of attachment needs.

Researchers hypothesize that the precise ways individuals differ in their desires and preferences for closeness in intimate relationships follow directly from two key functions of the attachment behavior system (e.g., see Bartholomew & Horowitz, 1991; Collins & Read, 1990; Hazan & Shaver, 1987; for reviews, see Cassiday, 1999; Collins & Feeney, 2004). The first function enables the individual to detect threats in the environment; feelings of anxiety cue the infant to seek proximity to the caregiver. But chronic exposure to a parent who is inattentive and unavailable, or inconsistent and unpredictable, will lead the child to develop internal working models resulting in chronic anxiety, insecurity, and sensitivity to rejection and abandonment. Such experiences may result in a low sense of self-worth and doubts about deserving love.

The second function concerns the degree to which the individual believes the caregiver is available, and the corresponding tendency to turn toward or away from other significant people in the face of distress. Infants typically aim

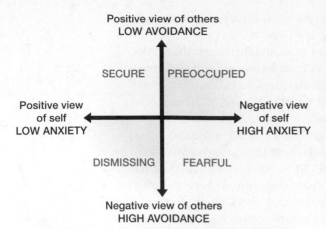

FIGURE 3.6 **The two dimensions of attachment.** Individual differences in internal working models are represented along two dimensions: anxiety, with generalized beliefs about one's value and self-worth; and avoidance, with generalized beliefs about the dependability and trustworthiness of others to meet one's needs. Four broad attachment styles result when these two dimensions are combined. People falling in the preoccupied, dismissing, and fearful quadrants are considered to have an insecure attachment style. About 60 percent of all people have a secure attachment style, with the rest distributed variously across the three insecure styles.

to restore proximity when they experience anxiety, but consistent exposure to a punitive and rejecting caregiver will lead the child to develop working models organized around the view that others are best avoided because they are not a reliable source of comfort. Such experiences may result in generalized expectations about the availability and support others are likely to provide (Hazan & Shaver, 1987).

Thus, in attachment theory, adults differ along two main dimensions: anxiety and avoidance. One tendency is to experience anxiety about perceived threats to the attachment relationship (and corresponds with a relatively negative view of the self). The other tendency is for avoidance in the face of attachment-related anxiety (and corresponds with a relatively negative view of others). Because the two dimensions of attachment—anxiety and avoidance—are assumed to be independent of each other, individual responses can be represented graphically (**FIGURE 3.6**).

An individual tends to fall into one of four quadrants, defined by the dimensions of anxiety and avoidance. The evidence is clear that attachment styles are better represented by continuous dimensions than by the neat categories Figure 3.6 suggests (Fraley & Waller, 1998). However, the four groupings illustrate how anxiety and avoidance combine to produce four broad **attachment styles:** secure, preoccupied, dismissing, and fearful.

1. **Secure attachment style**. Secure people are low in attachment-related anxiety and avoidance and have positive views of themselves and others. They feel worthy of others' love and confident that others will be responsive and dependable. Secure individuals are said to be comfortable with closeness and intimacy. They value relationships, but they can maintain their sense of independence and autonomy away from relationships.

2. **Preoccupied attachment style**. Like secure individuals, preoccupied people have a positive view of others and thus are low in attachment-related avoidance. They value closeness, but their low sense of self-worth leaves them chronically high in anxiety. Preoccupied with their own insecurities and perceived inadequacies, such individuals can come across as needy, depending on others to prop up their uncertain sense of who they are, and to reassure them that they are worthy of attention.

Rejection is especially painful for preoccupied individuals because it confirms doubts about their self-worth, while robbing them of the security they need others to provide for them.

3. **Dismissing attachment style**. Dismissing individuals are also like secure individuals, but on the other dimension: They have a positive view of themselves, and thus are low in attachment-related anxiety and view themselves as worthy of others' care and attention. The problem, as perceived by dismissing individuals, is that others are unlikely to be caring and available. Having formed internal working models with a negative view of others, dismissing individuals value independence and self-sufficiency. Dismissing individuals do not experience attachment-related anxiety or dwell on the possibility of rejection. But to maintain their positive self-view alongside their negative view of others, they tend to avoid closeness, minimize its importance, and dismiss their own need for intimacy.

4. **Fearful attachment style**. Fearful people have negative views of themselves and others, causing high anxiety. Their quest for intimacy begins with the expectation of being unworthy of caring and consideration; this view pushes them to seek validation from others. At the same time, they struggle with the internalized sense that others are unlikely to provide the affirmation they need. Because they expect others to be a source of pain and rejection, fearful individuals tend to avoid intimacy and the discomfort it brings.

Self-report measures of attachment typically assess the two main dimensions along which working models of attachment can differ. For example, the Experiences in Close Relationships Scale uses responses on items like those in TABLE 3.1 to index anxiety and avoidance (Brennan, Clark, & Shaver, 1998).

A key point to remember in thinking about how people differ in their attachment styles—and where you might fall along the dimensions in Figure 3.6—is that the attachment behavior system motivates virtually everyone to seek comfort and closeness. Evolution dictates that this behavior is not optional. Individuals high in attachment-related avoidance are just as likely as others to desire close, intimate relationships. However, the way they accomplish this central task will differ compared to the behavior of those low in avoidance: Highly avoidant people may be less emotionally forthcoming, or more tentative, or more indirect in expressing their need for closeness. Thus, some people are equipped to have a relatively easy time negotiating the complex terrain of human intimacy, while others must find ways to adapt who they are to the many challenges intimacy affords (FIGURE 3.7). In short, according to attachment theory, each of us is "making do" in our intimate relationships with the psychological apparatus—the internal working model—that resulted from our early interactions with caregivers.

TABLE 3.1 **The Experiences in Close Relationships Scale**

Indexing anxiety:	Disagree strongly				Agree strongly		
I worry about being abandoned.	1	2	3	4	5	6	7
I worry a lot about my relationships.	1	2	3	4	5	6	7
I worry that romantic partners won't care about me as much as I care about them.	1	2	3	4	5	6	7
I need a lot of reassurance that I am loved by my partner.	1	2	3	4	5	6	7
Indexing avoidance:	**Disagree strongly**				**Agree strongly**		
I prefer not to show a partner how I feel deep down.	1	2	3	4	5	6	7
Just when my partner starts to get close I find myself pulling away.	1	2	3	4	5	6	7
I want to get close to my partner, but I keep pulling back.	1	2	3	4	5	6	7
I prefer not to be too close to romantic partners.	1	2	3	4	5	6	7

Source: Adapted from Brennan, Clark, & Shaver, 1998.

How Attachment Theory Guides Research

Once Hazan and Shaver (1987) pointed out the links between infant attachment and adult attachment, researchers were eager to test whether the basic predictions of Bowlby's theory held true for adult intimate relationships. Largely, they did. Consistent with the way the attachment behavior system is expected to work in adulthood, for example, people do in fact seek closeness with, and benefit from, attachment figures when they are threatened in some way (Fraley & Shaver, 1998). Also, individuals experience greater feelings of security in relationships when the partner is viewed—even by outside observers—as more supportive and responsive (e.g., Collins & Feeney, 2000). And partners who describe themselves as secure experience happier (Simpson, 1990), more trusting (N. L. Collins & Read, 1990), and longer-lasting relationships (Kirkpatrick & Hazan, 1994) than those who describe themselves as insecure.

The next wave of research examined specific behaviors that help maintain the relationships of people with secure attachment styles and contribute to relationship problems for those with insecure attachment styles. For example, to the extent that people with insecure attachment styles have doubts about whether other people will love them, then they should be more alert to signs of problems in their intimate relationships and get more agitated when discussing those problems with their partners, compared to secure people.

To test this prediction, dating couples were asked to complete nightly surveys about their daily experiences and feelings in the relationship, every night for 14 nights (Campbell, Simpson, Boldry, & Kashy, 2005). As expected, those with insecure attachment styles seemed to have a heightened sensitivity to signs of conflict. They reported conflicts more often overall, and significantly more often than their partners reported in the same relationships. On days when they experienced conflicts, insecure partners were more gloomy about the relationship as a whole, in contrast to more secure individuals whose experience of specific conflicts were less likely to affect their opinions about the entire relationship. Finally, when these same couples were recorded talking about an area of disagreement, observers rated the less secure individuals as significantly more upset by the conversation than the secure participants, regardless of their partner's attempts to soothe them. The irony is that the tendency of insecure people to attend to and escalate conflicts weakens the long-term prospects for the relationship (Kirkpatrick & Hazan, 1994). Their excessive concerns about threats to the relationship appear to make those threats more damaging. These same processes appear to operate regardless of the gender of the attachment figure: Same-sex and different-sex couples are indistinguishable with respect to the way they describe their attachment styles and their attachment-related behaviors (Roisman, Clausell, Holland, Fortuna, & Elieff, 2008).

Another goal of research on attachment has been to examine the stability of attachment styles over the lifespan. To date, research supports Bowlby's original idea that attachment styles are generally stable. For example, when studied over intervals from 8 months (Scharfe & Bartholomew, 1994) to 4 years (Kirkpatrick & Hazan, 1994), most adults report the same attachment styles over time. In one study, young adults were interviewed about their attachment styles 20 years after they had been characterized during infancy. The researchers found that 72% of them received the same classification both times (Waters, Merrick, Treboux, Crowell, & Albersheim, 2000). Approaching the same phenomenon from the other direction, psychologists Eva Klohnen and Stephan Bera (1998) examined data from a longitudinal study that assessed women several times over the course of 31 years. Their analyses revealed that women who described themselves as avoidant at age 52 had been less committed to getting married at age 21, less likely to be married at age 27, more likely to be divorced at age 43, and less trusting and confident at every phase of the study than women who described themselves as secure. Across a number of similar studies,

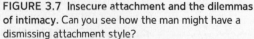

"I'm not saying that I don't have intimacy issues. I'm just saying that I prefer to work on them by myself."

FIGURE 3.7 Insecure attachment and the dilemmas of intimacy. Can you see how the man might have a dismissing attachment style?

around 70% of people seem to have stable attachment styles over time, lending considerable support to Bowlby's theory (Baldwin & Fehr, 1995).

Yet Bowlby argued that attachment styles can change when disruptions occur in the caregiver's availability and behavior, such as when a parent dies, becomes seriously ill for a prolonged period, or leaves the family (Bowlby, 1969). This prediction has also received support. For example, although attachment assessed in the first year of life (using a standard observational procedure) can predict attachment assessed around age 19, the continuity of attachment between childhood and early adulthood is significantly lower for children exposed to many difficult life events (e.g., Weinfield, Sroufe, & Egeland, 2000). People whose relationships end are likely to become less secure than people who remain in the same relationships over time (Ruvolo, Fabin, & Ruvolo, 2001). In contrast, people who get married tend to become more secure (Crowell, Treboux, & Waters, 2002). Adolescence seems to be a time when attachment styles are especially likely to change, as the transition from family-based attachment figures to romantic attachment figures might shake up a person's expectations about the care he or she can expect from others (e.g., W. A. Collins, 2003). Attachment theory predicts exactly this pattern. Overall, then, research on attachment styles over time reinforces Bowlby's theory of working models as generally stable but responsive to important experiences involving trust and intimacy throughout the lifespan.

Evaluating Attachment Theory

For a time after Hazan and Shaver introduced relationship researchers to Bowlby's work, attachment theory was the most popular approach to studying intimate relationships around. To this day, the theory continues to influence this field. Several strengths may account for the enduring interest in attachment and relationships. First, attachment theory adopts a developmental perspective lacking in other theories of intimate relationships. Clinical psychologists and practitioners, exposed as they are to clinical case studies, have an intuitive sense that our early experiences with intimacy affect the way we express intimacy as adults; but attachment theory provides researchers with a framework for thinking about and studying the continuity of experiences across the lifespan. Second, attachment theory offers an explanation for how this continuity may come about. Early experiences give rise to our models of attachment, and these models subsequently guide our expectations and behaviors in new relationships. Third, attachment theory begins to explain variability in the values and expectations people bring to their relationships. Why do some people demand a lot from their partners, while others tolerate neglect and even abuse? Attachment theory points out that our standards as adults may be the lasting consequences of our experiences as infants. Finally, attachment theory suggests that intimate relationships, parent-child relationships, and even relationships among primates are all manifestations of a single behavioral system. The economical nature of that idea has great appeal.

In focusing on continuity over the lifespan, however, attachment theory has thus far offered a somewhat limited explanation of how a specific relationship develops between two people. Presumably, people begin their relationships feeling optimistic that their specific needs for security will be fulfilled. Attachment theory is only now beginning to specify what happens within relationships to change the way those expectations develop over time. Similarly, the fact that most people rate themselves as securely attached would suggest that most people's relationships should be more successful and satisfying than they seem to be. How might relationships between secure people nevertheless fail? For that matter, how might relationships among people who are insecure sometimes succeed? Research on attachment has yet to explore these questions.

MAIN POINTS

>> Attachment theory proposes that humans have evolved an attachment behavior system, consisting of behaviors that ensure close proximity to caregivers during infancy and early childhood.

>> From different experiences with caregivers, individuals develop internal working models of attachment, which vary along two dimensions: anxiety (how much people worry about whether others will provide care) and avoidance (how much people seek out others or keep to themselves).

>> The two dimensions of attachment suggest four broad attachment styles: secure, preoccupied, dismissing, and fearful.

>> Research confirms the general stability of attachment styles over the lifespan and across different relationships, and demonstrates that partners describing themselves as secure experience closer and more long-lasting relationships than those describing themselves as insecure.

>> Attachment theory explains how previous experiences in relationships may affect each new relationship, by shaping the working models people use to interpret and evaluate their partner's behaviors.

Social Exchange Theory

The evolutionary perspective and attachment theory look to the past to understand adult intimate relationships. In contrast, social exchange theory is anchored firmly in the present. While acknowledging that relationships take place within a historical and personal context, social exchange theory centers on how individuals make decisions and evaluate their relationships in the

> " The interdependence between persons is specified by how they control one another's outcomes, which include on the one hand rewards and benefits and on the other hand costs and punishments."
>
> —Harold Kelley, *Personal Relationships* (1979, p. 13)

moment. This approach to understanding human relationships was developed in the late 1950s and early 1960s as part of a broader movement in psychology, sociology, and anthropology that combined principles of Skinner's behaviorism—especially the idea of rewards and punishments—with elementary economics (Homans, 1958). The result was an emerging set of theories that described social interactions in economic terms. Just as partners in a business transaction try to maximize their outcomes (or get the most they can from each transaction) by exchanging material goods, **social exchange theory** suggests that partners in all social interactions try to maximize their outcomes through the exchange of social goods like status, approval, and information. By identifying the perceived payoffs of specific behaviors, social exchange theory predicts what people will do in any given situation, and how they will feel about the outcomes of their actions.

The principles of social exchange theory have been applied to understanding human behavior in a wide variety of domains, from bureaucracies to jails to hospitals (e.g., Blau, 1954; Homans, 1961), and they have been especially productive as applied to intimate relationships (Thibaut & Kelley, 1959). For example, relationship satisfaction can be considered an evaluation of the outcomes a partner is receiving from the relationship at a given time. How do partners evaluate their outcomes in relationships, and how do they decide if they are satisfied with those outcomes? Relationship stability can be considered the result of each partner's decision whether to leave the relationship or stay and maintain it. How do partners make these decisions, and how can we predict when people will elect to leave or stay? In addressing these questions, social exchange theorists suggest that "relationships grow, develop, deteriorate, and dissolve as a consequence of an unfolding social-exchange process, which may be conceived as a bartering of rewards and costs both between the partners and between members of the partnership and others" (Huston & Burgess, 1979, p. 4). How influential has this approach been? Consider that, in 1992, Gary Becker, a University of Chicago professor who analyzed marital decisions in terms of rewards and costs, received the Nobel Prize in Economics (Becker, Landes, & Michael, 1977).

Psychologists John Thibaut and Harold Kelley laid out many of the central tenets of this perspective in their classic book *The Social Psychology of Groups* (1959). As their title suggests, they had planned to write a book about the behaviors of small groups of people, but they thought it wise to begin their analysis by focusing on the smallest group possible: two individuals, or a **dyad**. They expected that after figuring out the relationship between two people, they would move on to studying progressively larger and more complex groups. What began as a preliminary task in fact occupied both men for the rest of their lives.

Thibaut and Kelley (1959) were the first to propose, as noted in Chapter 1, that the defining feature of any relationship is interdependence, the extent to which the behaviors of each partner affect the outcomes of the other. This idea was so important to Thibaut and Kelley that they referred to their version of social exchange theory as **interdependence theory**. Because this version has been applied to intimate relationships most often, it is the one we emphasize here. Although in Chapter 1 we discussed the different ways two people might be interdependent with each other, Thibaut and Kelley were more interested in figuring out the effects of interdependence. Specifically, they wanted to understand the rules that predict how interdependent partners will behave toward each other, and how the partners will evaluate the outcomes of their actions.

Fundamental Assumptions

A fundamental assumption of social exchange theory as applied to intimate relationships is that people evaluate and make decisions about their relationships in the same way they approach economic decisions—by rationally analyzing the rewards and costs. The theory defines rewards and costs broadly: **Rewards** are any of the ways the relationship may fulfill the needs and desires of each partner, and **costs** are any of the consequences of being in a relationship that prevent partners from fulfilling their needs or desires. In line with elementary economic principles, the theory assumes that human beings are driven to maximize their rewards and minimize their costs whenever possible. The theory further assumes that people generally have good instincts about the likely rewards and costs of a situation.

What are the potential rewards of an intimate relationship? A relationship may ensure that partners have adequate food and protection, which are known as **material rewards**. As discussed in Chapter 1, however, some primary functions of relationships are to fulfill emotional and psychological needs (e.g., R. S. Weiss, 1973). Companionship, validation, and security are considered **social rewards**. Both types of rewards are important elements in social exchange theory. What are the potential costs of an intimate relationship? In a distressed relationship, these costs are fairly obvious. They can include the financial drain of an unreliable partner, the emotional pain of jealousy or frequent arguments, and even the threat of physical harm. Even a generally satisfying relationship, however, is likely to involve costs. Maintaining a relationship takes time and energy that are consequently unavailable to pursue other interests. Most relationships require some exclusivity, thus costing each partner the opportunity to explore alternative relationships. Costs associated with not pursuing these other possible sources of reward are called **opportunity costs**—as in "By sticking with this relationship, I missed the opportunity to do something else really cool" (e.g., take that job in Chicago; get to know that attractive member of the wedding party).

Of course, most relationships are neither perfectly rewarding nor perfectly costly. You probably find some aspects of your relationship rewarding (it's nice to have a hand to hold at the movies; there is something intoxicating about the way your partner smells) and some aspects costly (your partner's obsession with a television show you can't stand; the fact that you no longer have time to watch the television show you prefer). Given all the positives and negatives, how do partners evaluate the relationship as a whole? Social exchange theory suggests that partners evaluate the overall outcomes they receive in their relationship according to this very simple formula (Thibaut & Kelley, 1959, p. 13):

$$\text{OUTCOME} = \text{REWARDS} - \text{COSTS}$$

According to this formula, if the rewards you are receiving from the relationship are greater than what it is costing you to remain in the relationship, then your net outcome is positive. If the costs of the relationship outweigh the rewards, then your net outcome is negative.

This may seem like a straightforward idea, but comparing rewards and costs in relationships is not at all straightforward, because there are no set standards for comparing the degree to which certain rewards are rewarding and certain costs are costly. Suppose, for example, you are trying to decide whether to pursue a relationship with a potential partner. It makes more sense to pursue the relationship if the predicted outcome is positive; but in advance, you cannot know exactly what the rewards and costs of the relationship will be. Social exchange theory says your decision about whether to move forward will depend on your guesses about those rewards and costs. Moreover, the impact of any particular reward or cost on your guesses will be modified by **subjective probability**—your own sense about the likelihood of its occurrence (Levinger, 1976). A reward or cost that seems very probable carries more weight in calculating potential outcomes than one that may never happen. This is why, for example, even though relationships with celebrities may potentially be rewarding, most of us do not pursue them: We prefer the more modest but more probable rewards of relationships pursued within our own social circle.

Even if the outcome of a relationship is positive, the partners are not necessarily satisfied. What if the rewards of a relationship just barely outweigh the costs? How positive do the outcomes have to be before partners are satisfied? According to social exchange theory, evaluating satisfaction with a relationship requires that partners compare their perceived outcomes to a certain standard of what they think they deserve (Thibaut & Kelley, 1959). Thibaut and Kelley called this standard the **comparison level (CL)**. They suggested that different individuals have higher or lower comparison levels, based on their prior experiences in relationships. By this way of thinking, satisfaction in a relationship is not merely the result of experiencing positive outcomes, but of experiencing outcomes exceeding the level we think we deserve. When we get less than that comparison level, even if our outcomes are still positive, we are unlikely to be satisfied. Expressed as an equation:

$$\text{SATISFACTION} = \text{OUTCOME} - \text{CL}$$

The ideas expressed in this equation are more complicated than they look. By accounting for the different comparison levels of different individuals, social exchange theory helps explain how different individuals can reach very different conclusions about the same set of outcomes in the same relationship. Have you ever met someone who appears to be in a high-reward/low-cost relationship (e.g., good-looking partner, not a lot of arguing) but still complains and seems dissatisfied? Social exchange theory predicts that such an individual must have a high comparison level—so high that the outcomes that might be satisfying to other people are not positive enough to satisfy this person. On the other hand, maybe you know someone who seems content in a relationship that appears to have few rewards and many costs (e.g., with a partner observed to be inconsiderate or obnoxious). That person may have a low comparison level—so low that even negative outcomes are still greater than expected.

Social exchange theory has been applied not only to how people feel about their relationships, but also to how they behave in their relationships. One of the most important behaviors is also the most basic—the decision to remain in the relationship or end it. More satisfying relationships are usually more enduring, but not always. In fact, the association between being satisfied and remaining together is weaker than you might expect. Across multiple studies, the correlation between how satisfied partners are and how likely they are to stay together over time ranges from .14 to .44 (Karney & Bradbury, 1995). This is considered a small to moderate correlation (Cohen, 1983), suggesting that the two concepts are best treated independently.

Social exchange theory identifies precisely how satisfaction with a relationship and the decision to maintain a relationship can be separated. Evaluations of whether a relationship is satisfying are logically distinct from decisions about whether to remain in a relationship. If satisfaction is OUTCOME – CL, then it is entirely a function of how each partner evaluates what goes on within the relationship. In contrast, **dependence** on the relationship—that is, how free a person feels to leave the relationship—should be a function of how the relationship compares to the available alternatives outside of the relationship. Thibaut and Kelley (1959) called partners' perceptions of their potential options the **comparison level for alternatives (CL_{alt})**, and they pointed out that this standard may be entirely independent from an individual's CL. Whether partners have high or low standards for their current relationship, and whether they are satisfied with that relationship or not, they will be dependent on the relationship to the extent that the outcomes are greater than the outcomes available elsewhere. Expressed as an equation:

$$DEPENDENCY = OUTCOME - CL_{alt}$$

To understand the difference between satisfaction and dependence, consider the intimate relationships of some famous celebrities. The actor Brad Pitt, for example, was in a well-publicized marriage with the actress Jennifer

Satisfaction

	High	Low
High	Attracted and mutually committed relationships	Abusive relationships; "empty shell" marriages
Low	Uncommitted lovers	Strangers; pairs that are now dissolved

Dependence

FIGURE 3.8 Relationship satisfaction and dependence.
Social exchange theory suggests that satisfaction in, and dependence on, a relationship are two separate and distinct concepts. DIfferent combinations of each one characterize various types of relationships.

Aniston. To many outside observers, a relationship with a talented and beautiful actress like Jennifer Aniston would be satisfying and worth maintaining, and maybe it was. Brad Pitt, however, left her and ended the marriage. Why? Social exchange theory provides a possible answer. Brad probably had an exceptionally high CL_{alt}. No matter how high his satisfaction was (or how positive his outcomes were) in his marriage with Jennifer, he probably knew that equally positive or even more positive outcomes were available to him elsewhere; as a wealthy and attractive celebrity, he had more access to alternatives than an average guy does. As a result, Brad may never have been very dependent on the relationship, even though it may have been extremely satisfying. In fact, after the breakup with Jennifer, Brad quickly struck up a relationship with another talented and attractive actress, Angelina Jolie, suggesting that his high CL_{alt} was probably justified. In contrast to the average celebrity, however, many people have a far lower CL_{alt}. This helps explain why people may remain in unsatisfying or even abusive relationships. The implications of dependence and satisfaction for intimate relationships are summarized in **FIGURE 3.8**.

Although most people think of CL_{alt} in terms of alternative relationships, the concept of alternatives is much broader than that. Thibaut and Kelley (1959) thought of **alternatives** as being all of the likely consequences of leaving a relationship, including being alone. Psychologist George Levinger (1966, 1976) broadened the concept to include not only the alternatives to remaining in a relationship, but also the obstacles, or barriers, to overcome by ending it. **Barriers** can be defined as all the forces external to a relationship that act to keep partners together. In many cultures, for example, getting a divorce means facing strong disapproval from family and friends. The threat of negative judgments can be a powerful barrier that makes leaving a current relationship seem less appealing. Similarly, some people have no source of income and must rely entirely on their partners to provide for their basic needs. The threat of homelessness or poverty is another barrier reducing the perceived alternatives to an existing relationship.

Another perspective on the forces keeping people together is the idea of **investments**, "the number and magnitude of resources that are tied to a relationship" (Rusbult & Martz, 1995, p. 560), that would presumably be lost if the relationship were to end. Children, a shared home, and even the time spent in a relationship are all investments that may be lost or threatened when a relationship ends. Rather than lose their investments, some people elect to remain in relationships that may otherwise be unsatisfying. Barriers and investments may be considered elaborations of Thibaut and Kelley's CL_{alt}

BOX 3.2 SPOTLIGHT ON . . .

The Endurance of Abusive Relationships

Violence or abuse is surely one of the worst experiences a person can have in an intimate relationship. Yet women who have been abused often remain committed to their relationships. Even women who have sought help from shelters for battered women return to their partners at alarming rates of up to 40 percent by some estimates (e.g., Snyder & Fruchtman, 1981). Why do battered women frequently return to those who battered them? Many attempts to answer this question have focused on the personality of the victim. It has been suggested, for example, that women who remain in abusive relationships must be masochistic, have low self-esteem, or believe they deserve to be abused (e.g., Shainess, 1979). Social exchange theory offers what is perhaps a simpler explanation: Abused or battered women may be extremely dependent on their relationships. They return to their abusive partner because the alternative of leaving that partner would be even worse.

This view has considerable support. For example, women who return to their abusive partners are far less likely to have their own incomes than women who leave for good (Strube & Barbour, 1983). They usually have been in the relationship longer (Strube, 1988), and perhaps as a result they are likely to feel more invested in the relationship (Rusbult & Martz, 1995). What alternatives are available to these women if they decide to leave their partners? Research on the most extreme cases of intimate partner violence has shown that many batterers deliberately isolate their partners, separating them from friends, family, and other sources of support (Pence & Paymar, 1993). So for women in this situation, the likely consequences of leaving the relationship could be poverty, loneliness, and perhaps even a dangerously vengeful partner. From this perspective, the decision to remain committed makes perfect sense.

Which theory is believed has profound implications for which intervention would be most helpful to battered women. If women remain because they are masochists or feel they deserve the abuse, then a reasonable treatment would be to focus on helping women understand why they feel this way. If women stay because they have no other choice, however, then that type of intervention would be at best a waste of time and at worst dangerous. Social exchange theory suggests that effective interventions for intimate partner violence should focus on providing victims with acceptable alternatives, thereby reducing their dependence on the abusive relationship.

to the extent that high barriers and substantial investments both reduce the attractiveness of leaving a current relationship.

Social exchange theory has been accused of painting a cynical picture of intimate relationships, and indeed the idea of people staying with their partners to avoid costs or preserve rewards seems at odds with our ideals of romance. However, Levinger (1976) points out that the external forces keeping couples together become noticeable only when the partners are considering leaving the relationship. In satisfying relationships, partners generally focus on love and companionship (i.e., rewards) as the reasons they remain together. When the attractions of the relationship are powerful and satisfaction is high, the two people might not measure their investments and pay less attention to their alternatives (e.g., Miller, 1997a). In unsatisfying relationships, however, where the rewards are few and the costs are high, leaving the relationship becomes a real possibility. Under such circumstances, partners may be especially aware of all their reasons, other than satisfaction, for staying in the relationship. In this way, social exchange theory helps explain why some people remain in relationships that are distressing or abusive (BOX 3.2).

Drawing this distinction between satisfaction and dependence suggests two possible reasons for remaining in an intimate relationship (Levinger, 1976; Lewis & Spanier, 1979, 1982): because the partners want to (they are satisfied) or because they have to (they are dependent). The sum of all the forces, internal and external, that keep a relationship going gives rise to **commitment**—defined as the intention to remain in, and feel connected to, a relationship (M. P. Johnson, 1973; Rusbult, 1980). Expressed as an equation:

$$\text{COMMITMENT} = \text{SATISFACTION} + \text{DEPENDENCE}$$

In looking back over the equations we have described so far, you might notice that satisfaction, dependence, and commitment are all theoretically distinct. However, each of these constructs is in some way a function of the outcomes in the relationship. Thus, the more positive the outcomes, the more everything goes right. In other words, the more likely those outcomes are to meet the partners' standards of what they deserve (i.e., exceed their CL), the more likely those outcomes are to be better than the available alternatives (i.e., exceed their CL_{alt}); consequently, the more likely the partners are to be committed to the relationship.

How Social Exchange Theory Guides Research

The simple equations of social exchange theory have guided a great deal of research on how people behave in different kinds of relationships. Some of the largest contributions made by this theory are toward understanding the circumstances under which people will remain in or leave their relationships. For example, over periods from as short as 6 weeks (Drigotas & Rusbult, 1992) to as long as 15 years (Bui, Peplau, & Hill, 1996), partners who perceive fewer comparable alternatives to their current relationships prove significantly more likely to remain together. Sociologists Scott South and Kim Lloyd (1992; 1995) have used archival census data to make a similar point. They compared marriage and divorce rates across census tracts nationally and found that people are more likely to marry and divorce when they live in neighborhoods containing larger numbers of eligible partners. In neighborhoods with fewer eligible partners, people are naturally less likely to marry, but they also are less likely to divorce if they are married. Social exchange theory explains why: Where there are fewer alternative partners, people are more dependent on their current relationship.

In these studies, social exchange theory makes predictions that may seem obvious in retrospect. Of course people are more likely to stay together if they have nowhere better to go. However, it is worth noting that before the development of this theory, relationship scientists usually focused exclusively on the qualities of romantic partners, figuring that relationships ended if the partners had fatal character flaws and endured when partners were well balanced (e.g., Burgess & Cottrell, 1939). Social exchange theory led researchers to broaden their focus to include variables outside the partners that serve to keep them together or draw them apart.

Another focus of research guided by social exchange theory has been an examination of how people behave when they are committed to their relationships, because they are either satisfied or dependent. Social psychologist Caryl Rusbult and her students identified numerous ways partners act to protect and maintain their relationships when they are committed. For example, when asked to rate the physical attractiveness of a potential alternative partner, those in a committed relationship tended to rate the alternative as less physically attractive than single people did (Johnson & Rusbult, 1989). By devaluing possible alternatives, these individuals presumably protect their satisfaction with their current relationships. Similarly, committed partners express more willingness to make sacrifices on behalf of their relationships (Van Lange et al., 1997), a greater tendency to forgive their partner's transgressions (Finkel, Rusbult, Kumashiro, & Hannon, 2002), and a greater tendency to respond constructively when they are feeling dissatisfied with the relationship (Rusbult, Verette, Whitney, Slovik, & Lipkus, 1991). In each of these studies, promoting the relationship involves some costs. Social exchange theory holds that people should be willing to endure those costs when the costs of leaving the relationship would be even worse, or when the rewards of remaining are even greater.

Evaluating Social Exchange Theory

A beauty of social exchange theory is the broad framework it provides for addressing a wide range of different variables, yet it still draws fine distinctions that help explain how intimate relationships may succeed or fail. The major elements of social exchange theory—rewards, costs, alternatives, investments, and barriers—encompass psychological variables like perceptions of the partner and feelings of love, contextual variables like the presence of available alternatives, cultural variables like social norms and standards, and demographic variables like socioeconomic status. Thus, the theory can be applied to almost any specific question to suggest how different variables combine to affect relationships. At the same time, by distinguishing between satisfaction and dependence, social exchange theory provides a language for discussing complex relationship outcomes. Perhaps the greatest contribution of this theory to our understanding of intimate relationships is the recognition that being satisfied with a relationship is only one element influencing whether that relationship lasts, and that relationships may endure regardless of whether they are satisfying to the partners.

Yet despite the power of this theory to distinguish between different kinds of relationship outcomes, social exchange theory has little to say about how initially satisfied couples reach those outcomes. Presumably, relationships begin because both partners perceive many rewards, few costs, and outcomes that are greater than their comparison levels. Social exchange theory acknowledges that all of these perceptions are likely to change over time, suggesting that when relationships decline, "one or both partners find the old rewards less probable, and unanticipated costs are now discovered" (Levinger, 1976, p. 25). But how do these perceptions change? How do couples who begin as satisfied and committed draw apart? Why are some couples able to maintain a sense of their relationships as rewarding, while other couples gradually appreciate that better alternatives may lie elsewhere? The theory is mostly silent on these questions. Social exchange theory may be better at addressing how distressed couples confront the decision of whether to end the relationship than at explaining how initially satisfied couples become distressed in the first place.

MAIN POINTS

>> Social exchange theory proposes that partners evaluate their relationship by weighing perceptions of the rewards and costs they are experiencing at the moment.

>> A given level of outcomes is satisfying if it is greater than the person's comparison level (CL), a standard for what is expected from any relationship; a set of outcomes may be very satisfying to someone with a low CL but unsatisfying to someone with a high CL.

>> In deciding whether to remain in a relationship, partners compare their outcomes to a different standard—the comparison level for alternatives (CL_{alt}), the level of outcomes a person expects to receive outside the current relationship.

>> By distinguishing between CL and CL_{alt}, the theory suggests that satisfaction (liking the relationship) and dependence (needing the relationship) are independent ideas.

>> The main limitation of social exchange theory is that it tends to focus on rewards, costs, and alternatives at a single moment, which suffices for predicting breakups within a short time, but cannot explain how perceptions of rewards and costs may change over time, nor how relationships that start out satisfying may deteriorate.

Social Learning Theory

If theories of intimate relationships were a family, social exchange theory and social learning theory would be brother and sister. The parent of both theories is behaviorism, and both draw heavily on principles of reinforcement and punishment. Both approaches describe partners in intimate relationships as trying to maximize their outcomes by pursuing rewards and avoiding costs. The two theories differ in how those rewards and costs are typically translated into concrete terms. Social exchange theory defines rewards and costs broadly as anything that an individual perceives to be good or bad about being in a relationship. Thus, rewards and costs are "aspects of perception, not action" (Gottman, 1982, p. 950; see also Newcomb & Bentler, 1981).

> " Distress results from couples' aversive and ineffectual responses to conflict. When conflicts arise, one or both partners may respond aversively by nagging, complaining, distancing, or becoming violent until the other gives in, creating a coercive cycle that each partner contributes to and maintains."
>
> —Koerner & Jacobson (1994, p. 208)

Social learning theory, in contrast, takes a more interpersonal approach. Rather than defining rewards and costs in terms of individual perceptions, social learning theory defines them in terms of the behaviors partners exchange during their interactions with each other. One partner's behavior in the other's presence (e.g., expressing affection or criticism, touching or not touching, smiling or frowning) may be rewarding or punishing to the other partner, and this will lead to some rewarding or punishing response, which is responded to in turn. Thus, social learning theory is a more narrow approach than social exchange theory, focusing almost entirely on what goes on between the partners.

At the heart of social learning theory is the straightforward idea that exchanging rewarding or positive behaviors contributes to the quality of intimate relationships, and exchanging costly or negative behaviors does harm (e.g., Stuart, 1969; Weiss, Hops, & Patterson, 1973). The rest of social learning theory elaborates on this basic premise. What, specifically, are the behaviors that distinguish satisfied from unsatisfied couples? How do partners' reactions to each other's behaviors lead to changes in their feelings about the relationship? What are the skills that help partners in initially satisfying relationships to stay satisfied over time?

This emphasis on behaviors and skills arose as a response to the needs of clinical and counseling psychologists working with couples in the mid to late 1970s (e.g., Jacobson & Margolin, 1979). From their experiences with couples seeking counseling, therapists observed that couples often complain about the quality of their communication, about arguing too much, or about the presence of conflicts that seem to come up again and again without being resolved. Other theories may help explain why these problems exist, but they offer no easy answers for how to resolve them. An approach that focused on specific behaviors, in contrast, promised therapists concrete tools that could directly modify the aspects of intimate relationships that unhappy couples complained about most. It is no accident that the behavioral focus of social learning theory has been the foundation of many self-help and popular psychology books on intimate relationships. When people are suffering in their relationships, they often want recommendations for which behaviors to adopt to improve the relationship and which behaviors to avoid. Those recommendations are what social learning theory offers.

Fundamental Assumptions

Social learning theory grows out of the initial assumption that the ongoing exchange of behaviors between partners is the essence of any interpersonal relationship (Thibaut & Kelley, 1959). Why are behaviors so central? As Kelley et al. (1983) pointed out, it is only through interaction, through the on-going sequence of action and reaction between partners, that two individuals make contact. Certainly, a wife may find her husband pleasing or distressing, but it is really his behavior she is responding to. Other variables—like a partner's personality, values, and experiences—are important only insofar as they affect the way partners treat and react to each other. This is where social learning theory focuses our attention.

A second assumption of social learning theory, following directly from behavioral principles, is that partners learn from their experiences in each interaction about the quality of their relationship. This is the "learning" part of social learning theory. When a couple has a rewarding interaction, both partners learn that they can trust each other, that they can communicate effectively, and that they are loved and respected. All these messages contribute to and strengthen each partner's satisfaction with the relationship, making future rewarding interactions more likely. Difficult interactions, however, can erode confidence in a relationship. By itself, a single argument may be ignored, forgotten, or explained away. But as memories of unresolved conflicts and negative exchanges accumulate, partners may eventually begin to doubt their ability to communicate effectively. The presence of doubt, unfortunately, makes future negative interactions more likely. Thus, social learning theory describes a cyclical relationship between behavior and relationship satisfaction (**FIGURE 3.9**). The confidence of satisfied couples leads to rewarding interactions, strengthening their confidence and satisfaction in the relationship. The doubts of less satisfied couples lead to negative interactions, confirming their fears and contributing to distress in the relationship.

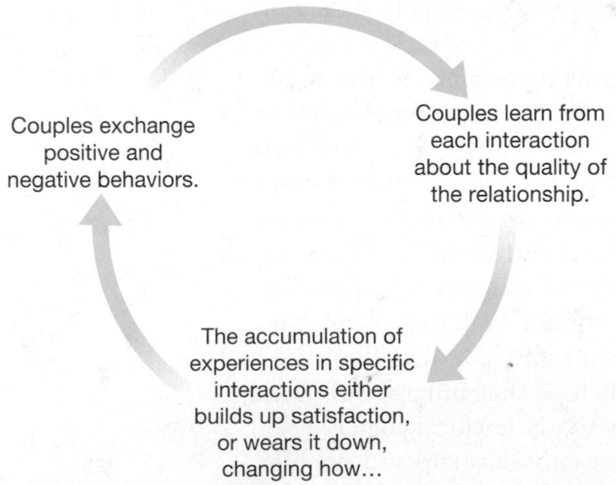

If negative interactions are so destructive for relationships, then why do partners engage in them? Why do partners who sincerely love each other sometimes treat each other poorly?

Couples exchange positive and negative behaviors.

Couples learn from each interaction about the quality of the relationship.

The accumulation of experiences in specific interactions either builds up satisfaction, or wears it down, changing how...

FIGURE 3.9 The cyclical relationship between behavior and relationship satisfaction, according to social learning theory.

A strictly behavioral approach assumes that people engage only in behaviors that are reinforced or rewarded in some way. Within intimate relationships, the primary source of reinforcement and reward is the partner. Thus, to explain the presence of negative behaviors in intimate relationships, social learning theorists explore ways partners may reinforce each other's undesirable behaviors unintentionally. **Coercion theory**, an offshoot of social learning theory, describes one way this kind of reinforcement can happen (Patterson & Hops, 1972). In the typical example of coercive processes in action, one partner wants the other to do some unpleasant chore, like taking out the trash. The requesting partner asks nicely at first, and is ignored. Then the partner asks a little less nicely, but is still ignored. Finally, the partner is reduced to nagging and demanding, whereupon the other partner might say "Okay, okay! I'll take out the trash already!" What has happened? When one partner has to nag before the other partner agrees to a desired change, that partner is reinforced for nagging. Thus nagging, a behavior nobody likes, will probably recur.

A similar approach to understanding how negative behaviors arise is the idea of escape conditioning (Gottman, 1993; Gottman & Levenson, 1986). In **escape conditioning**, behaviors are reinforced if they lead to the end of an aversive or painful stimulus. Imagine an argument that goes on and on, ending only when one partner finally breaks down crying, says something hurtful, or throws a plate against the wall. Nobody likes these behaviors, but to the extent that they lead to the rapid end of the argument, they can be reinforced. They will probably recur whenever interactions get difficult. The problem, of course, is that even if negative behaviors are rewarded in the short term, they can be extremely destructive over the long term. The short-term rewards of coercive and escape conditioning processes, however, can make these negative behaviors very hard to change.

The theorists who first applied social learning theory to intimate relationships during the late 1970s and early 1980s focused primarily on communication, specifically the explicit verbal and nonverbal behaviors partners exchange during discussions of marital issues (e.g., Gottman, 1979; Jacobson & Margolin, 1979; Markman & Floyd, 1980). As work in this area developed, however, theorists considerably broadened their definition of behavior. In particular, they expanded their exclusive emphasis on observable behavior to include partners' cognitive and emotional reactions to each other's behaviors as well (e.g., Baucom & Epstein, 1989; Fincham & O'Leary, 1983; Jacobson, McDonald, Follette, & Berley, 1985). The rationale for this development was the gradual realization that the implications of observable behaviors depend on how each partner interprets those behaviors. FIGURE 3.10 illustrates how behaviors and interpretations might accumulate to determine the outcome of a dyadic interaction. Imagine, for example, that your partner comes home from work distracted and does not seem interested in hearing about your day. By itself, that is a negative behavior; it is certainly less rewarding than if the partner came home interested and eager to talk. Still, there are several different ways of thinking about that behavior, and some interpretations (e.g., "My

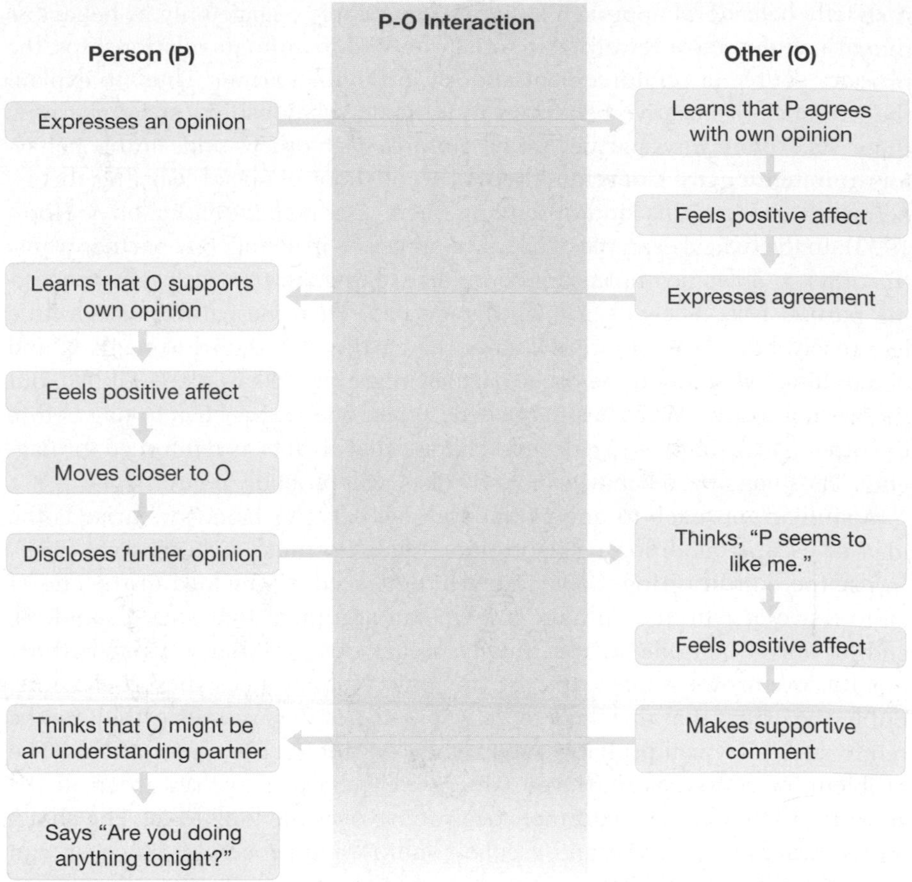

P-O Interaction

Person (P)   **Other (O)**

Expresses an opinion →   Learns that P agrees
                                                                     with own opinion

                                                                          ↓

                                                                     Feels positive affect

                                                                          ↓

Learns that O supports ←   Expresses agreement
own opinion

     ↓

Feels positive affect

     ↓

Moves closer to O

     ↓

Discloses further opinion →   Thinks, "P seems to
                                                                        like me."

                                                                          ↓

                                                                     Feels positive affect

                                                                          ↓

Thinks that O might be ←   Makes supportive
an understanding partner   comment

     ↓

Says "Are you doing
anything tonight?"

FIGURE 3.10 **The chain of an initial dyadic interaction.** Later versions of social learning theory focused on perceptions and interpretations.

partner does not care about me" or "My partner might be having an affair") make it seem a lot worse than others (e.g., "My partner must be experiencing a lot of stress at work"). Later versions of social learning theory acknowledged that initially satisfying relationships may encounter problems not only when partners exchange negative behaviors, but also when partners begin to perceive and interpret each other's behaviors negatively. In both cases, however, the end result is the same: Partners learn from their experiences of each interaction about the quality of their relationship.

How Social Learning Theory Guides Research

The development of social learning theory had a major impact on how research on intimate relationships was conducted. Early researchers relied exclusively on self-report data from surveys and questionnaires (e.g., Burgess, Wallin, & Shultz, 1954). The sole source of information on how intimate relationships developed was the partners themselves. These data were adequate for studying perceptions of relationships, but researchers realized early on that "studying what people say about themselves is no substitute for studying how they behave" (Raush, Barry, Hertel, & Swain, 1974, p. 5). Indeed, a great deal of early research on how couples behave confirmed that, in general, partners were poor reporters of their own interactions. They frequently disagreed about even recent behaviors occurring within the last 24 hours (Christensen & Nies, 1980; Jacobson & Moore, 1981). To identify what was really going on, researchers informed by social learning theory looked to observational studies (e.g., Gottman, 1979). In the late 1970s and early 1980s, researchers for the first time began to record couples talking to each other. Doing so allowed them to describe what partners were actually doing, independent of the partners' own interpretations. After nearly 30 years of this type of research, methods for observing interactions have become increasingly sophisticated, incorporating analyses of behavioral sequences (e.g., Bakeman, Quera, McArthur, & Robinson, 1997) and physiological measures (e.g., Gottman & Levenson, 1992).

The initial goal of these studies was to identify the specific behaviors associated with satisfying relationships and effective problem solving. To accomplish this, early studies in this vein recorded satisfied and distressed couples attempting to resolve significant issues in their relationships (e.g., Margolin & Wampold, 1981). Not surprisingly, the researchers found that when talking about sources of difficulty in their relationships, satisfied couples displayed more positive and fewer negative behaviors than distressed couples did. Simple self-report measures probably could have revealed this much as well. However, close observation of the behaviors of the two types of couples revealed additional, less obvious distinctions between their behaviors. For example, distressed couples were not only more negative in general but also demonstrated a greater tendency to respond to each other's negativity with more negativity—a behavioral sequence known as **negative reciprocity**. Satisfied partners, in contrast, were able to break out of negative cycles relatively quickly, accepting the occasional negative statement without necessarily firing back another negative statement. Negative reciprocity turns out to be an important predictor of unhappy relationships (Smith, Vivian, & O'Leary, 1990), even though couples are likely to be unaware they are doing it.

More recent observational studies of couple interactions have expanded the focus of this research beyond problem solving, helping researchers identify the specific behaviors and behavior patterns that characterize effective support (e.g., Cutrona & Suhr, 1994) and intimacy (e.g., Roberts & Greenberg, 2002) as well. For example, rather than observing couples trying to solve a problem, psychologist Alexandra Mitchell and her colleagues (2008) asked partners to write about and then take turns sharing with each other a time when their feelings had been hurt by someone outside the relationship. Trained coders watched recordings of these conversations and rated the amount of disclosure and empathy exchanged by the partners while discussing their emotional wounds. The researchers wanted to answer this question:

In a situation designed to reveal partners' vulnerabilities, what specific behaviors teach partners about the level of intimacy in their relationship? They
found that, in this situation, both men and women were especially responsive
to the behaviors of the male partner. So, after the men shared their experiences, the more that men had shared personal and emotional details, the
closer both partners felt. After the women shared their experiences, the more
that men had shown care and understanding, the closer both partners felt.
In other words, the men and women in this study were learning more about
their relationship from the way men behaved in this situation—something
that couples probably could not tell you if you asked them.

Evaluating Social Learning Theory

Social learning theory has been a powerful lens through which to explore
intimate relationships, for several reasons. First, by highlighting the ongoing dynamics between partners, social learning theory appropriately adopts
the couple (the dyad) as the basic unit of analysis. Other theories, in contrast—even though they are applied to couples—often focus on qualities and
perceptions of the individual partners. Second, social learning theory offers
a perspective on change in intimate relationships that other theories lack.
Certainly every theory acknowledges that partners' feelings about each other
may change or remain stable over time. Only social learning theory, however,
suggests a specific mechanism through which change may come about—that
is, through the repeated experience of unrewarding interactions and the
gradual accumulation of unresolved conflicts. Third, to record these interactions, researchers have been inspired to develop new techniques and procedures for observing and describing couples. These methodological advances
have had widespread influence on areas of social science beyond the study
of relationships, including education (e.g., Stoolmiller, Eddy, & Reid, 2000),
organizational behavior (e.g., Adair, Weingart, & Brett, 2007), and even pri-
matology (e.g., Bard, 1992).

　　These unique features of social learning theory may account for its lasting popular appeal. As mentioned earlier, social learning theory may have
influenced public opinion about intimate relationships more than any of the
other theories discussed so far. Outside of academic circles, it is relatively
rare to hear people talk about their evolved psychological mechanisms, their
attachment styles, or their comparison levels. It is common, however, to hear
people talk about how they and their partners communicate and the behaviors they wish their partners would change. Social learning theory is so influential that even people with no research training agree with its fundamental
assumption: Understanding couple interactions is central to understanding
relationships.

　　The strong focus on interaction is also the most significant limitation of
social learning theory. Although several decades of observational research
have resulted in a wealth of details about how couples interact, important

questions about how partner interactions fit into the broader context of intimate relationships remain unanswered. For example, why are some couples more effective at communicating than others? Communication problems are probably the result of larger issues in the relationship, but social learning theory provides no direction for determining what those might be. While pointing out that the partners' skills at communicating should directly affect their feelings about the relationship, so far this theory has been silent about the origins of those skills and why they might vary across couples. For practitioners interested in helping couples maintain their relationships over the long term, this can be a frustrating oversight. As one researcher put it, for developing therapies and interventions "a conceptualization of 'the husband is unhappy because he doesn't communicate well' is about as useful a conceptualization as 'the patient died because his heart stopped beating'" (Heyman, 2001, p. 6).

A second limitation of social learning theory is its inability to explain certain very common patterns of relationship development. As noted earlier, social learning theory explains how relationships may change; but it accounts for changes in only one direction. Happy couples are expected to treat each other well, maintaining their initial satisfaction, and less happy couples to treat each other more poorly, leading to gradually deteriorating satisfaction. But what about couples who go through bad patches and then get better on their own? What about couples who never dissolve but have dramatic ups and downs over time? Social learning theory focuses on the consequences of each interaction for subsequent interactions, but it has difficulty explaining how the nature of a couple's interactions can improve *and* decline over time within the same relationship. While social learning theory points out that how couples behave is an important mechanism of relationship development, the links between behaviors and other variables affecting relationships have yet to be explored.

MAIN POINTS

>> Social learning theory proposes that people learn about their relationships from their experience of each interaction with their partners, such that positive interactions strengthen initial satisfaction, whereas negative interactions and unresolved conflicts decrease satisfaction.

>> By closely analyzing what partners actually do when they communicate with each other, social learning theorists explore how partners may inadvertently reinforce each other's ineffective or punishing behaviors.

>> By identifying negative behaviors, researchers hope to teach couples more effective ways of communicating, thereby improving their relationships.

>> Social learning theory does not address the broader context of dyadic interactions, that is, where behaviors come from or how they may change over time.

Social Ecological Models

In understanding how intimate relationships work, the theories we have discussed so far focus mainly on how partners develop to form a relationship (e.g., evolutionary psychology and attachment theory) and how they interact and behave within their relationship (e.g., social exchange theory and social learning theory). What about the environment where the relationship takes place? Can a relationship be affected by anything outside of the relationship itself? You would not think so, from the preceding discussions. Only social exchange theory, by accounting for alternatives to the current relationship, explicitly acknowledges a world outside the couple. Even this theory, however, treats alternatives mainly as barriers or inducements to ending the relationship; social exchange theory still considers relationship quality to be a function of each partner's own perceptions and values. All these theories seem to assume that if we could know everything about two individuals and everything about the way they treat each other, then we might know everything important there is to know about their relationship.

> " We as a nation need to be reeducated about the necessary and sufficient conditions for making human beings human. We need to be reeducated not as parents—but as workers, neighbors, and friends; and as members of the organizations, committees, boards—and, especially, the informal networks that control our social institutions and thereby determine the conditions of life for our families and their children."
>
> —Urie Bronfenbrenner (1977)

Social ecological models of relationships reject this assumption. *Social ecology* refers not to a single theory, but to a range of approaches emphasizing the interplay between people and their environments. Arising from sociology and anthropology rather than psychology, this perspective recognizes that every intimate relationship develops within a specific context, or ecological niche. The nature of this context affects more than just whether relationships persist or dissolve. A **social ecological model** explains how the stresses, supports, and constraints in the environment of a couple may affect the way partners think, feel, and act in their relationships. This idea has clear precedents in ecology, ethology, and anthropology. Just as our understanding of a tree depends on whether it grows in the desert or the rain forest, our understanding of an intimate relationship depends on what we know about its circumstances. Some couples have plenty of free time and disposable income to spend together; others must endure long-distance separations or confront serious health or financial problems. No matter how securely attached two people are, and no matter how effective their communication skills, social ecological models point out that some relationships may be easier than others strictly because of the different environments in which they develop.

At the simplest level, the environment of the relationship consists of everything that does not reside within and between the partners themselves. Psychologist Urie Bronfenbrenner proposed a detailed model of social ecology, describing how multiple levels of context affect individuals and couples simultaneously (Bronfenbrenner, 1977, 1979, 1986). As shown in **FIGURE 3.11**, the most immediate environmental level is the **microsystem**, which contains the couple's family and friends. When Shakespeare's Romeo and Juliet were forced to deal with the disapproval of their friends and families, for example, they were being affected by the microsystem. The next level is the broader social context, the **mesosystem**, which contains the neighborhood, social system, and culture in which the relationship takes place. The differences between intimate relationships in a small Colombian village and those in midtown Manhattan show the mesosystem at work. Most removed from the couple's direct experience, but still influential according to Bronfenbrenner, is the **macrosystem**—the national and historical forces affecting the relationship. The differences between relationships in today's world of cell phones and instant text messaging compared to earlier times exemplify the influences at this level.

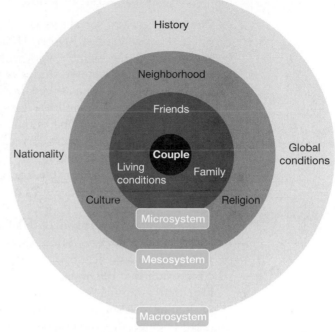

FIGURE 3.11 The couple in context. This social ecological model represents the many levels that define the environment of a relationship. (Source: Adapted from Bronfenbrenner, 1979.)

Although Bronfenbrenner emphasized social factors, ecological models also consider how physical features of the environment—weather, population density, the homes in which couples live, and so on—play a role in intimate relationships as well. A study from Sweden, for example, linked survey data on the relationship histories of 3,851 cohabiting couples with real estate data from the 21 counties where those couples lived (Lauster, 2008). While you might not think your relationship is affected by the housing market, these results showed significant links between the outcomes of cohabiting couples and changes in the cost of housing in that country over 20 years. As prices fell and housing became more affordable, the relationships of these couples were less likely to end and more likely to progress toward marriage.

After identifying the important environmental influences on a couple, social ecological models explore how they can interact to affect relationships. Under what circumstances do relationships thrive? How are relationships changed by the experience of stressful events? For couples who are vulnerable to experiencing problems, in what context are those problems most likely to arise? In addressing these questions, social ecological models link couples' ongoing experiences in their relationships to the physical and social features of their environments.

Fundamental Assumptions

One of the earliest social ecological models of intimate relationships was developed by sociologist Reuben Hill, who was an army psychologist during World War II. Through his work with military families, he became interested in understanding why the strains and challenges of war brought some families closer together even as they tore many families apart. The **ABC-X model**, which he developed to address this question, has served as the foundation of most social ecological models that followed (Hill, 1949). The ABC-X model is named for the four letters corresponding to the four elements Hill considered crucial to understanding the effects of external challenges on relationships. The A represents a **stressor**, defined as any event requiring some sort of behavioral response, such as having a baby, losing or changing jobs, or contracting a disease.

The B represents **resources**, defined as all the assets a couple may use in coping with a stressor. Some resources are material, like money; others are social, like having a supportive family, a close circle of friends, or a strong connection to a religious group. An important premise of the model is the idea that a family's level of resources (B) changes how they experience a particular stressor (A). For wealthier couples (couples with plenty of material resources), stressors like fixing the car, replacing a broken appliance, or maintaining a home may not be serious concerns. For poorer couples (those with fewer material resources), each of these things may be a major obstacle that can affect other areas of their lives. Similarly, the birth of a new baby has a different impact on couples with a close and available network of friends and family to call on for childcare (plenty of social resources) than on those who lack ready access to family and friends (fewer social resources). Couples who have these connections may turn to them for help if they need it; couples who are isolated may have fewer options when their own resources fail them.

The C in Hill's model represents the couple's **interpretation of the event**—that is, whether the couple defines the stressor as a challenge to be overcome or a catastrophe to be endured. Hill (1949) observed that families who viewed their stress as manageable seemed to adapt more effectively; they summoned their resources and banded together. In contrast, families who viewed the same stressors as tragedies or punishments did not cope as well; sometimes they failed to take advantage of the resources available to them.

Together, the nature of the stressor (A), the couple's level of resources (B), and their interpretation of the event (C) lead to X—**crisis**, or the couple's experience of and response to the stressful event. If the stress is severe, the level of resources is low, and the interpretation is negative, Hill predicted that couples will find it hard to adapt effectively, and the experience of the stressor should thus lead to weaker relationships. However, even if the stressor is severe, adequate resources and a positive interpretation can allow effective adaptation that "preserves family unity and enhances the family system and member growth and development" (McCubbin & Patterson, 1982, p. 45). In other words, a couple's external stresses may lead to relationship problems, but if resolved effectively, those stresses may also bring couples closer together.

Hill's ABC-X model, also known as crisis theory, proved influential, but it had some critics. For example, Hamilton McCubbin and Joan Patterson (1982) noted that Hill's original model was pretty static: Every element of the ABC-X model addresses the state of the relationship at a single moment—the moment a stressful event occurs. Responses probably change over time as the situation unfolds, however, and the experience can have implications for how couples and families react to future difficulties. To acknowledge the development of a couple's responses to stress over time, McCubbin and Patterson proposed a revision of Hill's original ABC-X model and called it the **Double ABC-X model** (FIGURE 3.12). This revision suggested that each element of Hill's model has an initial meaning as well as a meaning that emerges over time. For example, the consequences of an initial stressful event, like having a bad case of flu, can lead to additional stressful events over time: missing an important job interview, getting behind at work, or spreading the illness to loved ones. McCubbin and Patterson (1982) called this phenomenon **stress pile-up**, and they pointed out that the domino effect of a stressful event can be as stressful or even more stressful than the event itself. Besides the couple's initial level of resources, the Double ABC-X model accounts for resources the couple can develop or summon in response to an event. When one partner is diagnosed with a chronic disease, for example, the couple may not know

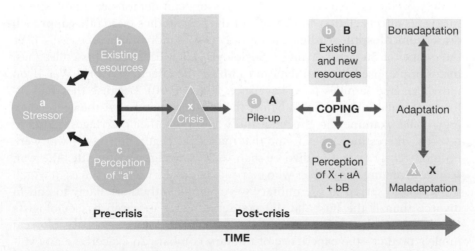

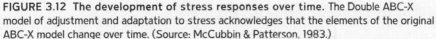

FIGURE 3.12 The development of stress responses over time. The Double ABC-X model of adjustment and adaptation to stress acknowledges that the elements of the original ABC-X model change over time. (Source: McCubbin & Patterson, 1983.)

how to respond or how to adjust to the effects of the disease on their lives. Over time, however, the couple may become educated about the disease, join a support group, or connect with family and friends. In this way, they are developing resources that were not in place initially. Further, although the original model emphasized interpretations of the initial event, the Double ABC-X model suggests that couples' interpretations of their ongoing coping efforts will also affect the relationship. Given the same stressful event, for example, a wife who believes her husband is trying his best to support her is likely to adapt more effectively than a wife who believes her husband is unwilling or unable to help. Finally, the Double ABC-X model considers not only the initial outcomes of a particular crisis but also the ongoing process of adaptation within the couple. This process ranges from coping that brings the couple closer to coping that drives partners apart.

How Social Ecological Models Guide Research

The ideal design for studying how intimate relationships respond to and affect their environments would be to compare relationships before and after some significant external event or change. In practice, however, this is hard to do. It would be unethical for researchers to create real stress in couples' lives and impossible to create real changes in their circumstances. Instead, researchers informed by social ecological models have found more creative ways of revealing the effects of environments on relationship processes.

One route is to follow couples over long periods of time and hope that important stressors or changes occur (i.e., perform longitudinal studies). Even if only some of the couples experience major stressors, comparing them to those who did not experience major stressors can demonstrate how stressful events affect relationships. Some of the best studies taking this approach draw from **lifespan studies**, which may assess individuals repeatedly over the course of 50 years or more. Sociologist Glen Elder and his colleagues, for example, used lifespan data to examine the effects of World War II on marriages and families (e.g., Pavalko & Elder, 1990). Because they had information about their sample before the war began and after the war ended, they could examine the effects of the war on whether marriages ended in divorce. Interestingly, they found that marriages begun during the war were no more likely to end in divorce than were marriages begun after the war. However, among the couples who married before the war, marriages in which the husband served in the military were significantly more likely to end in divorce than if the husband did not serve. Later research by sociologists Cynthia Gimbel and Alan Booth (1994) revealed that—as social ecological models predict—the experience of military combat can exacerbate any vulnerabilities and personality problems existing before military service, and it can have additional consequences (e.g., disabilities, post-traumatic stress disorder) that make life difficult even after the military service ends. In this way, lifespan research supports the idea that relationships that might otherwise endure can suffer greatly when the couples experience difficult times.

Problems with the lifespan approach include its expense and duration, especially if only a few couples experience some of the most interesting and important stressors. For a researcher interested in how couples react when one partner suffers a heart attack, for example, it is not cost-effective to begin with a sample of healthy couples and then wait for some of them to go into cardiac arrest. For researchers with a specific stressor in mind, an alternative approach is to find samples of couples who have experienced the event and then examine how different coping responses help account for different relationship outcomes. Most research on the effects of the transition to parenthood takes this approach, beginning with couples who are pregnant for the first time and examining the variables accounting for those who cope most effectively after their baby is born (e.g., Belsky & Pensky, 1988; Cox, Paley, Burchinal, & Payne, 1999). This research generally finds that couples who are pregnant for the first time are extremely happy and excited about the future, and then experience a precipitous decline in relationship satisfaction after their baby is born and the reality of childcare proves more taxing than they expected (Cowan & Cowan, 1992).

Another method is to identify couples who are likely to experience lots of daily variability in their stress levels, and then examine their relationships across days that are more or less stressful. For example, to examine the effects of daily stress on the nightly interactions of married couples, psychologist Rena Repetti (1989) studied a sample of air traffic controllers and their wives across three consecutive days. On days when traffic was especially high, husbands tended to withdraw and wives tended to be more supportive, and this pattern reflected happier marriages overall. Studies like these focus less on the effects of stress itself than on how different ways of coping with stress affect the course of an intimate relationship.

Social ecological models highlight not only stressful events, but also the broader effects of the various social and physical environments in which relationships unfold. Researchers typically compare intimate relationships across different environments. For example, to determine the effects of socioeconomic status on relationships, researchers have used census data to show that divorce rates are far higher among low-income than among upper-income marriages (e.g., Kreider & Fields, 2001). Other researchers have shown that rates of divorce are higher in disadvantaged neighborhoods than more affluent ones (e.g., South, 2001), and higher among blacks than whites (e.g., Orbuch, Veroff, Hassan, & Horrocks, 2002). Still others have shown that the links between the quality of couples' communication and their relationship satisfaction are consistent across American, Asian, European, and Latin American countries (e.g., Christensen, Eldridge, Catta-Preta, Lim, & Santagata, 2006).

Because all these studies are necessarily correlational (meaning they study naturally occurring associations among variables), none of them proves that different environments lead intimate relationships to be more or less successful. Still, the consistent finding that couples living in more demanding or challenging environments experience worse relationships than do those living in more supportive environments has been taken as strong support for the social ecological perspective.

Evaluating Social Ecological Models

In thinking about intimate relationships, it is easy to forget about how they are affected by their environments. The way partners and their behaviors affect relationships is far more vivid and easier to observe, which may explain the general tendency to believe that the course of a relationship depends mostly on who the partners are and how they treat each other. The great strength of social ecological models is that they encourage us to resist this tendency. By focusing directly on the ways environments facilitate or constrain what goes on in relationships, social ecological models substantially broaden the scope of research on intimate relationships.

Social ecological models address questions about intimate relationships that other theories overlook. For example, each theory discussed so far helps identify which of the couples who start out happy and satisfied risk having relationship problems. But exactly when are those problems likely to occur? Some couples, despite significant vulnerabilities, seem to be happy for many years before their relationships go bad. Other couples experience declines in satisfaction even without obvious vulnerabilities. Still other couples go through bad times but then improve. Social ecological models help explain these patterns by proposing that declines in a relationship usually occur when the environmental demands rise above a couple's ability to cope effectively. Until forced to confront a stressful event or challenging situation, even couples with many vulnerabilities may remain relatively happy. If their circumstances change, however, and they suddenly have to face a challenge, that is when vulnerable couples may experience declines. Similarly, some stresses (e.g., the death of a child, a debilitating accident) may be so great that even couples with many resources may experience declines when they occur. And some unhappy couples may even become more satisfied over time if their lives improve substantially (e.g., getting a better job, moving into a bigger house, making new friends). By acknowledging the effects of the environment external to a relationship, social ecological models account for the ups and downs of relationships in a way that other theories do not.

The limitations of social ecological models stem from a failure to specify exactly how some of the associations come about. For example, most social ecological models describe links between relationships and environments without explaining how demands outside a relationship affect processes within the relationship. An explicit goal of recent social ecological models has been to fill this theoretical gap. For example, research on the effects of economic hardship on African American families has built on Hill's early work by showing how financial stress outside the family increases the likelihood of negative interactions within the home (e.g., Conger, Rueter, & Elder, 1999). Similarly, although most social ecological models acknowledge that environments, resources, and coping behaviors all change over time (e.g., McCubbin and Patterson's Double ABC-X model), they have been slow to elaborate on how these constructs change and why some couples develop skills to meet their challenges while others do not. In general, most thinking informed by social ecological models has focused on identifying environmental forces affecting relationships, rather than on explaining how those forces interact or how they change.

MAIN POINTS

>> Social ecological models emphasize that the environment of a couple can support or damage their relationship.

>> The ABC-X model draws links between stressors (A), or events requiring behavioral change; the resources (B) a couple can bring to bear in coping with the stressor; the couple's interpretation of the event (C); and their successful or unsuccessful adaptation to the crisis (X).

>> The Double ABC-X model, a revision of these ideas, acknowledges that each element in the original model changes over time.

>> Most social ecological models share the focus on stressors, resources, and coping—thus suggesting that the same event may have different implications for relationships, depending on the level of resources available and the quality of a couple's coping efforts.

>> The limits of this approach lie in the failure to specify how resources and coping styles may change over time, and to explain why some couples develop skills to meet their challenges when others do not.

Underlying Themes in Theories of Intimate Relationships

TABLE 3.2 captures the main ideas, strengths, and limitations of each theoretical perspective reviewed in this chapter. As the table suggests, each theory helps identify some important pieces of the puzzle of intimate relationships. While each piece seems crucial for understanding intimate relationships and how they function, no single theory or perspective is complete by itself. Indeed, at this point in the history of scholarship on intimate relationships, there is no unified theory that addresses every possible question. In the attempts to explain what makes relationships satisfying and enduring,

TABLE 3.2 **Influential Theories of Intimate Relationships**

	Evolutionary Perspective	Attachment Theory	Social Exchange Theory	Social Learning Theory	Social Ecological Models
Main Idea	Mating behaviors are evolved solutions to reproductive problems that humans faced in ancestral times.	Adult relationships are shaped by the kinds of bonds we form with caregivers during infancy.	In relationships, partners seek to maximize rewards and minimize costs.	The behaviors that partners exchange with each other determine their satisfaction with the relationship.	The environment of a relationship can enhance or constrain relationship processes.
Key Variables	Gender differences Mate preferences	Attachment styles Internal working models	Comparison level Comparison level for alternatives Barriers Investments Commitment	Problem solving Communication Negative reciprocity	Stress Resources Social networks Culture
Strengths	Examines adaptive functions of mating behaviors Links current behaviors to biological and historical forces	Accounts for relationship patterns across the lifespan	Distinguishes between satisfaction and dependence Encompasses a wide variety of variables	Provides a specific mechanism for change in initially satisfying relationships	Accounts for when vulnerable couples may experience declines
Limitations	Can overlook more immediate causes of relationships	Does not address sources of variability among couples with the same attachment style	Does not explain how perceptions of rewards and costs may change over time	Does not explain where relationship skills and behavior come from	Does not provide a mechanism to link environmental demands to relationship processes

however, the theories described in this chapter highlight three broad themes, or classes of variables:

1. *Dyadic interaction.* If the interaction between two people is the heart of any relationship, then any general understanding of intimate relationships must take the way partners behave and respond to each other—their dyadic interaction—into account. Within the theories we

have discussed, the nature of partner interactions comes up repeatedly. Social learning theory addresses interactions within couples directly, suggesting that chains of behavior and interpretation are the mechanism of change and stability in relationships. Attachment theory also refers to rewarding, supportive interactions as a foundation of secure attachment, and blames unresponsive interactions as a source of insecurity. Social ecological models similarly point out that the way couples cope together with external stress is a crucial determinant of the impact that stress has on the relationship.

2. *Individual differences.* Partners do not enter their relationships as blank slates. Rather, they bring the sum of all their previous experiences, in the form of each partner's personality, values, history, ethnicity, culture, and socioeconomic status—all of which amounts to a lot of individual differences. Several of the theories discussed acknowledge that the characteristics of each partner, and the way they combine with the other's, probably affect the course of an intimate relationship. This comes up in attachment theory, which highlights the models and beliefs about relationships that individuals carry throughout their lives. It comes up also in the evolutionary perspective, with its focus on the evolved mechanisms thought to be stable qualities of human beings. Each individual brings different comparison levels to the relationship, according to social exchange theory. We can also think of the resources emphasized by social ecological models as an individual difference, in that partners vary in their ability to cope with stressful circumstances when they arise.

3. *External circumstances.* Relationships are affected not only by what goes on within them, but by the external circumstances around them, including social, physical, cultural, and historical forces. Of the theories described in this chapter, social ecological models place the most emphasis on a couple's external circumstances, but other theories refer to the environment of a relationship as well. Social exchange theory, for example, argues that the alternatives available outside of a relationship should play an important role in determining whether the relationship endures. Even the evolutionary perspective acknowledges that psychological mechanisms are sensitive to environmental cues.

These three broad themes—dyadic interaction, individual differences, and external circumstances—capture most of the independent variables studied in research on intimate relationships to date. Yet the most potential for advancing our understanding of intimate relationships may lie in examining how the variables within each of these themes combine and interact. Throughout the rest of this book, we emphasize research that is already moving in this direction.

>> The prevailing theories of intimate relationships all address three broad themes that capture most of the independent variables that have been studied by relationship scientists.

>> Most theories acknowledge the centrality of dyadic interaction, or the way couples behave and respond to each other.

>> Most theories also recognize that each partner brings to a relationship a set of individual differences that make each person unique.

>> Most theories address the powerful role that circumstances external to the relationship can play in shaping experiences within the relationship.

CONCLUSION

When two such influential psychologists as Sigmund Freud and B. F. Skinner disagree about a phenomenon as fundamental as intimate relationships, it is tempting to ask who was right and who was wrong. Yet, as we have seen throughout this chapter, there is no need to choose among the theoretical perspectives that have shaped relationship science. Each theory directs attention toward specific facets of human intimacy that other theories overlook. The perspectives endure because the directions they point in have proven useful, by identifying order in emotions and experiences that might otherwise appear chaotic and complex. As relationship scientists continue to pursue a greater understanding of intimate relationships, these theories have been a valuable starting point for inspiring new research and organizing the results.

As we turn toward examining that research in detail in the next chapters, these theories will serve the same function for us, and we will refer back to each of them again and again. The discussions will encourage you to try on multiple theories as lenses for interpreting the same experiences. It is good practice to ask yourself how a social exchange theorist might approach the issue differently from an evolutionary psychologist, or how the questions an attachment theorist would ask might differ from those inspired by a social ecological perspective. Maybe you will notice aspects of intimate relationships that no theory has yet explained. There, in the cracks between what current perspectives claim to know, lie the seeds of the next generation of relationship theories.

4

Men and Women, Gay and Straight

Comic Wisdom

Popular culture would have us believe that men and women are fundamentally different, that their basic differences destine them to disagree, and that intimate relationships are fraught with turmoil because of these differences and disagreements. Any number of YouTube clips shows that comedians are pithy observers of our everyday quirks and foibles; they summarize popular views of men and women particularly well, as do cartoonists (**FIGURE 4.1**).

Dylan Moran notes that men and women have fundamentally different styles of arguing: "All male arguments are early 1970s, Soviet-made, unidirectional, trundling behemoths that say the same thing again, and again, and again: 'I told you I would be late on Tuesday. I told you. I said it. I heard my own voice. I did say it. I told you.' Whereas women seem to have these amazing slinky stealth bombers designed by Jaguar with a lovely cream-leather interior with infinite torque. That's why they can respond by saying, 'Yes, maybe, all right—but why is the fridge door open?!'"

John Heffron notes that, even more basically, men and women have different inclinations to communicate: "My wife recently said we need to talk about our relationship, which was weird because I'm like 'But we're married. I thought that we were done with that. I thought we did the thing that would end all this talk.' I was misinformed—it's like declaring bankruptcy and still having bills to pay, right?" These widespread beliefs impel us to delve deeply into theory and research on the supposedly opposite sexes, so we can achieve a workable understanding of the interconnections and variations in intimacy between men and women.

QUESTIONS

Are men and women different creatures? At the most basic level, the answer must be yes—men and women are different biologically. But are they

"Sex brought us together, but gender drove us apart."

FIGURE 4.1 Distinguishing sex and gender. The term *sex* refers to whether someone is biologically male or female, and it can also refer to physical intimacy. *Gender* refers to a wide range of beliefs, values, and behaviors considered acceptable or typical for women and men. The two do not always align.

behavior is a necessary consequence of his or her biological sex, that would seem to justify and reinforce sex-related stereotypes. And if men and women are inherently different, that would be a rationale for promoting child-rearing practices that prepare boys for "the male role" in relationships and girls for "the female role." Thus, when we ask whether there are consistent and meaningful differences between men and women, a great deal is at stake—so much that it would be unwise to entrust the debate solely to the popular media, as entertaining as that might be.

In this chapter we focus on leading theories and research studies that help us understand men, women, and intimacy. This work addresses critical questions, such as: How much do men and women differ? If they do in fact differ, where are those differences most apparent and important? Are men and women destined for misunderstandings because of their sex? As you will see, most of these studies focus on different-sex relationships. However, examining same-sex relationships is important as well, for understanding intimacy in its various guises. And doing so has the added benefit of letting us ask new kinds of questions: Are gay and lesbian relationships different from straight relationships? If so, how? What happens when relationships are formed between two men, or two women, rather than one man and one woman?

fundamentally different in what they seek from and contribute to intimate relationships? Major ramifications would follow if they were. For example, if biology determines the success or failure of a relationship, then why bother working hard to fix things that do not seem to work? If a mate's

Sex and Gender

The term **sex** refers to whether an individual is male or female biologically. The term **gender** refers to a person's nonbiological and nonphysiological attributes, characteristics, and behaviors that are viewed as masculine or feminine. Gender refers to how people dress; their feelings and expressions; their attitudes, values, and interests. A person's biological sex is fixed; you are either male or female, and that usually does not change. (Of course, the word also refers to physical intimacy.) Gender, on the other hand, is more fluid. The attributes and behaviors linked to gender are many and diverse, and they can vary depending on the historical time period, the culture in question, and an individual's age and stage in life (**FIGURE 4.2**).

FIGURE 4.2 **Masculinity and femininity.** (a) Today's well-groomed "metrosexual," epitomized by the soccer player David Beckham, can easily be considered masculine; this same sense of style would have been considered as quite feminine in the 1950s. (b) Power-dressing women climb the corporate ladder and redefine cultural stereotypes of what it means to be feminine in the twenty-first century.

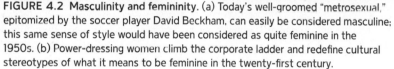

Profiles on social networking websites, such as Facebook and Twitter, allow us to see the many elements people use to identify and define themselves—their age, ethnicity, education, occupation, and income, of course, but also the cars they drive, the music they like, their favorite movies and TV shows, song lyrics and poems, their friends and partners, number of piercings and tattoos, how they prefer to spend their time, celebrities they admire, schools they attend, and so forth. Although these elements come together in endless and fascinating combinations to reveal each person's unique identity, no element is more basic, more encompassing, or more informative than the individual's sex.

The first thing we usually know (or want to know) about another person—is his or her sex. Even in this age of widespread electronic communication, it is oddly disconcerting to interact with someone without knowing whether that person is male or female. Millions of people use social networking sites regularly, and the profiles they create readily reveal their sex—even before you see the photographs. Computer scientists James Caverlee and Steve Webb (2008) analyzed nearly 2 million MySpace profiles and identified the words that distinguished profiles created by users. Some of the words are shown in **TABLE 4.1.** Is there any doubt which are from women and which are from men?

TABLE 4.1 **MySpace Profiles**

Profile Type I	Profile Type II
single	love
guitar	dancing
sport	shopping
metal	hearts
football	favorite
s***	people
wars	life
band	family
f***	being

Source: http://faculty.cs.tamu.edu/caverlee/pubs/caverlee08alarge.pdf. Adapted from Caverlee & Webb, 2008.

The human species is perpetuated by sexual reproduction, when the X or Y chromosomes provided via the male sperm joins with the X chromosome in the female egg. In the womb, females and males develop **primary sex characteristics** (i.e., different chromosomes, sex hormones, internal structures, and external genitalia) that are needed for sexual reproduction. Different **secondary sex characteristics** (e.g., breasts, finer skin, and more subcutaneous fat for females; facial hair, a deep voice and greater musculature for males) develop later. They further distinguish the two sexes anatomically, and facilitate courtship and mate selection. The story becomes more interesting when we consider that these primary and secondary characteristics are embedded and experienced within historical and cultural circumstances, which produce the social behaviors men and women typically learn and the situations in which they are permitted to display them. These behaviors are referred to as **tertiary sex characteristics** (e.g., Birdwhistell, 1970). Because these behaviors (and the perceptions of these behaviors) are the essence of intimate relationships, in this section we aim to clarify how males and females differ in their tertiary sex characteristics, and we offer some conceptual frameworks scientists have used to understand sex and gender.

Beyond its importance for individual identity, biological sex is also important in intimate relationships. Most of us choose partners first and foremost on the basis of whether the other person shares or does not share our identity as a male or female. Rare is the individual who says, "You know what? I don't care much whether my partner is male or female, as long as we get along well and as long as he or she is basically a good person. Isn't that what really matters?" (Men and women may differ in the strength of this tendency, however, as **BOX 4.1** describes.) Although the field of eligible partners is usually determined by biological sex, once that criterion is fulfilled, many other factors then determine which partner we form a relationship with (see Chapter 5). And once a stable relationship has formed, we might start asking some pointed questions about where sex ends and where gender begins: Are men less likely to commit? More likely to have sex with people outside the relationship? Are women more emotional? Less inclined to have sex? What are the appropriate roles for women and men in relationships?

The informal hunches and speculations you have about males and females in response to questions like these are a lot like the hypotheses social scientists test routinely and more formally in their research. Because sex is an important aspect of our identities and our social experiences, and because sex can be measured quickly and reliably, literally hundreds of studies have

---

BOX 4.1 SPOTLIGHT ON . . .

Thinking Outside the Boxes

Psychologists Amy Lykins, Marta Meana, and Gregory Strauss (2008) asked straight men and women to don special glasses that recorded exactly what they looked at as they watched a videotape of a woman and man having foreplay. The findings from this study—that men watched the woman far more than they watched the man, whereas women watched the man and woman about equally—are consistent with an emerging body of research indicating that the psychological basis of sexuality differs for men and women (Baumeister, 2000). Men seem to adopt a far more categorical or "either-or" sexual orientation than women, who show greater flexibility in what they find attractive sexually

If a group were asked to rate how sexually attracted they are to men and, separately, how attracted they are to women, you would discover a negative correlation; that is, with increasing attraction to men there is decreasing attraction to women, and vice versa—and this

holds true for both sexes. But the effect is far stronger for men than women (e.g., Lippa, 2007), suggesting that women's sexual attraction is not nearly as rigid or categorical as men's. Women are also more likely than men to fluctuate over time in their attraction to both sexes, and they are more likely to switch between relationships with male and female partners (Diamond, 2000, 2008).

Finally, studies physiologically measuring genital arousal show that straight men respond mainly to sexual images of women, but straight women are aroused by sexual images of men *and* women (e.g., Chivers, Rieger, Latty, & Bailey, 2004). Women, like men, can still be exclusively straight or gay in their sexual orientation, of course; but their orientation does not appear as closely tied to their patterns of physiological arousal as does men's. Thus, "most men can figure out their sexual orientation by monitoring their genitalia; few women can do so" (LeVay & Valente, 2006, p. 228).

been conducted to examine how males and females compare on a wide range of traits and characteristics.

Sex Differences, Sex Similarities

Because a study-by-study review of the large body of literature comparing males and females is impossible, we focus on quantitative summaries, or meta-analyses, in which many research findings are collected and synthesized (e.g., Rosenthal, 1991; also see Chapter 2). In a meta-analysis, researchers combine all known studies relating one variable—in this case, biological sex—to another variable or characteristic (e.g., empathy, aggression, sex drive), and reduce the findings to a single number indicating the degree of similarity or difference between males and females on one particular characteristic. So, for example, dozens of independent studies might be conducted to compare women and men on how empathic they are. Each study would produce an average empathy score for males and an average empathy score for females. All of these averages could themselves be averaged, producing a kind of grand average for males and another for females, and then those could be compared directly.

Because any one study can be unusual or biased in some unique way, averaging scores from many studies will provide a more reliable estimate of male-female differences in empathy. This new average is called a d **statistic**. When $d = 0$, it means men and women do not differ on the characteristic in question. But when d deviates from zero, we can conclude that men and women do differ. And the further d deviates from zero, the more confident we are that these differences are robust and meaningful. Negative d values indicate that females score higher than males on the specified dimension; positive values indicate the opposite. For example, you will not be surprised to learn that males can throw objects faster and farther than females ($d = 2.18$ and $d = 1.98$, respectively; Thomas & French, 1985). An even more extreme example, based on a study of 714 college students (Lippa, 2005), is that men are more sexually attracted to women than women are ($d = 3.52$), and women are more sexually attracted to men than men are ($d = -3.99$). Again, this will not surprise you; but it does give you an idea of the range within which d can vary. These examples are significant exceptions, though—as we will soon see, d values rarely exceed 1 in the literature on sex differences.

With these important technical details behind us, we can now put the powerful tool of meta-analysis to work and attempt some answers to the questions at hand: In what ways, and to what degrees, do males and females differ? **TABLE 4.2** provides d statistics comparing women and men in several areas in which social scientists have long suspected differences. Several specific variables are listed in each category. As you scan the d statistics associated with these variables, you might check whether your earlier predictions about male-female differences hold true.

TABLE 4.2 Meta-Analytic Studies Comparing Male and Female Behaviors and Experiences

Variable	*d* statistic[a]	Number of times this comparison was found in the scientific literature
Aggression		
Provoked aggression	.17	57
Verbal aggression	.35	35
Physical aggression	.66	44
Communication		
Skill in expressing emotion	−.52	35
Skill in decoding nonverbal behavior	−.43	64
Self-disclosure	−.18	205
Interruptions in conversation	.15	53
Intrusive interruptions	.33	17
Coping and Support Seeking		
Emotional support seeking	−.41	12
Rumination	−.39	10
Problem-focused coping	−.26	22
Mate Selection		
Importance of partner's social class	−.69	15
Importance of partner's ambitiousness	−.67	10
Importance of partner's character	−.35	13
Importance of partner's physical attractiveness	.54	28
Personality		
Tender-mindedness	−1.07	18
Agreeableness	−.25	11
Openness	.13	12
Assertiveness	.49	25
Sexuality		
Anxiety, guilt, or fear toward sex	−.35	11
Number of sexual partners	.25	12
Frequency of intercourse	.31	11
Attitude toward intercourse in a relationship	.49	10
Attitude toward casual intercourse	.81	10
Incidence of masturbation	.96	26
Well-Being		
Happiness	−.07	22
Self-esteem	.13	97

[a] Within a category, *d* statistics are ordered from those showing higher scores for women (i.e., larger negative values) to those showing higher scores for men (i.e., larger positive values).

Sources: Adapted from a variety of meta-analyses. Aggresion: Archer, 2004; Bettencourt & Miller, 1996. Communication: Anderson & Leaper, 1998; Dindia & Allen, 1992; Hall, 1984; LaFrance et al., 2003. Coping: Tamres et al., 2002. Mate selection: Feingold, 1990, 1992. Personality: Feingold, 1994. Sexuality: Oliver & Hyde, 1993. Well-being: Major et al., 1999; Wood et al., 1989. For valuable summaries, see Hyde, 2005; Lippa, 2005.

Here are some of the things we learn from Table 4.2:

- Men are more physically and verbally aggressive than women. These differences diminish to $d = .17$ when the participants are provoked in some way.

- Women are more skilled at expressing emotions than men; men are more prone to making intrusive interruptions.

- Women are more likely than men to seek out emotional support as a means of coping, and to dwell (or ruminate) on the difficulties they are facing.

- When selecting mates, women are more likely to emphasize the partner's social class and ambitiousness; men are more likely to prioritize physical attractiveness.

- Women are more likely to feel anxious, guilty, and fearful about sex. Men tend to have more positive orientations toward sexual intercourse in an established relationship and, to an even greater degree, in casual relationships.

- In contrast, men and women are rather similar in their reported levels of happiness and self-esteem.

Based on this vast set of studies, can we conclude that males and females differ? Yes, indeed we can, though we must also acknowledge that the magnitude of these differences varies with the characteristic in question, and with the specific variable being considered within that characteristic. We can also make a more encompassing observation: *Regardless of the domain, differences between women and men are not large.* Certainly the differences in Table 4.2 are far smaller than the earlier example regarding throwing distance and velocity, where d was about 2.

Thus, we can fairly easily distinguish between males and females on the basis of their physical primary and secondary sex characteristics. But among tertiary sex characteristics—behaviors, attitudes, and experiences—the differences are not as readily apparent, because they are not that large. When it comes to social behaviors, women and men differ more in degree than in kind. Males and females are more similar than dissimilar, and strong claims to the contrary are not warranted. At the same time, we cannot lose sight of the differences that do exist, particularly when we consider many differences simultaneously. Thus, the real but slight tendency for one-half of our species to be more physically and verbally aggressive, and more assertive, and more inclined to hold permissive attitudes about sex can,

> " I met this guy at a singles party. We talked for maybe 20 minutes, and then he said he'd like to go 'circulate.' I said, OK, fine. I didn't see him again that night. Then I got a call from a mutual friend the next day; she said that this guy had called her asking for my telephone number, was it OK to give it to him? I said, sure, why not? Next day he called; we talked for maybe 20 minutes and he asked me out. . . . He picked me up at my apartment, and we drove to a restaurant which is, oh, 20 minutes away. That makes a total of an hour we've known each other. We get a table, and then, while we're standing at the salad bar, he turned to me and asked, 'Am I going to get laid tonight?' So I said to him, 'I don't know—it depends on who you go out with after you say goodnight to me.' "
>
> —Goode (1996, p. 141)

in the aggregate, create overlapping but distinct spheres in which males and females conduct their daily lives.

The characteristics listed here and in Table 4.2 give us a panoramic view of some key similarities and differences between males and females. But missing from the picture is an attempt to explain them. Even though social scientists have come to a reasonable degree of consensus on the validity of the similarities and differences described here, great controversy persists over how best to understand them. Take, for example, the finding that the average male is more aggressive than the average female. Recalling what you learned about the evolutionary perspective in Chapter 3, you might ask: Is this because males are biologically predisposed to be aggressive in defending their mate and offspring? That is one possible explanation, and it takes us down the path of evolution and **nature**. Or, following social learning theory, is it because aggression is more likely to be rewarded by parents of male children than by parents of female children? Or is it because societies and cultures afford more opportunities for men than women to be aggressive, as a social ecological perspective would lead us to think? These are also plausible explanations, and they take us down the path of socialization and **nurture**.

The "Nature" Explanation: Sex Differences from the Inside Out

As humans, we have a lot going for us: opposable thumbs, color vision, a gag reflex, an upright posture, and sweat glands. We possess these features because we were given them by "nature": At some point in our distant evolutionary past, a series of random genetic mutations occurred that enabled these capacities to come into being, however gradually. They proved advantageous to our ancestors in confronting important problems, such as the need to grasp objects, to spot prey, to resist choking, to see distant predators, and to adjust body temperature in response to changing environments. Organisms with these capacities were more likely to survive and reproduce than organisms without them.

Males and females faced many similar adaptive problems in the past, and consequently they now share many similar abilities and capacities. However, as noted in Chapter 3, women and men also had to adapt to some different problems, and according to evolutionary psychology, those adaptations contributed to differences between the sexes. To understand these differences, it is crucial to remember that males and females differ in how they invest in their offspring (recall the theory of parental investment; Trivers, 1972). For women, offspring require the use of limited reproductive resources, a significant investment in time, and a tremendous amount of energy (from the actual birth and beyond). Men, in contrast, donate from a limitless supply of sperm with no comparable obligations and encumbrances. Males can and do contribute to child-rearing and protecting the child and mother, of course; but females bear the greater burden in reproduction, as is the case with all 4,000 species of mammals (Buss, 1994).

According to the evolutionary perspective, these reproductive realities have important implications for the kinds of mates that males and females prefer. Females will prefer males who are willing and able to provide resources for their protection and that of their offspring. Males, because the success of their reproductive efforts is limited primarily by the availability of healthy and fertile females, will tend to select mates on the basis of physical attraction and youthfulness. And because they fail to benefit from investing resources in children fathered by others, males will seek mates who are likely to be trustworthy and faithful.

Several lines of evidence converge to support the idea that nature, in the form of evolved adaptations, explains differences between the sexes. Go back to the meta-analyses in Table 4.2. Do you see how males and females do in fact differ in the ways that can be explained by the evolutionary perspective? In a study of mate preferences reported by over 10,000 subjects, ages 17–28, from 37 samples collected in 33 different countries, Buss (1989) demonstrated that women rated "good financial prospects" as significantly more important in a potential mate than men did in 36 of the 37 samples; women rated "ambition and industriousness" significantly more highly than men did in 29 of the 37 samples; and in all 37 samples, men preferred younger mates and women preferred older mates. Thus, even against a backdrop of remarkably diverse cultures, this study shows that males and females express preferences for mates that are consistent with the different investments they make in reproduction: Women want status and resources, and men are attuned to cues of fertility.

Social psychologist David Schmitt and his colleagues conducted an even larger study (2003) of 16,288 college-aged students from 52 countries. The results showed that across all regions, males would like to have more sex partners than would females (in the next month and over their lifetimes, with the d-statistic value = .45), that males would be more likely than females to have sex after knowing the partner for one month (d = .80), and that more males than females were actively looking for a short-term mate, regardless of their current relationship status (d = .45). An unusual study by social psychologists Margaret Clark and Elaine Hatfield (1989) helps round out this point. Attractive male or female research assistants approached members of the other sex on campus, stated "I have been noticing you around campus. I find you very attractive," and then randomly asked the person one of three questions: "Would you go out with me tonight?" "Would you come over to my apartment tonight?" or "Would you go to bed with me tonight?" In response to the first question, about half the participants agreed to a date, regardless of their sex. In response to the second question, 6 percent of the women agreed to go to the man's apartment, while 69 percent of the men agreed to go to the woman's apartment. And in response to the third question, 0 percent of the women agreed to go to bed with the man and 75 percent of the men agreed to go to bed with the woman (FIGURE 4.3).

Even across an array of remarkably diverse cultures, males and females express mate preferences consistent with the different investments they make in reproduction. Data collected in the Netherlands, Germany, and the United States indicate that men are more likely to experience jealousy when their partner has been *sexually* unfaithful compared to when they have been *emotionally* unfaithful; for women, the opposite pattern holds (Buunk, Angleitner, Oubaid, & Buss, 1996; Edlund et al., 2006). When understood from an evolutionary viewpoint, these findings indicate that men are oriented toward ensuring that they are investing resources in a child who will carry their genes into the next generation, whereas women are oriented toward ensuring that the mate will invest his resources in her (and their offspring) and not someone else.

FIGURE 4.3 **Mating strategies.** Men and women have different agendas and risks when it comes to short-term mating goals, and evolutionary theory argues that these result from the different investments they will make in producing offspring.

Other observed differences between men and women may stem not from how they attract and retain mates but from how they compete with other members of their own sex to gain some advantage in the mating marketplace. This behavior is known as **intrasexual competition**. Aggression, for example, probably proved advantageous for males when jockeying for the attention of the relatively discriminating females. Being more aggressive would enable males to take resources that belonged to competitors, to defend against similar attacks on their own resources, to inflict physical injury on their rivals, and to establish and elevate their status within a dominance hierarchy (Buss & Shackelford, 1997). Women are certainly not free from using tactics that will attract mates, but instead of aggression they rely on enhancing cues that signal their youth and health (via cosmetics, clothes, exercising, dieting, tanning, plastic surgery, etc.) or putting down other females by insulting their appearance or calling them "promiscuous" or a "tease" (Buss & Dedden, 1990). Males also put down their same-sex competitors, though they are more likely to do so by outperforming them in sports, commenting on their lack of resources and goals, or putting down their accomplishments.

In short, the evolutionary perspective explains human gender differences by highlighting the different problems males and females faced in our ancestral past (e.g., Buss, 1995; Buss & Kenrick, 1998). As we have seen, numerous findings support this contention, and these findings allow evolutionary

> ❝   Telling men not to become aroused by signs of youth and health is like telling them not to experience sugar as sweet.❞

—David Buss (1994, p. 71)

psychologists to make some rather encompassing assertions about sex differences in human mating behavior. For example, David Buss has observed that "Men and women differ in their tactics to attract mates, to keep mates, and to replace mates. These differences between the sexes appear to be *universal* features of our evolved selves. They *govern* the relations between the sexes" (1994, p. 211; italics added). Knowing about these evolved differences in human sexual behavior does not doom us to rigid roles and unfulfilling relationships—"biology is not destiny"—but is in fact a prerequisite to adopting new roles and engaging in behaviors most likely to promote enduring intimacy (Buss, 1994). We can expect many of these behaviors to be beneficial in relationships regardless of the participants' gender—males and females are both likely to remain in relationships in which they feel understood, cared for, and validated, as we will learn in Chapter 7. But nature-based explanations also cue us to the possibility that males and females may well differ in what they need from relationships.

The "Nurture" Explanation: Sex Differences from the Outside In

Even a cursory glance at the world around us shows that males and females often occupy different roles in society. Why do men and women differ in the responsibilities they take on in the home, at work, and in the community? And what difference does it make to intimate relationships if males and females do tend to have distinct social roles? We have seen that evolutionary psychology provides one valuable perspective for answering these questions. We turn next to an alternative theoretical framework that aims to explain differences between women and men based on how people are distributed in various roles and positions in society.

According to **social structural theory**, male-female differences in the division of labor are profoundly important for two reasons (Eagly & Wood, 1991, 1999; Eagly, Wood, & Johannesen-Schmidt, 2004). One reason focuses on how differences in the division of labor affect expectations for the roles in society that men and women should fill, and the second focuses on the steps men and women then take to meet these expectations.

First, given that there are differences between males and females in the division of labor, we form expectations regarding how people of each sex should behave. To the extent that women are more likely than men to occupy roles characterized by communal or domestic behaviors—kindergarten teachers, flight attendants, hairdressers, nurses, or caretakers in the home—then it follows that the female role will be identified with caretaking, selflessness, and friendliness. This is our expectation, or stereotype, of what the female role should involve; and new generations of girls and women are socialized into these roles—that is, they learn about the rules and norms that people in their society are expected to follow. Similarly, to the extent that men are more likely than women to occupy roles in which they are action- and task-oriented or are authority figures—that is, when men become college professors, airplane pilots, mechanics, police officers, or wage earners—then the male role is defined accordingly, and we expect men to behave in ways that are consistent with those roles (Eagly & Wood, 1999). Further, when people go outside these prescribed roles, they may encounter friction. For example, what would your initial reaction be if your sister aspired to be a mechanic or your brother aspired to be a hairdresser? When our expectations are violated, we tend to view those people and their actions less favorably (e.g., Anderson, John, Keltner, & Kring, 2001; Eagly, Makhijani, & Klonsky, 1992). In this way, gender-linked expectations associated with the division of labor channel people down particular avenues and not others.

A second way the division of labor contributes to sex differences involves the idea that males and females recognize the roles that are available to them in a given culture, and they learn or acquire the skills and experiences that will qualify them to compete for and fulfill these roles. It follows that those people who tend to be oriented toward roles that involve the accumulation and control of resources—money, ideas, control over others—are more likely to gain status and display dominant behaviors that will perpetuate their superior position, whereas those who tend to be oriented toward roles involving cooperation and bringing less power will tend to become subordinate and subservient. In our society, and in virtually all societies in which males and females have a hierarchical relationship with one another, males adopt the dominant role and females adopt the subordinate role (Whyte, 1978). The idea of **power**—which can be defined as an individual's capacity to alter the behavior and experiences of others, while also resisting the influence of others (Keltner, Gruenfeld, & Anderson, 2003)—crops up in a variety of ways when we discuss intimate relationships. Here we see that power can flow from the resources a person controls, some of which are embedded in societal roles. Below, and again in Chapter 8, we will discuss how power can be understood as an aspect of the transactions that happen in relationships, as when partners try to influence or exert control over one another.

Different male and female behaviors (see Table 4.2) can now be understood from a perspective that differs sharply from the evolutionary argument we summarized earlier: Viewed through the lens of social roles, men engage in behaviors that establish and reinforce their superior position in the social hierarchy; in contrast, women engage in behaviors that promote cooperation, nurturing of others, and adaptation to the inferior role to which they are assigned. Men and women differ in their social behavior not because of their differential investment in offspring, according to this view, but because of how the division of labor is organized in a society and the expectations following from that division. To the extent that men and women do differ, it is because they are responding to social worlds that present different opportunities and constraints on their behaviors.

Social structural theory holds that men and women differ because we have been led to expect them to differ. Based on these expectations, men and women seek out the experiences and gain the resources to equip them to take on the roles that are available and acceptable for their sex. These expectations themselves are hypothesized to flow from the stereotypic division of labor that people see around them.

Why is there a difference in the division of labor in the first place? Social structural theorists argue that males and females are distributed differently across various tasks and occupations because their physical attributes push them toward certain ones and away from others (**FIGURE 4.4**). Because only females can give birth to children, they are first in line to raise children, especially when the children are very young. And because of the heavy demands of these roles, women are discouraged from taking on duties that keep them away from their children for extended periods, thereby interfering with successfully fulfilling the caregiving role. Males, by contrast, tend to have greater size and strength than females do; consequently, they are likely to take on activities that benefit from these characteristics

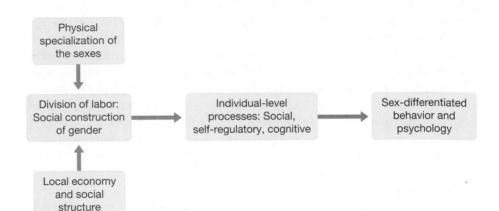

FIGURE 4.4 The social structural theory of sex differences and similarities. According to this model, the division of labor and the social construction of gender are a result of two factors: (1) the differing physical capacities of men and women, which produces specialization in specific roles; and (2) the ways a given society or the local economy represent gender (e.g., relative degree of equality between men and women). The socialization resulting from the division of labor and from the consensually understood roles for males and females in turn produces individuals who possess certain ways of interacting socially, regulating their behavior, and interpreting the world around them. Because males and females differ in how they are socialized and the contexts they are socialized in, they subsequently display differences in how they seek mates and behave.

(Wood & Eagly, 2002), such as building things, moving large or heavy objects, and acquiring and defending resources. Tasks of daily living are divided accordingly between males and females, and this division of labor can influence how small social groups like families can adapt to their surroundings. Because women and men naturally "play to their strengths," they often end up taking on different roles. According to social structural theory, this fact proves pivotal in how children are socialized and in how males and females come to think and behave differently. Figure 4.4 summarizes these ideas. As you look over this diagram, think about how it applies in the case of Carla and Frank, described in BOX 4.2.

You will notice that Figure 4.4 adds a new idea, which turns out to be crucially important in social structural theory: The division of labor and how we make sense of gender are also affected by the demands of the local economy as well as the social structure of a given society. This means the roles adopted by males and females can vary and change, depending on such

BOX 4.2 SPOTLIGHT ON . . .

Beliefs About Gender Roles and Parenting

This case study shows one way people's beliefs about gender roles might influence behavior in intimate relationships (from Barnett & Rivers, 2004, pp. 208–209):

Carla is a thirty-nine-year-old OB-GYN; she is married to Frank, a research scientist. They have a six-month-old child, Dana. They live in the Boston area and have been married for four years. Carla has been working hard for the past decade to complete medical school, finish her residency, and build her practice. Frank works long hours in a research lab, but his schedule is more flexible than hers. He can come home and work on the computer when he needs to. Carla has very little control over her schedule. "Hey, when a baby's ready to be born, I have to be there. I can't say 'How about we reschedule for Tuesday?'" It makes sense for Frank to take on greater child care responsibility—and he's willing to do so. But Carla, believing that only she has the innate capacity to mother, doesn't see any other option but to do it herself. "I don't think I have any choice. I don't want to cut back, but I don't want my child to suffer because of my career."

Asked why she couldn't take Frank up on his offer, she shakes her head. "He'd have one eye on his laptop and the other on the baby. I'm afraid he wouldn't be totally there for Dana." *So, Carla cuts way back on her practice, disappoints her patients, and leads her medical partners to doubt her commitment to medicine. While she adores Dana, she misses the challenges of full-time medicine—and is unhappy when Frank starts to work even longer hours to make up for her lost income and appears to enjoy it. She once thought she was part of an ideal couple; now Carla has begun to wonder about the health of her marriage. Frank sees that Carla is unhappy and finds himself becoming anxious and depressed. Carla created this problem because of her rigid beliefs about what the sexes can and can't do, and now she and Frank are suffering the consequences of her rigidity.*

This case illustrates how Carla's decisions about work and parenting are influenced by her belief about how children should be raised and the different roles men and women should take in raising a family. Can you imagine yourself in a similar situation? What would it take for you to modify your viewpoint about differences between men and women as parents? Why do you think Carla holds this belief? What is your speculation on why she holds it so strongly? What would happen if she were to relinquish her point of view?

> Does a woman remember the birthday of her mother-in-law because her brain is wired for emotion? Or because it is her job to buy the present?"
>
> —Barnett & Rivers (2004, p. 188)

factors as how many women and men are available to take on particular tasks at a given time, and how they are treated in a particular culture. So even though women do give birth to children and men are physically stronger, circumstances can arise to change the behaviors men and women typically display. Psychologists Alice Eagly and Wendy Wood (1999) conducted a clever study to test this idea. They reasoned that the sex differences reported by evolutionary psychologist David Buss (1989) and interpreted as supporting the evolutionary perspective—that men prefer younger and more domestic women, whereas women prefer older men with more resources—would in fact depend on how empowered the women were within a particular culture and on how equally men and women were viewed within that culture. The researchers supplemented the 37-culture data set used by Buss with data collected from these same cultures by the United Nations to assess gender empowerment and gender equality. The United Nations data captured such factors as the proportion of women in elected governmental positions and relative degree of education attained by men and women.

What do we learn from an analysis of the demands of local economies coupled with the extent of female empowerment? In cultures where women experience higher levels of empowerment, differences between how much men and women emphasize a mate's earning prospects and domestic abilities are reduced. As female empowerment and gender equality increase across cultures, women show less of a preference for older men and men show less of a preference for younger women. In short, where predictions from evolutionary psychology would lead us to expect mate preferences to be relatively consistent across cultures, Eagly and Wood demonstrate that these preferences actually fluctuate depending on how males and females are treated in these cultures. They conclude that sex differences in what people prefer in a mate are "by-products of a social and family structure in which the man acts as a provider and the woman acts as a homemaker" (1999, p. 420). Two studies by psychologists M. Zentner and K. Mitura, using improved measures of gender equality, replicate this finding, leading the authors to suggest that "gender differentiation may be bound to erode across a broad range of psychological attributes in societies where women and men are treated equally" (2012, p. 8).

A key implication, of course, is that as these social and family structures change, so do behavioral differences between men and women. Changes in local cultures can bring about changes in the behaviors of males and females. When World War II sent large numbers of men to battle Hitler in Europe, the image of Rosie the Riveter was used to recruit American women into factory jobs that would provide munitions and equipment for the war effort. Overalls and wrenches hardly fit the feminine image of the time, but economic circumstances dictated a new division of labor (FIGURE 4.5).

We have already noted that men are more likely than women to make intrusive interruptions in conversation (d = .33; see Table 4.2). However, a rather different conclusion emerges when we consider the relative power of the people speaking. In a classic study of same-sex and different-sex roommates varying in whether they were equal or unequal in the perceived balance of power between them, sociologists Peter Kollock, Philip Blumstein, and Pepper Schwartz (1985) showed that men and women interrupted their partners to equal degrees, but that the more powerful person in the unequal-power dyads was more likely to try to interrupt the partner—and succeed in doing so. In a detailed analysis of several similar studies, Aries (1996) showed that when women have more power (e.g., by virtue of their higher level of earnings in the family or by the position they hold within a company), they exert more control over conversations than women without these resources. Thus, power may derive not from gender, but from the roles males and females inhabit. When women are granted more power, their behavior changes accordingly.

FIGURE 4.5 New social roles and untapped capacities. Images like this were used during World War II to recognize and encourage the millions of women who were contributing in new ways to the war effort.

Women are more skilled than men in expressing emotion (d = –.52), and in decoding or interpreting nonverbal behavior (d = –.43; see Table 4.2). This suggests a general advantage for women in **empathic accuracy**, the capacity for one person to be accurate in knowing what someone else is thinking or feeling (e.g., Ickes, 1993). But are men really clueless when it comes to inferring others' internal states? When social scientists are confronted with questions like this, they often wonder: If women outperform men, is it because they possess truly superior *abilities* or is it simply because they perform with heightened *motivation*? For empathic accuracy, the latter turns out to be the case. When men and women in experimental studies are instructed to infer another person's thoughts and feelings, women outperform men if the instructions make it clear that the task is about emotion and empathy (Ickes, Gesn, & Graham, 2000). Empathy is part of the stereotype of being a woman, and when this aspect of the study is made obvious the stereotype is activated more for women than for men; they are motivated to represent their gender well (Eisenberg & Lennon, 1983). However, when participants are paid for accurately perceiving others' thoughts and feelings (Klein & Hodges, 2001), and when men are instructed that empathic accuracy increases their romantic appeal to women (Thomas & Maio, 2008), men and women no longer differ. Psychological differences between men and women in the capacity for empathic responding may have less to do with enduring evolutionary

"For one million dollars, what have I been talking about for the past ten minutes: the upcoming election, my mother, my job, or an article in the Home section about kitchen makeovers?"

FIGURE 4.6 Penny for your thoughts? Although women have been shown to be better than men at expressing, interpreting, and decoding emotions, research shows that with sufficient motivation, men can be as accurate as women in these domains. Thus, offered significant financial incentive, this husband should be capable of answering his wife's question.

changes and more to do with the social situations in which men and women operate (**FIGURE 4.6**).

Men and women appear to have different orientations to sexuality in relationships (see Table 4.2). Our earlier discussion suggested an evolutionary explanation of these differences: Women incur more costs than men do in reproducing and thus are more discriminating when selecting mates, whereas men invest less but will orient toward young, attractive mates who are most likely to achieve reproductive success. However, examination of how sexual behavior and attitudes have changed indicates that these differences are not static. **FIGURE 4.7**, representing changes over four recent decades, shows not only that more young people are sexually active and more accepting of premarital sex now than previously, but that women have changed more than men in these ways. For example, in the 1950s only 13 percent of young females (average age = 17) had engaged in sex; by the 1990s, the number had risen to 47 percent. The percentage for young males dropped slightly over this same period (Wells & Twenge, 2005), suggesting that sexual behavior is responsive to changes in the broader culture. Data such as these have also been interpreted as evidence that female sexual behavior is more malleable or "plastic" than male sexual behavior (see Box 4.1).

Joining Nature and Nurture

The evolutionary perspective, proposing the nature explanation, and social structural theory, offering the nurture explanation, are the two leading theories on the root causes of observed differences between men and women. Which explanation one favors has great consequences for public policy and what men and women are allowed, encouraged, and expected to do as individuals and as relationship partners. At the same time, it is important to recognize that each perspective acknowledges the need to incorporate aspects of the other in order to achieve a reasonably complete account of how men and women differ. The nature explanation assigns greatest weight to evolutionary and biological forces, yet it does not deny that social factors operate on biological dispositions to produce behaviors and experiences characteristic

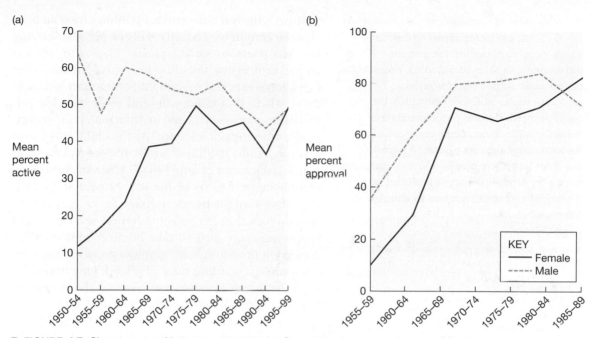

FIGURE 4.7 **Changing sexual behavior and attitudes.** Reports from women and men on (a) being sexually active, and (b) approving of premarital sex, show that women's behavior and attitudes have changed more than men's. Data were pooled from 530 studies consisting of over 269,649 participants, ranging in age from 12 to 27, with an average age of 17.

of men and women. And we have seen how the nurture explanation assigns greatest weight to social roles while not denying that biological differences affect how the roles come to be established and maintained. Thus, as evolutionary and social structural theorists continue arguing for the primacy of their perspective in explaining why men and women differ, we can see that some sort of integration of the two viewpoints is needed to fully articulate the wide range of factors contributing to sex differences and the development of gender.

Such an integration is not easily achieved, in part because a host of complex factors contribute to the gender-related development of any person, and they influence one another in complex ways (e.g., Lippa, 2005). Gender-related development begins with the direct genetic effects of sex chromosomes early in life, along with the effects of the mother's hormones and the unique fetal environment experienced before birth. Later in life, typical male and female hormonal influences contribute to development of the secondary sex characteristics up through puberty and early adolescence. But beyond biology and evolution (nature), gender development is at the same time affected by the influence of one's family, one's peers, and one's society and culture

> If we are determined to discover some 'core' explanation for gender differences, such as social roles, hormonal differences, or peer-segregated interactions, we will most certainly be disappointed. No one process exists in isolation and all exert influences on others. As with many aspects of human behavior, the truth has many facets, and our attraction to one or another theory is affected by the historical and social context in which we function."

—Leslie Brody (1999, p. 283)

(nurture). Early on, parents and siblings treat an individual a certain way based on his or her sex—buying toys that boys or girls typically play with, for example, or dressing the child in a way that conforms to society's expectations for how boys and girls will dress. Then, that child will tend to be exposed primarily to same-sex peers in informal play groups before entering adolescence. As the child grows into a young adult, media, schools, the workplace, and social groups can channel him or her in certain directions based on his or her sex: Movies and television shows might be more likely to show males as superheroes than as sensitive types; schools might encourage more girls to take home economics than computer programming; employers might inadvertently punish working moms while rewarding men who work long hours.

Even beyond social influences, gender is also manifested at the individual psychological level, in how people think and feel, in what they believe and value, and how they behave toward others. The individual's thoughts and beliefs include perceptions of the defining features of males and females learned early in life, along with stereotypes about what it means to be masculine and feminine. The individual also develops emotions and attitudes toward members of the same sex versus the other sex. He or she displays overt behaviors, such as playing with toys and developing interests that may or may not be consistent with his or her sex. And finally, the individual initiates intimate relationships with members of one sex or the other in adolescence and early adulthood and adopts a particular gender role in adulthood.

> The heredity and environment of an organism can be completely separated only in analytic thinking, for in actual nature such separation would lead to instant death of the organism, even though the philosopher himself making the analysis might himself survive."

—Arnold Gesell and Helen Thompson (1934, p. 293)

We learn two important lessons about sex and gender from this analysis. First, although the distinction between nature and nurture makes sense in the abstract, it breaks down when we think more deeply about how they combine to influence gender development. (Some say that asking whether nature or nurture is more important in social behavior is like asking whether the bow or the violin is more important for determining the music that is produced.) Though the arrival of secondary sex characteristics is clearly due to biological factors, which themselves have roots in our evolutionary past, the operation of these biological factors for a given individual appears to depend on social processes evident within the family earlier in life. Here and elsewhere, it is difficult to see where nature ends and nurture begins.

Second, we can see how easy it is to overestimate the importance of one's sex when attempting to understand a particular individual. Yes, the individual you dated in high school, or the person you are snuggling with in college, is either male or female. And, as we have seen, males and females do indeed differ in some important ways. However, we have also seen that they are more similar than different, and sex is an imperfect indicator of how people will behave. A diverse range of factors contribute to human development—that is, the ways in which individuals might become similar or different. But these factors also combine in countless ways to produce distinct individuals. There are many, many ways to be male and to be female. As we will see in the next section, considering the possibility that males and females can be masculine and feminine is a useful way to think about diversity in behaviors that might bear upon human intimacy.

Sex Role Identity: Finding the Individuals in the Categories

The way people view themselves in terms of masculine and feminine traits is referred to as their **sex role identity**. We can think of sex role identity as one key aspect of gender, which we defined earlier as a person's nonbiological and nonphysiological attributes, characteristics, and behaviors. Decades ago, psychologists believed that people could be lined up on a dimension ranging from masculine on one end to feminine on the other. This means that as you look across the spectrum of increasingly masculine people, by definition they would become less and less feminine (and vice versa, so that more femininity meant less masculinity). Later, in the 1970s, psychologists Sandra Bem, Janet Spence, and their colleagues observed that masculinity and femininity might be better understood as two distinct dimensions, with any given individual identifying himself or herself as relatively high or low in stereotypically masculine qualities and, separately, as relatively high or low in stereotypically feminine qualities; that is, men and women were understood to have both masculine and feminine traits. To make this observation more concrete, common traits used to characterize masculinity and femininity regardless of one's sex are shown in TABLE 4.3, along with some neutral traits for comparison.

As you look over these lists, it probably occurs to you that you may know people, men and women alike, who are warm and compassionate *and* who are competitive and decisive. For that matter, you probably know people who are high in masculine traits and low in feminine traits or vice versa, or people who are low in both. Moving away from the early unidimensional conception of masculinity and femininity lets us see how any person can have both masculine and feminine traits to varying degrees. FIGURE 4.8 takes this idea one step further and shows how the dimensions that represent masculine and feminine traits can be combined to produce four general classifications of people.

One of the more interesting ideas to emerge from research on sex role identity is that individuals who are high in both masculine and feminine traits are hypothesized to be competent in a wide range of situations and are less constrained by the roles and expectations associated with either gender.

TABLE 4.3 Common Masculine, Feminine, and Neutral Traits

Masculine Traits:	Feminine Traits:	Neutral Traits:
Acts as a leader	Affectionate	Likable
Forceful	Sympathetic	Conceited
Willing to take risks	Warm	Sincere
Self-reliant	Loves children	Happy
Competitive	Compassionate	Truthful
Defends own beliefs	Loyal	Secretive
Makes decisions easily	Gentle	Moody
Independent	Cheerful	Helpful
Analytical	Childlike	Unpredictable

Note: The words were derived by asking undergraduates to rate the desirability of some 200 personality attributes for a man and for a woman. Attributes were deemed masculine if they were judged as significantly more desirable for American men than women, and feminine if they were judged to be significantly more desirable for American women than men. Neutral traits are equally desirable for women and men.

Source: Reproduced by permission of the publisher, Mind Garden, Inc., www.mindgarden.com, from the Bem Sex Role Inventory by Sandra Bem. Copyright 1978, 1981 by Consulting Psychologists Press, Inc.

Thus, they have an advantage over those who are stereotypically masculine or feminine. Individuals who are high in both masculine and feminine traits are referred to as **androgynous**, a word derived from the Greek roots for male (*andro*) and female (*gyn*). Androgynous individuals do in fact appear to enjoy higher levels of self-esteem (e.g., Flaherty & Dusek, 1980), lower levels of anxiety (Williams & D'Alessandro, 1994), and higher levels of emotional intelligence (Guastello & Guastello, 2003). When compared to masculine or feminine individuals, androgynous people express their emotions more readily (Kring & Gordon, 1998). They are also more likely to adjust their behavior according to the demands of a situation, changing the situation via direct action when possible but accepting it when it is out of their control (Cheng, 2005). If, for example, a problem were to arise in an intimate relationship, an androgynous individual would be able to take an assertive stance if necessary ("I think it would be good for me to talk with your parents about why you and I want to take this trip together; maybe that would help them see that I am trustworthy") or a more passive approach if that is warranted ("I kind of see

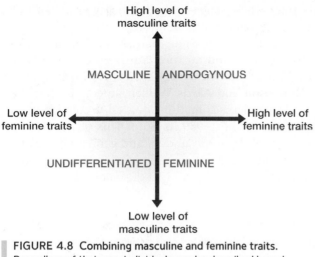

High level of
masculine traits

MASCULINE | ANDROGYNOUS

Low level of
feminine traits ← → High level of
feminine traits

UNDIFFERENTIATED | FEMININE

Low level of
masculine traits

FIGURE 4.8 Combining masculine and feminine traits.
Regardless of their sex, individuals can be described based
on their levels of feminine and masculine traits, yielding the
four classifications noted here. Androgynous individuals are
high in masculine and feminine traits; individuals are said to be
undifferentiated if they endorse few of both traits.

where your parents are coming from on
this; they barely know me, and after all
we want them to help us out with your
airfare. Let's wait until later in the summer to take the trip"). Perhaps as a result, androgynous individuals are more
desired as relationship partners (Green
& Kenrick, 1994). They also experience
higher levels of attachment security in relationships (Shaver et al., 1996), and they
appear least likely to need help for relationship difficulties (Peterson, Baucom,
Elliott, & Farr, 1989). Of course, masculine and feminine traits are valuable
separately; indeed, the former predict
objective indicators of career success
while the latter predict a greater propensity to form lasting relationships (Abele,
2003). Still, individuals who have task-
oriented masculine attributes as well as
other-oriented feminine traits are likely
to possess emotional and behavioral repertoires that serve them well in many
situations (**FIGURE 4.9**).

Finally, and perhaps most significantly, there is growing recognition that
sex and sex role identities represent more
than simply key aspects of our own and others' identities. They also serve as **schemas**—
cognitive categories that organize ideas and
beliefs about certain concepts, in this case sex
and gender. Schemas alter our perceptions
of others and how we relate to them (Bem,
1981). For example, we tend to like individuals more if they are described as androgynous than if they are masculine or feminine,
and we expect them to be better adjusted as
well (Major, Carnevale, & Deaux, 1981). If
men are led to believe they are negotiating
a division of labor with a person they cannot
see, they will negotiate harder and assign the
partner more feminine tasks if they believe
the person to be a female rather than a male
(Skrypnek & Snyder, 1982). Remarkably,
when women were incorrectly perceived to
be males in this study, they were less likely to

"Sometimes it would be helpful if you were a bit more androgynous."

FIGURE 4.9 The rewards of androgyny. Research
indicates that people prefer androgynous partners, and
that relationships with androgynous partners tend to be
more rewarding than those involving individuals who are
high in either masculinity or femininity.

choose feminine tasks for themselves—suggesting that being *perceived* to be of a certain gender can affect our behavior as well.

Findings like these have led theorists to argue that conceptions of sex and gender emerge not only from nature and nurture, but from our immediate yet ordinary everyday social interactions (Deaux & Major, 1987). As developmental scientists Linda Thompson and Alexis Walker stated: "Rather than an individual property or role, gender is something evoked, created, and sustained day-by-day through interaction" (1989, p. 865). This observation reminds us that as much as we might strive to understand gender and sex role identity as characteristics of individuals, their ultimate importance can be understood only by considering them in the context of social relationships.

MAIN POINTS

>> Meta-analytic studies identify several reliable differences between men and women; for example, men are more aggressive and more interested in sex; women are more agreeable and more skilled in communication.

>> Although these differences are often explained as arising from the different investments men and women make in their offspring, or from the different roles into which they are socialized, it is the combination of these two explanations that yields the most complete account of female and male behaviors.

>> Differences *among* men and *among* women might be at least as important as differences *between* men and women.

>> Attributes stereotypically associated with women and men can describe individuals regardless of their sex. Those with feminine and masculine attributes appear to enjoy benefits not experienced by those who are predominantly feminine or masculine.

>> Sex and gender are important categories, or schemas, that we use to anticipate, interpret, and evaluate others in our daily interactions.

Sex, Gender, and Intimacy

We can now revisit the sex similarities and differences listed in Table 4.2 with the recognition that they arise from a surprisingly intricate interplay of forces operating from the inside out and from the outside in. The ideas and research findings covered thus far should encourage you to reject simplistic notions about sex and gender, yet they leave unaddressed some tantalizing questions: What do men and women want from their intimate relationships? Are there systematic differences in how men and women make sense of and pursue intimacy?

We now move to the implications of sex similarities and differences for day-to-day functioning in intimate relationships. While keeping in mind the subtleties underlying *why* women and men differ (and do not differ), we now consider how knowing about these similarities and differences facilitates making predictions about how relationships unfold and change. To start, consider a well-substantiated view put forth by social psychologists Roy Baumeister and Kristin Sommer (1997) that males and females both need to feel they belong socially, but women meet the need through their connection with a few close others, whereas men meet the need more through their connection with larger collectives or groups.

Several studies by psychologists Shira Gabriel and Wendi Gardner (1999) support this view. For example, when asked to report on a single emotional event in their lives, women spontaneously described interpersonal events among a couple of people more than events involving a group of people; men did the opposite. After reading diary-like material containing equal numbers of dyadic and group-oriented activities, women recall the former more and men recall the latter more. And when men and women are forced to choose between putting aside their own personal interests to help a friend versus a group they belong to, women do the former while men do the latter. Further, men tend to trust another person more if they share memberships in groups with that person, whereas women tend to trust another person more if they share personal acquaintances (Maddux & Brewer, 2005). Finally, relationship disagreements elicit a stronger physiological response among women, whereas men react more when their competence or dominance is threatened (Smith, Gallo, Goble, Ngu, & Stark, 1998). In short, males and females appear to have different "default settings" when it comes to orienting toward their social bonds. Let's see where this synopsis takes us when we think explicitly about intimate relationships.

Relationship Awareness

Imagine that you and your different-sex partner of 2 years are out with a group of your old friends from high school. As your friends get to know your partner, the conversation turns to how you two met and what happened on your first date. Knowing what you now know about how males and females are oriented toward social relationships, can you predict whether you and your partner will remember these events the same way? Chances are good that there will be some discrepancies in your accounts. The woman is likely to recall more details, with greater accuracy and vividness, and to express them with more emotional range than the man. Women are also more likely to take the perspective of the couple (rather than themselves) in telling the story, and they are more likely to correct men's accounts than vice versa (Acitelli, 1992; Cate, Koval, Lloyd, & Wilson, 1995; Holmberg, Orbuch, & Veroff, 2004; Martin, 1991; Ross & Holmberg, 1992). In other words, women tend to have more relationship awareness than men do. The following interview excerpt, taken from a study conducted by psychologists Diane Holmberg, Terri Orbuch, and Joseph Veroff, helps illustrate these differences (2004, pp. 124–125):

> **Interviewer:** *How did the two of you become interested in each other?*
>
> **Fred:** *Ah, well, I suppose as we went out more, we found out what I like and what she likes. She was always pretty athletic herself. So I suppose we shared a lot in common.*
>
> **Sue:** *It was real easy, because we could talk a lot. We just hit it off. I think we went out and one night just sat and we talked the whole time. We went to a show and it was really easy to communicate with each other. At first, it was kind of weird, because I thought, I bet we're just going to end up being friends, because you know, usually friends can talk really well together.*

Women develop more differentiated and complex cognitive representations of relationship events, allowing them to recall prior experiences with the partner with greater ease and more emotional richness (**FIGURE 4.10**). Because they are capable of accessing a greater store of relationship knowledge, women might be inclined to see connections among relationship events that are not as obvious to men. In fact, divorcing men are 8 to 10 times more likely than their wives to say they do not know why their relationship ended (Kitson, 1992). Regardless of the validity of wives' explanations for their divorce, this and other findings suggest that women are more likely than men to try to understand their relationships. In turn, women also might be inclined to see their male partners' relatively impoverished memory as a sign of being less interested in the relationship than, say, sports—for which they can remember countless statistics. A more accurate interpretation might be that men and women seek out different kinds of information about relationships, and different kinds of information come to them more readily.

FIGURE 4.10 Social orientation. Although they are equally sociable, women and men may orient to different aspects of their social worlds. As this cartoon suggests, the average woman assigns greater priority to social relationships and the emotional well-being of others than the average man.

Quality of Interaction

Think about the last dozen or so interactions you had with same-sex friends, and then think about the last dozen or so interactions you had with different-sex friends. Which, if either, felt more superficial to you? Which felt more intimate or meaningful? A summary of eight studies (see Reis, 1998), all using a diary method and a rating scale where 1 = superficial and 7 = meaningful, shows that men tend to rate same-sex interactions around 3.4 whereas women tend to rate same-sex interactions around 4.2—a reliable difference yielding a relatively large d value of .85. Men and women do not differ in how they rate their different-sex interactions—reporting scores of 4.2 and 4.3 respectively (d = .05). This shows that men's interactions with men are *less* meaningful (or more superficial) than those with women, whereas women's interactions are equally meaningful regardless of the partner's gender. Along with evidence that women are more skilled than men in expressing emotion and decoding nonverbal behavior (see Table 4.2), this finding suggests that women are contributing more than men to the level of emotional connection in different-sex interactions.

With these findings in mind, you might be surprised to learn that married men and women, when instructed in a laboratory setting to provide social support to one another in whatever way they ordinarily would, are virtually identical in the rates of positive, neutral, and negative behaviors they are observed displaying (Neff & Karney, 2005). Yet when these same spouses reported on how much stress they experienced and how much partner support they received each day over the course of a week, husbands' stressful days were met by increases in support, whereas wives' stressful days were met by increases in support *and increases in criticism*—hardly a supportive experience (e.g., "I know your boss can be hard on you, and that must be rough, but seriously, you knew going into that job that he was a bit of a jerk, and I told you to quit that job months ago"). How can we make sense of these results? This study shows that men and women are equally capable of displaying supportive behaviors; it is not as though men lack the basic skills for being supportive or emotionally expressive (Reis, Senchak, & Solomon, 1985). In daily life, however, women tend to offer higher quality support than do men. "Perhaps husbands, more than wives, resent their role as support provider and thus act out these feelings of resentment by engaging in detrimental behaviors when providing support" (Neff & Karney, 2005, p. 88). This suggestion is very much in line with Baumeister and Sommer's contention (1997) that women show a greater inclination to invest in close dyadic relationships, whereas men are more likely to orient toward relationships in larger groups.

Further evidence for this difference between men and women comes from research on couples when one partner has been diagnosed with cancer. Knowing what you now know about how men and women think about and manage their relationship, how do you think they differ in their level of psychological distress when they have a partner who has a life-threatening

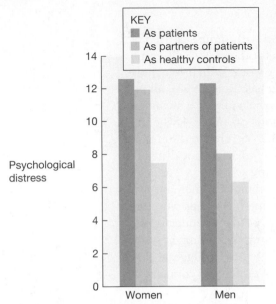

KEY
■ As patients
■ As partners of patients
■ As healthy controls

Psychological
distress

Women   Men

FIGURE 4.11 Women and men as caretakers.
Women and men are similar in their levels of
psychological distress, regardless of whether they
are cancer patients or healthy control participants.
But as partners of patients, women experience far
more psychological distress than men do. In fact,
men who are partners of patients do not differ
from men who are in healthy control couples. The
observation that women experience more distress
than men as caretakers may reflect the greater
investment women make in their close dyadic
relationships. (Source: Adapted from Hagedoorn et al., 2000.)

illness? Will the woman or the man be more upset? **FIGURE 4.11** answers this question, highlighting
the different experiences men and women have
when taking care of a partner who is ill (Hagedoorn et al., 2000).

Meanings of Intimacy

Do men and women differ in what it means to
have an intimate experience with a member of
the other sex? Do they set out to achieve different
things in relationships? If so, this might help explain why men and women seem to differ in their
approaches to intimate relationships. When asked
to rate the importance of 30 different standards or
expectations for a successful long-term relationship (e.g., respect, acceptance, demonstrations of
affection), adult men and women do not differ.
Women, however, are more likely than men to
state that their current relationship does not meet
their standards (Vangelisti & Daly, 1997). Men and
women seem to enter relationships with similar
standards in mind; however, perhaps by virtue of
women's greater sensitivity to the emotional tenor
of dyadic relationships, men end up being closer
to having their standards met.

A similar conclusion comes from a study in
which male and female undergraduates were
asked to describe an intimate experience, and researchers then analyzed those responses without
knowing the respondent's sex (Helgeson, Shaver, &
Dyer, 1987). On balance, this study found clear similarities in how men and
women understood intimacy. Women understood intimacy to mean feeling
and expressing appreciation and enjoyment (100 percent of them listed this),
feeling and expressing love (38 percent), feeling mutual interest and attraction (31 percent), and receiving support (28 percent). Men were similar in
that they listed feelings of love and enjoyment (at least 92 percent of them
did), mutual interest and appreciation (54 percent), and mutual support
(28 percent). While men and women were also quite similar in their mention of physical contact (44 percent and 46 percent, respectively), men were
seven times more likely than women to mention sex (21 percent versus 3 percent). In fact, as part of this 3 percent, women sometimes mentioned *not* having physical sex as evidence of their feelings of closeness. For example, one
woman wrote, "We finally kissed and got more intimate but did not have sex.
Just being with him makes me feel particularly close to him." In addition,

although men and women were equally likely to mention appreciating or valuing the partner as an element of intimacy, men were much less likely than women to think of *expressing* appreciation as part of their intimate experiences (19 percent versus 44 percent).

We might conclude that young women usually equate intimacy with expressions of appreciation, whereas young men tend to associate intimacy with sex. But such a conclusion misses some important facts: Women and men both define intimacy in terms of positive feelings. And even though women generally valued expressing appreciation and men generally valued sex, these views were expressed by fewer than half the people in both groups. So are men and women similar or different when it comes to how they understand intimacy? The similarities probably outweigh the differences (see also Burleson, Kunkel, Samter, & Werking, 1996). As we'll see in the next section, however, the differences tell us something important.

Sex and Physical Intimacy

The idea that sex is more central to men's than women's conceptions of intimacy barely hints at the consistently greater sex drive that men possess (or, perhaps, that possess men). This difference in sex drive is supported by every measurement and study (Vohs & Baumeister, 2004; also see Vohs, Catanese, & Baumeister, 2004). As the old joke goes, women want one man to satisfy their every need, while men want every woman to satisfy their one need. What are the various ways this "need" might play itself out in intimate relationships?

Men are younger than women when they first have sexual intercourse; and 90 percent of men say they wanted to have intercourse when they first had it, whereas that is true of only 70 percent of women (Michael, Gagnon, Laumann, & Kolata, 1994). Of those people who wanted to have intercourse their first time, 51 percent of the men did so out of curiosity, and 48 percent of the women did so because they felt affection for their partner. Seven percent of all men, but 21 percent of all women, have sex for the first time on their wedding night (Michael et al., 1994).

Early in different-sex relationships, men and women are similar in how much sex and closeness they desire. Men's desire for sex does not decline much as time passes, but their desire for closeness does. Women desire less sex as time passes, but their desire for closeness increases (Klusmann, 2002)—creating a kind of "perfect storm" in which men and women must negotiate their differing and changing needs for physical and emotional intimacy. Men are more likely to initiate sexual contact in their intimate relationships, and women are more likely to refuse this contact (Byers & Heinlein, 1989).

Couples commonly argue about sex, and when they do, it is nearly always the men who want more sexual interaction (Byers & Lewis, 1988). Men and women both express discontent with their sexual relationship to an increasing degree as their relationships progress. However, dissatisfaction with sexual

"Oh yeah, baby, I'll listen to you—I'll listen to you all night long."

FIGURE 4.12 Intimate exchanges. Evidence suggests that unmet sexual needs motivate married men to have affairs, and women enter affairs in the hope of greater emotional connection.

intimacy tends to be more closely associated with relationship satisfaction for men than for women (Storaasli & Markman, 1990).

Men's sexual dissatisfaction in their marriage increases the chance that they will engage in extramarital affairs (Atkins, Yi, Baucom, & Christensen, 2005). More men than women engage in extramarital sex at least once—approximately 25 percent versus 15 percent (Laumann et al., 1994)—and men's infidelity appears to be motivated more by sex than by the desire for emotional closeness with another person. The opposite is the case for women's infidelity; and, in turn, women are more likely than men to fall in love with their extramarital partner (Glass & Wright, 1985, 1992). For men, but not for women, dissatisfaction with sex in their relationship increases the likelihood that they will take active steps to seek relationship counseling, even more than their overall level of satisfaction with the relationship (Doss, Atkins, & Christensen, 2003).

In short, men's greater desire for sex helps organize a lot of information about relationships. It leads to valuable insights about why couples argue, why people stray, and why people seek relationship counseling. (It also inspires funny cartoons about the kinds of intimacy women would be willing to pay for; **FIGURE 4.12.**)

Relationship Dissolution and Its Aftermath

If men invest in and orient toward social groups more than dyadic relationships, and if their sex drive leaves them more likely than women to seek mates outside their primary relationship, does it follow that men will be more likely to want to dissolve their intimate relationships? The answer is no. To return to what is now a familiar theme, men appear to benefit from women's tendency to be more closely attuned to the emotional climate in the relationship, and men probably have more to lose by ending their intimate partnerships. Where men might operate like thermometers in a relationship—the information they provide is a reasonable indication of what is happening at the moment—women appear to be more like barometers in the sense that their experiences enable them to forecast what will happen to the relationship in the future.

Consistent with this observation, large surveys show that eventual marital disruption is better predicted by data collected from women than from men (South, Bose, & Trent, 2004)—though this disparity tends to weaken as spouses describe their relationship as less traditional and more egalitarian

(Heaton & Blake, 1999). When problems do set in, women lead the way in seeking therapy by recognizing problems earlier, accepting the need for counseling earlier, and initiating contact with practitioners (Doss et al., 2003). Early in treatment, women report more reasons for seeking help, they express these reasons with more negative feelings and fewer positive feelings, and they hold the partner more responsible for the problems they are confronting (Doss, Simpson, & Christensen, 2004). While we cannot know the validity of these claims that husbands are more responsible for their relationship difficulties, ex-husbands and ex-wives agree that women are more likely to want a divorce, to be first to talk about getting a divorce, and to actually file for a divorce (e.g., Amato & Previti, 2003; Braver, Whitley, & Ng, 1993; Hewitt, Western, & Baxter, 2006). In dating relationships as well, women tend to be the "last in and first out," whereas men tend to be the "first in and last out" (Hatfield & Walster, 1978).

As the dissolution unfolds (see Chapter 12), the period of greatest stress for women occurs before the relationship dissolves; for men, their stress peaks after the relationship has ended (e.g., Albrecht, 1980). Once their relationship has dissolved, men report relatively stable incomes but larger drops in life satisfaction and well-being; women report the opposite—relatively large decreases in income but smaller drops in life satisfaction (e.g., Andreb & Brockel, 2007; Williams & Umberson, 2004). This helps explain the puzzle of why women initiate divorce, knowing that it will be financially difficult for them and their children: These costs are offset by the gains in well-being. Consistent with what we have learned here, women appear to fare better through these difficult transitions because they tend to be the ones initiating the divorce, and they are more likely to marshal support from their friends and relatives as they cope with the transition. Also, as psychologists Sanford Braver, Jenessa Shapiro, and Matthew Goodman note:

> With divorce, women often gain higher status, within-family roles (e.g., head of the household, bread-earner), whereas men often gain roles lower in status (e.g., they gain domestic roles in new house) in addition to confusion and frustration by the new role as a noncustodial parent. (2006, p. 327)

The differing experiences of men and women in intimate relationships also predict patterns of remarriage; men enter new partnerships more quickly, and in higher numbers, than women (e.g., Sweeney, 2002; FIGURE 4.13). Divorce and dissolution are not the only transitions in which

"Oh, perfect. I can't remember what I wanted from the basement, and you've remarried."

FIGURE 4.13 Differing responses to divorce. Following divorce, men form new relationships more quickly than women do. This is consistent with the idea that women can draw upon stronger support networks than men, and that men benefit a great deal from being in relationships with women.

we can see the differing dependencies of men and women on their intimate partnerships: The death of a spouse takes a greater toll on men than women, and this effect is stronger at older ages (e.g., Williams & Umberson, 2004). When we use Baumeister and Sommer's (1997) core premise—that women orient to and invest in dyads to a greater degree than men, who focus more on socialization within larger groups—we find corroborating evidence in how men and women dissolve relationships, seek help for solving problems, respond to the end of their partnerships, and form new ones. As BOX 4.3 describes, one journalist went deep undercover to explore the very different emotional experiences men and women have in their daily lives.

BOX 4.3 SPOTLIGHT ON . . .

Changing Places

What would it be like to change your gender, if only temporarily? The author Norah Vincent did just that for a period of 18 months (Vincent, 2006; FIGURE 4.14). Hers was not a surgical transformation, but a complete cosmetic change in which she went from Norah to Ned with the help of a voice coach, makeup artist, and personal trainer.

FIGURE 4.14 A man's life through a woman's eyes. After changing her typical appearance to that of a man, Norah Vincent set out to learn more about men and the relationships between men and women. She discovered that women and men adopt very different approaches to emotion and status.

Norah, as Ned, spent a lot of time on the dating scene but also spent a great deal of time casually with men, in bars, on a bowling team, at a monastery, and in a "balls-to-the-wall sales job in a testosterone-saturated environment" (p. 184). On balance, and to her surprise, Vincent did not enjoy her time as a man. Her observations are fascinating, particularly those about emotional expression, generally and in the context of intimate relationships:

> I couldn't be myself, and after a while, this really got me down. I spent so much time worrying about being found out, even after I knew that nobody would question the drag, that I began to feel as stiff and scripted as a sandwich board. And it wasn't being found out as a woman that I was really worried about. It was being found out as less than a real man, and I suspect that this is something a lot of men endure their whole lives, this constant scrutiny and self-scrutiny.
>
> Somebody is always evaluating your manhood. Whether it's other men, other women, even children. And everybody is always on the lookout for your weakness or inadequacy, as if it's some kind of plague they're terrified of catching, or, more importantly, of other men catching. . . .
>
> And that, I learned very quickly, is the straitjacket of the male role, and one that is no less constrictive than its feminine counterpart. You're not allowed to be a complete human being. Instead you get to be a coached jumble of stoic poses. You get to be what's expected of you. (p. 276)

>> The idea that females gravitate toward and specialize in the tasks associated with intimacy in dyadic contexts, whereas men orient toward and invest in social relationships within larger groups, seems undeniable and consistent with what we know about the roles evolution mandates for males and females.

>> Focusing on the average woman and man leaves a lot of room within these categories for individuals to behave differently from their same-sex peers.

>> Males appear to benefit from being in close contact with females, but not all females are alike in their ability to produce this effect. Likewise, men vary in their inclination to nurture their partners and their children, and in their capacity to negotiate hierarchical relationships external to the relationship.

>> Natural differences in their social predispositions should not restrict how men and women actually behave, nor should it constrain our expectations for what people can do, inside or outside their relationships.

Same-Sex Relationships

Does the traditional arc of a relationship—boy meets girl, boy and girl fall in love, and boy and girl then stay together happily/stay together miserably/go their separate ways—change if boy meets boy or if girl meets girl? Are relationships between members of the same sex and relationships between members of different sexes more similar than different, or more different than similar? A complete understanding of human intimacy requires consideration of these questions, and attempting to answer them provides us with two very useful kinds of information. First, we can learn whether the theories and principles typically derived from and applied to different-sex relationships need to be modified when we consider same-sex relationships. Second, we can learn whether different-sex dyads are uniquely difficult to manage, or whether relationships are difficult in general, regardless of their composition. The case could be made that gay couples (involving two men) and lesbian couples (involving two women) have an advantage over different-sex couples because partners have the same biological sex. After all, if similarity promotes successful relationships (see Chapter 5), what could be better than having a partner who shares your biological sex and all that comes along with it?

As we set out to address the similarities and differences among same-sex and different-sex relationships, you might think this is an easy distinction to make: You either want to be with a partner of the same sex or you want to be with a partner of the other sex, period. But this distinction becomes a bit murky upon closer inspection. What if a person thinks about himself or herself as unambiguously straight but has had sex in the past with a person

❝

It is always a choice whether to be completely honest with yourself and admit you are not in the majority and are attracted to the same sex. I wasn't able to admit this to myself until a few weeks before my 28th birthday. The *choice* is to live your life as best you can. The question 'Why are you gay or lesbian?' is a small part of a much bigger question: 'Why are you You?'"

—C. F., Louisville, KY, *The Advocate* (July 17, 2001)

of the same sex, and occasionally fantasizes about having a gay or lesbian lover? What if a person is currently in a same-sex relationship but desires partners of the other sex—and does not consider him- or herself to be bisexual (attracted to both men and women)? For most people, the sexual label they apply to themselves, the target of their sexual fantasies, the focus of their sexual attraction, and their sexual behavior all cohere to produce a single sexual identity or sexual orientation. But for many other people, these phenomena do not overlap.

In a survey of about 8,000 college students, for example, about 87 percent said they were attracted exclusively to members of the other sex, and about 1 percent said they were attracted exclusively to members of the same sex, leaving about 12 percent in the middle—even though only about 1 percent identified themselves as bisexual (Ellis, Robb, & Burke, 2005). In a representative interview survey of more than 3,000 men and women, 2.8 percent of the men and 1.4 percent of the women identified themselves as homosexual, 6.2 percent of the men and 4.4 percent of the women reported being attracted to members of their own sex, and 4.9 percent of the men and 4.1 percent of the women reported having had at least one sexual contact with a member of their own sex since the age of 18 (Laumann et al., 1994). Thus, in the same way that we know there is great variability in what it means to be male or female, there is variability in who we are sexually attracted to. Most of the studies introduced here use the individual's self-identification when characterizing them as gay or straight. However, it is important to recognize that sexual orientation can sometimes defy simple labels.

Similarities and Differences in Same-Sex and Different-Sex Relationships

Comparisons between same-sex and different-sex relationships are relatively few in the scientific literature, but the studies that do exist make it clear that these relationships are more similar than different. Same-sex and different-sex partners experience comparable levels of satisfaction in their relationships, argue about similar issues, communicate their feelings and opinions in similar ways, and appear to change for largely similar reasons (for reviews, see Kurdek, 2005; Peplau & Fingerhut, 2007). Even so, there are some important differences between these two types of couples. Some can be summarized pretty easily: Perhaps because they value equality more and have fewer built-in power differences associated with their sex, same-sex couples divide household tasks more equally than different-sex couples do (e.g., Kurdek, 1993), and they display more effective problem solving (Kurdek, 2004;

Roisman et al., 2008). But other differences require deeper reflection. We next focus on three of the most consistent and important differences between same-sex and different-sex couples, involving the contexts in which relationships occur, sexual activity and attitudes toward exclusivity in relationships, and how relationships dissolve.

Context

Contextual influences—that is, the forces existing beyond the partners and their interactions—shape and guide our intimate relationships. We will discuss contextual influences on relationships in more detail in Chapter 11, but here, we focus specifically on the dramatically different contexts in which same-sex and different-sex couples live their intimate lives. According to the 2004 U.S. Census, same-sex couples make up 12 percent of the 5.84 million households headed by unmarried partners (**TABLE 4.4**). There is good reason to believe that these figures underestimate the number of same-sex households in the United States, given the fear that some have in divulging their sexual orientation. In any case, the fact that gay and lesbian partners are **sexual minorities** brings with it several implications.

TABLE 4.4 Facts About Same-Sex Couples

▪ In 2005, there were approximately 8.8 million gay, lesbian, and bisexual people living in the United States. This represents about 4.1% of the U.S. population between the ages of 18 and 45.
▪ Not all these people are in relationships. In 2005, there were 776,943 same-sex couples in the United States. This reflects a 30% increase from 2000, when 594,391 same-sex couples were counted.
▪ Same-sex couples make up about 1% of all households with couples in them.
▪ About 20% of all same-sex couples in the United States are raising children under the age of 18. About 48% of all married couples in the United States are raising children under 18. The average number of children in both types of couples is two.
▪ An analysis of data from four states—Vermont, Massachusetts, New Jersey, and California—shows that about half or fewer of all same-sex couples involved two women. At the same time, lesbians made up about two-thirds of all same-sex couples who married or sought legal recognition for their relationship.

Sources: U.S. Census Bureau; http://williamsinstitute.law.ucla.edu/. Accessed December 26, 2012.

First, whereas virtually all adolescents are confronted with the anxiety-provoking task of understanding how they are going to develop as participants in romantic relationships, gays and lesbians have the additional challenges of discovering and establishing—for themselves and the people around them—that they are gay or lesbian, and that their experiences in developing an intimate identity will take place outside the mainstream. Ritch Savin-Williams, a specialist in human development and clinical psychology (1996), notes that "Sexual-minority youth struggle with issues of identity and intimacy because important impediments rooted in our cultural values and attitudes deter them from dating those they love and instead mandate that they date those they cannot love" (p. 168). Indeed, most same-sex adolescents engage in different-sex relationships of one form or another in an effort either to mask or test their interest in same-sex partners (e.g., Herdt, Cohler, Boxer, & Floyd, 1993). Once two same-sex individuals are in a partnership, they may differ in the extent to which they have informed others about their sexual orientation, possibly adding to their relationship a further source of tension that different-sex partners do not feel (Peplau, Veniegas, & Campbell, 1996).

A second contextual difference is that gay and lesbian people must come to terms with having a sexual orientation that may be the subject of scorn and ostracism. For example, 48 percent of all American adults view same-sex relations between consenting adults as morally wrong (2008 Gallup Values and Beliefs Survey), and 19 percent of lesbians and 28 percent of gay men have been victimized because of their sexual orientation (Herek, Gillis, & Cogan, 1999). High levels of stress arising from victimization and other forms of discrimination (e.g., stigma, prejudice, internalized homophobia) appear to contribute to a host of mental health problems (e.g., Balsam, Beauchaine, Mickey, & Rothblum, 2005; Cochran, Sullivan, & Mays, 2003; Feinstein, Goldfried, & Davila, 2012; Herek & Garnets, 2007; Meyer, 2003) and lowered relationship quality (Otis, Rostosky, Riggle, & Hamrin, 2006; Todosijevic, Rothblum, & Solomon, 2005). This suggests that unique contextual influences conspire to make intimate relationships difficult for gays and lesbians. Moreover, same-sex couples are often deprived of even the simplest and most routine ways of expressing intimacy in public, such as holding hands or kissing good-bye. Marnie, a lesbian investment broker in her mid-40s, commented on how she and her partner Janet think about public places where it is acceptable to express intimacy: "You have to be careful. We have a little joke about [hugging in] airports. Sometimes we feel just like going out to the airport" (Blumstein & Schwartz, 1983, p. 499).

A third, related contextual difference is that gay and lesbian couples do not receive the same level of societal and familial support. As of 2014, except for 11 countries (Argentina, Belgium, Canada, Denmark, Iceland, the Netherlands, Norway, Portugal, South Africa, Spain, and Sweden) and a few U.S. states, same-sex marriages are not legally recognized. The lack of legal barriers to relationship dissolution, along with the fact that another common barrier to divorce—children—is more common among different-sex than same-sex couples (Kaiser Family Foundation, 2001, p. 31), suggests that same-sex couples have fewer external reasons for keeping their relationship intact. Along similar lines, 34 percent of all gays and lesbians, or about 1 in 3, report that their family or a member of their family has refused to accept them because of their sexual orientation (Kaiser Family Foundation, 2001, p. 29). Several studies show that gays and lesbians receive less support for their relationships from family members compared to different-sex couples and, perhaps to compensate for this reduced support, are more likely to turn instead to their friends and peers (e.g., Kurdek, 2004). The close social ties characterizing the support networks of same-sex couples differentiates them in yet another way from different-sex couples: When gays and lesbians dissolve their relationships, they are more likely to remain connected to their ex-partner, to see them socially, and to maintain a friendship with them (Harkless & Fowers, 2005).

Sexual Activity and Monogamy

Regardless of sexual orientation, relationship happiness is higher when partners are more sexually active, and sexual activity typically declines the longer a relationship continues (for reviews, see Diamond, 2006; Sprecher, Christopher, & Cate, 2006). However, gay, lesbian, and straight sexual relationships do differ regarding sexual activity in at least three key ways (see Peplau, Fingerhut, & Beals, 2004, and Peplau & Fingerhut, 2007, for reviews). First, as you might predict based on men having a stronger sex drive, sexual activity is higher in relationships involving two gay men than for different-sex partners, particularly in the first few years of the relationship.

Second, perhaps for similar reasons, gay men are more accepting of open (nonexclusive) relationships and are more likely to participate in them. In a study conducted before the outbreak of AIDS in 1981–1982, only 36 percent of gay men considered **monogamy**, or sexual exclusivity with their partner, to be important. Compare this to 62 percent of unmarried cohabiting men, 70 percent of unmarried cohabiting women, 71 percent of lesbians, 75 percent of married men, and 84 percent of married women who felt that way (see Blumstein & Schwartz, 1983). A short while later, a 1988 survey of 560 gay men—nearly all of whom were in highly committed partnerships—showed that 42 percent had sex outside their main relationship in the past year; 22 percent had nonmonogamous sex in the past month, typically once (Bryant & Demian, 1994). A 1994 survey of 2,500 gay men indicated that 48 percent had engaged in sex outside their relationship, though 70 percent indicated a preference for long-term, monogamous relationships (Lever, 1994). In a 2005 study of 195 gay men, about 60 percent reported having sex outside their primary relationship after becoming a couple; in about 45 percent of all relationships, the partners agreed that outside sex was acceptable under some circumstances. Comparable figures for straight married men were 15 percent and 3.5 percent, respectively (Solomon, Rothblum, & Balsam, 2005). Although it is clear that gay men experience less jealousy than straight men when confronted with jealousy-evoking situations (e.g., your partner has an affair; your partner kisses someone at a party; Bringle, 1995), not much is known about the various ways gay men manage to maintain a primary relationship with one partner while engaging in sex with others (see Adam, 2006; LaSala, 2004).

The third way sexual activity differs involves the flip side of the greater sex drive in men—the comparatively reduced sex drive in women. You would be right if you predicted that sex is less frequent in relationships involving two women (lesbian couples) than it is in relationships involving one woman (different-sex couples). Among couples who have been together more than 10 years, for example, sex occurs once a month or less for 15 percent of married couples, 33 percent of gay couples, and 47 percent of lesbian couples (Blumstein & Schwartz, 1983). A more recent study is consistent with this pattern. The 378 lesbians participating in a 2005 study by Solomon et al. reported having sex about twice a month, whereas the 219 straight married women reported having sex about twice a week. However, lesbians are not necessarily unhappy with the quality of their sexual lives (e.g., Kurdek, 1991), perhaps because they find satisfaction in intimate behaviors not typically defined as being sexual (e.g., hugging, caressing) or because they experience higher rates of orgasm compared to straight women (see Peplau et al., 2004).

Relationship Dissolution

Despite all the adverse contextual constraints operating on same-sex couples, their relationships are typically as fulfilling as those of straight couples (Roisman et al., 2008). And, as with straight couples, their feeling of satisfaction is highest earlier in the relationship and then declines with the passing of time (Kurdek, 1998, 2001). Some evidence suggests, however, that same-sex relationships are less stable than those of married couples, especially married couples with children (Kurdek, 2004). We might infer that relationships with fewer institutional supports—whether legal, social, or religious—are more vulnerable to dissolution. Even among different-sex couples, we know that cohabiting couples do not stay together as long as married couples, and married couples without children do not last as long as those with children. But the story gets a bit more interesting when we look at data from two countries—Norway and Sweden—where same-sex couples are able to form registered partnerships granting them the same legal rights as different-sex couples. Nevertheless, a comparison of dissolution rates indicates that same-sex relationships are more likely to dissolve than different-sex relationships, and that lesbian relationships are more likely to end than gay male relationships, even after equating the groups statistically across a host of demographic differences (Andersson, Noack, Seierstad, & Weedon-Fekjaer, 2006). For example, 13 percent of the different-sex relationships in Sweden ended within 5 years, compared to 20 percent of the gay relationships and 30 percent of the lesbian relationships, even though lesbian partners were more similar to one another than were gay partners in age, nationality, education, and income.

How can we interpret these findings? First, to understand why same-sex and different-sex couples differ in this regard, we can look at context. Although a transformed legal status may well provide same-sex partners with new rights, "this group's lower exposure to normative pressure to maintain lifelong unions" may explain their higher dissolution rate (Andersson et al., 2006, p. 95). Second, to understand why gay and lesbian couples differ, we can look at biological sex and related factors. For example, if women are more attuned to the quality of emotional connections in their relationships and more likely to take steps to end the relationship when problems arise, we could predict that relationships involving two women are more likely to end than are relationships involving two men. Lesbians appear to desire more intimacy than gay men do (Kurdek, 1998); when it is not forthcoming, they may look to other relationships to fill that need. Because sexual exclusivity is more the norm among lesbians than among gay men, these women may prefer to make a clean break from their current relationship to reestablish sexual exclusivity with another partner.

A third possibility is that gay and lesbian couples—due to the high value they place on autonomy and equality (e.g., Kurdek, 2004)—approach their committed partnerships with very high standards, which, if they go unmet, might prompt them to bring their relationship to an end.

> " I'd thought lesbian life would be easy, that love would come smoothly, that the whole of my living from the moment I declared my new self would be gravy. The reality was that real love, regardless of who it's with, is at once the most magical and the most difficult of undertakings. The great struggle of love is to reach a balance between what we want, what we imagine we deserve, what is offered to us, and what we accept."
>
> —Gretchen Legler (2005, p. 80)

MAIN POINTS

>> Although same-sex and different-sex relationships are more alike than different, and can be understood using similar principles, there can be distinguished in at least three important ways.

>> Profound differences in the social context in which gay and lesbian people discover their sexual identity, form connections with partners, and present their relationship to others affect their well-being and their chances for successfully managing their relationship.

>> Levels of sexual activity differentiate gay, lesbian, and straight relationships; higher levels of sex with the partner and outside the relationship correspond with the number of male

partners in a relationship. Biological sex and male-female sex drive variations are more important than same-sex orientation in explaining this difference.

>> Higher rates of dissolving relationships for same-sex couples may be due to the absence of the legal and cultural supports that help different-sex couples stay together when they have problems.

CONCLUSION

The fact that relationship scientists can identify meaningful differences in how men and women approach their intimate relationships would seem to prove the wisdom of comedians and cartoonists. Our analysis demonstrates, however, that sex, gender, and intimacy are far more complex than the stereotypes presented in the popular media. Differences between women and men can be easily exaggerated, and doing so distracts us from the social norms and expectations that affect our behavior—as well as from the inadequacy of using simple "male/female, gay/straight" categories to describe people and relationships.

Stepping back from the wealth of material presented here on sex, gender, and sexual orientation allows us to identify two themes to remember. *First: We cannot understand intimate relationships without taking into account the sex of the partners involved.* Our biological sex is hardwired into us—it is hard to change, and it captures a large part of who we are and how others perceive us. Our sex also consistently accounts for how we think about intimacy, pursue and maintain intimacy, repair rifts in our intimate relationships, and respond when intimacy is threatened or lost.

Second, and more importantly: We cannot understand intimate relationships unless we go beyond the sex of the partners involved. Careful quantitative analyses of male and female characteristics demonstrate relatively small differences between them. Investigation of masculine and feminine traits shows that men can be feminine, women can be masculine, and both can be androgynous. Two people of the same sex will behave quite differently depending on situational demands; given the chance, men will be wonderful fathers and women will be terrific CEOs. The point is that over and over, we have seen that hard categories do not serve us well. To understand sex, gender, and sexual orientation in relationships, we have to value these categories while simultaneously recognizing that they fail to capture the tremendous variety existing within them.

5

Attraction and Mate Selection

Matchmaker, Matchmaker

A woman asked a rabbi, "How long did it take God to create the universe?" The rabbi answered: "Six days." The woman considered this, and then asked: "So what has he been doing since then?" The rabbi answered: "Arranging marriages" (Cohen, 1949, p. 163).

He is not the only one. For most of recorded history, finding a partner was not a job that anyone was expected to do alone. People from cultures around the world have employed professional matchmakers, who are responsible for pairing up partners who they believe will be compatible. From biblical times to the present day, across Western and Eastern cultures, the tradition continues, as people from all walks of life seek help in finding a suitable mate. In 2007, there were 1,600 registered matchmakers in the United States, up from 1,300 in 2004. Far from an outdated custom, matchmaking is a growth industry (FIGURE 5.1).

Imagine you were given this job. How would you go about it? You might take some advice from Patti Stanger, the self-proclaimed "Millionaire Matchmaker" and the host of a reality television show of the same name. Ms. Stanger targets wealthy men who need a private club where they can find beautiful and intelligent partners. Noticing that highly desirable women may not feel the need for a matchmaking service, the Millionaire Matchmaker recruits attractive, eligible females and offers them membership for free. To the males, who have to pay a considerable fee to participate, she offers not only access to partners but also the services of a dating coach, personal trainers, hair stylists, dentists, and even plastic surgeons. Why do the wealthy clients of the Millionaire Matchmaker need all this help? "If a man wants to woo and win a 'Perfect 10' female," says the website, "he must himself become a 'Perfect 10' both internally and externally in order to reach his objective."

Not everyone can afford such personal treatment. For the rest of us, there is the Internet. Whereas

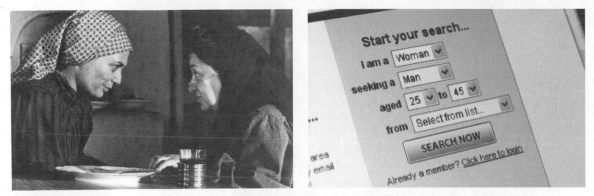

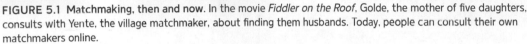

FIGURE 5.1 **Matchmaking, then and now.** In the movie *Fiddler on the Roof*, Golde, the mother of five daughters, consults with Yente, the village matchmaker, about finding them husbands. Today, people can consult their own matchmakers online.

Ms. Stanger creates matches based on her own intuition and experience, dating websites claim to do the same thing using the latest technology. For example, eHarmony.com promises to match you with a "highly select" group of available partners, chosen through a "compatibility matching model." Members complete an extensive survey that measures 29 dimensions of compatibility. Based on "rigorous scientific research" the site's patented algorithm—a closely guarded secret—matches its members with suitable partners. Is this approach more effective than the old-fashioned way? Perhaps, but the success rate of eHarmony's matches is also a closely guarded secret.

Maybe you are not willing to let someone choose your partner for you. Maybe you want to choose your own partner. Through the miracle of social networking, the Internet allows singles to communicate and interact with potential partners who might have been unknown or inaccessible years ago.

Match.com, for example, lets users search through millions of profiles for individuals who meet whatever criteria you specify. Do you harbor an attraction to dark-haired ice fishermen who read Jane Austen? Latin American gourmet cooks who vote libertarian? There is a profile to suit every taste, so you might think everyone should be able to find someone suitable. Yet, despite these technological breakthroughs, the problem of finding a mate remains, and the growing market for matchmakers—human and digital—shows no sign of slowing down.

QUESTIONS

People fall in love and form intimate relationships every day. Yet the endurance of professional matchmakers suggests that the beginnings of intimacy are mysterious. How is it that two individuals, once living independent lives, can come to mean so much to each other that they become inseparable, live their lives together, or break each other's hearts? In other words, how do intimate relationships get started?

Let's consider three separate questions. First, what draws us to other people in the first place? Friendships and intimate relationships, unlike family relationships, are relationships that we choose. Why do we choose to spend time with some people but not others? Is there any reason why an individual finds another person appealing?

Second, among all the people we might find to be pleasant company, why are we drawn to some people romantically, whereas others remain just friends? When you walk into a room full of new people, why is it that some people make your heart beat faster and your pupils dilate, whereas others

turn you off? Why does the person your best friend thinks would be perfect for you leave you cold, but you can't stop thinking about the blue eyes of the person who served you coffee this morning?

Third, how do two people actually form a committed relationship? Of all the people we might feel sexually or romantically attracted to, most of us will develop intimate relationships with very few.

Why do these two people end up in an intimate relationship, but not those other two?

In this chapter, we address the stages of relationship formation, starting by exploring the forces that make people appealing to one another. We then examine the sources of romantic and sexual attraction specifically, and finally discuss the processes through which relationships are formed.

Attraction: The Basis for Liking Someone

If we are lucky, most of us spend most of our time surrounded by people we like and by people who like us. But where does liking come from? Why do we like some people but not others? This is the question of **attraction**, which we define as the experience of evaluating another individual positively. In this section we focus on the aspects of a person that tend to make him or her appealing to others. Initially, most of these **bases of attraction** will seem pretty obvious, but in each case, research has revealed that even the simplest reasons for finding someone attractive can mask hidden complexities.

Personality: What Do We Like About Others?

Think of the people in your life you like a lot—your best friend, a favorite professor, or someone whose company you enjoy at work. What do you like about those people? Maybe they have a good sense of humor, or are good listeners, or seem trustworthy. In each case, you would be responding to personal qualities of those individuals—their **personality**. Indeed, early research on what makes people attractive assumed that some people simply had a better personality than others, and they were generally more attractive. This makes sense, but what exactly are the traits that constitute a good personality?

Social psychologist Norman Anderson (1968) gave a list of 555 traits to 100 college students and asked them to rate how likable they would find someone who possessed each trait. In general, his results confirm what you might have guessed: We are attracted to people who have positive personality characteristics and dislike people with negative ones. TABLE 5.1 lists the top 10 positive and negative traits. What's more interesting is to examine the specific types of words that appear at the extremes of likability. Notice, for example, how many words about honesty and dishonesty appear in the top 10 and bottom 10. Being fun is also positive but not quite as positive. Friendly appears on the list at number 19, good-humored at 25, and humorous at 27. In other words, we appear to be more attracted to people who are good than people who are fun.

One could draw from Anderson's findings and speculate that the more positive traits a person has, the more attractive that person should be. But

TABLE 5.1 **The Top 10 Most Likable and Least Likable Personality Traits**

Most Attractive Traits	Least Attractive Traits
1. Sincere	546. Deceitful
2. Honest	548. Malicious
3. Understanding	547. Dishonorable
4. Loyal	549. Obnoxious
5. Truthful	550. Untruthful
6. Trustworthy	551. Dishonest
7. Intelligent	552. Cruel
8. Dependable	553. Mean
9. Open-minded	554. Phony
10. Thoughtful	555. Liar

Source: Adapted from Anderson, 1968.

here's where the real world gets complicated. Some evidence suggests that people are not necessarily more attractive because of the wonderful qualities they have. For example, in a classic study of what makes a person likable, social psychologist Elliot Aronson and his colleagues asked college students to listen to an audiotape of someone supposedly auditioning for the chance to compete in a trivia contest (Aronson, Willerman, & Floyd, 1966). Each participant listened to one of four tapes. In the first tape, they could hear someone having a pretty mediocre audition. The person describes himself as an average student and gets most of the sample questions wrong. The second tape is the opposite, a great audition. The person describes his many honors and awards and answers nearly all the sample questions correctly. The third and fourth tapes are exactly like the first two, except that they end differently. At the end of both of them, the person is heard to spill his drink on himself and is clearly embarrassed. Participants listened to one of these tapes and then rated how much they liked the person they heard.

Which one was the most likable? If people are liked the more wonderful they are, then the person on the second tape with the nearly perfect audition should have been the most attractive, but this is not what the researchers found. Although that person was rated highly, the perfect person who spilled his drink received the highest ratings (fourth tape). In other words, participants were most attracted to the person who did a great job on the audition but also seemed to be a bit clumsy. The researchers labeled this the **pratfall effect**, and they suggested that this explains why self-deprecating humor works (FIGURE 5.2). Although we may admire people who possess wonderful qualities, we are even more attracted to people whose wonderful qualities are tempered by a few endearing flaws.

Similarity: Liking People Who Are Like Us

Why does the pratfall effect work? It turns out that the person on the third tape—basically wonderful but with the flaw of spilling his drink—is similar to how most people see themselves. Thus, what we find attrac-

FIGURE 5.2 Goofy, gorgeous, or both? Why are we attracted to movie stars (like Ben Stiller) who are routinely humiliated in their films? One possible explanation is the pratfall effect, the tendency for a few endearing flaws to make an otherwise wonderful person even more attractive.

tive about other peoples' personalities may not be how many positive qualities they possess but, more specifically, how much their qualities resemble our own (Newcomb, 1961). We may identify more with someone who generally does a good job but messes up once in a while more than we identify with someone whose performance is invariably excellent.

A great deal of research supports the general claim that we find people to be more attractive the more similar they are to ourselves. Clinical psychologist Donn Byrne and his students were among the pioneers in this area of research (e.g., Byrne, 1961; Byrne & Nelson, 1965). Many of their studies used a procedure called the **phantom other technique**. In one version of this design, participants whose attitudes on a variety of topics have already been measured are asked to make judgments about another person based on that person's responses to an attitude survey. Of course, there is no other person. The survey has been especially created so that the "phantom other" shares a certain number of attitudes with the participant. Using this procedure, the researchers can manipulate whether the other person shares all, some, or none of the participant's attitudes. In study after study using this technique, the more that people have in common with someone else, the more they find that person attractive. The findings hold true even when the other person is not a phantom. For example, randomly matched pairs of people who are left alone together report liking each other more to the extent that they have more things in common (Byrne, Ervin, & Lamberth, 1970). Perhaps as a result, friends and relationship partners do tend to be more similar to each other than they are to randomly matched strangers (Kupersmidt, DeRosier, & Patterson, 1995; Warren, 1966).

The effects of similarity are clearest when considering similarity in attitudes, values, and background (Simpson & Harris, 1994). The effects of other kinds of similarity, however, are much less clear. In studies of personality, for example, the degree to which partners have similar personalities has no consistent association with whether or not they are satisfied with their relationship (Montoya, Horton, & Kirchner, 2008). This is probably because some personality traits (like being disagreeable, depressed, or neurotic) are distinctly unattractive. It is easy to imagine that happy well-adjusted people are more attracted to other happy well-adjusted people (e.g., Botwin, Buss, & Shackelford, 1997), but there is no reason to expect that depressed, neurotic people are more attracted to other depressed, neurotic people. Indeed, couples who are similar on unappealing traits are less successful than couples that are dissimilar on these traits (Cuperman & Ickes, 2009). (We discuss this topic again in Chapter 6, in the context of individual personality differences.)

Some have suggested that when it comes to personality, it is **complementarity**, not similarity, that matters. Sociologist Robert Francis Winch (1958) suggested that, far from being attracted to similar others, we are instead attracted to people who possess qualities we lack. There is some intuitive appeal to this idea. For example, it is not hard to imagine couples who seem to be pairs of opposites: She is the social one and he is the quiet one, or he is the dominant one and she is the submissive one (e.g., Dryer & Horowitz, 1997). It is notable, therefore, that nearly all attempts to find support for this hypothesis have failed (Buss, 1985). Introverts, for example, show no signs of being especially attracted to extroverts (Hendrick & Brown, 1971). More generally, people do not report being more attracted to individuals who they think have personality traits that they lack themselves (Klohnen & Mendelsohn, 1998; Till & Freedman, 1978).

Why, then, is there the common belief that opposites attract? One possibility is that some happy couples adopt complementary patterns of behavior when they are together, even if they are both more similar to each other than they are to other people (Levinger, 1986). So, for example, an actress who is married to a famous comedian might let her husband take center stage when they are in public, even though both partners are far more outgoing and expressive than most people around them (**FIGURE 5.3**). Although a degree of situational complementarity appears to facilitate effective interactions within couples (Markey, Lowmaster, & Eichler, 2010), the basis of their attraction is still probably their similar tendencies rather than their complementary ones.

Why should similarity in values and interests be so attractive? Research on this question has identified at least three reasons. First, similar people are validating. Being with people who share our beliefs and interests reinforces the idea that our beliefs and interests are justified and worthwhile, making us feel better about ourselves (Byrne & Clore, 1970). Second, people who are similar to us are easy to get along with (Davis, 1981). The more someone else shares our values, the less likely we are to have disagreements and arguments with that person. Third, we might be attracted to similar people because we expect they are probably going to like us. To test this last idea,

FIGURE 5.3 Similar couples. *Left:* Marc Antony and Cleopatra (played by Richard Burton and Elizabeth Taylor) may have been from two different countries, but they were both powerful leaders, accustomed to having their orders obeyed. *Right:* The married celebrities Emily Blunt and John Krasinski are both talented comic actors. In general, partners in intimate relationships have more in common with each other than with randomly matched strangers. There is no concrete evidence that opposites attract, yet birds of a feather do seem to flock together.

social psychologists John Condon and William Crano (1988) conducted a variation of a phantom other study in which they presented people with another person's attitudes and supposed evaluations of the participant. Being liked accounted for a lot of the effects of similarity on attraction, leading the researchers to conclude that what makes similarity attractive is the expectation that people who are like us will respond well to us.

With all the evidence for the positive effects of similarity, it's worth mentioning one condition where increased similarity leads to less liking. A study by psychologists David Novak and Melvin Lerner (1968) used the same phantom other technique, manipulating the number of values that someone else supposedly shared with the participant. However, half of the phantom others had written at the bottom of their surveys: "I don't know if this is relevant or not, but last fall I had kind of a nervous breakdown and I had to be hospitalized for a while. I've been seeing a psychiatrist ever since. As you probably noticed, I'm pretty shaky right now." When the other person was recovering from a mental breakdown, the more that person shared values with participants, the *less* participants liked them. In other words, although we generally like similar others, we do not like them as much when they are suffering or in pain, perhaps because they remind us of our own vulnerability. When people are suffering, reminders of dissimilarity are more comforting than reminders of similarity.

Familiarity: Liking What We Know

All else being equal, humans and other animals prefer stimuli they have been exposed to over stimuli they have never experienced (Bornstein, 1989). For example, in 1968 psychologist Robert Zajonc (pronounced "zi-ence" as in "science") described a series of studies in which participants were exposed to different stimuli a number of times. Some of the stimuli were presented many times, and some only a few times. Whether they were exposed to the faces of strangers, Turkish adjectives, or Chinese pictograms, participants reported favoring the stimuli they were exposed to more frequently (Zajonc, 1968). Zajonc labeled this the **mere exposure effect**—the idea that simply being exposed to something can make that thing intrinsically reinforcing.

The mere exposure effect apparently explains people's feelings about their own face. In an ingenious study, social psychologists Theodore Mita, Marshall Derner, and Jeffrey Knight (1977) presented women with photographs of themselves side by side with mirror image versions of the same picture. When asked to choose which one they preferred, participants tended to choose the mirror image, the version of themselves they see in the mirror every morning. However, when presented with the same photos, close friends of these women preferred the original image, the version they are exposed to when they interact with their friend. Both sets of women seem to be demonstrating the mere exposure effect, expressing a preference for whatever stimulus they see more often. This effect accounts for some of the pleasure we take in going to school or family reunions. In a crowded world where we are often surrounded by strangers, reunions bring us together with familiar faces, and that familiarity can be comforting.

It is important to keep in mind, however, that the mere exposure effect assumes that the exposure has been relatively neutral. Repeated exposure to negative stimuli or repeated exposure to neutral stimuli accompanied by a negative one (e.g., every time I see a certain face I also smell a nauseating odor), does not lead to increased preference (Perlman & Oskamp, 1971). Although mere exposure might make our inoffensive habits endearing to others, we cannot (alas!) count on this effect to render our more annoying habits lovable.

Reciprocity: Liking People Who Like Us

The attractive effects of personality, similarity, and familiarity all presume that we know something about the people to whom we are exposed. Sometimes what we know about another person includes what that person thinks of us. Knowing that someone likes us and holds us in high esteem is a powerful reason to find that person appealing. After all, if someone has the good taste and keen insight to appreciate how wonderful we are, they are likely to be rewarding in other ways as well.

Sociologists Carl Backman and Paul Secord (1959) provided early confirmation of this idea by arranging for experimental participants to work on a project together with a "confederate," a member of the research team who was trained to treat all the participants the same way. After the project was completed, the participant and the confederate were taken to separate rooms, where they would ostensibly be completing questionnaires about their experiences. The key part of the experiment happened while participants were waiting alone for their questionnaires. Through an open door, they could hear the researchers asking the confederate in the other room what they thought of the participant. The overheard feedback was manipulated: Half the participants heard that their partners thought well of them, whereas the other half heard their partners had been critical of them. When all participants finally received their questionnaires, they had a chance to express their opinions of their partners. The results were clear: Even though all the confederates had behaved the same way, people reported more liking for their partners when they knew their partners had thought well of them, and far less liking when their partners had been critical. Since this early demonstration, the same basic finding has been replicated many times: The effects of being liked on feelings of attraction are far stronger than the effects associated with the qualities of the individuals (Kenny & la Voie, 1982).

Does this mean that we like people more the more they like us? Not necessarily. It turns out that not all liking is equally rewarding. For example, in a classic study, psychologists Elliot Aronson and Darwyn Linder (1965) examined how our attraction to someone is affected by the way their opinion of us develops over time. They set up a situation much like the Backman and Secord study: Real participants were working on a project with a confederate. In this study, however, participants worked with the confederate on a series of exercises spread out over the course of an experimental session. After each exercise, participants overheard their partner (the confederate) talking about them to the researcher in one of four possible conditions. In the first condition, participants overheard nothing but positive feedback. The partner seemed to like them from the very beginning of the study, and kept liking them until the end. In the second condition, participants overheard consistently negative feedback. Here the partner expressed an initially negative reaction to the participant, and that impression remained negative over the course of the experiment. So far, these two conditions are very similar to the two conditions of the Backman and Secord study, but Aronson and Linder added two additional types of feedback. In the third condition, the confederate started out by expressing positive feelings about the participant, but as the series of exercises wore on, began to express increasingly less positive feelings about the participant. By the end, the confederate was expressing a negative opinion about the participant. In the fourth condition, participants received the opposite pattern of feedback. In this case, the confederate began by expressing negative opinions about the participant but, by the end of the study, expressed opinions that were as positive as those in the first condition.

In which situation did participants like the confederate the most? If people are more attractive to us the more they like us, then the confederate in the first condition should be the most attractive because that is the person who was the most positive for the longest time. However, the results of the study indicated that the consistently positive person received only the second-highest ratings. The most-liked person was the person in the last condition, whose opinions started out negative but who was gradually won over as the experimental interaction progressed. Why should this be? It appears that approval from another person, while generally rewarding, is most rewarding when it seems to be contingent on our own behavior. Someone who likes us without even knowing us, as in the first condition, might well be a person who is very easy to please. Kind words from such a person may be flattering, but they are hard to take personally. Someone who grows to like us over time, as in the last condition, may be harder to please. When that person comes around, however, we can feel certain that the approval we are receiving reflects our own wonderful qualities (Eastwick et al., 2007).

MAIN POINTS

>> Research has identified several bases of attraction that account for why we like some people more than others.

>> Among personality traits, honesty and trustworthiness are rated as the most attractive, perhaps because they indicate how an individual is likely to treat us.

>> We tend to be more attracted to people who are similar to ourselves, especially in terms of values and interests.

>> All else being equal, we are more attracted to people who are familiar, that is, people to whom we have previously been exposed and who have thus proven themselves to be harmless.

>> We are attracted to people who we know are already attracted to us, especially those who have shown themselves to be selective and discriminating.

Romantic and Sexual Attraction

It is one thing to find another person fun and pleasant to be around. But as we discussed in Chapter 1, it's quite another matter to want to pursue a sexual or intimate relationship with someone. In many cases, the people we are attracted to romantically or sexually are a subset of the broader group of people we generally like. What's the difference between "I like you" and "I *really* like you"? What are the elements that make us want to go from just friends to more than friends? This is the question of **romantic attraction** or **sexual attraction**, which we define as the experience of finding someone desirable as a potential intimate partner.

Physical Appearance: How Much Does It Matter?

To address these questions, researchers have asked college students what they are attracted to in a potential romantic partner. Their responses seldom include the bases of attraction we have mentioned so far. Shared values come up, but few respondents say they are looking for someone to whom they have been exposed repeatedly, or someone whose positive traits are tempered by a few endearing flaws. Instead, one of the first qualities they list is physical appearance (Regan & Berscheid, 1997). Physical appearance is one of the first and easiest things we can know about other people. We cannot walk into a room and tell immediately whether a stranger is honest or intelligent, but we can certainly tell whether we like the way that person looks. To the extent that a sexual element distinguishes potential intimate partners from close friends, it makes sense that our reactions to a person's physical appearance play a unique role in romantic attraction.

How much of a role does physical appearance play? To answer this question, social psychologist Elaine Walster and her colleagues asked 752 members of the incoming freshman class at the University of Minnesota to participate in what the students thought was a test of a new computer dating service (Walster et al., 1966). To enroll in the service, students were asked to complete a number of questionnaires about their personality, their background, and their self-esteem. The researchers also had access to high school grades and SAT scores. Finally, based on photographs, the researchers rated the physical appearance of each student on a scale from "extremely attractive" to "extremely unattractive." When students were submitting these materials, they thought the school would be using the information to match each person up with an appropriate date for a Freshman Week mixer. In fact, the researchers assigned partners randomly. After the mixer, they asked each person whether he or she would want to go out with his or her assigned partner again.

Which variable predicted whether people were romantically attracted to their dates? You might guess that physical appearance would play a role here, and you would be right. People who were assigned to physically attractive dates were more likely to want to go out with them again, whereas people assigned to less attractive dates were less likely to want to go out with them again. But which of the other variables helped predict attraction in this situation? *None of them.* Whether the two people shared interests, came from similar backgrounds, had good social skills—none of these variables seemed to matter. The only thing that predicted the desire for a second date was physical appearance.

Much of the early research on the effects of physical appearance on attraction was conducted on samples of men, perhaps because researchers expected that physical attractiveness would be more important to men than to women. Lots of evidence from self-report data suggests they were right. For example, evolutionary psychologists David Buss and Michael Barnes (1986) asked college students and

> " I am in love—and, my God, it is the greatest thing that can happen to a man. I tell you, find a woman you can fall in love with. Do it. Let yourself fall in love. If you have not done so already, you are wasting your life."
>
> —D. H. Lawrence (1885–1930)

married couples what kinds of attributes they found attractive in a potential partner. Whereas most attributes were valued similarly by women and
men, men rated physical appearance as significantly more important to
them than women did. Since then, this gender difference has been replicated
in many different cultures (Buss, 1989) and across age and ethnic groups
(Sprecher, Sullivan, & Hatfield, 1994).

Does this mean men are more influenced by physical appearance than
women? Not necessarily. Although women consistently *report* they find physical appearance less important than men, studies that directly examine romantic attraction don't always find differences in the extent to which men
and women are affected by physical appearance (Feingold, 1988). For example, social psychologist Susan Sprecher (1989) presented male and female
undergraduates with different kinds of information about potential romantic
partners (e.g., their physical attractiveness, their personality, their earning
potential) and then asked them to indicate how attracted they were to each
person. Participants were asked to estimate how much each type of information affected their attraction ratings. Just as an evolutionary psychologist
would have predicted, the men in the study reported that physical attractiveness played an important role for them, whereas the women said they were
more affected by the person's earning potential and emotional expressiveness. Despite these explanations, however, by far the largest predictor of attraction was physical appearance, for women and men alike. Thus, studying
the effects of physical appearance is one case in which what people think they
want may be less informative than observing what people actually prefer.

It's hard to belive that romantic attraction might be as simple as how someone looks. If everyone is drawn to only the most physically attractive people
around, then how would the rest of us ever find partners? A casual glance at
the couples we pass every day suggests that people of widely varying physical appearance do indeed get asked out once in a while. People talk about
partners being "out of my league," suggesting they are aware of their own
appearance and seek partners who are not too far above or below their own
level (White, 1980). In fact, research confirms that people who are dating or
about to get married tend to be rated as similar to each other in physical appearance (Feingold, 1988). This tendency for people to pair up according to
similarity in appearance is called the **matching phenomenon** (Rosenfeld,
1964).

The matching phenomenon suggests that, at least in some circumstances,
we do not always pursue the most physically perfect specimens we can find.
When do we go for the most beautiful person in the room and when do we
compromise? Early research on the effects of physical appearance explored
one possible answer: Our own physical appearance might affect the kinds
of people we find attractive. People who are very attractive and accustomed
to being admired might feel comfortable approaching other physically attractive people. People who are more on the plain side might reasonably be
concerned about rejection, and therefore would probably approach potential

partners who are also less than gorgeous. One way to test this idea would be to ask men and women of various appearances to choose from partners of various appearances and see whether people's own appearance and the threat of rejection affect their choices.

This is exactly what social psychologist Ellen Berscheid and her colleagues did (1971). Berscheid's team asked male and female college students to participate in another test of a supposed computer dating service. After completing questionnaires and having their own photos taken, each student was presented with six photographs of potential different-sex dates, ranging from very physically attractive to physically unattractive, and were then asked to choose one date from among them. To evaluate the effects of the threat of rejection, the researchers varied the extent to which participants were aware of the possibility of being rejected. Students in one condition were told that the potential dates in all the folders had expressed an interest in them. Thus, the participant could choose any of the six potential dates without fear of being rejected. In the other condition, the students did not know what the potential dates thought of them, which is usually the case in real life. The researchers predicted that the matching phenomenon would be stronger for the people who knew they could be rejected and that there would be less evidence of matching for the people who were not thinking about being rejected. This was a reasonable idea, but it was not confirmed. Being aware of the possibility of rejection made no difference to the students' choices.

Even more surprising was the fact that a person's own attractiveness made very little difference in who that person wanted to date. The physical appearance of all participants was rated on a scale of 1 (extremely unattractive) to 8 (extremely attractive). The most attractive people in the study, who themselves had been rated between 6 and 7, picked dates who on average had been rated 6.84. The least attractive people in the study, who themselves had been rated between 1 and 2, picked dates who on average had been rated 6.26, only slightly lower than the desired dates of the first group. In other words, on average everyone in the study wanted to date attractive people. Even the least attractive students indicated a desire to date potential partners whose physical attractiveness (as rated by objective observers) far exceeded their own (Kalick & Hamilton, 1986).

Did the least attractive people in the study really think they had a chance with the most attractive of the potential dates? Probably not. When psychologist Matthew Montoya asked students to predict whether individuals pictured in photographs would go out with them, he found a clear relationship between the physical appearance of the student and the expectation of being rejected (Montoya, 2008). When less physically attractive students viewed pictures of more physically attractive individuals, they understood that they would probably be rejected as potential dates, and the students in the earlier computer dating studies probably understood this too. They just didn't care. And who could blame them? They had no expectations of ever really meeting the dates, and they were not deeply invested in starting a dating relationship

FIGURE 5.4 Are you hot or not? On the popular website HOTorNOT.com, people post their photos and invite visitors to rate their physical attractiveness. Millions of people have accepted this invitation, providing researchers with a treasure trove of data.

in the first place. With little to lose, they might as well choose the most attractive possible person.

How does our own physical appearance affect our preferences when we really are hoping and planning to date someone? To address this question, marketing professor Leonard Lee and his colleagues teamed up with the people who run the popular website HOTorNOT.com (Lee et al., 2008). When it was originally developed in 2000, HOTorNOT.com served as a place for people to post photographs of themselves and to rate, on a scale of 1 to 10, the "hotness" (i.e., physical attractiveness) of others who uploaded photographs to the site (**FIGURE 5.4**). As a source of information on what people find physically attractive, these ratings are themselves a goldmine, because the site has recorded over 12 billion ratings since it began.

HOTorNOT.com added a function allowing members to communicate with each other and ask each other out. Lee and his team recognized that, together with the attractiveness ratings, the data on who was eager to meet whom allowed them to address two questions about the role of physical appearance in romantic and sexual attraction using a vast amount of data from real people who are actually trying to find a date. First, does one's own physical appearance affect the sort of people one is willing to pursue? Based on over 2 million dating decisions made by over 16,000 people, the answer is unequivocally yes (Lee et al., 2008). People looking for dates tended to request dates from potential partners who matched them on physical attractiveness. As you might imagine, people were especially sensitive to negative differences between themselves and potential partners; nobody wanted to date someone much less attractive than they were. Yet the researchers also found evidence of sensitivity to positive differences: When looking for a real date, there seems to be reluctance to approach potential partners who might be out of one's league.

The second question: To the extent that less attractive people are less selective about the physical appearance of the people they ask out, are they also less aware of physical appearance? In other words, does one's own appearance affect the attractiveness ratings of others? Based on nearly 450,000 observations, the answer is no (Lee et al., 2008). Less attractive individuals on the site (as rated by the other members) had no illusions about the attractiveness of the people they asked out. Although they were willing to date less attractive partners, their ratings of those potential partners reflected an understanding that they were indeed less attractive.

Here we have an explanation for how we observe the matching phenomenon on physical appearance in real-world couples. It is not because some people are less interested in attractiveness than others. On the contrary, in the context of intimate relationships, physical attractiveness exerts a powerful pull. However, there are also countervailing forces, such as the desire to avoid rejection and the desire to pursue relationships likely to be successful. These forces are stronger in the real world of dating and relationships than in the laboratory, which is why we observe the matching phenomenon among people who are dating and seeking relationships and not among college students participating in research.

Physical Appearance: Why Does It Matter?

Whether we like it or not, physical appearance plays a large role in the initial experience of attraction, in some cases dwarfing the effects of all other aspects of the person. Why? When someone is physically attractive, we tend to assume other aspects of the person are positive as well. In an early study testing this idea, researchers asked people to make judgments about strangers based only on a photograph (Dion, Berscheid, & Walster, 1972). When the face in the photo was more attractive, people generally assumed the person was also more interesting, more kind, more sensitive, and more likely to be successful than when the face was less attractive. As BOX 5.1 describes, the content of the beauty stereotype varies somewhat across cultures (Wheeler & Kim, 1997). People everywhere seem to agree, however, that beautiful people have it made in many ways. Thus, one reason physical attractiveness may be so powerful is that people think that it is a cue for other desirable traits in a partner.

Do the beautiful people have it made? In a number of ways, they do. Certainly within the realm of social interactions, people who are more attractive have several concrete advantages (Langlois et al., 2000). People tend to smile more and feel more positive when they interact with attractive people (Garcia et al., 1991). More attractive men, in particular, have a greater number of interactions with members of the opposite sex than less attractive men, and more attractive women get more dates than less attractive women (Reis, Nezlek, & Wheeler, 1980). All this favorable attention may lead more attractive people to become as sociable as everybody thinks they are. In a clever test of this idea, social psychologist Mark Snyder and his colleagues tape-recorded telephone conversations between unacquainted men and women (Snyder, Tanke, & Berscheid, 1977). The men had been given a photograph of either an attractive or an unattractive woman and were told this was the woman they were going to be interacting with. It's not surprising that observers who listened to only the men's side of the conversation found that men were more animated and friendly when they believed they were talking to a more attractive woman. The interesting part is that observers who listened to only the women's side of the conversation found that women who were believed to be attractive also behaved in a more sociable and friendly manner. In other words, the stereotype that attractive people are more sociable lead men to engage in interactions that encouraged their partners to fulfill the expectation. When women are talking on the phone to allegedly attractive or unattractive men, the effects are the same (Andersen & Bem, 1981). This suggests that physical appearance can have a powerful effect on the social interactions of both women and men.

One can imagine that a lifetime of such experiences might have effects that extend beyond the realm of personal relationships. Indeed, more physically appealing people have a greater chance to be hired after a job interview (Hamermesh & Biddle, 1994), and they tend to have a higher salary in their first jobs (Frieze, Olson, & Russell, 1991). Physically attractive people are less likely to be convicted of crimes, and when they are convicted, they receive shorter sentences (Mazzella & Feingold, 1994).

There are also negative consequences of being attractive. For example, along with all of the positive assumptions made about them, more attractive

BOX 5.1 SPOTLIGHT ON . . .

Components of Facial Attractiveness

Do people from different cultures agree about the features that make someone physically attractive? Or is beauty, as they say, in the eye of the beholder? In general, if you ask any two people to rate the physical attractiveness of people in a wide range of photos, the agreement between them will be low (Diener, Wolsic, & Fujita, 1995). This accounts for our sense that individuals do differ in the kinds of features they find attractive. However, if you ask many people to rate photographs, there appears to be overall agreement about the components of physical attractiveness.

When men and women from a variety of different cultures were asked to rate photos of women, they tended to agree that women with large eyes, a small nose, and high cheekbones are especially attractive (Cunningham et al., 1995). There is less cross-cultural consistency in opinions about men's faces (Jones, 1995), but a wide smile and a broad jaw seem to be reliably attractive across cultures (Cunningham, Barbee, & Pike, 1990). Even infants, who have had limited access to media or cultural images, seem to prefer gazing at faces that are characterized by these features (Langlois et al., 1991). They can distinguish between faces rated as attractive and those rated as unattractive (Ramsey et al., 2004).

Why is there such agreement about these particular combinations? The question inspires controversy even among researchers. Developmental psychologist Judith Langlois and her colleagues suggest that the features people find attractive are characteristic of average faces. In support of this idea, they find that people rate computer-generated composites of many different photographs to be more attractive than any of the individual photos that make up the composites (e.g., Langlois, Roggman, & Musselman, 1994). (See for yourself in FIGURE 5.5.) Others suggest that what people find attractive is symmetry—the extent to which paired features on both sides of the face are aligned (Grammer & Thornhill, 1994). Still others report that, although average and symmetric faces are attractive, faces rated as *extremely* attractive are not necessarily average or symmetric (Perrett, May, & Yoshikawa, 1994).

Although the question is far from settled, the striking degree of consensus about which faces are attractive and which are not lends support to the perspective of evolutionary psychology suggesting that our preferences for mates may reflect evolved tendencies, rather than culturally specific standards (see Chapter 3).

people are also judged to be more vain and more likely to be promiscuous than less attractive people (Dermer & Thiel, 1975). People tend to lie about themselves when they are talking to more attractive people (Rowatt, Cunningham, & Druen, 1999), and perhaps as a result, very attractive people sometimes find it hard to trust the positive feedback they receive from others (Major, Carrington, & Carnevale, 1984).

Do the drawbacks outweigh the benefits of being physically attractive? Probably not. Despite any additional challenges they may face, a number of studies of the way people describe their own lives conclude that more physically attractive people are slightly but significantly happier with their lives than less attractive people (Burns & Farina, 1992; Diener et al., 1995).

Evolutionary psychologists have argued that humans might have developed a preference for physical appeal because, in our ancestral past, the features we now find attractive were markers of good health in a potential mate. It is ironic, then, that, in modern times, health is one domain in which nice-looking people are no different from anyone else. Psychologist Michael Kalick and his colleagues examined the health status of men and women who

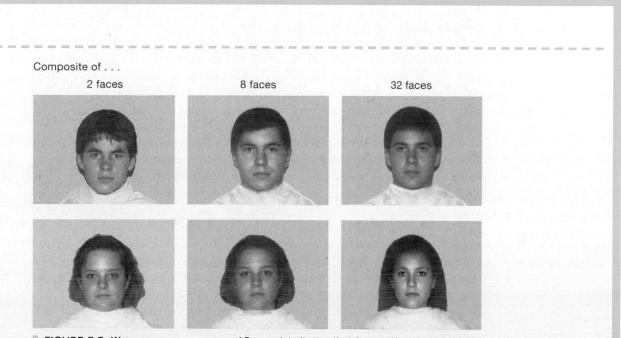

Composite of . . .

FIGURE 5.5 **Wow, you sure are average!** Research indicates that faces with average features are perceived as more attractive than faces with distinct features. These composites of 2, 8, and 32 faces were created with photography software. What do you think? (Source: Langlois, Roggman, & Musselman, 1994.)

had been followed through late adolescence and into older adulthood (Kalick et al., 1998). Observers looked at photos of these individuals as teenagers and were asked to rate their facial attractiveness. Raters guessed that the people they rated as more physically appealing were also more physically healthy, but they were wrong. In fact, the attractiveness ratings were unrelated to the health of the teenagers and did not predict health later on in life either. Thus, although being handsome or pretty no longer corresponds to the physical health of a potential mate, our preference for physical attractiveness nevertheless lives on.

Romantic Attraction in Long-Term vs. Short-Term Relationships

Physical appearance may be the first thing we notice about a person, but some would argue that finding someone physically appealing is by itself not a strong foundation for a long-term relationship. When asked directly about this, even college students agree. In one study, college students were asked to describe the attributes of an ideal partner for two kinds of romantic relationships: a short-term fling and a long-term involvement (Buss & Schmidt, 1993). When thinking about a short-term fling, male and female students both said that physical attractiveness was extremely important, as we have seen. When thinking about a long-term relationship, however, women and men agreed that they have to be attracted to their partner's personality as well. Psychologist Duane Lundy and his colleagues also found that, when asked about the kinds of people they would choose as marriage partners, men and women value personality characteristics, like a good sense of humor, as much as physical appeal (Lundy, Tan, & Cunningham, 1998).

The fact that men and women report different preferences for different types of relationships reflects what evolutionary psychologists call **strategic pluralism**, the idea that humans have developed the capacity to pursue long-term relationships or short-term involvements as their circumstances warrant (Gangestad & Simpson, 2000). Mountain gorillas, although closely related to humans, do not appear to have this capacity (Robbins, 1999). In their male-dominated groups, most pairings between male and female gorillas are short-lived. This suits the dominant males, who have access to a wide range of female partners, and it suits the females, who have access to the protection of the dominant male (the subordinate males are out of luck). For humans, in contrast, there are distinct reproductive advantages associated with both short-term and long-term relationships, so we appear to have evolved unique preferences for each.

Sexual strategies theory is an attempt to explain and predict what sorts of qualities men and women tend to look for when they pursue long-term versus short-term relationships (Buss, 1998; Buss & Schmidt, 1993). A premise of the theory is that, under the right circumstances, both kinds of relationships can be beneficial, although women and men may benefit in different ways. Consider, for example, the rewards of a short-term, no-strings-attached sexual relationship, such as a one-night stand. As we discussed in Chapter 3, males have much to gain reproductively by pursuing multiple short-term relationships with as many available females as they can find because they do not have to invest much time and energy to reproduce. From the perspective of evolution, it makes sense for men to devote disproportionate energy toward pursuing these relationships, and this seems to be the case. When college students were asked the number of sexual partners they hoped to have over the next couple of years, men said eight and women said one (Buss & Schmidt, 1993) (FIGURE 5.6). According to a study of 14,059 people across 48 nations, this gender difference in desire for short-term relationships is found pretty much everywhere (Schmitt, 2005).

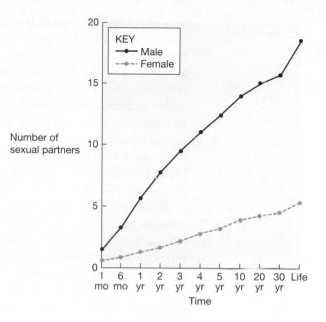

FIGURE 5.6 **Expected number of sexual partners.** Male college students desire far more partners than female students. According to sexual strategies theory, this stems from the fact that men devote more of their energy to short-term relationships than women do. (Source: Adapted from Buss & Schmidt, 1993.)

Sexual strategies theory predicts that, given the many benefits and few costs of short-term relationships for men, they would have evolved relatively low standards for short-term partners. Indeed, when asked about their minimum standards for partners in different kinds of relationships, men reported lower standards (less intelligence and less physical appeal) for a one-night stand (a hookup) than for a marriage partner and far lower standards than women overall (Kenrick et al., 1990). It follows that men rate evidence of sexual promiscuity desirable in a potential short-term partner because it signals accessibility and receptivity to a hookup, whereas the same traits are rated as highly undesirable in a long-term partner (Buss & Schmidt, 1993).

Short-term sexual pairings between men and women could not happen unless some women were willing to participate too. Sexual strategies theory explains that, even though women may devote more of their energy to long-term relationships, they may also pursue short-term strategies, but for different reasons. Specifically, the theory suggests women may benefit from a short-term relationship if it promises them access to resources or high-status men who were otherwise not accessible as long-term partners. To test this idea, women were asked to imagine a choice between an attractive but not very reliable partner and a dependable and loyal but not as physically appealing partner. Women who were looking for a short-term relationship went for the more attractive guys, and women who were more interested in a long-term relationship went for the more dependable ones (Simpson & Gangestad, 1992). Moreover, in their short-term relationships, women prefer partners who are physically strong and who are willing to spend money (Buss & Schmidt, 1993). In other words, whereas men are willing to *lower* their standards to engage in short-term relationships, women in several ways have *higher* standards for short- than long-term relationships, at least with respect to resources, status, and physical appearance. This might explain why teenage girls hang around backstage at rock concerts, even though rock stars generally do not leave their spouses for groupies. What groupies give up in terms of commitment, they gain in terms of contact with attractive and talented partners they might never connect with otherwise.

Sexual strategies theory brings a similar analysis to male-female preferences in long-term relationships. As we discussed in Chapter 3, females should be especially motivated to invest in long-term mating. Because having a child costs women much more than it costs men, women are motivated to find partners willing to invest in them and their offspring over time. It follows that women prefer signs of ambition and status in their intimate partners, and indeed that has been shown to be true in both developed and developing countries worldwide (Buss, 1989). But in long-term relationships, there is the potential of a trade-off between a partner's current resources and the likelihood that he will stick around and invest those resources in the relationship. When thinking about a long-term relationship, women indicate a willingness to settle for a less physically attractive partner if he will be a good provider in the future (Buss & Schmidt, 1993).

In contrast, when men commit to a long-term relationship, they are forgoing other opportunities for sex and reproduction. Given the relatively low costs of short-term relationships for men, why would men ever limit themselves in this way? Sexual strategies theory proposes that long-term relationships may serve for men a purpose similar to that of short-term relationships for women: to gain access to the most desirable partners, where desirability is defined not only by attractiveness and fertility but also by qualities that indicate good parenting and loyalty. It follows that men should have especially high standards when they are considering a long-term mate, and indeed that seems to be the case. In fact, when asked to report their standards for long-term relationships, the responses of men and women look nearly the same (Kenrick et al., 1990).

Romantic Attraction in Different Contexts

Our preferences for intimate partners are not necessarily consistent all the time; they can vary according to the context of different situations. In a classic study demonstrating this fact, social psychologists Donald Dutton and Arthur Aron sent an attractive female research assistant to the Capilano

Suspension Bridge in Vancouver, British Columbia (Dutton & Aron, 1974). The 450-foot bridge sways and bounces 230 feet above the Capilano River (**FIGURE 5.7**). Even if you are comfortable with heights, walking across it can be a nerve-racking experience (we've done it). Imagine, then, the reactions of the young men crossing alone who were approached by the pretty research assistant in the middle of this bridge and asked to participate in a brief study. She showed each man a picture, asked him to make up a story about it, and then gave him her number with an invitation to call her if he had any questions. Other young men were asked the same things by the same research

FIGURE 5.7 Is it love, or fear of heights? Sometimes sexual arousal can be mistaken for romantic attraction, when in fact it comes from another source entirely.

assistant, only these men were approached while walking alone on a wide, low, and sturdy bridge not far away. The researchers compared the responses of the two groups of men in two ways. First, they looked for the presence of sexual or romantic imagery in the stories the men were asked to make up. Second, they observed which men were more likely to take up the woman's invitation to call her. With respect to both of these outcomes, where the men were approached made a big difference. The men who were stopped high above the river told stories that had significantly more sexual themes and images, and they were more likely to call the woman back, compared to the men who had been stopped on the low bridge.

Why did the location make such a difference? The researchers argued, and subsequent research has confirmed, that sometimes we are pretty poor at recognizing the source of our own excitement or arousal. It's easy to envision that the men on the suspension bridge were, at the time they were approached, probably more aroused than the men on the low bridge. Their hearts were probably beating a bit faster, they were probably sweating a bit more. Then here comes an attractive woman. Talking to her in the moment, it would have been easy for the men to forget they were aroused from the swaying bridge and to assume they were actually aroused by the woman before them. The men on the low bridge, not being aroused in the first place, were less likely to make this error, known as the **misattribution of arousal**. The fact that we make this mistake explains all sorts of situational effects on attraction. Why does an amusement park make an excellent date? Because you get to be the first thing your date sees at the end of an exciting roller coaster ride.

A similar phenomenon takes place in singles bars as it gets closer to closing time. Legend has it that, in bars, as evening wears on, individuals that we would not be attracted to in daylight gradually start looking better and better (a transformation also known as "beer goggles"). Is there any truth to this legend? To find out, psychologists Brian Gladue and Jean Delaney (1990) went to bars and asked men and women to rate, on a 10-point scale, the physical attractiveness of other people. To examine the effects of time spent in the bar, they asked the same people to make their ratings several times over the course of an evening, at 9:00 P.M., 10:30 P.M., and midnight. Sure enough, as the hours passed, men's average ratings of the appeal of the women at the bar went up significantly. Women's ratings of men also went up, but by only half as much. It appears that men were more likely to misattribute changes that they were going through themselves as it grew later to changes in the attractiveness of the members of the opposite sex around them.

Situational effects on romantic and sexual attraction do not depend on misattribution of arousal alone. Different contexts also affect how we are attracted to others by supporting different mating strategies. Consider, for example, your own minimum criteria for having a one-night stand. Perhaps you are open to this sort of experience, perhaps not. But do you think your standards change depending on whether you are in a bar, at the library, or at the gym? Sexual strategies theory predicts that they do. A singles bar is a place that promotes brief sexual encounters. If hooking up is your goal, as is often the case for men, then being in a bar may lead to more relaxed standards and a wider range of people to whom you are attracted. Being in a library, however, might remind you of higher standards, even for a short-term partner. On the other hand, if short-term relationships are more of a stepping-stone to a long-term relationship, as is often the case for women, then being in a bar may lead to higher standards and a narrower range of people to whom you are attracted. The library might be the context in which women can relax their standards because it is a place where the pool may be deeper for finding partners who might be willing to let a long-term relationship develop from a one-night stand.

To test these ideas, psychologist Matthew Montoya (2005) asked women and men to imagine themselves in a range of locations—such as a bar, a fraternity party, a café, a classroom, a library, and a church—and then asked them to describe their minimum criteria for selecting a partner for a one-night stand in each place. As predicted, men reported lower standards for places most likely to promote one-night stands (i.e., the bar and the party) and higher standards for places least likely to promote them (i.e., the library and church). Women did the opposite, reporting higher standards for the bar and the party and lower standards for the library and church. To make sure these results described how people actually behaved in these places, Montoya also went to all of them, asking men and women in each locale to describe their standards for a brief encounter, and found the same results. When it comes to a short-term relationship, some situations allow for more selectivity than others, and the effects appear to be different for women and men. In other words, there are times when the objects of our romantic attraction really are different depending on the situation.

Unrequited Love

Consistent with social exchange theory (see Chapter 3), the research we have discussed so far can be summarized in terms of rewards and costs. We tend to be attracted, romantically or otherwise, to people who we think have the capacity and motivation to benefit us in some way (Berscheid & Reis, 1998). The problem with this generalization is that it seems to exclude an important and poignant category of experiences. Despite everything research has revealed about the role of rewards in attraction, sometimes we can be powerfully attracted to people who do not seem to reward us. An example of this kind of attraction, familiar to many of us, is **unrequited love**—attraction, or love, that is not returned. If attraction is exclusively about being rewarded, then being attracted to someone who has no corresponding interest in us should almost never happen. At the very least, those feelings of attraction should fade away the moment it becomes clear that the object of our affections has no intention of returning them. Unfortunately, for many people, this is not at all how unrequited love develops. On the contrary, feelings of attraction can persist even though those feelings cause a person anguish and heartache. It is possible to be attracted to people who reject us, ignore us, or even abuse us. Let's explore how research that focuses mostly on the rewards of attraction helps explain unrequited love or fatal attraction.

Resolving the apparent paradox of unrequited love may require an expanded definition of the kinds of rewards that being attracted to someone can bestow. For example, one research team asked 907 college students if they had ever experienced unrequited love (Aron, Aron, & Allen, 1998). More than 80 percent of their sample said they had. The unrequited lovers were then asked to evaluate various reasons for feeling the way they did. Results indicated that unrequited love was in fact rewarding for the lover in three areas. First, they tended to believe that the object of their attraction was exceptionally desirable. Thus, in terms of rewards, the perceived capacity of the person to reward the lover was very high. Second, the lovers tended to believe that, although their feelings were not currently being returned, they were likely to be returned eventually. For the lovers, then, the costs of not being loved today might have been outweighed by the potential rewards of possibly being loved in the future. Finally, the lovers strongly endorsed the view that simply being in love was rewarding, even if their feelings were not returned. In other words, they tended to agree with the statement: "It is better to have loved in vain than never to have loved at all."

Another way of thinking about unrequited love is to refer to the Aronson and Linder (1965) study of reciprocated interest we discussed earlier. It is relevant that, at the start of that study, the most attractive condition (a partner whose opinion of you starts out negative but grows positive) looks identical to one of the least attractive conditions (a partner whose opinion starts out negative and remains negative). In other words, at the beginning of that study, when your partner seems to be judging you negatively, you do not yet know

FIGURE 5.8 Unrequited love in the movies. Gérard Depardieu as Cyrano de Bergerac and Anne Brochet as Roxanne.

if you will end up in the most or least attractive condition by the end. The unrequited lovers in the study by Aron and his team (1998) appear to believe that they are in the most attractive condition, that if they work hard enough and love faithfully enough they may in fact eventually win the affection of the person they desire. Books and movies are full of messages that support the likelihood of this possibility. For example, in the classic play *Cyrano de Bergerac*, Cyrano suppresses his lifelong love for Roxanne because he is afraid of being rejected for his appearance (**FIGURE 5.8**). By the end of the play, however, the purity of his devotion succeeds in winning her heart (although Cyrano dies seconds later, unfortunately). Similarly, in many modern-day romantic comedies, the characters who are initially rejected frequently win over the objects of their affections by the end of the film. Given these messages, it is reasonable that people can maintain an attraction to someone who does not return their feelings. The expectation of possibly winning someone over in the future may, for many people, be a reward that more than compensates for the relatively small cost of being rejected today.

Taking into account the potential rewards of being attracted to someone may help explain the phenomenon of stalking. Recent evidence suggests that a large percentage of college women have been the victims of **stalking**, defined as unwanted and disturbing attention from someone seeking a romantic relationship (e.g., Fremouw, Westrup, & Pennypacker, 1997; Sinclair & Frieze, 2000). What makes stalkers dangerous is their insistence that they can win over the object of their affections (i.e., that they are in the most attractive condition of that study), despite increasing evidence and clear messages that their attentions are unwanted (i.e., the consistently negative condition of that study). The fact that early in an interaction with someone these two conditions look identical puts the object of unwanted affection in a difficult position. Outside the laboratory, it may be difficult to communicate the message that initially negative feelings about a person are going to remain negative no matter what.

To demonstrate this point, social psychologist Roy Baumeister and his colleagues asked people to describe their experiences of being the object of unrequited love (Baumeister, Wotman, & Stillwell, 1993). You might expect that it would be rewarding, or at least flattering, to be on the receiving end of someone's romantic attention. In fact, these reports suggested that any rewards are mostly outweighed by the considerable costs of having to reject someone. On one hand, the objects of unrequited love wanted to communicate their lack of interest clearly. On the other hand, they did not want to be in the position of having to hurt someone's feelings, which would have made them feel unpleasantly guilty. Perhaps as a result, the reasons people usually offer for not returning someone else's affections are often less than completely honest (e.g., "It's not you, it's me"), raising the possibility that they will be misinterpreted (Folkes, 1982), or worse, that the unwanted suitor will interpret their reluctance to cause pain as a sign of reciprocated attraction.

Making life even harder for the objects of unwanted attention is the fact that some people communicate mixed messages on purpose. For example, how are we to understand the attractiveness of playing hard to get? In an early study that addressed this question, the researchers initially supposed that there may be something intrinsically desirable about someone who does not express any interest in us (Hatfield et al., 1973). To test this idea, they conducted an artificial test of a computer dating service. The research team presented male participants with a set of folders, each describing a different (fictional) potential partner. Within the folders, the men could see some information about the selections the women had already made, and these were varied to indicate different levels of choosiness. The choosiest woman indicated she was not interested in anyone (presumably the hard-to-get woman). The least selective woman indicated she would date anyone at all. Then the researchers asked the men to rate how much they would like to go out with each woman. To the researchers' surprise, but perhaps to no one else's, the woman who indicated no interest in anyone was rated least attractive. After several unsuccessful efforts at pinning down this phenomenon, the researchers determined that men were most attracted to women who seemed quite choosy, rejecting most *other* men, but who simultaneously indicated an interest in *them*. In other words, playing hard to get was attractive only when combined with the message that the game could possibly be won. As in the most attractive condition of the Aronson and Linder study, people who successfully play hard to get are communicating that, although they currently have no interest in us, they could be won over with a little effort.

The possibility that the objects of our affection are playing hard to get, the presence of hard-to-read messages, and the hope that we might convince people who do not currently love us to love us in the future all help explain why unrequited love does not represent an exception to the reward theory of attraction after all. Unrequited lovers are indeed pursuing very desirable rewards. In contrast to other people, however, the rewards of attraction are, for the unrequited lover, more hypothetical than real.

MAIN POINTS

» Although men report a greater interest in physically attractive partners than women do, the physical appeal of a potential partner strongly predicts romantic and sexual interest for both women and men.

» Sexual strategies theory proposes that people are attracted to different characteristics in a partner depending on whether they are pursuing a short-term or a long-term relationship. For brief encounters (one-night stands or hookups), men lower their standards for partners, and women raise theirs.

>> What we find attractive in a potential romantic partner varies across different contexts, such that feelings of attraction inspired by a particular situation may be mistakenly attributed to the person we happen to be near.

>> In general, research on romantic and sexual attraction supports the idea that people are attractive as partners the more they appear able and willing to provide us with rewards.

>> Research on unrequited lovers suggests that, even for these people, the costs of being rejected are outweighed by the potential rewards of being accepted sometime in the future.

Mate Selection: From Chemistry to Connection

Many discussions about the beginning of relationships refer to romantic attraction and mate selection as if they are interchangeable. Indeed, in the Western world, there is an expectation that they should be related; we hope the people we select as mates are the people we initially find attractive. Over the course of a lifetime, however, most people are sexually and romantically attracted to many more people than they ever connect with intimately. Thus, there is a vast gulf between wanting to be with someone and actually being with that person. How do two people ever cross that gulf, and move beyond attraction to become a couple? This is the question of **mate selection**, which we define as the process through which a committed relationship is formed.

Predicting Partner Choices

Most research on romantic attraction assumes that preferences for romantic partners predict who people pursue as partners and they eventually end up with as mates. Those who express a preference for redheads should be more likely to end up with a partner who is a redhead, and people who express a preference for partners who can quote Judd Apatow films should be more likely to end up with a partner who can quote Judd Apatow films. This assumption is so basic and intuitive that it is rarely made explicit. Yet researchers have found this assumption difficult to demonstrate.

Consider the research of social psychologists Paul Eastwick and Eli Finkel. As a convenient way of studying what people want in a relationship partner, they set up a **speed dating** event where a group gets together in a large room, and over the course of an evening, each participant talks one-on-one with every other potential romantic partner in the group for a brief period (say 4 minutes) before switching partners (Finkel, Eastwick, & Matthews, 2007). At the end

> All tragedies are finished by death, all comedies by a marriage."
>
> —Lord Byron (1788–1824)

of the evening, each person gets to indicate which of the other people in the room he or she wishes to see again; if that wish is reciprocated, a real date can be scheduled. You can appreciate the efficiency of this sort of event: It allows you to interact quickly with a wide range of possible partners without having to spend a long and expensive evening out with each one.

Eastwick and Finkel (2008) drew on this efficiency to examine how men's and women's explicit romantic preferences, measured before the speed dating event, predicted who they wanted to date after the event. In their study, male and female college students filled out questionnaires rating the importance of physical attractiveness, earning potential, and friendliness in their ideal romantic partner. As you might have predicted from reading this chapter so far, men rated physical attractiveness as more important than women did, and women rated earning potential more importantly than men did. All participants subsequently attended another speed dating event, in which they had an opportunity to interact with between 9 and 13 members of the opposite sex in a single evening. After each 4-minute conversation, they rated each person on physical attractiveness, earning potential, and friendliness. At the end of the evening, participants indicated which of those people they would like to see again.

The researchers tested a very reasonable prediction: People who had indicated before the event that a particular quality (physical attractiveness, earning potential, or friendliness) was important to them should probably want to date those participants they had rated highly in that quality. But this was not the case. In fact, there was no relationship between what people said they wanted before the event and who they wanted to date after the event. People who said they cared about physical attractiveness or earning potential, whether they were male or female, were *not* more likely to want to date those that they had rated as most physically appealing or highest in earning potential. The researchers were understandably puzzled by their results. They speculated that, if our romantic preferences do not guide whom we pursue as dates, perhaps it's because dates have relatively few consequences, allowing us some freedom to go out with people who don't match our ideals very well. In the case of potential marriage partners, though, the researchers predicted observing stronger effects of romantic preferences because of the higher stakes of marrying someone who fails to meet our ideals.

A study by behavioral geneticist David Lykken and psychologist Auke Tellegen (1993) had already addressed this issue. Lykken and Tellegen had been studying the lives and preferences of twins. In particular, their research compared two kinds of twins: fraternal twins (also known as dizygotic twins), who grew from two different fertilized eggs, and identical twins (monozygotic twins), who grew from a single egg. Comparisons between these kinds of twins can be instructive because identical twins raised together share the same environment and the same genes (identical twins are essentially clones of each other), whereas fraternal twins raised together share only the same environment. Thus, the degree to which identical twins are more similar in a particular feature of their lives than fraternal twins has been treated as an index of the degree to which that feature has a genetic basis. These kinds of comparisons have revealed that identical twins are more similar than fraternal twins in their choice of wardrobe, household furnishings, vacation activities, and jobs, suggesting that preferences for each of these things has some genetic component, a premise that few behavioral geneticists dispute. Using this logic, Lykken and Tellegen wondered whether preferences for romantic partners may also have some genetic basis. To address this possibility, they did not measure twins' romantic preferences directly. Instead, they examined the spouses of identical and fraternal twins. If our choices of life partners are in any way a function of our own preferences, they argued, then the spouses of identical twins should be more similar than the spouses of fraternal twins because the romantic preferences of identical twins should be more similar to each other than the romantic preferences of fraternal twins. Furthermore, each twin in an identical twin pair should be more attracted to their co-twin's spouse than each twin in a fraternal twin pair. Finally, the spouses of identical twins should be more attracted to the co-twin of their partners (who are, after all, identical to their partners) than the spouses of fraternal twins.

What made the Lykken and Tellegen (1993) study provocative is that, as in the Eastwick and Finkel study, none of their predictions came true. Even though identical twins tend to have similar preferences in many aspects of their lives, their spouses were no more similar to each other than were the spouses of fraternal twins. Identical twins reported no increased tendency to be attracted to their co-twins' spouses, nor did spouses of identical twins report a greater attraction to their partners' twins, compared to the reports from fraternal twins and their spouses. Their analyses led these researchers to the conclusion that our preferences have little bearing on who we ultimately end up with as mates. They wrote: "Whereas much human choice behavior is undoubtedly lawful and, to some extent, predictable, mate selection is to a surprising extent random and unpredictable" (Lykken & Tellegen, 1993, p. 56).

The results of the speed dating and twin studies are remarkable because they fly in the face of most people's sense of their own lives. Far from being random, many people report that their relationship with their partner feels as if it were destined, as if their partner were the only individual in the world with whom they could have formed a lasting bond (e.g., Knee, 1998). Happy couples describe themselves as a perfect fit, implying that each has the exact qualities the other desired in a mate. How can we reconcile people's experience of deep meaning in the process of mate selection with research suggesting that our choice of mates may be essentially random?

The answer may lie in the kinds of variables that these researchers examined. Look again through the bases of attraction. For the most part, research on attraction has focused on what is or is not attractive about people's stable traits: how they look, what they value, and what benefits they can provide us.

Knowing about the qualities of a person may be enough to understand attraction because, as we have said, being attracted is something a person can experience as an individual. It follows that, when we ask people about the sources of their romantic attraction to others, as Eastwick and Finkel (2008) did, the answers almost always focus on the qualities of the individuals they prefer.

But people do not really select their mates the way they select their clothes, their jobs, or their vacations. Mate selection is a dyadic process; relationship partners must select each other. Before the speed dating event, the participants in that study may have considered the general qualities they hope for in their romantic partners. During the event, however, they learned about how each person made them feel, whether he or she responded well to jokes, and their own level of arousal. None of these things was measured by the researchers after each interaction, but each of them may play a role in how enjoyable the interaction was and whether the participants felt a sense of chemistry. Lykken and Tellegen (1993) also focused exclusively on the enduring traits of each twin and his or her partners. Together, these studies suggest not that mate selection is random, but that knowing only about the qualities of the two individuals who have selected each other may not be enough to explain the process through which their relationship was formed. Explaining how people actually form intimate relationships requires understanding how people who are initially attracted to each other interact.

Proximity: Making Interaction Possible

We can be attracted to someone from afar. We can admire, respect, and even dream about someone we have never met. But to have a relationship with someone, we must first have the opportunity to interact with him or her. Thus, it makes sense that a prerequisite for relationship formation is **proximity**, or being near. We are most likely to form relationships with people who are physically close to us because these are the people with whom we are most likely to interact.

Social psychologist Leon Festinger and his colleagues conducted the classic test of this idea. They asked 270 people living in campus housing to list their three closest friends, and then the researchers mapped the answers according to where each person lived (Festinger, Schacter, & Back, 1950) (FIGURE 5.9). The results were strong and clear: The closer together people lived, the more likely they were to have formed a friendship. Not only did students who lived in buildings next to each other tend to be friends, but within the same building the chances of being friends with someone increased considerably as the distance between the doors to their rooms decreased.

> And if you can't be with the one you love, honey, love the one you're with."
> —Stephen Stills (1970)

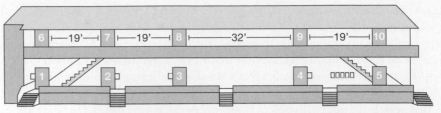

FIGURE 5.9 **Liking who is nearby.** This diagram of a college dormitory shows the effect of proximity on forming friendships. Students usually make friends with those in neighboring or nearby rooms. The numbers are the distance (in feet) between the doors to different rooms. The shorter the distance, the greater the likelihood a friendship would develop. (Source: Adapted from Festinger, Schacter, & Back, 1950.)

Does being nearby make someone intrinsically more attractive? It would not seem so, although people who are nearby are certainly more familiar, and they may be more similar as well. The more logical explanation for these results is that people who are physically closer to each other simply have more opportunities to interact than people who are farther away. In this way, proximity should be a prerequisite for the formation of any relationship, not just friendships and intimate relationships. Indeed, social psychologist Ebbe Ebbesen and his colleagues found, in a study of relationships among residents of a condominium complex, that although most people tended to live near their closest friends, they tended to live close to their enemies as well (Ebbesen, Kjos, & Konecni, 1976). While proximity provides more opportunities for positive interactions with people, it also creates more opportunities for conflict.

With respect to intimate relationships, the power of proximity may be to limit the field of eligible partners. Thus, most people end up marrying someone who lives nearby because the people who do not live nearby tend to be people we never meet. This fact actually provides support for some family wisdom that was passed down to one of the authors of this book. One of our grandmothers was fond of advising that one should never marry for money. Instead, she suggested, "Go to where the rich people are, and fall in love!"

In the modern age, of course, improved communication technologies have changed the meaning of proximity. A century ago, there were few opportunities to interact with anyone who did not live within a day's horseback ride. Today, the Internet makes it possible to interact regularly with people around the globe. Although there may be no substitute for face-to-face communication, the ability to be psychologically close to someone through electronic communication suggests that relationships should form through online contact—and with increasing regularity, they do. Conducted in 2009, one survey found that 22 percent of different-sex couples who had recently formed relationships had met their partners over the Internet, making it the second most popular way to meet a partner, after being introduced by friends (Rosenfeld & Thomas, 2012).

First Moves: Signaling Availability and Interest

Attraction and proximity can be thought of as setting the stage for a relationship. But once the stage is set, how does that connection begin? Where does attraction between two individuals become a mutual process of mate selection?

Aron and his colleagues explored this question by asking 50 college students who had fallen in love within the past 6 months to describe how their relationships began (Aron et al., 1989). As the research we have described so far would suggest, the first element that people mentioned was noticing the other person and noticing that the person had desirable qualities. The next most frequently mentioned element, however, was that the other person behaved in some way that indicated the attraction might be mutual. After reading all of the accounts, the researchers concluded that "people are just waiting for an attractive person to do something they can interpret as liking them" (Aron et al., 1989, p. 251). In other words, the difference between feeling attraction and starting a relationship lies in someone making the first move.

One thing that makes a consideration of first moves interesting is that they are a requirement of eventual mate selection not only in humans but also in all animals that use sexual intercourse for reproduction. Recognizing this common theme has led animal behavior scientists to search for patterns of behavior that characterize the beginnings of mate selection across species and cultures (Eibl-Eibesfeldt, 1979). For example, among most animals and all primates, mate selection begins with a sequence of three kinds of behaviors: behaviors that alert potential mates to one's presence, behaviors that establish one's sex, and behaviors that advertise one's availability and interest in a relationship.

Do these same kinds of behaviors characterize first moves among humans? To address this question, anthropologists have observed human behaviors in a context in which many successful and unsuccessful first moves are likely to occur—singles bars (Givens, 1978, 1983). Although it may seem like a crude comparison, the behaviors that anthropologists observe in singles bars seem very similar to the behaviors they observe among animals in the wild. For example, every interaction in a singles bar begins with behaviors designed to attract notice from potential partners. Of course, simply showing up at a bar is a central behavior toward this goal, but so is laughing or speaking loudly or bumping into someone. The researchers also observed behaviors designed to emphasize gender identity. For men, these include demonstrations of dominance (e.g., punching a friend in the shoulder as a way of saying hello) or competence (e.g., winning at pool or darts). For women, sexual characteristics can be emphasized through dress or makeup, long hair can be tossed or flipped, and hips can be swayed. Together, these kinds of behaviors send a necessary first message: "I am here, and I am a potential partner."

Whereas these behaviors tend to be broadcast widely, behaviors that indicate sexual interest tend to be directed at particular individuals. The message of these behaviors is: "Out of all of the people around us right now, I am interested in starting up an interaction with *you*." Who is most likely to initiate an actual interaction? Widely held stereotypes suggest that men are the first to express sexual interest; therefore, men are the initiators in our culture. The truth, as usual, is more complex. Observation of behavior in singles bars indicates that, although men are indeed the ones who tend to initiate conversations with women, their attempts are almost always preceded by nonverbal behaviors from the woman that indicate her receptiveness to an approach (Perper & Weis, 1987). Sex researcher Timothy Perper (1989) coined the term **proceptivity** to refer to these sorts of anticipatory behaviors. For example, in sweeping her gaze across a room, a woman might catch the eye of someone she finds attractive and hold his gaze for just longer than normal. This is frequently taken as a signal that it would be acceptable for him to come up and start a conversation.

Once two people have actually begun an interaction, partners can do other things to indicate more or less interest in taking it further. In a study designed to identify these behaviors, clinical psychologist Charlene Muehlenhard and her colleagues (1986) showed college students a variety of videotapes of a man and woman having a conversation in a public place, and after each tape the observers were asked to rate the likelihood that the woman would accept the man's invitation for a date. By comparing responses to the different tapes, the researchers could determine which specific behaviors on the part of the women were interpreted as signs of interest and which were not. Among the weaker signs were leaning forward, speaking with animation, and not looking at other members of the opposite sex who were passing by. The stronger signs included standing less than 18 inches away, touching while laughing, and—most significant—touching while not laughing. As two people become more involved and interested in each other during a conversation, they tend to demonstrate **behavioral synchrony** (FIGURE 5.10); they mimic each other's movements unconsciously, leaning forward when the other person leans forward, stretching when the other person stretches, looking directly into each other's eyes, and so on (Crown, 1991). Lack of interest is shown by opposite behaviors, such as avoiding eye contact, leaning away, or crossing one's arms (Grammer, 1990). The more two people demonstrate behavioral synchrony during an interaction, the smoother that interaction goes, and presumably the easier it is for them to build on that interaction to develop a relationship (Chartrand & Bargh, 1999).

It may appear from the discussion so far that many of the behaviors that indicate initial interest in another person are nonverbal. One

FIGURE 5.10 Behavioral synchrony. When an interaction is going well, partners tend to unconsciously mimic each other's behaviors and postures.

methodological reason for this emphasis is that animal behavior researchers use the same observational techniques to study animals and humans. Naturally, researchers who adopt these techniques will tend to focus on the nonverbal behaviors that animals and humans may have in common. A psychological reason, however, is that the start of a romantic interaction can be a tricky situation, opening up each person to possible rejection and the loss of self-esteem that goes with it. In contrast to direct, explicit expressions of interest, nonverbal behaviors give people a chance to express their interest in ways that are subtle enough that the interest can be denied if it is not returned.

A willingness to approach someone you are interested in may depend on whether the situation allows you to be somewhat ambiguous about your motives. In a clever test of this idea, social psychologist William Bernstein and his colleagues (1983) asked male college students to participate in what they thought was a movie-rating exercise. When they arrived at the research rooms, participants found they could squeeze into a narrow booth and watch a movie next to an attractive female, or they could have their own booth and sit alone. The researchers found that choice of where to sit was strongly affected by whether the same movie was playing in the two booths. When both booths featured the same movie, the only reason for the men to squeeze in next to the attractive woman would be as a nonverbal expression of interest. When the situation was this explicit, only 25 percent of the men chose the occupied booth. However, when each booth featured a different movie, the men had an excuse for sitting next to the woman (perhaps that was the movie they really wanted to see). Regardless of which movie was actually playing, over 75 percent of the men in this condition chose to sit next to the woman. In other words, when they could plausibly claim to have a nonromantic reason for starting up an interaction, three times as many men were willing to do so.

Although communicating interest nonverbally may help avoid rejection, the obvious disadvantage of this nonverbal behavior is that it leaves room for miscommunication. Misunderstandings may be especially likely during initial conversations because women and men often interpret the same behaviors differently. For example, social psychologists Lance Shotland and Jane Craig (1988) asked college students to watch videotapes of men and women interacting and then to rate the amount of sexual interest demonstrated by each partner. Regardless of whether the two people on the tape were actually friends or in a romantic relationship, men were more likely than women to interpret both partners' behaviors as expressions of sexual interest. Furthermore, this tendency is strongest when asking women and men to interpret nonverbal behaviors (Abbey & Melby, 1986). Thus, nonverbal communication is a mixed bag. Between two people who really are interested in each other, nonverbal behaviors may provide a safe way to express that interest. However, between two people whose interest in each other is not mutual, a reliance on these less direct avenues of communication may lead to hurt feelings or worse. For more on the implications of being vague about your intentions, see **BOX 5.2.**

Self-Disclosure: Knowing and Being Known

Once a conversation between two people has begun, whether a relationship develops between them may depend on what they actually talk about. According to **social penetration theory**, the development of a relationship is associated with the kind of personal information partners exchange with

Hooking Up in College

So there you are at the party, it's getting late, and the person you have been desperately flirting with seems to be flirting back. What's your next move?

On college campuses, the next move can be **hooking up**, which sociologists Norval Glenn and Elizabeth Marquardt define as when two people "get together for a physical encounter and don't necessarily expect anything further" (2001, p. 4). You might notice that this definition of hooking up is pretty vague, especially the part about the "physical encounter." In interviews about their experiences, college students report that hooking up can refer to a wide range of sexual behaviors, from kissing to intercourse to anything in between (Bogle, 2008). The vagueness of the term may be part of its appeal: You can tell a friend that you hooked up with someone without being specific about what actually went on. What is not vague about hooking up is that in all cases, the physical encounter does not imply any ongoing commitment or future relationship between the two participants. Hookups are a physical, and usually impulsive, way for two people to connect sexually without the complications of an emotional involvement.

They also seem to be an increasingly common form of social interaction on college campuses. One survey of 555 undergraduate students in northeastern colleges in the United States found that 78 percent of women and men had experienced a hookup at least once (Paul, McManus, & Hayes, 2000). For nearly half the men and a third of the women, the hookup involved sexual intercourse. Of the many variables that have been examined as predictors of experience with hookups, intoxication seems to play the largest role, with 65 percent of college students in one survey reporting that their hookups were preceded by alcohol or drug use (Grello, Welsh, & Harper, 2006).

Uncommitted sex is hardly a new invention, of course, but the idea that a sexual encounter might be an acceptable way to get to know someone is a relatively recent development (**FIGURE 5.11**). For most of the last century, college students who wanted to get to know each other would go out on dates, and the scripts for those dates were fairly rigid; that is, the man did the asking, decided on the activity, and paid (Bailey, 1988). Through going on dates, young people decided whether they wanted to enter into a relationship. Sex, if it happened at all, was the culmination of that formal, scripted courtship process. Today's college students also go on dates, but dates are now something that people do *after* they are already established as a couple and often after they are already sexually intimate (Bogle, 2008). The idea of getting to know potential partners by asking them out on a date (e.g., "Hey, Susie, would you like to go to a movie with me Friday night?") has been replaced by activities in which groups of unattached, available individuals all go out together (e.g., "Hey, Susie, a bunch of us are getting together to watch movies Friday night. Why don't you come along?").

Are today's college students happy about their social and sexual flexibility? As you might expect, men are happier than women about their own hookups, but both each other (Altman & Taylor, 1973). The theory categorizes self-disclosures along two dimensions: breadth, or the variety of information shared, and depth, the personal significance of the information shared. During an initial conversation, people tend to exchange information that is neither broad nor deep (e.g., "What do you think of the music they play here? What do you do for a living?"). Over the course of multiple interactions, however, self-disclosures tend to spread over a wider range of areas and gradually deal with increasingly personal issues (e.g., "I've been depressed because my parents are getting divorced"). This approach to relationships suggests that we might be able to classify the people in our lives by the kinds of information

men and women believe that other people are having a better time hooking up than they are (Lambert, Kahn, & Apple, 2003). What makes a hookup a bad experience? Asked about their worst hookups, college students mention being drunk, feeling used or pressured to have sex, and feeling regret or embarrassment afterward (Paul & Hayes, 2002). What makes a hookup a good experience? Asked about their best hookups, the same college students mention being attracted to the partner, enjoying the sexual experience, and—oh yes—the fact that, in over a third of their best hookups (38 percent), the no-strings-attached, no-commitment-implied sexual encounter did lead to the development of a romantic relationship after all.

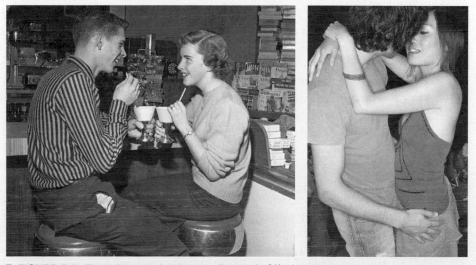

FIGURE 5.11 From dating to hooking up. For most of the last century, young people got to know each other by going out on dates, a process that may or may not have culminated in an emotional or sexual relationship. Contemporary young people are not doing much dating. Instead, they are hooking up.

we share with them—from casual acquaintances, with whom we share only the superficial details of our lives, to intimates, with whom we share our most profound joys and sorrows.

Research on social penetration theory confirms many of these ideas. Several studies have shown that not only do we tend to like people who disclose personal information to us, but we also generally like people more after we have disclosed personal information to them (Collins & Miller, 1994). Among strangers, the information disclosed is usually pretty factual, lacking breadth and depth, but as people get to know each other better, they share a broader range of topics, and then increasingly deeper and more personal information about themselves (Hornstein & Truesdell, 1988). Furthermore, consistent with the theory, the rate that people disclose personal information about themselves seems to change over the course of a relationship. Conversations between strangers are characterized by **disclosure reciprocity**, such that when one person shares something personal, the other person immediately shares something equally personal (Derlega, Wilson, & Chaikin, 1976). In dating couples, partners disclose a great deal of information in a fairly short span of time. In a study of couples in which partners were dating exclusively and had been together for an average of 8 months, for example, nearly 60 percent of all respondents reported that they had disclosed fully to their partner across 17 different areas (Rubin et al., 1980). As you would expect, "My feelings toward my parents" was disclosed fully by more than 70 percent of the participants, whereas "The things about myself that I am most ashamed of" was disclosed fully by fewer than 40 percent.

Exchanging personal disclosures at an escalating level of depth is a way for two people to gradually increase the intimacy between them. Each exchange of information is a sign that the last exchange was appreciated. Once two people get to know one another better, however, the pressure for each person to match the other's disclosures appears to level off. For example, among friends and spouses who have known each other for years, the pattern of reciprocal exchange of information is not as rigid (Morton, 1978). Thus, the function of self-disclosures may change as the relationship develops. People who are getting acquainted may disclose personal information as a way of figuring each other out, whereas people who already depend on each other may disclose personal information as a way of getting validation and support (as we shall see in Chapter 7).

Although the association between disclosure and liking between two people is generally strong, it is clear that not all personal disclosures help bring people closer together. As with expressions of romantic interest, there are socially prescribed levels of disclosure that are appropriate for different stages of a relationship, and violating those norms can hinder the development of a relationship as much as following them can help (FIGURE 5.12). For example, people who disclose highly personal information too early in an interaction are viewed more negatively than people who wait for a more appropriate moment (Wortman et al., 1976). Similarly, people who disclose personal information about themselves are liked less when they give the impression of self-disclosing to anyone who will listen (Jones & Archer, 1976).

Sometimes we reveal something we later regret, or we may sense that certain topics are simply off-limits. What topics do couples avoid? In a study by communication researchers Leanne Knobloch and Katy Carpenter-Theune (2004), the six general topics shown in **TABLE 5.2** were nominated as most likely to be avoided by college students in romantic relationships who, on average, had been dating just over a year. The researchers found the surprising result that avoiding topics such as these is greatest when partners report a moderate level of intimacy. Uncertainty about the relationship is greatest during this time, and thus partners are more inclined to avoid topics that they believe will threaten the relationship.

"I wonder if there is ever a perfect time to tell someone his hands are sticky."

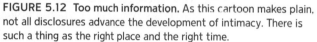

FIGURE 5.12 Too much information. As this cartoon makes plain, not all disclosures advance the development of intimacy. There is such a thing as the right place and the right time.

TABLE 5.2 Common Topics Avoided by Partners in Romantic Relationships

The State of the Relationship *"Where do we stand? Are we friends or more than friends?"*
Extra-Relationship Activity *"When I have conversations with other girls, then I don't really tell her about it."*
Prior Romantic Relationships *"How many partners we have had sex with in the past."*
Conflict-Inducing Topics *"Drinking alcohol. He does it, and I don't agree with it."*
Relationship Norms *"Sex. We're not to that point yet, but we will probably talk about it when the time is right."*
Negative Life Experiences *"My past experiences with an eating disorder."*

Note: Topics identified as most avoided are listed first.
Source: Adapted from Knobloch & Carpenter-Theune, 2004.

Paradoxically, a retreat from potentially risky topics can signal increased concern for the relationship and deepening intimacy on the horizon.

Overall, then, it may not be self-disclosure itself that makes a difference in the development of a relationship. Rather, it is the association between two people's self-disclosures, the tendency for two people to match and then escalate and then match again in what they reveal to each other, that propels a new relationship forward.

Courtship: Developing Commitment

Meeting someone and having a great conversation is one thing; establishing an enduring bond is another. How do couples progress from casual dating to a serious relationship to a lifelong partnership? Early attempts to address this question led to various types of **stage theories**, which describe relationships as developing through steps that proceed in a specific sequence. For example, in their staircase model of relationship formation, communication researchers Mark Knapp and Anita Vangelisti (1991) described relationship formation as a process of rising through a series of five steps. The first four steps—initiating, experimenting, intensifying, and integrating—are marked by increasingly personal disclosures across a widening range of topics. In the fourth step (integrating), friends and family members view the two partners as having formed a committed partnership, and the couple themselves begin to plan for a future together. In the fifth and final step, bonding, these plans are formalized in some form of public ceremony or ritual, as in a wedding or a commitment ceremony.

The problem with stage theories is that intimate relationships rarely follow the orderly pattern of development that they describe. When recently married couples, for example, are asked to chart the development of their relationships from the time they first met, some people describe a steady increase in involvement over time, but others describe relationships that progress from strangers to marriage very rapidly, and still others describe relationships that experience many ups and downs before reaching marriage (Huston et al., 1981). Some people marry before they ever discuss their values and attitudes, whereas others know each other intimately for years before deciding whether to move the relationship forward.

Rather than thinking of relationship development in terms of stages, researchers who have examined how relationships actually develop think instead of turning points, or specific events or behaviors that increase or decrease the level of commitment between two people (Bullis, Clark, & Sline, 1993). In one study that examined these behaviors, couples who were dating each other exclusively were asked to describe the turning points in their relationship, and the descriptions from each partner were compared (Baxter & Bullis, 1986). Most of the time, both partners agreed on what the major turning points were. Whereas the behaviors that characterize the beginnings of relationships tend to be indirect and ambiguous, the behaviors that couples described as characterizing the development of their relationships tended to be direct and explicit. In fact, in over half the cases, the turning point was a conversation in which the two partners talked openly about their feelings and intentions for the relationship. Other research confirms that the first time partners exchange the words "I love you" is a major event that affects the way both partners feel about the relationship (Owen, 1987).

Among more established relationships, development is marked by other behaviors that indicate increased commitment, like moving in together, accepting jobs that allow partners to remain in the same city, or buying a house together. Thinking about turning points in this way suggests that a relationship can become more or less committed for reasons that have little to do with the enduring qualities of the two partners. Factors that are entirely external to the couple, like when they graduate from school or what opportunities they are offered professionally, can lead to decisions that affect the future course of a relationship. The difference between relationships that become committed and those that do not may lie in how couples respond to the choices presented to them.

MAIN POINTS

>> Because forming a lasting relationship involves both selecting a mate and being selected, relationship formation requires that partners have attractive qualities and that they interact in a certain way.

>> Mate selection is strongly affected by the proximity of different types of partners, and people generally form friendships and relationships with people who live nearby.

>> Researchers have identified three behaviors that characterize the start of relationships: behaviors that indicate one's presence, behaviors that identify one's sex, and behaviors that express one's interest and availability.

>> Once two people are having a conversation, their relationship develops as a function of the breadth and depth of the personal information they exchange. The matching of self-disclosures propels a relationship forward.

>> At specific turning points, each partner's commitment to the relationship is made explicit, either through a conversation or through the choices he or she makes in response to the opportunities offered.

CONCLUSION

Let's consider the relative value of the accumulated research on attraction and mate selection for a budding young matchmaker hoping to arrange long-lasting relationships. Studies on attraction focus primarily on stable qualities of individuals that make them more or less appealing as potential partners.

The power of these variables to explain the success or failure of relationships over the long term may be limited. After all, people who start out physically attractive to us will probably remain physically attractive. People who are similar to us will tend to get more similar as they stay with us, and they will certainly become more familiar. If all we know about are the bases of attraction, then people who are mutually attracted initially should remain or even become more attracted to each other over time. The fact that early attraction frequently fades has an important implication: The forces that initially attract two people cannot be the same as the ones that keep them together.

Research on the behavioral exchanges that lead to mate selection may have more potential for predicting which couples might stay together and which ones will not. To the extent that an exchange of behaviors can lead to an escalation of feelings, an exchange of different kinds of behaviors may lead to changes in those feelings over time. We shall return to these topics in later chapters.

6

Personality and Personal History

What a Difference a Day Makes

In Richard Linklater's movie *Before Sunrise*, a young American named Jesse meets Celine, a young French student, while riding on a train in Europe. They connect immediately, share a meal, and converse at length about the future and their philosophies of life and love. Jesse convinces Celine to get off the train and explore Vienna with him for the day (FIGURE 6.1). While wandering around sightseeing, talking,

and enjoying the day, they gradually become infatuated with each other and end up spending an intimate night together. As they separate the next morning—Jesse catching a flight home, Celine returning to Paris—they make a plan to meet again in Vienna in 6 months. The movie leaves us wondering whether either person will follow through on the plan.

In the sequel, *Before Sunset*, we learn that the meeting did not take place. Jesse did return to Vienna, but Celine, to her regret, could not be there due to a death in her family. Never thinking to exchange phone numbers or even last names in the midst of that intense day together, they have had no contact for the past 9 years. Now, in Paris, they meet again. Jesse is there to promote a novel he wrote about that romantic day in Vienna, and Celine, having

learned of Jesse's visit, goes to meet him. Jesse and Celine talk about many things as they stroll around the city, particularly about the stability of identity. Celine says she recently reread her journal from her teenage years, discovering that, although she was a bit more hopeful and naïve back then, she is really exactly the same person now. Jesse comments that "no one really changes," saying that what really matters are the commitments we make in life.

These observations are interesting because they directly contradict what Jesse and Celine later say about how the events of 9 years ago affected them. Celine talks about how the unrealized hope and optimism of that night has left her devastated and miserable in her love life, and she prefers keeping her partners at arm's length. Her current boyfriend is a

FIGURE 6.1 Powerful characters. In the movies *Before Sunrise* (left) and *Before Sunset* (right), Jesse (Ethan Hawke) and Celine (Julie Delpy) invite us to speculate about the power of enduring personality traits in the context of an intimate relationship. To what extent is relationship success due to the partners' personalities or to their unique chemistry?

photojournalist, regularly dispatched to document distant wars, and this arrangement suits her, rather than a relationship in which she sees her partner every day. Meanwhile, Jesse had married his pregnant girlfriend and now feels as though he "runs a small nursery with a woman he used to date." He loves his son but is miserable in his marriage and longs for a relationship with more depth and intensity. He wonders whether there is more to love than commitment, and he worries that he gave up on the idea of romantic love on that December day in Vienna, when Celine was nowhere to be found.

QUESTIONS

If Jesse and Celine had reconnected in Vienna, would their relationship—some 9 years later—still be going strong because of the initial spark between them? Or would it have ended by now, after being weakened by the same things that are contributing to their current relationship problems? Is it possible that, because of who they are as people, Jesse and Celine would be unhappy with almost any partner they found? Or are they wise to trust their intuitions, and thus accurate in their belief that the misery they are now experiencing is a result of their failure to reconnect in Vienna and of having the wrong partners?

The formation, course, and quality of an intimate relationship are in some way determined by

each partner's personality and unique personal experiences. We might see our roommate struggle through a series of short and intense relationships, for example, and wonder what it is about him that produces such a pattern. Perhaps having weathered the storms of our parents' unhappy marriage, we might be motivated to ask whether these experiences destine us for a similar fate as we look to settle down with a steady partner. Or, after reflecting on our own intimate relationships, we might come to the uncomfortable realization that we tend to be jealous, or insecure, or needy, regardless of who we are with—prompting us to figure out a way to prevent these strong feelings from sabotaging our next relationship.

In all these instances, we are assuming that intimate bonds are affected by the partners' enduring characteristics and experiences. In this chapter, we focus on how preferences and tendencies in relationships are rooted in early life experiences. This focus is intriguing because it implies that who we are as intimate partners in adulthood cannot be understood without considering earlier relationships, especially those we witnessed or participated in while growing up. Before turning to that rich vein of material, however, we first examine a different proposition: that our personalities can be captured with a small set of traits, a few of which are believed to be especially damaging for intimate bonds.

The Effect of Personality Traits on Intimate Relationships

What do you most want in a relationship partner? Most of us tend to be pretty choosy (e.g., Kenrick et al., 1993), hoping our partner will be above average in all the crucial areas. Physical attraction is important, of course. However, we also want a partner who is kind and compassionate, trustworthy and reliable, open and expressive, and has a good sense of humor (e.g., Sprecher & Regan, 2002). But when choosing a partner for a long-term relationship, most of us opt for an average-looking person with a great personality over a great-looking person with an average personality (e.g., Scheib, 2001). Scholars define **personality** as those distinctive qualities that characterize an individual, that are relatively stable over time and across situations, that have some coherence or internal organization to them, and that influence how the person behaves in and adapts to the world (e.g., Revelle, 1995). From the wide variety of possible personality characteristics, which ones are especially beneficial or costly in relationships? And how, exactly, do they affect intimacy?

The earliest efforts to understand the causes of relationship success and failure focused precisely on this issue of partners' personalities and temperaments. Psychologist Lewis Terman, who achieved fame by studying the lives of gifted people, sought to understand genius of a different sort by identifying the factors that differentiated between happy and unhappy married couples (**FIGURE 6.2**). As Terman and his colleagues wrote in 1938:

> We wish to propose a theory regarding the role of temperament as a determiner of marital happiness or unhappiness. We believe that a large proportion of incompatible marriages are so because of a predisposition to unhappiness in one or both of the spouses. Whether by nature or by nurture, these persons are so lacking in the qualities that make for compatibility that they would be incapable of finding happiness in any marriage. (p. 110)

Clearly, this is not a theory that prioritizes interpersonal communication. Instead, according to this view, enduring characteristics of the partners are the driving force in intimate relationships. This means that efforts to understand relationships—including what happens between the partners—must begin by considering each partner's personal qualities.

Terman was primarily a trait theorist. Researchers using the **trait approach** to study relationships (or anything else) identify a core set of personality traits by

FIGURE 6.2 Lewis Terman (1877–1956). Terman was a pioneer in the study of the role of personality in marriage.

TABLE 6.1 **Personality Traits in the Big Five Model of Personality**

Trait	Definition
Neuroticism	Inclination to experience unpleasant emotions
Extraversion	Preference for social interaction and lively activity
Openness	Receptiveness to new ideas, approaches, and experiences
Agreeableness	Selfless concern for others; generous, trusting
Conscientiousness	Degree of discipline and organization

conducting extensive statistical analysis of the adjectives people use to describe themselves and others. For example, when we say that someone is "extraverted," we are usually saying he or she is more extraverted compared to another person or to the average person; and in doing so, we are employing the language of traits—and a definition of extraversion that we all share, more or less. Dozens of traits have been identified using this approach, but an emerging consensus holds that just five traits are needed to capture personality differences between individuals. These five traits, shown in **TABLE 6.1**, are known as the **Big Five** (Costa & McCrae, 1985; McCrae & Costa, 1990). These are encompassing traits that include many other specific aspects of personality. Neuroticism, for example, refers to a predisposition to experience unpleasant and disturbing emotions. It is considered a "higher-order" trait that includes specific descriptors like anxiety, hostility, self-consciousness, and pessimism. The Big Five traits can be measured reliably, and the information required is easily gathered by administering brief questionnaires.

> " The mechanisms of personality exist to help the individual regulate behavior in important life activities, and there are few activities more significant to the individual's well-being and survival than those involved in relating to other persons, especially those persons with whom the individual has an ongoing, interdependent relationship."
>
> —Reis, Capobianco, & Tsai (2002, p. 841)

Personality, Emotion, and Intimacy

Many research findings linking personality to interpersonal functioning concern traits that govern how emotions are experienced, regulated, and expressed. If a bridge can be built between enduring traits and human intimacy, then surely the planks are predominantly emotional in form.

One surprising aspect of this evidence is that even measures of personality taken in childhood predict relationships later in life. For example, children who display frequent and severe temper tantrums before the age of 10 are twice as likely to divorce years later, compared to their counterparts with a more even temper, and women with a history of childhood tantrums are more likely than their even-tempered counterparts to marry men with lower occupational status (Caspi, Elder, & Bem, 1987). Even when children are assessed at a very young age, their dispositions forecast their interpersonal adjustment years later. Children who are judged at age 3 to be "undercontrolled"—that is, restless, impulsive, easily frustrated, and moody—are more likely to go on to experience more turbulent relationships with others and more interpersonal conflict at age 21, and people who know them well at that point judge them to have more problems and social difficulties (Newman, Caspi, Moffitt, & Silva, 1997).

FIGURE 6.3 "Life is full of misery, loneliness, and suffering—and it is over much too soon." Director-writer-actor Woody Allen typifies the personality trait of neuroticism, or negative affectivity. People who have this trait tend to be less satisfied in their relationships, more likely to divorce, and appear to be more difficult as relationship partners.

When personality is assessed later, in adulthood, again we see associations between enduring emotional dispositions and the experiences people have in intimate relationships. Individuals high in **neuroticism** or **negative affectivity**, who tend to dwell on their own negative qualities as well as those of other people and the world in general (Watson & Clark, 1984), appear to be particularly vulnerable to poor relationships (**FIGURE 6.3**). For example, in a study of marriage conducted over five decades, psychologists E. Lowell Kelly and James Conley (1987) demonstrated that neuroticism—as judged by five acquaintances—in partners who were engaged to be married was greater in those who became unhappy in their marriage and those who later divorced. Among unhappy couples who eventually divorced, the husbands were more outgoing and more impulsive than husbands in unhappy couples who did not divorce. Thus, unhappy spouses are more likely to proceed toward divorce (rather than remain unhappily married) if the husbands have personality traits that make them prone to engage in behaviors that undermine the relationship, such as infidelity, financial irresponsibility, and excessive drinking. Kelly and Conley concluded: "Neuroticism acts to bring about distress, and the other traits of the husband help to determine whether the distress is brought to a head (in divorce) or suffered passively (in a stable but unsatisfactory marriage)" (1987, p. 34).

Less is known about the association between personality traits other than neuroticism and relationship outcomes. However, as you might expect, partners who are more agreeable or more conscientious tend to be happier in their relationships (Heller, Watson, & Ilies, 2004). Personality factors appear to operate by determining the general range of functioning individuals experience in a relationship. Couples in which partners have low levels of agreeableness—and high levels of neuroticism—tend to experience lower levels of satisfaction over time, compared to couples with higher levels of agreeableness and lower levels of negativity. Then, within this broad range of functioning, how well the two partners communicate with each other appears to determine whether their relationship will deteriorate (Belsky & Hsieh, 1998; Kurdek, 1999).

How do personality traits operate within relationships to make them more or less satisfying, more or less durable? Where, within relationships, do we find evidence that personality traits matter? We know that partners' personalities are tied to the problems and complaints they confront. Partners of people low in agreeableness complain of being treated with condescension and a lack of consideration, and partners of people high in neuroticism are more likely to cite self-centeredness, jealousy, and dependency as difficulties in their relationships (Buss, 1991; **FIGURE 6.4**). Individuals relatively high in neuroticism tend to interpret their partner's negative behaviors in a more critical light than those who are low in neuroticism (Karney, Bradbury, Fincham, & Sullivan, 1994), and their interpretations appear to be more stable and rigid over time (Karney & Bradbury, 2000). You can imagine the emotional challenge of being in a relationship with a person who tends to exaggerate your flaws and rarely gives you the benefit of the doubt when you make a mistake. By actually watching couples in a laboratory as they discuss the strengths and weaknesses of their relationship, we can see that conversations tend to be harsher and more hostile when partners are higher in neuroticism and lower in agreeableness (Donnellan, Conger, & Bryant, 2004; McNulty, 2008).

Another way of thinking about personality and relationship outcomes involves considering both partners' traits simultaneously. It is pretty well established that individuals do not tend to pair up with those who have similar personality traits. Partners are far more similar in religiousness, age, political orientation, and general intelligence than they are in personality (Watson et al., 2004; see also Chapter 5). Birds of a feather do flock together, it seems, but the decision to flock together has very little to do with personality. Even

FIGURE 6.4 An imperfect match. People who are less agreeable and more negative treat their partners less favorably than people with agreeable, cheerful personalities. By complaining about his date's personality, Dilbert may be saying at least as much about his own personality as he does about hers.

so, to the degree that partners are similar in their personalities, they tend to have happier relationships—particularly when they are similar in agreeableness and openness (Luo & Klohnen, 2005). This fact is central to the computer programs used by various online matching services in suggesting potential mates to their clients.

Taken together, we can see from this work that partners' personality traits—when measured in childhood, long before their intimate relationships have formed, or in the early stages of intimate relationships, when they are still happy—are relatively stable forces operating continuously in the background. Personality traits seem to set the boundaries within which a relationship unfolds, while also affecting the ways the two partners perceive and communicate. Knowing this confirms the common intuition that partners' personalities do indeed matter in relationships. But more important, it helps to identify agreeableness and negative affectivity as particularly influential traits.

Consequences of Negative Affectivity and Low Self-Esteem

What is it about a person who is high in negative affectivity that produces difficult relationships? Social psychologist Sandra Murray and her colleagues conducted a series of studies focusing on one aspect of negative affectivity, low self-esteem, that have yielded new insights. Their **dependency regulation model** demonstrates that individuals with low self-esteem underestimate how favorably their partner views them. That faulty estimation sets off a series of psychological processes—being excessively cautious and self-protective in the relationship, over-reacting to the partner's interpersonal slights, dismissing genuine praise, feeling and expressing strong negative emotions like anger—that combine to contribute to the unintended demise of the relationship. Four key phases in this model are outlined below, with sections of a case study illustrating each phase.

1. *Low self-esteem.* Although experiences of rejection produce day-to-day fluctuations in anyone's feelings, high or low self-esteem tends to be much more like a personality trait than a mood state (Orth, Robins, & Widaman, 2012; Trzesniewski, Donnellan, & Robins, 2003). As the following example shows, chronic low self-esteem can create difficulties for a relationship:

    Jamaal, 25, has been in a relationship with Katya, 26, for just over 2 years. Katya considers herself to be even-keeled, as do her many friends and customers. As a creative hairstylist she has a growing clientele, and she is saving money so she can realize her dream of owning a salon. Jamaal loves his work as a veterinarian's assistant, and he plans to apply to veterinary school after he takes some courses in chemistry and biology. Although well-liked by his co-workers, Jamaal lacks self-confidence and he struggles with feelings of low self-worth. Even after his boss commends him for his hard work, Jamaal cannot help wondering whether his boss is simply saying this to make him feel better for mistakes he has made. Katya often finds herself reassuring Jamaal, propping him up and trying to convince him that he is a good and worthwhile person.

2. *Underestimating the partner's regard for self.* Individuals low in self-esteem typically assume their partners do not regard them highly, and also that others share the pessimistic view they hold of themselves. This perception is inaccurate, however; studies show that insecure individuals with low self-esteem consistently underestimate their partners' positive impressions and their confidence in the relationship. As a result, they are overly cautious in their approach to relationships—often to reduce the risk of rejection—thus creating a distance that makes them even less likely to feel secure with the partner (Murray, Holmes, & Griffin, 2000). These unwarranted doubts can grow to the point where they detract from the relationship:

   Katya finds Jamaal to be articulate, supportive of her dreams, and as passionate about jazz as he is about the animals he treats. Sure, he can be moody and reclusive, but on balance Katya adores Jamaal and believes they have a pretty good relationship. Jamaal thinks the world of Katya, revels in her ability to cook amazing Brazilian food, and likes the fact that Katya's flexible work schedule leaves a lot of time for them to be together. Jamaal hears the reassuring words that Katya says to him, but deeper down he has serious doubts about whether she "really" loves him. How could she, given his moodiness and all his baggage? Jamaal harbors suspicions that Katya is biding her time in this relationship until someone better comes along. When Jamaal expresses these feelings, Katya reassures him that they are a good match and that she is entirely content with the relationship. Jamaal wonders why she is trying to reassure him so much, because it deepens his suspicions even more.

3. *Perceiving the partner in an unfavorable light and expressing discontent.* The mistaken belief that the partner does not truly love them leads individuals with low self-esteem to be ever vigilant for evidence that the partner does care for them. At the same time, they tend to see rejection even where it does not exist and to devalue their partner—probably as a self-protective strategy for believing they will have less to lose if the relationship ends. Confident people, high in self-esteem, are less sensitive to threats to the relationship and tend not to "make mountains out of molehills" (Murray, Rose, Bellavia, Holmes, & Kusche, 2002; also see Downey & Feldman, 1996; Downey, Freitas, Michaelis, & Khouri, 1998). Feeling hurt and ignored, insecure people express anger and sadness, particularly after disagreements (Murray, Bellavia, Rose, & Griffin, 2003), which in turn perpetuate arguments, promote disengagement, and prevent the partners from apologizing or reconnecting.

Katya's success as a hairstylist continues to grow, and she is recruited to work at a large salon where she could earn more money. One of her new clients is looking for an investment opportunity and offers to help Katya start her own salon. Katya jumps at the chance. Although Jamaal was supportive at first, Katya's long hours as a hairstylist and her new role as a business owner keep her away from home far longer than usual. Katya comes home exhilarated but tired and sometimes stressed out, and she finds she has less energy than usual for the relationship—and for the pep talks Jamaal needs. Katya feels she is spending more time worrying about Jamaal's feelings than her own, at a time when she really could use some support. Shortly thereafter, a new employee at Jamaal's veterinary clinic offers some well-intentioned but critical feedback on Jamaal's work. Katya, perhaps a little less compassionate than usual given her fatigue, tries to reassure Jamaal, but he cannot accept her encouragement, and the conversation deteriorates into an argument:

> **Jamaal:** *Look, this guy could have my job in a month and you tell me not to worry about it?! Listen to what you are saying!*
>
> **Katya:** *No Jamaal, you listen to what I am saying—your boss loves you, everything is going to be fine, trust me on this!*
>
> **Jamaal:** *Trust you? You want me to trust you? I barely see you anymore, and when I do you basically ignore me!*
>
> **Katya:** *OK, OK Jamaal, all I am saying is that you might be blowing this whole thing at work out of proportion, that's all . . .*
>
> **Jamaal:** *How can you ignore my feelings like that?!*

4. *Perceiving the relationship in an unfavorable light.* Do these processes foretell the future of a relationship? To find out, Murray and her colleagues (2003) used data from a 21-day diary study—in which spouses reported on self-esteem, perceived regard, perceptions of rejection, felt acceptance, and relationship behaviors—to predict changes in relationship satisfaction over a 12-month period. They found that the *partners* of people who were especially sensitive to rejection became less happy with the relationship as time passed, thus highlighting the interpersonal costs of the heightened sensitivities of the mate with low self-esteem. Recent studies corroborate this finding and suggest that being in a relationship with an insecure partner is challenging because so much effort must be invested in protecting that person's feelings (Lemay & Dudley, 2011).

While Jamaal thought he and Katya might work things out if her work schedule settled down, he came across as distant and cool with her. Just as the lease on their apartment was about to end, Katya told Jamaal that things were not going the way she hoped they would, and that she thought now would be a good time to make a clean break of it. Though not unexpected, Katya's departure came as a huge blow to Jamaal, and after Katya

BOX 6.1 SPOTLIGHT ON . . .

Relationships Influencing Personality

As people develop through adolescence and into early adulthood, negative affectivity tends to decline and they become more conscientious (e.g., Robins, Fraley, Roberts, & Trzesniewski, 2001). Are these changes a consequence of some intrinsic and perhaps genetic process by which individuals mature, as some have argued (e.g., Costa & McCrae, 1994)? Or, are the changes possibly a result of relationships during this period, as others contend (e.g., Caspi & Roberts, 1999)? In a large 4-year longitudinal study of 489 young adults in Germany, Neyer and Asendorpf (2001) showed that personality changes are more dramatic for people who enter a new intimate relationship in this period than for those who do not form one (also see Aspendorpf & Wilpers, 1998). People who began a relationship increased in self-reported conscientiousness, extraversion, and self-esteem; neuroticism and shyness decreased. Thus, personalities seem to be responsive to interpersonal experiences. On balance, however, the effects on personality of participating in a relationship are weaker than the effects of personality traits on a relationship.

Beyond the effects of mere participation, do relationships involve particular experiences that can push personality in one direction or another? The answer appears to be yes, and the results are strongest for negative affectivity. Relationships at age 21 that are marked by relatively low levels of satisfaction, high levels of disagreement, and more physical abuse tend to increase feelings of hostility, anxiety, irritability, and alienation—all facets of negative affectivity—over the next several years (Robins, Caspi, & Moffitt, 2002). These effects, particularly those involving disagreements, are evident when individuals remain in the same relationship over this time span, as well as when they form a relationship with a new partner.

Finally, if in reading the story of Jamaal and Katya you predicted that Jamaal's self-esteem would decrease over the course of the relationship, you are correct. An interesting corollary of the dependency regulation model is that, as a result of underestimating the positive regard and admiration their partners hold for them, individuals low in self-esteem actually come to incorporate this misperception into the image they hold of themselves. Insecure people start to view themselves in the way they assumed (mistakenly) the partner viewed them. In contrast, confident people probably build relationships that affirm their basic sense of self-worth, further bolstering their self-image. Evidence collected over a 12-month period supports this claim (Murray et al., 2000), thus indicating that relationships and individuals alike pay a price when partners defensively misperceive each other's positive sentiments.

---

politely dismissed his pleas to continue the relationship, Jamaal felt more down and depressed than usual. He reluctantly renewed the lease on the apartment, started working extra hours, and advertised for a new roommate. Katya's impressions of Jamaal finally matched the impressions Jamaal had of himself, and they went their separate ways.

Whereas Terman drew attention to "predispositions to unhappiness," and Kelly and Conley demonstrated that neuroticism foretells later relationship problems, the dependency regulation model specifies key psychological pathways by which such a predisposition brings about relationship discord and discontent (FIGURE 6.5). This line of work leaves important questions unanswered. How is it that many individuals with low self-esteem can have good relationships? Why do confident people sometimes have poor relationships? Still, the dependency regulation model provides convincing evidence that enduring traits capture reliable information about the quality and course of intimate relationships and the emotions partners experience within them. In the case study we presented, what do you think happens to Jamaal's self-esteem over the course of his relationship with Katya? The accompanying BOX 6.1 helps address this question.

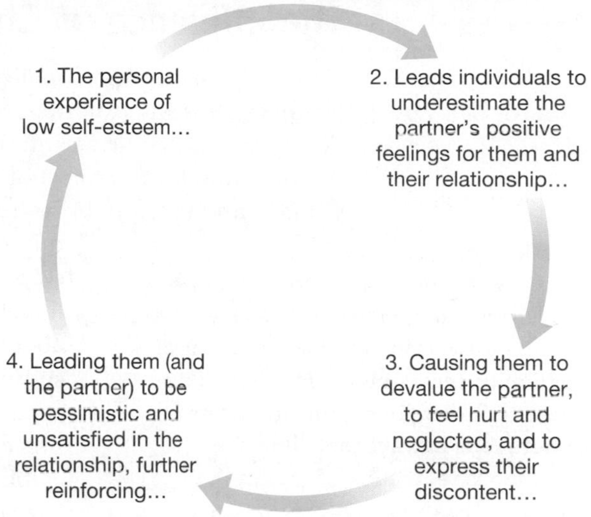

>> Personality refers to an individual's enduring and distinctive qualities.

>> Relationship scientists are interested in partners' personalities because they are presumed to influence how they adapt to each other and to the circumstances they encounter.

1. The personal experience of low self-esteem...

2. Leads individuals to underestimate the partner's positive feelings for them and their relationship...

3. Causing them to devalue the partner, to feel hurt and neglected, and to express their discontent...

4. Leading them (and the partner) to be pessimistic and unsatisfied in the relationship, further reinforcing...

FIGURE 6.5 **The dependency regulation model.** An enduring personality characteristic, low self-esteem, can affect how partners perceive and communicate with one another.

>> One approach to studying personality focuses on a few discrete personality traits that all people possess to some degree.

>> The traits that appear to matter most in relationships reflect how individuals regulate or manage different emotions. These traits include negative affectivity (or neuroticism), agreeableness, and conscientiousness.

>> The dependency regulation model states that one particular facet of negative affectivity—low self-esteem—is particularly corrosive in relationships. According to this view, people with low self-esteem underestimate the positive feelings their partner has about them and the relationship. Doing so leads the insecure person to inadvertently devalue the partner and the relationship, leading to hurt feelings and tension.

The Influence of Childhood Family Experiences

Although partners' personality traits provide powerful information about the intimacy they will experience and share, this is not the only place to look for evidence that enduring interpersonal differences can affect the course of a relationship. Indeed, most of us recognize implicitly that who we are as individuals, and presumably as relationship partners, derives from how we were raised and nurtured. To what degree are the relationships we form in adulthood related to our early family relationships? How might such associations come about? In this section we tackle these questions, by summarizing what scholars have learned about how each new generation in a family partially resembles preceding generations.

" We look to the family as the context for negotiating the problems of continuity and change, of individuality and integration, between and within generations in ways that allow the continuous recreation of society."

—Bengston, Biblarz, & Roberts (2002, p. 168)

Maybe you have had this experience. You are dating someone, generally having a great time getting to know your partner, while also trying to figure out what kind of person he is and whether the two of you have any kind of long-term future together. Your relationship develops to the point where you meet his family, and after just a few minutes with them, many things become clear: Your partner has a goofy sense of humor because his father has a goofy sense of humor! Your partner likes to hug you in public because his parents can't keep their hands off each other! Your partner is a lovable nerd because he spent the last 12 years playing Trivial Pursuit every Friday night with his family! Apart from whether you want these people to be your in-laws, you now have some new insights about who your partner is and how he came to be that way.

Social scientists call the family you were raised in the **family of origin**. The effects your family of origin has on who you are as a person, as well as on who you are as a relationship partner later in life, are referred to as **intergenerational transmission effects**. These effects turn out to be quite reliable in the scientific literature, and we can learn a great deal about partners in intimate relationships by studying the families in which the two people were raised.

The Impact of Conflict and Divorce on Relationships

Of all the changes occurring in families in developed countries over the past century, few have attracted as much attention as the rise in divorce, and for good reason. Although the divorce rate has held steady since the early 1980s, about half of all first marriages—and an even higher proportion of remarriages—end in divorce or permanent separation (Bramlett & Mosher, 2002). Not all divorces involve children, of course, yet it is staggering to consider that more than 1 million children experience the divorce of their parents every year in the United States, and that approximately 40 percent of all children will experience the divorce of their parents before becoming adults (Bumpass, 1990; U.S. Bureau of the Census, 1998). Thus, when considering factors in the family that influence the development of individuals in general and as eventual relationship partners, divorce and the conflicts surrounding it must take center stage.

The experience of divorce varies markedly for different people and families. However, five key conclusions have emerged from research into the ways parental conflict and divorce affect individuals as they develop through childhood to adolescence and into adulthood.

First, the adverse effects of marital discord and divorce on children are evident in a range of domains, including academic achievement, conduct and behavior, psychological adjustment, self-esteem, and social relationships (Amato & Keith, 1991).

Second, the magnitude of these effects can be interpreted in different ways. On one hand, studies show that parental divorce approximately *doubles the risk* of adverse consequences for the offspring (e.g., McLanahan & Sandefur, 1994; Simons, 1996). This sounds ominous, especially to those people whose parents divorced, but it does not mean that divorce guarantees unhappiness in children. On the contrary, although about 20–30 percent of children from divorced families experience adverse outcomes, about 10–15 percent of children from *intact* marriages do so, as well. This means that children from these two groups are far more alike than different, and that most children—regardless of their family background—can be found in the normal or healthy range of functioning (Hetherington & Kelly, 2002).

> " I couldn't remember a time when I had been content. I still can't. And compared to my divorce-free peers, I have needed more time and space to grow. I had more work to do: I had to overcome the past and create a path for myself. For the most part, my friends with divorced parents had contended with their situations. But I couldn't get over it because for years and years there seemed to be no real end, no closure."
>
> —Priluck, *Split: Stories from a Generation Raised on Divorce* (2002, p. 64)

Third, children are affected by conflict and divorce because the dissolution of a marriage jeopardizes the family's economic circumstances and parental mental health, reduces the amount and quality of the child's contact with one parent (typically the father), and makes the family vulnerable to new kinds of stresses. For example, raising a family in two households is more expensive than doing so in one home, and situations that were managed doing so easily before divorce—family get-togethers, or one parent moving on to a better job in a new location—can be a source of conflict after the parents have separated. Despite the best intentions, the quality of parenting often suffers following a divorce, and family instability increases the chances that a child will not receive the monitoring, emotional support, and discipline he or she needs (Hetherington & Clingempeel, 1992; Simons, 1996). Ongoing conflict between parents and additional family transitions—moving to a new home or school, for example, or adjusting to a stepmother or stepfather—can undermine the child's adjustment following divorce (e.g., Buchanan, Maccoby,

& Dornbush, 1996). These adverse effects are offset when children employ active coping skills, avoid blaming themselves for the divorce, and develop supportive relationships with parents, peers, and other family members (see Amato, 2000, and Emery, 1999, for reviews).

Fourth, it is important to recognize that children can have difficulties in the absence of divorce, and that high levels of conflict between parents are often correlated with these effects (Cummings & Davies, 1994; Grych & Fincham, 2001). For example, in families where parents eventually separate or divorce, children show behavior problems—being verbally hostile, or becoming sad and withdrawn—long before the breakup actually occurs (Cherlin et al., 1991). The same appears to be true even if separation or divorce never takes place. Looking over a longer time span in continuously intact marriages, for example, sociologists Paul Amato and Alan Booth (1997) showed that children exposed to higher levels of parental conflict in adolescence had lower self-esteem, happiness, and life satisfaction in early adulthood compared to children exposed to low levels of parental conflict. Can you see how this connects with our earlier discussion of self-esteem?

Fifth, following on this last point, the well-being of adult offspring depends on a complex combination of whether the parents divorced and what the marriage was like before the divorce (e.g., Amato, Loomis, & Booth, 1995; Jekielek, 1998). **FIGURE 6.6** graphs the psychological well-being of nearly 700

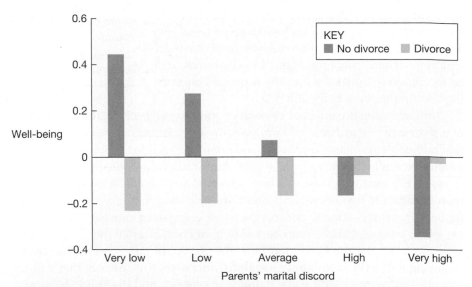

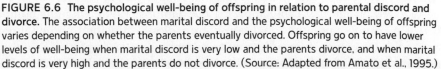

FIGURE 6.6 The psychological well-being of offspring in relation to parental discord and divorce. The association between marital discord and the psychological well-being of offspring varies depending on whether the parents eventually divorced. Offspring go on to have lower levels of well-being when marital discord is very low and the parents divorce, and when marital discord is very high and the parents do not divorce. (Source: Adapted from Amato et al., 1995.)

27-year-old adults in 1997, in relation to whether their parents had divorced at some point between 1980 and 1997 and how much conflict and turbulence there was in the marriage between 1980 and 1997. As you can see, the well-being of adults is lowest when marriages very low in discord end in divorce *and* when marriages very high in discord do not end in divorce (Amato et al., 1995). Not surprisingly, children are better off when a highly conflicted marriage is terminated. But you may be surprised at the harmful consequences of dissolving marriages that don't have much conflict. Why might this be? One possibility is that unexpected divorces strike children particularly hard in the short term and undercut their capacity to develop trusting relationships over the long term. If dissolving low-conflict marriages and maintaining high-conflict marriages can both be detrimental to the well-being of offspring, what does this tell us? What are the implications for clinical interventions and designing constructive social policies? Certainly these findings suggest that preventing divorce is at best an incomplete strategy for improving children's well-being, and that promoting nurturing, low-conflict, two-parent families is a better way to reach this goal. (We will have more to say about conflict and aggression in Chapter 8.)

Children of Divorce

We have seen that individuals raised in different family environments differ across a range of domains. Parental marital discord and dissolution appear to contribute to these differences to a small but discernible degree, and the differences are evident in childhood and adulthood. These are important conclusions because they show that a complete understanding of intimate relationships begins not when two people meet, but when their parents meet and create a new family. As we outline below, early family experiences affect a wide range of phenomena that will bear upon the formation and development of intimate relationships later in life.

Children of divorce excercise more caution toward marriage and are more accepting of divorce. Some studies show that children of divorce marry earlier than others, perhaps reflecting their desire to leave difficult family situations (e.g., McLeod, 1991). Other studies demonstrate that children of divorce are more likely to live together without marrying, and to delay getting married, suggesting they are just as motivated to form partnerships as children from intact families but are more pessimistic about marriage as the means of accomplishing this goal (Tasker & Richards, 1994). Further evidence for parental divorce reducing commitment to marriage comes from studies showing that unhappily married offspring with divorced parents are more likely to contemplate divorce as an option than are equally unhappy offspring from intact family backgrounds (Amato & DeBoer, 2001). Differences between individuals from differing family backgrounds seem to be magnified "when the going gets tough" in their own relationships. How much they get magnified is a matter of debate, as BOX 6.2 illustrates.

BOX 6.2 SPOTLIGHT ON . . .

Science and the Politics of Divorce

The state of the American family can be a contentious political issue, and debates over the effects of divorce crystallize divergent views on whether the family is deteriorating or merely evolving as a social institution. Those on the conservative end of the political spectrum tend to view divorce and other shifts away from two-parent families as undermining the foundations of society, whereas those on the liberal end of the spectrum tend to be more accepting of divorce and the emergence of diverse family forms. What does science have to contribute to this debate? Consider the conclusions drawn from the following two long-term studies of divorce.

In 2000, clinical practitioners Judith S. Wallerstein, Julia M. Lewis, and Sandra Blakeslee published *The Unexpected Legacy of Divorce: A 25 Year Landmark Study*. In this book, they wrote:

> At each developmental stage divorce is experienced anew in different ways. In adulthood it affects personality, the ability to trust, expectations about relationships, and ability to cope with change. . . . The impact of divorce hits them most cruelly as they go in search of love, sexual intimacy, and commitment. Their lack of inner images of a man and a woman in a stable relationship . . . badly hobbles their search, leading them to heartbreak and even despair. . . . Their fear of abandonment, betrayal, and rejection mounted when they found themselves having to disagree with someone they loved. . . . All had trouble dealing with differences or even moderate conflict in their close relationships. (p. 298)

In 2002, developmental psychologist Mavis Hetherington and writer John Kelly published *For Better or for Worse: Divorce Reconsidered*. In this book, they wrote:

> The adverse effects of divorce and remarriage are still echoing in some divorced families and their offspring twenty years after divorce, but they are in the minority. The vast majority of young people from these families are reasonably well adjusted and coping reasonably well in relationships with their families, friends, and intimate partners. . . . Most parents and children see the divorce

as having been for the best, and have moved forward with their lives. (p. 252)

How could experts disagree so profoundly about whether divorce has lasting effects on children? How could one analysis sound a grim warning about the lasting effects of divorce, while the other depicts divorce as a serious but manageable crisis that most families resolve and put behind them? One answer can be found in the methodological differences of the two studies. Wallerstein emphasized intensive interviews, conducted at several points with a small, nonrandom sample of families undergoing divorce; she did not use a control group of intact families studied over the same interval. Hetherington used standardized questionnaires and direct observation with large samples of families, including those who were divorced, intact, and remarried.

The differing methods tilt this comparison decidedly in favor of the Hetherington study, particularly because it shows that some children from intact marriages, generally overlooked in the Wallerstein study, can encounter difficulties much like those of children from divorced families. However, we cannot dismiss the Wallerstein study. It provides a rich portrait of individuals as they struggle to form relationships in adulthood, and in several respects it corroborates key findings from the larger literature on divorce (see Amato, 2003).

Are divorce and the attendant rise in single-parent families the source of many social ills? Or are these transitions desirable, and even beneficial, because they remove children from adverse living arrangements and give adults new opportunities for contentment and individual freedom? The answer lies somewhere in between. Sociologist Paul Amato (2000) summarizes the literature in the following way:

> Both of these views represent one-sided accentuations of reality. The increase in marital instability has not brought society to the brink of chaos, but neither has it led to a golden age of freedom and self-actualization. Divorce benefits some individuals, leads others to experience temporary decrements in well-being that improve over time, and forces others on a downward cycle from which they never fully recover. (p. 1282)

Children of divorce have less money and weaker social networks as they enter and negotiate adulthood. Because offspring from divorced family backgrounds are more likely to drop out of high school and are less likely to attend college, they enter adulthood with fewer socioeconomic resources (e.g., McLanahan & Sandefur, 1994). Children exposed to divorce and marital distress also tend to have less fulfilling and supportive relationships with their parents, even later in life, and father-child relationships are particularly fragile following family dissolutions (e.g., Zill, Morrison, & Coiro, 1993). As you might expect, having fewer economic and social resources can put relationships at a disadvantage, particularly when couples undergo important transitions, such as the arrival of a child or the diagnosis of chronic health problems (see Chapter 11).

Children of divorce experience more relationship distress and dissolution. As children mature through adolescence and into adulthood, the experiences they have in their relationships can be linked to what happened in their parents' relationship. For example, children whose parents were unhappy in marriage are likely themselves to go on to form relatively unhappy marriages (e.g., Feng, Giarusso, Bengston, & Frye, 1999). This tendency appears to be true regardless of parents' education, income, religious views, and whether they subsequently divorced (Amato & Booth, 2001). And compared to children from intact family backgrounds, children exposed to parental divorce are more likely to divorce as adults (e.g., Glenn & Kramer, 1987). So potent are these effects that divorce in one generation has been shown to reverberate through the next generation and into the intimate relationships of grandchildren some 40 years later (Amato & Cheadle, 2005).

How can we make sense of these connections between our parents' relationships and the way we negotiate relationships as we enter adulthood ourselves? The most compelling explanation holds that children learn about relationships from seeing how family members relate to one another, so the interpersonal styles they learn while growing up carry forward into adulthood to affect later intimate relationships. Following the principles of social learning theory (see Chapter 3), we can assume that, by observing and interacting with their parents and family members, children acquire emotional and behavioral models that then generalize to relationships outside the family (e.g., Furman & Flanagan, 1997; O'Leary, 1988). For example, when observed in the laboratory discussing relationship difficulties with their spouse, individuals with a history of parental divorce are more likely to disagree, express disrespect and disdain for their partner, and withdraw in unproductive ways from the conversation (e.g., Sanders, Halford, & Behrens, 1999) (FIGURE 6.7). In short, social learning theory encourages us to think of families as a kind of training ground for the next generation of intimate relationships. Who we are as intimate partners is shaped by the ways our parents managed their emotions and conversations while we were growing up. And the effects of these experiences are apparent, even to outside observers, in the conversations we hold now with our intimate partners.

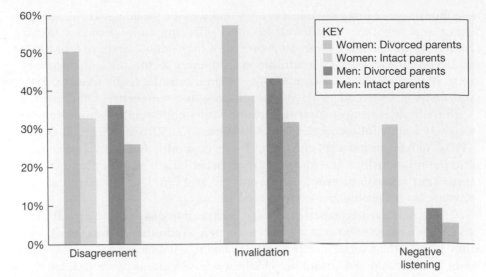

FIGURE 6.7 Parental divorce and couple communication. Compared to engaged women and men with intact family backgrounds, women and men with divorced parents express more disagreement and invalidation toward their partner when discussing problems in the relationship. When their partner is speaking, women and men with divorced parents show more negative facial expressions and gestures as listeners. The percentages represent the speaking intervals in which the specified behavior occurred. (Source: Adapted from Sanders, Halford, & Behrens, 1999.)

MAIN POINTS

>> Close, intimate bonds are fundamentally important to the welfare of individuals and to their children. The weakening of those bonds affects the development of children and their subsequent relationships, continuing into adulthood.

>> Understanding how people manage their interpersonal lives in adulthood requires information about the family relationships they were exposed to when growing up.

>> The family of origin perspective highlights how people are molded by various family structures (e.g., parental divorce, parental remarriage) and family processes (e.g., parental conflict, the quality of parent-child relationships following divorce).

>> Stable, warm family relationships promote healthy interpersonal relationships later in life, compared to unstable, harsh family relationships. At the same time, these effects are small and varied; many of the people who grow up with conflicted or divorced parents experience few lasting scars.

Early Experiences with Caregivers

While staying with the theme of what makes individuals different as relationship partners, we continue to pursue the idea that the family is a crucial source for establishing those early differences. Now we focus on caregivers and the very first relationships developing children experience.

The scene is familiar: Your partner will be flying off for a few days to be with friends and family while you stay home to finish up some important work. The two of you have arrived at the airport, your partner has checked in, and you approach the gate beyond which only passengers are allowed. You whisper your feelings to one another, kiss, snuggle a little, kiss again, start to walk away, then return for one last hug, and then watch and wave as your partner goes through the gate. As you leave, you notice several others doing the same thing—sharing tender thoughts, caressing, staying together until the last possible minute, promising to reconnect as soon as possible.

> **"** If monkeys have taught us anything, it's that you've got to learn how to love before you learn how to live."
>
> —Harry Harlow, Psychologist (1961)

Where most people might see nothing more than the parting exchanges of family members and intimate partners, proponents of **attachment theory** see something different (e.g., Fraley & Shaver, 1998). To them, these behavioral exchanges are outward indications that an **attachment behavior system** is at work, an innate, biologically based system shaped by evolution to help ensure our safety and survival. As you learned in Chapter 3, this system governs our capacity to form emotional bonds with others, motivates us to stay near our attachment figures, and impels us to restore our connection with attachment figures when the relationship is threatened or temporarily disrupted, or when we personally feel threatened, anxious, ill, or otherwise distressed. Restoring the connection reduces anxiety and allows us to feel calm, soothed, and supported. This is exactly what your behavior in the airport is designed to achieve, if only temporarily, as you manage the stress of separating from your partner.

According to this view, evidence of the attachment behavior system is all around us: in day-care centers, when parents drop off and pick up their infants; in cemeteries, where families and friends mourn the deceased; in hospitals, where patients long to be close to children and partners; and in times of great calamity, as in the chaotic aftermath of the 9/11 tragedy, when partners and family members posted hundreds of pictures and notes in the desperate hope of locating lost loved ones (**FIGURE 6.8**).

Surprisingly, the motivating nature of love and affection was not always recognized, nor were these emotions viewed as being beneficial to children's development. In the first half of the 20th century, behaviorism reigned supreme in the early days of academic psychology. Dispassionate objectivity and principles of learning were held up as the surest avenues to understanding and modifying human behavior. Human emotions were viewed as problems

FIGURE 6.8 Attachment behavior systems at work. After 9/11, families and friends created a makeshift memorial at the World Trade Center in the hopes of locating lost loved ones.

to be controlled, and the proper way to raise children was to shape their behavior by judiciously selecting rewards and punishments. Nurturing children, it was thought, only made them spoiled, needy, and dependent. Psychologist John Watson (1878–1958), father of behaviorism and an early president of the American Psychological Association, was particularly keen on separating children from their parents and then raising them without genuine affection but according to "scientific" principles (see Blum, 2002).

Pioneering studies by astute clinical observers and dedicated scientists—most notably Harry Harlow, an American psychologist and a graduate student of Lewis Terman in the 1920s; John Bowlby, a British psychiatrist; and Mary Salter Ainsworth, a developmental psychologist working in Canada—eventually overturned this view. Collectively, their work drew attention to the profound importance of caregiver-child attachments and to the enduring effects of these bonds on how individuals viewed themselves and others over the course of their lives. Attachment theory provides another perspective on why people differ as partners and how these differences come to affect their intimate relationships.

Recall from our discussion of attachment theory in Chapter 3 that the quality of the caregiver-child bond contributes to the developing child's internal working model of attachment. Because each caregiver-child relationship is unique, each person's working model—or style—is also unique. These early relationships and the working models they generate become our personality and the foundation of who we are. Attachment theory maintains that individual differences arise from early connections, and it goes further by stating that the working models of attachment develop along two dimensions—reflecting our impressions of ourselves and of others.

When caregivers are consistent and available to meet our needs, we develop a confident, positive sense of who we are. When caregivers are inconsistent and unavailable, we feel anxious, insecure, inadequate, and unworthy of others' care and attention. This becomes encoded as a *self-relevant dimension of anxiety* in our internal working model. Our working model contains representations of others as well. When we aim to restore proximity to a caregiver and are met with love and comfort, we come to believe that others are trustworthy and we are valued; punishment and rejection, on the other hand, lead us to conclude that others are unreliable and are best avoided. This becomes encoded as an *other-relevant dimension of avoidance* in our internal working model. People who are low in anxiety and avoidance are considered to be securely attached, whereas people who represent themselves as low in self-worth and others as unapproachable or not trustworthy are considered to be insecurely attached.

Suppose your partner doesn't respond when you want to cuddle. Why might this be? Or what if your partner doesn't say nice, supportive things to you when you're feeling down. How do you make sense of this? There are many ways to interpret the same event, and these various interpretations can take our conversations down different emotional pathways (as you will see in Chapter 10). Like politicians, relationship partners can "spin" a given event in a way that benefits the relationship: "She did not comfort me because she knew I could handle the situation myself; she really is considerate and has faith in me"—or damages it: "She did not comfort me because she still holds a grudge about that time I refused to help her with the chem lab assignment; she's trying to get back at me." A direct implication of Bowlby's notion of internal working models is that they affect how we view interpersonal events like these (Bowlby, 1980).

Interpretations made by individuals with secure attachment styles will tend to minimize the impact of negative events, and interpretations made by insecure individuals will magnify the impact of these same events. Research supports this point (e.g., Collins, 1996) and confirms the more specific prediction that those with the most negative models of themselves and others—that is, fearful individuals—typically offer the most pessimistic interpretations for relationship events. People who typically keep tighter control over their emotions as a means of denying the importance of intimacy—that is, those higher in avoidance—do in fact express less emotion in response to relationship events, and they report being less aware of their physiological cues of anger, such as heart rate or muscular tension (Mikulincer, 1998).

Corroboration of attachment theory requires evidence that individuals with different attachment styles behave differently in their intimate relationships, and a host of studies show just this. For example, children rated as having secure attachment in infancy go on to have more secure friendships at age 16; by the time they reach their mid-20s, they say they experience more positive emotion in their relationships and display less negative emotion when communicating with their partners (Simpson, Collins, Tran, & Haydon, 2007). Similarly, adults identified as being securely attached (based on a detailed interview) report a greater likelihood of talking openly with the partner after the partner has done something potentially destructive to the relationship, and a lesser likelihood of thinking about ending the relationship. Individuals identified as fearful show the opposite pattern, closing off contact and perhaps jumping to conclusions about the relationship's demise (Scharfe & Bartholomew, 1995).

"Can you spare a few seconds to minimize my problems?"

FIGURE 6.9 Insecure attachment and partner communication. This women's insecure attachment style causes her to use an ineffective strategy when seeking support from her partner.

Direct observation (e.g., Collins & Feeney, 2000) of newlywed couples discussing their relationships demonstrates that secure partners are more likely than insecure partners to signal their needs clearly, to expect that the partner will help address these needs, and to make good use of the partner's efforts to help (**FIGURE 6.9**). And, when on the receiving end of these signals, secure individuals are more likely than those who are less secure to show interest, express willingness to help, and display sensitivity to the partner's distress (Crowell et al., 2002; also see Kobak & Hazan, 1991; Paley, Cox, Burchinal, & Payne, 1999). Consider the signals being exchanged in the following conversation. How do they keep both partners engaged despite the distress Carol is experiencing?

Kim: *Hey, how was your day?*

Carol: *Not so great. How about you?*

Kim: *Good enough I guess, but what's up?*

Carol: *You know the story—lousy commute, Elaine needs the budget for that duplex project a week earlier than she said, and my assistant Josh is now telling me he might have to move to Peoria if his partner accepts a job there.*

Kim: *Yikes. Sounds rough—not the Peoria part, but the fact that all this is coming down at once on you. Where are you going to go with all this?*

Carol: *Well, Josh will at least be around to help with the budget—he has already committed to that—and I called Carter to let him know I may have to set aside the pro bono work I am doing. So I will survive; I just have a few long nights coming up. All I know is that I am exhausted.*

Kim: *I'm sure you will survive—you always do. Sorry to hear about the project with Carter—that sounded a lot more interesting than the duplex budget. Can you work from home tomorrow and avoid the commute?*

Carol: *You know, that's a good idea. I'll check with Elaine but I'm guessing she would probably rather have me working than stuck in traffic.*

Kim: *Great. Maybe we can order in some dinner then.*

Carol: *OK, whatever. All I know is that I am really beat.*

Now compare that exchange with this one, in which Carol is not quite so clear in expressing her needs—a tendency that characterizes individuals with insecure attachment styles. Notice how Kim has difficulty finding opportunities to offer any kind of support, despite her best intentions:

Kim: *Hey, how was your day?*

Carol: *You know, same old same old.*

Kim: *You look a little beat.*

Carol: *I am, but I'm not sure your saying that is going to make me feel any better.*

Kim: *Yeah, sorry. So anything interesting happen today?*

Carol: *Interesting? Yeah, my commute sucked, my boss is giving me grief about a duplex project, I had to tell Carter I have to delay a pro bono project I want to do, and Josh is probably moving to Peoria. Other than that it was a great day. And frankly I am not sure there is much anybody can do about it.*

Kim: *You mean about Josh?*

Carol: *No, about this crappy job and this damn commute.*

Kim: *Yeah, I hear you. Is there anything I can do to help?*

Carol: *Not unless you know how to do an Excel spreadsheet with about a zillion macros.*

Kim: *Sorry, I wish I did but I can't help you there. But let me know if there is something I can do to help.*

We can see from such examples that attachment theory does more than help articulate differences in internal working models. It also provides important clues about the specific kinds of communicative behaviors likely to promote and discourage successful relationships.

Differences in attachment styles also appear to be magnified in times of stress. Recall that the attachment behavior system is not always operating; it is activated when a person is challenged or when access to the caregiver is threatened. Attachment theory predicts that in times like these, individuals will naturally signal the need for comfort and strive to maintain or restore felt security with the attachment figure. But remember, too, that differences in attachment should lead secure and insecure people to fulfill their needs in different ways. For example, secure individuals will appraise the situation confidently and cope well, either by mobilizing others' support or by resolving the difficulty themselves. Those prone to anxiety will compensate for their lack of self-confidence by overusing the support available to them and perhaps not feeling satisfied with that support. And individuals prone to avoidance will adopt a defensive position, denying the need for support and using distancing strategies to cope with their distress.

To test these ideas, social psychologist Jeffry Simpson and his colleagues assessed the attachment styles of both partners in 83 dating relationships among different-sex couples. Each woman was told: "You are going to be exposed to a situation and set of experimental procedures that arouse considerable anxiety and distress in most people" (Simpson et al. 1992, p. 437). The researchers showed her a small, dark, equipment-filled room that looked like an isolation chamber. She was then escorted to a waiting room where her partner was seated, and their interaction was videotaped with a hidden camera for 5 minutes. The couple was then told that due to an equipment malfunction, the study could not proceed. All the couples involved were told about the true purpose of the study, and all granted permission for their videotapes to be used for the research.

Detailed coding of these videotapes showed that secure and avoidant women differed rather dramatically in their behavior. As secure women became more fearful of the experience, they generally turned to their partners for comfort and reassurance. Avoidant women, however, did not necessarily turn to the partner for comfort and reassurance as their anxiety and fear increased, and they were less likely than secure women to even mention the impending stressful event to their partner. (Results were mixed for anxious women.) **FIGURE 6.10** shows this finding.

The men's behavior was also associated with their attachment styles. Secure men gave more support and reassurance to the partner the more her

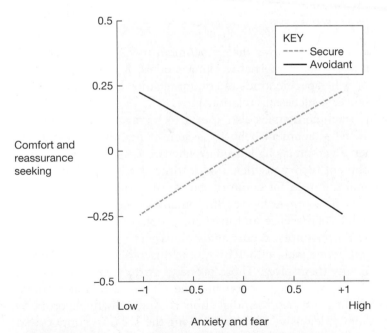

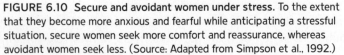

FIGURE 6.10 Secure and avoidant women under stress. To the extent that they become more anxious and fearful while anticipating a stressful situation, secure women seek more comfort and reassurance, whereas avoidant women seek less. (Source: Adapted from Simpson et al., 1992.)

anxiety and fear increased, while support and reassurance offered by avoidant men dropped off as the partner displayed more distress. In other words, when confronted with exactly the same stressful situation, secure individuals reach out to their partner when needing or providing support, whereas avoidant individuals retreat—presumably because they have learned through earlier experiences with caregivers that little comfort is to be gained from others who are close to them.

MAIN POINTS

>> Attachment theory assigns primary significance to the bond between caregiver and infant, and to the internal psychological structures—the working models—that arise from this bond.

>> Attachment theory provides a framework for understanding the forces that motivate us to seek closeness with others and that differentiate us from others in our orientation toward intimacy.

>> Devised initially to understand how children develop and navigate their social world, attachment theory has been extended to explain similar phenomena in adult intimate relationships.

>> The attachment perspective teaches us that the degree of warmth and sensitivity a caregiver shows to a distressed infant results in internal working models that persist into adulthood, thereby affecting the diverse ways people face the challenges and dilemmas of intimate relationships.

>> Whereas the family of origin perspective emphasizes how our individuality stems from, and probably perpetuates, a particular family lineage, the attachment perspective reminds us that we are, in fact, participating in an even more fundamental and primitive process.

CONCLUSION –

When this chapter began, Jesse and Celine were trying to come to terms with their personal identities and with the unhappiness they experienced in their relationships with other people. Hearing their stories led us to ask questions about whether *who we are* dictates *how happy our relationships will be*. Naturally, we wonder whether the relationships we create with others are like chemical reactions, yielding products with special and surprising qualities that are unpredictable from the personalities of the two people involved. But another possibility is that those personalities—the characteristics and experiences that define us and make us who we are—will continue to affect our choices and behaviors in reasonably predictable ways, with various relationship partners.

Analysis from three perspectives indicates that the latter possibility is more plausible. Whether defining individual differences primarily in terms of personality traits (like negative affectivity), or in terms of the effects of our parents' relationships on how we approach our own, or with regard to the working models of attachment that arise from exchanges with our caregivers in childhood, the message is consistent. Personality traits, and life experiences, especially early relationships with others, affect our intimate relationships in diverse ways. In addition, the personality differences that matter tap how we experience, express, and manage emotion, including the emotion we direct toward ourself (as in self-esteem), the emotional styles we learned from seeing our parents' conversations, or the emotional consequences of being raised by a responsive caregiver. Any confusion Jesse and Celine are confronting about their lives, then, is likely to have its resolution in how they contend with emotion and how they respond to the emotional needs of their partners.

While it is clear that who we are as individuals shapes the intimate relationships we go on to form, our relationships are not determined solely by our personality traits or prior experiences. Our feelings and behavior in relationships are not a perfect reflection of our personalities, if only because two people can adjust to each other, and even create entirely new experiences that affect how they feel about themselves and others. A person, for instance, who initially fears conflict because of chronic hostility between his parents can be soothed and reassured by a loving partner.

Having completed our analysis of the ways individuals matter in intimate relationships, we now delve more deeply into the actual interaction processes that connect two partners. Foremost among these are the strategies partners use to nurture their relationship and communicate closeness, which we examine next.

7

Communicating Closeness

A Soldier's Last Letter to His Wife

Reading letters exchanged between soldiers and their partners during wartime gives us a glimpse at the intimate bonds these couples have formed and the forces that maintain them. The following letter (from collections by Carroll, 2001, 2005) is from the Cold War period between the end of the Korean War and the beginning of the Vietnam War. Commander Jack Sweeney was a pilot flying reconnaissance missions from Hamilton Air Force Base in Bermuda. He wrote this letter in November 1956 to his wife Beebe, who was pregnant with their fifth child at the time:

To the best wife a man ever had:

Honey, I am writing this letter to you to say a few things that I might leave unsaid if I should depart this world unexpected-like. In this flying business you can never tell when you might all of a sudden get mighty unlucky and wake up dead some morning.

Even if I should die the day after writing this, I still claim I am one of the luckiest people who ever lived, and you know it. I've got a lot to live for, as I write this, but when I count up all

the blessings I've had, I can see that I have already lived a lot. When you come right down to it, I've done just about everything I've wanted to do and seen about everything I've wanted to see. Sure, I'd like to stick around while the boys are growing up, and to have fun with you again when we have time after they grow up. But you and I agree so closely on how to raise a family, the boys are going to be all right; I'm sure of that. And I've had enough fun with you to last anybody a lifetime.

Don't let the memories of me keep you from marrying again, if you run across somebody fit to be your husband, which would be hard to find, I know. But you're much too wonderful a

237

wife and mother to waste yourself as a widow. Life is for the living. (That's not original, I'm sure.)

So get that smile back on your face, put on some lipstick and a new dress, and show me what you can do toward building a new life. Just remember me once in a while—not too often, or it'll cramp your style, you know—and as long as I'm remembered, I'm not really dead. I'll still be living in John, and Bill, and Al, and Dan, bless their hearts. That's what they mean by eternity, I think.

> *My love as always,*
> *Jack*

This is the last letter Jack Sweeney wrote to his wife; he was killed with his crew a few days later when his airplane went down in the Atlantic Ocean.

QUESTIONS

The human virtues depicted so vividly in Jack Sweeney's letter—love, dedication, humor, trust, commitment, concern, kindness, compassion—reveal the powerful connections that intimate partners can forge and the qualities of relationships we often aspire to. For the science of human intimacy, these letters prompt important questions about how these virtues develop and endure in successful relationships. What are the forces that bind people together in intimate relationships and inspire feelings of gratitude and affection, as evidenced by Sweeney's comment, "Even if I should die the day after writing this, I still claim I am one of the luckiest people who ever lived, and you know it. . . . I've had enough fun with you to last anybody a lifetime"? What experiences might happen in a relationship that would lead Sweeney to selflessly encourage his wife to find a new partner if he dies? These expressions could simply be a characteristic of who Jack Sweeney is as a person; perhaps he would share these feelings with anyone he might have married.

But there seems to be something more here—something special about the relationship between Jack and Beebe that has evoked these feelings and moved him to write this letter.

In Chapter 6 we examined the characteristics *within* individuals that can either hinder or promote the development of an intimate relationship. In this chapter, we focus more intently on the couple; we ask how intimacy *between* two people develops, deepens, and is maintained throughout the life of the relationship (**FIGURE 7.1**). How do the strong feelings that bring two people together evolve and change to keep the relationship strong?

FIGURE 7.1 A sailor and his girl. Soldiers and their partners are forced to develop and maintain intimate bonds during the stress and struggle of wartime.

How Communication Promotes Intimacy

As two people grow increasingly attracted to one another, they are transformed from strangers with no romantic connection into interdependent partners in an intimate relationship. Early on, this transformation can be exhilarating as they express their mutual newfound love, deepen their bond through shared activities, become recognized as a couple by family and friends, and possibly ponder a future together. How does a relationship proceed and develop from this point forward? Although the partners have established an intimate relationship, they now face the task of maintaining it. **Relationship maintenance** refers to the routine behaviors and strategies partners undertake to help ensure that their relationship will continue (e.g., Ballard-Reisch & Wiegel, 1999; Dindia & Baxter, 1987; Haas & Stafford, 1998). These strategies need not be intentional, of course; you may not think that going out at 5 A.M. to buy coffee and fresh doughnuts for your partner is an act of relationship maintenance, though it may well serve this purpose—especially if your partner has a sweet tooth or a long commute. Intentional or otherwise, relationship maintenance involves taking steps that will keep a good relationship strong, avert declines in a relationship, or repair a struggling relationship.

How do couples maintain their relationship? One essential starting point for answering this question focuses on the revelations, personal expressions, and disclosures partners make to one another. Sometimes this involves one partner revealing something about herself or himself that the other person did not know: *I am adopted. When I was 15, I got caught shoplifting. My dad has a drinking problem. My first boyfriend cheated on me with my best friend.* As a relationship matures and fewer of these details remain to be shared, more expressions and disclosures focus on daily life and future plans: *Your mom really irritated me at the picnic on Saturday. I would rather stay home with the baby than go back to work. I passed the bar exam!*

Regardless of what form they take, these expressions and disclosures provide a valuable window into how relationships deepen and how they are maintained. This is because intimate relationships, as you know from the definition in Chapter 1, are more than just personal relationships. They transcend superficial exchanges of information, and in doing so, the partners must reveal important aspects of who they are and how they are experiencing the world around them. What is it about these expressions and disclosures that makes them so informative? As the three examples in BOX 7.1 illustrate, the key resides not simply in what one person reveals but in how the partner responds.

Expressions and Disclosures: The Intimacy Process Model

Later in this chapter, we'll describe five common ways that partners communicate closeness and maintain their relationship. For now, we will outline the key elements underlying all these maintenance strategies, in a more

BOX 7.1 SPOTLIGHT ON . . .

Finding Keepers

Writers Linda Lee Small and Norine Dworkin (2003) documented dozens of experiences that led women to decide whether the person they were dating was, in their opinion, a "keeper" or a "loser." Here are some examples of what men did to become keepers:

The Final Good-bye. *When my sister passed away in 1978 I said good-bye to her at the funeral, sat shiva, went to the unveiling, and then never, ever returned to the cemetery to visit her grave. Over the years I would get very depressed and cry over the Fourth of July weekend, because that was the last weekend I spent with her before she died. When I met Sam, I told him all about my sister and how, although I had "officially" said good-bye at the cemetery, there was still some unfinished business in my heart. One of the first things he suggested after our first Fourth of July together was that we take a trip to the cemetery where Shelly was buried. At the cemetery I had a really good cry, introduced Sam to Shelly, and then finally said a proper good-bye to her. I knew he was a keeper on our first date, but his knowledge of my need to say farewell and close an open wound really sealed it for me.* —Laney, Omaha, Nebraska.

For as Long as You Need Me. *I had been dating Max for only about two months when my company sent me to Germany for a month. I didn't really want to go, and I felt very isolated because I didn't speak the language. By the time I arrived back home, I had really bad stomach pains. When I called the doctor, he said I probably had an ulcer, and he recommended I take some over-the-counter pills. The medicine didn't help, and when Max came over the next day he saw how much pain I was in. He found my address book and called my doctor, who said I needed to go to the emergency room. Max gathered up my purse and took me to the hospital. He listened to the emergency room doctor's directions because I wasn't able to pay attention. (It turned out I did have an ulcer.) Then Max took me home, went to the pharmacy, and filled the prescription. He stayed with me for the next two days. When I called my best friend, she said, "You went to the hospital and no one called me?" You see, my last boyfriend would always call her when I didn't feel good. He didn't do well with illness! The way Max took care of me made a huge impression.* —Janie, Los Angeles, California.

The Chosen One. *When I met my future husband, Len, I was dating other men, including a guy named Mark. In general, I felt that the guys I dated, although they had important jobs, became competitive when I talked about my own work experiences. I often deal with the most senior people in Fortune 500 companies and conduct off-site meetings in resorts around the world. Len, who I met when I worked as a consultant at his company, was quite different. A widower with two children, he had been married to a woman who helped him develop his sensitivity to women. He called me every night after his children went to bed and asked how my day was. In contrast, Mark called on Wednesdays to plan for Saturday night dates. On Saturdays we "reported" how our weeks went. With Len, it was "in the moment," with all the emotions and details. As I slowly shared my stories with him, I'd find that he was very supportive and encouraging, giving me more ideas as we talked. I always felt as if I was taken to another level with anything I shared. In contrast, with Mark, as I tested the waters—sharing my stories of the week—I found myself hearing cues to stop. My enthusiasm for my accomplishments went flat in his presence. This contrast was the defining moment regarding the type of person I wanted to be around. Len and I have been married for ten years now, and we're still sharing and adding to each other's ideas.* —Chris, Phoenix, Arizona.

In our daily lives, we often turn to people around us to share and manage the vulnerabilities evoked by events like these. Given a choice, we tend to pursue and deepen an intimate connection when responses to our disclosures leave us feeling *understood*, as it was for Laney, who benefited from Sam's recognition that she needed to grieve her sister's death; *cared for*, as it was for Janie, who appreciated Max's attention to her illness; and *validated*, as it was for Chris, who recognized the value of Len's patient listening. (Can you imagine the responses that would create the opposite experience in these three women?) In the end, partners maintain and develop intimacy by setting aside their own needs and expressing genuine concern and sensitivity for each other, particularly when one person feels exposed or vulnerable. Interpreted as a sample of what the future holds in store, these expressions can prove decisive in the development of an intimate relationship.

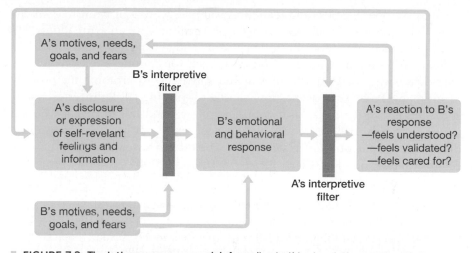

FIGURE 7.2 **The intimacy process model.** According to this view, intimacy arises from interactions in which person A discloses or expresses self-relevant thoughts and feelings to person B; based on B's response, A feels understood, validated, and cared for. The behaviors displayed by person A and person B, and the interpretive filters guiding their perceptions of each other's behaviors, are reflections of their motives, needs, goals, and fears. (Source: Adapted from Reis & Patrick, 1996.)

generalized form. The **intimacy process model**, proposed by social psychologists Harry Reis and Philip Shaver, provides a framework for thinking about intimacy in relationships—not in the sense that a relationship is either intimate or not, but in the sense that the daily exchanges between partners can be understood as either maintaining or thwarting the degree of intimacy in the relationship they have created (Reis & Patrick, 1996; Reis & Shaver, 1988).

The main components of the model include the expressions and disclosures discussed earlier, how the partner perceives and responds to them, and the judgments that the disclosing individual then makes about him- or herself and the relationship. Intimacy is best understood as a process, according to this model. And through this process, a person comes to believe that the partner understands core aspects of his or her inner self, including important needs, emotions, and beliefs; the partner validates, respects, or otherwise ascribes value to these core aspects of one's self; and the partner cares for and displays concern for his or her welfare. These three end points are shown on the right side of **FIGURE 7.2**. As we will outline shortly, the left side of this figure represents what must transpire between two people for this set of beliefs and experiences to arise.

According to this view, the intimacy process involves one person saying or doing something that reveals important information about himself or herself. Figure 7.2 shows further that these disclosures are themselves prompted by motives, needs, goals, and fears; for example, we might want to come to terms with the loss of a sibling; we need help dealing with an acute illness; we want to be recognized for our unique talents and accomplishments.

Though we attempt to reveal our inner self for countless reasons and in countless ways, not all disclosures are equally likely to promote the process of intimacy. Premature disclosures can be off-putting (Mikulincer & Nachson, 1991); dishonest disclosures mislead others and fail to reveal who we truly are (Prager, 1995); and factual disclosures reveal less than emotional disclosures about our inner self and hence afford fewer opportunities for relationships to develop (Clark, Fitness, & Brissette, 2001). As other researchers have observed:

> Self-revealing behaviors are those that reveal personal, private aspects of the self to another, or invite another into a zone of privacy. Both verbal behavior and nonverbal behavior (physical touch, sexual contact) can be self-revealing. Being self-revealing implies a willingness to drop defenses and invite the other to witness and to know private, personal aspects of the self. As a condition for an intimate interaction, then, some aspect of the self is willingly revealed or "exposed" to the other. (Prager & Roberts, 2004, p. 45)

Of course, inviting another person into our "zone of privacy" does not guarantee he or she will accept our invitation or respond the way we want to the feelings and information we have expressed. Our partner—who is motivated by his or her own set of motives, needs, goals, and fears—may either fail to pick up on the needs, feelings, and vulnerabilities we express, or dismiss them as trivial or unimportant. Thus, our partner's interpretive filter affects how he or she chooses to respond to our disclosures.

Responsiveness can be understood through the words our partner says, how they are said, and when they are said. For a person's behavior to be viewed as responsive, he or she needs to listen to the initial disclosure; understand the superficial meaning conveyed in the words, as well as subtle hidden meanings; respond in a way that reflects this understanding, perhaps including questions that encourage the discloser to elaborate; and know whether, when, and how to make the transition to another topic (Davis, 1982; also see Berg, 1987; Burleson, 1994; Derlega, Metts, Petronio, & Margulis, 1993; Miller & Berg, 1984). Can you infer which of these steps proved most difficult for the man in **FIGURE 7.3**? Relationship scientists often discuss responsiveness under the broad heading of **empathy**, the capacity to understand and share another person's thoughts and feelings.

As we've said, the sensitivity and empathy our partner displays when responding to our disclosures hinges on the interpretive filter guiding his or her responsiveness. This filter is itself influenced by the partner's motives, needs, goals, and fears. The following passage, taken from the book *Memoirs of a Geisha* by Arthur Golden (1998), illustrates this aspect of the intimacy

FIGURE 7.3 **When is support not support?** Individuals feel understood, validated, and cared for to the extent that their partner is responsive to their disclosures. The intimacy process model outlines this process and identifies where it can go awry.

process model. The passage describes how the main character, Nitta Sayuri, responds to her partner, Iwamura Ken, at the end of his workday. Iwamura Ken is the founder of a large company in Japan, and Nitta Sayuri refers to him as "the Chairman."

> Usually when he first came, the Chairman talked for a time about his workday. He might tell me about troubles with a new product, or about a traffic accident involving a truckload of parts, or some such thing. Of course I was happy to sit and listen, but I understood perfectly well that the Chairman wasn't telling these things to me because he wanted me to know them. He was clearing them from his mind, just like draining water from a bucket. So I listened closely not to his words, but to the tone of his voice; because in the same way that sound rises as a bucket is emptied, I could hear the Chairman's voice softening as he spoke. When the moment was right, I changed the subject, and soon we were talking about nothing so serious as business, but about everything else instead, such as what happened to him that morning on the way to work; or something about the film we may have watched a few nights earlier. . . . In any case, this simple process of first draining the Chairman's mind and then relaxing him with playful conversation had the same effect water has on a towel that has dried stiffly in the sun. When he first arrived and I washed his

hands with a hot cloth, his fingers felt rigid, like heavy twigs. After we had
talked for a time, they bent as gracefully as if he were sleeping. (p. 422)

Here we see how the Chairman's initial disclosure (stress at work) is filtered through Nitta's motives, needs, and goals (e.g., to comfort and relax him, to show him that she cares about him). In turn, Nitta's interpretive filter guides her behavioral response (listening closely, not judging or criticizing, gradually shifting the conversation to something besides work). The Chairman's own interpretive filter determines the impact and meaning of Nitta's gestures upon him.

According to the intimacy process model, partner responsiveness links self-relevant disclosures to the disclosing individual's feeling understood, validated, and cared for. Without responsiveness, this chain breaks, and the intimacy process is likely to falter; with responsiveness, the links in the chain remain connected. However, just as an interpretive filter comes between the initial disclosure and the partner's response, so, too, does an interpretive filter come between the partner's response and the discloser's tendency to experience that response as validating, understanding, and caring. (see Figure 7.2). In fact, this may be the most important filter in the intimacy process—because our empathic behaviors will not lead our partner to feel validated, understood, or cared for unless our partner encodes or experiences them as such.

Generally, we can expect that kindness and caring, and invalidation and criticism, are experienced in the way they were intended. Without some reasonably high correspondence between what our partner says and how we respond to it, for example, communication suffers and relationships falter. But this correspondence is not perfect. You have probably had the experience of trying valiantly to be responsive to your partner's needs, only to be rebuffed; even the Chairman might dismiss Nitta Sayuri's exquisitely sensitive approach to him by saying, "Can't you see that I need some time to myself?! Why are you smothering me? Why are you always trying to control me and my feelings?!" And you may have had the opposite experience of mumbling some superficial platitude ("When life gives you lemons, honey, make lemonade"), only to be told you are the most insightful and caring partner the world has ever known.

These examples show that there is not always a simple correspondence between what we say and whether our partner then comes to feel understood, validated, and cared for. If we feel we have been rebuffed, it may be because our partner needs to feel more self-sufficient, would rather not disclose certain feelings or actions, or does not want the relationship to develop too quickly. And when we are told we are the most insightful partner ever, it may be because our partner is feeling insecure, wants to be in a relationship where nice gestures are recognized, is worried about losing us, or simply wants to show his or her appreciation. The broader point is that interpretive filters are crucial in the intimacy process and to relationships in general. (We'll return to this in Chapter 9.)

Research Findings on the Process of Intimacy

Evidence supports the intimacy process model. For example, withdrawal and disengagement appear to be particularly detrimental to relationships, especially when one partner is expressing feelings of vulnerability (Christensen & Shenk, 1991; Roberts, 2000). This idea is illustrated in the following transcript, in which a wife expresses the emotional pain she experiences due to being overweight (Roberts & Greenberg, 2002, p. 138):

Wife: *I'm very insecure. . . . Everytime I walk into a room I know they're talking about me. I know those people are talking about me because I'm fat.*

Husband: (no response, 12 seconds, but he looks at her, kindly). *So . . .*

Wife: *I wonder, you know, if people really like me, personally.*

Husband: *Are you talking about your friends?*

Wife: *So called.*

Husband: (no response, 10 seconds)

Wife: (challenging, flicking a pencil at him) *Even you.*

We can presume that withdrawal and disengagement take their toll on relationships because disengagement severs the connection between disclosure, on one hand, and feeling understood by the partner, on the other. Rather than serving as opportunities for validation and connection, these moments of poignant disclosure lead the vulnerable partner to feel invalidated and alone. An opportunity for deepening the relationship has been lost.

More evidence comes from a diary study in which husbands and wives from 96 married couples reported on their conversations every day for 42 days. Increased self-disclosure predicted enhanced perceived partner responsiveness, which in turn predicted stronger feelings of closeness (Laurenceau, Barrett, & Rovine, 2005, also see Laurenceau, Barrett, & Pietromonaco, 1998; Lippert & Prager, 2001). An observational study —in which breast cancer patients and their intimate partners rated the levels of disclosure, partner responsiveness, and levels of closeness experienced while discussing important relationship issues—showed similar results, at least for the partners (Manne et al., 2004). Findings for the patients were different, and they suggested that patients' own disclosures were less important than those of the partner in determining their feelings of closeness.

What about the motives, needs, goals, and fears that figure prominently in the intimacy process model? Do they affect partners' disclosures and the ways they interpret one another's actions? Growing evidence suggests they do. For example, Asians and Asian Americans are more reluctant than European Americans to disclose their need for support from their partners, out of concern that this will burden the partner or cause embarrassment (Kim, Sherman, & Taylor, 2008). In one experimental study, individuals who rated themselves as either high or low in self-esteem were all told they had failed a standardized achievement test; half the people in each of these two groups were then instructed to disclose this failure in a videotaped message to their dating partner (Cameron, Holmes, & Vorauer, 2009). Individuals low in self-esteem felt *less* valued by their partner if they made the disclosure, and more valued by their partner if they concealed the disclosure. The exact opposite pattern emerged for those higher in self-esteem; they felt *more* valued by the partner after making the disclosure than after concealing it. Disclosure is not a uniformly beneficial experience, it seems. As discussed in Chapter 6, partners of individuals with low self-esteem have to work quite hard to overcome their mates' overly pessimistic interpretive filters if they are to convey their understanding and support.

MAIN POINTS

>> Relationship maintenance refers to all the ways partners keep their relationship strong, prevent it from deteriorating, and work to improve it when problems arise.

>> Disclosures are essential to relationship maintenance. To ensure the stability and quality of their relationship, partners must share their thoughts and have open exchanges about issues that matter to them.

>> The intimacy process model asserts that a healthy relationship requires partners to share their inner experiences, to respond with interest and compassion, and to recognize these responses as sympathetic gestures.

>> According to this model, a person feels understood, validated, and cared for to the extent that the partner responds to disclosures with genuine empathy and concern.

>> Approaching intimacy as an interactional process provides a platform for identifying a range of specific strategies people use to maintain their relationships.

Maintaining Intimacy

Depending on how they negotiate moments of disclosure, partners might fall more deeply in love, learn to trust each other more, and consider the possibility of a longer commitment to the relationship. As these transitions occur, interpersonal repertoires also change: For example, the partners confront major decisions about where to live and whether they should raise children, they require mutual support in dealing with the stresses of parenthood and work, they make mistakes and ask for forgiveness, and they talk about ways to keep their sex life fresh. In situations like these, what happens between partners that enables them to maintain positive feelings in the relationship, long after the intense early stages have become distant memories?

We'll discuss five ways partners facilitate and maintain closeness in their relationship, using the intimacy process model as our frame of reference. We focus not on what positive features are maintained (e.g., the feelings of love and commitment), but on the interpersonal processes that serve to keep them strong. The five strategies are shared activities, social support, capitalization, forgiveness, and sexual satisfaction.

Shared Activities

There is much we do not know about human intimacy, but we do know this: On average, relationships become less fulfilling as time passes. You might expect that when two people fall in love, settle down, and get on with the business of making a life together, they would take great pleasure in one another's company and their love would only blossom, flourish, and grow. For many couples, this does happen. As we become more familiar with our partner and more accustomed to our relationship, we settle into our routines and habits, and the special glow we once experienced can diminish. Even among newlyweds who go on to have stable marriages, initially high levels of love, expressions of affection, and perceptions of partner responsiveness drop off on average during the first 2 years of marriage (Huston et al., 2001).

Psychologists Arthur Aron, Elaine Aron, and their colleagues refer to this phenomenon as the "typical honeymoon-then-years-of-blandness pattern" (Aron & Aron, 1996; Aron, Aron, & Norman, 2001; Aron, Mashek, & Aron, 2004). To explain it, they proposed the **self-expansion model**, which is based on two assumptions. First, people naturally want to increase their capacity and effectiveness as individuals to achieve their goals—that is, people are motivated to "expand the self"—and thus they strive to acquire resources of various kinds, enrich their identities, and elaborate on what they know and what they can do. Second, intimate relationships are a common way individuals attempt to accomplish self-expansion. The two partners include or incorporate each other's resources, perspectives, and identities into how they define themselves. By doing so, they expand who they are as individuals. Thus, according to this perspective, relationships are marked by a merging of two individuals' possessions (partners might share music, or books, or clothes), resources (they might become friends with each other's siblings), and identities (they might begin to share hobbies and interests, and learn specialized expertise, skill, or knowledge).

What do these shared activities have to do with the fact that relationships decline? A key idea is that early in a developing relationship, partners typically disclose a lot of personal information, feel an intense sense of connection, and wonder with excitement about their future together. This is a time "in which the partners are expanding their selves at a rapid rate, gaining knowledge, feeling an increase in self-efficacy, and including the other in the self" (Aron, Aron, & Norman, 2001, p. 49). In fact, short-term longitudinal studies conducted over the period of a semester show that college students who fall in love feel more effective and include a wider variety of domains in their self-descriptions, compared to other semesters when these same students did not fall in love, and compared to other students who did not fall in love at all (Aron, Paris, & Aron, 1995). This period of exhilaration and self-expansion cannot be sustained, however, and an important transition occurs: Because partners already know a lot about one another, opportunities for further self-expansion tend to diminish, and the emotional highs (and lows) that marked the initial phases of the relationship typically become more moderate. In the first few weeks of a new relationship, you might be thrilled to stay up all night sharing life experiences and philosophies; but there are limits to how often you can do this. Eventually, you settle into a normal routine. Feelings of satisfaction and love begin to fade as the rate of self-expansion drops, and boredom and disappointment can set in.

What is a couple to do in the face of this depressing progression? It's important to recognize that we are talking about averages here, and many couples do not succumb to this change. But a logical implication of the self-expansion model is that many couples need to find ways to restore the energy and excitement—the self-expansion—that comes to them naturally when the relationship is just beginning. They need to find shared activities—create situations where they can reveal new aspects of themselves, thereby leading to new opportunities for understanding, validation, and care (**FIGURE 7.4**).

"Hey, I know—why don't we go on a little crime spree?"

FIGURE 7.4 Quality time. According to the self-expansion model, intimate relationships provide fewer rewards with the passing of time because the initially intense period, marked by rapid self-expansion, slows dramatically. Engaging in novel and challenging shared activities can reverse this effect and restore feelings of closeness.

Support for this notion comes from a series of short- and long-term experiments in which couples share novel, challenging, and exciting activities. In these studies, change in relationship satisfaction is measured before and after these activities and then compared to the satisfaction levels of couples in control groups (Aron, Norman, Aron, McKenna, & Heyman, 2000; Reissman, Aron, & Bergen, 1993). In the short-term studies, couples completed baseline measures of relationship satisfaction. Next, half the couples were randomly assigned to an activity in which partners were bound together on one side at the wrist and ankle with Velcro straps; instructed to carry a cylindrical pillow between them without using their hands, arms, or teeth; and asked to negotiate a padded obstacle course in a large room in less than 1 minute without dropping the pillow (**FIGURE 7.5**). This group was told that most couples could not accomplish this task, but if they succeeded, they would win a small prize. After a few attempts, all couples in this group were told they had successfully completed the task and were rewarded. Couples in the control group also were given a task, but partners took turns within the task (so it didn't require the same level of cooperation), they were instructed to proceed very slowly in completing the task (making it far less exciting), and there was no opportunity to win a prize or outperform other couples. At the conclusion, all partners made judgments about relationship satisfaction; only those couples who participated together in the novel and exciting task experienced an increase in relationship satisfaction (Aron et al., 2000). Additional studies showed that activities like these also improve observed communication (Aron et al., 2000), and that the novelty of the shared activity is the most important aspect in producing these effects (Aron et al., 2002).

FIGURE 7.5 Main squeeze. By engaging in new, fun activities, couples can keep their relationship fresh and energized. (Source: Aron et al., 2000.)

Before you rush out to buy Velcro straps and cylindrical pillows in the hope of improving your relationship, consider the results from another experiment (Reissman, Aron, & Berger, 1993). In a 10-week study, established couples were randomly assigned to one of three groups, in which they either participated in activities they had rated as "exciting" (e.g., hiking, skiing, dancing) for 90 minutes per week; participated in equally pleasant but not particularly exciting activities (going to dinner, visiting friends, attending church) each week for 90 minutes per week; or did not participate in any activities outside their ordinary routine. All couples completed measures of relationship satisfaction before and after the 10-week period. Consistent with predictions, levels of satisfaction for couples in the first group improved more than for couples in the second and third groups. This experiment indicates that exciting activities can produce reliable increases in relationship satisfaction, even outside laboratory settings, and that this effect is not due to the fact that couples may have found the exciting activities to be pleasant as well.

Social Support

In 1995, Christopher Reeve, known the world over for his starring role in four *Superman* movies, was paralyzed after sustaining a spinal cord injury when he fell from a horse. After a long and valiant struggle to recover from his injury—a struggle distinguished as much by his battle to regain lost functionality as by his mission to advance scientific understanding of the treatment of spinal cord injuries—Reeve passed away in 2004 at the age of 52 (FIGURE 7.6). In the following passage from his autobiography *Still Me* (1998), Reeve recounts a conversation he had in the hospital with his wife, Dana, moments after realizing the severity of his condition:

> *Dana came into the room. She stood beside me, and we made eye contact. I mouthed my first lucid words to her: "Maybe we should let me go."*

*Dana started crying. She said, "I am only going to say this once: I will sup-
port whatever you want to do, because this is your life, and your decision.
But I want you to know that I'll be with you for the long haul, no matter
what." Then she added the words that saved my life: "You're still you. And
I love you."*

*[W]hat Dana said made living seem possible, because I felt the depth of
her love and commitment. I was even able to make a little joke. I mouthed,
"This is way beyond the marriage vows—in sickness and in
health." And she said, "I know." I knew then and there that
she was going to be with me forever.*

*A crisis like my accident doesn't change a marriage; it
brings out what is truly there. It intensifies but does not
transform it. We had become a family. When Dana looked at
me in the UVA hospital room and said, "You're still you," it
also meant that we're still us. We are. We made a bargain for
life. I got the better part of the deal. (pp. 31–32)*

FIGURE 7.6 Still me, still us. After
being paralyzed in an accident, the
actor Christopher Reeve recounted
heartfelt conversations he had with
his wife Dana. His disclosures and her
responses revealed the depth of their
commitment—a key principle in keeping
an intimate relationship strong.

This touching exchange conforms surprisingly well with
the intimacy process model: a heartrending disclosure by
Reeve that perhaps he should be allowed to die so as not
to burden his family; the principled response by Dana that
she would permit him latitude in making this decision
but would be with him regardless of what he decided; and
Reeve's reaction, which (we infer) implies that he felt deeply
valued and cared for and was inspired to live and improve.
Indeed, it is difficult to imagine a more validating response
than to be told that, despite being stripped of all but one's
most basic bodily functions, "You're still you." Note too that
Reeve's response to Dana's statement seems to be strengthened by his interpretive filter: He sees her behavior as motivated not by obligation but by her genuine devotion to him
and their relationship.

Social scientists have long been interested in social support, especially following research showing that people who
have stronger **social integration**—that is, a higher number of social ties and
more connections among them—have lower levels of mortality (Berkman,
1985). They also have faster rates of recovery from coronary heart disease
(Williams et al., 1992) and coronary bypass surgery (King, Reis, Porter, &
Norsen, 1993). Other research looks less at the structural features of social
support networks and focuses instead on their supportive *functions*, especially from one's partner. A convincing argument has been made that one's
intimate partner has special status as a support provider, and that support is
unique and difficult to attain elsewhere within the social network (Coyne &
DeLongis, 1986). According to psychologist Carolyn Cutrona, a leading
scholar in this area, **social support** can be defined in this context like this:

> Social support is conceptualized most generally as responsiveness to
> another's needs and, more specifically, as acts that communicate car-
> ing; that validate the other's worth, feelings, or actions; or that facilitate
> adaptive coping with problems through the provision of information,
> assistance, or tangible resources. (1996, p. 10)

Supportive behaviors are indeed characteristic of more fulfilling relationships, and generally are a reliable way for couples to maintain strong partnerships. Such couples are more satisfied in their relationships and demonstrate
short-term improvements in their mood and their self-esteem because of
the support (Brunstein, Dangelmayer, & Schultheiss, 1996; Collins & Feeney,
2000; Feeney, 2004). And these effects seem to accumulate over time: Newlywed couples who experience more emotional and practical support report
increased relationship satisfaction 2 years later, compared to couples who
show lower levels of support (Pasch & Bradbury, 1998; also see Cutrona &
Suhr, 1994).

So support is good. Or is it? Before accepting this simple conclusion, we
must reconcile the previous findings with some counterintuitive results. For
example, wives are *more* likely to succeed in a weight-loss program when
their husbands are told to be as *uninvolved* as possible in their partner's attempts to adopt a healthier lifestyle, relative to husbands in a control group
(Pearce, LeBow, & Orchard, 1981). And individuals who have suffered from
a heart attack may actually recover *more slowly* when they receive more support from relationship partners (Helgeson, 1993). More generally, a large
body of literature shows that the support people *perceive to be available to
them* tends to be beneficial as they contend with various stressors, whereas
the support people *actually receive* is sometimes beneficial and sometimes
detrimental (Cohen & Wills, 1985; Rook, 1998; Stroebe & Stroebe, 1996;
Wethington & Kessler, 1986). How are the occasionally detrimental effects of
received support explained?

One answer lies with the realization that attempts at support intended
to be helpful may not actually have that effect on the partner. More specifically, even well-intentioned and skillful efforts to provide support may inadvertently convey the idea that the partner is overwhelmed and lacks the
skills or resources to resolve the stressful situation alone (Coyne, Wortman,
& Lehman, 1988; Fisher, Nadler, & Whitcher-Alagna, 1982; Rafaeli & Gleason, 2009). The recipient might also be put in the uncomfortable position of
feeling obligated to reciprocate when the roles are reversed. Thus, **visible
support**, which the recipient knows he or she has received, can be quite costly
to the recipient's self-esteem. This drawback can be avoided by offering **invisible support**, which the recipient does not notice.

Research backs up the provocative idea that support is more beneficial to
the recipient's emotional state when it is relatively invisible. Social psychologist Niall Bolger and his colleagues (2000) studied 68 couples in which one
partner was a law student preparing for the grueling 2-day New York State

Bar Exam. Each evening, for 32 days leading up to the exam, the law students reported on whether they had received support from their partners, and described how anxious or depressed they felt that day. The partners independently reported on whether they had provided support on each of these same days. On the days when the law students reported receiving support, anxiety and depression both *increased*—a finding consistent with the idea that visible support is costly to the recipient's well-being. However, when partners had provided more support than the law students reported receiving, anxiety and depression both *decreased*.

The surprising message here is that supportive gestures in relationships can be a boost to the partner's self-esteem and well-being, or they can have precisely the opposite effect. Just as the intimacy process model implies, this distinction hinges not on whether the gestures are well intended, but on whether they enable the partner to feel capable, competent, and free of any indebtedness to reciprocate.

Capitalization

As we have seen, social support occurs in an intimate relationship when at least one partner feels bad, anticipates difficulties, or is struggling somehow. Partners typically expect to be called upon to provide emotional and practical support to each other when times are rough. But maintaining an intimate relationship obviously involves far more than simply managing unpleasant and difficult situations: Exams are passed with flying colors, time spent with a childhood friend evokes fond recollections, an important project earns special praise, a complex computer program finally runs, the arrival of a child prompts wonder and delight, and so on. We might reasonably ask whether positive experiences like these have any bearing on the health of relationships and, if so, how.

Recent theorizing recognizes the importance of positive experiences and the ways that partners elaborate, and fail to elaborate, on them. The **broaden and build theory**, for example, maintains that the experience and expression of positive emotions serve two purposes: to expand and enhance how we attend to, think about, and respond to the countless events encountered in daily life; and to build or amass the resources—including physical health, intellectual and creative capacities, spiritual connections, and social relationships—for maintaining our well-being (Frederickson, 2001). Indeed, diary data show that disclosing positive events to our partner improves our mood, as does being on the receiving end of such disclosures (Hicks & Diamond, 2008).

How might positive emotions in intimate relationships build resources? What are the interpersonal processes by which positive emotions might enhance the resources we possess? Drawing from work by psychologists Christopher Langston (1994), Abraham Tesser (2000), and others, social psychologist Shelly Gable and her colleagues (2004) propose that **capitalization**, or the sharing of positive events in one's life, builds personal and interpersonal resources because it allows us to relive the events, to see that others are pleased for us, to connect a given event with prior events in a relationship, and to experience ourselves being viewed favorably by others. Thus, more than the mere experience of the good events themselves, the sharing of them yields important benefits. Of course, simply expressing our successes provides no assurance that benefits will accrue. As you might expect from the intimacy process model, this is primarily because how our partner responds is a crucial factor in the capitalization process. An example helps illustrate this point.

Imagine this: You see your partner at dinner, when you usually catch up on the events of the day. "Hey—what's up?" you ask. Barely able to contain her exuberance, she responds: "You will never believe what happened this afternoon. Do you remember that paper I was working on for my European history seminar? For Professor Campbell, who I'm hoping will supervise my senior thesis? Here it is—I got an A PLUS on it!! I think it was the highest grade in the class!" According to Gable, all of the possible responses that we might make in situations like this boil down to four basic types, based on whether they are active versus passive and constructive versus destructive:

- Active-constructive response: *Holy cats!! Show me that! I've never even seen an A+! Wow, Crystal, this is amazing. Look at these comments—"brilliant idea," "excellent writing style," "exemplary organization," "great argument"—and here it says, "Come see me next week, you could probably publish this with a bit more work!" Are you going to do that?! What were his exact words when he handed you the paper?*

- Passive-constructive response: *Wow, Crystal, great job. Have you thought about when you're going to ask him about supervising your thesis?*

- Active-destructive response: *A+ —way better than your last paper. Pretty impressive; too bad it's only worth 40 percent of your final grade. I don't want to burst your bubble, but I've heard that Campbell is one of the more lenient graders in the department.*

- Passive-destructive response: *I cannot write to save my life. The last history class I took, I got totally screwed. Maybe I should take a class with this Campbell guy.*

Gable's team conducted a series of studies (2004, 2006) to examine which of these responses, if any, relate to the quality of intimate relationships. In studies of married couples and couples dating an average of 14 months, these researchers found that people who perceive their partner to be primarily "active-constructive" in response to expressions of positive events also reported higher levels of intimacy in the relationship, even after taking into account the way the partner is perceived to respond to negative events in the relationship (Gable et al., 2004). Destructive strategies, whether active or passive, were more often reported by those experiencing lower levels of intimacy. What about "passive-constructive" responses, in which destructive sentiments are avoided but the degree of elaboration on the positive emotion is rather weak? Unfortunately, the passive part of these responses overshadowed the constructive part. Perceptions of passive-constructive responses correlated with lower levels of intimacy. Such responses, it seems, tend to make us feel as though we've been "damned with faint praise," as the expression goes (**FIGURE 7.7**).

"It was just that one time that you won the Nobel Prize, wasn't it, dear?"

FIGURE 7.7 Failing to capitalize. Responding to a partner's positive experience with passive or destructive comments could defeat an opportunity to strengthen the relationship. Active, constructive responses let partners express admiration, recognize shared resources, and deepen memories of positive events.

Forgiveness

Although intimate partners can nurture their relationship by sharing in new and exciting activities, by supporting one another in difficult circumstances, and by elaborating on positive experiences, much of the truly hard work in maintaining the relationship arises when one partner hurts or betrays the other. Hurts and betrayals can take many forms—cheating, divulging confidential information, breaking a promise, offending friends or family members—and they can threaten the basic assumptions partners hold about each other and their relationship (Vangelisti, 2001). The person who has been wronged or let down must contend with the feelings stirred up by the act of betrayal, with thoughts about the foundation and future of the relationship, and with choices about whether to forgive the partner.

Perhaps one of the most difficult transgressions for couples to deal with is infidelity. Infidelity is not rare; representative national surveys in the United States indicate that 13.3 percent of currently married people report having had extramarital sex (Atkins, Baucom, & Jacobson, 2001). This estimate could be higher if it included separated and divorced people. How do couples deal with such a major violation of their relationship? Is forgiveness even possible? What makes forgiveness more or less likely?

Common to most definitions of **forgiveness** is the idea that feelings of hurt and anger, and desires to retaliate, are transformed in such a way that the person who has been slighted adopts an altruistic orientation to the offender. Despite the offender's hurtful actions, the partner's motivation to seek revenge diminishes, and the desire to restore the relationship in some form increases (McCullough, Worthington, & Rachal, 1997). Social psychologist

Roy Baumeister and his colleagues (1998) add two important observations that help explain forgiveness in intimate relationships. Take a moment now to read **BOX 7.2**, a case based on the experiences of an actual couple. First, for complete forgiveness to occur, motivation has to shift on the *intrapersonal* level (Aaron's personal motivation would have to shift from anger and blame to charity and compassion) and behavior has to change on the *interpersonal* level (Aaron will somehow need to express and demonstrate these feelings to Jenny). When only the intrapersonal shift happens, it is known as *silent forgiveness*; when only the interpersonal change happens, it is *hollow forgiveness*. Second, forgiveness is a challenge in intimate relationships because partners adopt biased perspectives about the transgression. Offenders tend to minimize the adverse effects of their actions, and victims often fail to acknowledge mitigating circumstances and their own contributions to the problem. Because of these discrepant views, the process of forgiveness requires the victim "to cancel a debt that is larger than the one the perpetrator acknowledges" (Baumeister et al., 1998, p. 85).

Whether or not one partner forgives the other for a transgression occurring in their relationship appears to depend on at least four factors. First, relatively minor acts are more likely to be forgiven than more severe acts (McCullough et al., 1998; Ohbuchi, Kameda, & Agarie, 1989).

Second, victims who are generally more empathic, agreeable, and emotionally stable are more inclined to be forgiving as well (Brown, 2003; McCullough & Hoyt, 2002). Research also shows that victims with a secure attachment style (see Chapters 3 and 6), are more likely to forgive transgressions (Mikulincer, Shaver, & Slav, 2006).

Third, apologies and expressions of remorse by the offender tend to promote forgiveness (e.g., Weiner, Graham, Peter, & Zmuidinas, 1991), apparently because they encourage the victim to empathize with the offender (McCullough et al., 1997). As **FIGURE 7.8** shows, however, apologies are not always accepted, particularly if the person who has been wronged believes the apology is not sincere enough.

Fourth, forgiveness is more likely to occur if the levels of commitment and satisfaction are high between the offender and the victim (e.g., Van Lange et al., 1997). If partners have already invested a great deal in their relationship, then the offended partner will be motivated to preserve this investment by forgiving the misdeeds. And, similarly, if victims depend a great deal on the partner, or if they feel they have no good alternatives beyond the current relationship, then they have a great deal to lose by failing to forgive the partner.

Longitudinal research conducted over 6 months indicates that forgiveness—a willingness to forgo retaliation, on one hand, and a benevolent desire to achieve reconciliation on the other—is beneficial for relationships (Paleari, Regalia, & Fincham, 2005). These benefits might arise because partners reporting higher levels of forgiveness also report more effective

BOX 7.2 SPOTLIGHT ON . . .

Forgiveness and Infidelity

Jenny and Aaron, both in their late 30s, have been married for 8 of the 10 years they have known each other. By all accounts, the first several years of marriage were satisfying for Jenny and Aaron as they worked together to establish their careers, form a family, and immerse themselves in their neighborhood and community. Jenny is an advertising executive, and Aaron is an obstetrician. Their two daughters, ages 5 and 6, are energetic and precocious. (Names and identifying information have been changed.)

Jenny: In retrospect it does seem like we began to grow apart after our second daughter—Katie—was born. Nothing traumatic, just the feeling like our relationship was losing intensity and direction. When Katie was diagnosed with a brain tumor when she was three, we really rallied to her cause, and Aaron was really there for me. I remember thinking, "This is a terrible situation, but this is what a good relationship is really all about." In the end Katie was fine, but the tight bond that we had seemed to weaken all of a sudden, like it was just a temporary solution to this one problem. Aaron went back to focusing on his work, and so did I, and we seemed to be even worse off than when the whole ordeal with Katie started. I was incredibly grateful that my daughter was alive, but I felt like my marriage was dead. When I met Patrick, something clicked. He was coming off a bad divorce, figuring out how to stay in his kids' lives, trying to pick up the pieces. He is a nice guy, really sweet and sensitive. Yes, it is true that Patrick and I did spend a lot of time together; we would leave work and spend hours together, talking about everything and anything. The thought of seeing Patrick at work really gave me a reason to get up and get out of the house. There was a level of intimacy there that I really needed, and that I will continue to need. I don't really want to say that I have done something wrong, but I do see that I have hurt Aaron and that I have done things that might lead him to not trust me. So maybe I did do something wrong, and that is just something I will learn to live with. But I do hope Aaron will forgive me. When all is said and done, I know the right thing is for me to stay with Aaron. Something needs to change, though, for this relationship to work out. Aaron and I have tried talking about it ourselves, and we tried going to counseling for a few sessions, but that's all it is—talk, talk, talk, and not very pleasant talk at that. I need more than that.

This is not about talking, it is about us supporting one another, and being there for one another. I hope Aaron can see this situation with Patrick for what it was, so we can move on and try to build something better now.

Aaron: Before the kids arrived we traveled whenever we could, we spent a lot of time together, we had fun planning for the future. But thinking back on it now, I can see that that could not last, not if we wanted to have kids. Jenny really pushed to have kids; I was a bit less enthusiastic but I knew that this was something that she really wanted. Our kids are beautiful, and I think they are even more precious to me now after Katie's surgeries. We managed Katie's crisis really well, but in front of the marriage counselor Jenny said that I did not love her as much after that, which strikes me as bizarre. Yes, I was working long hours, I was on-call a lot, and the fact is I did not have that much time for our marriage, much less myself. I see that now. Maybe I did take on more work than I should have, but it seemed like the right decision at the time, and Jenny did not disagree. When I found out about this thing with Patrick, I was stunned. She tried to cover it up at first, and minimize it and all, but I knew something was going on. Her work hours changed, she was volunteering to do projects with this guy, and all of a sudden she had a new wardrobe and a spring in her step. I am not sure how this is going to play out between us, and in fact I do not even know if Jenny had an affair with this guy. Jenny denies it, but then she does not really seem to want to talk about it. But even if she did not have sex with him, I feel like she has crossed a line. Married people just should not be doing this kind of thing except with their spouse. If I find out she was screwing around with this guy, I am not sure what I will do. I hope I have it in my heart to forgive her, but I also know I have been hurt bad. I hope I can learn how to trust her, because—who knows?—what happens if someone better than Patrick comes along, and sweeps her off her feet? Then I end up looking like a doormat. My parents divorced when I was 8 and I want no part of that, though it is not really up to me. My heart is in this 100% but I can't speak for Jenny. Personally I think we need to get into counseling and get back on track. We could do it, and I keep telling her this. She knows I love her. Our kids deserve nothing less than our absolute best effort.

Can Aaron forgive Jenny? Should he?

problem-solving skills, even after adjusting for their overall level of satisfaction with the relationship (Fincham, Beach, & Davila, 2004).

Let's return to Jenny and Aaron (see **BOX 7.2**). Were they able to reap the benefits of forgiveness? Three months after Jenny's involvement with Patrick was revealed, they were not. Although Jenny said she was not sexually intimate with Patrick, Aaron had difficulty accepting this claim. Jenny expressed no remorse for her actions, sexual or otherwise, nor did she see a need to cut off her relationship with Patrick. She did not apologize for hurting Aaron's feelings or disrupting the family, and Aaron, who refused to be treated so poorly, was deeply confused about Jenny's actions. As both of them held their ground, Jenny felt more and more like she needed someone to talk to, and Aaron felt less and less inclined to be that someone. "She has made my life very, very hard," Aaron would say, "but she has made my decision about whether to stay in this relationship very, very easy." Aaron was left more bewildered and saddened than angry, and Jenny took steps to form a new identity for herself and a new relationship with Patrick. After signing the divorce papers, Aaron and Jenny both vowed that they would not allow this change in their relationship to affect their children.

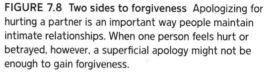

"I don't want your apology -- I want you to be sorry."

FIGURE 7.8 Two sides to forgiveness Apologizing for hurting a partner is an important way people maintain intimate relationships. When one person feels hurt or betrayed, however, a superficial apology might not be enough to gain forgiveness.

Although Jenny and Aaron did not achieve forgiveness and reconciliation within their marriage, it is important to recognize that forgiveness is a process that can unfold over a long span of time. Aaron's forgiving Jenny might arise much later, after both of them have moved on to new relationships. Recent theorizing suggests that forgiveness for intimacy betrayals progresses through three stages. (Gordon & Baucom, 1998). In the **impact stage**, partners learn of the transgression and begin to recognize the effect it has on them and their relationship. This is a time of great disorientation and confusion—filled with anger, recrimination, and withdrawal—as the offended partner tries to absorb what has happened and the offending partner engages in some form of damage control. As the impact stage gives way to the **meaning stage**, the offended partner tries to make some sense of why the transgression happened. Having some understanding of the incident enables the victim to explain what the offending partner has done, and perhaps predict what that partner might do next to protect himself or herself, as well as contend with feelings of powerlessness. The offended partner may also try to extract a confession in an effort to restore the balance of power in the relationship. The transition to the **moving on stage** occurs as the victim finds a way to adjust to, and move beyond, the incident. The offended person might recognize that further hostility directed toward the partner may not be productive and may hinder his or her own adjustment. Feelings of forgiveness might ensue at the intrapersonal level, and interpersonal gestures of forgiveness might be made toward the offending partner, in hopes of restoring the relationship in some form. Aaron's current task is to make sense of this incident in his life, and how he does this will determine whether he will ever be able to forgive Jenny.

Sexual Satisfaction

People define closeness in relationships in part on the presence of sexual intercourse and other forms of physical intimacy (Helgeson, Shaver, & Dyer, 1987). Evidence is clear that the nature of one's sexual relationship marches hand in hand with the quality of one's relationship in general, that judgments of sexual satisfaction correlate more strongly with relationship quality than with sexual frequency, and that changes over time in sexual functioning correlate with changes in relationship functioning (Byers, 2005; Edwards & Booth, 1994; Sprecher, 2002; for reviews, see Christopher & Sprecher, 2000; Sprecher & Cate, 2004).

But which factor—sexual functioning or relationship functioning—is leading the march? In keeping with the focus of this chapter, can we claim that sexual functioning maintains and promotes relationship satisfaction? Adopting this position would lead us to believe that it is because of their relatively high degree of satisfaction with their sexual relationship that some couples are happier in their relationships overall than couples with lower levels of sexual satisfaction. This position would also lead us to assume that engaging in sexual interactions with our partner is likely to at least solidify or perhaps even improve our relationship. But it is just as likely that a good sex life itself is a consequence of a fulfilling relationship. Findings in support of this idea would lend credence to the notion that good sex is a by-product of a healthy relationship, and that a couple's sexual relationship can be improved by enhancing the quality of the relationship broadly. As we will soon see from a review of longitudinal studies, evidence can be lined up in support of—and in opposition to—both of these positions.

> "Sex is not everything, of course, but it is a catalyst for many other things and, since so many other things must be right for it to function well, also a touchstone for the quality of the total relationship. When it is good, people look different. The emotional atmosphere one senses in a house where it is right is one of calm and peace, yet also of lightness, fun, and humor, and everything moves easily."
>
> —A. C. Robin Skynner, *One Flesh; Separate Persons* (1976)

Let's pose the first question: Does better sex promote a better relationship? Although there is some evidence to the contrary (e.g., Byers, 2005; Felmlee, Sprecher, & Bassin, 1990), at least five longitudinal studies answer this question in the affirmative. In a study of 101 dating couples, men with higher sexual satisfaction scores were less likely to dissolve their relationships over a 12-month period; no such association was observed among women (Sprecher, 2002). In a study of 103 individuals in dating relationships, men and women reporting lower levels of conflict over sex (e.g., one partner not being in the mood for sex, discussions about previous sexual partners) reported smaller declines in satisfaction in the following 4 months (Long et al., 1996). In a study of 106 newlywed couples, wives who reported having sex and initiating sex were more satisfied in their relationship 2 years later (Huston & Vangelisti, 1991). Comparable reports of sexual activity by their husbands did not predict their satisfaction over this same interval. However, in a recent study of 101 newlywed couples, husbands reporting higher quality of sexuality and sensuality in their marriages reported more favorable changes in relationship satisfaction over the next 3 years. This was not the case for their wives, for whom better communication and conflict management predicted better relationships (Lawrence et al., 2008). And finally, a study of 72 newlywed couples studied over 6 months showed that men's satisfaction with the relationship fluctuated with how often they had sex; this was not the case for women (McNulty & Fisher, 2008).

Now let's pose the second question: Does a better relationship promote better sex? Although some longitudinal studies reveal no such association (e.g., Huston & Vangelisti, 1991; Sprecher, 2002), at least three others indicate that better relationships produce better sexual experiences. According to a study of 87 individuals in established relationships, higher levels of relationship satisfaction and reports of more effective communication both predicted higher levels of sexual satisfaction 18 months later (Byers, 2005). In a study of 70 couples planning for marriage, wives' reports of open communication and husbands' reports of empathic communication predicted wives' reports of sexual satisfaction 1 year later. Wives' open communication and perceptions of relationship stability predicted husbands' reports of sexual satisfaction 1 year later (Larson et al., 1998). In a study of 44 distressed couples, a five-session therapeutic intervention focusing on improving marital communication produced increases in relationship satisfaction and sexual satisfaction (O'Leary & Arias, 1983).

In sum, sexual functioning *does* predict the quality and stability of relationships, and better relationships and improvements in relationships *also* forecast better sexual functioning. It is tempting to conclude that sexual functioning in relationships and global perceptions about relationship quality are reciprocally linked, but no study has yet demonstrated this. Instead, some of the studies hint at the idea that we cannot meaningfully discuss sexuality and the quality of intimate relationships without also discussing a third factor that is likely to influence both sets of phenomena: the quality of communication between partners. It is not unusual for partners to disagree on their sexual agendas, desires, and timing (Miller & Byers, 2004). Thus, it follows that successfully negotiating the sexual realm of an intimate relationship requires a great deal of communication skill and sensitivity in, for example, initiating sexual contact, turning down a partner's request, managing one's own feelings after a sexual advance is rejected, or requesting specific kinds of sexual interactions and behaviors. Studies show that the quality of a couple's sex life is in fact associated with how well partners understand each other's sexual preferences (Montesi et al., 2010; Purnine & Carey, 1997). In addition, the quality of communication predicts changes in relationship satisfaction and sexual satisfaction (Byers, 2005).

To this point in the discussion, we have assumed that sex is a positive experience in intimate relationships. Leaving aside situations in which one partner coerces the other to have sex, there are times when even consensual sexual encounters are an indicator that all is not well in the relationship. How might this be? At several places in this book, including our discussion of the intimacy process model earlier in this chapter (see Figure 7.2), we make the point that the effects of behaviors on relationships are typically determined by how those behaviors are understood and interpreted (see also Chapter 10). Sex is no different. If a partner in an established relationship engages in sex to avoid adverse outcomes (e.g., to avoid conflict, to prevent the partner from getting upset, to prevent the partner from losing interest in the relationship), the relationship is more likely to dissolve (Impett, Peplau, & Gable, 2005). This is also true for the partner's *perception* that the mate is engaging in sex to avoid undesirable outcomes. (This perception might be unrelated to whether the partner is actually having sex for that reason; Impett et al., 2005). Thus, the meaning of sex, and the reason for it, appear to matter. A good relationship might promote sexual satisfaction, and in so doing help maintain the partners' bond. But in a less stable situation, significant concerns (e.g., that your partner is no longer interested in you or that your partner will get angry with you) might motivate sexual encounters in an effort to repair the relationship, which could backfire and thereby weaken it.

MAIN POINTS

>> Partners can use several strategies to keep their relationship healthy and strong.

>> Shared activities counteract a natural tendency for relationships to stagnate over time. New activities create opportunities for couples to discover unfamiliar aspects of their identities and grow closer as a result.

>> Social support, or responsiveness to another's needs, involves one partner assisting the other during times of personal stress. Support strengthens trust and commitment, but it can be costly if partners call attention to the support they are providing.

>> Capitalization refers to the sharing of positive events. Active, constructive discussion of the good things that happen to partners strengthens their bond, enabling both to feel validated and successful.

>> Forgiveness can occur after one person has mistreated the partner in some way. Forgiveness helps maintain relationships because the offended partner sets aside natural inclinations to retaliate, promoting compassion and sincere apologies.

>> Sexual interaction, a defining feature of an intimate relationship, brings partners together in ways that are not usually shared with others. Relationships that are satisfying in general also tend to be sexually fulfilling, and vice versa.

CONCLUSION

We began this chapter with the last letter that Jack Sweeney, a military pilot, wrote to his wife Beebe. Jack wrote the letter in anticipation of the possibility that he would die in service, but rather than dwell on his fears, or regrets, or disappointments, he focused on the wonderful life he and Beebe shared. Grateful for the time they had together and obviously proud of the four boys they had raised, Jack even encouraged his wife to find a new husband in the event of his death. Jack's selfless and relentlessly upbeat letter gave us a glimpse into some of the qualities that define a stable and fulfilling relationship, and it prompted us to ask a crucial question about how two people sustain that kind of bond. In the context of relationship maintenance, the intimacy process model outlines partner exchanges that link disclosures and responses, thereby creating feelings of understanding, validation, and caring. The five specific strategies a couple can use to keep their relationship healthy and strong are: shared activities, social support in times of stress, capitalization of positive events, forgiveness in the face of behaviors that might threaten the relationship, and sexual satisfaction.

To a large extent, the ability of a couple to use these strategies will determine how fulfilling they will perceive their relationship to be. But is it merely the absence of these kinds of selfless acts and gestures that makes a relationship deteriorate? Or are there other kinds of exchanges that undermine the feelings of closeness between two people? The next chapter addresses these questions.

Public Personas, Hidden Hostility

A classic Hollywood image: The actress Marilyn Monroe, in *The Seven Year Itch*, stands over a sidewalk grate in New York City and the rushing air from a passing subway train blows her white skirt above her waist. Less familiar is the fact that Marilyn Monroe was recently married at the time this movie was made, and that looking on during the repeated takes of this shot was her husband, the recently retired baseball great Joe DiMaggio—together with dozens of other men (**FIGURE 8.1**). The next day, Monroe would tell her hairdresser and wardrobe assistant that DiMaggio, in a jealous rage, attacked her in their hotel suite later that evening. Bruises on her back and shoulders confirmed the abuse. The couple divorced 6 weeks later, after 9 months of marriage; Monroe filed to end the relationship on the grounds of DiMaggio's mental cruelty toward her. "Your honor," she said to the court, "my husband would get in moods where he wouldn't speak to me for five to seven days at a time—sometimes longer, ten days. I would ask him what was wrong. He wouldn't answer, or he would say, 'Stop nagging me!' I was permitted to have visitors three times . . . on one occasion, it was when I

was sick. Then, he did allow someone to come and see me. . . . I hoped to have out of my marriage love, warmth, affection and understanding. But the relationship was mostly one of coldness and indifference" (Cramer, 2000, p. 371). There were reports that this was not the first time DiMaggio had injured Monroe, and apparently he wanted her to give up her career in acting and adopt a more traditional role as his wife. DiMaggio's love for Monroe did not end with their marriage, however. After she died unexpectedly in August 1962, DiMaggio, crying, kissed the corpse as it lay in the casket, whispering, "I love you." He arranged for fresh roses to be delivered to her crypt, 3 times a week, for more than 20 years.

FIGURE 8.1 Behind the scenes. The baseball star Joe DiMaggio and the Hollywood legend Marilyn Monroe were married in January 1954 and divorced in October that same year. Enraged during the filming of the famous "skirt scene" in *The Seven Year Itch*, DiMaggio allegedly later struck her when they were alone.

QUESTIONS

It is easy to imagine why we might beat up a stranger who threatens us or why we might shout obscenities at someone who has cut us off in traffic, but it is harder to explain why we sometimes hurt the ones we love the most. What was DiMaggio trying to accomplish with his acts of aggression? By limiting Monroe's contact with others, was he controlling her, or protecting her? Was this a momentary angry outburst or part of a larger strategy to ensure that Monroe would abide by his wishes in their relationship? To complicate matters further, how do we make sense of the fact that Monroe had agreed to remarry DiMaggio in the months before she died, knowing that he was physically aggressive in the past?

For this one couple, we can only speculate about the answers to these questions. But decades of systematic research now provide us with important insights about how it is that many couples simply want "love, warmth, affection and understanding,"

yet find themselves faced with "coldness and indifference" or even outright physical abuse.

Few relationships achieve the iconic status of Monroe and DiMaggio, but disagreements and the expression of strong negative emotions—jealousy, rage, frustration, anger, contempt—are anything but rare between intimate partners. Recognition of this fact leads us to ask several specific questions: What sparks disagreements and conflict in couples? What happens when partners disagree? How do happy and unhappy couples differ in the ways they approach their disagreements? Does the way in which a couple works out their disagreements tell us anything about how fulfilling their relationship is likely to be years later? What forms does aggression take, what causes it, and when and why does aggression escalate into physical violence? This chapter addresses these questions, focusing first on verbal disagreements and then moving on to consider disagreements that erupt into physical aggression.

> The process of selecting a partner for a long-term relationship should involve the realization that you will inevitably be choosing a particular set of unresolvable problems that you will be grappling with for the next ten, twenty, or fifty years. . . . [A] relationship is, in some sense, the attempt to work out the negative side effects of what attracts you to your partner in the first place."
>
> —Dan Wile, clinical psychologist (1988, p. 263)

Verbal Conflict

By their very nature, relationships consist of two people, and by *their* very nature, the two people have unique sets of goals, needs, and preferences. Often partners share these perspectives and gain strength and a sense of connection from them. But relationships at any stage are rife with opportunities for misunderstanding and miscommunication, and the discussions and debates that ensue can sometimes pose a threat to the partners' feelings for one another—and to their own well-being. When relationships are in their early stages, disagreements can stem from not having had the opportunity to discuss certain issues or from the discomfort caused by doing so. Even in established relationships, however, disagreements can be part of a couple's regular exchanges. At the most fundamental level, this is because situations arise in which both partners cannot simultaneously have what they want. But other factors can make the situation even more complex. For example, the two people themselves may not be aware of the depth of their feelings on a particular topic, they may not always articulate their expectations, and their changing goals and preferences might necessitate new and difficult negotiations.

Let's start by defining conflict. In 1948, Kurt Lewin, a well-known social psychologist, proposed that a definition of **conflict** begins with the recognition that participants in social interaction have goals. These goals need not be conscious, they may be specific or general, and they may be short-term or long-term in nature. According to Lewin, conflict arises when one person pursues his or her goals in such a way that it interferes with the other person's goals. The goals can be trivial or monumental, and the people can be keenly aware of them or barely able to articulate them, but the main idea is that conflict arises from goal interference. The interference can be direct or indirect, and crucially, the people involved can respond to this interference in a host of different ways.

Lewin's definition was about conflict in general, but it has two key implications for our analysis of intimate relationships. First, it means that conflicts between people—what we might think of as "conflicts of interest"—are inevitable, and are particularly likely when the two people are highly interdependent and in frequent contact. Second, responses to conflicts can vary. While we might not always recognize it in the heat of an argument, as intimate partners we have some control over how to respond when our partner interferes with our goals—and when our partner claims we are doing the same. Relationship scientists have recognized the natural and inevitable presence of disagreements between intimate partners, and they typically undertake their studies of conflict with the assumption that it is *how* couples disagree, more than *whether* they disagree or *what* they disagree about, that is most consequential for their relationship. This is a pivotal assumption, because with it comes the idea that couples can strengthen their relationship by learning specific skills and strategies for managing their disagreements well.

What choices should partners be making when they are talking about instances when their goals conflict? Most people believe that clear and honest communication is a key ingredient for relationship success, and indeed it comes as little surprise that communication is identified by couples therapists as the leading reason couples seek counseling (Doss, Simpson, & Christensen, 2004; Whisman, Dixon, & Johnson, 1997). But what, exactly, must two people communicate if their relationship is to thrive? Even a moment's reflection shows that it is not enough to say that couples must "communicate well" if they are to remain happy. After all, if two people are exquisitely clear in communicating their disdain for one another, then it is difficult to see their relationship as having a bright future. So effective communication must mean more than expressing our goals and desires clearly. What do you think are the key elements of good communication in intimate relationships, in general and when partners disagree? More so than any other topic, these very questions have attracted the attention of relationship scientists. As you will see later in this chapter, the journey toward answering these questions has taken some interesting twists and turns.

We noted above that Lewin's original definition in 1948 did not refer to conflict in couples. But even if it had, it is doubtful whether anyone would have paid much attention: Aside from a spike in divorce rates immediately after World War II, divorce tended to be relatively rare and problems in marriage rarely became public concerns. Although the Second World War allowed women to take on new and important jobs in the workforce, society still assigned men and women to relatively rigid roles in relationships, and this probably tipped the balance of power in problem-solving toward men (see Chapter 4). When problems did arise in a marriage, they were assumed to stem from one individual's family history and personality, rather than anything that might have transpired between relationship partners (e.g., Eisenstein, 1956). There was a great deal of stigma associated with divorce— divorced men were viewed as unreliable employees, for example—and the few people seeking professional help for relationship problems would likely be met by a therapist who assumed that character flaws in one or both partners were the source of all the turbulence.

Conflict from the Perspective of Social Learning Theory

All this would change dramatically over the next three decades. Divorce rates would rise sharply, reaching a peak around 1980, and couples struggling to keep their relationships intact turned with increasing frequency to mental health professionals who had growing expertise in helping couples and families. It was no longer reasonable to blame all divorces on flaws in individuals' personalities, nor was it particularly fruitful to do so. How, after all, could you change a person's personality? A small group of professionals—including Robert L. Weiss, Gerald Patterson, John Gottman, Gayla Margolin, and Neil Jacobson—had one foot in the marital therapy clinic and one foot in the research laboratory, and they sought to establish a rigorous scientific basis for the interventions they would undertake with distressed couples. They would focus not on individual personalities and family backgrounds but on the unproductive ways partners talked about their differences of opinion.

Social exchange theory, with its emphasis on the bartering of rewards and costs, had immediate relevance to understanding the punishing exchanges that typified unhappy couples. Knowing what you do about this theoretical approach from Chapter 3, you can easily see how a couple's evaluations of the nature of their exchanged behaviors could affect future conversations and their overall judgments of how fulfilling the relationship is. But because these professionals spent much of their daily clinical work listening to partners argue with each other while struggling to restore some semblance of intimacy, the researchers were interested less in the partners' perceptions of what was happening and more interested in the actual statements that generated the exchanges. The perceptions themselves were important because there was a lot of validity to them; partners really were treating each other poorly. Moreover, the perceptions were difficult to measure well, whereas the words partners were saying were directly observable and could be recorded for careful analysis.

Early scholars were therefore influenced to an even greater degree by the principles of behaviorism and social learning theory (see Chapter 3). Here the focus is on how the behaviors expressed by one person—a critical statement, for example—would serve to punish the statement that came before it. And if a negative statement by one partner was followed by the other partner giving in, then the person making that negative statement would be rewarded by way of negative reinforcement. Accordingly, to test this perspective, a high premium was placed on direct, objective, and repeatable observation of interaction, and the statements that spouses made were recorded, quantified, and analyzed in detail. Because partner interaction is a central feature of intimate relationships, we will focus on how relationship scientists typically quantify interaction, thus expanding on the introduction to observational methods provided in Chapter 2.

A key assumption of social learning theory is that marital distress arises because partners have simply not learned the skills required to manage an intimate relationship in general (e.g., Weiss, 1978) and to solve their disagreements in particular. As unresolved conflicts accumulate, negative exchanges begin to outnumber rewarding ones, and partners experience increasing dissatisfaction with the relationship (Koerner & Jacobson, 1994). For the social learning perspective to be viable as an approach to understanding and repairing distressed relationships, it was necessary to demonstrate—at minimum—that unhappy couples, compared to happy couples, did in fact differ

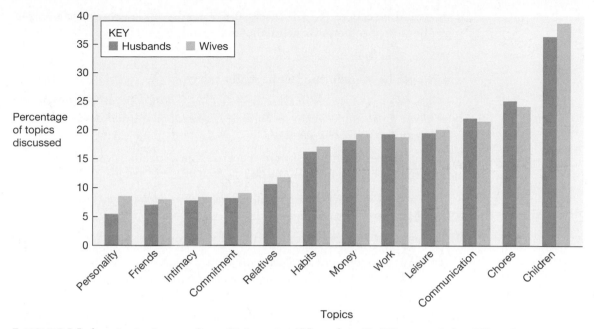

FIGURE 8.2 **Agreeing to disagree.** Over a 15-day period, 100 couples with children reported on 748 conflicts. Husbands and wives gave independent reports, but provided similar information about the topics of their disagreements. Totals can exceed 100% because more than one topic can be endorsed to describe a conflict. (Source: Papp, Cummings, & Goeke-Morey, 2009.)

in how they talked about their disagreements. Couples varying in their levels of marital satisfaction were brought to a laboratory setting and asked to discuss—and work toward resolving—an important marital disagreement for a specified length of time, usually 10 or 15 minutes. These discussions spanned a wide range of topics, and as **FIGURE 8.2** shows, most disagreements in established relationships involve children, followed by chores, communication, leisure time, work, and money (Papp, Cummings, & Goeke-Morey, 2009). Research assistants were provided with audiotaped or videotaped recordings of couples as they conversed. After intensive training to sharpen their powers of observing and classifying interaction behaviors, the assistants analyzed the tapes using a detailed **coding system**, which outlined how specific codes were assigned to observed behaviors.

For example, if a wife began the discussion by saying:

> *I think a lot of our squabbling comes down to one thing: not enough money.*

Her speaking turn would be coded as a "Problem Description." The husband could respond in one of several ways. For example, he might say:

> *I get anxious just thinking about money problems.*

This would be coded as "Self-Disclosure" because he is expressing his feelings about the problem. Or he might say:

> *Yep. That's it in a nutshell. Money.*

This would be "Agreement." Or he might say:

> *I've been thinking about that. Joe asked me to help him out installing floors for about five hours on Saturdays, and I think I want to take him up on that. It's decent money.*

This would be a "Positive Solution" because it is a specific, constructive solution to the problem. Or he might say:

> *You think so? I think we are always squabbling about trivial stuff, like whose turn it is to wash the dog.*

This would be "Disagreement." And, finally, he might instead say:

> *Are you kidding me? We have more money coming in now than we've ever had. The problem does come down to one thing though: your out-of-control spending.*

This would be coded as "Criticism" because it ascribes responsibility for the problem solely to the other partner and because it expresses disapproval for what she does.

Recognizing that the content of partners' speech acts carried only part of the information in a speaking turn, the coding systems were also designed to classify the same speech acts on the basis of whether they were delivered with a positive, negative, or neutral emotional tone. We can see, for example, that the statement coded as Disagreement ("You think so? I think we are always squabbling about trivial stuff, like whose turn it is to wash the dog.") would have a completely different effect on the partner if it were delivered with a smile and a humorous tone of voice, versus with a scowl and an angry tone of voice. The coding of emotional tone for each speaking turn helps resolve this ambiguity.

Identification of verbal content and emotional tone—also known as **affect**, such as sadness, or affection, or anger—would be done for each speaking turn expressed by each couple in the study. Research assistants typically were not told if the couples were happy or unhappy, so that the coding would reflect only the behaviors observed rather than global impressions of how happy and unhappy couples were. In addition, a subset of the discussions was coded independently by at least two research assistants; their **interrater reliability** was then computed to determine whether the coding process was in fact objective and verifiable. If interrater reliability was low, for a particular couple or for a particular code, it meant the two assistants were not seeing the same things in the conversations. Additional training to achieve high reliability would ensure that consensus could be achieved on the variables to be analyzed. This painstaking work enabled investigators to have reasonable assurance that the coding system they used could be duplicated by a different investigative team.

ANALYZING COUPLE INTERACTIONS. In this type of study, data analyses are designed with one main objective: to compare groups of happy and unhappy couples and thereby determine whether they differ in their use of any of the behavioral codes. Relative happiness is the independent variable because it is assumed to be the cause of the behaviors; the behaviors are the dependent variables in the sense that how they vary is assumed to depend on the happiness of the relationship. BOX 8.1 provides additional details. Note that this is a nonexperimental study design because none of the variables is manipulated by the researchers. Both variables are simply measured, and their degree of association or covariation is then examined. We cannot infer from this design that the degree of relationship happiness is the cause of the observed behaviors, a fact that takes on considerable importance later in this chapter.

BOX 8.1 SPOTLIGHT ON . . .

Quantifying Couple Communication

When relationship scientists conduct detailed analyses of couple communication, they typically study two kinds of dependent variables. The first are called **unconditional probabilities** because they reflect how often a coded behavior would occur, disregarding any other behaviors. If a husband expressed disagreement 22 times out of the entire set of 220 speaking turns, his unconditional probability for disagreement is 22/220 or 0.10. Using this information, we can see that his relationship is probably better than one in which a husband has an unconditional probability of 110/220 or 0.50 for this same code.

Notice, however, that the unconditional probabilities of all the codes for both partners are unlikely to tell you everything you want to know about how a couple is discussing their disagreement. For example, your reactions to those 22 expressions of disagreement would be affected by whether the statements came after neutral problem descriptions or disagreement statements made by the wife. In the former case, you might conclude that the husband was instigating a conflict (wife's problem

description → husband's disagreement), whereas in the latter case, you might conclude that he is perpetuating a conflict (wife's disagreement → husband's disagreement). We know intuitively that the sequence of behaviors is powerful; after all, a kiss followed by a slap is entirely different than a slap followed by a kiss (Hinde, 1979)—even though the unconditional probability of kissing and slapping in the two sequences is identical.

By analogy, we know that a tennis match is much more than the total number of times the two players hit various shots; the dynamic flow of the match is captured better by the sequence of strokes that make up the exchanges. **Conditional probabilities** address exactly this situation and represent the relationship between partners' unconditional probabilities: the likelihood, for example, that the wife's problem descriptions are followed by the husband's disagreements. With the full set of behavioral codes, and the unconditional and conditional probabilities that describe them, investigators have the statistical tools that enable them to achieve a strong understanding of how conflicts unfold.

In a particularly elegant series of studies, clinical psychologist John Gottman (1979) built on the seminal observational work by psychologist Harold Raush and his colleagues (1974) by demonstrating that the problem-solving conversations of unhappy couples do indeed differ from those of happy couples in three specific ways. According to Gottman's **structural model of marital interaction**, the interactions of unhappy couples can be characterized by the following:

■ *Less positive behavior and more negative behavior*. This comes as no surprise, of course. Less obvious, however, is the finding that *how* couples communicate about disagreements is a good predictor of whether they are happy or unhappy. Unhappy couples are 10 times more likely to use a negative tone of voice as are happy couples in these situations. What we say and how we say it are indeed different channels of interpersonal communication, and while we can never disentangle them completely, the latter is probably more important than the former in our relationships. Can you imagine what tone of voice the woman in **FIGURE 8.3** is using? And which is more important, the request she's making or the way she's making it?

"How did Operation Remember to Pick Up Milk go?"

FIGURE 8.3 Operation Don't Say What You Really Mean. The emotional tone a person uses to express his or her complaints has a powerful impact on how the partner will respond. Here, the woman's sarcastic comment could easily prompt an angry response from the man, much more so than a matter-of-fact statement ("Honey, did you have a chance to pick up the milk?") or an understanding statement ("You forgot the milk—is everything OK?"). Her use of language that mocks his occupation may make it even harder for him to respond without anger or defensiveness.

■ *Greater predictability of behaviors between partners*. Unhappy couples, generally, show more predictable patterns and structure in their conversations than do happy couples. How an unhappy partner behaves tends to be limited or governed by what has already been said, more so than is the case of happy partners. This probably parallels the feeling of being stuck in a rut when it comes to relationship disagreements, so that no matter how disagreements start, they seem to unfold the same way and end in the same place.

■ *Longer cycles of reciprocal negative behavior*. Unhappy partners are more likely to reciprocate negative behaviors and remain mired in longer cycles of this negative reciprocity than happy couples. Some of the specific ways unhappy couples get stuck in these cycles—and the ways happy couples exit them—are shown in **TABLE 8.1**. As you read them, see

TABLE 8.1 **Strategies for Conflict Resolution**

Destructive Strategies	Constructive Strategies
Linking the current issue to other problems in the relationship.	Staying focused on the problem at hand.
Blaming your partner for the problem.	Recognizing one's own contributions to the problem.
Listening to devise a new attack on your partner.	Listening to understand what your partner is saying.
Asking hostile and closed-ended questions.	Asking open-ended questions.
Assuming you know what your partner is thinking and feeling about the issue.	Asking your partner about his or her thoughts and feelings about the topic.
Summarizing your own position and opinions.	Summarizing your partner's position and opinions.
Following your partner's complaint with your own complaint.	Following your partner's complaint with requests for more information.
Working to show that your partner is wrong.	Working toward consensus and agreement.
Prescribing what your partner must do to solve this problem.	Offering constructive suggestions about what you can do to solve the problem.
Delivering ultimatums.	Remaining flexible and offering possible solutions.
Emphasizing points of disagreement.	Looking for points of agreement.
Raising issues with an accusatory or hostile tone.	Raising issues in a neutral and gentle way.
Rejecting your partner's views as invalid or misinformed.	Accepting your partner's views as important.
Displaying negative nonverbal behaviors while listening.	Listening with genuine interest.
Interrupting your partner.	Letting your partner finish his or her thoughts.

whether there is any rule or principle that summarizes the constructive strategies. Can you see how they all serve to keep the lines of communication open, whereas the destructive strategies close off communication?

Guided by principles of social learning theory, and armed with little more than cameras, coding systems, and trained research assistants, relationship scientists have been able to observe and analyze conversations between intimate partners and discover a surprising degree of organization and quantifiable structure. This line of work gave researchers a new and more precise language for articulating the communication difficulties that unhappy couples were having. The strategies shown in Table 8.1, for example, put a far more specific point on the kinds of things relationship partners could do to make their disagreements more constructive. Psychological approaches that promote effective conflict management to improve relationships will be discussed in Chapter 12. For now we stay focused on conflict itself, for one simple reason: Hour after hour of direct observation of couple communication was merely the starting point for even deeper insights about conflict between intimate partners.

Partner Perceptions of Conflict

Initially, social learning theorists would have simply liked to offer unhappy partners a behavioral recipe for getting their relationship on track. Established principles of good communication do exist, but studies would soon show that a complete explanation for why some couples struggle to connect required analyses that went beyond the words they exchanged. Even the observational work itself gave important clues that researchers would have to delve deeper, into partners' perceptions; happy spouses, for example, were assumed to engage in **cognitive editing**, whereby they would hear something negative but respond back in a neutral or even a positive way (Gottman, 1979). Similarly negative behaviors in unhappy relationships would spark ever-escalating cycles of hostility. What was going on here? Our behaviors do not speak for themselves, it seems, and the same behavior can have dramatically different meanings in two different relationships or for two people in the same relationship.

It turns out that disagreements arise in our relationships not simply because of differing goals and agendas, as Lewin suggested, but because we and our partners are operating on the basis of remarkably different perceptions and experiences of our relationships. Diary studies have been valuable for showing that there is greater correspondence or linkage between daily events and daily satisfaction ratings for unhappy couples than for happy couples, *regardless of whether the events are positive or negative* (Margolin, 1981; Wills, Weiss, & Patterson, 1974). One explanation for this, the **reactivity hypothesis**, suggests that unhappy spouses are more sensitive to the tone of immediate events in their relationship—they might be "on guard" and ready to find meaning in the things their partner said and did, good and bad, as a way of gauging how the relationship was going (Jacobson, Follette, & McDonald, 1982). Perhaps the radar for happy spouses is less sensitive, and because they feel pretty good about how the relationship is going already, their judgments of relationship quality do not fluctuate so much from day to day as a result of their verbal exchanges.

More interesting still is the finding that, when comparisons were made between husbands' and wives' reports of daily events, the level of agreement between them was quite low; about half the time or less, spouses did not agree on specific events that one partner said had occurred (Christensen & Nies, 1980; Christensen, Sulloway, & King, 1983; Jacobson & Moore, 1981). This was true in all relationships, though more pronounced among the unhappy couples. To make matters worse, the biases unhappy spouses have tend to put the partner in an unfavorable light. In one study, unhappy couples seeking therapy agreed less than 60 percent of the time about whether or not their relationship was marked by physical aggression in the previous year (Simpson & Christensen, 2005). In general, both partners report a lower level of aggression for themselves than the partner attributes to them.

We learn, then, that any analysis of partner interaction is incomplete without considering how the partners themselves make sense of the behaviors they send and receive. It is not an easy task to devise tools that permit real-time glimpses inside the heads of relationship partners actively engaged in a disagreement, but some creative approaches have been developed to do so. One procedure, called the **talk table**, pinpoints the source of a couple's miscommunication by structuring a problem-solving discussion (Gottman et al., 1976). For instance:

- Partner A begins the conversation and then pushes a button that rates the *intended impact* of his or her message, ranging from "super negative" to "neutral" to "super positive."

- On the receiving end of this message, partner B rates the *actual impact* of the message as he or she experiences it, using the same scale. Partner B then generates a response, rates its intended impact, and then delivers it to partner A.

- Partner A is now on the receiving end and rates the actual impact of the message partner B just delivered, generates his or her own response, and rates its intended impact.

- This pattern continues for an entire 10- or 15-minute conversation. Partners can see each other at all times, but they cannot see each others' ratings.

Results from this classic study show that happy and unhappy couples are similar in that they both send messages that they intended to be positive in their impact. However, only happy couples rate the actual *impact* of these messages as positive; unhappy couples, in contrast, rate the actual impact of the partner's messages as relatively negative (Gottman, 1979; also see Markman, 1981). So, one partner might say, "Honey, you really do need to be less of a slob around home" and intend this to be a positive and even constructive statement. A happy partner might see the positive intent ("Point well taken"), whereas an unhappy partner might see it as an attack.

> " The fact that two spouses living in the same environment perceive such different worlds suggests that in functional terms, spouses are operating in vastly different environments."
>
> —Neil Jacobson and Danny Moore, clinical psychologists, (1981, p. 276)

To overcome the fact that our perceptions, much less our goals and agendas, are not always shared, one of our tasks as intimate partners is to clarify verbal information and strive for mutual understanding of day-to-day events, and be prepared to acknowledge that our perceptions are often just subjective impressions, rather than objective representations of the events around us. The demonstrated lack of agreement between partners, together with evidence for the reactivity hypothesis, would generate volumes of research on cognition in relationships (i.e., perceptions and interpretations of relationship events; see Chapters 9 and 10). For now, however, we have to recognize that much of the work described thus far highlights small building blocks of intimate communication, such as partners' specific speaking turns in conversation and how they are perceived by trained coders and the participants themselves. As valuable as this perspective is, you might also wonder whether these building blocks can be combined to capture larger patterns of behavior that unfold over longer periods of time. The answer is yes.

Broad Behavior Patterns in Arguments

German philosopher Arthur Schopenhauer's parable of the porcupines, in the margin on the next page, provides a classic illustration of the changing dynamics of intimate relationships. It suggests that there is a delicate balance in the behaviors exchanged by partners, and that it can take effort and co-ordination to maximize the benefits of intimacy while minimizing the costs. For an example of how this delicate balance unfolds, consider the following case study (Christensen & Jacobson, 2000, pp. 1–7):

Debra: *After eight years of marriage and almost two years of courtship before that, I still cannot communicate with Frank. The problem is, he doesn't listen to me. He never shares his feelings, just turns off, withdraws. I hardly ever can figure out what's going on with him. In many ways I'm just the opposite: I have a lot of ups and downs. But most of the time I'm energetic, optimistic, spontaneous. Of course I get upset, angry, and frustrated sometimes. . . .His lack of communication bothers me most when we disagree about something. I want to discuss our differences and try to work out a solution. I expect conflict in a close relationship; I'm not threatened by it; and I want to deal with it openly. But Frank won't even discuss it. At the first sign of tension, he runs. He offers some feeble platitude like "Things will work themselves out." I think the root of our problem is Frank's sensitivity to criticism and anger.*

Frank: *Debra never seems to be satisfied. I'm never doing enough, never giving enough, never loving enough, never sharing enough. You name it, and I don't do enough of it. I think she must be insecure. She wants constant reassurance. Maybe she's bored with her life. She's always looking for high drama and excitement in the relationship. It's really a* *soap-opera view of love, where everything has to be heavy and emotional. But I want our relationship to be a place where I can retreat from the stresses and strains of my life, not one more addition to them. I don't put down Debra for being the way she is. I'm basically a tolerant person. . . .So I don't take offense at little annoyances; I don't feel compelled to talk about every difference or dislike; I don't feel every potential area of disagreement has to be explored in detail. I just let things ride. When I show that kind of tolerance, I expect my partner to do the same for me.*

This case depicts one of the best-recognized patterns of conflictual communication in couples, the **demand/withdraw pattern** (Wile, 1981; also see Napier, 1978). Debra and Frank both see Debra as the more engaged person in the relationship and as the person who wants more emotional closeness, and they agree that Frank likes the status quo and is less inclined to engage with Debra in an emotional way. What's interesting is that each downplays his or her own contributions to this recurring conflict, and each finds fault with the other person's characteristic response ("He is too sensitive to criticism." "She wants drama all the time."). We might say that the two partners punctuate the conversation in different ways. Debra feels justified in pursuing Frank *because* he is disengaged and unwilling to discuss important issues; Frank feels he must disengage from Debra *because* she is so demanding. From their individual perspectives, each one is being reasonable and is simply the innocent victim of the partner's unreasonable ideas about what it means to be close in an intimate relationship. The self-perpetuating quality in this pattern of interaction is obvious: Debra's requests for change in the relationship might cause Frank to become more defensive and disengaged, reactions that might, in turn, cause Debra to become more demanding and insistent, thereby causing Frank to pull back still further—or to dig in his heels and explode. In cases like this the couple is **polarized**, in the sense that they have adopted different viewpoints, or opposing positions, in the conflict they have created. And, beyond simply having different positions in the dispute, each makes the problem worse for the other by doing what each sees as reasonable and justifiable—merely responding to the behavior of the other! They are in a reciprocal trap, and the more one behaves in ways considered reasonable, the more the other becomes unreasonable, and thus the gulf between them widens.

You can see from this example that the cognitive processes outlined earlier are at work in full force. You can also see that we are now considering conflict at a broader level, compared with the closer level of focusing intently on each person's speaking turns in the conversation. Now we are looking at the

> " On a cold winter day, a group of porcupines huddled together closely to save themselves by their mutual warmth from freezing. But soon they felt the mutual quills and drew apart. Whenever the need for warmth brought them closer together again, this second evil was repeated, so that they were tossed back and forth between these two kinds of suffering until they discovered a moderate distance that proved tolerable. . . . To be sure, this only permits imperfect satisfaction of the need for mutual warmth, but it also keeps one from feeling the prick of the quills."
>
> —Arthur Schopenhauer, philosopher (1851)

forest, where before we saw only the trees. Is there a larger pattern that can give meaning to all the specific statements the partners are making? This is generally how professionals working directly with couples address relationship problems, in terms of broad patterns rather than specific reciprocation sequences. Couples themselves might find it more intuitive to think about their interaction style in terms of hot button issues and dynamics or patterns that emphasize the interdependence of each partner's actions.

Two main factors converge to produce the demand/withdraw pattern (Eldridge et al., 2007). First, when discussing difficulties perceived in their relationship, women tend to want more change than men do. This is true in general, and it is true even when couples discuss topics that are not problems in the relationship. The difference is exaggerated, however, when women are given the opportunity to air their complaints in laboratory studies. So, when couples' videotaped conversations about relationship problems are analyzed for demanding and withdrawing behaviors, women tend to do more of the demanding and men more of the withdrawing. When the situation is reversed, and men are given the chance to air their complaints, men and women are more or less equal in how much they demand and how much they withdraw.

Our discussion of sex role identity and male-female differences in Chapter 4 sheds some light on why this might be. After highlighting the idea that men and women are far more similar than different, we reviewed the idea that gender differences add up to suggest that women orient more toward dyadic connections, whereas men orient more toward hierarchical connections. The average woman is more attuned to the quality of the intimate bond than the average man, and the average man is more aware of whether he is in a one-up or a one-down position than the average woman (Sommer & Baumeister, 1997). Men are seeking to maintain or improve that position—to assert or expand their power, as it were—while women are seeking to maintain or improve the intimate connection. Men may hear demands for change as a threat to their status and therefore resist; women may hear resistance to change as a threat to their intimacy and therefore push for more change. The expected demand/withdraw pattern becomes apparent only when the women's desires for change are under discussion, presumably because they have more to gain from pursuing change, whereas men have more to gain by avoiding it (Jacobson, 1989).

Second, this pattern will be more extreme in relationships where people want a lot of change—unhappy couples. An unhappy wife's demand for closeness is therefore greater than that of a happy wife, but this could have the unintentional effect of strengthening the husband's desire for autonomy, resulting in his withdrawal, avoidance of confrontation, and distancing—and the perpetuation of the pattern. (Recall how this pattern was apparent in the interactions between Marilyn Monroe and Joe DiMaggio.) FIGURE 8.4, from a study by clinical psychologist Kathleen Eldridge and her colleagues (2007), summarizes how relationship problems produce the demand/withdraw pattern

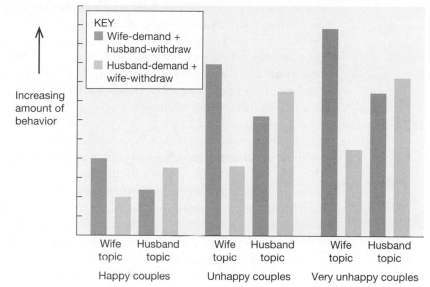

FIGURE 8.4 The demand/withdraw pattern. Direct observation of couples discussing relationship problems lets researchers measure how much husbands and wives display demand behaviors (e.g., pressuring the partner for change, nagging) and withdraw behaviors (e.g., avoiding the topic, denying the problem). This figure shows that wives demand and husbands withdraw more than the opposite pattern, particularly during discussion of wives' problem topics and among unhappy couples. (Source: Adapted from Eldridge et. al., 2007.)

during conflict. Studies conducted in Brazil, Italy, and Taiwan replicate these basic effects (Christensen et al., 2006).

What implications does this have for Frank and Debra? Think about what advice you might give them. You're on the right track if you're thinking you would first want to help them see the recurring pattern and recognize how each of them contributes to it, before working to change it. For her part, Debra needs to see that Frank wants the relationship to be a place of refuge, which she threatens with her criticism and anger. Frank needs to see that Debra wants the relationship to be a place where they both share and express their feelings, which he threatens by closing down and turning away from her. And both might need to accept the real possibility that their partner will never be perfect. Paradoxically, Debra might be able to get more closeness by demanding less of it from Frank, and Frank might get more solace by not insisting on it so much.

Mismanaged Conflict as a Cause of Relationship Distress

The research findings presented thus far do not address whether the ways in which couples approach and manage their disagreements determine, in a causal sense, the quality of their relationship. There is little doubt now that distressed relationships are routinely *characterized by* poor communication, but we have not yet addressed whether these deficits are *the means by which* relationship distress might arise. Relationship distress may be the cause of communication problems, or some other variable (such as a troubled family background or poor judgment in mate selection) may cause poor communication *and* unfulfilling relationships.

Relationship scientists have sought this missing clue by following couples over time in longitudinal studies, typically by inviting them to participate in an observational assessment at one point, and later asking the partners if they are still married; if they are, they are then asked to complete questionnaires measuring relationship satisfaction (see Chapter 2). First-time newlywed couples are particularly valuable for this type of study because they are almost uniformly happy with their relationship, thereby permitting analysis of how much their satisfaction level changes, as well as tracking couples whose relationships eventually dissolve. Longitudinal studies of newlyweds are interesting because census data show that divorce is most common in the first few years of marriage (Bramlett & Mosher, 2002). Couples often start families in these early years, and couples on average undergo a rapid decline in judgments about relationship satisfaction (**FIGURE 8.5**). So change is clearly happening, and the question is whether these changes are somehow

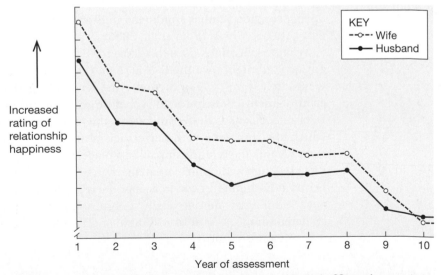

FIGURE 8.5 **Declining satisfaction during a marriage.** In this study, 93 couples reported on the level of happiness in their relationship over 10 years. On average, their satisfaction decreased at first, then stabilized, and then declined again. (Source: Adapted from Kurdek, 1999.)

a consequence of the ways in which couples discuss their conflicts. Some newlyweds are quite good at resolving differences, while others struggle mightily with this basic task. Does it matter?

Couples who express a lot of strong negative sentiments and emotions during their arguments—hostility, name-calling, verbal abuse, angry accusations, and the like—do indeed experience unhappy and unstable relationships, especially if they do these things regularly (Rogge et al., 2006). But the effects of more ordinary bad communication—such as listening poorly; being defensive, disagreeable, or stubborn; not being able to generate or sustain reasonable solutions—are usually weaker and a bit more subtle to see. For example, anger and poorer problem-solving skills have been shown to predict both *lower* levels of satisfaction (Gill, Christensen, & Fincham, 1999) and *higher* levels of satisfaction (Gottman & Krokoff, 1989; Karney & Bradbury, 1997). How could this be?

One possibility is that some unskilled forms of communication are relatively direct and clear while others are ambiguous, and that only the direct expressions bring about the desired change in the relationship. Consider the following two statements; assume they are delivered with an identical tone of voice and expression of emotion, and that they are intended to achieve the exact same change in the partner:

- "Look, I'm going to have to insist that you start cleaning up the kitchen right after dinner. I'm exhausted when I come home from work, and you have to pitch in. Wrap up the leftovers, wipe down the table, and load the dishwasher. I am not asking much, but I'm not giving you a choice in the matter, either. Are you with me on this?"

- "Look, after work I'm stressed, and you know that. You should be ashamed of yourself for not helping me out more. Can you see that I'm stressed, and that I'm already doing more around the house than you?"

Which approach is going to work?

Carefully distinguishing between direct and indirect strategies, and between positive and negative strategies, allowed social psychologists Nickola Overall, Garth J. O. Fletcher, Jeffry Simpson, and Chris Sibley (2009) to show that direct statements work best, even if they are negative. Not all negative communication is counterproductive. Negative messages may be painful to hear and deliver, but if they are direct, specific, and reasonable, they can benefit the relationship over time. Negative but vague statements, in contrast, might elicit defensiveness or counterattacks. In the example above, the first statement represents the direct approach, whereas the second statement is nonspecific and might not lead to the desired result.

The expression of positive emotions—such as gentle humor, interest, and affection—is another factor that can influence whether negative communication behaviors are detrimental for relationships. We might expect that warm and positive emotions expressed during an important discussion could soften any adverse effects of the negative statements partners make, while the absence of warmth and positivity would allow those negative statements to register with a painful sting. Longitudinal research supports this claim. When newlywed spouses display *high* levels of positive emotion, poor communication skills appear to have little effect on how much the marriage changes in the next 4 years. But when levels of positive emotion are *low*, then negative skills emerge as potent predictors of rapid declines in relationship happiness (Huston & Vangelisti, 1994; Johnson et al., 2005; Smith, Vivian, & O'Leary, 1990). As findings from this line of research become clearer, relationship scientists naturally wonder whether they can predict the fate of marriages by observing how couples discuss disagreements. **BOX 8.2** introduces some of the complexities that arise when they attempt to do so.

Observing the emotions partners display in problem-solving discussions has proven valuable for describing and predicting relationship distress, and to learn more in this area, researchers have collected biological measures presumed to reflect emotional processes during problem-solving conversations. In one study by psychoneuroimmunologist Janice Kiecolt-Glaser and her colleagues (2003), couples checked into a special hospital wing for a 24-hour stay. With permission, blood samples were taken at regular intervals. The samples were analyzed for the presence of hormones—epinephrine (or adrenaline), norepinephrine, cortisol, and adrenocorticotropic hormone— that indicate stress levels and how the body responds. Following a 90-minute baseline observation period, the couples began a 30-minute discussion with instructions to work toward resolving two or three important relationship problems. Their stress hormone levels were then monitored for several hours.

The negative behaviors partners display in these discussions are important when predicting the status and quality of the relationship 10 years later, but higher levels of the stress hormones are far more useful in predicting which newlywed couples will divorce and which marriages will become distressed (**FIGURE 8.6**). Conflict may well be important for the longevity of marriages, but perhaps not for the reasons we expect. Observable features of conflict may reveal only a few clues for understanding relationship deterioration. On the other hand, discussions that stir up couples biologically may be quite potent in taking their toll on the well-being of intimate relationships, despite evidence that these biological responses are largely outside of conscious awareness most of the time. Chronic exposure to conflict produces biological changes that gradually have a negative effect on health and well-being.

Here is a good way to summarize all the findings we have covered. When discussing their differences of opinion, couples will thrive when they communicate that the relationship is a safe, secure, and even nurturing place, and when they eliminate any sense that they are a threat to each other. Social learning theory helps identify some strategies people use to create feelings of security and minimize threat. This goal itself is actually not within the boundaries of social learning theory, but it may sound familiar because it is part of another major theoretical framework we discussed in Chapter 3

BOX 8.2 SPOTLIGHT ON . . .

Predicting Marital Outcomes

Is it possible, in 9 cases out of 10, to predict the state a marriage will be in several years later? Relationship scientists have quantified the behaviors displayed by couples, typically when resolving relationship conflicts, and have linked these data with whether the couples later divorced and, if not, with spouses' later judgments of how satisfied they are in their relationship. In a series of studies using different groups of couples and a variety of ways of measuring couple communication, they report surprisingly high levels of accuracy in predicting these outcomes: 95 percent accuracy over 15 years (Hill & Peplau, 1998), 94 percent over three years (Buehlman, Gottman, & Katz, 1992), 92.7 percent over 4 years (Gottman & Levenson, 1999b), 84 percent over 2 years (Gottman, 1994; Larson & Olson, 1989). These findings received a great deal of attention in the popular media. If they were true, they could lead to early identification of couples at risk for divorce. Could it be true that a detailed analysis of a 10- or 15-minute conversation can foretell the fate of intimate relationships with this degree of precision?

Strong claims require strong data, and these findings have attracted scrutiny by other relationship scientists (Heyman & Slep, 2001; Rogge & Bradbury, 1999). Scholars identify several factors to suggest that these prediction studies overestimate the amount of information contained in the observed behaviors, and that the reported levels of prediction are inflated. For example:

- Some studies involve couples who have been married several years. We might expect that if higher levels of anger predict dissatisfaction or divorce, the anger spouses are expressing may be in part a *consequence* of existing levels of dissatisfaction rather than a cause of it.
- Some studies involve only couples who are extremely high or extremely low in relationship satisfaction. Use of extreme groups makes prediction appear stronger than it might be. By analogy, we might be successful in predicting very hot and very cold days according to the month of the year, but prediction will suffer when we add in all the remaining days of medium temperatures. And indeed, by definition most couples fall in the middle range of satisfaction, rather than at either extreme.
- The statistical methods used to analyze these data are designed to extract as much predictive information as possible from the independent variables. This has advantages, but when a high number of variables is collected from small samples of couples (few of whom, typically, go on to divorce), applying these procedures results in different information being extracted from the samples. High levels of prediction are achieved, but the specific nature of this prediction can differ from study to study. Sometimes, researchers take the predictive solution they discover in one data set and then apply the same solution to another similar data set. This is known as **cross-validation**. In principle, if prediction is valid, it should work well across the different data sets. But when attempts cross-validate one set of predictive results on a new sample of couples, the prediction levels drop dramatically (Heyman & Slep, 2001). The key task is not to achieve maximally high levels of prediction but to establish an appropriately high level of prediction that will be robust across many couples.
- A true prediction study has not yet been undertaken. This would require collecting data, making a prediction on the basis of these data, then waiting a certain amount of time to see whether the prediction was correct. Instead, marital outcomes are already known at the time the "prediction" is made, thus allowing investigators to revise their predictions depending on the results they obtain. Research typically proceeds in this fashion, though several independent replications are needed to conclude that prediction has been achieved.

Can marital outcomes be predicted with greater than 90 percent accuracy? The answer is yes, but this is not the most important question. The answer to the important question—Can marital outcomes be predicted with greater than 90 percent accuracy, with identical procedures, across diverse samples of couples?—is no, at least not yet.

As you read about findings such as these in the popular media, bear in mind that reporting and science are often odd bedfellows: Reporting tends to emphasize one-night stands (provocative findings perceived to be breakthroughs, reported once, without much context or analysis), whereas science tends to emphasize long-term committed relationships (repeated tests of trustworthiness, daily attention to mundane details, a fair amount of consistency).

and again in Chapter 6. We now find ourselves at the doorstep of attachment theory, which offers a different explanation for why couples vary in how they mismanage conflicts.

ATTACHMENT THEORY AND COUPLE CONFLICT.   Because children receive different kinds of care, they develop various working models of attachment, the two basic dimensions of anxiety (reflecting positive versus negative views of one's self) and avoidance (reflecting positive versus negative views of others). These working models guide relationship behavior well into adulthood. Extended specifically to the domain of conflict, attachment theory makes some specific predictions about how individuals with various working models will behave (Mikulincer & Shaver, 2007):

- Secure individuals, confident in the knowledge that they are worthwhile and that others are generally trustworthy and well-intentioned, are skilled problem solvers; they are unlikely to be threatened much by the partner's emotions or by the idea of having to discuss problems, nor will they be a threat to the partner.

- Individuals relatively high in attachment-related anxiety, with a negative view of themselves in relationships, are threatened by conflict because it can get in the way of the high level of approval and support they need from a close partner. They will assume the worst about their conflicts, obsess about them, and express their feelings of anxiety and hostility because they feel threatened.

- Individuals relatively high in attachment-related avoidance see others as unreliable, unavailable, and uncaring. Conflict threatens their need to keep some distance from intimacy and emotion, particularly because it calls attention to the unpleasant possibility that they are vulnerable or need something from another person. As a result they strive to regulate their emotions by keeping the conflict and the partner at bay; they work to avoid conflict and minimize the concerns the partner might raise. When conflict cannot be avoided, they do all they can to defend themselves and to create distance between themselves and their partner.

At this point you might well ask: Are our recollections of the early caregiving environment actually related to how we manage problems and conflicts with intimate partners in adulthood? Are there observable differences between securely and insecurely attached spouses? Yes, there are. Generally speaking, compared to secure individuals, insecure people tend to be poorer problem solvers, and they display less positive emotion and more negative emotion. Whereas secure people are good at fostering security in their closest relationships, insecure individuals seem to create friction in a variety of ways, such as by expressing less empathy and affection, escalating conflicts, neglecting to compromise, or disengaging (Alexandrov, Cowan, & Cowan, 2005; Campbell et al., 2005; Crowell et al., 2002; Feeney, 1998). Are there observable

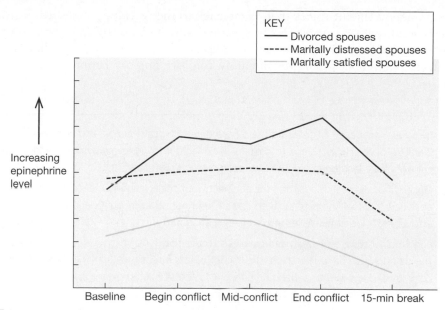

FIGURE 8.6 Stress hormones and marital satisfaction. Epinephrine, the fight-or-flight hormone, is released from the brain into the bloodstream when danger threatens, thus preparing the body for action by boosting the supply of oxygen and glucose to the muscles. The epinephrine levels of the newlyweds in this study were compared across couples, who 10 years later were either divorced, unhappily married, or happily married. Epineprine levels were higher in couples who went on to divorce or have unhappy marriages, compared to those who went on to have happy marriages. (Source: Adapted from Kiecolt-Glaser et al., 2003.)

differences among insecure individuals? For the most part, no, although evidence from a few studies indicates that avoidant people are more disengaged, closed off emotionally, and contemptuous compared to individuals with other insecure classifications (Creasey & Ladd, 2005).

Early social learning theorists were probably justified in rejecting prevailing models of personality and marriage in the 1970s, but it is now abundantly clear that attachment insecurity, and the early family relationships that give rise to it, shape the manner in which intimate partners approach, manage, and recover from conflict. From this large body of evidence we can draw a somewhat surprising conclusion: Factors that seem to be far removed from our current relationship—whether our parents divorced, whether our parents pushed and shoved each other in the heat of conflict, how our parents treated us, and our sense of how we were cared for as children—may well shape how we think, feel, and act when confronting problems and difficulties daily with our intimate partner. Thus, whereas research conducted from the social learning perspective encourages us to evaluate couples in conflict on the basis of rewards, costs, and ultimately the many specific ways in which partners create security and contain threat, attachment theory sees these same behaviors but traces their roots back to the working models the partners acquired early in life. Neither perspective is obviously right or wrong, yet it is significant that both draw attention to the powerful need we have for interpersonal bonds that provide safety, comfort, and protection.

MAIN POINTS

>> Disagreements arise because partners have different goals, needs, and interpretations. Because of their importance to couples seeking counseling, disagreements and verbal conflicts have long been of interest to relationship scientists.

>> Observational research adopting the perspective of social learning theory reveals several specific ways that intimate partners reward and punish each other, and how they can inadvertently lock themselves into communication patterns that are difficult to escape.

>> Longitudinal studies of newlywed couples indicate that harsh negative behaviors hasten the deterioration of relationships. The impact of less intense negative behaviors is more complex and appears to depend on how direct and specific they are, and whether they are accompanied by positive emotions like humor and affection.

>> Along with evidence that negative behaviors during conflict cause the release of fight-or-flight stress hormones, these findings lead to the observation that conflict management in intimate relationships is effective to the extent it conveys security while eliminating any sense of threat. Research on conflict derived from attachment theory shows continuities between insecure attachment and a wide array of problem-solving deficits.

Physical Aggression

Just after midnight on February 8, 2009, in Los Angeles, a 19-year-old man named Chris was driving with Robyn, his girlfriend of 18 months, when she noticed a long text message on his cell phone from a woman with whom he had previously had a sexual relationship. The police report, based on Robyn's recounting of the episode, noted that "a verbal argument ensued," and Chris opened the passenger door and tried to force Robyn out of the car. He was unable to do so because she was wearing her seatbelt. "He took his right hand and shoved her head against the passenger window . . . he punched her in the left eye . . . and continued to punch her in the face with his right hand while steering the vehicle with his left hand." Blood filled Robyn's mouth and spattered on her and in the car. Chris then said "I'm going to beat the shit out of you when we get home!" Robyn attempted to call a friend, Jennifer. Unable to reach her, Robyn pretended to talk to her and said, "I'm on my way home. Make sure the cops are there when I get there." Chris then stated, "You just did the stupidest thing ever! Now I'm really going to kill you!" Chris continued to punch, bite, and choke Robyn as she struggled to defend herself. At one point, his grip around her neck almost resulted in her losing consciousness. Eventually she put her back against the car door and, with her legs, pushed him away. Someone heard Robyn's screaming and called 911; the police responded and took her to a nearby hospital for treatment. Chris walked away but was later arrested for making criminal threats.

The young man in this case is singer Chris Brown, and the young woman is better known as Rihanna, internationally acclaimed pop singer and model. Both were nominated for Grammy Awards in 2009, and together they were planning to attend the awards ceremony later that same day. Images of Rihanna's badly bruised face were leaked to the media, and what is usually a private drama became a very public event. Subsequent news stories focused on Brown's apology, Rihanna's apparent willingness to take him back as her boyfriend, and the subsequent ups and downs of their relationship.

Incidents like this prompt some important questions about human intimacy. How is it that the very person to whom we turn for solace and compassion can sometimes become a source of verbal abuse, physical abuse, and even torture? And how is it that verbal sparring with an intimate partner—an experience familiar to many of us—can spin wildly out of control, as it apparently did in this case? By building on our preceding discussion about conflict, we can explore these questions.

We know from media reports and from extensive research that the aggressive physical contacts occurring between intimate partners vary widely in severity and form—from incidents of pushing, shoving, and slapping that almost always remain hidden behind closed doors, to murders, beatings, and burnings reported on the evening news. These exchanges all involve aggressive contacts between partners, but do they represent the same phenomena or different phenomena? Is it appropriate to develop theories and interventions using a single perspective on domestic violence, or are different approaches needed, depending on the nature of the aggressive acts?

Initially, more and less severe acts of aggression were assumed to fall along a single continuum. As studies accumulated, however, scholars with differing perspectives on relational aggression would produce findings that proved contradictory and difficult to integrate. One group, pursuing a **family sociology perspective** to understanding violence, tended to discover, for example, equal rates of aggression by women and men, or even *greater* rates of aggression by women than men. Another group, pursuing an **advocacy perspective** and seeking to understand aggression against women in particular, found that acts of aggression *almost always* involved men as perpetrators and women as victims. Far from being a mere academic debate, this discrepancy had drastic implications for the well-being of victims of domestic violence. If it were true, for example, that men and women were equally likely to be victimized and to comparable degrees, a case could be made that state and federal funding devoted to battered women would have to be shared with battered men (Straus, 1999).

The ambiguity was resolved when it was discovered that the two groups of scholars were sampling aggression in different ways. Family sociologists, by emphasizing data from large national surveys, were probably not studying the most aggressive couples in large numbers. The more extreme acts of aggression are rare by comparison, and survey respondents might be less likely to divulge them. Scholars in the advocacy tradition, in contrast, by emphasizing data specifically from national crime surveys and from battered women who had come into contact with emergency rooms, shelters, and police, were probably undersampling the less severe acts of aggression (Dobash & Dobash, 1990; Johnson, 1995; Lloyd & Emery, 1994; Steinmetz, 1978).

There is now growing consensus that these two approaches tap distinct types of aggression. In **situational couple violence**, typically a tense or heated exchange escalates to the point at which one or both members of a couple engage in some form of assault. More severe acts can happen in situational couple violence (e.g., beating up the partner, threatening with a knife or gun), but less extreme acts (e.g., pushing, grabbing, slapping) are most likely. Women are just as likely as men to engage in situational couple violence, and in some studies are shown to be more likely than men to do so.

In **intimate terrorism**, by contrast, aggression is one of several means used by one member of the couple (almost always the man, in different-sex relationships) to dominate and subjugate the partner (Johnson, 2008, 2011; Johnson & Ferraro, 2000). While situational couple violence tends to be used to control a specific dispute that erupts in the course of a relationship, intimate terrorism tends to be used to control the partner and hence comes to be a defining feature of the relationship. Situational couple violence can be thought of as being *reactive*, in the sense that it reflects frustration and hostility displayed in the midst of an argument; in some couples, under some conditions, verbal conflicts give way to hostile acts of pushing and shoving, and worse (TABLE 8.2). Intimate terrorism can be viewed as *proactive*, in the sense that it reflects a systematic and sustained strategy to intimidate another person and control what he or she is allowed to do (Chase, O'Leary, & Heyman, 2001; Tweed & Dutton, 1998). Perpetrators of intimate terrorism are sometimes called *batterers*, a term that captures the severity of this abuse and its one-sided nature.

Our primary focus is on situational couple violence, not because intimate terrorism is unimportant, but because intimate terrorism reveals far more about the individual psychopathology of the perpetrator, many of whom suffer from personality disorders and drug abuse problems, than about the relationship dynamics that give rise to aggressive acts (Moore et al., 2008). The dynamics that lead battered women to leave their abusive partners are quite interesting, however, and BOX 8.3 examines this issue.

Before discussing situational couple violence in detail, it will be helpful to examine the Conflict Tactics Scales (CTS), a commonly used set of questions designed to measure, over the span of the previous year, what happens when partners disagree (Straus et al., 1996). Although other indices are also

TABLE 8.2 Common Warning Signs of an Abusive Relationship

Victims and potential victims of domestic violence can feel afraid and confused. Do you . . .

> Feel afraid of your partner much of the time?
> Avoid certain topics out of fear of angering your partner?
> Believe that you deserve to be hurt or mistreated?
> Wonder if you're the one who is crazy?
> Feel emotionally numb or helpless?

Victims and potential victims are subjected to invalidation and belittling. Does your partner . . .

> Humiliate, criticize, or yell at you?
> Call you harsh names?
> Treat you so badly that you're embarrassed for your friends or family to see?
> Blame you for his or her own abusive behavior?
> See you as property or as a sex object, rather than as a person?

Perpetrators of domestic violence attempt to control their victim. Does your partner . . .

> Act excessively jealous and possessive?
> Control where you go or what you do?
> Keep you from seeing your friends or family?
> Read your mail or look at your personal papers?
> Limit your access to money, telephone, or car?

Perpetrators of domestic violence make threats and display aggressive acts. Does your partner . . .

> Have a bad and unpredictable temper?
> Hurt you, or threaten to hurt or kill you?
> Threaten to commit suicide if you leave?
> Force you to have sex?
> Destroy your belongings?

If you answered yes to one or more of these questions, you may be in an abusive relationship or be at risk for abuse. It is recommended that you speak with a domestic violence advocate.

Source: Adapted from www.helpguide.org (accessed February 5, 2013).

used to study aggression (e.g., arrest records, homicides, interviews), data from the CTS are a common source of evidence for testing hypotheses in this domain.

As you can see from **TABLE 8.3**, the CTS questions reflect negotiation strategies, psychological aggression, physical assault, sexual coercion, and the extent of resulting injuries. The CTS does not provide much information about the context of the aggression, such as what provoked a particular act, who initiated the aggression, or whether the act was in self-defense. This lack of attention to contextual details is a common criticism of the CTS (Kurz, 1993; Schwartz, 2000). For example, some abused women fight back, even to the point at which they kill the man who committed the abuse. This form of aggression, known as **violent resistance**, occurs in a small number of cases

BOX 8.3   SPOTLIGHT ON . . .

The Cycle of Intimate Terrorism

The problem of domestic violence in general, and intimate terrorism in particular, was thrust into the national spotlight in 1994 when O. J. Simpson was accused of murdering his former wife, Nicole Brown Simpson, and her friend Ronald Goldman outside her home. In the controversial "trial of the century," Simpson was acquitted of those charges in 1995, though in a civil trial 2 years later he was found "responsible" for the two murders. Though this incident raised public awareness about domestic abuse, the topic itself had been a focus of study for nearly two decades (Straus, Gelles, & Steinmetz, 1980; Walker, 1979).

We have seen that studying intimate relationships over time is essential to understanding them. This is also true with intimate terrorism because one important clue about physical abuse is that it does not occur all the time and in all situations. Clinical psychologist Lenore Walker (1979), in an early and influential study of battered women, identified a **cycle of violence** in which partners repeatedly go through three phases:

- The *tension-building phase*, in which the man's hostility escalates and emerges in the form of angry outbursts, often in response to his feelings of jealousy and a desire to control and contain the woman.
- The explosive, *acute battering phase*, in which the tension from the earlier stage is unleashed in the form of uncontrollable rage and aggression perpetrated by the man against the woman, often in the context of some disagreement or otherwise frustrating moment.
- The *contrition phase*, in which the man apologizes, promises to change, and tries to convince the woman and anyone else involved that the severe abuse will never happen again. A temporary calm is restored, but the promises are soon forgotten and the man's

desire to re-establish control soon reappears as the tension-building phase begins again.

This depiction appears to capture well the dynamics of battering, but some have criticized it because it fails to acknowledge how women often play an active role in extricating themselves from relationships in which they are abused (Kirkwood, 1993). The virtue of this view is evident in recent studies showing, contrary to popular wisdom, that battered women do leave their abusive relationships in large numbers. In a longitudinal study of women and their severely abusive husbands, 39 percent of couples had separated or divorced over a 2-year period (Gortner et al., 1997). This is a much higher rate of relationship dissolution than among couples in the general population.

These separations and divorces were all initiated by the women, and they were all more common among women subjected to degrading *emotional* abuse than those subjected to physical abuse. Emotional abuse is powerful because it is common in such relationships, and because it is a constant reminder of the physical abuse the women have also suffered. Virtually all physically abusive husbands also engage in some form of degrading emotional abuse, including unrelenting public insults, humiliation, and ridicule.

A batterer can decrease his illegal behavior (i.e., physical abuse) and substitute a legal behavior (i.e., emotional abuse and threats) and still be able to control his wife. Severe emotional abuse therefore prompts many women to leave their abusive marriages, particularly after they realize that their husband is a pathetic and fragile character, and that a relationship with him no longer allows her to achieve any of her dreams (e.g., raising a healthy, secure family; see Jacobson & Gottman, 1998).

involving intimate terrorism and is therefore quite rare (Johnson, 2006; see also Swan & Snow, 2002). But without recognizing that the woman's violence occurred in response the man's abuse, her actions would be misrepresented as intimate terrorism. Interpretation of findings generated with measures like the CTS must take this lack of contextual details into account. The creators

TABLE 8.3 Measuring Aggression in Relationships: The Conflict Tactics Scales

Instructions: No matter how well a couple gets along, there are times when they disagree, get annoyed with the other person, want different things from each other, or just have spats or fights because they are in a bad mood, are tired, or for some other reason. Couples also have many different ways of trying to settle their differences. This is a list of things that might happen when you have differences. Please circle how many times you did each of these things in the past year, and how many times your partner did them in the past year.

How often did this happen?

1 = Once in the past year	5 = 11–20 times in the past year
2 = Twice in the past year	6 = More than 20 times in the past year
3 = 3-5 times in the past year	7 = Not in the past year, but it did happen before
4 = 6-10 times in the past year	0 = This has never happened

I showed my partner I cared even though we disagreed.	1 2 3 4 5 6 7 0
I suggested a compromise to a disagreement.	1 2 3 4 5 6 7 0
I insulted or swore at my partner.	1 2 3 4 5 6 7 0
I called my partner fat or ugly.	1 2 3 4 5 6 7 0
I destroyed something belonging to my partner.	1 2 3 4 5 6 7 0
I threatened to hit or throw something at my partner.	1 2 3 4 5 6 7 0
I twisted my partner's arm or hair.	1 2 3 4 5 6 7 0
I pushed or shoved my partner.	1 2 3 4 5 6 7 0
I grabbed my partner.	1 2 3 4 5 6 7 0
I choked my partner.	1 2 3 4 5 6 7 0
I beat up my partner.	1 2 3 4 5 6 7 0
I used a knife or a gun on my partner.	1 2 3 4 5 6 7 0
I used threats to make my partner have sex.	1 2 3 4 5 6 7 0

Note: The actual items are not presented in this order on the CTS. For each item on the scale, another item asks about the partner's behavior. For example, the first item has a corresponding item that reads: "My partner showed care for me even though we disagreed."

Source: Adapted from Straus et al., 1996.

of the instrument note that their goal was to develop a measure of broad applicability in this field, and the CTS is intended to be used alongside other information that can clarify the circumstances in which the aggression arises (Straus et al., 1996). Some studies do include these details, yet it is important to remember that the CTS provides a narrow range of information for a wide variety of aggressive acts that can occur in relationships.

Characteristics of Situational Couple Violence

Having made the distinction between situational couple violence and intimate terrorism, we can now see that the incident in which Joe DiMaggio struck Marilyn Monroe was probably situational couple violence. We cannot be certain, because many details are not available; we don't know, for example, whether DiMaggio's jealous rage was part of an effort to control Monroe, how frequently similar events may have happened in the past, or whether Monroe was afraid of DiMaggio. But based on Monroe's comments, we can infer that DiMaggio was not intending to subjugate Monroe but was instead reacting to a specific situation in an outburst of jealous anger. How would you characterize the altercation between Chris Brown and Rihanna? These incidents highlight typical dimensions of situational couple violence: how it can begin, what happens, the nature of resulting injuries, and whether one or both partners are physically aggressive. However, because no single example can capture broader trends and themes about aggression, we aim to round out these illustrations by detailing the key characteristics of situational couple violence.

Let's begin with prevalence. Among engaged couples, more than half (57 percent) report either husband-to-wife or wife-to-husband aggression (or both) in the year before marriage (O'Leary et al., 1989; also see McLaughlin, Leonard, & Senchak, 1992). Pushing, grabbing, or shoving the partner tends to be the most common act of aggression, but slapping and throwing objects at the partner are also reported. Comparable data among a wider range of married couples reveal lower rates of aggression—16 percent (Straus & Gelles, 1990) and 19 percent (Kenney & McLanahan, 2006)—because divorce and separation take aggressive couples out of the population of married couples, thereby reducing the rate. Along similar lines, results from an anonymous survey administered to more than 42,000 members of the U.S. military indicated that 12.9 percent of the men and 15.1 percent of the women perpetrated intimate partner violence (Foran, Slep, & Heyman, 2011).

Rates of prevalence for dating couples are slightly lower than those for newlyweds, perhaps because of the lower levels of contact dating partners have, or the lower levels of control they exert on one another. For example, a study of more than 20,000 adolescents in grades 10–12 indicated that about 16 percent reported ever being a victim of dating violence (Marquart et al., 2007). In a random sample designed to be representative of 18- to 30-year-olds in dating relationships, 30 percent reported mild aggression against the partner in the previous year, and 11 percent reported perpetrating severe aggression (Stets, 1992). And a large study of more than 11,000 young adults ages 18–28 showed that about 24 percent of all relationships involved some type of physical aggression in the previous year (Whitaker et al., 2007).

Slightly higher overall rates of aggression are observed for couples living together than for those who are married—35 percent (Stets & Straus, 1990) and 31 percent (Kenney & McLanahan, 2006), respectively. The percentages vary from study to study because methods and samples are different, but the important and unvarying conclusion is that situational couple violence is very common.

Many people are surprised to learn that women in different-sex relationships display slightly more situational couple violence than men, and that women are more likely to initiate aggressive acts than men (Whitaker et al., 2007). By virtue of their greater size and strength, however, men are significantly more likely to injure women (**FIGURE 8.7**; Archer, 2000). This innate ability on the part of men to inflict greater harm on women than vice-versa is an essential qualification in any discussion of gender and physical aggression; ostensibly identical acts by men and women (e.g., a slap) are far more likely to result in greater pain and injury when committed by men (e.g., six times more likely; Cantos, Neidig, & O'Leary, 1994). Situational couple violence is not limited to different-sex relationships, of course; comparable rates and experiences of aggression are reported for intimate relationships between women and between men (Cruz & Firestone, 1998; Lie et al., 1991; Turell, 2000).

Few formal distinctions are made within the domain of situational couple violence, but couples can be distinguished on the basis of the severity of the aggression in their relationship, and according to whether acts of aggression are perpetrated solely by one partner, **unilateral aggression**, or by both partners, **bilateral aggression**. Milder acts tend to be more common than severe acts, and the aforementioned tendency for women to be more aggressive than men is evident at

FIGURE 8.7 Physical aggression. In situational couple violence, women are about as aggressive as men, and sometimes more aggressive. As this image suggests, because of larger size and greater strength, male acts of aggression usually cause more injury.

both lower and higher levels of severity (Williams & Frieze, 2005). Aggressive relationships are divided about equally between those characterized by bilateral and those by unilateral aggression, and the reciprocation of aggression appears to be especially important in determining the severity of any resulting injuries (Marcus, 2012).

Antisocial acts of all kinds decline with age, and this finding extends to situational couple violence (Kim et al., 2008; O'Leary, 1999). Nonviolent couples tend to stay nonviolent as their relationship develops, and aggressive couples tend to stay that way. About 60–80 percent of all young partners who are aggressive early in their relationship (e.g., during an engagement period) are likely to be aggressive again in the following 30 months (Capaldi, Shortt, & Crosby, 2003; Lorber & O'Leary, 2004). High levels of aggression tend to signal persistent violence over time (Lawrence, 2002; O'Leary et al., 1989). These situations are particularly difficult to change, even with therapy (Woodin & O'Leary, 2006).

If aggressive behavior tends to persist, does that mean a person who is aggressive in one relationship is destined to be aggressive in the next relationship? If the initial level of aggression is high and persistent, then the answer is probably yes. But, in general, when young adults form new relationships, the level of physical (and verbal) aggression in the new relationship is almost completely unrelated to how aggressive they were in the original relationship (Capaldi et al., 2003). Unlike intimate terrorism, this suggests that situational couple violence is less a product of individual personalities and more a consequence of how a specific couple communicates, and miscommunicates, when their tempers are flaring. The same people in different relationships, and in different situations, may well respond in more productive ways.

Situational couple violence might be viewed logically as an outgrowth of a deteriorating relationship and escalating frustration with the partner. Two people could grow disenchanted with each other and their relationship, become frustrated at their inability to get things back on track, and then behave aggressively at some particularly tense moment. As reasonable as this scenario sounds, we have already presented reasons suggesting that it is inaccurate: The high proportion of engaged and newlywed couples reporting violent behavior in the previous year indicates that it is in place early in relationships, and findings suggest that the aggression tends to decline thereafter, especially in milder cases. Does the aggression take a toll on the quality of the relationship? Yes. Couples whose aggression is more severe and persistent begin their relationship with lower levels of satisfaction and become even less satisfied over time (Heyman, O'Leary, & Jouriles, 1995). Aggressive behavior is generally associated with poor communication in intimate relationships (Schumacher & Leonard, 2005). In addition, aggression reveals something uniquely important about which couples are going to become unhappy and dissolve their relationship (Rogge & Bradbury, 1999; Testa & Leonard, 2001).

Oddly enough, many couples do not view the episodes of aggressiveness in their lives to be a significant problem, even when they are in a distressed relationship. When wives seeking marital therapy are asked to list their most important problems, only 6 percent list physical aggression, despite the fact that 56 percent of couples report aggression in interviews and 67 percent indicate its presence on the CTS (O'Leary, Vivian, & Malone, 1992). How could this be? A follow-up study shows that husbands and wives often discount the importance of aggression in their relationship because it is infrequent; they see it as a consequence of some other problem, such as poor communication (Ehrensaft & Vivian, 1996). Thus, as with verbal conflicts, there is a disparity between acts of aggression and the meaning spouses assign to them. Once again we are reminded of the need for multiple avenues of assessment when seeking to understand phenomena in intimate relationships.

Explaining Situational Couple Violence

Julie and Zack, in the fall semester of their junior and senior years, respectively, met in an advanced political science class. They shared a major (economics) and career aspirations (law), and after 4 months of low-key dating realized they had several mutual friends, common interests in Thai food and Dave Matthews, and a fascination with Nicolas Cage. Neither knew where the relationship was headed—they hadn't really talked about it and didn't see much need to—but they liked each other well enough and enjoyed the time they spent together, studying or relaxing over a few beers, fretting about graduate school. The start of school in January brought with it two important events: Julie and Zack slept together for the first time, and Zack's ex-girlfriend returned from a semester abroad in Spain. Contrary to what he had told Julie, Zack was hoping he might get back together with his ex-girlfriend, but he accepted Julie's invitation to go bar-hopping anyway and was happy they ended up having sex at his apartment. The next morning, Julie thought the moment was right to talk with Zack about the future of their relationship. To her shock and surprise, Zack balked, saying he wasn't ready to talk about it or make any kind of commitment. Julie suspected immediately that he wanted to resume his relationship with his ex-girlfriend. Feeling jealous and betrayed, she berated Zack for using her "like a toy" until his ex-girlfriend returned. Zack angrily denied this and felt falsely accused. He would later claim that he grabbed Julie by the wrists and pushed her onto a table only in self-defense, after she moved to slap him; she did not deny wanting to slap him but would claim that he grabbed (and bruised) her wrists and shoved her to prevent her from leaving. As she was storming out of his apartment, Zack's cell phone rang; on an impulse Julie answered it, and discovering Zack's ex-girlfriend on the line, hurled the phone at him, swore at him, and left in tears.

Why are any intimate partners aggressive? Why are some aggressive while others are not? Why are they violent at certain times but not others? To understand and explain situational couple violence, relationship scientists work at three broad levels of analysis to establish conceptual frameworks that can

FIGURE 8.8 Aggression in context. Theorists adopting a sociocultural perspective on aggression recognize that violence is common in many arenas of life.

organize research and inform interventions. These levels of analysis can be viewed as interconnected layers of explanation, each one adding detail where the others come up short.

According to the **sociocultural perspective on aggression**, violence in relationships must be understood with reference to the aggressiveness found in many realms of human behavior, such as warfare instigated in the name of religious or political agendas; violence depicted in movies, television shows, and video games; or aggression sanctioned in such sports as mixed martial arts, wrestling, and ice hockey (**FIGURE 8.8**). Elaborations on this view emphasize that people with limited access to valued resources (e.g., stable jobs, decent homes in good neighborhoods, education) have less invested in existing social structures and therefore less to lose from violating norms, that there are subcultural differences in the acceptability of violence, and that deadly weapons can be readily acquired and are often used in the home to harm family members. Feminist variants on the sociocultural perspective focus on how society is organized along gender lines, the greater institutional power men have in many arenas of social life, and men's use of aggression and threats to maintain the status quo. (An emphasis on the male-dominated organization of society takes on much greater weight in explaining intimate terrorism by men against women than it does in explaining common couple violence; see Dobash & Dobash, 1979; Dutton, 1995; Lloyd & Emery, 2000). A broad level of research support exists for the view that the causes of aggression can be found in social and cultural institutions (Geen & Donnerstein, 1998). At the same time, it is important to bear in mind a limitation of this approach: If most people are exposed to violent images in the media, for example, why is it that only some relationships are marked by aggressive behavior?

The **interpersonal perspective on aggression** acknowledges the role of these broad cultural and subcultural influences, and goes further. The association between sociocultural forces and aggression must be moderated by other potent forces; that is, interpersonal factors, such as the private and passionate nature of intimate relationships, the high degree of partner interdependence, the inevitable presence of disagreements and differing perceptions, and variations in the behavioral and cognitive capacities partners express in their interactions. If Zack, for instance, had been more skilled he could have seen that he was misleading Julie and could have clarified things. Acknowledging his true feelings for his ex-girlfriend, he might have responded differently to Julie's invitation to go bar-hopping: *"You know, I think I want to take a raincheck on that. But are you up for coffee in the morning* *tomorrow? There are some things I want to talk with you about, about how our relationship is going."* Julie might have been more suspicious of Zack and his ex-girlfriend, and she might have responded differently when Zack resisted talking about the future of their relationship, and so on.

Like interpersonal models of relationship communication in general, and social learning theory in particular, the interpersonal perspective on aggression focuses on the moment-by-moment details of dyadic exchanges (O'Leary, 1988). Can violent and nonviolent couples be distinguished on the basis of their communication in problem-solving situations? Indeed they can, even when they do not differ in their degree of dissatisfaction with the relationship. Aggressive partners tend to show more negative behaviors and more escalation of negative behaviors over the course of their problem-solving conversations, tend to report more intense feelings of emotional upset (Margolin, John, & Gleberman, 1988), and reciprocate partner behaviors that lead to further negativity (Burman, John, & Margolin, 1992). Distressed spouses tend to see the partner's negative behaviors as intentional, selfish, and blameworthy (Holtzworth-Munroe & Hutchinson, 1993), and these biased perceptions presumably fuel the negative exchanges. The key point is that the basic principles of distressed relationship communication can be extrapolated to encompass situational couple violence; aggressive couples appear to be more extreme in their behaviors and cognitions than those who are unhappy in their relationship but not aggressive. Although physically aggressive acts are not observed in these interactions, the assumption is that daily, ordinary disagreements, particularly those involving jealousy, rejection, and criticism, escalate into aggressive episodes because people misperceive their partner's behaviors and lack the competence to generate more effective responses, particularly when they are in riskier situations (Holtzworth-Munroe & Hutchinson, 1993). For example, alcohol consumption, which impairs the ability to control emotional responses and reduces inhibitions, intensifies poor communication skills in relationships, particularly when men are drinking (Leonard & Quigley, 1999; Leonard & Roberts, 1998; White & Chen, 2002).

The **intraindividual perspective on aggression** focuses on the fact that partners differ in ways that might cause them to contribute differently to the aggression that occurs between them. Although partners can differ in many important ways, such as general degree of hostility, attitudes toward and tolerance of aggression, history of psychopathology, education and job status, and preference for traditional versus egalitarian relationships, the strongest intraindividual models trace the roots of aggression back to the family of origin. Recall from Chapter 6 that early family environments are the training grounds for how people behave in their later relationships. Early exposure to aggression (and lack of exposure to relatively calm, productive discussions of differences of opinion) provides developing children and adolescents with models of hostile and harsh behaviors that shape how they respond when difficult situations arise in their own relationships later in life.

Evidence for this view is impressive. Studies show that the degree of hostility displayed in families early in a child's life—including hostility in parent–child relationships, unskilled parenting, exposure to aggression between parents, and harsh discipline practices—predict the child's use of aggression in intimate relationships in early adulthood (Andrews et al., 2000; Capaldi & Clark, 1998; Ehrensaft et al., 2003; Magdol et al., 1998). The fact that intergenerational transmission of aggression occurs is largely beyond doubt (Stith et al., 2000). It is important to emphasize, however, that there is not a perfect correlation between aggression in early caregiving environments and aggression in later intimate relationships. Many individuals exposed to aggression as they are growing up will not be aggressive later, and many who are aggressive later were not exposed to aggression while they were growing up.

We began this section by emphasizing an important distinction, between situational couple violence and intimate terrorism. We close by emphasizing a different kind of distinction: the difference between analyzing why someone is aggressive versus excusing the individual for the aggressive actions. Through research, we continue to learn about aggression and the factors that increase the chances that it will occur: a troubled family background, poor skills for handling difficult interpersonal situations, frustrating experiences associated with school or work, drug and alcohol use, and so on. Research might even identify how behaviors displayed by victims can increase the likelihood that they will be abused, or that individuals who have been victimized once are likely to be victimized again in other relationships. Aggressors often use these and many other excuses to excuse their violent behavior, yet we must not confuse an understanding of why someone is aggressive with freeing them from responsibility. Except in very rare cases, such as when spouses resort to violence in self-defense or as the only way out of a relationship in which they and/or their children are being terrorized, aggression in relationships is never acceptable, and responsibility must be placed squarely and completely on the shoulders of the aggressor.

MAIN POINTS

>> The most common form of physical agression in intimate relationships is situational couple violence, which typically arises when a verbal conflict escalates to the point of pushing, slapping, shoving, or more severe types of physical contact.

>> Couples who engage in situational aggression tend to be less happy in their relationship, are more likely to end their relationship, and are generally less effective in how they communicate.

>> Three distinct but overlapping theoretical perspectives explain situational couple violence, focusing on exposure to aggression in society, on immediate deficits in interpreting actions and regulating emotions during verbal conflicts, and on individual personalities and personal histories of the partners involved.

>> Whereas men and women both engage in situational couple violence, intimate terrorism, or battering, is generally committed by men against women in an effort to control and subjugate them.

CONCLUSION –

In an intimate relationship, disagreements and conflicts can cast a long shadow over the good will and positive feelings we have for our partner. Rarely does someone say, "Sure we fight like cats and dogs every day, but basically our relationship is strong and stable, and we are happy to be together." As the iconic and tempestuous relationship between Marilyn Monroe and Joe DiMaggio demonstrates, unresolved negative feelings generated by conflict seem to absorb the positive feelings we once held for our partner, to the point that it becomes difficult to see much else.

In this discussion, our point of entry into the intimate dyad has been the behaviors exchanged between partners, and we have seen how relationship scientists have developed tools to gain access to this essential feature of intimate relationships. Many of these tools involve direct observation, particularly in the case of verbal conflict; and others involve asking spouses to serve as reporters on the events in their relationship, especially in the case of physical aggression, which is rarely observed in laboratory settings. In both cases, scientists have sought to capture the objective reality of how different couples contend with their disagreements. Though the quest to understand objective features of relationships has proven to be unusually fruitful, several empirical findings raise doubts about whether this should be the only strategy. Partners themselves disagree on whether or not specific events have happened in their relationship in the previous 24 hours, talk-table studies reveal discrepancies between how messages sent by one partner are received by the other, and studies of relationship aggression show that couples seeking therapy are not particularly concerned with their aggression despite evidence that it is detrimental.

All these findings tell us that the objective, verifiable features of relationships do not speak for themselves, and that to understand intimate relationships fully we need to know more about what partners seek, value, and expect in their relationships. We explore these topics next.

9

Beliefs and Values

Summer of Love

During the summer of 1991, when she was 19, Minal Hajratwala marched in her first gay pride parade. As far as her parents knew, she was in New York for an internship at *Time* magazine. They had no idea that, as an undergraduate, she had come out as a "radical bisexual lesbian feminist." True, she had a boyfriend, but as she would later write: "I felt I was merely marking time with him until I figured out how to be with a woman." That summer was the perfect opportunity, and she took full advantage. The ravages of the ongoing AIDS epidemic had inspired an outspoken activist movement, and she was eager to participate. Within weeks, she had experienced her first lesbian affair, and she knew how she wanted to live the rest of her life.

It seemed like a different planet from the one she lived on back home. Born in San Francisco, Minal had spent her early childhood moving frequently for her father's academic career. When she was 8, the family settled in a suburb of Detroit, as one of the only Indian families in town. Acutely aware of her status as an outsider, she withdrew into her studies, and dreamed of a world where her peers could pronounce her name and she didn't have to worry about the smell of her mother's curries on her clothes. That summer in New York was a revelation; it was the first time she heard people referring to "us" and "we," realizing they were referring to her, too.

Minal's newfound freedom had consequences, however. As she described in her 2009 family memoir *Leaving India: My Family's Journey from Five Villages to Five Continents*, her parents had clear ideas about the life they hoped their children would live. They were Hindus, and they socialized exclusively with other Indian families. At these gatherings, the boys played in the yard while Minal and the girls were sent to the kitchen to learn how to make perfectly round rotlis. On a visit home from college, her parents, thinking ahead to Minal's graduation, had

FIGURE 9.1 Two worlds. In her family memoir *Leaving India: My Family's Journey from Five Villages to Five Continents*, Minal Hajratwala describes how her own emerging sexual identity clashed with the traditional Hindu beliefs of her parents.

brought up the marriage they fully expected to arrange for her. Minal had hinted long before that she might take a different path, declaring at a family dinner when she was 14 that she would never get married. But her parents had not taken such behavior seriously. Minal understood that the life she now lived would be hard for her parents to accept, so despite her activism she kept silent as long as she could.

The decision to come out was made for her when a box of papers she'd sent from college to her summer address in New York accidentally ended up, battered and opened, at her parents' house. Her writing samples had spilled out, including articles she'd written about her sex life for the campus feminist newspaper. Confronted by her parents, Minal confirmed that she was bisexual, and they in turn confirmed her fears by saying they would not be paying her college tuition any longer.

For Minal's parents, accepting their daughter's sexual identity took time, and that time was full of fighting and tears, withdrawal and hostility. Yet, despite the gulf she felt between her parents and herself, the adult Minal looks back on that period and understands what she did not understand then:

I can see now that my parents, like most parents, deeply loved us and wanted only the best for us. They were not engaged in a lifelong conspiracy to suppress our true selves, as it sometimes seemed to my brother and me in our adolescent fury; really they only wanted us to be happy. They believed our happiness would take the same shape as theirs: outward assimilation and material success in America, inward Indianness and hewing to tradition in private life.

But just as education separated my parents from their own families, something separated my brother and me from our parents. (Hajratwala, 2009, p. 332)

QUESTIONS

What was it that separated Minal and her brother from their parents? Why are parents who only want happiness and freedom for their children so often confused when the shape of that happiness and the expression of that freedom take unfamiliar forms?

From one generation to the next, and across cultures, standards for what makes a good or a bad intimate relationship may vary widely. Even within a single culture, aspects of human intimacy that may be acceptable and even desirable for some people can be intolerable to others. The sheer diversity of intimate relationships suggests that at least part of what makes them satisfying and fulfilling is not universal and fixed, but relative—a matter of context and interpretation. In other words, how people feel about their relationships may be a function not only of what they experience but also of how they think about those experiences. As hard as it is for Minal's (or anyone's) parents to understand, a relationship that satisfies one person may be very different from an intimate partnership that would satisfy someone else. Understanding this diversity requires an examination of beliefs and values.

What kinds of beliefs and values matter the most? What purpose do they serve in a relationship? How do they affect the way relationships develop, succeed, or fail? To the extent that our beliefs and values do affect our relationships, how much are our relationships all in our minds? Are there more or less healthy ways to think about intimacy? Where do these beliefs and values come from, and how can they change?

What We Already Know About Intimate Relationships

It does not take a formal education to accumulate a detailed and sophisticated body of knowledge and opinions about intimate relationships. Think of how much you already knew before picking up this book. How do people in love behave? What happens when couples disagree? What would your ideal relationship be like? You probably could answer these questions before reading this book, and so can most people. Most of us develop intricate ideas about how intimate relationships work and what we want from them simply by observing the relationships of those around us. Your own ideas probably share some features with those of your neighbors and friends, but they also have some aspects that are unique to you, a product of your specific experiences and observations.

> "Don't know much about history, don't know much biology. Don't know much about a science book, don't know much about the French I took. But I do know that I love you, and I know that if you love me, too, what a wonderful world this would be."
>
> —Sam Cooke, "Wonderful World" (1960)

Describing how different people's understanding of intimate relationships *might* vary requires that we first identify some of the broad ways that knowledge of intimate relationships *can* vary. Researchers have found it helpful to distinguish between beliefs and values. A **belief** is an idea or theory about what the world is actually like. A lot of our knowledge about relationships takes the form of beliefs, such as "Couples who fight a lot are probably unhappy" and "Blondes have more fun." Beliefs are simple descriptions of the world. In contrast, a **value** is an idea about what a person wants or what the world should be like. Values express opinions or attitudes, such as "I want a partner who shares my love for dogs" and "Infidelity is a good reason to leave a relationship." There is some overlap between beliefs and values. For example, the belief that members of a particular ethnic or racial group make better romantic partners is not exactly value-free. Nevertheless, the broad distinction between what people think is true and what they want to be true has some useful implications for understanding how people evaluate their relationships.

To describe how knowledge about intimate relationships can vary for different people, researchers distinguish among three dimensions: (1) beliefs vs. values; (2) knowledge targeting ourself, our partner, and our relationship; and (3) general vs. specific knowledge. We will discuss each of these in turn.

Applied to understanding intimate relationships, beliefs and values have three possible targets: ourself, our partner, and our relationship with our partner (Baldwin, 1992). Consider what you can know about your own relationship. You can have beliefs about yourself in the relationship (e.g., "I feel confident and secure here"). You can also have opinions about your partner (e.g., "I love the way her nose crinkles when she laughs"). Both of these types of knowledge are distinct from what you can know about the relationship itself (e.g., "We can talk about anything in the world, except politics").

Social psychologists Garth Fletcher and Geoff Thomas (1996) refer to all of this knowledge as **lay relationship theories**. They use the term *lay theories* to distinguish the informal beliefs and values that laypeople (i.e., people who do not study relationships for a living) accumulate from the explicit theories and empirical data gathered by researchers. To map the possible landscape of lay relationship theories, they developed the framework shown in **FIGURE 9.2**. Their model includes another way our knowledge of relationships can vary: We have beliefs and values about relationships in general—**general lay theories**, and we have beliefs and values about particular relationships we are experiencing or have experienced in the past—**specific lay theories**. **TABLE 9.1** has examples of beliefs and values targeting the self, the partner, and the relationship at general and specific levels. An important implication is that our theories about specific relationships may or may not correspond to our general beliefs and values about what relationships should be like.

With these broad distinctions, researchers have mapped ways that knowledge about intimate relationships can vary among people. Now we will explore different regions of this map in more detail.

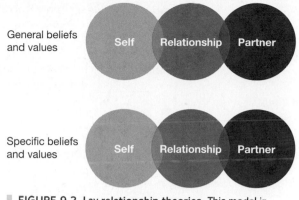

FIGURE 9.2 Lay relationship theories. This model is organized around two dimensions: beliefs and values about relationships in general, and specific beliefs and values about current and past relationships. There are three targets of that knowledge: self, partner, and relationship. (Source: Fletcher & Thomas, 1996.)

General Beliefs About Relationships

Advice about relationships often takes the form of general lay theories, as in "Never go to bed angry." Throughout recorded history, poets and songwriters have regularly expressed values and beliefs about romance and love. When Shakespeare wrote, in Sonnet 116, that "Love is not love / which alters when it alternation finds," he was expressing the general theory that true love remains constant even when confronted by challenges. When in 2008 the pop singer Beyoncé advised, "If you liked it, then you shoulda put a ring on it," she was expressing the theory that a formal engagement is an appropriate expression of commitment in a long-term relationship.

TABLE 9.1 Describing Knowledge About Intimate Relationships

Knowledge	Self	Partner	Relationship
General	Belief: *Most people find me attractive.* Value: *I like receiving compliments from my partner.*	Belief: *Partners who think I'm good-looking will treat me well.* Value: *Athletic types turn me on.*	Belief: *Relationships must be passionate and intense to be successful.* Value: *I want a relationship that sweeps me off my feet.*
Specific	Belief: *I have made a lot of compromises in this relationship.* Value: *I shouldn't let him put me down in public.*	Belief: *My partner is not that attracted to me.* Value: *I wish he would communicate better.*	Belief: *This relationship has fallen into a routine.* Value: *I need a change or I'm out of here.*

Source: Adapted from Fletcher & Thomas, 1996.

Although we did not refer to them as general lay theories, we have already discussed similar concepts throughout this book. In the context of attachment theory, for example, we noted that infants develop relatively stable internal working models of how relationships function and then apply them toward understanding their adult relationships (see Chapter 3). We also described research showing that different kinds of attachment predict different kinds of behaviors and relationship outcomes (see Chapter 6). Central to that line of research is the idea that people have general beliefs about relationships that shape their understanding of every specific intimate involvement they experience. In this section, we will broaden the focus to describe the wider range of beliefs individuals bring to their relationships.

As you might expect, people around the world have many different kinds of general beliefs about intimate relationships and how they function. As a preliminary step toward describing what people think about relationships, researchers simply tend to ask large numbers of people to describe their beliefs and then analyze the responses to see if any consistent themes emerge. For example, consider this question: What does it mean to have a successful intimate relationship? We have talked about researchers' answers in prior chapters, but what do people who are not researchers think?

Social psychologist Manfred Hassebrauck (1997) asked 120 university students in Germany to list as many features of a satisfying intimate relationship as they could in 4 minutes. The students named 352 different features, of which 64 were listed by more than two people. Those 64 items were then

TABLE 9.2 **Features of Satisfying Relationships**

Feature	Average Rating[a]
Trust	1.477
Love	1.660
Looking forward to seeing each other	1.790
Mutual respect	1.792
Honesty	1.832
Friendship	1.848
Listening to each other	1.864
Accepting partner	1.887
Tenderness	1.897
Taking time for each other	1.952
Taking interest in partner	1.972
Having and allowing for freedom	1.991
Understanding	2.057
Talking with each other	2.066
Openness	2.075
Being there for each other	2.093
Helping each other	2.104
Affection	2.152
Paying attention to partner	2.168
Knowing partner	2.290
Solving problems together	2.295

[a] Rating scale: 1 = excellent indicator of a good relationship. 7 = poor indicator of a good relationship.
Source: Adapted from Hassebrauck, 1997.

presented to a second group of students who were asked to rate how central each feature is to a good relationship. Students were remarkably consistent in making these ratings, and the 21 most central features are presented in **TABLE** 9.2. Before looking at the table, think about your own answers to this question: What do you think makes a good relationship? Most of the features listed in the table are what you'd expect; for example, no one would argue with trust and love being important parts of a good relationship. Perhaps what is surprising is what is missing from the top of the list. Love, care, and affection are there, but passion and excitement are not. The students in this study, at least, generally believed that passion is less important to successful intimate relationships than devotion and good communication.

Do you agree? Not everyone does. On the contrary, the passionate, exciting aspect of love is a recurring theme in relationships across the world (**FIGURE 9.3**). In fact, a review of anthropological studies of 186 societies found evidence of developed ideas about romance and passionate love in nearly 90 percent of them (Jankowiak & Fischer, 1992). To describe general beliefs about romantic love, researchers Susan Sprecher and Sandra Metts (1989) asked college students to rate how much they agreed with specific statements about the role of romance in relationships. Their analyses suggested that ideas about romantic love are composed of four separate beliefs: (1) the belief that loving someone means loving everything about them, (2) the belief that

FIGURE 9.3 An enduring theory of love. Throughout recorded history all over the world, artists have expressed the general belief that a mutual feeling of sexual or romantic attraction to a partner is desirable for a successful intimate relationship.

there exists only one suitable partner for every person, (3) the belief that love can overcome all challenges, and (4) the belief that it is possible to fall in love at first sight. For people who endorse such beliefs, an exciting, erotic feeling of attraction to a partner is a necessary element for a successful intimate relationship. For those who disagree, however, a relationship can be grounded in realities other than romantic or sexual attraction, such as duty, obligation, or friendship (**FIGURE 9.4**).

If someone who values passion and excitement is in a relationship that lacks these things, is the relationship doomed? Not necessarily. A second broad theme in general beliefs about intimate relationships concerns the capacity for partners and relationships to grow and change over time. Some people believe that the

"Gee, Jeffrey, an annual report on our marriage is a novel anniversary gift, but I was hoping for something a little more romantic."

FIGURE 9.4 It's the thought that counts. People vary in their general beliefs about the importance of passion and romance relative to practical concerns in intimate relationships. Jeffrey and his wife seem to have different beliefs about the best way to celebrate their anniversary.

qualities of a relationship are determined and set in stone from the start. Others believe that relationships develop and evolve, and the nature of the relationship today may not necessarily predict its future. Social psychologist C. Raymond Knee (1998) measured these aspects of general relationship beliefs, showing that people who believe that relationships can grow and change tend to agree with statements like this: "A successful relationship evolves through hard work and resolution of incompatibilities." People who believe that the nature of a relationship is fixed from the start disagree with such statements, instead endorsing items like this: "Relationships that do not start off well inevitably fail."

Thus far, most researchers have examined these two types of general beliefs about relationships separately, but those few studies that have examined both suggest that they may be relatively independent (e.g., Fletcher & Kininmonth, 1992; Rusbult, Onizuka, & Lipkus, 1993). In other words, what people believe about the role of passion in relationships may have nothing to do with their beliefs about the possibility of change and growth in relationships. With this in mind, social psychologist Caryl Rusbult and her colleagues (1993) developed a framework for four broad classes of beliefs about relationships, shown in **FIGURE 9.5**. Some people may believe in the importance of passion and also believe that passionate relationships are a product of fate or chemistry (upper right quadrant). Others who value passion equally may believe that passion can be nurtured and developed (upper left quadrant). Still others may minimize the role of passion, but emphasize the importance of other ways that couples grow closer and more interdependent over time (lower left

FIGURE 9.5 **Broad beliefs about relationships.** These four classes are based on combined ideas about the importance of passion and the capacity for relationships to develop and evolve.

quadrant). A final group may minimize the role of passion, but consider relationships to be more like business arrangements whose terms are not subject to negotiation (lower right quadrant).

Each of these beliefs can be considered a lay theory, because each one describes how regular people think intimate relationships work in general, regardless of their personal experiences. But people develop theories specific to their own relationships as well.

Specific Beliefs About Relationships

Every description or characterization that has ever been made about a particular relationship can be considered a specific lay theory or belief about that relationship. For example, when love songs are written in the first or second person, they typically are written to express a specific lay theory. When Taylor Swift sang to a former partner that "We are never ever ever ever getting back together," she was describing her own specific belief that the wounds inflicted in that relationship were extremely unlikely to heal.

Clearly, there are as many different specific beliefs about relationships as there are love songs, but research has shown some of these beliefs to be especially important. One type that has received a lot of attention from researchers is **expectations**—the predictions about what is likely to happen in the future in a particular relationship, often (but not always) based on general beliefs about how relationships function. For example, some people believe in general that passion and romance are critical to the success of an intimate relationship, yet they don't expect to experience romance and sexual passion in their own relationship. Partners have expectations—both spoken and unspoken—about all aspects of their relationship, from how frequently they expect to have arguments to how long they expect the relationship to last.

An especially relevant set of expectations is the ability of partners to bring about desired changes within their relationship, referred to as a **locus of control**. Early researchers described locus of control as a general belief, suggesting two different orientations (e.g., Rotter, 1975). People with an **internal locus of control** feel that the power to achieve their goals lies within themselves. People with an **external locus of control** believe their successes and failures are due to forces outside themselves.

After initial studies found weak or mixed evidence that a general locus of control affects relationships (e.g., Constantine & Bahr, 1980; Doherty, 1981; Doherty & Ryder, 1979), researchers began to redefine locus of control as a specific belief; that is, as an expectation likely to be unique to particular relationships. Social psychologists Phillip Miller, Herbert Lefcourt, and Edward Ware (1983), for example, developed a scale to assess spouses' expectations of the degree to which they can affect desired outcomes within their marriages. Spouses with an internal locus of control relative to their marriages believe they can effectively exert their will to bring about changes, and that they are responsible for the outcomes they experience in the marriage. Spouses with an external locus of control, in contrast, believe that their own actions are likely to be ineffectual, and that they have little responsibility for what happens in the marriage. In both cases, these are specific beliefs about the current relationship and may be unrelated to the couples' general beliefs about how intimate relationships change.

Let's return to attachment theory. The theory describes working models as ideas about how relationships function, developed in infancy and then applied throughout our lives. Psychiatrist John Bowlby (1969, 1973, 1980) described these models as general lay theories and suggested that we draw on basically the same beliefs to understand all of our specific relationships throughout life. Indeed, research that characterizes individuals in terms of their general comfort with closeness and dependence on others rests on this assumption. More recent work on attachment, however, has called this characterization of attachment into question. For example, social psychologists Jennifer La Guardia and her colleagues (2000) asked college students to describe the security of their attachments to a variety of different people in their lives (e.g., parents, best friends, teachers, romantic partners). If internal working models are general theories we apply to all our relationships, then participants in this study should have described more or less the same level of security across different relationships. This is not what the researchers found. Instead, participants described different levels of security in different relationships. In other words, people can have one set of beliefs about their romantic partners, quite a different set of beliefs about their mothers, and yet another set of beliefs about their fathers.

A similar study showed that the general working models people hold at any one time are largely a function of the specific relationships they are able to bring to mind easily (Baldwin et al., 1996). When people are prompted to think about a particular relationship, they tend to endorse general attachment

FIGURE 9.6 **Working models of attachment, general and specific.** Research suggests that we develop specific beliefs about closeness and dependence in different relationships. Being securely attached in one relationship does not mean we will necessarily feel securely attached in all other relationships throughout life.

beliefs that are consistent with that relationship. When prompted to think about a different relationship, they tend to endorse different attachment beliefs. Thus, attachment models, at least in adulthood, may be better characterized as specific lay theories, capturing the expectations that people have developed for particular relationships in their lives (**FIGURE 9.6**).

Attitudes, Standards, and Ideals

What people believe about relationships in general is often related to what they want from their own relationship. Those who believe, for instance, that passion is a critical element of a successful relationship are likely to value passion in their own relationship. Furthermore, people's values for relationships are often associated with their specific beliefs about what their own relationship is like (Fletcher, Simpson, & Thomas, 2000; Murray, Holmes, & Griffin, 1996). Some people believe their own relationship strongly resembles the best that an intimate relationship can be. Yet, despite the overlap between beliefs and values, there is good reason to distinguish between what people *think* is true about relationships in general and what people *want* to be true about their intimate relationship.

Ethnographers and sociologists Kathryn Edin and Maria Kefalas (2005) interviewed low-income single mothers about their values regarding marriage and their beliefs about the likelihood of marriage for themselves. Again and again, these researchers noticed a significant gap between the participants' values and their beliefs: Although most of them deeply *wished* to find partners they could depend on for support and assistance in raising their children, they generally *believed* that most of the potential partners available to them would be unreliable. Indeed, in most relationships there are likely to be some differences between what partners want from their relationship and what they believe they are actually getting. Keeping these differences in mind, we'll examine various kinds of values partners bring to bear in thinking about their intimate relationship. (The direct effects of those values on the relationship will be discussed in detail later and also in Chapter 10.)

Just as we distinguished between general and specific beliefs about relationships, we can also distinguish between general and specific values related to particular relationships. Another name for a general value is **attitude**, which we can define as a positive or negative evaluation of someone or something. General attitudes are what telephone surveys and public opinion polls tend to measure. With respect to intimate relationships, social leaders in recent years have devoted a great deal of attention to people's attitudes regarding marriage, sex, child rearing, and gender roles. Together, this set of attitudes has been broadly (and often vaguely) labeled as "family values."

Researchers have examined these sorts of general attitudes, although they have tended to address each one separately rather than as a group. For example, social psychologists Anne Peplau, Charles Hill, and Zick Rubin (1993) measured preferences for traditional versus egalitarian division of labor within male-female couples. People who score high in **sex role traditionalism** value a clear separation of the roles and responsibilities for men and women. In particular, they tend to believe that men should be responsible for the financial security of the family and women should be responsible for the home and children. People who score low in sex-role traditionalism value a more egalitarian approach. Not only do they reject the idea that women and men have different spheres of influence, they care about both partners having an equal role in making decisions as well. Other researchers have examined attitudes toward divorce and premarital cohabitation, revealing, for example, a strong trend toward increasing acceptance of nontraditional family forms in the United States over the last several decades (Thornton, 2009; Thornton & Young-DeMarco, 2001). What all of these attitudes have in common is that they are general values, reflecting what people want everyone's relationships to be like.

In contrast, people also have specific attitudes capturing what they value in their own relationships. In fact, it is hard to imagine any perceptions of a relationship or a relationship partner that do not have some evaluative element to them (Hampson, Goldberg, & John, 1987). We don't simply observe that our partner acts in certain ways; rather, we tend to express our perceptions as evaluative judgments, as in "She is passionate" (suggesting a positive attitude toward her level of expressed emotion) or "He is moody" (suggesting a negative attitude toward his level of expressed emotion). Thus, partners have specific attitudes about every aspect of the relationship, from each other's appearance, to the time they spend together, to the way they divide up responsibilities. From this perspective, one of the most important specific attitudes is one that we have been discussing throughout this book: relationship satisfaction—the way each partner evaluates the relationship as a whole. In the hierarchy of attitudes that one may have about a particular

"You'll do."

FIGURE 9.7 Crossing the threshold. People whose relationships meet or surpass their standards will be satisfied, and people whose relationships fail to meet their standards will not.

relationship, relationship satisfaction may be at the top.

Whereas an attitude is an expression of an evaluation, a standard is like a yardstick for making that evaluation. In the context of intimate relationships, a **standard** is the minimum set of qualities and attributes partners require to be satisfied with the relationship. As discussed in Chapter 3, social exchange theory features standards as a central element. When the social psychologists John Thibaut and Harold Kelley (1959), for example, coined the term *comparison levels*, they were referring to the standards a relationship had to meet for a given individual to feel satisfied. Partners are unlikely to complain when their relationships exceed their standards, but they become distressed when their relationships fall short (**FIGURE 9.7**).

Reports about distressed couples are a good place to learn about the standards that may be especially important in intimate relationships, because they reflect the issues of unhappy partners. Clinical psychologists working with couples in troubled marriages have identified standards in five areas that are frequent sources of problems (Baucom et al., 1996). In each area, couples may have different specific standards, but all of them feel unsatisfied when their standard is not being met. In the first area, couples have different standards about independence and boundaries. Some people want their partners to join with them in every aspect of their lives, whereas others care about maintaining some degree of independence. The second area in which couples differ is in their standards about exercising control. Some couples are comfortable exerting direct control, or making demands on each other, whereas others prefer to negotiate important decisions. The third area captures standards for sharing power. Some partners desire an egalitarian relationship, and others prefer that one or the other partner wields more influence. The fourth area addresses standards for how partners express their investment in the relationship, capturing the degree to which they desire more or less frequent expressions of love and affection from each other. The fifth area addresses standards about how much the relationship should require each partner to make sacrifices.

Clearly, this is far from an exhaustive set of relationship standards. Yet, because partners tend to think about the standards they are having difficulty meeting, perhaps these are five standards that play a significant role in evaluating intimate relationships. What all have in common is that they are issues specific to the partners' current relationship. The only standard that can make us happy or unhappy is the one we think the current relationship should be meeting.

Another kind of value, distinct from a standard, is an ideal. Whereas a standard expresses what a person would settle for, an **ideal** represents what a person wishes for. Put another way, standards represent a person's minimum requirements for happiness, and ideals represent a person's maximum hopes and dreams. Distinguishing between standards and ideals in this way suggests that the two kinds of values may serve very different purposes in relationships. Whereas Thibaut and Kelley (1959) proposed that people cannot be happy if their outcomes fall short of their standards, people can be perfectly happy if their outcomes fall short of their ideals. Ideally you might want to spend your life with a beautiful, independently wealthy, brain-surgeon/massage therapist, but realistically you would be happy with a partner who falls slightly short of that ideal. Ideals and standards may therefore represent the upper and lower boundaries of the region in which partners can be satisfied with their relationship.

Psychologists Steven Gangestad and Jeffry Simpson (2000) suggest that, in contrast to other relationship values and beliefs that vary widely across people, relationship ideals may be more or less uniform throughout the world. Drawing from evolutionary theory, these researchers note that humans should have evolved common desires for partners and relationships that maximize their reproductive fitness. At a broad level, therefore, the ideal relationship partner would reflect the common desires of the human species. For example, to the extent that health and physical attractiveness are usually indicators of good genes and above-average fertility, all people should imagine ideal partners who are relatively healthy and attractive. To the extent that one's children are more likely to live to have their own children if they are raised by a committed and attentive parent, all people should imagine ideal partners who are sensitive, responsive, and capable of intimacy. To the extent that the likelihood of raising children successfully is enhanced by social status and adequate resources, everyone should imagine ideal partners of relatively high status and material wealth. Indeed, these ideal preferences do seem to characterize men and women across the globe (Buss, 1989).

When thinking about the ideal relationship, as opposed to the ideal partner, the same logic applies. Humans should have evolved common desires for relationships that maximize their chances of reproducing successfully. To the extent that a passionate relationship offers more opportunities for sexual intercourse, the ideal relationship should always be characterized by high levels of passion. To the extent that a committed relationship offers the best context for raising children, the ideal relationship should be characterized by high levels of commitment and intimacy, in all cases. Cross-cultural research on relationship ideals has yet to be conducted, but studies of college students do confirm that their self-described ideals for their own relationships boil down to a desire for intimacy and commitment on one hand, and a desire for excitement and passion on the other (Fletcher et al., 1999).

One implication of this line of thinking is that when we are looking for ways that relationship values differ, we are more likely to find differences in standards than in ideals. Everybody may hope to get more or less the same general things out of his or her intimate relationship, but people may differ in what they are willing to settle for.

<hr>

MAIN POINTS

>> Although people bring various ideas to their intimate relationships, we can distinguish between beliefs, or ideas about what the world is like, and values, or ideas about how the world should be.

>> With respect to beliefs, we can further distinguish between beliefs about relationships in general, such as theories about the relative importance of passionate love, and beliefs about specific relationships, such as expectations about how events in a particular relationship will turn out.

>> Values can be classified as general attitudes about how relationships should be, and as specific standards and ideals people apply toward evaluating their own relationships.

<hr>

The Effect of Beliefs and Values on Relationships

You might wonder why researchers spend time documenting what people believe and value about intimate relationships. The reason is that beliefs and values matter; they play an important role in the way intimate relationships develop. Relationship scientists did not always believe this. For most of the 1970s and 1980s, the focus was on couples' behaviors. Indeed, it is easy to imagine how the observable characteristics of a relationship (i.e., the way partners treat each other, or the structure of their domestic environment) may affect its outcome. It is quite another thing to explain how the unobservable and intangible content of each partner's thoughts may affect the relationship as well. How does something that exists inside the heads of two individuals affect the development of a relationship between them?

Evaluating Our Relationships

One way that general ideas affect how we feel about particular relationships is by guiding our reactions to specific aspects of the relationship. In other words, differences in beliefs and values explain why different people have unique reactions to the same relationship experiences. In particular, Fletcher and Thomas (1996) suggest that the match between people's specific theories about their own relationships and their general beliefs about how relationships work helps them figure out whether they are in good relationships. The same experience should have different effects on our emotions and reactions, depending on how well it matches with our beliefs and values.

A number of studies of beliefs and values confirm this idea. In one study, college students described their beliefs about what makes an intimate relationship satisfying, and then specific aspects of their own relationships (Fletcher & Kininmonth, 1992). The researchers found that the association between relationship satisfaction and perceptions of any one aspect of the relationship depended on students' beliefs about that aspect. For example, for students who believed that good sex is a necessary element of a good relationship, evaluations of the quality of the sex in their own relationship were strongly associated with whether or not they were satisfied. However, for students who believed that good sex is less important for a successful relationship, the association between sexual intimacy and relationship satisfaction was nearly zero. In other words, students who might have been getting the same outcomes in their relationships (e.g., unexciting sex) had very different levels of satisfaction with the relationship as a whole, depending on their general theories about what makes relationships work.

The **ideal standards model** makes similar predictions for the role values play in evaluating relationships (Fletcher & Simpson, 2000; Simpson, Fletcher & Campbell, 2001). Acccording to this theory, the amount of discrepancy between values for relationships in general and perceptions of the current relationship in particular determines whether an individual will be satisfied. Several studies of college students confirm this prediction: The greater the discrepancy between partners' ideals and their perceptions, the lower their overall rating of the relationship (Fletcher et al., 1999) and the more distressed and anxious they feel (Lackenbauer & Campbell, 2012). The ideal, in other words, determines how each specific perception affects overall relationship satisfaction.

Longitudinal data on relationships show how these processes can have implications not only for relationship satisfaction but also for whether the relationship lasts or breaks up. College students were asked to describe their beliefs about whether successful relationships are a product of hard work or a product of luck and destiny (Knee, 1998). The students also reported on their satisfaction with their own relationships. After 4 months, they reported on whether their relationship had ended. Results indicated that the association between initial satisfaction and the length of the relationship depended on what people believed about destiny. For students who believed that a good relationship is either destined to succeed or destined to fail, initial satisfaction was a strong predictor of how long the relationship lasted. The less satisfied people, apparently figuring that their relationship was destined to fail, ended it quickly, whereas the more satisfied people, assuming the relationship was destined to succeed, stayed together. In contrast, for students who did not believe in the role of destiny, initial satisfaction was unrelated to whether the relationship survived. Perhaps because these students believed

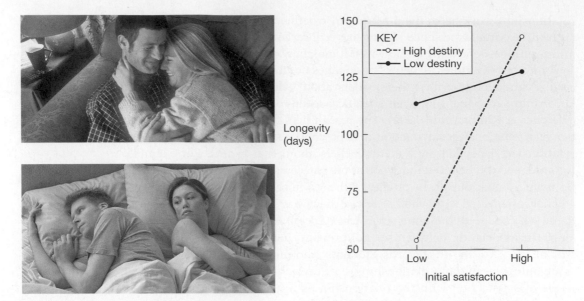

FIGURE 9.8 Clues to relationship longevity. In the two couples above, you might expect the smiling, cuddling couple's relationship will last longer than that of the withdrawn, angry couple. But research indicates that early satisfaction is an unreliable predictor of the success and longevity of any relationship. The graph shows that among couples who believe destiny plays a role in relationship success (high destiny: dashed line), the most satisfied couples stayed together longer than the least satisfied couples. Yet among couples who do not believe in the role of destiny (low destiny: solid line), satisfaction barely predicted the length of the relationship. (Source: Knee, 1998.)

that their relationships could develop over time, the state of the relationship at a single measurement did not play as large a role in the decision to stay or leave (**FIGURE 9.8**).

Interpreting Relationship Events

In studies described thus far, it is not the nature of people's ideas that is important but rather the gap between their ideas about relationships in general and their perceptions of their own relationships. However, our cognitions—thoughts, beliefs, attitudes—may do more than shape how we react to our experiences. What we believe and value may change our interpretations of those experiences as well (Baldwin, 1992).

In most of social life, but especially in intimate relationships, specific events are often subject to multiple interpretations. What does it mean, for instance, when out of the blue, your partner asks: "How are you feeling?" Is he genuinely concerned about your welfare? Is he trying to get you to return the question and thus have an excuse to raise a complaint? Or is the comment just an empty form of chitchat? Much of the time, an experience does not by itself provide enough information to answer these kinds of questions definitively. Yet they require answers so we can proceed with our conversations and social interactions. To lessen the inherent ambiguity of social life, we tend to interpret our experiences by drawing on our beliefs and expectations. Thus, if you believe your partner is sensitive and concerned for your emotional health, you are more likely to perceive that "How are you feeling?" is a genuine question and respond with gratitude and warmth. If you expect he is looking for an opening to complain about your behavior, you might perceive the same words as signs of an attack and respond with wariness and defensiveness.

An important consequence of the tendency to use our existing ideas to interpret ambiguous behaviors is that the resulting interpretations are probably going to be consistent with, and thus confirm, the ideas we already have. In other words, if you expect people to behave a certain way, you're more likely to perceive that they have behaved in that way. This process has been called **perceptual confirmation**, and it appears to be an important mechanism through which beliefs and expectations can affect intimate relationships.

Social psychologists Geraldine Downey and Scott Feldman (1996) examined how childhood experiences of rejection might have lasting effects throughout life. Elaborating on attachment theory, these researchers argue that significant rejection experiences should shape the beliefs and expectations adults bring to their intimate relationships, leading to a greater sensitivity to rejection than that experienced by adults who were not rejected as children. To evaluate the effects of these expectations, they conducted an experiment in which participants who had completed a self-report measure of rejection sensitivity were asked to interact with a confederate. After a brief conversation, the confederate left the room. Then the experimenter came in and informed the participant that the other person no longer wished to continue the experiment. How did participants react to this news? People scoring low in rejection sensitivity (i.e., people who did not generally expect to be rejected) did not react much at all, figuring perhaps that the other person had a pressing engagement elsewhere. However, those scoring high in rejection sensitivity (i.e., those who did generally expect to be rejected) were significantly upset by the news, perceiving the identical behavior as a personal insult to themselves. Because they expected rejection, they perceived rejection in an otherwise ambiguous experience.

Social psychologists Gina Bellavia and Sandra Murray (2003) found similar evidence for perceptual confirmation in a study that considered how self-esteem can affect perceptions of intimate relationships. Self-esteem has been described as a belief about the self that is shaped by experiences of rejection and acceptance from others (Leary et al., 1995). Thus, people with high self-esteem presumably expect people will like them, and people with low self-esteem expect others will not like them. In this study, students who had rated themselves high or low in self-esteem were asked to imagine that they encountered their romantic partners in either a positive or a negative mood and then to describe their reactions. Half the time, the participants were given a reason for their partner's mood (e.g., your partner just did well on an important exam), and half the time, the source of the mood was left unclear. The researchers found that when no other cause for a partner's negative mood was available, people with low self-esteem were more likely to see themselves as the cause of the bad mood and to perceive their partner's behavior toward them as a rejection (see also Murray et al., 2001). Here, as in the previous study, general beliefs about relationships appear to fill in missing information, so that ambiguous experiences are perceived to be consistent with existing beliefs.

Behavior in Relationships

The idea of perceptual confirmation draws attention to processes entirely within the individual. When I expect something from my partner, observe a behavior, and then interpret it so it is consistent with my expectations, each step of that process takes place within my own head. But, as social psychologists John Darley and Russell Fazio (1980) observed, there is more than one way an initial belief or expectation about a relationship can be confirmed. In contrast to perceptual confirmation, **behavioral confirmation** suggests that our beliefs or expectations can also shape the way we experience the world by affecting our behavior toward others. Numerous studies show that how someone expects to be treated affects how that person treats other people. In one study, spouses who had an internal locus of control, expecting that their own actions would be effective at bringing about desired changes in the marriage, communicated more productively about marital problems than those who expected that their own behaviors have no effect on the marriage (Miller et al., 1986). People with a secure attachment style (i.e., those who believe a degree of dependence is an appropriate part of an intimate relationship) provide more effective social support to their partners than those who believe that dependence is threatening to a relationship (Feeney & Collins, 2001).

What happens when people expect others to behave in a certain way, and then act in accordance with those expectations? Often, the result is that other people respond in kind, confirming the initial expectation. In a study described in Chapter 5, Mark Snyder and his colleagues provided a classic example of this process by audiotaping phone conversations between men and women who had never met (Snyder, Tanke, & Berscheid, 1977). The men were given a photo of either an attractive or a plain woman and were told that this was the woman on the line. Because people generally expect physically attractive people to be more friendly, the men who thought they were talking with an attractive partner behaved in a more friendly manner during the conversations. What makes this study interesting, however, is that the women on the other end of the conversation also behaved in a more friendly manner, even though they did not know which photo their partners had seen. In other words, the men's initial beliefs and expectations about physically attractive people created a **self-fulfilling prophecy**, wherein individuals act to bring about the experiences they expect to happen.

This sort of cyclical process, with beliefs leading to behaviors that lead back again to beliefs, lies at the heart of attachment perspectives on intimate relationships. For example, the reason Bowlby originally suggested that working models of attachment persist from the cradle to the grave was because he expected that secure and insecure attachment styles cause people to interact with their partners in ways that confirm and strengthen the original internal models. In an observational study of rejection sensitivity, Geraldine Downey and her colleagues (1998) showed how these processes may occur. Women who had completed a self-report measure of rejection sensitivity were videotaped discussing difficult issues with their partners. Observers then coded the videotapes for positive and negative behaviors. They found that women high in rejection sensitivity behaved significantly more negatively during the interactions than women low in rejection sensitivity. In other words, the expectation that they would be rejected seemed to lead women high on this measure to behave in ways that made rejection more likely. Indeed, after the interactions, the partners of women who scored high in rejection sensitivity reported being more angry about the relationship than partners of women who scored low in rejection sensitivity. Ironically, the women who feared rejection the most behaved in ways that converted their fears into reality.

Although most research on self-fulfilling prophecies has focused on beliefs, values can have similar effects on our experiences to the extent that they serve as goals that guide behavior. People tend to pursue what they want, so it makes sense to imagine that what people value about relationships will affect their behaviors in relationships. Thus, for example, college women who value intimacy in their dating relationships report behaving in ways that tend to promote intimacy (Sanderson & Evans, 2001). Those who value communal relationships (i.e., relationships in which each partner attends to the other's needs without expecting rewards in return) do seem to pay more attention to other people's needs than those who value exchange relationships (i.e., relationships in which partners give to each other only when they are likely to benefit in return; Clark, Mills, & Powell, 1986). People who behave according to these values will probably encourage others to do the same and thereby achieve the kinds of relationships they hope for. In this way, how we think about relationships appears to affect not only how we interpret and react to our relationship experience, but also the nature of the experiences themselves.

MAIN POINTS

>> Our general ideas about relationships shape our reactions to events within a specific relationship.

>> Ideas about relationships can lead to perceptual confirmation, such that people interpret ambiguous events in ways that are consistent with their prior expectations.

>> Ideas about relationships can lead to behavioral confirmation, such that people with particular ideas about relationships act in ways that turn those ideas into reality.

>> What people experience in their relationships is affected not only by the objective quality of the relationship, but also by the beliefs and values of the partners.

What Is a Healthy Way to Think About Relationships?

Understanding the ways our beliefs and values affect our intimate relationships suggests that some ways of thinking may be more beneficial than others. Is there a right way to think about relationships? Many people seem to think so. Popular books and advice columns often suggest that the key to more successful relationships lies in learning how to think about them differently. The problem for people trying to follow such advice, however, is that experts have different opinions. On one side are those who think that people who expect the best in life are more likely to achieve it. On the other side are those who believe that people who expect too much are more likely to end up disappointed. When it comes to our intimate relationships, should we expect the best or brace for the worst?

Research on intimate relationships has devoted considerable effort toward answering this question, but unfortunately the results have so far been mixed. For example, some research on married couples suggests that spouses with higher standards report higher marital satisfaction (Baucom et al., 1996). In contrast, other research on married couples shows that spouses with high expectations tend to report lower marital satisfaction (Epstein & Eidelson, 1981; Kurdek, 1992). Research on dating couples has generally failed to find any significant effects of beliefs and values on relationship satisfaction (Fletcher & Kininmonth, 1992; Knee, 1998). Each of these studies examined different kinds of couples and used different measures, so it is hard to compare across studies. Still, the wide range of results strongly suggests that the effects of various beliefs and values on relationship outcomes are complex and depend on the specific qualities of the relationship.

The Case for Positive Thinking

Given that positive expectations and high standards can lead to self-fulfilling prophecies, it makes sense to say that people with more positive expectations and higher standards should be better off in their relationships. Daytime television talk shows are full of this argument (FIGURE 9.9). Typically, the guest is a person who has accommodated to a neglectful or even abusive partner. The guest describes the compromises that maintaining the relationship requires, and the sacrifices the ungrateful partner has demanded. The host strolls through the audience, holding a microphone out to people with advice to offer. Often that advice is a strongly worded suggestion to dump the partner and develop higher standards. For these audience members, expecting more is a first step toward achieving more in a relationship. Young people are frequent targets of this sort of advice, urged by older people not to settle for the first partner that comes along but instead to pursue their ideals.

FIGURE 9.9 The power of positive thinking. Television talk shows, like the Jerry Springer Show above, frequently advise viewers who have settled for unsatisfying relationships to develop higher standards. Expect the best and you will achieve it! The truth is that the effects of positive expectations may be complex, and this advice may not work for everyone.

Considerable evidence supports the case for high expectations. As we saw in Chapter 6, people with a secure attachment style, who are confident that they are lovable and that other people can be trusted, do in fact behave in ways that seem likely to promote successful relationships. Compared to insecure people, secure people do have higher standards for their relationships (Hazan & Shaver, 1987), they generally seek support when they are stressed (Mikulincer, Florian, & Weller, 1993), and they resolve conflicts more effectively (Kobak & Hazan, 1991). Perhaps as a result, their relationships tend to be longer and happier than the relationships of people with insecure attachment styles (Kirkpatrick & Hazan, 1994; Klohnen & Bera, 1998). Partners with an internal locus of control tend to report fewer problems, higher satisfaction, and more stable satisfaction over time than partners with an external locus of control (Doherty, 1981; Myers & Booth, 1999).

What may be happening in these cases is that positive expectations and high standards motivate people to capitalize on relationship strengths and minimize weaknesses. To illustrate how this happens, social psychologists Sandra Murray, Gina Bellavia, Paul Rose, and Dale Griffin (2003) asked married couples to report on their relationships every day for 21 days. By examining how the events of one day were associated with each partner's feelings and behaviors on subsequent days, these researchers could identify the patterns that distinguish spouses who have positive beliefs from spouses who have less positive ones. These analyses revealed that spouses who believed they were highly regarded by their partners tended to behave especially constructively in the days after a serious argument. Perhaps because they expected that their partners would love and forgive them, they acted in ways that made love and forgiveness easier to express. In contrast, spouses who doubted their partner's feelings for them tended to behave especially negatively in the days after a serious argument. Expecting that conflicts can have severe implications, these individuals behaved in ways that intensified conflicts and drew out their aftermath.

Such studies suggest that positive beliefs and high standards are beneficial for relationships when they motivate behaviors and emotional reactions that strengthen the relationship. In contrast, negative beliefs and low standards are detrimental to the extent that they discourage relationship-enhancing behaviors and reactions.

The Case for Lowering Expectations

The problem with the preceding argument is that positive expectations and high standards do not always motivate beneficial behaviors and responses. Sometimes they can motivate emotional reactions that may harm relationships. For example, when people have experiences that contradict their expectations or fail to live up to their standards, they typically react with disappointment and even frustration or anger (Berscheid, 1983; Carver & Scheier, 1990). The more positive someone's expectations and the higher someone's standards, the more likely that a partner will eventually fall short, and over time the negative feelings that result may lead to negative feelings about the relationship.

Perhaps it is a little extreme to ask people to expect nothing. One approach to more successful relationships involves developing moderate expectations and reasonable standards, to avoid disappointment when the relationship is less than perfect. Several prominent authors have blamed the relatively high divorce rates in the United States over the past few decades on young people's excessively romantic and unrealistic expectations for marriage (Bennett, 2001; Thomas, 2002). The problem, these authors suggest, is that young couples expect their marriages to bring them nothing but love, passion, and fulfillment. When a lasting marriage turns out to be hard work, these couples are disillusioned and quick to abandon their partners in search of someone who may yet fulfill their unreasonable expectations (FIGURE 9.10).

Such modern couples are often contrasted with couples of the past, who expected that marriage would be hard work and therefore stayed with the relationship when this in fact proved to be the case (for a historical perspective, see Coontz, 2005). The result of this line of thinking is advice of the sort that social psychologist Roland Miller provided

"Couldn't you at least try and read my mind?"

FIGURE 9.10 Heading for disappointment. Sometimes we expect our partner to do the impossible. Researchers have shown some of the negative consequences of unrealistic expectations.

TABLE 9.3 **The Relationship Belief Inventory**

Instructions: The statements below describe ways in which a person might feel about a relationship with another person. Please mark the space next to each statement to indicate how strongly you believe that it is true or false for you.

0	1	2	3	4	5
Very False	False	Probably False	Probably True	True	Very True

Sub-scale I: Disagreement is destructive

I take it as a personal insult when my partner disagrees with an important idea of mine.   ____

I cannot tolerate it when my partner argues with me.   ____

Sub-scale II: Mind-reading is expected

People who love each other know exactly what each other's thoughts are without a word ever being said.   ____

A partner should know what you are thinking or feeling without you having to tell.   ____

Sub-scale III: Partners cannot change

Damages done early in a relationship probably cannot be reversed.   ____

A partner who hurts you badly once probably will hurt you again.   ____

Sub-scale IV: Sexual perfectionism

If I cannot perform well sexually whenever my partner is in the mood, I would consider that I have a problem.   ____

A good sexual partner can get aroused for sex whenever necessary.   ____

Sub-scale V: The sexes are different

Men and women probably will never understand the opposite sex very well.   ____

One of the major causes of marital problems is that men and women have different emotional needs.   ____

Source: Adapted from Eidelson & Epstein, 1982; Baucom & Epstein, 1990.

when he wrote that to avoid disappointment and frustration in our relationships, "we might be better off for expecting inattention and impoliteness from those who love us" (1997b, p. 24).

Some evidence supports this position as well. For example, Roy Eidelson and Norman Epstein (1982), clinical psychologists, developed the Relationship Belief Inventory to assess unrealistic beliefs about marriage. To create this measurement tool, they identified general beliefs and standards about relationships that couples in counseling had complained about. Selected items from the inventory are in **TABLE 9.3**. The authors argue that holding such beliefs will probably lead to disappointment and negative emotions because each belief expresses an expectation that is highly unlikely to be confirmed in an actual relationship. Thus, people who agree that "If you have to ask your partner for something, it shows that he/she was not 'tuned into' your needs" may be less likely to make the effort to express their own thoughts and feelings and may be more irritated and upset when their partners misunderstand them, compared to people who expect to have to explain themselves once in a while. We might imagine that sex is a much more stressful activity for someone who reports that "I get upset if I think I have not completely satisfied my partner sexually," compared to someone with more flexible standards for sexual performance. Indeed, spouses who score higher on this measure do report lower marital satisfaction (Eidelson & Epstein, 1982; Kurdek, 1992), consistent with the idea that excessively high standards give rise to emotional reactions that may harm relationships.

Expecting the Best, Bracing for the Worst

How should we interpret the seemingly contradictory findings about the effects of high expectations and standards? On one hand, positive beliefs and high standards appear to benefit relationships when they motivate positive behaviors. On the other hand, they seem to harm relationships when they inhibit active coping and promote negative reactions. Some researchers suggest that positive expectations and high standards are beneficial only when they are "realistic," but it is hard to define exactly what makes a belief or a value realistic; moreover, what is realistic for one couple may be unrealistic for another (McNulty & Karney, 2004). Thus, the existing research has left us where we started, wondering which positive thoughts motivate relationship maintenance and which positive thoughts discourage it. The jury is still out. There are, however, several intriguing possibilities for resolution that have yet to be explored.

Research on the effects of expectations on academic performance and achievement has distinguished between different kinds of positive beliefs and values. Social and developmental psychologist Carol Dweck (1986) and her colleagues (e.g., Elliott & Dweck, 1988) have distinguished between *learning goals*, which drive people toward mastery of a topic, and *performance goals*, which drive people to seek favorable evaluations and avoid negative ones. Within classroom settings, students with learning goals seek challenges and try to overcome them, whereas students with performance goals avoid difficult situations and freeze up when challenged (Elliott & Dweck, 1988). Within relationships, there may be similarly important distinctions between partners with positive expectations that focus on the process of the relationship and those with positive expectations that focus only on the outcome. Partners who have positive beliefs and high standards about relationship processes might resemble students with learning goals, in that they might seek ways to improve the relationship and not shy away from conflicts that need to be addressed. Because they expect positive results from their interactions, they are willing to devote efforts toward relationship maintenance. Partners who have positive expectations and high standards for relationship outcomes, however, might resemble students with performance goals, in that they might avoid potential conflicts and perhaps react poorly when conflicts do arise. Some have suggested that both kinds of goals work together (Barron & Harackiewicz, 2001) so that partners whose expectations and standards focus on process *and* outcomes might have more successful relationships than partners who focus on only one of these.

Other distinctions between types of positive beliefs and values may have similar functions. For example, some parts of a relationship are probably more subject to control by each partner than others; that is, people have more control over their own efforts in the relationship than they do over their partner's efforts. People have more control over how they resolve conflict than over whether they will have a lot of time to spend together. When an outcome can be controlled, perhaps that's when positive beliefs and values are the most beneficial, because that's when they motivate partners to take advantage of their control. When an outcome cannot be controlled, perhaps that's when it is best to cultivate more moderate expectations and standards, so that unanticipated negative events might be more readily accepted and addressed. Such advice would be consistent with that of the Serenity Prayer, which figures prominently in recovery groups like Alcoholics Anonymous: "Grant me the serenity to accept the things I cannot change, the courage to change the things I can, and the wisdom to know the difference."

Until further research examines some of these possibilities directly, the distinction between positive beliefs and values that benefit relationships and those that harm relationships remains unclear. For now, it is safe to conclude that couples should set their expectations and standards high enough to motivate their best efforts to maintain their relationships, but not so high that they risk frequent disappointments.

Similarity in Partners' Beliefs and Values

Some researchers have suggested that confusion over the effects of positive beliefs and values has been caused by asking the wrong question. Perhaps it is not the nature of each partner's beliefs and values that matter most in a relationship, but rather the level of agreement *between* partners' beliefs and values. This is an intuitively appealing idea. After all, it is easy to imagine that individuals with any set of values, no matter how unusual or extreme, may find happiness if they find partners who share those values. Political conservatives should be happy with other conservatives, vegetarians with other vegetarians, those who value passion with others who share that value, and those who favor independence with others who favor the same. While this is an appealing idea, it is not always true (FIGURE 9.11). The available supporting evidence is relatively weak, for several reasons.

FIGURE 9.11 Do similar beliefs matter? Republican Mary Matalin, a political consultant who has worked exclusively for conservative politicians, and Democrat James Carville, a campaign strategist who worked for Bill and Hillary Clinton, have been married since 1993. Even though their political affiliations differ, they share important values for raising a family together.

First, the effects of similarity between partners' beliefs and values tend to be small relative to the effects of beliefs and values within each partner. For example, although research has found that spouses who shared similar standards reported higher marital satisfaction than spouses who disagreed, that association was notably smaller than the effects of each spouse perceiving that his or her standards were being met in the relationship (Baucom et al., 1996). A similar analysis directly compared the power of discrepancies between perceptions and ideals within each partner and agreement between partners to account for differences in relationship satisfaction (Kelley & Burgoon, 1991). Once the significant effects of perceiving that one's ideals are being met were taken into account, the effects of the similarity between partners' ideals were negligible. Research on attachment models paints the same picture. Although people prefer partners with similar attachment styles to their own (e.g., Collins & Read, 1990; Frazier et al., 1996), this preference is significantly weaker than a more general preference for secure partners over insecure ones (Latty-Mann & Davis, 1996).

Second, although some couples are more similar than others, in general most people end up in relationships with partners who share their beliefs and values to a large degree. For example, as discussed in Chapter 5, similarity in attitudes is an important basis for personal attraction (Byrne, 1961; Byrne, Ervin, & Lamberth, 1970). Perhaps as a result, studies of married people reveal that husbands and wives tend to report quite similar beliefs and values (e.g., Baucom et al., 1996; Hill & Peplau, 1998). Thus, even the couples who disagree the most still tend to agree quite a bit, at least compared to the other variables. This problem may help explain the relatively weak effects of similarity on relationship outcomes.

Finally, not only are partners usually pretty similar to each other but, as psychologists David Kenny and Linda Acitelli (1994) have pointed out, to some degree everybody is pretty similar to everybody else. Personality psychologists call this the **stereotype accuracy effect**, referring to the fact that any two people are likely to agree, for example, that it is important to be kind to others simply because most people share this basic value. One implication of the stereotype accuracy effect is that, within a given couple, both partners may share many of their beliefs and values and still be no more similar to each other than they are to any other member of their population. When the effects of stereotypical agreement are controlled, the effects of agreement between partners on relationship satisfaction can be reduced or eliminated entirely (Acitelli, Kenny, & Gladstone, 1996).

Are there any beliefs or values on which it helps to agree with one's partner? Some research on engaged and newly married couples suggests that couples do better when partners agree about gender roles than when they disagree (Craddock, 1980, 1983). However, even this finding is complicated. It is true that, in these studies, couples were most satisfied with their relationships when husbands and wives shared traditional or egalitarian views about gender roles. Yet couples were just as satisfied on average when husbands had egalitarian views and wives had traditional views. In fact, the only problematic pattern was the pairing of traditional husbands with egalitarian wives. In other words, even in this domain, it may not be agreement by itself that makes a difference to relationships but rather the effects of specific patterns of partners' beliefs.

MAIN POINTS

>> To the extent that our ideas shape our experience of intimate relationships, some ideas may be healthier than others.

>> Some research shows that partners with positive expectations are more likely to act in ways that support the relationship and lead to positive outcomes.

>> Other research shows that partners who have unrealistically high expectations will probably be disappointed when inevitable conflicts arise.

>> Initial work on resolving these two positions suggests that couples should set their expectations high enough to motivate them to keep their relationship strong, but not so high that they aspire to goals that are truly out of reach.

Origins of Beliefs and Values

Understanding how different beliefs and values affect relationship outcomes is only the first step in understanding the diversity we can observe in relationships across the world and throughout history. The next step is to understand where different sets of beliefs and values come from. As discussed here and in Chapter 1, we may be born with a general set of relationship values hardwired into our brain, and some values and ideals seem to be universal (Jankowiak & Fischer, 1992; Rhodes et al., 2001). Yet different people also expect, and are willing to settle for, different things in their intimate relationships, so our common biological inheritance cannot be the whole story. Why are behaviors that indicate love and affection for some people frowned upon by others? Why do some people demand that their intimate relationships be simultaneously passionate, secure, and intellectually stimulating, whereas others seem willing to compromise or settle for relationships that fulfill some of their needs but not others? How can we account for this diversity?

In general, an individual's beliefs and values about relationships are determined by multiple factors, the product of an array of influences operating throughout the lifespan. To guide our consideration of some of these influences, it is useful to distinguish between influences that are more removed from the individual (e.g., culture, the media) and will therefore affect entire populations in the same way, and influences that are specific to the individual (e.g., family history, personal experiences) and will therefore help explain differences between individuals within a population.

Culture

Whereas love and romance are common to human experience everywhere, the ways that love and romance are expressed differ widely across societies. Take, for example, the association between courtship and eating. In Western societies, dining together is closely intertwined with romantic courtship. Inviting someone to share a meal is one way of indicating a potential romantic interest in that person; preparing a special meal for someone is even more intimate. This is not true for the Nuer, the indigenous society of southern Sudan. Among the Nuer, food and romance are so completely incompatible that a man will refrain from even mentioning food in the presence of a potential romantic partner. As anthropologist Sir Edward Evans-Pritchard observed: "Food must never be mentioned in the presence of girls, and a man will endure severe hunger rather than let them know that he has not eaten for a long time. . . . It is a strict rule of Nuer society that the sexes, unless they are close kin, avoid each other in the matter of food" (1951, p. 55). Instead of inviting her to dinner, a young Nuer man who wishes to express romantic interest in a woman might go to her village in the evening and loudly chant poems about her so her family knows his intentions.

Given that humans are basically similar with respect to their physical and emotional needs, why should there be such vast differences in the way they enact their intimate relationships? The key differences may not be what humans need but rather what they believe and value. In other words, diversity in intimate relationships may be the result not of biology but of culture. **Culture** can be defined as the shared attitudes, beliefs, norms, and values of

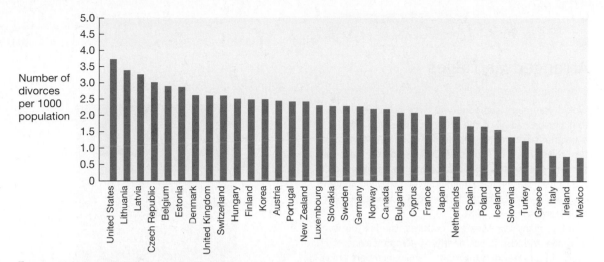

FIGURE 9.12 **Worldwide rates of divorce, 2005-2007.** Divorce rates vary widely throughout different countries. Of these, the United States has the highest divorce rate, and Mexico has the lowest. Across cultures, people differ in their standards for ending unsatisfying marriages. (Source: Organization for Economic Cooperation and Development, 2008.)

people who speak the same language and share a geographic area, during a specific period of time (Triandis, 1999). Culture is thus the repository for a society's knowledge about how intimate relationships ought to work. By conveying unique beliefs, expectations, standards, and ideals, culture affects how members of a society behave and react to each other in a wide range of situations, including intimate relationships (Gaines, 1995).

Thinking about cultures as collections of beliefs and values helps explain some phenomena that would otherwise be puzzling. For example, why do divorce rates vary so much across countries (**FIGURE 9.12**)? According to statistics compiled by the United Nations and the European Commission, the divorce rate in the United States is approximately 50 percent higher than in New Zealand, and 100 percent higher than in Mexico (Organization for Economic Cooperation and Development, 2008). It seems unlikely that marriages are actually much worse in the United States than in other countries or that spouses in other countries are somehow more capable of keeping their relationships satisfying. In fact, cross-cultural research has found few reliable differences between countries in feelings of love and fulfillment in intimate relationships (Sprecher et al., 1994). Rather, it may be that the unique cultures of different countries teach different standards for when divorce is or is not acceptable.

Cross-cultural research on what people believe about love and marriage support this idea. In one study (Levine et al., 1995), college students in 11 diverse cultures (India, Pakistan, Thailand, Mexico, Brazil, Japan, Hong Kong, the Philippines, Australia, England, and the United States) were asked to answer a single question: "If a man (woman) had all the qualities you desired,

BOX 9.1 SPOTLIGHT ON . . .

Arranged Marriages

Would you marry someone you were not in love with if that person had all of the other qualities you look for in a partner? For young people raised in Western societies, this is not a difficult question. During the past half-century, college students responding to this question in the United States overwhelmingly said they would never consider marrying someone they did not love (Kephart, 1967; Simpson et al., 1986).

Yet in many non-Western cultures, the link between marriage and love is not nearly as strong (Levine et al., 1995). In an **arranged marriage**, family members are responsible for selecting and approving potential mates for their children (**FIGURE 9.13**). From the outside, this can seem like a puzzling or even cruel practice, but it is important to keep in mind that arranged marriages differ widely around the world and even within specific communities. An arranged marriage is not necessarily synonymous with a forced marriage. Although there are parts of the world where children are still forced into marriages against their will, more often families at least consider their children's feelings when arranging their marriages (e.g., De Munck, 1996, 1998). In Japan, for example, where arranged marriage is still common, the families bring the potential bride and groom together, but then it is up to the couple to decide if they will proceed to marriage. Thus, love is not necessarily absent in an arranged marriage; it's just not the foundation of the relationship, as it is in a partner-selected marriage.

FIGURE 9.13 Circle seven times to say "I do." In the Kashmir region of India, a bride and groom whose marriage was arranged circle a ceremonial fire seven times. When the circles are completed, they are married. Studies of arranged marriages in India suggest that over time, couples in arranged marriages report greater satisfaction than couples who selected each other. How would you feel if your family decided who you would marry?

would you marry this person if you were not in love with him (her)?" Earlier research had shown that, in the United States, female and male students overwhelmingly said they would not marry without love (Kephart, 1967; Simpson, Campbell, & Berscheid, 1986), and that finding was replicated here. However, standards for marriage varied widely across countries. Especially in nations with lower economic standards of living and higher rates of fertility, love was viewed as less crucial to getting married and presumably less crucial to staying married as well. Thus, differences in divorce rates across countries may stem in part from cultural differences in standards for entering and leaving marriage. Where divorce rates are lower, it may not be that marriages have fewer problems, but rather that spouses simply react differently to the same old problems.

This seemingly fundamental difference has implications for the outcome of the relationship, but the implications seem to be different across cultures. Research on Chinese and Turkish marriages found what people from Western cultures might predict. Among Chinese women, those in partner-selected marriages were more satisfied than those in arranged marriages, and this held true regardless of the length of the marriage (Xiaohe & Whyte, 1990). Among Turkish couples, partner-selected marriages were characterized by greater marital adjustment and fewer reports of loneliness than arranged marriages (Demir & Fisiloglu, 1999).

However, studies of marriages in India tend to report the opposite results. In multiple studies, Indian spouses in arranged marriages report greater satisfaction with their relationships than spouses in partner-selected marriages (Kumar & Dhyani, 1996; Yelsma & Athappilly, 1988). The benefits of arranged marriage for Indian couples seem to depend on the duration of the marriage. Among newlyweds and the recently married, those in partner-selected marriages were happier than those in arranged marriages, just as in the Chinese and Turkish studies. Over longer durations, however, those in arranged marriages reported greater happiness than those in partner-selected marriages (Gupta & Singh, 1982).

The standards and expectations of couples in the two kinds of marriages may help explain this result. For the couples in partner-selected marriages, standards and expectations are probably high. The partners choose each other for love and passion, and they probably expect that love and passion will continue throughout the marriage. Some couples will get what they expect, but many others are likely to be disappointed. In contrast, couples in arranged marriages may have more modest or even low expectations for their marital relationships. After many years, some couples will experience the problems that they were prepared for, but others may be pleasantly surprised by their emerging depth of feeling for each other.

The difference may lie not in what happens to the couples, but in how different beliefs and values affect their reactions to what happens. Support for this idea comes from a study by communications researchers Paul Yelsma and Kuriakose Athappilly (1988), who asked Indian couples to rate not only their marital satisfaction but their satisfaction with their verbal, nonverbal, and sexual communication as well. The communication ratings were more strongly associated with marital satisfaction in the partner-selected marriages than in the arranged marriages, suggesting that the two kinds of couples had different standards for what it means to be happy in a marriage.

The tradition of arranged marriages raises similar issues. In cultures where spouses generally choose each other, the standards for what makes a suitable mate are likely to be quite different from what they are in cultures where third parties are responsible for pairing spouses together. BOX 9.1 describes research comparing the implications of these different standards for the eventual success of the marriage.

Cultural differences shape not only broad relationship outcomes but also the more concrete behaviors that make relationships more or less satisfying. Imagine, for example, you have a guest in your home and you wanted to make that person feel extremely comfortable. You might offer to bring your guest a drink or something to eat. Indeed, if your guest had grown up in a Western culture, that would be considered very thoughtful. However, when

Japanese psychiatrist Takeo Doi encountered this same behavior upon his first visit to the United States, he was taken aback. He wrote in his classic book, *The Anatomy of Dependence*:

> I visited a house of someone to whom I had been introduced by a Japanese acquaintance, and was talking to him when he asked me, "Are you hungry? We have some ice cream if you'd like it." As I remember, I was rather hungry, but finding myself asked point-blank if I was hungry by someone whom I was visiting for the first time, I could not bring myself to admit it, and ended by denying the suggestion. I probably cherished a mild hope that he would press me again, but my host, disappointingly said "I see" with no further ado, leaving me regretting that I had not replied more honestly. And I found myself thinking that a Japanese would almost never ask a stranger unceremoniously if he was hungry, but would produce something to give him without asking. (Doi, 1971/2002, p. 11)

Doi explains this misunderstanding as stemming from cultural differences in the way Westerners and Japanese express caring. In Western cultures, caring about someone involves respecting that person's autonomy and independence. In Japan, caring is grounded in *amae*, a word with no direct translation in English but which roughly means caring grounded in dependence and indulgence, like the caring between a mother and child. A love that expresses *amae* is not a love between partners or teammates but rather one in which each partner feels comfortable enough to expect that the other will grant every wish and meet every need without having to be asked. Doi uses the image of a puppy that rolls onto its back, hoping to be rewarded with a pat or a cuddle. Whereas Western couples may have little tolerance for that kind of passivity, the Japanese culture praises a love that allows that kind of trust in a partner's willingness to satisfy the other's needs. Thus, even though individuals in both countries and around the world wish to love and be loved, the specific behaviors that express or represent love may be shaped by beliefs and values that differ culturally.

Media Influences

If culture is the repository of a society's beliefs and values, then the mass media is one means through which the beliefs and values of a culture are transmitted to individuals. Especially in the Western world, where life is saturated with media of every description, the average person spends each day bombarded by countless messages about what the world is like and how it ought to be. Because intimate relationships are so fundamental to human experience, it is no surprise that they are the theme of many of those messages.

Exposure to media messages does not necessarily mean accepting or being affected by them. Are people's own beliefs and values influenced by the messages they are exposed to in the media? This has been a controversial question, especially in regard to media potrayals of relationships and sexuality. Some argue that people are able to separate what they see in the media from what they experience in their own lives, suggesting that media images should have no effect on what people expect or value in their own relationships. Others maintain that the media represents an important source of information about relationships, particularly for young people. In this view, the media is likely to have a powerful influence on how people think about their own relationships, especially over time.

Research on this question consistently supports the latter view (Allen, D'Alessio, & Brezgel, 1995; Collins et al., 2004). The way relationships are portrayed in the media has been shown to affect what people believe about relationships in general, how people evaluate their own relationships, and how they behave. Social psychologists Neil Malamuth and James Check (1981) used an experimental field study to examine how images of sexual violence in movies affect men's and women's attitudes toward sexual violence against women in the real world. They hypothesized that it is the outcome of the violence that sends the message: Depicting sexual violence as having positive consequences sends the message that violence against women is acceptable. To test this idea, they randomly assigned 271 male and female college students to watch one of two pairs of popular (i.e., nonpornographic) feature films. The first pair depicted sexual behavior within the context of a romantic relationship but did not feature aggression or sexual violence. The second pair featured sexual violence with positive consequences; that is, sexually aggressive behavior toward a woman who initially resists but ultimately falls in love with her aggressor. Several days later, all the participants completed a seemingly unrelated attitudes survey that included items about the acceptability of sexual violence.

If watching films has no effect on beliefs about relationships, then there should have been no average difference between the attitudes of the students randomly assigned to watch one kind of movie or the other. But the films did have an effect, especially on men (**FIGURE 9.14**). Compared to men who had watched the nonviolent films, those who had watched the films featuring sexual violence with positive consequences were significantly more likely to agree with statements such as, "Being roughed up is sexually stimulating to many women" and "If a woman engages in necking or petting and she lets things get out of hand, it is her own fault if her partner forces sex on her." Women, in contrast, were slightly *less* likely to agree with such statements after watching the more violent films. What makes this demonstration especially impressive is that the participants in this study had several days to digest, think about, or forget the films that they had seen. Moreover, they had no idea that the films were at all related to their answers on the survey several days later. Nevertheless, a few hours spent in a movie theater had measurable effects on beliefs about whether sexual aggression is acceptable behavior. It's not hard to imagine that the cumulative effects of a lifetime of absorbing such messages might be much greater.

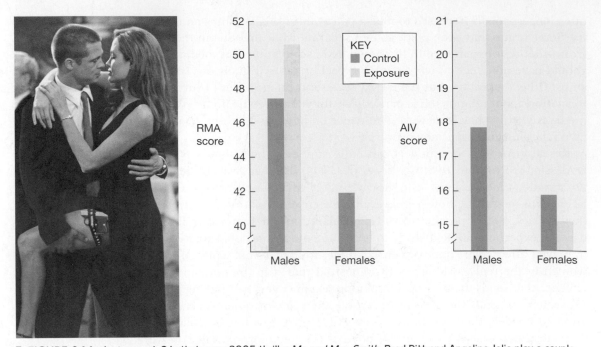

FIGURE 9.14 Just a movie? In their sexy 2005 thriller *Mr. and Mrs. Smith*, Brad Pitt and Angelina Jolie play a couple whose humdrum sex life is enhanced when they discover that each is secretly an assassin and they have been hired to target each other. Do popular films that combine sex and violence influence people's beliefs about sexual violence against women? Students were randomly assigned to watch popular films that either did or did not depict women getting aroused from sexual violence. As the graphs show, men who watched these films subsequently scored higher on scales of rape myth acceptance (RMA) and acceptance of interpersonal violence against women (AIV). In contrast, women who watched the violent films scored significantly lower on both scales. (Source: Malamuth & Check, 1981.)

The influence of media messages is not limited to general beliefs. Such messages can also shape the values and standards people apply toward evaluations of their own relationships. It is often argued, for example, that the media's relentless focus on exceptionally attractive celebrities leads to unrealistic standards of beauty in the broader culture. In research finding evidence for this sort of effect, women and men were shown slides featuring either abstract art or magazine centerfolds (Kenrick, Gutierres, & Goldberg, 1989). Then all participants were asked to rate of an average nude figure and their feelings of love for their current partners. As you might expect, regardless of the gender of the centerfold, they all rated an average nude as less attractive immediately after viewing the centerfold, compared to those who had viewed the abstract art. In addition, the more positive the men's reaction to the centerfold, the less they described themselves as being in love with their wives. If a single exposure to a centerfold in a research study can affect beauty standards immediately afterward (at least for men), it seems likely that the long-term effects of being exposed to extremely beautiful people on every magazine cover, billboard, and television screen may be powerful indeed.

Correlational research gives a sense of that power through analyses of the association between the sexual content of television shows and the sexual behavior of adolescents who watch the shows. Rather than examining the effect of a single exposure to a single message, one study analyzed the sexual content of a broad range of television shows and then related those data to adolescents' reports of the kinds of shows they watch and their sexual behavior over the subsequent year (Collins et al., 2004). The associations were powerful: Adolescents who watched the most television with sexual content were twice as likely to begin having sex during the next year than their peers who watched the least television with sexual content, even after controlling for several other variables known to predict early onset of sexual behavior. In general, teenagers who watched the most sexual behavior on television reported similar levels of sexual behavior as teenagers 2–3 years older who watched the least sexual behavior on television. One explanation for these findings is that young people learn from television about when they are expected to have sex, and that these expectations subsequently affect their choices and behaviors.

While pointing out the ways that media messages can influence beliefs and values in relationships, it is also worth noting that people are not merely passive recipients of such messages. On the contrary, people frequently have a vast range of media from which to choose, and they generally select the messages to which they are exposed. Moreover, people can think about what they read and watch and can reject negative messages if they have a basis for doing so. Some encouraging research suggests that educating people about the effects of media messages can have a substantial influence on their resistance to being persuaded by such messages (Check & Malamuth, 1984; Irving & Berel, 2001). Most people probably do not receive such education, however, and the media remains a powerful, if unreliable, source of information and values about intimate relationships.

Personal Experience

Throughout this chapter, we have described ways that beliefs and values help us understand how people experience their intimate relationships. It is also true, of course, that our personal experiences shape our beliefs and values. Indeed, this is the central idea of attachment theory. Whereas Bowlby emphasized the effects of our earliest experiences on our thinking about relationships, substantial evidence suggests that personal experiences across the lifespan continue to have effects.

One experience shown to be especially powerful in this regard is the divorce of one's parents. This follows directly from attachment theory. To the extent that one totally depends on one's parents in infancy, then the nature of the parents' relationship should be a powerful model for children of what relationships are like and how they should be. The disruption of that relationship ought to have severe consequences for children's views of what they can expect from relationships. A number of studies confirm that this is so (Franklin, Janoff-Bulman, & Roberts, 1990; King, 2002; Sprague & Kinney, 1997; van Schaick & Stolberg, 2001).

Psychologist Kathryn Franklin and her colleagues asked unmarried college students, some of whose parents had divorced and some of whose parents remained married, to describe their own views on marriage and their expectations for their own marriages (Franklin, Janoff-Bulman, & Roberts, 1990). Compared to students whose parents had remained married, students whose parents had divorced reported less optimism about marriage in general and lower expectations of trust in a future partner. It seems that, in the absence of any direct knowledge about their futures, children of divorced parents used their observations of their parents' marriage as a basis for their own expectations and, as a result, were more pessimistic than the children of parents who remained married. That pessimism about whether it is safe to trust another person may be one reason adult children of divorced parents also find it harder to discuss difficult issues with their romantic partners (Sanders, Halford, & Behrens, 1999). Without models of successful problem solving from childhood, it may be more difficult to develop successful problem-solving skills in later life.

Just as powerful as the breakup of a parents' relationship are the experiences we have in our own relationships. A passionate first love, a bad breakup, or the experience of abuse can affect what we believe about relationships in general, and shape the models we apply toward future relationships. Perhaps you have even met someone who cannot help but use an especially influential prior relationship as a standard against which all current and future relationships are judged. In some cases, this tendency to generalize from past experiences may lead to relationship problems, such as when beliefs shaped by a prior relationship prevent individuals from learning from and responding to their current partners. On the other hand, the fact that new experiences can change our beliefs and values offers hope to people whose experiences have led them to be pessimistic about relationships. As studies examining how attachment styles change over the course of multiple relationships have shown, the experience of a rewarding, dependable relationship can lead formerly insecure people to develop more secure models of relationships in general (Crowell, Treboux, & Waters, 2002; Ruvolo, Fabin, & Ruvolo, 2001).

MAIN POINTS

>> One source of diversity in ideas about intimate relationships is culture; culturally determined standards help explain the vast differences in divorce rates in countries around the world.

>> The media transmits ideas about intimate relationships to individuals, and has been shown to affect what people believe about relationships, standards of beauty, and sexual behavior.

>> Beliefs and values are also shaped by personal experiences; for example, children of divorced parents tend to have pessimistic beliefs about marriage, and partners in rewarding relationships grow more secure.

CONCLUSION -

When Minal Hajratwala came out to her parents in 1991, she faced a conflict that repeats every generation as parents and their children express different views about what makes intimate relationships worthwhile and satisfying. A look around the world suggests that the same disagreements can be found across cultures and historical periods. The elements that keep passion alive in a studio apartment in Manhattan are not the same as those that are important in a hut on the banks of the Amazon River. What made for a good relationship in 1917 may not be the same as what makes for a good relationship in the 21st century. The more we examine intimate relationships, the more it becomes clear that people's experiences in their relationships are affected not only by what happens but how they understand what happens. Understanding the diversity in intimate relationships around the world therefore requires understanding the specific beliefs and values people use to make sense of their relationship experiences.

Saying that intimate relationships are shaped by partners' beliefs and values is not the same as saying that relationships are all in the mind. Clearly, the events of an intimate relationship have an objective reality. In fact, as we have seen throughout this chapter, beliefs and values may guide how individuals find meaning in that reality, how they choose which events in their relationships to focus on, and how they interpret them. Thus, relationships are not purely cognitive; they result from an interaction between the relatively stable ideas individuals bring to their relationships and their daily experiences of the relationship. In the next chapter, we examine in more detail how this interaction plays out, exploring the ways people process information to reach conclusions about what their relationships are like.

10

Understanding Each Other

Remembering the Way We Were

"My name is Stuart, and I remember everything." So begins Julian Barnes' novel *Talking It Over* (1991), the story of a love triangle. The main characters are in their early 30s: Stuart, a bit dull and stodgy; his highly verbal, flamboyant friend Oliver; and the reserved Gillian, who falls in love with both of these men. What makes the novel unusual is its form:

a series of monologues by each character. Speaking directly to the reader, Stuart, Oliver, and Gillian try to convey their own interpretations of how their relationships unfolded and why events played out the way they did (**FIGURE 10.1**). Oliver and Gillian, like Stuart and perhaps like a lot of us, believe they remember everything, and each character assures us that his or her version of events is accurate.

The poignancy of the novel lies in the fact that none of the characters actually remembers anything in exactly the same way. Sometimes one of them describes in great detail an event that another one forgets or ignores as unimportant. Other times two of them describe the same event, but emphasize different details. For example, at the party where he first met Gillian, Stuart remembers telling

jokes and being unusually witty. Of the same night, Gillian recalls: "Stuart began by telling a couple of jokes, which fell rather flat because he was so jumpy, and I don't think the jokes were much good in the first place (p. 25)."

At another point, the three characters describe the day Stuart and Gillian got married. Here is Stuart's version:

It was a beautiful day. The sort of day everyone should have their wedding on. A soft June morning with a blue sky and a gentle breeze. . . . The registrar was a dignified man who behaved with the correct degree of formality. . . . I said my vows a bit too loud and they seemed to echo round the light oak paneling of the room; Gill

FIGURE 10.1 Three points of view in a love triangle. Comparing different points of view offers a window on how we make meanings in our intimate relationships.

seemed to overcompensate and whispered hers so the registrar and I could only just hear. We were very happy. (p. 8)

Oliver, who served as witness and who likes to use big words, provides a different perspective:

I remember the sky that day: swirling clouds like marbled end-papers. A little too much wind, and everyone patting his hair back into place inside the door of the register office. . . . Then we went in to face this perfectly oleaginous and crepuscular little registrar. A flour-bomb of dandruff on his shoulders. The show went off as well as these things do. . . . Stuart bellowed his words as if answering a court-martial and failure to enunciate perfectly at top volume would earn him a few more years in the glasshouse. Poor Gillie could scarcely vocalize her responses. I think she was crying, but adjudged it vulgar to peer. (p. 13)

And Gillian, the bride, what is her take on the day?

I met Stuart. I fell in love. I married. What's the story? (p. 41)

By asking "What's the story?" Gillian seems to be saying that an event should speak for itself, without needing elaboration. But, as the novel points out, that is almost never the case. Although Stuart, Oliver, and Gillian participate in the same events and conversations, they each remember and focus on different details—details that make the difference between a suave charmer and a nervous dullard, between a blissful wedding celebration and a rushed and formal proceeding. Far from events speaking for themselves, the three characters work hard to speak for each event, sifting through the details, minimizing or forgetting some and enhancing others. Through this work, they decide what each experience means for their overall sense of their relationships, and the interpretations they arrive at are very different.

QUESTIONS

Within an intimate relationship, understanding each other requires partners to recognize that specific events do not always have their own single, or objective, meaning. Rather, the meaning partners make of their experiences is the product of considerable work—selecting, constructing, and interpreting the information.

How does new knowledge about relationships get created? Every moment in a relationship provides us with a steady stream of new information—about our partner, about ourself, and about the state of the relationship. Given the tremendous complexity of that information, how do partners process, understand, and integrate their experiences to construct their general beliefs about what their relationships are like? Are people as objective about their relationships as they think they are? If not, what are the motives and biases that affect the way relationship experiences are interpreted? How flexible are those interpretations? Can we believe pretty much whatever we want to believe, or are there limits to understanding each other? If so, what are they? How do our beliefs change, even if we would sometimes prefer to resist that change?

Information Processing

How fundamental is a kiss? Is a sigh just a sigh? Can people just accept their intimate experiences without having to explain or interpret them? The classic song from the movie *Casablanca* suggests that they can, but research on intimate relationships proves otherwise.

> " You must remember this
> A kiss is still a kiss
> A sigh is just a sigh
> The fundamental things apply
> As time goes by."
>
> —Herman Hupfeld (1931)

In Chapter 8, we described the talk table, an approach to measuring how partners understand their interactions with each other (Gottman et al., 1976). As you may recall, partners using the talk table are asked to rate the intent of every statement they make as soon as they've made it. Each partner also rates the impact of each statement he or she hears from the other partner. By comparing each partner's ratings of intent with the other partner's ratings of impact, the talk table helps identify the extent to which each partner is successful at getting his or her point across.

The same technique has been used to compare how partners and outside observers interpret the same behaviors (Floyd & Markman, 1983; Hawkins, Carrère, & Gottman, 2002). For example, psychologists Melissa Hawkins, Sybil Carrère, and John Gottman (2002) asked 96 married couples to discuss a marital problem using the talk table. At the same time, trained outside observers, people who did not know the spouses and had no investment in their relationship, rated the impact of each partner's statements. If behaviors have their own meanings—if a kiss is just a kiss and a sigh is just a sigh—then we would expect observers and spouses to agree, at least roughly, on the positivity and negativity of each statement in the interaction. In fact, this was not the case. On the contrary, spouses and observers frequently disagreed about the meaning of the very same statements. Some statements that multiple observers reliably rated as negative were rated by spouses as positive, and vice versa. Somehow, the spouses in this study were doing more than simply perceiving each other's behaviors. They were interpreting those behaviors, and the result of that interpretation was that they understood each other in ways that outside observers could not (FIGURE 10.2).

It doesn't take research to recognize that many of our experiences are subject to multiple interpretations. Deciding what specific behaviors mean is one of the central challenges of an intimate relationship. For example:

- The hopeful lover watches the object of his affections for some sign that his feelings are returned. Aha! A glance his way! Is it an invitation, a dismissal, or just a coincidence?

- When Linda, under a lot of stress at work, asks Robert to be more supportive, he decides to get her car waxed. He gets home with her car, proud of himself for being such a good mate, and is soon puzzled and

FIGURE 10.2 **Interpreting each other.** We do not just record the events of our relationships, we actively interpret and construct meaning. One reason intimate relationships are challenging is that each partner may construct different meanings from the same events.

frustrated by her lack of appreciation. Was he being supportive or wasn't he?

- In marital therapy, a husband and wife each explain to the therapist how the other one is to blame for their marital difficulties. She says he withdraws and is unwilling to respond to her until she gets upset. He says she nags, forcing him to withdraw in order to avoid a fight. Who is right?

In each of these examples, there is little question about what specific behaviors occurred. Undoubtedly, there was a glance in the direction of a lover, a car was waxed, a couple had an argument. Every day of an intimate relationship is full of specific behaviors like these, but we are rarely satisfied with examining and understanding at this level. It is not enough to know that my partner looked at me, that she is quiet tonight, or that she cooked dinner. Rather, I want to know that my partner cooked dinner because she loves me, not because she feels obligated to do so. I want to know that my partner is quiet because she is tired, not because she is trying to avoid my company. In other words, we tend to want to know the meaning behind our concrete perceptions. To understand our relationship, it is not enough to simply observe what happens. We have to connect what we observe to some higher-order feelings and intentions.

How do we link experience to meaning? The term **information processing** refers to all the ways we organize our many perceptions, thoughts, and beliefs about the world. Consider that all knowledge about a relationship is not equal. The things we know vary in how specific or general they are. At the specific end, much of what we know consists of daily occurrences (we ate lunch together, we brushed by each other in the hallway). In the middle level, we have knowledge in the form of general beliefs about a partner's qualities (my partner is dependable, my partner is attractive). At the global, most abstract level, are broad feelings about whether the relationship is worthwhile overall (this is a person I want to continue to spend time with, this is the right relationship for me). None of this information would be very useful if we couldn't organize it into a coherent representation of the relationship as a whole. We do this quickly and often without conscious awareness, drawing connections between our specific observations and more general beliefs and feelings (Smith, Ratliff, & Nosek, 2012). The result can be described as a hierarchical structure. As **FIGURE 10.3** shows, specific observations provide the foundation for more general beliefs about a partner's qualities, and those beliefs in turn support global feelings about whether a relationship is satisfying or not (Hampson, John, & Goldberg, 1986).

Describing relationship knowledge hierarchically has a couple of important implications for how we think about information processing. First, any piece of specific information can be connected to different levels of the hierarchy. In other words, an experience can be considered solely for its concrete details (i.e., no connection to more general beliefs), as a sign of particular qualities of the relationship or the partner (i.e., the concrete experience is connected to a more general belief), or as an indicator of the quality of the relationship as a whole (i.e., the concrete experience links directly to satisfaction with the

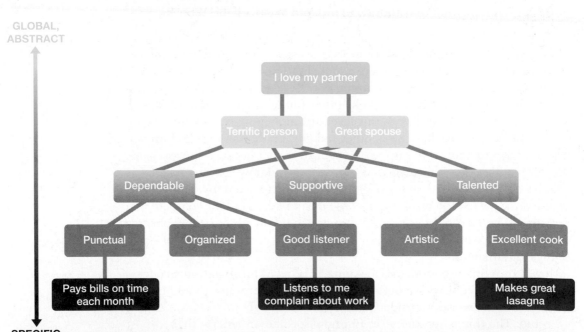

FIGURE 10.3 Hierarchical relationship knowledge. What we know about our partner varies from very concrete observations ("Makes great lasagna") to mid-level knowledge ("My partner is talented") to global, abstract feelings ("I love my partner"). The same specific observations can be linked to broader beliefs in different ways, with implications for the development of the relationship. (Source: Adapted from Neff & Karney, 2005.)

relationship). Imagine, for example, that you observe your partner drinking a beer. What does this behavior mean for the relationship? Figure 10.3 suggests that the same behavior may have different possible meanings depending on how that information is processed. The behavior can be taken for granted as a specific behavior that has no bearing on the rest of the relationship ("My partner must be thirsty right now"). Or the behavior can be understood as a sign of your partner's more general characteristics ("My partner sure loves beer"). Or the behavior can be viewed as a threat to the foundation of the relationship ("My partner may have a drinking problem").

When describing other people, we tend to gravitate toward labels and beliefs that are in the middle range of this hierarchy, broad enough to connect specific behaviors to some higher meaning but not so broad as to lack description (John, Hampson, & Goldberg, 1991). For example, thinking of your partner as "dependable" (a mid-level idea) lets you predict that he will be punctual, pay bills on time, and be there when you need him. Thinking of him as "good" (a more global impression) is more evaluative but less descriptive of any specific behaviors, so less useful for predicting what your partner will do at any given moment.

A second implication of this way of thinking is that it is possible to link most specific observations or perceptions to several different higher-level meanings. A partner who shows up on time to every appointment could be seen as dependable or compulsive. A lover who wants to be around you every minute of the day could be seen as affectionate or clinging. This flexibility helps explain why partners may each perceive the same events very differently, and why they might have very different views about their relationship than people outside. Even if everyone perceives the same specific behaviors, different people may process those observations differently, connecting them to different meanings and thus reaching different conclusions (**FIGURE 10.4**).

This process may also help explain how the same person can have different interpretations about the same behavior at different times. Consider how our impressions of a partner can change over the course of a relationship. After studying accounts of how relationships begin and end, sociologist Diane Felmlee (1995, 1998, 2001) documented a phenomenon she calls **fatal attraction**, wherein qualities that are initially attractive in a partner become the very same qualities that end the relationship. For example, the cool silence that is so attractive when seen as a sign of masculine self-confidence may not be attractive later if it becomes a sign

FIGURE 10.4 Needy is in the eye of the beholder. The fact that two people are sharing the same experience does not mean they are focusing on the same details or interpreting the experience in the same way.

(a)   (b)   (c)   (d)

> FIGURE 10.5 **Fatal attractions?** The same qualities that are attractive initially can turn into problems later. Does your partner's silence and reluctance to open up emotionally make him cool, like (a) Clint Eastwood, or brutish, like (b) Tony Soprano? Is your partner's impulsiveness the sign of a vibrant free spirit, like (c) Zooey Deschanel in *500 Days of Summer*, or a self-centered and uncontrolled person, like (d) Glenn Close in *Fatal Attraction*?

of brutal indifference. Similarly, the impulsive behavior that is so compelling when it's considered part of a passionate free spirit may eventually hurt the relationship, if it becomes evidence of an uncontrolled, self-centered personality (**FIGURE 10.5**). In several studies, Felmlee identified this sort of transformation in just under half the relationships she examined. To understand these cases, it is not necessary to believe that people change drastically over time or that observers initially misjudge their partner and later learn the truth. It is sufficient to understand that the same behaviors can have multiple interpretations and meanings, and that the process of linking a specific behavior to its meaning can change over time, even if the behavior itself remains relatively constant.

Recognizing that the broader implications of specific behaviors are somewhat flexible renders arguments about the "true" meaning of any behavior irrelevant. There may not be a single inherent meaning, but a variety of possible meanings. When partners argue about what really happened or what a behavior really implied, they may actually be arguing about whether each of their different ways of processing the same information is valid.

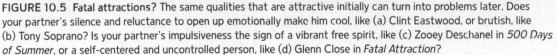

MAIN POINTS

>> Our perceptions, thoughts, and beliefs about a relationship and our partner vary from specific and concrete observations of behaviors to more general ideas about what our partner is like, to broadly global evaluations of the relationship as a whole.

>> Information processing refers to all the ways our perceptions, thoughts, and beliefs are organized.

>> A specific perception of the relationship can be used to support many different interpretations or meanings.

>> In a fatal attraction, a specific behavior that has a positive association early in the relationship comes to be associated with negative feelings later in the relationship.

Motivated Reasoning

Given some flexibility in assigning meaning to specific behaviors and experiences in relationships, why do we choose some interpretations over others? On a night when our partner is withdrawn and uncommunicative, how do we know whether the behavior is a symptom of a rough day at work or a sign of growing disenchantment with the relationship? One obvious answer is that we tend to assign the meanings that fit best with what we already know. For example, if we know that our partner is usually open and sensitive, we may be more likely to see the behavior as a temporary aberration. Silence that fits into a broader pattern of withdrawal, however, will probably be interpreted differently.

Sometimes the meanings we give to specific behaviors and experiences are shaped not only by what makes sense but also by the kind of sense we want to make. After all, the way we understand the specific events of a relationship has powerful consequences for our feelings about the relationship. Seeing evidence of positive qualities in our partner is rewarding, and seeing evidence of negative qualities is disappointing. Thus, when it comes to understanding relationships, we have conscious and unconscious preferences that lead us to favor particular beliefs and interpretations over others. A **motive** is a drive to reach a specific goal; a **bias** is a tendency to process information to protect a particular point of view. When we think about our relationships, our motive to believe certain things about our partner can lead to biases in how we perceive and understand our partner's behavior. **Motivated reasoning** refers to all the ways our motives, desires, and preferences bias the way information is selected, interpreted, and organized, for the purpose of satisfying specific needs and achieving specific goals (Kunda, 1990).

Motivated reasoning helps explain why outside observers of a relationship often evaluate it very differently from the participants. Observers can be dispassionate. Having no investment in any particular outcomes, they can weigh everything they know about a relationship equally and arrive at whatever interpretations make the most sense. The partners in the relationship, in contrast, do have an investment. Because some conclusions (e.g., this is a good relationship) are far more desirable than others (e.g., I'm wasting my time in this relationship), partners are motivated to process the same information in ways that favor beneficial interpretations.

What are the goals that drive motivated reasoning in relationships? What do people prefer to believe about their partners? What are the information-processing biases that help them achieve these goals? Numerous motives and biases affect how partners interpret their experiences in relationships, and we'll focus here on a few of the most important.

Enhancement: Believing the Best

The feeling of being in a loving intimate relationship is one of the best that human beings can experience. An unsuccessful relationship, in contrast, is one of the worst experiences. It is no surprise, then, that people want to believe that their intimate relationships are successful, that their partners are worthy of trust, and that their investments of time and energy in relationships are warranted. This powerful **enhancement motive** affects the way partners process information about their relationships, leading to an **enhancement bias**—a preference for information that supports and strengthens positive beliefs about a partner and a relationship.

Satisfied partners tend to view each other and their relationship in an exceedingly positive light. In a straightforward demonstration, social psychologists Sandra Murray, John Holmes, and Dale Griffin (1996) asked both partners in dating and married couples to rate themselves on a number of qualities, to rate the ideal partner on the same qualities, and finally to rate their actual partner on the same qualities. Comparing the results, the researchers found that people tended to idealize their loved ones; that is, participants viewed their partners as having more positive qualities than the partners perceived in themselves. Could it be that the self-ratings were simply modest and that partners' ratings of each other were in fact accurate? To address this possibility, the researchers also asked friends of the couples to rate each partner on the same set of qualities (Murray et al., 2000). Among those in satisfying relationships, each partner rated the other far more positively than their friends did, suggesting that the earlier findings stem not from modesty in self-ratings but from partners' tendency to idealize each other (FIGURE 10.6).

The same enhancement bias appears to characterize evaluations of a relationship as a whole. Social psychologist Caryl Rusbult and her colleagues have shown that people tend to believe their own relationships have more positive qualities and fewer negative ones than most other people's relationships (Rusbult et al., 2000; Van Lange & Rusbult, 1995). Perhaps as a consequence, social psychologists Tara MacDonald and Michael Ross (1999) showed that dating partners tend to be overly optimistic about their relationship's stability. In this study, dating partners were asked to predict whether or not they would still be together after 1 year. Friends and relatives of the couples were asked to make the same prediction. Even though the partners presumably knew more about the weaknesses of their relationships than their friends and families did, the partners nevertheless were far more optimistic (and far less accurate) about the future than the outside observers.

It makes sense that once people have committed to an intimate relationship, they should be motivated to view that relationship favorably. After all, entering into any relationship is a risky endeavor. Our partners, because they know us so well, are in the best position to hurt or betray us. To justify the effort and risk that intimate relationships require, it helps to be confident that

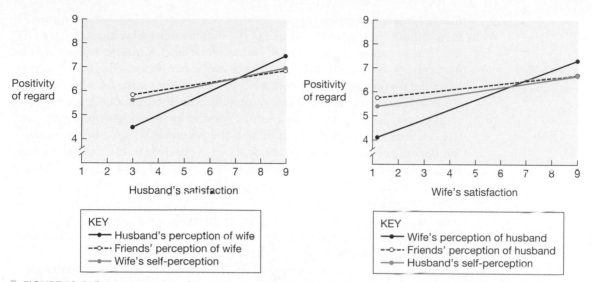

FIGURE 10.6 **Enhancement bias.** Researchers compared spouses' perceptions of each other's qualities to their friends' ratings of the same. Having little reason to perceive the spouses in any particular way, the friends tended to rate each partner as partners rated themselves. But spouses rated each other more positively than they rated themselves when they were happy with the relationship, and less positively when unhappy. The self-ratings matched those of an outside observer, but the spouses' ratings were colored by their overall feelings about the relationship. (Source: Murray et al., 2000.)

our partners are worthy of the trust and time we invest in them (Murray & Holmes, 1997). The enhancement bias serves to strengthen that confidence and thus functions to minimize doubts that might otherwise prevent us from starting a relationship at all.

Accuracy: Knowing and Being Known

Although it is always rewarding to believe one is in a satisfying relationship, there are times when an **accuracy motive**, the desire to understand a partner and be understood in turn, is more important (Gagne & Lydon, 2004). On a first date, for example, most people do not rush to idealize their companions. On the contrary, the initial stages of a relationship are more likely to be characterized by a desire for accurate information about the partner, so that the individual can judge whether a relationship is likely to be worth pursuing. Over the course of an intimate relationship, there may be other important choice points and transitions—Should we move in together? Should I pass up a career or educational opportunity to stay in the same city as my partner? Should I marry this person?—when partners are strongly motivated, not necessarily to strengthen an existing commitment but rather to find out whether they should make or deepen a commitment.

At times like these, information processing is likely to reflect not an enhancement bias but rather a **diagnosticity bias**, a preference for information that may indicate important qualities in a partner or a relationship (Vorauer & Ross, 1996). For the best example of the diagnosticity bias in action, try talking to a friend who has a crush on someone and wants to know if his or her feelings are returned. If you've ever had a conversation with a would-be lover (or if you've been one yourself), you're familiar with the way such lovers analyze the specific behavior of the object of their affection, scrutinizing each glance and every friendly greeting for deeper meaning. Given the potential rewards of returned affection, and the potential sting of being rejected, the desire for accurate information about a possible partner's true feelings makes a lot of sense. The problem, however, is that specific behaviors do not always indicate what another person is feeling (sometimes a sigh *is* just a sigh). Thus, just as the enhancement motive can lead people to make overly positive assessments of their ongoing relationships, the accuracy motive can lead people to read meanings and intentions into specific behaviors that may not actually be there.

Once a relationship has begun, there continue to be reasons for partners to prefer accurate information about each other. As social psychologist William Swann (1984) and his colleagues have argued, effective interaction with a partner requires that we understand him or her. Imagine, for example, being married to someone who is warm and funny in private but somewhat uncomfortable in social situations. Although it might be flattering, it would not be very functional to insist that your partner be the life of every party. Rather, understanding her real strengths and weaknesses would help you predict her behavior in different contexts and thereby contribute to a sense of control over events in the relationship. The benefits of prediction and control fuel a desire for accurate knowledge of a partner, even if this means recognizing faults and limitations. (For more on the desire to be known, see **BOX 10.1**.)

With respect to motivated reasoning, the desire to be accurate can lead to a **confirmation bias**, a preference for information that supports what is already known about a partner or a relationship. In a demonstration of this bias, spouses were asked to rate their partner's social skills and then were presented with a bogus psychological assessment of that partner, describing him or her as either socially skilled or socially inept (De La Ronde & Swann, 1998). Spouses then had an opportunity to interact with their partners, and these interactions were videotaped and coded by outside observers. The observers noticed that, when spouses disagreed with the feedback they had received about their partners, they actively rejected that feedback during the interactions, even when it was positive. In other words, for spouses who believed their partners to be socially inept, it was no comfort to read an assessment saying that their partners were more skilled than they thought. Rather, they actively tried to refute the assessment, seeking to restore the more negative perception they believed was more accurate. It is interesting that the partners of these spouses *also* behaved in ways that refuted the inconsistent feedback, even when that feedback was positive. Does it help relationships for partners to try to understand each other in this way? It seems

BOX 10.1 SPOTLIGHT ON . . .

Depressed People in Relationships

When partners feel good about themselves and about each other, the motive to feel positive about the relationship and the incentive to understand each other accurately go hand in hand. However, in the case of a partner who is depressed or suffering from low self-esteem, the two motives may be in conflict (Murray et al., 2001; Swann, 1990). Consider the dilemma of depressed people in relationships. They want to be loved by their partners, and they also want to be understood, which in this case means being known for having the negative qualities that depressed people often see in themselves. Recognition of this tension has led to a lengthy debate about whether the enhancement or accuracy motive is more important, with a number of scholars offering models that rank them in different ways (Sedikides & Strube, 1995; Swann & Schroeder, 1995).

Recently, however, researchers have begun to appreciate that enhancement and accuracy are not mutually exclusive at all and, in fact, are goals that can be pursued simultaneously (Gagne & Lydon, 2004; Neff & Karney, 2002). In research on college students, for example, clinical psychologists Thomas Joiner and Gerald Metalsky (1995) found that, compared to their nondepressed peers, depressed individuals were more likely to seek out negative feedback about their traits and abilities (e.g., "What is some evidence you have seen that your roommate doesn't have very good social skills?"). For depressed people, asking for negative feedback is consistent with an accuracy motive. At the same time, however, these depressed students were also more likely than nondepressed peers to engage in excessive reassurance seeking; that is, pressuring others to prove their positive regard for them (e.g., "Do you frequently seek reassurance from the people you feel close to as to whether they really care about you?"). Asking to be told how loved you are is consistent with an enhancement motive.

How can depressed people want positive and negative feedback at the same time? The hierarchy in Figure 10.3 suggests an answer. If beliefs about relationships vary in level, it's possible to seek one kind of feedback about one level and another kind of feedback about another level. This is what the depressed students in the Joiner and Metalsky (1995) study appear to have been doing. The negative feedback they solicited from others addressed the mid-level, the abilities and traits they thought they lacked (e.g., intellectual ability, artistic ability, physical attractiveness). However, the reassurance they sought addressed the more global level of their relationships with others (e.g., "Do other people care about me?"). In other words, they wanted to know that their failings and limitations were understood, and that overall they were accepted and appreciated by others. This may be all anyone wants from an intimate relationship: to be known by a partner, warts and all, and then to be loved and accepted anyway.

so: Both spouses were more satisfied with the marriage when their strengths and weaknesses were acknowledged than when their partners were willing to accept feedback that did not reflect their sense of themselves (Gill & Swann, 2004; Swann, De La Ronde, & Hixon, 1994). Thus, it appears that not only do we want to think highly of our partners, but we also want to feel like we understand them and are understood in return.

Justification: Being Right

Not all motivated reasoning serves to benefit intimate relationships. In a study described earlier, we noted that partners in satisfied relationships rated each other more positively than their friends did (Murray et al., 2000). What was also true in that study was that partners in *unsatisfying* relationships rated each other more *negatively* than their friends did. This sort of bias toward negativity is common in unsatisfying or distressed relationships. Just as partners who are committed to the relationship process information in ways that support their commitment, partners who are upset with each other, or who are contemplating leaving, process information in ways that support and justify these feelings (Fincham & O'Leary, 1983; Jacobson et al., 1985). Rather than minimizing faults and enhancing strengths, for example, unhappy partners do the opposite, exaggerating their partners' flaws and overlooking their positive qualities. This process is an example of sentiment override, which we defined in Chapter 2 as the tendency for partners' global feelings about their relationship to color their perceptions of specific behaviors and experiences (Weiss, 1980).

It is not hard to understand why partners who are satisfied would process information in a relationship-enhancing way, but why would dissatisfied partners process information in ways that contribute to disappointment? One reason is that there are times when the desire to protect the self outweighs the desire to feel positively toward the relationship. A large body of literature within social psychology documents the fact that people, especially people in Western countries like the United States, have a **justification motive**; that is, they generally wish to feel that they are moral and reasonable (Festinger, 1957; Rosenberg, 1979; Sedikides & Green, 2000; Swann, Rentfrow, & Guinn, 2003). In a satisfying relationship, feeling good about a partner reflects well on the self, so enhancing the partner makes the decision to pursue a relationship seem like a reasonable thing to do. In a troubled relationship, however, attending to a partner's negative qualities may, paradoxically, increase self-esteem by relieving the individual of any responsibility for the failure of the relationship. Imagine being in a seriously distressed relationship, full of arguments and conflict. If you believed your partner to be a terrific person, it would be possible that the problems in the relationship were your fault. If your partner is a terrible person, however, then at least you have the comfort of knowing that, despite the problems in your relationship, you remain the moral, reasonable, blameless person that most of us wish to be.

The desire to justify our own feelings and behaviors contributes to the **self-serving bias**, the tendency to take credit for our successes and to blame others for our failures (Miller & Ross, 1975) (FIGURE 10.7). Evidence for the self-serving bias comes from research in many domains, but some of the earliest demonstrations involved research on relationships. In one example, male college students were asked to describe how they ended up with their current relationship partner (Nisbett et al., 1973). The researchers also asked these students to describe how their best friends ended up with their current partners, and then the researchers compared the two accounts. Describing their own relationships, the participants focused on characteristics of their partners and aspects of their situation, seeing themselves as responding to

FIGURE 10.7 **Serving the relationship or serving the self?** When we love our partners, we look for reasons to praise them and elevate them. When our relationships are in trouble, however, we may succumb to the self-serving bias, looking for ways to protect our own self-esteem at the expense of the relationship.

circumstances. Describing their friends' relationships, in contrast, they focused more on their friends' traits and preferences, viewing them as responsible for their own fate.

Explanations for the self-serving bias have focused not only on the motive to take credit for success and avoid blame for failure, but also on the fact that actors have access to different information than observers do (Storms, 1973). When we observe our friends' relationships, we tend to focus on our friends and conclude that they are responsible for their outcomes. When we look out from our own eyes, however, the behaviors of other people and the role of the situation are more noticeable, and it's easier to conclude that we are not responsible for our occasional failures to live up to our good intentions.

It is not hard to see how the self-serving bias might contribute to conflicts even in generally satisfying relationships. People who love their partner do not want to feel they have caused pain or disappointment. When confronted with the possibility that something we did in fact caused our partner pain, the desire to feel justified can motivate a search for ways to avoid taking responsibility, either by blaming the situation or by casting blame back upon our partner. Furthermore, as observers of our own behaviors, we are aware of all the ways we may be constrained by our situation and surroundings, and thus prevented from acting the way we want. Our partner, however, is also affected by the self-serving bias. The partner focuses on our behaviors and not on the circumstances surrounding our behaviors. As a result, in any couple, what one partner sees as a reasonable explanation for a hurtful behavior may come across to the other partner as a defensive rationalization.

To study these processes at work, communication researchers videotaped 188 couples discussing an area of disagreement in their relationships, and then gave each spouse the opportunity to review the videotape individually (Sillars et al., 2000). While they watched themselves, spouses were asked to speak into a tape recorder and describe what they had been thinking and feeling during the discussion. By synchronizing the tapes from each spouse, the

TABLE 10.1 **Motivated Misunderstandings**

Her Thoughts	His Thoughts
I feel he . . . he uh . . . that it's up to him first to make up his decision because the household really revolves around him. So . . .	She's just trying to prove a point and what she's saying really isn't true. She's just saying that 'cause I think that's the best thing that she's got on me.
He's more or less upset, of course, that he lost his job, and he's under a lot of pressure but he's making it sound like it's my responsibility.	She's making up another excuse. She always uses excuses, just to get out of doing anything. Always somebody else. But never doing anything for herself.
He's more or less telling me, like, get a job, like, or else . . . where I don't feel it should be that way.	Can't resolve nothing. She's backed up in a corner and she just wants to push the blame off on . . . most likely me or anybody that she could at the time . . .
I feel again he's using me as a scapegoat because I know he's hurting inside and everything. . . . He also feels bad because he knows that I have someone to go to, to talk to and he really don't, except me.	Now she's backing down and she's almost ready to give up. She'd walk out if she got any more pissed off.
There I feel that he felt real bad, that maybe he was realizing what he was really saying.	I'll just keep pressing, to prove a point or just until she gives in.

Source: Adapted from Sillars et al., 2000.

researchers could compare their different perspectives on the same moments of the conversation. **TABLE 10.1** has a sample transcript, showing each spouse's thoughts at parallel points in the discussion. The husband had been unemployed for a period of time and was pressuring his wife to find a job. The wife, having full responsibility for taking care of their children, was reluctant to do so. As the table makes clear, a lot of this couple's thoughts revolve around blame. The wife thinks: "He's under a lot of pressure but he's making it sound like it's my responsibility." At the same moment, the husband is thinking: "She always uses excuses, just to get out of doing anything" (Sillars et al., 2000, p. 481). Each of them believes that the other is being unreasonable. In this case, the self-serving bias serves neither accuracy nor enhancement in the relationship, but it allows each spouse the comfort of blaming the other.

MAIN POINTS

>> Because they have flexibility in assigning meanings to experiences in relationships, people tend to gravitate toward interpretations of their relationships that have positive consequences for them.

>> Motivated reasoning refers to all the ways that motives, desires, and preferences shape the way information is selected, interpreted, and organized, in order to satisfy needs and reach goals.

>> The enhancement motive is the desire to support and strengthen positive views of the partner and the relationship. Partners driven by this motive seek out and focus on positive information about their relationships more than negative information, thus demonstrating an enhancement bias.

>> The accuracy motive is the desire to understand a partner and to be understood in turn. People driven by this motive overestimate how much their specific experiences actually reveal about their partners (a diagnosticity bias) and seek out information and feedback that supports what they already believe (a confirmation bias).

>> The justification motive is a preference for information that supports a positive view of the self, even if it does not support the relationship. Partners driven by this motive tend to take credit for their successes and blame each other for failures, thus demonstrating a self-serving bias.

>> None of these motives or biases is mutually exclusive. One partner can pursue enhancement of the relationship at the global level, while also seeking accurate information about the other partner's strengths and limitations.

Reaching an Understanding

Although we might want our relationship to be fulfilling, for our partner to be perfectly suited to us, and for all our interactions with them to be loving and open, our experiences do not always conform to our ideals. In even the best relationships, partners sometimes disappoint or hurt each other. Yet when disappointments happen, people do not immediately conclude that their relationships are worthless. On the contrary, people have a remarkable capacity to tolerate their partner's negative behaviors and still maintain an overall positive view of their relationships. In fact, some relationships endure despite behaviors such as infidelity and physical aggression. How do we reconcile positive feelings about a relationship with the specific disappointments, irritations, and hurts that are bound to occur when two people are deeply interdependent over significant lengths of time? How do partners reach an understanding of each other?

> " You can't always get what you want
> But if you try sometimes you just might find
> You get what you need."
>
> —Rolling Stones (1969)

Addressing this question requires us to recognize that there are different ways that beliefs about partners and relationships can be affected by new information. In his classic work on how children acquire knowledge, developmental psychologist Jean Piaget (1929) described these responses by differentiating between accommodation and assimilation. **Accommodation** occurs when existing beliefs change to integrate new information. Accommodation lies at the heart of learning from experience: The new information is processed to create a new understanding. **Assimilation** occurs when new information is integrated with existing knowledge without changing the original beliefs. Assimilation is what goes on most of the time in our interactions with people we know well: New experiences usually fit right into what we already know and are assimilated without any effect on our beliefs and judgments.

When people are in satisfying relationships, as most couples are at the start, new experiences are often positive, and assimilating them into a positive view of the relationship is relatively easy. What if my partner is warm and affectionate with me tonight? That fits perfectly with my image of my partner as a loving and affectionate person, so no accommodation is required (no change in my generally positive view of the relationship). If anything, my existing beliefs are strengthened by the supportive information. The challenge comes when our experiences in relationships are less than positive. When couples argue or hurt each other, must they accommodate (change their views of the relationship), or can they assimilate even negative experiences into an overall positive view of the relationship?

Relationship scientists have identified many ways that individuals process undesirable information to preserve their desired views of the relationship. Although the specific techniques vary widely, they generally pursue one of two broad strategies. First, specific negative information about a relationship can be ignored, forgotten, or denied. If a negative experience is effectively erased, then there is no need to accommodate to it, and the desired beliefs about our relationships are protected. Second, when specific negative information must be acknowledged, the implications of that information can be denied or minimized. If a negative experience has no implications for evaluations of a relationship, it may be recognized and assimilated without having to change any higher-level beliefs.

To distinguish between these strategies, it may help to consider them in terms of the hierarchical knowledge structure in Figure 10.3. If general beliefs about a partner and a relationship are supported by perceptions of concrete behaviors and experiences, then one strategy to preserve positive beliefs is to focus your attention on positive perceptions and experiences and avoid or ignore negative ones. For example, if you are asked whether there is conflict in your relationship, you might ignore or just refuse to think about those times when you and your partner have argued. This strategy keeps negative experiences out of awareness. A second strategy coming into play when a negative experience cannot be avoided or ignored is to sever the links between that experience and more general beliefs that would normally be associated with it. Let's return to the conflict example: When confronted with the memory of a specific heated disagreement with your partner, you might acknowledge that the event occurred, but deny that it was really a conflict, or insist that the discussion had no further consequences for the relationship. In this case, the negative information is recognized, but it is processed in such a way that it has no effect on higher-level beliefs and feelings. Researchers have identified a number of specific information-processing techniques that adopt each of these two approaches.

Keeping Negative Information Out of Awareness

There are ways to make sure undesirable information does not threaten positive views of a relationship. Researchers have identified two strategies: First, ignore the threatening information if you can, and second, if you have to recognize the threatening information, try to forget it quickly. We will discuss each of these approaches.

SELECTIVE ATTENTION. Think of how much information a person can have about an intimate relationship. Every behavior, every event, every day provides innumerable pieces of data that could contribute to an overall impression of a relationship and a partner. The human brain, though vastly capable, has only a finite capacity to attend to information. Thus, making sense of a complex world requires **selective attention**; of the total field of available information, we pay attention to only some of it. The process of selective attention is not entirely conscious. We do not pick bits of information like cherries, choosing and storing the ones that look good and leaving the rest on the tree. Rather, our desires and goals affect what information we notice in the first place, how long we pay attention, and what we overlook, and much of this happens without our conscious awareness (Srull & Wyer, 1986).

In an early demonstration of how selective attention might serve relationships, single college students viewed videotapes of three different people, one of whom they would eventually be paired with on a date (Berscheid et al., 1976). Naturally, the students spent much more time viewing the video of their potential date than the other two tapes. In an effort to reduce their uncertainty about someone they knew they would be spending time with, they devoted a great deal of attention to gathering information about that person, leaving less time to learn about people with whom they would not be interacting.

Once a relationship has formed, selective attention allows partners to focus on information that supports the relationship and pay less attention to information that threatens it. Social psychologist Roland Miller (1997a) explored this process when he studied how college students in relationships approach information about attractive alternatives to their current partners. Told that they were taking part in a study of advertising, participants were asked to review a series of slides, some of which featured highly attractive members of the opposite sex. Participants were allowed to review the slides at their own pace, and the researchers timed how long each slide was examined. Attentiveness to the attractive targets was associated with participants' feelings about their own relationships. Dating partners who were committed to their current partners and felt close to them spent less time reviewing photographs of opposite-sex people, presumably because they were less interested in information that might make their own partners look less desirable. In contrast, participants who responded positively to the statement "I'm distracted by other people that I find attractive" spent more time reviewing those photographs, and were the most likely to end their relationships within the subsequent 2 months. In some ways this study is the flip side of the previous study. When people want to start a relationship, the desire for accuracy and control drives selective attention toward a possible partner, but once a relationship is formed, the motive to protect the relationship drives reduced attention to possible alternatives.

The same sorts of processes appear to focus attention within the relationship itself. Building on the idea of selective attention, social psychologists William Ickes and Jeffry Simpson (1997) developed the **empathy accuracy model** to account for situations in which partners should be more or less motivated to attend to and understand what the other is thinking and feeling. According to the model, our level of attention to, and understanding of, our partner varies according to how threatening our partner's thoughts and feelings are likely to be. Most of the time during the course of daily events, our partner's thoughts and feelings are not threatening at all. In these situations, we should be motivated to pay attention to our partner to encourage effective communication and closeness. However, during conflicts or arguments, an accurate understanding of our partner's thoughts and feelings might reveal information we would rather not know. We might learn that we are misunderstood, or that we are not as loved as we wish to be. In such situations, the empathy accuracy model predicts that people will adopt a strategy of motivated inaccuracy; faced with the possibility of threatening information about our partner's feelings, we should be less motivated to try to understand those feelings accurately.

Support for the empathy accuracy model comes from research that looks a lot like the study by Alan Sillars and his colleagues (2000) described earlier (see Table 10.1). As in that study, social psychologists Jeffry Simpson, Minda Oriña, and William Ickes (2003) asked married couples to engage in videotaped problem-solving discussions and immediately afterward to describe their thoughts and feelings while reviewing the video. The researchers then asked each spouse to guess what his or her partner had been feeling at specific points during the discussion. Independent raters rated the extent to which each spouse's guesses matched what the partners had actually been feeling at that moment. Consistent with the empathy accuracy model, when the other partner's thoughts and feelings were not threatening (as coded by outside raters), couples felt closer after the discussion when they understood each other accurately. However, when the other partner's thoughts and feelings were rated as more threatening by the outside observers, couples felt closer after the discussion when they *misunderstood* each other. Selective attention to their partner's actual thoughts and feelings appeared to help these spouses protect their own feelings, at least in the short term, by allowing them to recognize only information consistent with their goals for the relationship. Put another way, selective attention ensures that the only information entering awareness is information that will easily be assimilated into our current understanding of our relationship.

MEMORY BIAS. Once we pay attention to an aspect of our relationship, what happens to that information? Stuart, the character in the novel at the start of this chapter, claims, "I remember everything." In other words, he believes that the information of his life is stored in memory as a perfect record of his experiences. Many people have this view of their memories, insisting that if they remember an experience a certain way, then that is the way it must have happened.

Yet research provides a very different picture of how autobiographical memory works (e.g., Bartlett, 1932; Loftus, 1979; Ross & Buehler, 1994). Just as we cannot attend to everything in the immediate environment, we can't possibly recall every detail of our past experiences either. Thus, far from being a recording of our life, memory appears to be a constructive process. When we remember the past, we weave together remembered information with knowledge of the present to construct a coherent narrative that makes sense to us. Because the process is constructive, we have the flexibility to leave out events we would rather not recall and to play up experiences that support our current view of our partner and our relationship.

> " He: We met at nine.
> She: We met at eight.
> He: I was on time.
> She: No, you were late.
> He: Ah yes! I remember it well."
>
> —Alan Jay Lerner and Frederick Loewe (1958)

To show how memories can serve the current interests of a relationship, social psychologists Cathy McFarland and Michael Ross (1987) asked dating couples to rate their relationships and their partners' personality. Two months later, the same individuals were asked to do the ratings again, and then to recall their prior ratings. Comparing partners' recollections with their actual ratings provided a window into how accurately they remembered what they used to feel about each other. The researchers found that people's memories of their past feelings tended to be distorted by their current feelings about their relationships. Such distortion is a type of **memory bias**. The partners whose satisfaction with the relationship had improved tended to remember that they had been more positive about the relationship in the past than they actually had been. Partners whose satisfaction had declined remembered being more negative about the relationship than they had been. In both cases, partners were affected by their memory bias, recalling the past in ways that supported and justified their current feelings about the relationship.

Flexibility within the memory process enables us to forget aspects of the past that might threaten our current feelings about our relationship. As mentioned throughout this book, intimate relationships usually start out satisfying and gradually become less satisfying over time (Johnson, Amoloza, & Booth, 1992; VanLaningham, Johnson, & Amato, 2001). This trend is not fatal to most relationships, but it's hard to reconcile with the common desire to believe that our relationship is growing and improving and will probably continue to do so in the future. How do partners assimilate declining satisfaction with an optimistic view of their relationship? Simple: Most partners fail to remember that their satisfaction has declined. Social psychologist Susan Sprecher (1999) observed this phenomenon in a study of dating couples that asked partners to rate their relationship satisfaction every year for several years, and to describe how their satisfaction had changed since the previous assessment. At every assessment, partners reported that their satisfaction had increased significantly since the last assessment a year earlier. However, direct comparisons of their satisfaction ratings at each assessment revealed no such improvements. These couples were not actually growing more satisfied over time; they only thought they were.

Memory biases like these serve the same purpose as selective attention, ensuring that the only information that enters awareness is information consistent with people's goals for their relationships. Whereas selective attention means that consistent information is noticed and inconsistent information is not, memory biases usually operate so that consistent information is remembered and inconsistent information is forgotten. The result is that the information in awareness is easily assimilated, and existing feelings and beliefs about the relationships are preserved.

Minimizing the Impact of Negative Information

Sometimes undesirable information about a relationship is so glaringly obvious that it cannot be ignored or forgotten, and yet partners manage to maintain optimism about their relationships anyway. As an extreme example, consider wives who catch their husbands having affairs. Although sexual infidelity is viewed as destructive to relationships in most cultures (Betzig, 1989), it does not always mean the end of a relationship, or even that a relationship must no longer be viewed as satisfying. When male celebrities or politicians are embroiled in extramarital scandals, it is not uncommon for them to hold a press conference during which their wives are close by their sides. Is the steadfast loyalty of those wives an act for the cameras, covering up crushing pain? It is certainly possible. Or could they be convinced that their husbands' infidelity is unimportant or less important than an outsider who has not experienced a partner's infidelity might believe?

If it is possible to assimilate a partner's infidelity into a general belief that a relationship is worthwhile, it should be easier to assimilate the more common hurts and disappointments that arise in an ongoing commitment. But how? How do we recognize the faults and limitations of our relationships but take pleasure in them anyway? Relationship scientists have identified a number of ways that partners can acknowledge negative information but minimize the extent to which it threatens the relationship.

ADAPTIVE ATTRIBUTIONS. What do we think about when our partners do something unexpected or negative? Clinical psychologists Amy Holtzworth-Munroe and Neil Jacobson (1985) addressed this question by presenting couples in distressed or satisfying relationships with a list of 10 positive and 10 negative behaviors likely to occur at least some of the time in most relationships (e.g., your partner comes home late, your partner criticizes something you say). For each behavior, partners were asked to list what they might think or feel if the behavior occurred today or tomorrow. Objective coders found that when the event in question was negative, distressed and satisfied couples were more likely to list thoughts that focused on explaining why the behavior occurred, compared to when the behavior was positive. This makes sense. If our partner does something nice for us, it is enough to enjoy it, but when our partner does something insensitive or hurtful, understanding why it happened is a first step toward being prepared if it should happen again.

The explanations we use to understand each other's behavior are called **attributions** because the explanation attributes a behavior to some more general cause. One way of visualizing this process is to return once again to the hierarchical structure in Figure 10.3. Our observations of our partner's specific behaviors (my partner mowed the lawn, my partner came home late, my partner kissed me) lie at the most specific level in the hierarchy of knowledge. An attribution links a specific observation to a broader cause or meaning (my partner mowed the lawn *because she is thoughtful,* my partner came home late *because he is insensitive,* my partner kissed me *because he is sorry for yesterday's argument*).

As we have been discussing throughout this chapter, there are many ways to link specific observations to higher-level meanings, and there are many different ways to explain a given specific behavior. Two dimensions that seem especially important are the locus and the stability of the attribution (Weiner, 1972). The **locus dimension** refers to the location of the cause of a behavior, distinguishing between causes that are internal or external to the actor. Blaming a partner's lateness on traffic, for example, would be making an external attribution for the behavior, whereas blaming the partner's thoughtlessness would be making an internal attribution. The **stability dimension** refers to the duration of the cause of a behavior, distinguishing between causes that are temporary (e.g., traffic) and those that are likely to affect behavior continuously (e.g., thoughtlessness). The locus and the stability of an attribution can be related, but, as FIGURE 10.8 makes clear, they are conceptually distinct. In other words, the cause of a behavior can be internal and stable, internal and temporary, external and stable, or external and temporary. Of course, these two dimensions are by no means exhaustive. For example, attributions also vary in the degree of intentionality they assign to a behavior: Did my partner intend to hurt my feelings or was it an accident? But this dimension

Locus

	Internal	External
Stable	"My partner was late because he is a thoughtless jerk."	"My partner was late because his crappy car broke down again."
Temporary	"My partner was late because he forgot to set his alarm."	"My partner was late because he got stuck in traffic."

Stability

FIGURE 10.8 Dimensions of adaptive attributions. When a partner does something perceived as negative, several attributions can explain the behavior. The two dimensions of locus and stability describe some of the ways explanations for the same behavior can vary.

overlaps a great deal with locus and stability (intentional causes are more likely to be internal and stable).

From the perspective of maintaining positive feelings about a relationship, you might imagine that some attributions for a partner's behaviors are more adaptive, or beneficial, than others. When behaviors are especially thoughtful or affectionate, seeing the cause of those behaviors as stable and internal to the partner (e.g., my partner loves me) supports a general belief that the relationship is worth pursuing. However, when a partner's behaviors are thoughtless or hurtful, we can still maintain faith in the quality of the relationship, as long as the negative behaviors are excused as the result of causes that are external and temporary (e.g., my partner must have had a hard day at work). Indeed, research comparing the attributions of couples in satisfying and distressed marriages confirms that satisfied couples tend to give each other credit for positive behaviors and excuse each other for negative ones, whereas distressed couples do the opposite, finding external reasons for each other's positive behaviors but blaming each other for negative ones (Fincham & O'Leary, 1983; Jacobson et al., 1985). In all of these cases, the *occurrence* of the negative behavior is not in question. What distinguishes between happy and distressed couples is how negative behaviors are linked to higher-level causes and meanings. The tendency to make adaptive attributions not only distinguishes between satisfied and distressed couples, but also predicts which couples are likely to stay happy and stay together over time (Bradbury & Fincham, 1990; Fletcher & Fincham, 1991). If you make a habit of excusing your partner's negative behavior, then your global feelings about the relationship are going to be pretty resilient over time, even when negative behaviors occur.

There can be a dark side to this process. Adaptive attributions can protect a relationship even if it is harmful to the individual, and nowhere is this clearer than in the case of battered women. As we discussed in Chapter 8, the vast majority of battered women rightly blame their partners for their abuse and struggle to free themselves from their relationships, often overcoming significant obstacles to do so (Strube & Barbour, 1983). However, some women, either because they have nowhere else to go or because they still love their partners, remain in relationships even when physical abuse continues (see **BOX 8.3**). How do they justify remaining in an abusive relationship? One way is to blame themselves for the abuse and excuse their partners, thereby minimizing the implications of their experience for their general faith in the relationship (Barnett, Martinez, & Keyson, 1996). People who work at shelters for battered women understand this tendency, and their guidelines for helping women exit these relationships include encouraging them to stop making attributions (explanations) that protect their abusive partners, and to understand that they are not to blame for being abused.

FLEXIBLE STANDARDS. In one of the studies described earlier, partners were found to be worse at predicting the future of their relationships than their friends and family were (MacDonald & Ross, 1999). The same study also asked the friends and relatives of each couple to judge the partners' satisfaction with the relationship. Then the researchers compared how well those judgments accounted for the future stability of the relationship, compared to partners' ratings of their own satisfaction. The results, given what we already know about this study, were unexpected. Although partners were worse than their friends and family at directly predicting the future of their relationships, their ratings of their own satisfaction were *better* at predicting the future than those of friends and relatives. In other words, partners had information (their own satisfaction) that would have allowed them to make good predictions about the future, but they did not appear to draw on this information when they actually made their predictions.

This result highlights the fact that even when we have processed and stored specific information about our relationship, we need not use all that information when we evaluate the relationship or make decisions about it. Nor must all of the information that we do use be weighted equally. Instead, as discussed in Chapter 9, we draw on our standards and ideals to determine which aspects of the relationship matter and which do not (Fletcher & Simpson, 2000; Simpson, Fletcher, & Campbell, 2001; Thibaut & Kelley, 1959). In terms of the hierarchy shown in Figure 10.3, standards and ideals can be thought of as the glue that links specific perceptions more or less strongly to more global beliefs and evaluations of a relationship. For those who have high standards for the physical attractiveness of their partner, specific perceptions of the partner's appearance will be closely related to global satisfaction with the relationship. For those who have high standards for open communication, perceptions of specific discussions and arguments may weigh more heavily in judgments of satisfaction. Indeed, research on dating couples confirms that partners are happier when their perceptions of the relationship more closely match their particular ideals and standards (Fletcher et al., 1999). This is consistent with the predictions of social exchange theory (see Chapter 3).

What happens to a satisfying relationship when specific perceptions of the partner change over time? What happens when a partner no longer meets our standards for what constitutes a good relationship? If we want to preserve positive feelings about the relationship, one option is to maintain **flexible standards**, so that whatever is currently perceived to be positive is considered important, and whatever is currently perceived to be negative is dismissed as unimportant. Of course, this is not how we usually think about our standards. Many people consider their standards toward relationships (and everything else) as stable aspects of their personality, guiding their behavior like a beacon. However, decades of research by social psychologists indicate that people's values and attitudes often change to justify their behavior (Festinger, 1957; Festinger & Carlsmith, 1959). For example, people with high self-esteem have been shown to change their standards in reaction to learning how they performed on exams. Those who scored well on the SAT were more likely to believe that the test is an important indicator of aptitude, thus bolstering their self-esteem (Shepperd, 1993). Those who scored poorly were more likely to dismiss the test as unimportant in predicting academic success, leaving their self-esteem unaffected by the negative feedback.

Some evidence suggests that people shift their standards in the same way to protect their beliefs about their intimate relationships. Social psychologists Garth Fletcher, Jeffry Simpson, and Geoff Thomas (2000), for example, examined ideal standards among dating couples and then assessed the couples that remained together 3 months later. They found that, over time, partners' ideals for their relationships shifted in the direction of their initial perceptions of the relationship. Thus, a partner who started off reporting that good communication was very important to relationships (but that the communication in the current relationship was not so great) was likely to report 3 months later that good communication was less important.

Over the course of a relationship, couples who can be flexible with their standards are usually resilient to ups and downs in their specific perceptions of each other. Social psychologists Lisa Neff and Benjamin Karney (2003) examined how spouses' standards for relationships and specific perceptions of each other changed during the early years of marriage. They found that when specific perceptions were changing, global satisfaction with the marriage was more stable if the spouses' standards were more flexible. The stably happy couples judged the current strengths of their relationships to be important for successful relationships, regardless of whether the relationship used to have different strengths. As the marriage developed and spouses began to perceive their partners' weaknesses, the stably happy couples judged those qualities to be unimportant, even if they had once deemed the very same qualities important. Thus, flexible standards allow partners to recognize faults and limitations in the relationship but dismiss them, while simultaneously emphasizing the relationship's strengths. In this way, both positive and negative specific information can be assimilated into a globally positive evaluation of the relationship.

COGNITIVE RESTRUCTURING. What if you know something about your partner that is unquestionably important and negative, and yet you are highly motivated to maintain a positive view of the relationship anyway? This is the dilemma participants were forced to confront in a study that asked people in dating relationships to write about their partner's greatest flaw (Murray & Holmes, 1999). Although most of the participants rated themselves as quite happy with their relationships, all of them were able to identify flaws in their partner without much trouble. For 89 percent of the participants, the greatest flaw was an aspect of their partner's personality (e.g., jealousy, immaturity, inexpressiveness), ruling out the possibility of excusing the problem by making an external attribution. Perhaps these were minor faults, easily ignored? Not according to the participants, who rated the flaws as significantly negative, with negative consequences for the relationship. How, then, were they able to assimilate their awareness of these flaws into their generally positive feelings about the relationship?

Sandra Murray and John Holmes (1994) suggested that partners address this challenge by constructing stories about their relationships that link their partner's acknowledged faults to more positive elements of the relationship, a process called **cognitive restructuring**. In the study we have been describing (Murray & Holmes, 1999), trained raters reviewed participants' written descriptions of their partner's flaws and searched for evidence of two specific ways that people can do this. First, the raters looked for **reinterpretations**, or statements that identified redeeming features even within an acknowledged fault in the partner. For example, one participant named her partner's stubbornness as his greatest fault, but then wrote: "I respect him for his strong beliefs, and it helps me to have confidence in the relationship" (p. 1237). Another named her partner's laziness but then added: "I think his laziness is actually kind of funny; it gives us a reason to laugh" (p. 1233). Neither of these women is denying that her partner is stubborn or lazy. Instead, both are recognizing their partner's limitations but connecting them to higher-level positive ideals (i.e., strong beliefs or a source of humor). The more that participants engaged in this sort of construction, the happier they were with their relationships.

Second, the raters looked for **refutations**, or statements that explicitly minimized the broader implications of the fault for the relationship. Murray and Holmes (1994) refer to these refutations as "yes, but" statements, as in "*Yes*, my partner has a noteworthy flaw, *but* I really don't think it affects us very much." For example, one participant in their 1999 study noted that her partner had difficulty discussing important issues in the relationship but then added: "I don't think this problem weighs too heavily on the relationship because he has no problem discussing other important items with me" (p. 1237). Another participant noted that her partner has a tendency to be impatient with her, adding: "But he tries to [be more patient] and that is really all that matters" (p. 1235). Again, each is aware that her partner is withdrawn or impatient, but each tempers her awareness by linking the fault directly to other positive behaviors (i.e., discussing other issues or making the effort to be more patient). Participants who engaged in this sort of construction were also happier with their relationships, and they were more likely to remain together over the next year. What both these ways of managing negative information have in common is that they focus not on the negative information itself, but rather on how that information fits within an overall picture of the partner and the relationship.

DOWNWARD SOCIAL COMPARISONS. Sometimes evaluations of a relationship can be affected by information from outside the relationship itself. Regardless of the status of your current relationship, imagine how you might feel if you encountered a couple who appeared to have a relationship that was passionate, fulfilling, stable, and otherwise ideal in every way. After hearing at length from the happy couple about their fabulous life together, you might be forgiven for feeling a little less satisfied with your own relationship. Given hard evidence of the best that a relationship can be, the imperfections in your own might be that much more obvious. On the other hand, imagine how you might feel after an afternoon watching the troubled relationships that are often featured on daytime television soap operas and talk shows. After listening to couples betray, berate, and abuse each other, you might take some comfort from a natural reaction such as: "Whatever the flaws in my own situation, at least we're better off than *they* are!"

Most of us live in a world full of relationships of every sort, and those relationships can inform our feelings about our own involvements. The process of using information about others as a gauge of our own attitudes and abilities has been called **social comparison** (Festinger, 1954). **Upward social comparisons**, or comparisons with others who are doing better than we are, can feel discouraging, especially if we do not have confidence that we can improve our own situation. **Downward social comparisons**, or comparisons with others who are doing worse than we are, can feel encouraging to the extent that people who are suffering more than we are put our own problems in perspective.

Thus, faced with stark evidence of problems in a relationship, one way of minimizing the broader implications is to engage in a downward social comparison: "We may have some issues, but at least we don't have serious problems like so-and-so." As we have already seen in this chapter, people in relationships generally do engage in downward social comparisons rather than upward ones (Van Lange & Rusbult, 1995; Van Lange et al., 1999). When asked to think about other people's relationships, people tend to think about those that have fewer positive qualities and more negative qualities than their own. Caryl Rusbult and her colleagues demonstrated that this tendency is particularly strong when people feel their relationship is threatened (Rusbult et al., 2000). They asked college students in dating relationships to list qualities that came to mind when they thought about their own relationships and those of other students. Some students were given these instructions and nothing else, but other students were told this additional piece of information: "We are especially interested in college students' dating relationships because previous research has demonstrated that in comparison to other types of relationships, college students' relationships are less likely to persist over time and tend to exhibit lower levels of overall adjustment" (Rusbult et al., 2000, p. 526). This was the "threat condition" of the experiment, meant to highlight in students' minds the vulnerabilities in their relationships. It seemed to work, because students who received the threatening instructions were significantly more likely to perceive that their relationships were superior to (i.e., had more positive qualities and fewer negative qualities than) the relationships of other college students. It appears that, when faced with evidence of potential flaws in a relationship, one way to continue feeling positive about the relationship is to compare it to relationships with even worse flaws.

The social world can affect evaluations of a relationship in another way: by determining the field of eligible alternatives to a current partner. Even people who are relatively satisfied with their relationship may be threatened by an attractive alternative to their current partner, for two reasons. First, as you may recall from social exchange theory in Chapter 3, relationship dependence is a function of the quality of a relationship compared to the quality of the available alternatives to the relationship. Thus, when attractive alternatives are available, people will generally be less dependent on their current relationship and therefore be less motivated to maintain it. Second, when people are deeply committed to their relationship, it may feel awkward and uncomfortable to admit to an attraction to someone other than their partner. That attraction could indicate that committing to the current partner was a mistake, or that their self-image as faithful and monogamous may be wrong.

To avoid these uncomfortable feelings and protect the relationship, committed partners can simply avoid attractive alternatives, as discussed earlier (Miller, 1997a). But when avoidance is not an option (e.g., when the attractive alternative approaches *you*), what can committed partners do to manage the threat and protect their relationships? One option is to decide that the alternative is not that attractive after all. By **derogating alternative partners**, people manage threatening information (the attractiveness of an alternative partner) by interpreting that information as less threatening (less attractive). In one demonstration of this phenomenon, social psychologists John Lydon, Gráinne Fitzsimons, and Loren Naidoo (2003) asked college students to rate photographs of highly attractive people of the other sex (the targets). The researchers manipulated the threat of these targets in two ways. First, half the participants were in committed dating relationships (high threat) and half were not (low threat). Second, half the participants were asked to rate how attractive they personally thought the target was (high threat) and half were asked to rate how attractive they thought their friends would rate the photograph (low threat). People who were committed to a current partner and who were asked to report their own attraction to the photograph (the most threatening condition) rated the same targets as significantly less attractive than did people who had no relationships to protect, or people who were simply reporting how they thought their friends would react. By devaluing the target's attractiveness, committed partners defused a potentially troubling situation, transforming potentially negative information into information more easily assimilated within their general feelings of commitment to their relationships.

>> When confronted with negative or undesirable information about their relationship, partners can find a way to assimilate the information, integrating it into their existing knowledge, or they can accommodate to it, changing their existing beliefs as a result.

>> Initially positive feelings about a partner can be maintained to the extent that negative information is ignored, through selective attention, or forgotten, through memory bias.

>> If negative information must be acknowledged, partners can minimize its impact on their feelings about the relationship through adaptive attributions, changing their standards, using cognitive restructuring, or engaging in downward social comparisons.

Ability and Motive: The Limits of Motivated Reasoning

So far in this chapter, we have reviewed several ways that partners who generally feel positive about their relationships can protect those feelings from specific negative information. It would be possible to leave this discussion with the idea that people can believe pretty much whatever they want to believe, ignoring or explaining away whatever fails to confirm their rosy views of their partner and their relationship. Clearly, this is not the case. If people did assimilate all negative information, then everyone who felt positive about their relationship would continue to feel that way regardless of specific experiences and observations. As we have seen throughout this book, most couples who begin their relationship feeling positively about each other in fact have serious difficulty maintaining their positive feelings over time. Far from believing whatever they want to believe, partners who begin their relationship full of love and optimism all too frequently reach conclusions they would very much prefer to avoid (e.g., "Committing to this relationship was a mistake," or "My partner is unworthy of the sacrifices I have made"). Thus, there must come a time when the techniques we have been discussing fail, when assimilation ends and accommodation begins.

Sadly, this is exactly what happens to Gillian, the new bride we met in the Julian Barnes novel *Talking It Over* at the start of the chapter. When she first meets Stuart, the somewhat conservative man who would become her husband, she is moved by how much effort he devotes to wooing her and trying to please her. After the wedding, she reminds herself about the reasons she found Stuart attractive: his character, his dependability, his love for her. Yet after she learns that Stuart's best friend, Oliver, loves her as well, she begins to doubt herself and her feelings. At first, Gillian brushes off Oliver's declarations of love, telling herself that Oliver is just insecure and certainly not serious. Gillian tries to convince herself that Stuart is right for her and that

Oliver is unsuitable. But none of this is enough. Eventually, Gillian leaves Stuart for Oliver, and all three end up devastated.

How does this happen? Under what circumstances do specific negative experiences affect global feelings about the relationship? Why do initially positive feelings so often change, even though the partners are desperate to resist this change? The answers rest on the observation that motivated reasoning takes effort. Making adaptive attributions, weaving a partner's faults into a positive story, derogating alternatives: Processing information in these ways is work, and engaging in this work requires ability and motivation. In other words, global feelings are protected when specific negative information *can* be assimilated and when partners *want* to do the work it takes to assimilate it. So when does assimilation stop? It stops when partners lack the ability or motivation to continue doing the work.

The Ability to Protect the Relationship

Earlier we discussed the study by Hawkins, Carrère, and Gottman (2002) which found that spouses interpreted each other's specific behaviors during a problem-solving discussion differently from outside observers. In fact, a closer look at the results of that study reveals that the differences between the spouses and the observers emerged only with respect to behaviors that were rated as mildly negative or mildly positive. When the behaviors were extremely positive (e.g., "I love you from the bottom of my heart") or severely negative (e.g., "I wish I had never married you"), spouses and observers were much more likely to agree. This aspect of the findings points out an important limitation of the motivated-reasoning techniques we have been discussing: Some types of negative information are simply easier to assimilate than others. The more obvious or severe a negative behavior is, the harder it will be for spouses to make sense of it within a positive view of the relationship. This is why some intimate relationships survive a partner's infidelity but most do not (Betzig, 1989). Infidelity is beyond the ability of most partners to ignore or explain away.

Furthermore, information that can be assimilated once may not be as easily assimilated when it keeps coming up again and again. Consider our discussion of adaptive attributions. When a partner behaves in a way that appears to be neglectful, it certainly protects the relationship to excuse the behavior as the result of a bad day at work or a lack of sleep. Yet if the behavior recurs repeatedly, such adaptive attributions may be harder to sustain (Kelley, 1967). Several of the techniques we have described may be similar in this way: effective in the short term but hard to sustain over time.

Social psychologist Carolyn Showers and her colleagues have demonstrated that this can be true. In research on how college students make sense of their partner's negative qualities (Showers & Kevlyn, 1999), they showed that people are happier when they can draw connections between those negative qualities and their partner's more desirable qualities (e.g., "He's not very ambitious but that just means he has more time to devote to our relationship"). Yet in a follow-up study that revisited the same individuals 1 year later, the integration that was initially associated with greater happiness predicted high rates of dissolution over the subsequent year (Showers & Zeigler-Hill, 2004). What changed? Perhaps the problem for these couples was what did *not* change. Integrating negative perceptions does not make them go away. Over time, those perceptions may become more prominent and harder to ignore, ultimately overcoming a partner's capacity to assimilate them.

Regardless of the kinds of relationships they have, some people may also be better or worse than others at processing information in ways that fulfill their motives and goals. Individual differences in information processing can be characterized in terms of **cognitive complexity**, or the extent to which a person's thoughts about particular subjects are well integrated and take multiple dimensions into consideration (Schroder, 1971). For example, people who have cognitively complex views of their relationships consider many aspects of their partner (e.g., my partner is a good friend, a source of support, a productive member of society) and acknowledge that the different aspects are related. In contrast, people who are low in cognitive complexity may view their relationships through a more simple set of lenses (e.g., the relationship is either all good or all bad).

FIGURE 10.9 shows the differences between levels of cognitive complexity. The more complex the understanding of a relationship, the more specific perceptions will be linked to a large number of higher-level ideas and the more those ideas will be linked to one another. In a less complex interpretation, specific information is linked to a smaller number of ideas, and these ideas are relatively independent from each other. To the extent that a more complex structure offers more flexibility in assimilating new information, more complex knowledge structures should be more resilient to negative information, and less complex knowledge structures should be more fragile. Indeed, people rated higher in cognitive complexity are less likely to change their minds when they encounter information that contradicts their existing beliefs (Streufert & Fromkin, 1972).

Within relationships, spouses whose thoughts about their marriages are more complex tend to be more satisfied (Crouse, Karlins, & Schroder, 1968; Neimeyer, 1984) and tend to be more effective at resolving problems (Denton, Burleson, & Sprenkle, 1995; Martin, 1992; Tyndall & Lichtenberg, 1985). It is easy to see why this should be true. If you have a complex view of a partner, then recognizing a failing in one area (my partner is a slob) leaves you with many other areas of strength to focus on (even if my partner is a slob, my partner still has a good heart, is supportive, is funny, etc.). During an argument, a more complex view of the relationship helps place a conflict in a broader perspective, too. For partners in lower cognitive complexity, the same challenges may loom larger. Partners who tend not to organize their

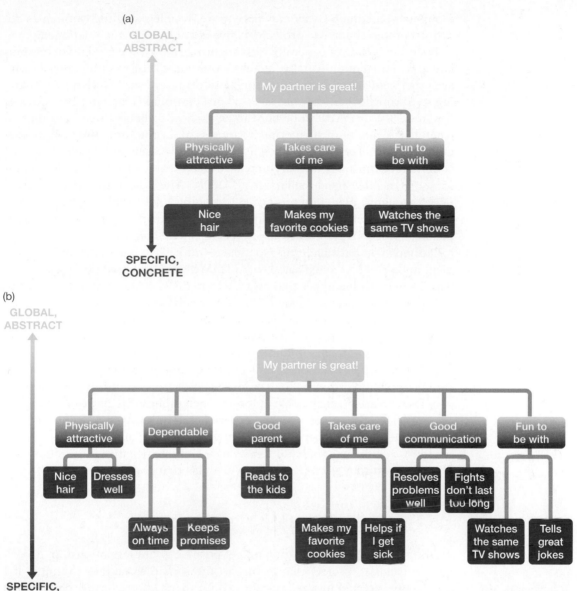

FIGURE 10.9 **High and low complexity: Two ways of organizing relationship beliefs.** Among people who love their partners, different people support their positive beliefs in different ways. (a) The beliefs of someone low in cognitive complexity: The conclusion that the partner is great rests on only a few specific beliefs. (b) The beliefs of someone high in cognitive complexity: The same conclusion rests on a richer set of specific ideas and observations. Which cognitive structure is likely to be more resilient over time?

thoughts in a complex way may have more trouble using the techniques de-scribed in this chapter to protect positive feelings about the relationship.

Even for people of generally high cognitive ability, the capacity to assimi-late new information usually fluctuates over time. For example, people who are otherwise adept at processing new information may have difficulty do-ing so at times when they are stressed or emotional (Fincham, Bradbury, & Grych, 1990). It may also be hard to know how to handle new information when there is a lot of it entering awareness all at the same time (Bavelas & Coates, 1992). The problem is that these are precisely the conditions most couples face during heated arguments, exactly when effective motivated rea-soning is needed most (Sillars et al., 2000). The constraints that an emo-tional exchange places on motivated reasoning might explain why normally thoughtful, rational people can find themselves, during a conflict with a part-ner, behaving in ways they would never otherwise behave.

Perhaps you have had this experience yourself, looking back on an argu-ment and thinking "What came over me? Why did I say that?" In these cases, what may be happening is that, when we are distracted or upset, the effort of excusing our partner and placing his or her behavior in perspective is simply impossible. Instead, we may react instinctively, responding to being hurt by striking back, only to regret it when the emotions subside and the ability to process new information effectively returns. By this point, however, the damage has often been done. Indeed, longitudinal research that examined couples' attributions under high or low levels of stress confirms that the same couples who are normally able to forgive each other for their negative behav-iors prove less able to do so when experiencing more stress than usual (Neff & Karney, 2004). In other words, effective processing of information in rela-tionships requires not only the ability to assimilate negative information but also a context that allows partners to exercise that ability.

The Motive to Protect the Relationship

Although it is always rewarding to feel positive about a relationship, not ev-eryone needs to protect that feeling to the same degree. For example, if I am deeply invested in a relationship (I am married and have a child), then I should be strongly motivated to protect the relationship from threats. In contrast, if I am not as invested in a relationship (I am casually dating), then I may be less strongly motivated to protect the relationship, even if it is rela-tively satisfying. Several studies have demonstrated that partners who have the most to lose are the ones most likely to engage in activities that protect and maintain the relationship (Finkel et al., 2002; Rusbult, 1983; Rusbult et al., 1991).

The motive to protect a relationship is influenced not only by the way partners feel about the relationship but also by the nature of the threat. This

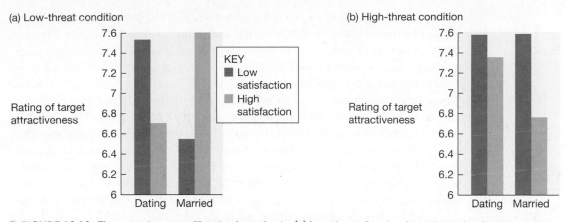

FIGURE 10.10 The commitment calibration hypothesis. (a) Low threat: People with different levels of commitment to their current partner rated photos of attractive members of the opposite sex. The least committed (unhappy daters) and the most committed (happily married) rated the target as quite attractive. The middle groups (happy daters and unhappily married) rated the same target at less attractive, perhaps because it represented a threat calibrated to their level of commitment. (b) High threat: The target was described as interested in a relationship with the rater; this changed the effects of commitment. Only the happily married people derogated the possible alternate partner; everyone else rated the target as highly attractive. (Source: Lydon et al., 1999.)

is the central idea of the **commitment calibration hypothesis**: Threats to a relationship should motivate activities to protect the relationship only if the threat is calibrated to the partners' levels of commitment (Lydon et al., 1999). In other words, for partners to think about protecting the relationship, a threat must be big enough to notice but not so big as to overwhelm partners' desire to protect the relationship (**FIGURE 10.10**). To test this hypothesis, John Lydon and his colleagues conducted a clever study that examined the tendency of committed partners to derogate alternative partners (Lydon et al., 1999). As in previous studies, the researchers told participants they were evaluating pictures for a new dating service, and presented them with photographs of attractive opposite-sex targets. There were four kinds of participants: married people in satisfying relationships, married people in unsatisfying relationships, dating people in satisfying relationships, and dating people in unsatisfying relationships. According to the commitment calibration hypothesis, these groups should not all react to a photo of an attractive alternative partner in the same way. The unhappy daters, with little investment in their own relationships, should not be threatened by the photos and so should not derogate them. The happily married people, secure in their own relationships, should not feel threatened and thus should also show no tendency to derogate. Instead, the researchers hypothesized that this threat was calibrated to the unhappily married and the happy daters. For those two groups, the attractive target might be just threatening enough to motivate an effort to protect the relationship. In fact, these hypotheses were confirmed: The unhappily married and the happy daters rated the targets as significantly less attractive than did the happily married and unhappy daters who, for different reasons, were not motivated to derogate (Figure 10.10a).

Then the researchers took their hypothesis a step further. What happens when the threat becomes more threatening? If people protect their relationships only in response to a calibrated amount of threat, then turning up the threat should change which groups are motivated to derogate. The researchers replicated their study using the same four types of people, only this time everyone was told that the attractive person in the picture had seen the *participant's* picture, and had expressed interest in the participant. That is quite a different matter from simply rating the attractiveness of a stranger. When threatened in this way, the unhappily married and the happy daters no longer engaged in derogating alternative partners. The increased threat of the interested stranger seemed to overwhelm their commitment, and their ratings of the attractiveness of the target were no longer any different from those of the unhappy daters (Figure 10.10b). Now it was the happily married who derogated. Apparently, the prospect of an attractive individual who was interested in them was threatening enough to require some effort to protect their relationships, whereas the prospect of merely looking at a photograph of an attractive person was not.

The results of this study capture an important truth about when partners may be more or less likely to feel comfortable talking about the attractiveness of people outside their relationship. As long as the person being discussed is not a real threat, then considering that person attractive is no problem. So, for example, you may hear couples commenting amiably on the attractiveness of celebrities or models, because it's unlikely that such people represent real alternatives to the current relationship. It is far less common to hear couples freely discussing their attraction to friends or co-workers; that would be a threat perfectly calibrated to motivate efforts to protect a committed relationship.

Acknowledging the role of motivation in information processing highlights the potential dark side of the techniques we have discussed. When relationships are going well, partners want to preserve their positive feelings and therefore will be motivated to process negative or threatening information in ways that protect their feelings. However, when relationships are not going as well, partners may be less motivated to engage in this sort of processing. The result can be a negative cycle, in which problems in the relationship lead to less assimilation of negative information, which in turn raises more doubts and makes the use of motivated-reasoning techniques even less likely. By the time partners are genuinely distressed in their relationship, any of the techniques can be turned around and used not to justify feeling good about the relationship but to justify feeling bad. Thus, for example, Sandra Murray and John Holmes (1999), in their study of how partners construct stories to explain their partners' faults, found that although satisfied partners magnified each other's strengths and minimized weaknesses, unsatisfied partners did the opposite, minimizing each other's strengths and magnifying faults. Similarly, whereas spouses in satisfied marriages give each other credit for positive behaviors and excuse each other for negative ones, distressed spouses tend to be suspicious of their partners' positive behaviors and blame them for their negative ones (Jacobson et al., 1985). The fact that satisfied and unsatisfied partners can use the same techniques to reach different ends reinforces the point made at the beginning of this chapter: The broader meaning of our specific experiences in relationships is not fixed, but rather a product of the way we associate those perceptions and experiences with what we already know.

MAIN POINTS

>> There must be limits to our flexibility in assigning meaning to relationship experiences, otherwise we could believe whatever we want and never make interpretations, or reach conclusions, that might be undesirable.

>> We are sometimes forced to make unwanted interpretations because engaging in motivated reasoning takes ability and desire, and sometimes we lack one or both.

>> With respect to ability, some negative information is too difficult to assimilate, and some circumstances limit our capacity to do the work that motivated reasoning requires.

>> With respect to desire, people will act to protect their relationship from threatening information only when they have something to lose.

>> In couples who are already doubting their relationship, motivated reasoning can be turned around and used to justify dissatisfaction.

CONCLUSION –

Imagine being a fly on the wall, observing the lives of Stuart, Gillian, and Oliver, the unhappy threesome at the beginning of the chapter. You would witness only one set of events, of course. And yet each player in the drama describes the events very differently, and each feels absolutely sure that his or her memory is accurate and the others' memories are hopelessly biased. How is it that different people in the same relationship, living through the same experiences, often remember it so differently? It seems that the meanings of experiences in relationships do not lie solely in the experiences themselves. Rather, understanding our relationships involves processing those experiences, making interpretations, and arriving at a higher meaning.

Still, there is something circular about the way information processing affects relationships. It seems that satisfied partners process information in ways that preserve and enhance their satisfaction, whereas unsatisfied partners process information in ways that justify their distress. Yet the rich do not always get richer in relationships, nor do the poor necessarily get poorer.

Rather, over the course of a long-term relationship, couples can have good times and bad times, and satisfaction can increase and decline and then increase again. Understanding these sorts of changes requires looking beyond the conditions of the relationship itself to recognize that forces external to a couple can affect what goes on between partners. In the next chapter, we examine the role the environment plays in the development and health of relationships.

11
Relationships in Context

Collateral Damage

John Zazulka, a New York City firefighter at a Staten Island firehouse, was one of the lucky ones on September 11, 2001. Just a few weeks before terrorists hijacked commercial jet planes and crashed them into the World Trade Center, the Pentagon, and a Pennsylvania field, John had been offered a transfer to a prestigious unit that responds to dangerous situations in the city of New York.

It was an appealing offer—John was trained in exactly that sort of work. Yet he had recently promised his colleagues at the Staten Island firehouse that he would not leave them for another position, so he recommended someone else for the job. That person, as well as 34 others John knew and worked with, died on September 11 as they were trying to rescue people inside the collapsing Twin Towers.

In the months after the attacks, John spent a lot of time in the rubble of the towers (or "the pit," as the firefighters called it) digging for the remains of the dead. In a *New York Times Magazine* story about the families of the surviving firefighters (Dominus, 2004), Rudy Sanfilippo, the Manhattan trustee for the firefighter's union, had this to say:

You have to understand, all those months at the pit was a way of life that changed our lives and made our lives seem uncontrollable. You work and you work, and the best thing you can do is call a widow to say we found the tip of your husband's pinkie? We lost control at the site, and we lost control at home. In both places we were doing the best we could, and it wasn't sufficient. Before this, we'd been good providers. (p. 39)

Family strife and marital discord were common in the homes of the surviving firefighters after September 11. The number of firefighters requesting couples counseling tripled. John and his family were not immune. Married for 18 years, John and

373

FIGURE 11.1 Devastation at Ground Zero. After the events of September 11, 2001, the firefighters and rescue workers who dug through the rubble of the Twin Towers faced day after day of emotional strain as they recovered the bodies of the dead. In what specific ways do you think that this experience might have affected their families?

Susan had four children. A year after the attacks, John announced he was unhappy and was leaving the marriage. The *New York Times* story quoted Susan's reaction to the news: "'Of course he was unhappy. Look what he'd just been through'" (Dominus, 2004, p. 38).

But John's unhappiness was not the only reason he had decided to end their marriage. It turns out that John had fallen in love with another woman. Debbie Amato was a widow whose husband, also a firefighter, had been killed in the line of duty on 9/11. She and John met and got to know each other at the many funerals, memorials, and ceremonies that took place in the months following the attacks.

It may seem like the most unlikely of coincidences that a firefighter who survived would become involved with the widow of a firefighter who had perished. In fact, the story of John and Susan is not unique (Hill, 2004). The New York City Fire Department knows of 10 or 11 triangles involving married firefighters and the widows of firefighters who died on September 11 (**FIGURE 11.1**). For Susan, who came to feel like a widow even though her

husband survived, all of this is evidence that her marriage was another victim of the attacks. "Her personal disaster, she seems to believe, is part of the bigger national tragedy" (Dominus, 2004, p. 40)." John, however, failed to see the connection. He claimed he was never happy in the marriage and that the attacks served merely as "a wake-up call." And what of the theory that his attraction to the widow of another firefighter is a sign of some sort of "rescue complex"? "John laughs at these theories. 'No, that's not it,' he said, looking at Debbie. 'It's the other way around. She saved me'" (p. 40).

QUESTIONS

John, like a lot of people, seems to believe the success or failure of his relationships depends on the qualities of his partner and how she treats him. Yet for an observer, it is hard to ignore the powerful ways that relationships seem to be affected by events and circumstances completely external to the couple. Had the attacks on September 11 never occurred, would John and the many other firefighters who entered couples counseling have been as unhappy? If not for the obligation to attend funerals and memorial services, would these men have had the opportunity to develop attachments to the widows of their fallen colleagues?

It is much easier to see how relationships are affected by partner behaviors than to identify the less visible ways that the environment can shape, facilitate, or constrain those behaviors. How do outside forces affect what goes on inside a relationship?

What sorts of environments support intimate relationships and which ones are the most challenging? What happens to relationships when couples experience stress? How are relationships affected by stable conditions, such as socioeconomic status and social structure? How is the relationship between two people affected by their relationships with everyone else in their lives? In the face of challenges beyond a couple's control, does love really conquer all?

Mapping the Context of Intimate Relationships

What does it mean to say a relationship is shaped by its context? At the simplest level, the context begins where the couple (the dyad) ends. The **context** can be defined as everything that affects a relationship outside of the couple and their interactions; it includes the physical surroundings as well as social, cultural, and historical elements. How can we make sense of the richness of people's environments without excluding anything that may be important? Relationship scientists have responded to this challenge by abandoning any attempt to list the particular contextual elements that might matter to relationships, and instead try to identify important dimensions for organizing the ones that have been studied.

From Direct to Indirect Effects

In Chapter 3, we described developmental psychologist Urie Bronfenbrenner's social ecological model of development, which depicts the context of a relationship as a series of concentric rings radiating outward (Bronfenbrenner, 1977, 1979, 1986). Important to this model is the idea that elements of the context can be organized according to how directly they affect the couple (**FIGURE 11.2**). Contextual elements that are parts of the couple's immediate environment, and therefore affect them most directly, comprise the **proximal context**.

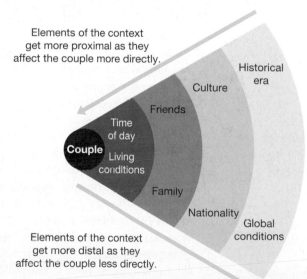

Elements of the context get more proximal as they affect the couple more directly.

Elements of the context get more distal as they affect the couple less directly.

Historical era

Culture

Friends

Time of day

Couple

Living conditions

Family

Nationality

Global conditions

FIGURE 11.2 The social ecological model applied to relationship context. All the contextual elements that affect a relationship can be arranged on a continuum from proximal, affecting a couple directly (e.g., timing of daily events, living conditions), to distal, affecting a couple indirectly (e.g., culture, global conditions). (Source: Adapted from Bronfenbrenner, 1977, 1979, 1986).

Elements of the proximal context include the time of day an interaction takes place, the room the couple interacts in, whether the lights are on or off, and whether each partner had a good day at work or a bad one.

To get a feeling for the effects of differences in the proximal context, try this thought experiment. Imagine you have a difficult issue to discuss with your partner, such as how each of you were going to have to cut back on activities you enjoy so your bills can get paid. Think of how that conversation might go on a Sunday afternoon, when both of you have just had brunch and read the paper, and the day stretches in front of you with no other appointments. Now think of how that same conversation might go at 11:30 on a Tuesday night, when you're both tired from washing the dishes and putting the kids to bed; you both have to get up early the next day for work. If you have a sense that these might be two very different conversations, then you have a sense of the profound effects that the proximal context can have on how an interaction unfolds. When a couple considers the ways they may be affected by forces outside themselves, this is the level of context they are probably thinking about, because it's the context that is most apparent to them.

Bronfenbrenner's model also highlights forces in the environment with which the couple has no direct contact. The elements that are more removed from them are known as the **distal context**. For example, as we discussed in Chapter 9, differences in beliefs and values regarding relationships often stem from the various social, religious, and cultural contexts within which relationships form and develop. On a daily basis, couples may not think much about how their beliefs are shaped by their culture, but that does not make the effects of this level of context any less profound. More distal still are global and historical conditions. The intimate relationships of the 21st century, for example, form and develop within a context that includes air travel, electronic communication, and routine vaccinations, removing many challenges intimate partners faced in the 18th century. This broadest level of context is essentially taken for granted by couples themselves, but it is the central focus for historians and sociologists interested in how the conduct of intimate relationships has changed over time (e.g., Coontz, 2005).

One implication of distinguishing between proximal and distal levels of context is that the effects of elements at any given level are likely to be influenced by elements at more distal levels. Consider, for example, the role that support from extended family members may play in the life of a couple. The presence or absence of such support is an element of the proximal context, a tangible element of a couple's immediate surroundings. Yet the extent to which they can draw on their families for support, and the kinds of support their families are willing or able to give, will be shaped by ethnic group differences in family structures and attitudes—in other words, by the distal cultural context within which the relationship is embedded. Similarly, the amount of time partners have to spend together (an element of the proximal context) is directly affected by the demands of working outside the home (an element of the distal context). Those demands will be constrained by the employment opportunities and childcare resources available in the neighborhood (even more distal), which will in turn be shaped by the economic conditions of the state and the country (still more distal). The point is that a complete understanding of the effects of any element in the proximal context usually requires an understanding of the distal context as well.

The reverse should also be true: Elements of the distal context, to the extent that they affect relationships at all, are likely to do so through their direct effects on more proximal elements. Policy makers, sociologists, and historians consider this sort of effect all the time. For example, the trend toward an increasing presence of women in the workforce during the 20th century mirrored a similar rate of increase in divorce rates over the same period (McLanahan, 2004). How did a change in the social structure of employment in the United States (an element of the distal context) affect the decision of so many couples to end their relationship? One possibility is that a social structure that allowed women control over their own income created proximal contexts in which those who were in unsatisfying or distressed marriages saw alternatives to staying married that had not existed when they depended on their husbands for survival (Wilson, 1987).

Proximal and distal contexts thus highlight the potential importance of variables that may have only slight direct effects on relationships. When distal and proximal elements are examined independently, the direct effects of the proximal context usually look larger than those of the distal context. For example, the household income of a married couple (a proximal element) is far more strongly associated with whether or not the marriage will end in divorce than the crime rate in the neighborhood (more distal) or the national minimum wage (more distal still). If you were trying to understand relationships and could choose only one variable to analyze, you might choose the most proximal one. Considered as a system, however, the more distal variables may be causes that partially determine the proximal context of a couple and therefore should not be overlooked.

Stressors and Resources

The context of a relationship contains some factors that make the relationship harder and some that make it easier. A **stressor** is an aspect of the environment that makes demands on the partners, leaving them with a reduced capacity to maintain their relationship. Losing a job, having a child, and recovering from an illness are examples of stressors that drain energy away from the relationship. Time spent recovering from an illness is time not spent engaging in rewarding activities, sharing intimacies, or working through disagreements. In contrast, a **resource** is a source of support outside the couple, something that contributes to their ability to interact effectively. For example, a close extended family, a satisfactory income, and a safe neighborhood are factors that function as resources because these aspects of the environment provide partners with the flexibility to devote time to each other. A good in-come and a safe neighborhood are associated with stronger relationships, perhaps because couples who do not have to worry about their security can spend more time and energy supporting each other (Cutrona et al., 2003).

What makes thinking about the context so complex is the fact that, as the following case shows, every level of the context, from proximal to distal, is likely to contain both stressors and resources.

> Sanjay, 24, has been married to Renee, 25, for 2 years. They began dating in college, married soon after they both graduated, and moved in together after their honeymoon. The search for the right apartment took several months, but in the end they found exactly what they were looking for: a cozy two-bedroom close to a charming commercial street lined with cof-fee houses, used bookstores, and boutiques. It's the lifestyle they always wanted, but it is expensive, and they struggle every month to pay their high rent.
>
> Although paying the rent is hard now, both Sanjay and Renee have con-fidence it will become easier in the future. Sanjay works as a programmer for a computer software company started by some friends from college. He loves the work, he's good at it, and if the company takes off, he expects to do very well financially. But if the new company is going to succeed, San-jay and his co-workers must put in long hours. Sanjay frequently works weekends, and on weekdays he often wakes up before Renee and comes home exhausted when she's already in bed reading. Fortunately for their relationship, Renee's job, as a freelance writer for magazines, gives her some flexibility, and she tries to be available whenever Sanjay can take a day off.
>
> Working as hard as they do, Sanjay and Renee have not had a lot of time to see friends, and this is especially hard on Renee, who was used to going out a lot when she was in school. Renee calls her closest friends when she has the chance, but many now live in other states, and she does not get to see them often. Sanjay keeps in touch with friends mostly through e-mail. He is not much of a phone person, except with his parents, whom he calls once a week, and with his two older brothers, both of whom are married with young children Sanjay adores. He is especially close to his mother and shares most of the details of his life with her. This is great for Sanjay but not so great for Renee, who sometimes wishes Sanjay's mother were slightly less generous with her advice.

This case study barely scratches the surface of the environment of a single relationship, describing only the neighborhood, employment, and social net-works of Sanjay and Renee. Yet even this small slice of their context reveals the complex effects of each of these elements. A great apartment in a safe neighborhood is a resource, but high rent on that apartment can be a stressor. A satisfying, well-paying job supports financial stability, but long hours take time away from activities that make romantic relationships rewarding. Close ties with family can be a source of support for one partner, but an annoying intrusion for the other. Describing the circumstances of Sanjay and Renee suggests that the environment of a couple contains a diverse field of forces, some strong and some weak, some binding partners together and others pulling them apart. Ultimately, the outcomes of a relationship are going to be affected by the sum of the supportive and the demanding external forces that act on it.

Chronic Conditions and Acute Events

Some elements in the environment of a relationship are stable, or at least they tend to change very slowly. For example, the historical period in which a relationship takes place plays an enormous role in shaping the way the relationship unfolds. Consider the many differences between American marriages from the 1940s and 1950s and marriages from the 2000s. For any relationship, the historical era can pretty much be taken for granted because it is the same for everyone and will remain more or less the same for several generations. In contrast, other aspects of the environment of a relationship are in constant flux. Partners change jobs and residences, friends and family members move closer or farther away, the economy booms and then it busts. Researchers have recognized that the stability of different contextual elements is likely to determine how those elements affect relationships. Accordingly, research in this area has frequently organized contextual elements according to how much they change over time.

The **chronic conditions** of a relationship are those aspects of the environment that are relatively stable and enduring. Unless a couple moves frequently, the quality of the neighborhoods they live in tends to be a fairly chronic condition of the relationship, as is the amount of money they earn, their general health, and the quality of their social networks. All of these things can and do change over time, but those changes tend to be slow relative to other changes that take place in relationships. Chronic conditions form the background of a couple's life, and are taken for granted as accepted parts of their daily experiences (Gump & Matthews, 1999). In contrast, **acute events**, such as a car accident, an illness, or a period of unemployment, have a relatively clear onset and the possibility of an end point. Particular acute events, like the death of a child, may occur infrequently but have a major impact.

As the last example points out, the distinction between chronic and acute elements is not black and white. Some events (e.g., the death of a loved one, a promotion at work) have a clear onset but no clear end point. Some conditions that are usually fairly stable (the presence of close family, the quality of the neighborhood) can undergo rapid and substantial change. Sometimes an acute event leads to a new chronic condition, such as when a car accident (an acute event) leads to a permanent disability (a chronic condition). Thus, rather than try to force specific elements of the context to fit into one category or another, it is usually more accurate simply to describe some elements of the context as more or less chronic or more or less acute than others.

Research on how chronic and acute stressors affect relationships confirms what you might expect: In general, stressors are associated with more negative relationship outcomes, whether they are chronic or acute (e.g., Bolger et al., 1996; Conger et al., 1990; Tesser & Beach, 1998). Yet researchers continue to distinguish between chronic and acute aspects of the context because they are likely to influence relationships in a different way. Chronic conditions are by definition relatively stable, so their influence on relationships tends to be relatively stable as well. As couples adapt to the chronic conditions of their environments, the effects of those conditions should persist and become enduring aspects of the relationship. Thus, research on chronic conditions often examines differences between couples in more or less stressful environments. For example, clinical psychologist Carolyn Cutrona and her colleagues (2003), in a study of African American couples, demonstrated that the marital quality of couples who live in economically disadvantaged neighborhoods tends to be lower than the marital quality of couples living in more affluent neighborhoods (**FIGURE 11.3**). The quality of the neighborhood tends to be a chronic feature of a relationship's context.

In contrast, acute events represent a relatively sudden change in the context. The temporary nature of acute events suggests that, unlike the lasting effects of chronic conditions, the effects of acute events may be reversible, fading away as people adapt and their lives return to normal. In a powerful demonstration of this process, a German study assessed over 1,000 individuals every year for 15 years (Lucas, Clark, Georgellis, & Diener, 2003). At each assessment, the participants were asked about events they had experienced since the prior assessment and rated their satisfaction with their lives on a scale of 1 to 10. It is not surprising that acute events, like getting married

FIGURE 11.3 Neighborhood as a chronic condition. A couple's neighborhood can affect their relationship. Imagine how an intimate relationship might be influenced by a high-crime neighborhood where few other couples live. How might the same relationship develop in a neighborhood of single-family homes?

or being widowed, predicted changes in life satisfaction, such that people got slightly happier on average when they married and a lot less happy on average when they were widowed. Over time, however, people seemed to adapt, and life satisfaction tended to return to where it was before the transition. Because relationships can bounce back from acute events the same way individuals can, measuring the acute events that couples face may be one way to account for the ups and downs people experience in their relationships. When the environment presents a couple with many demands, relationships may suffer and go through hard times; but when the circumstances of a couple improve, the relationship may recover as well.

In addition to their independent effects, sociologist Reuben Hill's (1949) ABC-X model of family stress suggested that chronic and acute aspects of the context may also interact to affect relationships (see Chapter 3). Hill believed that the presence or absence of resources (a chronic condition of a family's environment) should shape the way families respond to the acute events they experience. Imagine, for example, how two couples— one from a wealthy neighborhood and one from a poor neighborhood—might react differently if their cars were to collide in an accident (**FIGURE 11.4**). The wealthy couple, confident in the availability of alternative transportation and covered by adequate insurance, might find the accident a significant hassle, but

FIGURE 11.4 An annoyance or a serious problem? When an acute event, such as a car accident, happens to a couple, the extent to which it affects the relationship depends on chronic conditions, such as the resources the couple has for dealing with the incident.

nothing more. In contrast, the less financially stable couple might not have adequate car or health insurance. The partners may not have jobs with flexible hours, making it difficult to find the time to get their car fixed, assuming they could afford the repairs. For this couple, the same accident might be experienced as a major stressor, requiring significant adaptation from all members of the family. Indeed, research on physiological reactions to acute stress indicates that people react more severely to an acute stressor when they are dealing with other ongoing problems at the same time (Gump & Matthews, 1999).

Controllable, Predictable vs. Uncontrollable, Unpredictable Conditions

Although we have defined the context as being outside a relationship, some of its elements are nevertheless affected by the behavior of the partners. Graduating from college or being offered a major promotion at work, for example, are presumably rewards for good performance, just as being arrested is usually a punishment for criminal behavior. Often, these events can be predicted, or at least couples can behave in ways that make them more or less likely. Similarly, couples have some ability to choose the chronic conditions of their lives (Berscheid, 1998). Sanjay and Renee, in the case presented earlier, chose to live in an expensive apartment in a great neighborhood, but they might have taken a cheaper apartment in a less desirable neighborhood, thereby improving their financial security at the expense of their personal security. In fact, selecting a supportive environment and avoiding challenging ones may be an important way for a couple to maintain their relationship. A couple with children may choose to live near relatives who might help with childcare or choose jobs with flexible hours that afford opportunities for family time. The decision to move together to a new environment is one way to increase partner interdependence. In contrast, other acute events and chronic conditions, such as natural disasters or political and economic upheavals, are unpredictable and beyond partners' control. Even with respect to aspects of the environment that can be controlled, not every couple has the same range of options from which to choose. The lower their socioeconomic level, for example, the more limited their ability to affect and change their own context.

This distinction matters because elements of the context that can be controlled and predicted may have fewer effects on relationships than those that are unpredictable or beyond control. Sociologist Elizabeth Menaghan (1983) drew on longitudinal data from a large sample of married couples to identify those who had experienced 1 of 10 common family transitions (e.g., first child enters school, first child leaves home, last child leaves home). She compared the changes experienced by those couples to the changes experienced by couples who did not experience those transitions. By all accounts, such transitions are quite stressful for families, so Menaghan expected that the satisfaction of couples who experienced them would decline over time compared to couples who did not experience the changes. In fact, there were few significant differences between the two groups. Why? Menaghan speculated that when a stressor is controllable and expected, the spouses have time to prepare for it. As a result, the event is less disruptive, and they quickly return to baseline levels of functioning. It follows that events that are unpredictable may be more disruptive because couples don't have time to gather their resources together and prepare to cope effectively.

MAIN POINTS

>> The context of an intimate relationship encompasses everything that affects it outside of the partners and their interactions.

>> Elements in the context range from proximal (nearby, such as living arrangements, friends, and stressful experiences) to distal (removed, such as the culture, historical era, and climate).

>> Elements of the context can operate as stressors that require the couple to adapt, or as resources that contribute to their ability to interact effectively.

>> Some conditions of the environment are chronic, or likely to persist over time (e.g., being poor, being the victim of oppression), and some are acute, characterized by a specific onset and potential end point (e.g., a car accident, a period of unemployment).

>> Controllable stressors, such as moving for a new job or having children, may have fewer negative effects on a relationship than stressors that are uncontrollable and unpredictable, like a natural disaster or an illness.

Stress: When Bad Things Happen to Good Relationships

Nobody gets married expecting to get a divorce. On the contrary, newlyweds report tremendous optimism about their future, expecting that the difficult parts of their lives will improve and the rewarding parts will get even better. One reason for this optimism is that newlyweds, like most people, greatly underestimate the chance that unanticipated negative events will happen to them (Helweg-Larsen & Shepperd, 2001). The truth, however, is that over the course of any long-term relationship, at least a few bad things are very likely to happen, things that are unpredictable and beyond the partners' control. Some may be mild irritants, like a flat tire or an increased load at work. Others may be catastrophic, like the sudden death of a family member, the diagnosis of a serious illness, or a natural disaster. The fact that couples will have to face challenges is one reason relationship outcomes can be hard to predict. Even if a couple seems to have everything going for them, there is always the chance that they will experience unexpected stressors that overwhelm their ability to adapt effectively.

The ways that events outside a couple make their way inside the relationship are not always easy to see. In the story that started this chapter, John, the New York City firefighter, denied that the end of his marriage had anything to do with his devastating experiences after the 9/11 terrorist attacks. Research on college students shows the same thing: People generally attribute the success or failure of their relationship to their own and their partner's qualities, minimizing or even ignoring the context of the relationship (Berscheid et al., 2001; Lamm, Wiesmann, & Keller, 1998). Yet, whether they are recognized or not, events outside a relationship can have profound effects on how it develops and changes over time.

Concrete Effects of Stress

Many of the resources people draw upon to maintain their relationships are limited. There are only 24 hours in a day and only so much money in the bank. One of the ways that demands outside the relationship affect what goes on inside the relationship is the draining of such resources as time, energy, and money, leaving fewer reserves for the things that make the relationship satisfying and fulfilling. Imagine a couple in which both partners suddenly face increased demands at work. Even if all their interactions are exceptionally rewarding and fulfilling, when they are spending more time at their jobs, they will be having fewer of those interactions.

Most research on how external stress affects time in intimate relationships has focused on time married couples spend on household chores. As you might expect, the more that either spouse faces demands outside the home, the less time is available for chores within the home (Pittman, Solheim, & Blanchard, 1996; South & Spitze, 1994). Yet it seems likely that the concrete effects of stress on the allocation of resources in relationships are far broader. All the activities of a relationship—from making a home to sharing intimacy to solving problems—occupy a space that is limited by the other demands in partners' lives. Under stressful circumstances, that space may be severely limited, even for the happiest couples.

Moreover, the demands of the world outside a relationship are rarely left at the door when couples are together. On the contrary, external stress often means that couples must spend more of their time within that relationship dealing with that stress. The impact of external stressors was revealed in a survey that asked 1,010 newlywed husbands and wives about the most problematic areas of their marriage (Schramm et al., 2005). The responses are shown in TABLE 11.1. The most frequent problems for newlywed husbands and wives came from outside: paying off debts and balancing the demands of their jobs and their relationship. Thus, even at the beginning of a marriage when the relationship is presumably at its most positive, the outside world can intrude, raising issues that couples must find time to address. Moreover, as we discussed in Chapter 7, partners usually serve as each other's most important source of social support when they are experiencing stress (Coyne & DeLongis, 1986). The more stress partners are experiencing, the more they will expect each other to provide support when they are together. If a problem is especially severe or unmanageable (e.g., a chronically ill relative, an impending transfer to a new city), then couples will be required to spend their time together coping with the problem rather than sharing their feelings or enjoying each other's company. In married couples, a lack of shared leisure time is a powerful predictor of divorce, in one study second only to the duration of the marriage (Hill, 1988). Thus, stress outside the relationship not only limits the time a couple can spend together but also changes the nature of that time.

Finally, as discussed in Chapter 3, stressful events can lead to consequences that are themselves stressful, causing a **stress pile-up** (McCubbin & Patterson, 1982). A car accident on the way to work is stressful by itself; if the accident makes you late for an important meeting, you now have two stressors to deal with instead of one. Severe chronic stress is associated with health problems (e.g., Taylor, Repetti, & Seeman, 1997), which themselves

TABLE 11.1 **Intrusion of the Outside World**

Wives		Husbands	
Stressor	% Indicating Problem	Stressor	% Indicating Problem
Debt brought into marriage	19	Balancing job and marriage	19
Balancing job and marriage	18	Debt brought into marriage	18
Frequency of sexual relations/In-laws	13	Husband employment	14
Expectations about household tasks/Financial decision making	13	Frequency of sexual relations	14
Communication with spouse	13	In-laws	12
Resolving major conflicts/ Time spent together	12	Financial decision making	12
Husband employment	12	Expectations about household tasks	12
Wife employment	11	Wife employment	11
Birth control	10	Communication with spouse/Resolving major conflicts	11
Constant bickering	8	Time spent together	10

Source: Adapted from Schramm et al., 2005.

require coping and resources (e.g., trips to the doctor, money for medical bills).

Physiological Effects of Stress

Because the concrete effects of stressful circumstances are relatively obvious, we can often anticipate and prepare for them. Other effects of stress are more subtle. In particular, experiencing a stressful event has immediate, powerful, but usually invisible physiological effects on body chemistry.

Imagine that while driving to meet your partner for a date, your car is struck from behind by another driver. Even if the collision is a mild one and you have no obvious injuries, the shock of the incident will cause numerous physical changes you cannot see. For example, before your conscious mind even processes what happened, two systems in your body are activated by the brain. One of these, the sympathetic adrenal medullary (SAM) system, triggers your adrenal glands to pump epinephrine (adrenaline) and other hormones into your bloodstream. The other system, the hypothalamic pituitary adrenocortical (HPA) axis, adds steroids, such as hydrocortisone, to the mix. These hormones signal your body to accelerate your heart rate and increase your blood pressure. Your sweat glands are activated, your pores open up, and your cells start processing oxygen and other nutrients more effectively. In moments, you are transformed. Whereas a split-second ago, you were relaxed and looking forward to your date, now your body is aroused, completely focused, and ready for action. This is the **fight-or-flight response** (FIGURE 11.5).

Behavioral and Cognitive Effects of Stress

The physiological responses to stress have psychological consequences that are useful for dealing with crises. Psychologists Robert Yerkes and John Dodson (1908) were the first to provide evidence that physiological arousal affects performance on tasks. The **Yerkes-Dodson law** suggests that, with respect to simple tasks or reflexes, increased arousal enhances performance. Running away is a simple reflex, and when you are aroused by a potential threat, you can run faster and longer than normal. Cognitive tasks are affected in a similar way. When you are physically or emotionally aroused, your attention tends to focus on the key details of an event, and your memory for those details improves (Christianson & Loftus, 1991). If you need to remember a threatening stimulus in order to avoid it the next time you see it, this can be an essential response.

From the perspective of intimate relationships, the problem with stress is that the tasks that keep partners feeling connected and satisfied are rarely simple or governed by reflex. On the contrary, even straightforward couple interactions require complex cognitive processes, such as empathy, perspective taking, and forgiveness. Unfortunately for couples experiencing stress, while arousal enhances performance on simple and reflex tasks, it diminishes performance on complex and deliberative tasks (Matthews et al., 2000). In other words, stress enhances your ability to do what comes naturally but diminishes your ability to do things that are difficult or new. Therefore, people who are physically aroused are more likely to rely on stereotypes to understand other people (Bodenhausen, 1993). They also take longer to solve complicated thought problems (Adam et al., 1997). Although they have better memory for the central details of events, they have poor memory for the peripheral details; that is, they demonstrate "tunnel vision" (Brown, 2003).

Consider how these effects might affect your interactions with your partner when you show up late for your date after being rear-ended. Your partner, unaware that you have been in an accident, might be a little short with

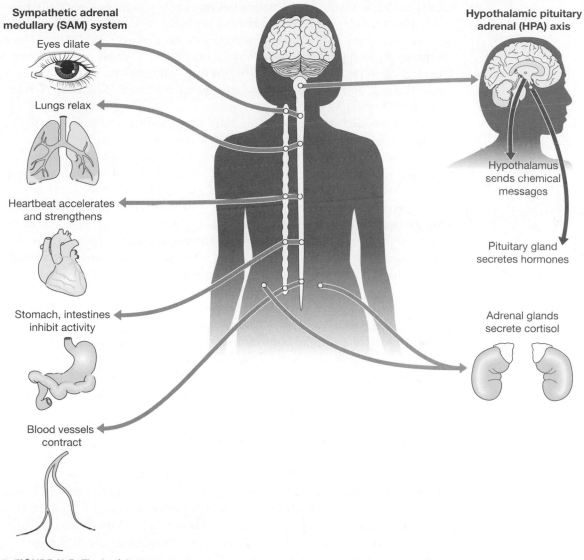

**Sympathetic adrenal
medullary (SAM) system**

Eyes dilate

Lungs relax

Heartbeat accelerates
and strengthens

Stomach, intestines
inhibit activity

Blood vessels
contract

**Hypothalamic pituitary
adrenal (HPA) axis**

Hypothalamus
sends chemical
messages

Pituitary gland
secretes hormones

Adrenal glands
secrete cortisol

▌ **FIGURE 11.5 The body's response to stress.**

you: "What took you so long? I've been waiting 20 minutes!" How do you respond? If you have fully recovered from the stress of the accident, perhaps you are able to adopt your partner's perspective. You might be able to step back and think: "My partner is understandably irritated at having to wait but will surely embrace me when I explain what has just happened." On the other hand, taking the broader context of a partner's actions into account does not come easily to most people. If you are still aroused from the shock of the accident, the tendency of people under stress to ignore peripheral details (i.e., the fact that your partner does not know about your accident) may make it impossible to take your partner's perspective. Instead, you might rely on a stereotypical judgment to understand your partner's behavior: "There you go again with your nagging!" Feeling hurt, and still tense from the crash, you might lash out with a negative retort, like: "You have no idea what I have been through, and already you are getting on my case? Why don't you try listening for once?"

The difference between a simple misunderstanding and a long negative interaction often lies in the ability of one partner to resist the urge to reciprocate negative behaviors (see Chapter 8). Stress-induced physiological arousal can determine when partners have this ability and when they do not. Through observational research on married couples, psychologists Robert Levenson and John Gottman (1983, 1985) demonstrated that physiological arousal during marital interactions is associated with increased negative reciprocity between partners. The more aroused a couple is when they communicate with each other, the more likely they are to reciprocate each other's negative behavior and to experience declines in their relationship satisfaction over time.

To clarify the effects of stress on couple interactions, social psychologists Lisa Neff and Benjamin Karney (2004) contacted newlyweds every 6 months for the first 3 years of marriage. At every contact, spouses completed a measure that asked them to imagine what they would think if their partner acted in an insensitive way (e.g., failing to listen, acting cool or distant). Spouses were also asked to describe the sorts of stresses they had experienced outside the relationship since the last assessment. Over time, the explanations for their partner's behaviors varied in relation to the stress they had been experiencing. Couples with relatively low levels of stress on average avoided blaming their partners for their negative behaviors, excusing them as the product of demands external to the relationship (such as stress). Yet paradoxically, when outside stress was high, *these same couples* were more likely to blame their partners for their negative behaviors. In other words, the ability to see the broader context of a partner's negative behavior, and therefore excuse it, seems to be diminished during the very times that partners need it most.

In terms of maintaining a relationship, stress seems to present couples with a double dilemma. External stress forces them to spend resources on coping that they might otherwise have spent on more rewarding activities. Yet at the very time they most need to come together and interact effectively, stress renders partners less capable of cognitive processes that support the relationship, such as understanding, restraint, and forgiveness. It might be expected, then, that couples under stress should experience more negative relationship outcomes than couples not under stress, even if the stress is entirely external to the relationship, and that seems to be the case. Research on a wide variety of external stressors, including financial strain (Conger, Rueter,

& Elder, 1999), employment insecurity (Larson, Wilson, & Beley, 1994), a child with a chronic illness (Dahlquist et al., 1993), and a severe illness in one partner (Giese-Davis et al., 2000), reveals that, on average, satisfaction with the relationship tends to decline and the risk of breaking up increases, after partners are exposed to external stressors.

Stress Spillover and Stress Crossover

When Bronfenbrenner (1979) first started writing about the effects of the environment on human development, he was thinking about the environment surrounding an individual. Once we start thinking about couples or families, identifying the effects of the environment becomes more complicated because the environment of each partner overlaps with, but is not identical to, the environment of the other partner. Some stressors affect both partners at the same time, such as being physically separated, as described in **BOX 11.1**. Some stressors affect only one partner directly but still influence the other partner indirectly. Researchers have begun to tease apart this complexity by distinguishing between different routes through which stress can affect individual outcomes in relationships.

Thus far, most of the examples we have used refer to the simplest situation: A stressor that someone experiences outside the relationship affects the way that person functions within the relationship. This is a specific case of a general phenomenon called **stress spillover**, which occurs whenever the effects of stress in one domain of a person's life are transmitted to other domains. Research on stress in relationships frequently addresses spillover, showing that people who experience various kinds of stressors outside the home report less satisfaction with their relationships (Gracia & Herrero, 2004; Harper, Schaalje, & Sandberg, 2000; Larson et al., 1994), display more negative emotions during problem-solving interactions (Krokoff, Gottman, & Roy, 1988), and are less accepting of each other (Crouter & Bumpus, 2001) than people who have not experienced those stressors.

Stress spillover can travel in multiple directions at once. Sometimes external stress can spill over into relationships, but relationship problems can also spill over into domains outside the relationship, as anyone who has tried to take an exam the night after a big fight with a partner knows. If the stress and the relationship are measured only once, it is impossible to know what kind of spillover is really happening. One promising method that overcomes this concern, introduced in Chapter 2, is the daily diary approach, which involves asking individuals to report on aspects of their life at regular intervals (e.g., once or twice a day), usually by responding to brief survey questions. With repeated assessments of the same people over time, individuals act as their own controls, allowing the researcher to examine how changes in one domain of a person's life are associated with subsequent changes in other domains.

BOX 11.1 SPOTLIGHT ON . . .

Long-Distance Relationships

Relationship scientists usually assume partners either live together or live in such close proximity that they have frequent opportunities for face-to-face interaction. But this is not always the case. Sometimes people pursue **long-distance relationships** with partners they cannot see regularly. Young adults may enter long-distance relationships when high school sweethearts find themselves going to different colleges, or when college couples accept jobs in different states. Even married couples do not always live together. Between 5 and 7 percent of white spouses and 12 to 20 percent of African American spouses ages 18–24 live apart from their partners, most often due to one partner's military service or incarceration (Rindfuss & Stephen, 1990). With the rise of the Internet and global communications, it is even possible for intense and passionate relationships to form between individuals who have never met in person.

What happens in these relationships? Conventional wisdom suggests that absence makes the heart grow fonder. Indeed, one might argue that couples living apart get to preserve their most positive beliefs about the relationship, protected from the disappointments and irritations that may arise through daily contact. Moreover, separation might serve to make the times that partners do spend together that much more special.

These may be comforting thoughts for those forced to endure long-distance relationships, but research offers no support for them. On the contrary, physical distance between partners appears to be a significant source of stress for intimate relationships, for several reasons. First, like other external demands, long distance severely restricts face-to-face interaction, thereby minimizing opportunities for disappointment but also limiting the shared activities that contribute to closeness and intimacy (Aron et al., 2000). Second, long distance increases the cost of maintaining the relationship. Couples who live in close proximity can take for granted

that they will be able to interact in person regularly. For these couples, relationship closeness can be reaffirmed with a touch, a gesture, or a look. In contrast, couples in long-distance relationships must expend more effort simply to keep in contact. During stressful periods, when couples are most likely to turn to each other for support, those in long-distance relationships may have trouble mustering the time and resources necessary to affirm their connection. Third, long distance means that partners will of necessity spend significant amounts of time in the company of other people, creating opportunities for jealousy and infidelity that couples living near each other may not have.

Among college students, those in long-distance relationships score higher on measures of psychological distress (Guldner, 1996) and lower on measures of closeness and relationship satisfaction (Van Horn et al., 1997) than those who live near their partners. Among married couples, one study found that spouses living apart were three times more likely to divorce than were spouses living together (Rindfuss & Stephen, 1990). Moreover, the negative consequences of physical distance do not end when couples reunite. Adjusting to a partner's presence after an extended period of separation can be a stressor in itself, as partners who have adjusted to independent living must remember old routines and establish new ones. Couples separated by one partner's military service, for example, frequently report problems after the service member's tour of duty ends (e.g., Elder & Clipp, 1989). After a long separation, the high expectations of both partners can be hard to fulfill, leading to disappointments and resentments.

None of this suggests that successful long-distance relationships are impossible, only that they are especially challenging. Couples in this situation must be aware of the ways that their circumstances place stress on the relationship.

Clinical psychologist Rena Repetti (1989) used the daily diary approach to examine how stress at work affects the home life of air traffic controllers. Air traffic controllers are an ideal group for studying stress because their daily stress at work can be quantified precisely and objectively by examining traffic volume at the airport, rather than relying on the controllers' own subjective assessments. Each day for 3 days, Repetti gathered data on traffic conditions and then asked the controllers and their spouses to report on the kinds of marital behaviors they engaged in during the evenings. Because there is no way that behaviors exchanged at night can affect traffic conditions during the day, any links between work stress and home stress has to be evidence for spillover in only one direction—from work to the relationship. Indeed, that is what Repetti found. When their day at work had been more stressful, the controllers and their spouses reported that the controller was more socially withdrawn at home compared to less stressful days. This seemed to be a coping strategy, allowing the controllers, overloaded on the busiest days, to unwind without encountering other stressful stimuli from their families.

Although this strategy might work for the air traffic controllers, what about their partners and children? Because couples and family members are interdependent and their actions affect one another's outcomes, it seems likely that stress affecting one member may be transmitted to other members, a phenomenon called **stress crossover** (Larson & Almeida, 1999). In contrast to stress spillover, which takes place entirely within an individual, stress crossover occurs whenever stress experienced by one partner in a relationship affects the outcomes and functioning of the other partner. In an early study of stress crossover, researchers interviewed 1,383 wives about the stresses their husbands were experiencing at work and their own experiences of depression and other emotional problems (Rook, Dooley, & Catalano, 1991). The wives' level of symptoms was not associated with their own parenting and work demands, or with the level of support they received from their husbands. In a clear example of stress crossover, it was associated with the amount of job stress their husbands were experiencing: The wives reported more symptoms when their husbands were experiencing more job stress. It is interesting that this association was strongest for wives in the most satisfying marriages and weakest for wives in the least satisfying marriages. For stress to cross over between partners, there may have to be a strong bond between partners to act as a bridge. The less partners are invested in each other's outcomes, the less they may be affected by the stress in each other's lives.

NOTICING A STRESSOR CHANGES ITS EFFECTS. When partners experience stress spillover and crossover, do they know it is happening? Probably not. The moment that two partners who are arguing with each other think "Hey, we are both just irritable because we've had really stressful days at work," a lot of the blame that motivates arguments ought to evaporate. Instead, it seems more likely that the failure to recognize how stressful events affect partner interactions is exactly what allows spillover and crossover to happen.

In a study exploring this possibility, psychologists Abraham Tesser and Steven Beach (1998) proposed that stress outside of a relationship might have complex and indirect effects on judgments of the relationship. Low levels of external stress can easily escape our awareness, but they make us irritated and put us in a bad mood, affecting the way we evaluate anything, including our relationship (Schwarz & Clore, 1983, 2003). At higher levels of external stress, however, the cause of the stress becomes more obvious, and we are able to compensate for the effects of the stressor. Thus, if you have had a mildly bad day at work, you might be in a bad mood at home, not know why, and get irritated with your partner. However, if you have had a *very* bad day at work, you might still be in a bad mood at home, but you would know why, and probably not let your mood affect your interactions.

In fact, people do correct for the effects of their mood on their judgments, if they are reminded that their mood can have this effect (Clore, 1992). The problem, as other research has shown (Martin, Seta, & Crelia, 1990), is that this sort of correcting takes effort, and when people are extremely stressed or distracted, they might be unable to correct their judgments even if they want to. With this in mind, Tesser and Beach hypothesized that, overall, stress and relationship satisfaction should be inversely related. This is not surprising, but they also predicted that the people in between the lowest and highest levels of stress become aware of the stress and make adjustments for it. Because of the adjustments and corrections, their satisfaction would be relatively high. As people experienced yet higher levels of stress, however, they would be unable to sustain these adjustments, and relationship satisfaction would then plummet.

To test their ideas, the researchers estimated stress spillover in three samples of people experiencing varying levels of stressful life events: mothers with adolescent children, eighth-grade students, and newlywed couples (Tesser & Beach, 1998). In all three samples, they found evidence of the changes in judgment they expected (**FIGURE 11.6**). At the lowest and highest levels of stress, there was a clear correlation between external stress and evaluations of the relationship (parent–child relationships for the mothers and eighth-graders, marital relationship for the newlyweds). The more stress experienced, the more negative the evaluations of the relationship. Somewhere in the middle, however, there was a point in each sample when the relationship between stress and evaluations of the relationship dropped sharply. This is the point, the researchers argued, that the stressors in people's lives are obvious enough to be within awareness but not so overwhelming that spouses lose their ability to correct for their stress.

Awareness of the stressor may play a similar role in stress crossover. One problem with a lot of research on stress is that different people are exposed to different stressors that are not really comparable. Social psychologists Anne Thompson and Niall Bolger (1999) avoided this problem by studying a sample of couples that all included one partner who was preparing for the same stressful event: the New York State bar examination. The bar exam is

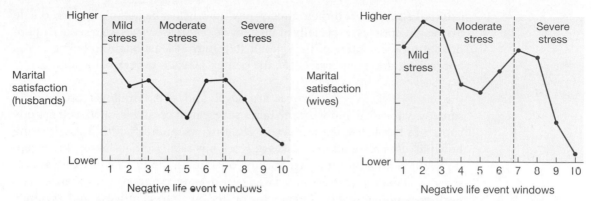

FIGURE 11.6 Stress levels and relationship satisfaction. With increasing levels of stress, partners in this study were less satisfied with their marriage. But after the fifth negative life event window, they were more satisfied as stress increased. This change was seen as evidence that, when stress is serious enough, couples become aware of its effects, thus helping protect their feelings about the relationship. This correction takes effort, and the researchers found that when stress gets severe and persistent, the ability to make the change is defeated, and stress spillover returns. (Source: Adapted from Tesser & Beach, 1998.)

the test that law school graduates must pass before they can practice law; preparing for and taking the exam is extremely stressful for most who take it. Thompson and Bolger wanted to see how stress crossover from the examinee to the other partner changed across the weeks preceding the exam. They asked 68 couples to complete reports of their mood every day for 35 days. The study period covered 4 weeks before the exam and 1 week after the exam. Consistent with Tesser and Beach's (1998) description of spillover, the researchers predicted that crossover from the examinee to the partner would be strongest when the test was still 4 weeks away. However, as the day of the test got closer, they expected that partners would make allowances for the stressed other partner, thereby diminishing the effect on their own mood. This is exactly what happened. The association between the examinees' mood on one day and their partners' mood on the next day started out strong, but got weaker as the test got closer, finally dropping to near zero the day before the exam. Presumably, when the exam was the next day, the examinees were extremely anxious, but their partners understood why, so their own moods were unaffected. This understanding allowed the partners of the test-takers to make a correction that was harder to make when the exam was farther away and they were less aware of the exam's role as a stressor.

Understanding the role of stressor awareness in stress spillover and crossover has several important implications for treating couples who are experiencing relationship difficulties. First, stressful experiences completely external to the relationship can affect partners' experiences within the relationship, even if they are unaware that they are being affected in this way. Second, being aware of how external stressors may affect relationships is a first step toward weakening the spillover and crossover effects. Awareness of external stressors and their effects may not always be sufficient to reconcile distressed couples, especially at high levels of stress, as we have seen. But appreciating the context of the relationship may at least begin to help couples appreciate, and then correct for, the context of each other's behaviors.

GENDER DIFFERENCES. Do stress crossover and stress spillover operate the same way for men and women? In most research on stress, such as the study shown in FIGURE 11.6, the answer is yes. But research specifically addressing how partners respond to stresses at work has identified an important exception. When both partners are working outside the home, the possibilities for stress spillover and stress crossover become more numerous, because each partner is potentially affected by his or her own stress at work and at home, plus the other person's stress at work.

To compare the relative strengths of these sources of influence, Niall Bolger and his colleagues asked dual-income married couples to complete brief nightly surveys about their home and work experiences for 42 days in a row (Bolger et al., 1989). The surveys included checklists of various kinds of stressors that spouses might have experienced outside the home during the previous 24 hours (e.g., "tensions or arguments with coworkers") as well as measures of stress in the home each evening (e.g., "tensions or arguments with spouse/children"). Because the researchers had so many days of data from each partner, they were able to examine how stresses experienced on a given day were associated with interpersonal tensions on subsequent days, controlling for the general level of tension within the marriage, and they were able to examine these associations within each partner (stress spillover) and across partners (stress crossover). The researchers reasoned that wives, socialized to invest more of their identities in their families, would be more affected by problems at home than their husbands, leading to impaired functioning outside the home. In fact, the results indicated exactly the opposite. Whereas both spouses experienced worse outcomes at home after having more stressful days at work, spillover from home to work was significant only for husbands, who were more likely to report problems at work after having problems at home the previous night. Wives, in contrast, reported the same sorts of experiences at work regardless of their problems at home the night before (FIGURE 11.7).

What explains the unexpected gender difference in spillover? The answer may have something to do with differences in the way women and men generally respond to their partners'

"Look, it's silly for you to come home from work miserable every day. Why don't you just stay there?"

FIGURE 11.7 Home is where the heart is? Home can be a refuge from the demands of the workplace, but not if partners bring their stress from work home with them.

stress. In the Bolger et al. (1989) study, wives tended to increase their involvement at home on days when their husbands had experienced elevated stress at work. Husbands were significantly less likely to do this. Other studies have found similar differences, showing that wives accept more responsibility at home when their husbands have been stressed at work, but husbands are less likely to change their home behaviors when their wives have been stressed at work (Doumas, Margolin, & John, 2003; Pittman et al., 1996). As a result, stressed men, like the air traffic controllers in the Repetti (1989) study, may be shielded from home stress in a way that stressed women are not.

This difference has two implications for stress spillover from home to work. First, because husbands are often shielded from stress at home by their supportive wives, they may be more negatively affected by home stress when they do experience it directly. This would explain why, when they perceive stress at home, they are affected even at work the next day. Second, because wives cannot expect to be shielded from stress at home by their husbands, they may be better prepared to cope with it. This might explain how wives prevent stress at home from affecting their experiences outside the home.

The Benefits of Crises

Thus far, our discussion of stress has focused on its negative consequences, and it is true that most research suggests that, all else being equal, couples should try to avoid stress when they can. But not everyone thinks this way. For example, one of the authors was once discussing his research with his optometrist during an eye exam, and the optometrist broke in with this statement: *"I'll tell you what makes a relationship successful: experiencing a crisis together."* Pressed to explain, the optometrist described the early years of his own marriage. Shortly after he was married, his wife was diagnosed with a rare and virulent form of cancer. The doctors informed the couple that, because the cancer had been detected early, she had a chance of surviving it but that the treatments would be aggressive, lengthy, and debilitating. Indeed, the period of her treatment was as awful as they had been led to expect, but it was also successful. With the disease in full remission, the optometrist and his wife went on to have three sons and a long and satisfying marriage. "You see," he concluded, "getting through my wife's cancer was the hardest thing that either one of us would ever do in our lives, but we got through it together. That gave us a confidence that couples who don't experience crises never feel. Nothing could touch us after that."

Can the stress of a crisis be good for an intimate relationship? In fact, the effects of crises on relationships may be more complex than this experience suggests. Some sense of the complexity comes from research that looks at how natural disasters and terrorist attacks affect rates of marriage, childbirth, and divorce. For example, in the last week of August 2005, Hurricane Katrina, a

FIGURE 11.8 **City under water.** When Hurricane Katrina struck the Louisiana coast in 2005, the city of New Orleans was devastated after the levees broke, flooding entire neighborhoods. How do you think living through this disaster affected people's intimate relationships?

class 3 hurricane, struck southeastern Louisiana, creating over $100 billion in damage, the worst natural disaster in the history of the United States. By far the hardest hit area was New Orleans, where the levees that usually protect the city from flooding failed catastrophically, leaving swaths of the city underwater and wiping out entire neighborhoods (**FIGURE 11.8**). How might the experience of this disaster have affected relationships? On one hand, most of the research discussed so far suggests that the stress of the hurricane should have led to problems. After all, those affected suddenly found themselves having to put their homes and their lives back in order, draining away time, money, and energy that might have been spent on the relationship. On the other hand, the crisis of Hurricane Katrina was an opportunity for partners to come together and support each other in a time when support was sorely needed. From this perspective, relationships that survived the hurricane should have been stronger than ever.

To figure out which of these perspectives has a greater claim on the truth, psychologists Catherine Cohan and Steve Cole (2002) studied the effects of an earlier disaster, Hurricane Hugo, a class 4 storm that struck South Carolina in 1989. At the time it was the fourth worst natural disaster on record in the United States: 40 percent of the residences in the affected areas were damaged, and no one escaped unscathed. Cohan and Cole drew from public records to examine rates of marriage, childbirth, and divorce in South Carolina from 1975 through 1997, that is, 14 years before the hurricane and 8 years after. If the hurricane damaged families, then these data would reveal increases in divorces after the hurricane hit, especially in the counties that were hit hardest. If the hurricane brought couples together, then these data would reveal increases in marriage and childbirth rates after the hurricane, reflecting couples' decisions to increase their commitment after enduring the disaster. What really happened? Both, as shown in **FIGURE 11.9**. Relative to the trends in the years before Hurricane Hugo, the years immediately after the storm saw marked increases in rates of marriage, childbirth, *and* divorce, and only in those counties affected by the hurricane. After a couple of years, the effects of the hurricane appeared to fade away, and prior trends in all three indicators resumed. In other words, surviving a natural disaster together seems to have led some couples to decide to get married and have children at the same time that it led other couples to break up.

How can we understand these contradictory responses to the same stressful event? One answer lies in Hill's (1949) original theory of family crisis, the ABC-X model. As discussed earlier, this model proposes that the impact of a crisis on a couple or a family depends on the resources available and the kind of coping that occurs. When couples encounter stress that is too great

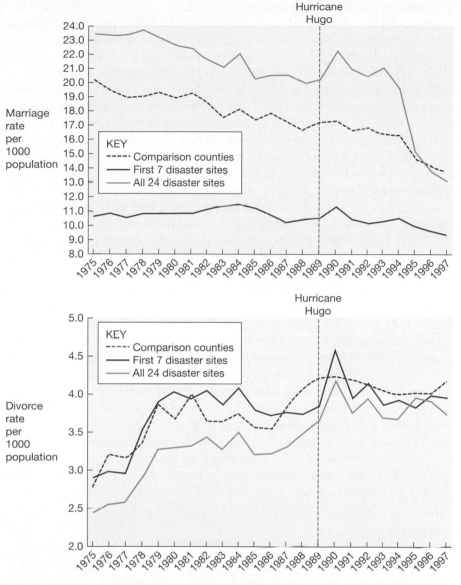

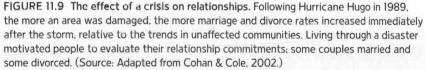

FIGURE 11.9 The effect of a crisis on relationships. Following Hurricane Hugo in 1989, the more an area was damaged, the more marriage and divorce rates increased immediately after the storm, relative to the trends in unaffected communities. Living through a disaster motivated people to evaluate their relationship commitments; some couples married and some divorced. (Source: Adapted from Cohan & Cole, 2002.)

for their resources and coping ability, that level of stress leads to the deterioration of the relationship. However, Hill was careful to note that for couples with adequate resources and coping skills, a stressful episode can engender growth in the relationship, thereby laying a foundation for resilience when facing challenges in the future.

In the decades since Hill proposed his theory, considerable evidence has accumulated to support the idea that the way couples cope with a stressful event determines the impact of that event on the relationship. Sociologist Rand Conger and his colleagues, for example, observed couples with varying degrees of economic strain discussing problems in their relationship (Conger et al., 1990, 1999). The researchers followed the couples over time, to see how their relationships progressed. On average, as we have seen, financial strain predicts declines in satisfaction, but couples demonstrating the most effective problem-solving skills appear able to resist these declines. Other longitudinal research on newlywed couples has found a similar association between stress and the ability to solve problems. For the couples with the least effective skills, experiencing stress predicted declines in satisfaction, but for the couples with the most effective problem-solving skills, experiencing stress early in the marriage predicted more satisfying relationships 18 months later (Cohan & Bradbury, 1997). Married couples who are effective at solving problems and providing support have even been shown to experience better outcomes in samples in which one partner is suffering from cancer (Halford, Scott, & Smythe, 2000).

The optometrist was partly right. For any couple, experiencing a crisis is a challenge. For couples who lack the resources or skills to meet the challenge successfully, extremely stressful experiences may highlight vulnerabilities in the relationship that would never have come up otherwise. In such cases, stress can prove to be the catalyst that leads to the demise of the relationship. The optometrist and his wife, however, seem to have had adequate resources. Perhaps they were able to communicate so effectively that they managed to connect even when their communication was in the context of the most difficult period in their lives. Maybe they were surrounded by family and friends who provided support when they were too drained to support each other. For couples who possess such advantages, encountering stress provides an opportunity to grow together and may make the relationship stronger as a result. The success or failure of the coping efforts makes the difference.

MAIN POINTS

>> The concrete effects of stress on a couple not only drain time, energy, and resources that might otherwise be devoted to the relationship; they also change the nature of time spent together, because the couple must cope with difficult issues.

>> Stress often has unseen physiological effects, including a heightened level of arousal that interferes with complex tasks, rendering a couple less able to interact effectively during the precise times when effective interaction is most sorely needed.

>> Stress spillover is the transfer of stress in one domain of life into other domains. Stress crossover is the transmission of one partner's stress to the other partner.

>> Although persistent levels of stress generally lead to relationship declines, if a stressful experience is handled effectively, a couple might become stronger and more resilient than before.

Socioeconomic Status

Having money cannot guarantee you will find someone to accept you and support you throughout an enduring intimate relationship. However, once you have found someone to love, a little money never hurts.

This point was made glaringly obvious in 1999, when newspapers around the United States reported what many considered a startling finding. Census data collected the previous year revealed that Alabama, Arkansas, Oklahoma, and Tennessee had the highest divorce rates in the country, around 50 percent higher than the national average. Many people found this surprising because these four states constitute the heart of the Bible Belt, a region of conservative values and strong connections to religious organizations, which many predicted would have led to lower divorce rates, not higher ones.

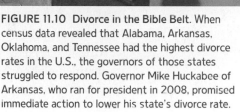

FIGURE 11.10 Divorce in the Bible Belt. When census data revealed that Alabama, Arkansas, Oklahoma, and Tennessee had the highest divorce rates in the U.S., the governors of those states struggled to respond. Governor Mike Huckabee of Arkansas, who ran for president in 2008, promised immediate action to lower his state's divorce rate.

Initial efforts to explain the puzzling finding focused on expectations and education. For example, Jerry Regier, Oklahoma's secretary of health and human services at the time, suggested to the press that children do not have a realistic view of marriage. Governor Mike Huckabee of Arkansas declared a "marital emergency" and promised support for educational programs designed to lower his state's divorce rate (**FIGURE 11.10**). Relationship education began to be written into high school curricula, in the form of required classes teaching communication skills and relationship values. The theory underlying these efforts seemed to be that high divorce rates are the result of a general misunderstanding of the challenges of marriage. Correcting this misunderstanding should, therefore, lower divorce rates and presumably lead to happier marriages.

> " I don't care too much for money, money can't buy me love."
>
> —John Lennon and Paul McCartney (1964)

The problem with this line of reasoning is that it is hard to explain why misunderstandings about marriage should be more prevalent in the Bible Belt states than elsewhere in the country. Explaining why Alabama, Arkansas, Oklahoma, and Tennessee have higher divorce rates than the other 46 states requires, as a first step, some effort to identify how these four may differ from others. To this end, the same data that revealed state-by-state disparities in divorce rates also pointed out other ways in which these four states are distinct. According to the National Center for Health Statistics (2003), these states ranked near the bottom of the 50 states in terms of employment rate, annual pay, household income, and health insurance coverage. At the same time, they had among the highest rates of murder, infant mortality, and poverty in the nation. Thus, while it's possible that couples in Alabama, Arkansas, Oklahoma, and Tennessee misunderstand the challenges of marriage, it is a certainty that life in general is more challenging in those states. The observation that divorce rates are higher in states where the overall quality of life is poorer suggests an alternative explanation for high divorce rates: Relationships that might survive and even thrive elsewhere may struggle in the face of unstable working conditions, neighborhoods beset by crime, poor education, and low wages.

Socioeconomic status (SES) is a blanket term that refers to all the ways that individuals differ in their ranking within a social structure. In the United States, SES is often measured as a composite variable that takes into account an individual's household income, level of education, and occupation. Most research on the links between SES and intimate relationships has focused on marriage, and the evidence that SES affects relationship outcomes is extensive. Here are a few examples:

▪ Women who have less than a high school education or who live in low-income neighborhoods are as likely as, or slightly more likely than, more affluent women to marry by the time they are 30 (Bramlett & Mosher, 2002). Yet rates of divorce for low-income women are substantially higher, nearly twice as high for women who live in low-income neighborhoods compared to those in high-income neighborhoods (Bramlett & Mosher, 2002; Raley & Bumpass, 2003). Moreover, marriages end earlier in low-income neighborhoods than in more affluent neighborhoods (**FIGURE 11.11**).

▪ Even among marriages that remain intact, low-income spouses report significantly higher levels of marital distress than do middle- or

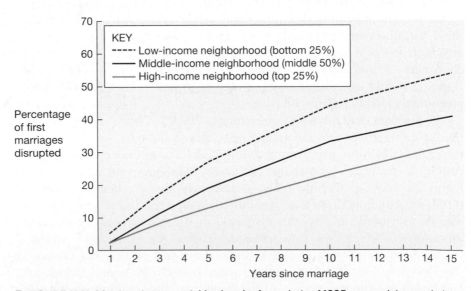

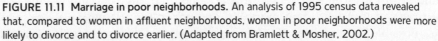

FIGURE 11.11 Marriage in poor neighborhoods. An analysis of 1995 census data revealed that, compared to women in affluent neighborhoods, women in poor neighborhoods were more likely to divorce and to divorce earlier. (Adapted from Bramlett & Mosher, 2002.)

high-income spouses (Amato et al., 2003). Relative to more affluent couples, low-income couples tend to experience more physical abuse and domestic violence (e.g., Amato & Previti, 2003).

- Compared to more affluent couples, low-income couples are four times more likely to have their first child before getting married, and they have additional children more rapidly after marriage as well (Elwood & Jencks, 2004).

Because marital disruptions among poor couples frequently involve children, they are a matter of great concern to policy makers. In 2006, the federal government committed unprecedented amounts of money—$750 million over a 5-year period—toward efforts to promote and strengthen marriages among the poor, mostly through classes designed to teach couples communication skills and family values. Whether or not this was a good use of federal funds depends in large part on understanding why intimate relationships seem to be more difficult to maintain in poor communities compared to wealthier communities. Yet, whereas the differences in rates of disruption across levels of socioeconomic status are beyond dispute, the reasons for these differences remain a subject of some controversy.

Do the Poor Value Marriage Less?

Some people believe that high rates of marital disruption reflect moral decay, or a lack of dedication to the institution of marriage. When David Popenoe (2001), professor of sociology and head of the National Marriage Project at Rutgers University, testified before a subcommittee of the U.S. House of Representatives as part of a hearing on welfare and marriage issues, he went so far as to suggest that the breakdown of marriage was at its heart a problem of declining values. "Our national goal," he told Congress, "should be no less than to rebuild a marriage culture" (Popenoe, 2001). Other notable scholars and social leaders have echoed this call, suggesting that high rates of out-of-wedlock pregnancy and increasing rates of divorce are directly attributable to society's failure to appreciate the value of stable, healthy marriages and its failure to teach this value to each new generation (Waite & Gallagher, 2000; Wilson, 2002). To the extent that maintaining marriages is more challenging for low-income couples, this perspective suggests that an appreciation of the value of marriage is especially lacking in these groups.

Is there any evidence that attitudes toward the institution of marriage are in fact declining? On the contrary, surveys throughout the U.S. reveal that, in the country as a whole, people's attitudes about marriage have remained highly positive over the last several decades (Axinn & Thornton, 1992; Thornton & Young-DeMarco, 2001). Young adults, ages 20–24, continue to value marriage very highly. A recent national survey showed that 83 percent of men and women in this age range believe it is important or very important

FIGURE 11.12 Valuing marriage. Some have argued that modern culture has devalued marriage, but there is no evidence for this claim. On the contrary, getting married continues to be an explicit goal for most young people.

to be married some day (Scott et al., 2009). Furthermore, some 90 percent of young adults in the same study expected they would be married by the time they are 40 years old. Although in most states same-sex marriage is still illegal, nearly 80 percent of gays and lesbians want to be married as well (Egan & Sherrill, 2005) (**FIGURE 11.12**).

Social psychologists Thomas Trail and Benjamin Karney (2012) extended this work by directly comparing responses from more and less affluent respondents in a telephone survey of 6,012 people living in Florida, Texas, California, and New York. Their analyses paint a similar picture, suggesting that on some attitude scales, poorer men and women report more positive attitudes toward the institution of marriage, and less approval for divorce than wealthier men and women. For example, the wealthiest respondents in this study were significantly more likely than the poorest respondents to agree that divorce can be a reasonable solution to an unhappy marriage. In contrast, the poorest respondents were more likely to agree that for the sake of children, parents should remain married even if their relationship has declined. Researcher Jane Mauldon and her colleagues examined responses to the same sorts of items among women who were receiving public assistance (Mauldon et al., 2002). Again, these women reported high levels of agreement with statements expressing positive attitudes toward marriage (e.g., "People who want children ought to marry") and strong desires to marry themselves.

Thus, on average throughout the United States and within low-income populations in particular, there is no evidence that marriage has lost its value. In fact, as sociologist and professor of public policy Andrew Cherlin (2004) has observed, marriage in the early 21st century appears to have developed into a symbol of status and prestige, and this is even more true for low-income populations than for more affluent groups.

If people from all walks of life and all levels of socioeconomic status actually agree about the value of marriage, then where does the sense of a declining culture of marriage come from? What appears to have changed is not the value of marriage per se but rather the tolerance and acceptance of family forms other than marriage (e.g., cohabitation, divorce, premarital pregnancy). For example, when sociologists Arland Thornton and Linda Young-DeMarco (2001) examined four decades of survey data from 1960 to 2000, they noticed that while attitudes toward marriage did not change much during that time, attitudes toward divorce, premarital sex, unmarried cohabitation, remaining single, and choosing to be childless all became more acceptable.

Obstacles to Marriage for Low-Income Mothers

Interviews with low-income single mothers suggest why acceptance of alternatives to traditional marriage might be especially pronounced within poor communities. Kathryn Edin and her colleagues conducted a series of studies in which they spent long periods of time with low-income single mothers, talking with them in detail to get a sense of the way they think about marriage and relationships (Edin, 2000; Edin & Kefalas, 2005; Edin, Kefalas, & Reed, 2004; Edin & Reed, 2005). Over and over, their interviews revealed women who take marriage very seriously, who value marriage for themselves and for their children, and who fully intend to get married at some point (**FIGURE 11.13**).

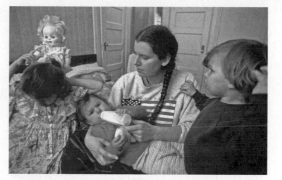

FIGURE 11.13 Single mothers. Low-income single mothers value marriage, but they perceive obstacles to getting married, such as the lack of available, appropriate partners.

Quantitative data support this view. Research on unmarried, low-income couples who had just had their first baby revealed that over 80 percent of mothers and fathers plan to marry each other. Between 70 and 80 percent of these couples rate their chances of marriage as "good" or "almost certain." Unfortunately, when these same couples were followed up a year later, only 11 percent had actually married, and 32 percent had broken up (Carlson, McLanahan, & England, 2004). What comes between the value of traditional marriage and the plan to marry, on one hand, and the fact that many low-income couples engage in nontraditional practices, on the other? Talking to low-income families reveals that, despite their strong desire to get married eventually, low-income mothers see several reasons why marriage might involve more costs than benefits, especially relative to the available alternatives (Edin & Kefalas, 2005).

Edin identified several obstacles to marriage that came up repeatedly in the interviews (Edin, 2000; Edin & Reed, 2005). The first and most important obstacle was affordability. Low-income women, and especially African American women, said that an absolute requirement for marriage is that the man contributes economically to the household. The women felt caught between two forces. The men available to them may not be employed in jobs that pay enough to support children, or might not be able to find employment at all. In addition, these women, who are already supporting their own children, are living on such tight budgets they clearly can't afford to allow a man into their lives who they would also have to support. As one woman said: "I can do bad by myself. I don't need no one helping me [do bad]" (Edin, 2000, p. 119).

A second obstacle for these women was the fear of divorce. These mothers, like most people, want marriage to mean marriage for life. Yet given the economic burdens they currently faced, they felt any marriage would probably collapse under the strain, and this was a risk they were unwilling to take. Edin wrote: "It is not that mothers held marriage in low esteem, but rather the fact that they held it in such high esteem that convinced them to forgo marriage, at least until their prospective partner could prove himself worthy economically or they could find another partner who could" (2000, pp. 120–121). For these mothers, getting married is not a step toward respectability, it is something to accomplish once they feel they have achieved respectability. Given the economic constraints that they face, this becomes a difficult hurdle to cross.

A third obstacle was the fear of losing independence and autonomy. As single mothers supporting themselves and their children, the women Edin interviewed had, within the context of their considerable financial constraints, a great deal of autonomy and control over their own lives. In the interviews, they expressed the belief that they would lose that control if they got married. For example, one mother who was living with her partner said: "If we were to marry, I don't think that would be so ideal. [Husbands] want to be in charge and I cannot deal with that" (Edin, 2000, p. 121). Other research supports the idea that differences in what men and women think about the acceptable roles for women are widest among low-income groups (Scanzoni, 1970). African American men in particular report more traditional views about gender roles than do African American women or white men (Blee & Tickamyer, 1995). For mothers who are already supporting themselves, the expectation that they should defer to a husband who may not be contributing to the family financially is simply unacceptable.

A fourth obstacle to marriage was the fear of domestic violence. Although Edin did not ask directly, she was surprised by how often it came up anyway, and far more often with white women than African American women. For these white women, marriage meant the threat of physical abuse, and that is something they were unwilling to accept. When asked if there were advantages to being a single mother, one woman said the advantage was "not living with someone there to abuse you. I'm not scared anymore. I'm scared of my bills and I'm scared of when I get sick, what's going to happen to my kids, but I'm not afraid for my life" (Edin, 2000, p. 126). Researchers are increasingly recognizing that domestic violence may play a large role in the family decisions people make. Sociologist Andrew Cherlin and his colleagues analyzed data from 2,500 welfare families and found that women in this population had high rates of physical abuse in their childhoods, and that those who experienced abuse were the least likely to be married (Cherlin et al., 2004).

You may find it puzzling that these women, who seem to value the institution of marriage, are so accepting of raising children outside of marriage or cohabiting without being married. It is even more puzzling in light of the fact that "these same respondents generally said that one should be married before having children" (Edin, 2000, p. 123). What Edin's interviews revealed, however, was that even though these women believed that marriage before children was ideal, it was not perceived as practical given their situations. They wanted to get married and they wanted children, but whereas marriage was out of their reach, they could have children and, given the numerous models of successful single-parenting they grew up with, they felt confident that they could raise a child alone. Instead of trying to find men to rely on, these women were having their own families and hoping that a life partner would come later.

In sum, high divorce rates and high rates of unmarried births in low-income communities do not seem to be the result of people lacking respect or value for the institution of marriage. Low-income families report exceptionally high respect for marriage. Instead, decisions regarding marriage, families, and relationships seem to be a response to real challenges and obstacles that people face in their lives. People want to get married and to stay married, but many women do not feel that they have the resources to do so. The result appears to be increased tolerance for alternatives to marriage.

Relationship Challenges in Low-Income Communities

By focusing attention on the daily challenges in their lives, interviews with low-income mothers begin to suggest why maintaining successful relationships may be more difficult in low-income communities than in more affluent communities. Low-income relationships form and develop in what may be a fundamentally different context than the one in which more affluent relationships form and develop, and the differences extend far beyond income. On each of the predictors of relationship outcomes we have discussed so far in this book, low-income couples are likely to differ from more affluent couples in ways that reduce their chances of having successful and enduring intimate relationships.

Being poor is associated with a host of other challenges that have a negative impact on relationships. Members of low-income communities are far more likely than those in more affluent communities to experience significant health problems (e.g., Gallo & Matthews, 2003). Because income is strongly associated with level of education, partners in poor couples generally have less formal education than more affluent partners (Fein, 2004). With respect to personal history, they are more likely to have been raised in a single-parent home (McLanahan & Sandefur, 1994) and to have been exposed to physical and sexual abuse during childhood (Cherlin et al., 2004). Perhaps as a consequence, rates of psychopathology, criminal behavior, and substance abuse are all higher in low-income communities than in more affluent communities (Costello et al., 2003; Cutrona et al., 2005). For all these possible reasons, people raised in poor communities are more likely to contend with personal challenges quite apart from maintaining a relationship with another person. Given that their partners are also more likely to be experiencing personal challenges, their relationships start out at a significant disadvantage.

Throughout this chapter, we have been discussing how couples are affected by their environment. For low-income couples, the environment contains more demands than resources. By definition, low-income couples must cope with higher levels of financial strain than more affluent couples. Moreover, low-income neighborhoods generally have more social disorder (e.g., crime, drug use, delinquency), and the residences of low-income families are likely to be more crowded, noisier, and in poorer condition (Evans, 2004). There is some evidence that low-income couples may benefit from extended families and well-developed social and religious networks (e.g., Anderson, 1999; Henly, Danziger, & Offer, 2005; Moore, 2003). However, these networks can be a further drain on couples as well (Cattell, 2001). For example, the working poor spend more time caring for disabled and elderly family members than do more affluent groups (Heymann et al., 2002). Poor working mothers are also twice as likely to have a child with a chronic health condition (Heymann & Earle, 1999). Thus, low-income couples must expend considerable effort simply to survive and care for those who depend on them, all within a context that does not provide much support.

Time is another resource that is scarce for poor couples. As a result of demands outside the home, poor couples usually have less time to spend together. Sociologist Harriet Presser and her colleagues have documented work patterns among poor working families (Presser, 1995; Presser & Cain, 1983). What they found in several studies is that members of low-income couples are more likely than middle- and high-income couples to be forced to work nonstandard hours. In other words, during the evenings and weekends, when middle- and high-income couples are communicating, being intimate, and sharing leisure time, low-income couples are probably at their jobs. Even when poor couples do have time outside of employment, they cannot really choose how to spend that time. Analyses by the National Longitudinal Survey of Youth have shown that working poor families are less likely to have paid sick leave, vacation leave, or flexible work hours (Heymann, 2000). So low-income families are unable to devote time to taking care of their children, attending school meetings, or catching up with each other's lives because they are unable to choose when their free time will be. It is not hard to imagine that these conditions affect the emotional well-being of couples, and that's precisely what the research demonstrates. Presser (2000) has shown that when married women with children work nights, their chances of divorce are three times higher than women who work the same number of hours during the day. When married men with children work nights, their chances of divorce are six times higher. These findings make sense when we stop to consider what makes marriage and intimate relationships fulfilling. All couples need time to interact, to be intimate, to share with each other their feelings. Poor couples don't have this kind of time because they are working nonstandard hours and double-shifts just to keep food on the table. When they do have time to talk, they are likely to have difficult things to discuss when they are together. When low-income married couples file for divorce, they complain about their communication like everyone else (Amato & Previti, 2003), but it may not be communication itself that is at the heart of their problems.

Helping Low-Income Couples

Given the unique challenges that low-income couples face, what kinds of public policies or interventions might be most effective in helping them? The research described here does not point to any simple answers, but it does have implications for the general kinds of programs with the potential for success. First, efforts to improve the lives of low-income couples will be most effective if they acknowledge the real challenges that low-income couples face. This is not always easy to do. Earlier, we described how the governors of four states reacted with shock when they learned that their states had the highest divorce rates in the country. In one of those states, Oklahoma, couples were offered classes in relationship skills. The problem for low-income couples interested in this sort of assistance was that the materials for the classes had been developed for middle-class, college-educated couples. To describe better and worse ways of resolving problems, the initial materials described examples that included fights over who gets to use the home computer and who has to clean the guest bedroom (Boo, 2003). These are issues that seldom come up in the lives of poor couples. Indeed, although hundreds of millions of dollars have been spent on programs that administer skills-based relationship education to low-income couples, the results of two national evaluations that randomly assigned couples to treatment or control conditions indicate that such programs have almost no power to make low-income relationships more stable or more satisfying (Hsueh et al., 2012; Wood et al., 2012).

Second, to the extent that the success of relationships depends upon the general quality of couples' lives, any programs that improve the lives of low-income individuals are likely to benefit their relationships as well. An example from Norway makes this point. In 1999, that country began offering subsidies to families who elected not to use government-run daycare services for their 1- to 3-year-old children, essentially paying couples to stay home with their children. The policy did not mention marriage, nor did it target marriages directly. Nevertheless, analyses of divorce rates in Norway before and after the policy took effect revealed that divorce rates dropped significantly among couples who were eligible for the subsidies (Hardoy & Schøne, 2008). It appears that simply allowing families more time to spend together strengthened their marriages on average. We might imagine that many other policies that do not immediately look like relationship enhancement programs—like offering job training, health care, or a higher minimum wage—may also turn out to be as effective at helping couples as programs that target relationships directly (Johnson, 2012).

MAIN POINTS

>> Maintaining successful intimate relationships appears to be much more difficult in low-income communities compared to more affluent communities, as demonstrated by higher rates of divorce and lower reported relationship satisfaction among poorer couples.

>> The source of these difficulties does not seem to be related to values or attitudes; members of poor communities report more positive attitudes toward marriage and stable families than do members of more affluent communities.

>> Couples who are poor face concrete challenges (e.g., health problems, inflexible work schedules, lack of social support) that increase the demands on their relationship.

Social Networks: The Ties That Bind

Consider all of the things that Romeo and Juliet had going for them. Both were the favored children of wealthy families. Neither had any obvious personality problems. In their short time together, they enjoyed each other's company and communicated beautifully (it helps to have your interactions scripted by Shakespeare). And yet, their romance did not go smoothly. What was the source of their tragic situation? Reading Shakespeare's play suggests that the sad fate of this couple had little to do with the partners and the way they related to each other, and almost everything to do with the complex web of relationships in which they were involved. As we are told in the prologue to the play, the two lovers' families feuded over an old grudge. Fearing their families' disapproval, Romeo and Juliet were forced to keep their relationship a secret, leading to the series of accidents and misunderstandings that ultimately ended in the death of the two lovers.

The tragedy of Romeo and Juliet points out that an important part of the context of any relationship is not physical and concrete but social. An intimate relationship does more than unite two people; it also links their **social networks**—the families, friendships, neighborhoods, clubs, and institutions to which those two individuals are connected (Lee, 1979). Today, when we hear people talking about social networks, they're usually referring to connections maintained online, through Internet services like Facebook, LinkedIn, and Twitter. These online networks are mostly unrelated to the offline networks of people we talk to, face to face, and depend on every day (Pollet, Robert, & Dunbar, 2011). The offline networks are the topic of interest here. In the Verona that Shakespeare described in *Romeo and Juliet*, those networks were strong and diverse, affecting nearly every aspect of life. Romeo, for example, had close ties to his own extended family (including aunts, uncles, and cousins), to his peers, to the local militia, and to his church. Over the last century, in contrast, social networks in the United States have generally become smaller, weaker, and less diverse. For example, as described in the book *Bowling Alone: The Collapse and Revival of American Community* (Putnam, 2000), the last several decades have witnessed Americans interacting far less frequently with their extended families, being less likely to join clubs and sports leagues, and less inclined to invite friends to their homes for dinner. Whereas centuries ago an intimate relationship formed and developed within a dense web of other relationships and affiliations, now there are far fewer strands of that web, with consequences both good and bad for couples (Amato, 2004).

Attributes of Social Networks

Researchers interested in studying how social networks affect people's lives have generally adopted one of two approaches. The first approach was developed in the 1930s by the Viennese psychologist Jacob Moreno, a contemporary of Sigmund Freud. Moreno (1951) wanted to be able to describe patterns of interaction within small groups, and to do so he developed **sociometry**, a method of graphically displaying the strength and number of relationships within a collection of individuals. In its simplest form, a sociometric map requires asking all members of a group about the quality and quantity of their interactions with every other member of the group. By mapping out the relationships among group members, this approach has been used to identify more or less influential people within a group, and highlight sources of potential communication breakdown (Hoffman et al., 1992; Widmer & LaFarga, 2000). Creating these maps, however, is extremely time-consuming and labor-intensive, requiring access to every individual in the network, as shown in FIGURE 11.14. As a consequence, most relationship scientists have used a second approach, which is simply to ask partners about their perceptions of the social networks that surround them.

Research adopting this second approach has generally focused on three attributes of social networks (Sprecher et al., 2002). The first is the size of the network—the number of separate people to whom an individual is connected. Some researchers distinguish between the **psychological network**, those who play important roles, and the **interactive network**, those with whom a person interacts regularly (Milardo & Allan, 1997; Surra, 1988). Psychological and interactive networks are likely to overlap somewhat but not completely, in that there are some people with whom we interact regularly, but who do not play significant roles in our lives (e.g., the mail carrier), and others with whom we may interact far less often, but who we perceive as more relevant (e.g., a good friend who lives in another state). Regardless of which kind of network has been studied, research consistently suggests that couples with more network connections do better than those with fewer (Widmer, Kellerhals, & Levy, 2004). For many couples, the strongest ties outside of the dyad are with each partner's friends and family of origin. When those ties are close, marriages are happier and less likely to end in divorce (Timmer & Veroff, 2000; Timmer, Veroff, & Hatchett, 1996). Very early research on marriage showed that couples who were members of social organizations and clubs (e.g., country clubs, sports leagues) experienced better outcomes than couples who were less involved in community activities (Burgess & Cottrell, 1939; Burgess, Wallin, & Shultz, 1954). In recent decades, with membership

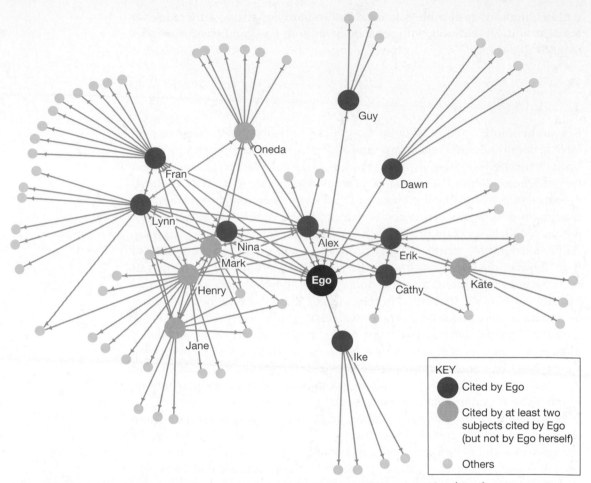

FIGURE 11.14 A sociometric map. To represent the social network of a 55-year-old woman ("Ego"), researchers had her name important members of her family and asked her to describe how they influence one another. Then each one was interviewed and asked the same question. Combining all answers, the researchers created a sociometric map showing the relative extent of influence each relative had on Ego and on each other. Arrows indicate which people are able to change the minds of others, based on their level of influence. (Source: Widmer & La Farga, 2000.)

in clubs and organizations on the decline, attending religious services represents one of the few remaining community activities that families engage in, and indeed couples who attend religious services regularly experience more stable marriages than those who do not (Call & Heaton, 1997).

The second attribute is **network density**, the degree to which members of an individual's social network are themselves connected to other people within the network. The density of a network is independent of its size. For example, one person might feel connected to 100 people in a religious congregation, all of whom know and interact with each other (a high-density network), while another person might feel connected to 100 different people, none of whom know each other (a low-density network). Although the role of network density has not been studied extensively in regard to intimate relationships, this example suggests that a high-density network is also a fragile network, in that a problem with one relationship in the network is more likely to affect relationships with all the other members of the network through their relationships with each other. In contrast, a low-density network of multiple smaller groups may allow individuals to remain connected to most of their network, even if their relationships in one group come to an end.

The third attribute of particular interest to research on intimate relationships is **network overlap**, the extent to which partners in a relationship consider the same individuals to be part of their personal networks. In a system with the maximum degree of overlap, both members of a couple feel connected to the same degree with all of the same people. They love each other's families, they have all the same friends, and they draw on the same sources of social support. In a system with the minimum degree of overlap, each partner in a couple is connected to an entirely separate social network, with no common members and no contact between each partner's networks. A number of studies have examined the role of network overlap in predicting relationship outcomes, and all have found that when couples know each other's friends and share associates, they are happier and more likely to stay together over time than when they do not (Kearns & Leonard, 2004; Kim & Stiff, 1991; Parks, Stan, & Eggert, 1983). This seems to be true cross-culturally as well. An anthropological analysis of 62 societies around the world found that divorce rates tend to be lower in communities where people marry within their own social networks than in communities where people marry outside of their networks (Ackerman, 1963).

How Social Networks Benefit Relationships

If two people care for each other, why should it make a difference whether they are surrounded by friends and family or lost on a desert island? There are a number of very concrete ways in which strong connections to people outside the relationship can be beneficial.

One benefit may seem obvious, but it remains worth pointing out: If you had no social networks, you would never meet anyone with whom to form a relationship. Among college students, most people report that they knew a close friend of their current romantic partner before they ever met their current partner, highlighting the role of overlapping friendship networks in providing the context for new relationships (Parks & Eggert, 1991). Moreover, the sorts of people that make up a person's social network determine the kinds of partners available to that person. So, for example, people whose social networks are ethnically diverse are more likely to have experienced an interracial relationship than those whose social networks are more homogeneous (Clark-Ibáñez & Felmlee, 2004) (FIGURE 11.15).

FIGURE 11.15 A diverse social network. The types of people you know determine the types of people with whom you will probably form intimate relationships. Those with a diverse social network tend to have relationships with a variety of different types of people.

Close ties with people outside the relationship can also serve as an important resource for couples, one that is comparable to the financial and material resources discussed earlier. Economists coined the term **social capital** to refer to the benefits individuals derive from their relationships with others. Some of these benefits are tangible: The people around you can provide support and help out when you are in need. Some of these benefits are intangible: Being surrounded by people who know you means it is easier to make yourself understood and make your needs known. For all couples, it helps to have a supportive network to turn to, especially during times of stress or crisis (Julien & Markman, 1991; Veroff, Douvan, & Hatchett, 1995). For low-income couples, lacking in other resources, the support of a strong social network can be the difference between successful coping and a life of unending struggle (Henly et al., 2005).

Shared networks can also provide incentives for staying in relationships and barriers to leaving them. The way two partners are treated by members of their social networks can have a significant effect on how the partners feel about their relationship. Imagine, for example, how you might treat a friend who has just entered into a new romantic relationship. If you like the new partner, perhaps you will be more likely to ask your friend about him or her. You might encourage your friend to include the new partner the next time you get together. You might go out of your way to treat the new partner well and make him or her comfortable when you are hanging out with the new couple. Research on college students suggests that parents do just these sorts of things when they approve of their children's new relationships (Leslie, Huston, & Johnson, 1986). All of this makes being in the relationship more pleasant for both partners and provides an environment that makes it easier for them to allow intimacy and commitment to develop. This may be why a number of studies have found that, when they are surrounded by a social network that approves of the relationship, partners are more satisfied (Bryant & Conger, 1999; Parks et al., 1983), more committed (Lehmiller & Agnew, 2006), and less likely to break up over time (Lehmiller & Agnew, 2007; Sprecher & Felmlee, 1992).

There is a drawback to social approval of a relationship, however. When partners in an intimate relationship are very closely tied to each other's social networks, then breaking up with the partner may involve severing those ties, thereby increasing the cost of leaving the relationship. With respect to a socially valued relationship like marriage, the social network can raise barriers to leaving the relationship even if neither partner wishes to remain. Indeed, for most of human history, the fear of disapproval from the social network has kept many couples together in severely distressed or abusive relationships, prolonging suffering that would have ended had partners felt able to leave without being stigmatized.

How Social Networks Can Challenge Relationships

Although there are several ways that strong social networks can benefit intimate relationships and keep partners together, the tragedy of Romeo and Juliet reminds us that couples obtain these benefits only when two specific criteria are met: (1) the social networks of the two partners overlap, and (2) the social networks of both partners approve of and support the relationship. The problem for Romeo and Juliet was that they were powerfully tied to their social networks, and yet neither of those criteria was true. Research sides with Shakespeare on this point: When partners have independent networks or networks that fail to support their relationship, close ties with others do far more harm to the relationship than good.

One way that social networks present a challenge is by providing alternatives to current partners. The key issue is the extent to which each partner's network provides **substitutability**, the degree to which different members of a social network fulfill the same needs for a person (Marsiglio & Scanzoni, 1995). For example, in dating relationships, partners who feel closer to their own best friends are more likely to end their relationships (Felmlee, 2001). Why? Because a best friend can provide companionship and emotional support similar to that provided by a romantic partner, reducing dependence on the relationship to meet those needs. If the partners' networks overlap, substitutability is less of a threat, because members of the network are likely to consider both partners as part of a couple. However, when each partner maintains separate networks, then members of those networks can represent alternative sources of companionship.

Demographic research has tested these ideas by drawing from census data to quantify the effects of social networks on divorce. In neighborhoods with high numbers of eligible singles, where geographic mobility is high (and couples do not have ties to the community), and where women are more likely to be employed outside the home (and tend to develop independent friendship networks), divorce rates are significantly higher (South & Lloyd, 1995; South, Trent, & Shen, 2001).

Social networks can also be a challenge for an intimate relationship more directly (FIGURE 11.16). Earlier, we discussed all the ways that friends and family can make a relationship more rewarding if they approve of the relationship. When friends and family do not approve of the relationship, however, they can make life for a couple pretty miserable in ways that range from subtle to obvious. When parents disapprove of their child's relationship, they can simply ignore the partner, treat the partner poorly, or refuse to recognize the

"I invited a few friends over who think you should see a psychiatrist."

FIGURE 11.16 The downside of friendships. People with more friends generally have better intimate relationships, but not always. When the friendship networks of each partner do not overlap much, interference from friends outside the relationship can exacerbate problems within the relationship.

couple as being in a relationship (Leslie et al., 1986). Just as friends are a frequent route through which people meet their relationship partners, friends who disapprove of the relationship can take steps to introduce alternative partners. When partners in a relationship are in conflict, they often turn to their friends and family for support (Julien & Markman, 1991). This is a good thing for the partners, but to the extent that each partner's friends validate and strengthen that person's side of the argument, the involvement of friends outside the relationship can intensify problems within (Julien et al., 1994). Finally, even if a relationship is intact and satisfying, the friends and family of each partner compete for a finite amount of time. Although relationships are more satisfying and stable when couples are connected to strong social networks, a relationship can suffer when partners spend too much time with friends or relatives (Blood, 1969; Felmlee, 2001).

> **MAIN POINTS**

>> Intimate relationships are stronger when the couple has close ties to their social networks, and when the networks of each partner overlap (i.e., when each partner feels close with the friends and family of the other partner).

>> When the social network of a couple approves of the relationship, network members can make life easier for the couple by treating both partners as a unit and supporting the couple during difficult times.

>> When the social network disapproves of the relationship, network members can help pull couples apart by providing alternative partners, exacerbating conflicts, or competing for time that partners might spend together.

CONCLUSION

When the New York City firefighter in the chapter opening tried to understand the changes in his relationships after September 11, 2001, he focused exclusively on characteristics of the relationships themselves. When he was unhappy in his marriage, he blamed his feelings on failings in his wife. More satisfied in his new relationship, he attributed those feelings to the superior qualities of his new partner. When we consider our own relationship, or those of others, it is easy to do the same, imagining that the success or failure of these relationships lies entirely in the hands of the partners and how they treat each other. Indeed, partners typically do rely on such information to predict their future, and this may account for the optimism of people who have fallen in love. If we know ourself and we know our partner, and if the relationship is a good one, why should anything change?

The problem with this reasoning is that no relationship takes place in a vacuum. On the contrary, the environment of a couple can play a significant role in supporting the relationship or challenging it. Some of these effects can be predicted, but because so much of the environments lay beyond anyone's control, many cannot. Recognizing the effects of context on intimate relationships underscores the limit of our ability to predict the future of any relationship.

Yet it would be wrong to suggest that we are entirely victims of a relationship's context. Although it is clear that aspects of the environment affect couples, sometimes without their knowledge, it is also true that environments themselves can be changed. Sometimes couples play a role in determining their environments, by deciding whether to move or to put down roots or whether to take a job or continue their education. Sometimes the context is changed by policy makers passing new laws or by businesses opening or closing. Acknowledging how the context can change and be changed raises the question of how best to intervene to make relationships stronger. What are the appropriate targets: aspects of the couple or aspects of their environment? These are some of the questions we will take up next.

12
Improving Relationships

Help Wanted:
National Czar on Intimate Relationships

Imagine you have risen to the heights of power and are a member of the cabinet of the president of the United States, as the new Secretary of Health and Human Services. Your job description—to protect and promote the welfare of the American people, especially those least able to help themselves—encompasses a broad range of issues.

You were appointed to this position by a president who campaigned hard on the importance of two-parent families; the significance of stable intimate relationships to the social fabric of the country; and the enduring value of nurturing the development of happy, healthy children (**FIGURE 12.1**). First and foremost, you know you are responsible for realizing the president's vision.

You have done your homework in your first several months on the job: You commissioned surveys, read dozens of reports, reviewed all the leading programs and therapies, and organized conferences with well-chosen experts. Tomorrow you will brief the president on how you propose to put his plan into action. You drift off to sleep as you

run confidently through your 5-point plan, only to awaken several hours later with nagging doubts about each one:

1. *Abolish no-fault divorce laws to make it harder to divorce, and impose a 6-month waiting period before a divorce is issued so that couples can seek therapy and reconsider.* This is sure to lower divorce rates. But what if it keeps adults and children in miserable relationships? Exposure to conflict conflict is bad for kids; this will just set some of them up to perpetuate the problem in future generations, right? What if people simply abandon their partners and children, without divorcing?

FIGURE 12.1 Promoting healthy relationships. In the United States, the Secretary of Health and Human Services oversees a wide range of institutes and resources that affect couples and families. In 2014, the Secretary of Health and Human Services was Kathleen Sebelius, shown here with President Barack Obama.

2. *Make relationship education mandatory for adolescents in school.* Won't relationship education detract from what kids learn in other areas? Can we really teach teenagers things now that will help them have a better marriage? And if we promote abstinence, kids might tune out and teachers might resist. If we promote safe sex, parents will be up in arms, and this is tacit approval for teenagers to have sex, right?

3. *Require all couples to learn a specific set of skills before getting married.* Many people will like this idea. But if we make it harder to get married, *fewer* people will do it, right? Is that okay, or does it mean more kids born to unmarried parents? Even if this went forward, how would we implement such a program? And doesn't this recommendation assume that poor relationship skills are the reason people have bad marriages? Is this a fair assumption? What if bad marriages are caused by low wages, poverty, poor health care, stressful working conditions, and inadequate child care?

4. *Encourage workplace reform, so people will have higher wages, safer working conditions, access to good childcare, and better health care for themselves and their children.* Do I really want to meddle with private businesses? Would this lead to businesses offering fewer jobs? Is there evidence that general changes in the workplace have specific payoffs for couples and families of the kind I want to demonstrate? Won't I have to extend these benefits to all people, even if they don't have kids? How expensive will this be?

5. *Require insurance companies to help pay the costs for couple and family therapy.* Sounds good, but employers and couples will have to pay more for insurance under this plan. Besides, do people go to professionals for couples therapy in large enough numbers for this proposal to make a difference in the divorce rate? Does couple therapy really work?

Your alarm clock reads 3:57 A.M. Your meeting is in 6 hours. You turn on your laptop, pull up the file with your presentation in it, and wonder what to propose and how the president will respond.

QUESTIONS

Interventions usually refer to specific kinds of educational and therapeutic experiences individuals and couples can have that might enhance their communication, facilitate mutual understanding, and generally improve their relationships. However, interventions can also involve harnessing broader social forces and institutions with the goal of bringing about stronger relationships on a much larger scale. Interventions can involve changing laws, working to create healthier environments in which couples and families can flourish, developing better educational and therapeutic programs, and making those programs widely available.

As you can see, simple solutions to problems involving relationships might be difficult to come by. Further, a range of solutions operating at different levels may be needed to help people realize the potential of their intimate partnerships. In this chapter we address a host of questions that would help you, as the hypothetical Secretary of Health and Human Services, grapple with these solutions as you set about to revise your 5-point plan. Given all the complex forces operating on and within re- lationships, what hope do we have for improving relationships and preventing adverse outcomes? Do we know enough about relationships to intervene? What is the state of the art in intervention programs?

Experiencing Distress and Seeking Help

At several points in this book we have looked at some of the interpersonal characteristics and probable signs of relationship distress. Now we'll examine how distressed partners experience their troubled relationships. The follow- ing excerpts from interviews conducted with 50 highly disaffected spouses help show what happens as relationships unravel (Kayser, 1993).

A 31-year-old female, married 3 years:

> *He wasn't intimate. . . . That is something I need—I need to have some- one I can share time with—all of me—my thoughts, feelings, everything. He just stopped doing that, and the whole marriage got mechanical. He wanted his physical needs to be met—feeding him, sex, take care of him and wash his clothes—just all of that. And there was no more romance, and I think that has to be there—at least a little bit. (p. 100)*

A 30-year-old male, married 7 years:

> *Do I really love her? I know I care for her; she was a very good friend of mine. I considered her on that basis, but I really questioned in my mind if I really loved her. She wasn't what I wanted, but does everybody get exactly what they want in a relationship? I've got a lot of good things here. Basi- cally [I'm] just trying to weigh things out. (p. 54)*

A 34-year-old female, married 12 years:

> *It's such a gradual thing. I don't think I ever wanted to admit that I wasn't in love with him. . . . But romantically I didn't want him to touch me, and we fought continuously. And I preferred not to be around him unless we were with a group of people, and then we couldn't fight. I think all of a sudden I realized, "I'm just not in love with this man." (p. 51)*

Relationship difficulties like these are a leading reason people seek any kind of professional assistance (Swindle et al., 2000). Professional help comes in many forms, and people often turn to familiar channels (a religious adviser, for example, or a family physician or attorney) and not necessarily to an agency or individual with expertise in treating distressed relationships (Veroff, Kulka, & Douvan, 1981). There is also evidence that couples often wait a long time to seek out any kind of help for a struggling relationship. When asked at the start of treatment about when problems began in their re- lationship, couples commonly note that several years have passed since they first realized something was wrong (Doss & Christensen, 2004). Why might this be? Although relationship distress can be precipitated by specific events, as in the first outburst of physical aggression or the discovery of one partner's infidelity, more typically the onset of distress is gradual, with no obvious starting point and thus no urgent need to seek help. However, as a relationship spirals downward, often a specific event will occur (the death of a parent, a financial crisis, a severe illness, discovery of an affair) that can outstrip a couple's ability to cope, sending them seeking help for their relationship.

For practitioners, the fact that couples who seek their services are commonly entrenched in their problems, and close to separating, means that relationship therapy is an uphill struggle (**FIGURE 12.2**). Therapists must contend

"Brad, we've got to talk."

FIGURE 12.2 Sink or swim. Couples therapy can be difficult because partners might wait a long time before seeking help, and because they might seek help during a time of crisis.

with the long-standing maladaptive strategies that spouses have used to cope with their distress, such as arguing unproductively, blaming each other, avoiding sexual intimacy or otherwise withdrawing, working more, drinking or taking drugs, staying away from home, and involving children in their disputes. The therapist might have to help manage an acute crisis that precipitated the decision to seek help, as well as uncover the factors that caused the relationship difficulties in the first place. **TABLE 12.1** presents the 10 most common, the 10 most damaging, and the 10 most difficult problem areas that couples therapists report encountering in their practices (Whisman, Dixon, & Johnson, 1997). Five of the problems (printed in boldface in the table) appear on all three lists and provide a broad outline of the challenges that couples therapists face: deficits in communication, power struggles, unrealistic expectations of the relationship or partner, lack of loving feelings, and serious individual problems. Practitioners use theoretical models to organize these indicators and mobilize their efforts to treat relationship problems.

Couples Therapy:
Interventions for Distressed Relationships

Where does one begin in developing an intervention for rescuing couples from a state of distress and enabling them to maintain a stronger relationship in the future? The very complexity of relationships leaves open many possibilities. What is needed are theories that describe principles thought to govern relationship distress, provide leverage for altering these governing forces,

TABLE 12.1 **Relationship Problems Seen by Couples Therapists**

Most Common Problems[a]	Most Damaging Problems	Most Difficult Problems to Treat
Communication[b] (87%)	Physical abuse	Lack of loving feelings
Power struggles (62%)	Extramarital affairs	Alcoholism
Unrealistic expectations (50%)	Alcoholism	Extramarital affairs
Sex (47%)	Lack of loving feelings	Power struggles
Solving problems (47%)	Incest	Serious individual problems
Demonstrations of affection (45%)	Communication	Physical abuse
Money management and finances (43%)	Power struggles	Communication
Lack of loving feelings (40%)	Unrealistic expectations	Unrealistic expectations
Children (38%)	Serious individual problems	Other addictive behaviors
Serious individual problems (38%)	Other addictive behaviors	Incest

[a]Therapists' reports of the proportion of treated couples identifying the problem in the past year are shown in parentheses. Thus, for example, on average, 87% of treated couples identified problems with communication, as estimated by the therapists.

[b]The five problems appearing in all three lists are shown in boldface.

Source: Adapted from Whisman, Dixon, & Johnson, 1997.

and specify the steps and techniques for working with couples to bring about change in their relationship. Most theories of therapeutic intervention are a combination of established principles of human behavior (drawn, for example, from theories of social development, learning, emotion, and cognition); findings from basic and applied research on relationships, such as those you have read about in this book; and, typically, a healthy dose of clinical experience regarding what seems to work in strengthening couples' relationships (FIGURE 12.3).

In this section, we discuss the leading theoretical models that have been developed in the service of treating distressed relationships. Different models of couples therapy focus on modifying different aspects of relationships according to which of these aspects they identify as the main cause of distress. Four main types of models, summarized in TABLE 12.2, are outlined in this section. In practice, most professionals draw from a range of perspectives when conducting couples therapy, and these four sets of models form the basis for much of their work.

Psychodynamic Models

Psychodynamic models of couples therapy emphasize how a person's very early experiences with a parent result in unconscious psychological processes that, in adulthood, can form the basis for misunderstanding between partners, uncontrolled negative emotions, and ineffective attempts at intimacy. The most prominent version of psychodynamic treatment for couples is known as **object relations couples therapy** (e.g., Dicks, 1967; Sager 1976; Skynner, 1976; see Scharff & Bagnini, 2002, for an overview). In this context, the word "object" refers to an internal representation a person forms of someone who has taken care of him or her, often called a *caregiver,* and it is this representation that guides and influences the nature of the relationships that person has throughout his or her lifetime. You would be correct to note that this emphasis on caregiving and internal representations shares features with attachment theory (see Chapters 3 and 6). Recall in particular that these internal representations are referred to as working models in attachment theory. Regardless of their label, the point is that who we are as an intimate partner is guided by how we have been treated in important relationships in our past, particularly when we were very young.

FIGURE 12.3 On neutral ground. Couples therapy usually involves a weekly meeting with one therapist for several months to help the couple achieve a new understanding of each other and of their relationship.

This perspective begins with the idea that parents and other caregivers will vary in their ability to meet the basic needs of the developing infant, and that even the best caregivers will leave the infant frustrated and disappointed at times. Hunger is not satisfied immediately, for example, and discomforts are not always soothed. These negative experiences are registered by the infant,

TABLE 12.2 **Common Models of Couples Therapy**

Model	Primary Emphasis
Psychodynamic	The role of unconscious forces in how partners perceive each other's behaviors
Systems	The rules or principles that govern and restrict the exchange of behaviors
Behavioral	The rewarding and punishing properties of exchanged behaviors and their associated thoughts
Emotion	The manner in which different emotional expressions can inhibit and promote intimate bonds

"I'm not quite ready yet. Why don't you come in and make us a drink while I figure out how not to project all my hopes and fears onto you?"

FIGURE 12.4 Turning off the projector. Object relations couples therapy emphasizes how unconscious thoughts and feelings projected by one partner onto the other can interfere with the ability to have an authentic intimate connection.

and because the experiences are painful, the infant copes with them by *repressing* them, banishing them to the realm of the unconscious. Repressed material has strong emotions associated with it, including anger and rage for the slights that have been suffered, but these emotions also include the feelings of longing and craving for a more satisfying connection to the caregiver.

Fast-forward ahead to adulthood. How do these forces operate in relationships? In our daily exchanges, aspects of who we are and the early experiences we've had, especially aspects of the self that have been repressed and split off from consciousness, are projected onto others. Here, **projection** refers to an unconscious tendency for a person to deny his or her own flaws, locating them instead externally—including attributing them to the partner. For example, an unconscious and unresolved need for closeness might lead us to select a partner who we believe will satisfy this need for us, or a partner who will accept those unfavorable parts of ourself that we have repressed. (**FIGURE 12.4**). Once in a relationship we might dwell on some inadequacy or flaw in our partner; this is understood to be a projection motivated by the feelings associated with the inadequate care we received as an infant. Or the feelings of anger that we experience are erroneously assumed to be emanating from the partner, which in turn justifies our own feelings of anger.

You may have had this experience: You accuse your partner of being grouchy, only to have your partner respond *"I* am not grouchy, *you* are grouchy, but now you are *making me* grouchy!"* And later you might realize your partner is right, that something outside the relationship did make you grouchy, and that your own feelings of grouchiness *projected onto your partner* initiated the unpleasant interaction. In this sense you are not responding to your partner as he or she truly is; instead you are responding to your partner as you make him or her out to be. Conversely, on the receiving end of such a sequence, you might wonder why you feel tense or moody suddenly, only to realize that you are picking up signals about your partner's emotional state that are leading you to feel this way.

How the partner responds to these projections, a process known as **projective identification**, turns out to be pivotal to the well-being of the relationship (Scharf & Bagnini, 2002). Let's say Cathy projects some negative emotion onto Joe. Joe can then identify with that projection—that is, Joe can acknowledge Cathy's distress and show he is not threatened by it, in much the same way that a mother can absorb a child's distress. The term used to describe what Joe is doing when he holds onto Cathy's distress is **containment**; he is taking a part of Cathy's unpleasant experience of herself and reducing the intensity of that experience. An object relations therapist would say that Joe is "detoxifying" the experience, or removing its most disturbing elements, by containing it for Cathy. This is a good deal for Cathy: now, through **introjective identification**, she can take back her original projection in a better, detoxified form, and she can merge this new experience into the image she holds of herself. The mother-child relationship is instructive again, in the sense that a distressed child first *projects* those feelings onto the mother, the mother *identifies* with this projection and *contains* it for the child, enabling the child to take back that experience and incorporate it— through *introjection*—into his or her identity.

Thus, according to this view, to the extent that partners can identify with, contain, and detoxify the needs and feelings they are expressing, then relationships have the power to enable individuals to become more mature and well adjusted. The partners are really interacting with each other in an authentic way, rather than through the fog of the angry and repressed feelings from earlier relationships. Of course, these processes can also go awry and become destructive, which leads us to consider how the psychodynamic therapist then intervenes.

The primary aim of a couples therapist operating from the object relations perspective is to weaken the harmful effects that projection, projective identification, and introjective identification have on the relationship, in part by improving the way in which partners contain each other's projections. That all sounds terribly complex, so let's take a simple example. When Nancy speaks to Joe and thereby *projects* certain needs, emotions, and experiences on him, the therapist's task is to help Joe *identify with* these projections. More than this, the therapist would encourage Joe to respond to Nancy's expressed needs and emotions in a way that is affected not by his own unresolved feelings from past relationships, but by his understanding of Nancy and what will benefit her. Nancy, for her part, must work to accept rather than reject what Joe offers in response to what she has said. Nancy eventually realizes that Joe is not merely a convenient screen on which she can project her repressed feelings and unresolved experiences from childhood. He is instead a separate individual who merits love and affection because of who he is rather than who she needs him to be, and because he enables her to develop as an individual who is less bound by her unresolved early experiences. (In the same way that Joe helps Nancy gain a deeper appreciation of herself, so, too, does Nancy identify with and contain Joe's projections so that he understands himself better as well.) As Nancy and Joe help each other differentiate between the issues that each brings to the relationship from early childhood and those from the relationship itself, both partners achieve a greater capacity for experiencing the love of the partner and for expressing love toward the partner.

By identifying the ways partners bring unresolved early experiences into their interactions, object relations therapists try to help partners recognize

how those experiences cloud their abilities to provide a nurturing environment. They also learn how they can free themselves from these constraints in
order to have a healthy, mature relationship.

One interesting implication of the object relations approach is that treatment can be viewed as successful even if the relationship ends. As the two
partners develop new identities for themselves, one or both may find that
the relationship was initiated under false (but newly clarified) pretenses, that
one person is more open to changing than the other, or that their experiences
of insight and independence leave them seeking either no relationship or a
relationship with a different person.

Systems Models

Whereas psychodynamic models of couples therapy locate the source of relationship functioning in early caregiving experiences, **systems models** down-
play these individual experiences and emphasize instead repetitive patterns
of partner interaction and the typically unspoken rules and beliefs that govern them. A systems perspective suggests that problems arise between people
not because of any deficiencies or pathologies in the partners, but because the
recurring patterns of behaviors in the relationship are too rigid or are ineffective for meeting new demands confronting the pair (Haley, 1963; Madanes,
1983; Minuchin, 1974; Watzlawick, Weakland, & Fisch, 1974). A robbery in
the neighborhood, for example, might prevent a partner from taking a nightly
walk to relieve stress, which is instead directed at the partner. Or a change
in a partner's work hours leads to a change in sleeping habits and in turn decreases opportunities for sexual interaction for the couple, thereby disrupting the existing balance of intimacy and creating a new source of tension.

Systems models recognize that couples fall into regular patterns of interaction when they deal with various stressors. For example, when a new
challenge arises, Partner A might express feelings and concerns about the
problem, while Partner B might offer support, solutions, or a logical analysis
of the problem. These patterns and the unstated rules that produce them will
be effective under some circumstances but not others. For example, Partner
B's parent might have an incapacitating illness, forcing Partner A into the
unfamiliar supportive role and Partner B into the foreign "feeling" role, highlighting the possibility that changing the basic pattern of "A feels, B analyzes"
will enable the system to thrive rather than collapse. Much like the benefits
of psychological androgyny (see Chapter 4), therapeutic change might mean
that *both* partners recognize their capacity to express concerns *and* to provide reassurance at different times, as the situation dictates.

From this perspective, key tasks for intervention include interrupting the
repetitive pattern of harmful interaction, helping partners see that the problems they are experiencing stem from the system of unstated rules governing
their relationship rather than flaws in themselves, and inducing the partners

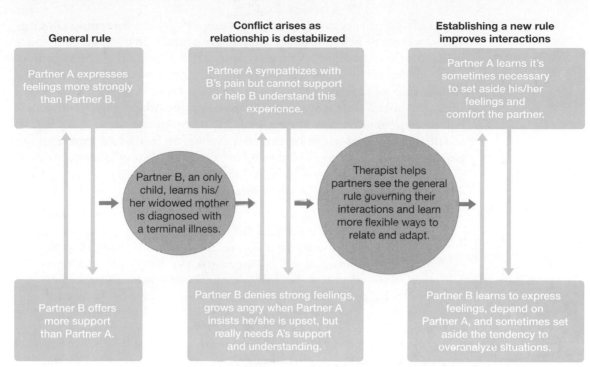

General rule	Conflict arises as relationship is destabilized	Establishing a new rule improves interactions

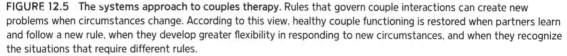

FIGURE 12.5 **The systems approach to couples therapy.** Rules that govern couple interactions can create new problems when circumstances change. According to this view, healthy couple functioning is restored when partners learn and follow a new rule, when they develop greater flexibility in responding to new circumstances, and when they recognize the situations that require different rules.

to interact under new rules, typically by mobilizing underused strengths and untapped resources available to them. In the earlier example, this might involve encouraging Partner A to develop a more analytic perspective and encouraging Partner B to focus more on his or her emotions (**FIGURE 12.5**).

Unlike psychodynamic models of couples therapy, insight about why partners engage in repetitive, counterproductive patterns is insufficient for bringing about constructive changes from a systems perspective. Systems-oriented interventions are designed to make the unspoken rules of a relationship explicit, to help the couple establish new rules that allow both partners greater flexibility and range in their behavior (Lederer & Jackson, 1968). One important set of therapeutic techniques involves helping couples redefine their problems, so that they bypass their usual patterns of behavior. Thus, the therapist might **relabel** a specific behavior: "Joe, now that Ellen is working more, can you see how your feelings of jealousy might be a sign that you are worried about her?" The therapist can **reframe** the problem so it can be understood in a more positive and productive light: "You both seem concerned that having sex less often means your relationship is not as strong as it once was, and that you are drifting apart. But this might just be a temporary stage you happen to be going through, and it might actually be a signal that you are ready to 'drift together' more on an emotional level. Without having sex more often, can you think of things you might try together that might make your relationship more enjoyable?" One of the advantages of all forms of couples therapy is that a third party, the therapist, can provide a couple with a new and more productive way of interpreting their circumstances.

Other techniques are used to make explicit the rules that contribute to counterproductive patterns of interaction. For example, in the following case, adapted from psychologist Thomas Todd (1986, pp. 81–82), a husband and wife married for 35 years sought marital counseling:

> *The husband had been forced to retire at age 62 after a corporate takeover, and although this was a difficult and abrupt transition in several ways, both partners were looking forward to realizing their dream of going into the antiques business together. The dream soon turned into a nightmare, however, because the couple bickered incessantly over which antiques shows they should go to, which antiques to bring to each show, how to arrange their display, and so on. Arguments erupted in other areas of the relationship as well, leading the couple to doubt the future of their marriage, even to the point at which they wondered whether they had not really loved each other all along and whether they had simply been too busy with work earlier in their marriage to realize how much they hated one another. An interview revealed numerous enjoyable times together, many pleasant vacations, and a great deal of mutual support, suggesting that their current arguments were a response to the transition they were making to retirement. Building on a strategy that the couple used very effectively to manage their finances, the therapist instructed the couple to divide up the scheduled antiques shows between them; the "off-duty" partner was allowed to attend the shows only as a helper and was not allowed to spend too much time at the show. Instituting this rule was easy and effective, and the couple themselves went on to use a similar rule to work out problems in other areas of their relationship (e.g., spending time alone while both were present in the house).*

The original rule that governed this repetitive exchange was made explicit—"Because we are partners in our marriage and in this business, we are both in charge at all times"—and a new rule was introduced that built on existing strengths in the relationship: "We are both in charge but at different times, and we defer to the person who is in charge." As a result, the behaviors exchanged under the new rules were experienced as positive and rewarding, and the original problem was alleviated. We do not know how the therapist reframed the problem for this couple to facilitate the changes, but we can imagine they were told it was wonderful that they were both so passionately and deeply committed to making their new joint venture work, and that perhaps with a few small changes in how they each channeled their passion into the business, they could achieve their dreams more readily.

Behavioral Models

As the divorce rate rose during the 1960s, there was an increased demand for couples therapies and decreased stigma associated with seeking help for personal and interpersonal problems. Couples sought the assistance of psychodynamic and systems-oriented practitioners, but these two perspectives suffered from a significant limitation: Their basic concepts—projective identification, for example, or the unstated rules that governed the display of couples' distressing interactions—were notoriously difficult to measure and study directly. Growing need for treatment and for evidence that treatments really worked prompted some scholars to reject approaches to couples therapy that emphasized abstract concepts and to embrace aspects of couple relationships that could be observed directly and reliably. This approach led to **behavioral models** of couples therapy.

Social learning theory provides a useful foundation for this new and more rigorous approach to treating distressed couples (see Chapters 3 and 8). Applied to intimate relationships, the social learning view holds that distress between partners arises because they are insufficiently rewarding toward each other, and because they engage in behaviors that serve to magnify, rather than contain or resolve, their differing goals and desires. A key point in this approach is that behaviors are shaped and maintained by their consequences in the natural environment, and that the most salient and potent consequences in the natural environment are delivered typically by our intimate partner.

In the classic work that outlined the behavioral perspective on marriage, clinical psychologists Neil Jacobson and Gayla Margolin (1979) theorized that as we engage in and reward negative behaviors and neglect or punish positive behaviors, the quality of our communication deteriorates. As this happens, our judgments of how happy we are with the relationship also decline. BOX 12.1 illustrates how this type of miscommunication can happen in common daily exhanges.

Conceptualizing partners' exchanged behaviors in terms of their rewarding and punishing properties would prove to be revolutionary. For the first time, scholars had testable hypotheses about why relationships deteriorated, solid targets for measurement (i.e., the rewarding and costly aspects of couple communication itself), and specific ideas for what had to be changed in order for a relationship to improve.

BEHAVIORAL COUPLES THERAPY. The main form of couples therapy, known as **behavioral couples therapy**, incorporates the principles of social learning theory. This approach has evolved over the past few decades, thanks to a wealth of experience in delivering this form of couples therapy and a wealth of evidence on whether it really helps.

In contrast to psychodynamic and systems models, behavioral couples therapy does not view the behaviors exchanged by partners as a sign of some other hidden problem. Rather, it is the dysfunctional behaviors themselves

BOX 12.1 SPOTLIGHT ON . . .

How Partners Reward and Punish Each Other

Chris asks Keith to wash the dishes but Keith settles in to watch his favorite TV show instead, Chris could either drop the original request to wash the dishes or repeat and perhaps strengthen that request. If Chris drops the request, Keith's inaction has been rewarded. An aversive situation—having to listen to the partner nagging—has now passed, and Keith will be more inclined to ignore Chris when similar situations arise in the future. After all there are real benefits and few costs to doing so. This is a good deal for Keith, but Chris might grow to resent Keith's failure to contribute to the household chores.

There are two kinds of reinforcement. The removal of an aversive stimulus is called **negative reinforcement**. **Positive reinforcement** is the introduction of a positive consequence following some behavior. For example, if Keith turned off the TV, and Chris said "Thanks, do you want me to record that show for you next week, so you can watch it before you go to bed?" the chance of Keith turning off the TV would presumably increase in the future.

Suppose Keith continues to watch TV but Chris doesn't let him off the hook. Chris voices the original request in even stronger terms: "Look, I cooked dinner for you, and the very least you can do is clean up the kitchen!" Keith complies. Now Chris has been rewarded; the escalated request (but not the less-intense original request) produced the desired response. Chris, having been rewarded, might be more vigilant and vociferous in the future when Keith leaves the kitchen after dinner, which could lead to further conflicts. The next time Chris cooks dinner he might say, "Now don't go plopping yourself in front of the TV, you've got dishes to do!" and you can imagine how Keith would respond to Chris's assumption that he will not help.

By getting up to do the dishes, Keith is negatively reinforced. Chris' nagging has ended and the aversive encounter is over. This is a good thing, right? Maybe, in the short term, because the dishes will get done. But Keith is likely to be resentful of how Chris is always nagging him, in which case he will experience this exchange as punishing. Repeated with sufficient frequency, in the longer term this sort of exchange will weaken the couple's feelings of happiness.

that are the problem, and they are the primary target for therapeutic change. Thus, the task of the behaviorally oriented couples therapist is not to delve into the history and circumstances that led to the problem the couple now faces, because the assumption is that this information is not reliably known or readily retrieved. Instead, the therapist strives to (1) define the problem in the present in terms of the specific behaviors the partners find troubling or aversive, and (2) understand the rewards and punishments that maintain these behaviors and thus perpetuate the couple's interpersonal difficulties (Lieberman, 1970; Stuart, 1969). The therapist collects information from the couple in order to develop testable hypotheses about the circumstances that precede the unwanted behaviors and the events that happen immediately after. In doing so, the practitioner seeks to clarify the *function* that a particular behavior or set of behaviors serves in a relationship. By understanding the circumstances surrounding troublesome behaviors, the therapist identifies environmental conditions or other partner behaviors which, if changed, may result in reducing or eliminating the problem.

The behavioral approach to relationship distress proposes that partners are initially sources of powerful rewards to each other, but that over time they become used to these rewards to the point where they feel their relationship has become routine and boring. Behavioral therapists help identify the nature of this problem and suggest new behaviors (or old behaviors that are no longer displayed) that couples can exchange to enhance their relationship. This is very much in keeping with the idea that relationships benefit when couples engage in novel and arousing activities (see Chapter 7). Similarly, differences of opinion between partners, which early in a relationship are often avoided, ignored, or difficult to discern, typically become more apparent as the relationship grows more serious and the couple encounters more opportunities for disagreements. Behavioral couples therapy is designed to tip the balance of rewards and costs exchanged between partners, by expanding the range of positive experiences and neutralizing the behaviors that might damage the partners' views about their relationship.

Consistent with the emphasis on observable behavior, practitioners make use of interviews, direct observations of the couple (e.g., while attempting to solve a problem), daily diaries completed by spouses to capture day-to-day behaviors that are pleasing and displeasing, and questionnaires about what specific behaviors partners most want to change. One such tool is the Spouse Observation Checklist (SOC), introduced in Chapter 2 (Willis, Weiss, & Patterson, 1974). With the SOC, partners independently indicate which of 409 relationship events occurred in the past 24 hours and, if they did occur, whether the reporting spouse experienced them as pleasing, displeasing, or neutral in their impact (**TABLE 12.3**). By examining responses, the therapist can gain a sense of the behaviors that are and are not exchanged in a relationship (e.g., if the one or both partners is deficient in displaying pleasing behaviors), how partners react to those behaviors, and which behaviors appear to contribute to or detract from relationship satisfaction.

This initial stage of traditional behavioral couples therapy, known as **behavior exchange**, provides the practitioner with important diagnostic information regarding the extent to which partners can generate new, positive experiences in their relationship, and it conveys to the partners that improving their relationship can be enjoyable rather than painful (Jacobson & Margolin, 1979). Once this foundation is established, treatment then turns to **communication training**, in which partners receive very practical advice on how to listen (e.g., listening to understand the partner's point of view instead of listening to develop a response to what the partner has said) and how to talk to each other productively (e.g., avoiding blame and accusations, using softer emotions like hurt and sadness instead of harder emotions like anger, responding nondefensively). Finally, in **problem-solving training**, couples learn to apply their communication skills to specific problems in their relationship, following a series of guidelines. For example, partners are encouraged to always begin with something positive when stating a problem, to specify in precise terms the behavior that is most bothersome, to

TABLE 12.3 **The Spouse Observation Checklist**

Affection:	
We held each other.	____ pleasing ____ displeasing behavior
Spouse greeted me affectionately when I came home.	____ pleasing ____ displeasing behavior
Consideration:	
Spouse called me just to say hello.	____ pleasing ____ displeasing behavior
Spouse was sarcastic with me.	____ pleasing ____ displeasing behavior
Sex:	
We engaged in sexual intercourse.	____ pleasing ____ displeasing behavior
Spouse rushed into intercourse without foreplay.	____ pleasing ____ displeasing behavior
Communication Process:	
We had a constructive conversation about family management.	____ pleasing ____ displeasing behavior
Spouse read a book or watched TV and wouldn't talk to me.	____ pleasing ____ displeasing behavior
Employment–Education:	
We figured out ways to meet new job demands.	____ pleasing ____ displeasing behavior
Spouse complained I spent too much time at work.	____ pleasing ____ displeasing behavior
Personal Habits and Appearance:	
Spouse dressed nicely.	____ pleasing ____ displeasing behavior
Spouse left the bathroom in a mess.	____ pleasing ____ displeasing behavior

Please rate your satisfaction with your relationship today:

1	2	3	4	5	6	7	8	9
Very Unsatisfied				Neither Satisfied Nor Dissatisfied				Very Satisfied

Source: Adapted from Willis, Weiss, & Perry, 1974.

acknowledge his or her own role in the problem, to discuss only one problem at a time, and to generate solutions in which both partners must make behavioral changes (Jacobson & Margolin, 1979). By teaching couples new skills for communicating, behavioral couples therapy aims to steer couples away from influencing one another with nagging and disengagement, shift the balance of rewarding and punishing exchanges, and give them the tools they need to manage their relationship in the future.

COGNITIVE-BEHAVIORAL COUPLES THERAPY. When asking questions about why a partner behaves in a certain way in a relationship, traditional behavioral couples therapists look for answers in the immediate environment generally and, in particular, whether the partner's responses to that behavior are rewarding or punishing. When you think about why your partner displays behaviors you dislike, what answers do you come up with? Chances are you might say something like: "Gary's not as interested in me sexually anymore because our wedding is next month and I think he is scared" or "Jane can get pretty pessimistic sometimes, so she thinks we'll never have enough money to buy our own place" or "Larry's changing the baby's diaper now so I have to be the one getting up at 3 A.M." or "Caroline almost never calls when she's going to be late; she can be insensitive that way." These explanations are rather different from those highlighted in traditional behavioral models in that they reveal interpretations of the partner's behavior. **Cognitive-behavioral couples therapy** shares many of the principles and goals of behavioral couples therapy—especially the importance of changing the way partners behave with each other—but the cognitive approach maintains that the focus on observable behaviors is too restrictive. Therapists working from this perspective recognize that behaviors can be the product of the thoughts and feelings experienced in response to one partner's behavior. They note that the exact same behavior expressed by one partner can lead to very different responses by the other partner, depending on interpretation.

Noted clinical psychologists Donald Baucom and Norman Epstein (2002) summarized the cognitive-behavioral view well:

> A major premise of this approach is that partners' dysfunctional emotional and behavioral responses to relationship events are influenced by inappropriate information processing, whereby cognitive appraisals of the events are either distorted or extreme ("You stayed late at the office because you don't really love me. I know you have an annual report due tomorrow and the network went down, but if you wanted to, you'd find a way to be home with me"), or are evaluated according to extreme or unreasonable standards of what a relationship should be ("If you really cared, you'd want to spend all your free time with me. That's the way a marriage should be"). (p. 28)

The idea that cognitive processes can operate in powerful ways to modify the impact of behaviors is not new. In *The Enchiridion*, Greek philosopher Epictetus (**FIGURE 12.6**) wrote "People are disturbed not by things but by the view they take of them," (1888, p. 381). Shakespeare's Hamlet said "for there is nothing either good or bad, but thinking makes it so" to Rosencrantz and Guildenstern (1917, p. 60). Cognitive-behavioral couples therapists have built on these basic observations to delineate different types of thoughts and strategies for changing them. In Chapter 10, we discussed how the ways people make sense of the world around them in general, and their relationships in particular, can affect how they converse with their

FIGURE 12.6 Epictetus (55–135 B.C.E.), Greek philosopher. Even today his wisdom echoes basic tenets of cognitive-behavioral couples therapy.

"Can you spare a few seconds to minimize my problems?"

FIGURE 12.7 Expecting the worst. According to cognitive-behavioral couples therapy, the ways partners perceive and organize the world around them will affect how they feel and how they communicate. This woman's expectation that her partner will dismiss her problems instigates a conversation that probably won't go well: regardless of whether he answers yes or no, her pessimistic expectations have put him in a difficult position.

partners and how they judge relationship satisfaction. As the following examples illustrate, these interpretive processes can be slanted toward *enhancing* the relationship or *maintaining distress* in the relationship (Holtzworth-Munroe & Jacobson, 1985):

- *Selective attention* is the tendency of partners to focus on certain behaviors displayed by their mate while overlooking or ignoring others ("Thanks for making my coffee this morning!" versus "When you made my coffee this morning, you forgot to put in the milk!").

- *Attributions* are interpretations or explanations for the behaviors and events ("You forgot to put milk in my coffee; did I forget to buy milk?" or "You forgot to put milk in my coffee; I think you are overreacting to what I said about your mother at dinner last night!").

- *Expectations* are predictions about what the partner will do or about what will happen in the relationship in the future (**FIGURE 12.7**).

Other thoughts are broader in nature and are not linked to specific events in relationships:

- *Assumptions* reflect beliefs about how relationships and people actually operate ("Men and women are more similar than different; they have the same basic needs, though they might have different ways of trying to satisfy them" or "Men and women are inherently different; it's a wonder we ever get along at all!").

- *Standards* refer to the way relationships and partners should be ("Relationships should really be about give and take. The two people in a relationship really need to have a say, even if they disagree, otherwise one feels alienated" or "One partner, me, really needs to be in charge of the relationship, otherwise life is too chaotic and no one is really in control").

The cognitive-behavioral therapist's task is to modify these thoughts and interpretations, and the resulting emotions and behaviors, by sharpening the capacity of partners to observe and evaluate how they gather and analyze information, and by making them aware of their assumptions and standards. **BOX 12.2** takes you inside the cognitive-behavioral therapist's office to show how this works in practice.

BOX 12.2 SPOTLIGHT ON . . .

A Therapy Session

The following excerpt from a cognitive-behavioral therapy session, adapted from Baucom and Epstein (1990, pp. 303–304), illustrates how a therapist would work with a couple to help them recognize how their interpretations affect their feelings and the ways they subsequently converse.

Husband: *I had been out playing softball with friends and had told Julie that I'd be home after dark. . . . When I pulled my car into the driveway, it had been dark for a while. I knew that Julie must be furious, because all the lights in the house were out except one upstairs in our bedroom. When I walked into the bedroom and asked her why she didn't leave a light on for me downstairs, she just blew up and said that I only think about myself.*

Wife: *Well, what did you expect when you didn't even say hello and started grilling me about the lights?*

Therapist: *Bob, what was it that you figured had Julie so upset with you at the time?*

Husband: *That I was late and hadn't kept my word.*

Wife: *No, Bob, I was upset at the way you charged into the room and started questioning me about the lights. You usually end up playing later than you think you will, so I figured you'd be late and planned to get some chores and reading done.*

Husband: *Then why were all the lights off if you weren't angry about the game?*

Wife: *When I decided to read in bed it was still light out, and I got involved in the book and didn't even realize it had gotten dark! . . .*

Therapist: *What seems to have happened is that the two of you had very different interpretations about what was going on between you, and each of your views got you pretty upset with the other person. . . . Cognitive-behavioral marital therapy is designed to help you take an approach to marital problems somewhat similar to the approach a scientist takes to answering questions. The basic approach is to gather evidence to discover which of your views about problems that occur in your relationship are accurate or reasonable, and which may not be the most accurate or reasonable ways to interpret what you see happening. Then your approach to solving a problem will be based on a clear picture of what is contributing to the difficulties between the two of you.*

This example focuses on one specific type of thought, a destructive attribution. Yet it illustrates the more general point about how cognitive-behavioral therapy is designed to link specific thoughts to strong negative emotions and potentially destructive interactions, so couples themselves can anticipate and sidestep these experiences in the future.

INTEGRATIVE BEHAVIORAL COUPLES THERAPY. Behavioral couples therapy and cognitive-behavioral couples therapy both focus on prescribing new rules for how partners behave together. The new behaviors are said to be "rule-governed," and the rules sound like this: "Here is the way to listen, here are the specific things you should be doing to make each other happier, here are the guidelines for solving problems, here are the kinds of attributions you should be making. If you follow these rules, then your relationship will improve." Practitioners' experiences with these models, and data collected to test them, soon revealed important cracks in their foundation. For example, inducing people to change would sometimes backfire, producing defensiveness and resistance instead.

What was happening? After considering these data, clinical psychologists Neil Jacobson and Andrew Christensen (1996) surmised that traditional behavioral models were inadequate because they aimed to impose change where it might be difficult to achieve, and because they hoped to help couples for whom significant change was unlikely, despite their commitment to improving the relationship. They devised **integrative behavioral couples therapy** to address these problems, by combining the standard behavioral interventions—behavior exchange, communication training, and problem-solving training—with interventions that helped couples see that it was beneficial to tolerate and even accept aspects of the partner and the relationship that were displeasing. As they noted, "When direct efforts to change are blocked by incompatibilities, irreconcilable differences, and unsolvable problems, the only way to generate relationship improvement is by promoting acceptance of what seems at first glance unacceptable" (Jacobson & Christensen, 1996, p. 11). Thus, for example, if your partner is not as affectionate as you would like, and this proves difficult to change, the goal of this therapy would be to provide you with the tools for adjusting. It is interesting that when the pressure for more affection is lifted and the partner's natural level of expressing affection is understood and validated, then that partner may actually come to be more loving and affectionate.

As this example shows, far greater emphasis is put on the offended partner's capacity for accommodating the mate's behavior than on changing the offending behavior itself. Rather than aiming to increase the number of affectionate behaviors by a certain amount (as would be the goal in traditional behavioral couples therapy), the intervention seeks to promote affectionate behaviors because the partner actually *feels* affection for the partner and the mate responds naturally to this behavior with appreciation (Dimidjian, Martell, & Christensen, 2008). Thus, on one hand, this approach builds on tried-and-true behavioral strategies for changing interaction patterns in relationships, but on the other hand, it is a radical departure from behavioral strategies in that couples learn to accept the bothersome behaviors that are not readily changed.

Integrative behavioral therapists make use of three primary techniques for promoting acceptance. In **empathic joining**, the practitioner aims to define the problem in terms of a theme that takes both partners' perspectives into account without blaming either of them. Thus, by encouraging partners to see a broader and more constructive theme for the interpersonal pattern that is troubling them, they come to empathize and join together to find a solution. For example, two partners might differ in that one prefers a very conventional lifestyle while the other prefers a free-spirited, unscripted life. The more the conventional partner imposes structure on their lives, the more the unconventional partner rebels, and the more this partner rebels, the more the conventional partner tries to impose more structure, resulting in ever-increasing dissatisfaction for both partners (Jacobson & Christensen, 1996). Neither partner is right or wrong, but the partners do differ, and they are not managing their differences well. Helping the partners see their problems as stemming from a kind of dance or reciprocated process to which both contribute takes the blame off any one person, while emphasizing that they are both responsible for improving the situation. To achieve this, both partners will need to see themselves and each other as playing a role in the difficulties they face. This new formulation then sets the stage for the couple to talk about their experiences at a deeper and more intimate level, avoiding accusations, and encouraging more mutual empathy. Acceptance is promoted further through a second technique, **unified detachment**, whereby both partners learn to view their problems with less charged emotion and to talk about them in more neutral, descriptive terms.

If acceptance interventions are designed to bring partners closer together by reorienting their views on their conflicts, then **tolerance building** interventions are designed to help them relinquish the idea that additional negotiations and conflict will prove beneficial, and instead contend with the real possibility that some undesirable aspects of the relationship will not change (Dimidjian et al., 2008). One way tolerance is accomplished is by helping a partner recognize the positive aspects of an otherwise undesirable or unpleasant behavior. Thus, a thrifty partner who gets upset about the other partner's careless spending habits might learn to acknowledge that it is important to have some luxuries and pleasures in life. In essence, integrative behavioral couples therapy encourages partners to change what they can change, but to stop trying to change everything in the partner and the relationship that they dislike, and to learn to accept or at least tolerate those aspects that they cannot change (**FIGURE 12.8**).

"No, I don't want to change you, Darryl. But sure, it would be great if you were completely different."

FIGURE 12.8 Future imperfect. Integrative behavioral couples therapy aims to produce behavioral change when possible and to encourage acceptance or tolerance when it is not. This woman professes to not want to change Darryl, but her tolerance of his quirks appears to be in short supply.

Emotion Models

Notable by its absence from our discussion thus far is explicit consideration of emotion as a central focus in couples therapy. Emotion warrants attention, because emotional expression distinguishes happy from unhappy couples, and helps predict whether a successful relationship will become distressed. Anger, despair, grief, sadness, and hope are frequent companions to those seeking relationship counseling, and **emotion models** fill the gap.

Emotionally focused couples therapy was developed in the early 1980s by clinical psychologists Leslie Greenberg and Susan Johnson. They observed that helping partners gain insight about early caregiving experiences, and develop skills for solving their problems, failed to address the strong emotions often displayed during therapy sessions (Johnson, 2004; Johnson & Denton, 2002). Something more was needed: a focus on the feelings being expressed. By drawing out the emotional moments in couples' conversations, emotionally focused couples therapy aims to create "bonds" instead of the "bargains" that typified traditional behavioral approaches (Johnson, 1986).

A cornerstone of emotionally focused couples therapy is the idea, originating with John Bowlby and formalized in attachment theory (see Chapters 3 and 6), that we as humans have a built-in need for safe and secure connections with other people. As we saw in our earlier discussions of attachment, if these basic needs go unmet in a relationship, then we feel vulnerable and exposed, and we experience distress and anxiety as a consequence. Unmet needs produce strong **primary emotions**, such as feelings of abandonment, fear of rejection, shame, and helplessness, but these are often masked by **secondary emotions**, such as anger (Greenberg & Johnson, 1988). Negative interactions between partners tend to involve repeated displays of secondary emotions, thereby gradually eroding their mutual trust and making the expression of primary emotions less likely. Can you think of instances in which you or another person you were close to expressed anger, a secondary emotion, but deeper down you knew a more painful emotion, like shame or feeling hurt or betrayed, was really at work?

The emotionally-focused couples therapist works through the secondary emotions to bring the primary emotions into the open, explores and expands on these emotions, and encourages empathic responses to them. Couples are thus encouraged to express their emotions differently and therefore have different, and more constructive, conversations. Improvement comes not from guiding couples toward a deeper understanding of their past relationships or teaching them a better set of problem-solving skills, but from giving them a new awareness of the kinds of emotional experiences they can have.

> " Change occurs not through insight into the past, catharsis, or negotiation, but through new emotional experience in the present context of attachment-salient interactions."
>
> —Johnson & Denton (2002, p. 229)

Attempting to capture and modify something as abstract as emotion might seem like it would produce a vague treatment model; the opposite is actually the case with emotionally focused couples therapy. Therapists follow three distinct stages in this model (Johnson & Greenman, 2006; Johnson & Denton, 2002; Johnson, 2004).

1. *De-escalation of negative cycles.* The therapist brings the couple to the point where they can acknowledge that they both contribute to the problems in the relationship, that the underlying interaction cycle and not the partner is really the problem, and that this cycle can be understood in terms of emotions and unmet attachment needs. More generally, the goal of the first stage is to help couples see that their negative interaction cycle is

fueling their insecure attachment and blocking a deeper level of emotional connection.

2. *Shaping new cycles of responsiveness and accessibility*. A crucial transformation occurs as partners learn to use more positive ways of approaching and responding to each other. A withdrawn partner is encouraged to engage more by expressing deeper primary emotions, and an overly critical partner is likewise encouraged to express vulnerabilities rather than the secondary emotions that have been masking them. As a result of this new understanding, partners feel more compelled to respond more compassionately, and new interactional cycles will begin to form (**FIGURE 12.9**).

3. *Consolidation and integration*. The therapist works with the couple to reflect on the changes they have made, to establish a story or narrative that helps them understand how their relationship deteriorated and then improved, and to solve specific problems they have not yet addressed. No formal problem-solving training occurs at this stage, unlike in the behavioral models of therapy. Instead, the expectation is that partners will be able to resolve problems largely on their own because they are no longer attacking and counterattacking as in their original destructive cycle of interaction.

"*Since we're both working on the same marriage, I thought it would be a good idea to get together and compare notes.*"

FIGURE 12.9 Comparing notes. In emotionally focused couples therapy, partners learn to approach each other honestly and candidly. If we assume this couple is working on their marriage because it has not been going well, we might infer that the most impressive part of the woman's statement is what she refrains from saying. Instead of expressing a strong secondary emotion like anger, she offers a friendly invitation to her husband to iron out any problems that might exist between them.

Evaluating the Models of Couples Therapy

Because couples typically seek treatment to improve their relationship and establish a more rewarding partnership, it is logical to examine whether treatment fulfills these goals. Psychodynamic and systems models are underrepresented in the studies described below, and behavioral and emotion models are overrepresented. Far fewer studies of the effects of psychodynamic and systems therapies have been conducted, for two reasons. First, these models were developed and practiced largely in private clinical settings, where the inclination and resources for research are lower than in academic settings (Keim & Lappin, 2002). Second, some proponents of these models reject the idea that the effects of treatment can be measured in any meaningful way (e.g., Sander, 1998). With these considerations in mind, we'll review the available evidence on whether couples benefit from participation in couples therapy. This evidence comes from **outcome research**, so named because the purpose in conducting it is to determine what kinds of therapeutic interventions produce the best possible outcomes for couples. The two basic types of outcome research are efficacy studies and effectiveness studies.

LABORATORY STUDIES OF INTERVENTIONS. The use of experimental methods renders some beliefs and explanations less plausible while others remain viable, at least until additional experiments indicate otherwise. Scientists interested in understanding the effects of couples therapy have used this principle to design **efficacy studies**, in which they randomly assign some couples to one or more forms of relationship therapy and other couples to some nontherapeutic condition, and then examine how the differing groups compare in relationship functioning months or years later.

In a typical study, couples completing a specific form of relationship therapy are compared with those who do not receive any intervention for the duration of the study. In a meta-analysis, the results of many such studies are carefully combined using quantitative methods (see Chapter 2). They reveal rather consistently that couples who receive treatment experience a higher level of relationship satisfaction at the end of treatment than the control couples. More specifically, we learn from these studies that the average treated couple is functioning better in their relationship than 72–80 percent of the control couples (Lebow et al., 2012; Shadish & Baldwin, 2003, 2005). These effects are typically obtained with 10 to 15 one-hour sessions of counseling.

At first glance this would appear to be pretty good news: Most of the couples who receive relationship therapy improve, whereas most of the couples not receiving treatment fail to improve. And given our earlier observation that unhappy couples often wait a long time before seeking help, these results are impressive indeed, and may underestimate the benefits of couples therapy for those who seek it out before their relationship is in serious trouble. Should we accept this summary as an enthusiastic endorsement of relationship therapies? Not yet, because three more considerations temper this general conclusion. First, the discussion focuses on *improvements* without specifying whether couples were actually *happy* with their relationship at the end of treatment. For purposes of this analysis, let's define *happy* as improved to the point at which a couple is indistinguishable from those couples in the general population who report a satisfying relationship. When this stricter criterion is applied, 40–50 percent of treated couples actually change from being distressed to describing their relationship as satisfying and rewarding (Christensen et al., 2006; Jacobson et al., 1984; Shadish et al., 1993). Comparable improvements are rare among untreated couples, suggesting that relationship distress rarely goes away on its own accord.

Second, if therapy does improve a relationship to the point where partners are happy, do those improvements last? After all, most couples seeking treatment are hoping for more than immediate relief from their problems, and the interventions themselves are designed to make fundamental rather than temporary alterations in the ways partners treat each other. Unfortunately, the vast majority of studies in this area do not follow couples long enough to answer this question. But we do know from longer-term studies of behavioral couples therapy that approximately 70 percent of those couples who are satisfied in their relationship at the end of treatment maintain these gains over the next 2 years, whereas 30 percent do not (Christensen et al., 2006; Jacobson, Schmaling, & Holtzworth-Munroe, 1987). About 15 percent of couples receiving behavioral couples therapy divorce within 2 years (Christensen et al., 2006), and roughly 28–38 percent do so within 4 or 5 years (Christensen et al., 2012; Snyder, Wills, & Grady-Fletcher, 1991). Thus, many but not all couples do achieve lasting benefits with behavioral couples therapy. Over a 2-year span, emotionally focused couples therapy also produced lasting benefits and lowered divorce rates (Cloutier et al., 2002).

Third, do the various interventions differ in how effective they are? When considering measures of relationship quality and examining a host of studies, the answer to this question tends to be no. In the largest study of marital therapy conducted to date, for example, the original version of behavioral couples therapy produced results that were very similar to those obtained with integrative behavioral couples therapy 5 years after completion of treatment, both in terms of the proportion of couples who either recovered fully or improved significantly in their level of relationship satisfaction (about 48 percent) and in terms of the proportion of couples deteriorating in relationship satisfaction (about 38 percent) (FIGURE 12.10). Included in this group of deteriorating couples were those who dissolved their relationship; overall about 27 percent of the couples chose to do so (Christensen et al., 2010). When considering measures of couples' behavior, the various tested interventions also produced comparable results, though change in cognition is greater in cognitive-behavioral than in traditional behavioral couples therapy (Dunn & Schwebel, 1995).

FIELD STUDIES OF INTERVENTIONS. To this point we have discussed experimental tests of couples therapies that are characterized by a high degree of scientific rigor and control. These efficacy studies are well suited to address whether an intervention *can* produce improvements in relationships, but they don't resolve the issue of whether interventions *do* produce improvements when delivered by practitioners in the real world. **Effectiveness studies** are designed to answer this question. Unlike efficacy studies, effectiveness studies are undertaken in the more typical contexts where couples therapy takes place, and as a result they are less scientifically rigorous. Practitioners might not be as well trained, the incentives for staying in treatment might be weaker, the treatments themselves might not be as well-defined or systematically administered, and initial evaluations of couples might be less detailed or informative.

Effectiveness studies indicate that large numbers of couples drop out of therapy, that about 30 percent of treated couples show improvement after treatment (with 20 percent achieving a score in the satisfied range of relationship functioning by the end), that success rates in effectiveness studies are lower than those in efficacy studies (Hahlweg & Klann, 1997), and that

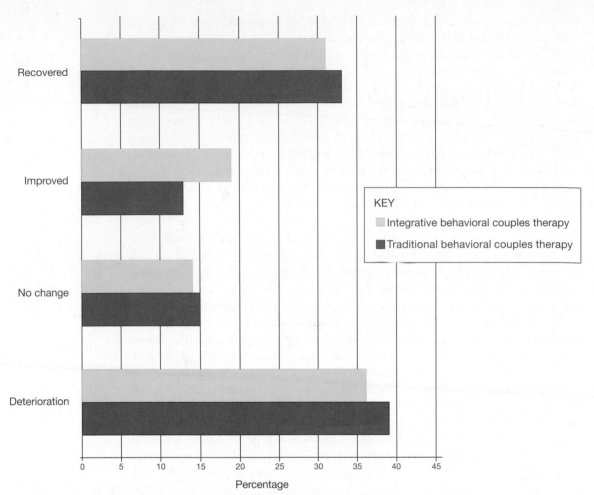

FIGURE 12.10 The relative success of couples therapy. Outcome research focuses on improving upon the best available form of intervention. In this study, researchers tested whether couples receiving integrative behavioral couples therapy were more satisfied and less likely to divorce than couples getting traditional behavioral couples therapy. The results, 5 years later, were largely the same for both types of treatment. (Source: Adapted from Christensen et al., 2010.)

treatments for couple problems are not as effective as treatments for individual disorders (Seligman, 1995). Though the number of studies in this area is small and perhaps not representative of couples therapy as it occurs naturally, we can conclude from effectiveness studies that relationship difficulties are hard to treat, and that relatively few couples receiving treatment benefit from the intervention.

MAIN POINTS

» Relationship problems are a leading reason why people seek professional counseling. Four broad models of couples therapy are used to address the communication problems and power struggles that partners experience.

>> Psychodynamic models help couples achieve a more authentic bond that is unclouded by feelings that arise from unmet needs in childhood.

>> Systems models emphasize the way communication between intimate partners can be hampered by the unstated rules or tendencies that create rigid patterns of interaction.

>> Behavioral models focus on the rewarding and punishing behaviors partners exchange. Some versions focus on the perceptions and interpretations that underlie behavior exchanges, and others focus on accepting or tolerating behaviors that cannot be changed.

>> Emotion models focus on how strong feelings like anger can be divisive. The expression of underlying feelings of vulnerability, in contrast, can bring partners closer together.

>> The long-term benefits of behavioral and emotion models of couples therapy have been examined. Roughly half the couples receiving these therapies experience lasting improvements in their relationships.

Enhancing Relationships, Preventing Distress

Of all the couples who become dissatisfied with their relationship, we know that a small minority seeks treatment in one form or another (Halford & Moore, 2002), that a smaller number benefit from the treatment, and that a smaller number still are able to sustain their improvements over a long span of time. This unfortunate reality leaves many couples, even couples who have undergone treatment, unhappy with their relationship, and unable to reap the rewards that a healthy relationship can provide. In contrast to this **clinical model** of treating relationship distress once it has developed into a major problem, some professionals adopt a **public health model**, with the goal of enhancing relationships and preventing relationship distress before it happens. This approach typically entails helping couples identify strengths and weaknesses in their developing relationship, and perhaps teaching them skills and capabilities considered necessary for a strong partnership. In the public health model, the aim is to help large numbers of couples and encourage their participation proactively, long before serious problems arise, usually by building on their strengths, often in the cost-effective context of educational groups (Johnson, 2012). It might seem strange for couples to participate in intervention programs when their relationship is still strong; if they are happy, why should they seek any kind of help? As you have learned throughout this book, one reason is that relationships change and often deteriorate. Well-functioning couples participate in these programs to learn more about themselves and their relationship, and to anticipate and negotiate changes successfully; they appear to find great value in their participation (Sullivan & Bradbury, 1997).

Despite the differences between the clinical and the public health models, the two perspectives can be arranged along a single timeline. **Primary**

"
    The time to fix the roof is when the
sun is still shining."
—President John F. Kennedy (1962)

prevention is undertaken *before it happens* to reduce new cases of relationship dysfunction in the population at large. **Secondary prevention** is undertaken *before it gets worse* to assist relationships that are identified as vulnerable in some way to subsequent difficulties. **Tertiary prevention** (the clinical model, and also called therapy) is undertaken *before it is too late* in order to treat and rehabilitate relationships that are already in trouble (L'Abate, 1990). Even if we focus only on those primary and secondary interventions designed to enhance intimate relationships, we can envision numerous segments of the population that, in principle, could benefit from learning more about relationships and how to keep them strong. Indeed, various programs have been developed to address the unique concerns and interests of individuals and couples before they begin dating, after they begin dating, around the time of marriage, as they make the transition to parenthood, as step-families are forming, and so on. Because a large proportion of these programs are designed to help couples as they are deepening their commitment and formalizing their relationship, it is here that we will focus our discussion.

Public Health Approaches

Although dozens of programs have been developed for the purpose of enhancing relationships and preventing their deterioration (Berger & Hannah, 1999), prevailing approaches take one of three forms (Halford & Moore, 2002). The first form, which is widespread, provides couples with information about relationships and makes them more aware of potential challenges, such as managing finances and becoming parents. The second form builds on the first form by administering self-report questionnaires and inventories that assess key dimensions of interpersonal functioning. Couples then receive feedback on their responses and recommendations on the steps they can take to strengthen their relationship. For example, with the PREPARE/ENRICH program (e.g., Olson & Olson, 1999), each partner completes a 165-item questionnaire that assesses personality dimensions (e.g., assertiveness, avoidance), intrapersonal issues (e.g., spiritual beliefs, relationship expectations), interpersonal issues (e.g., communication), and external issues (e.g., family and friends). Partners can compare themselves to each other and to a large database of responses from others. Couples then participate in a series of exercises either on their own or with guidance from a counselor. The exercises focus on exploring relationship strengths, strengthening communication skills, resolving conflicts, understanding each partner's family background, developing a workable budget and financial plan, and developing goals for the future.

The third form of intervention emphasizes teaching couples specific interpersonal skills for maintaining the relationship. Although skills are also addressed in the other two forms of intervention, here skill training takes center

TABLE 12.4 Programs to Strengthen Relationships by Improving Communication Skills

---

Compassionate and Accepting Relationships Through Empathy (CARE)
Based on integrative behavioral couples therapy. Aims to strengthen relationships by teaching couples supportive and empathic skills, including skills in acceptance. (Rogge et al., 2002)

Couple Communication (CC)
Based on systems theory. Focuses on increasing awareness of the self and the partner, and on viewing the relationship as a system. Teaches partners to understand boundaries in the relationship and recognize how information flows between them. (Miller et al., 1991)

Couples Coping Enhancement Training (CCET)
Focuses on the effects of stress on couples and builds coping and support skills. Helps partners improve their ability to manage stress, as individuals and as a couple. (Bodenmann & Shantinath, 2004)

Prevention and Relationship Enhancement Program (PREP)
Based on social learning theory. Partner communications are understood as being rewarding or punishing. Educates couples on effective conflict management and the construction expression of strong negative emotions. (Markman, Stanley, & Blumberg, 1994)

Relationship Enhancement (RE)
Based on a wide range of theoretical perspectives. Focuses on teaching couples skills for expressing their needs and desires, and empathizing with each other. (Guerney, 1987)

Self-Regulatory Prevention and Relationship Enhancement Program (Self-PREP)
Variant of PREP, based on social learning theory. Emphasizes helping couples develop the ability to monitor and modify how they communicate. Includes self-appraisals, goals for changes, and self-evaluations. (Halford, 2001)

---

stage. Instruction involves lectures on principles of partner communication, live demonstrations of good and poor communication, videotapes of couples interacting, and opportunities for couples to practice newly learned skills.

All skill based programs focus on communication in general and often cover similar topics, but they have slightly different theoretical emphases that lead them to prioritize different aspects of communication. Many of these aspects will be familiar to you, as they have appeared in various chapters in this book. Six such programs are summarized in TABLE 12.4. These interventions vary in format, but they are typically delivered in small group settings, with 15–25 hours of program content distributed over the course of a weekend workshop or over a period of 1–2 months.

Strengthening Healthy Relationships

> *... [P]reliminary research shows that marriage education workshops can make a real difference in helping married couples stay together and in encouraging unmarried couples who are living together to form a more lasting bond. Expanding access to such services to low-income couples, perhaps in concert with other services already available, should be something everybody can agree on.*"
>
> —President Barack Obama, *The Audacity of Hope* (2006)

The issues of efficacy and effectiveness, introduced earlier in the context of relationship therapies, apply with equal force to programs intending to enhance relationships and prevent relationship distress and dissolution. How do the different forms of intervention stack up? Because their content and goals are not well documented, programs designed only to inform couples and increase their awareness about relationships have proven difficult to test; their "lack of standardization means they cannot readily be evaluated in scientific research" (Halford & Moore, 2002, p. 401). And despite their widespread use, interventions involving the administration of inventories and subsequent feedback sessions have not been the subject of careful experimental testing, particularly over longer spans of time. As a result, we cannot know whether couples randomly assigned to participate in these kinds of programs experience better relationships over time than those assigned to a control group. Though a strong case can be made for the intrinsic value of these interventions, a competing position is that helping couples understand strengths and weaknesses in their relationship will be insufficient unless they also learn a wide array of communication skills that they can put to use when difficult circumstances arise.

We can state several things about programs designed to teach couples skills for their relationship. First, compared to control couples, couples participating in skill-based interventions show modest gains in relationship satisfaction after going through treatment (Hawkins et al., 2008). Second, couples who undergo treatment show improvements in observable relationship skills, and these improvements are larger than those found for self-reported relationship quality (Blanchard et al., 2009). This may reflect genuine improvements in communication, though it is also possible that couples are on their best behavior when their communication is assessed, and thus outperform control couples on this dimension. Another possible explanation for this result is that assessments of communication appear to change more with treatment because relationship satisfaction is already quite high (e.g., for newlywed couples) and cannot change much more.

Third, very few studies examine whether the effects of enhancement and prevention programs are sustained over a significant span of time (Christensen & Heavey, 1999). This is a serious shortcoming, because claims about preventing adverse relationship outcomes require, by definition, longer-term follow-up data. In some studies that were conducted with longer-term follow-up data, couples were not assigned randomly to treatment and control groups (Hahlweg et al., 1998), and many couples declined to participate (Markman et al., 1993). As a result, these studies are not true experiments, and they are open to the criticism that couples receiving treatments outperform those who do not because they are more motivated and eager to participate. Fourth, evidence demonstrates that the effects of interventions weaken with time (Hawkins et al., 2008). This indicates that prevention programs are likely to be most effective when they incorporate some form of follow-up booster sessions. Failure to produce long-term changes in communication skills may be more than merely a lost opportunity to help couples; it might bring about other problems as well. For example, helping couples understand the problems in their relationship may harm them in the long run if they do not improve their ability to resolve those problems (Butler & Wampler, 1999).

Finally, in line with the importance of individual personality traits and experiences, the effects of preventive treatments appear to vary, depending on the qualities and characteristics partners bring to their relationship (see Chapter 6). You might expect that couples in which the partners had more risk factors (i.e., characteristics that increase the probability of relationship difficulties, such as a family history of divorce) would benefit *less* from prevention programs than those with fewer risk factors, but there is some evidence that higher-risk couples actually benefit more. In an experimental test of the Self-PREP program (see Table 12.4), about half the couples were assigned randomly to the Self-PREP intervention and the remainder were assigned to a control group in which couples read a book about relationships and met twice with a counselor, who facilitated a small-group discussion of the book (Halford, Sanders, & Behrens, 2001). Couples in both groups were designated as high-risk if the woman's parents had divorced and the man's father had been violent toward his mother, or as low-risk if they possessed neither of these characteristics. Four years later, high-risk couples in the Self-PREP group were more satisfied with their relationship than high-risk couples in the control group. In contrast, low-risk couples in the control group were more satisfied with their relationship than low-risk couples in the Self-PREP group. In other words, the effects of treatment on outcome were affected by risk status.

Two important conclusions can be drawn from this study. First, we cannot assume that all couples will respond in the same way to a given intervention. The risk profile of each couple matters, and there are likely to be some advantages to delivering prevention programs to couples with more risk. Second, matching the intensity of an intervention to a couples' level of risk might be most beneficial. High-risk couples appear to benefit from more intensive instruction in communication skills (so that any less intensive intervention produces a weaker effect), whereas low-risk couples already have strong skills and might need minimal intervention to build on them (so that any more intensive intervention produces a weaker effect). Why might this be? One possibility is that preventive interventions might disrupt the effective communication habits healthier couples have established.

Dissemination and Public Policy

Although few would deny the value of educating couples about basic principles for improving their relationship and teaching them good communication skills, the available evidence does not yet support claims that preventive interventions produce enduring effects on the stability or quality of intimate relationships. (Bradbury & Lavner, 2012). We anticipate that research will continue to unravel this puzzle, however, and couples will be able to learn reliable strategies for keeping their relationship healthy and strong. Let's assume that this day has arrived. Can we expect that divorce rates will plummet and that relationships will flourish? Probably not, because not all couples will take advantage of these services, no matter how effective they may be. Though we might hope that couples at high risk for eventual problems might be especially likely to participate in early intervention programs, evidence shows that this does not happen. Indeed, at least on some indicators, low-risk couples—those who probably have relatively satisfying relationships even in the absence of any kind of formal intervention—are more likely than high-risk couples to take part in premarital counseling (Sullivan & Bradbury, 1997). Current recommendations therefore favor taking active steps to identify at-risk couples early in their relationships and to disseminate programs specifically to that population (Halford et al., 2003). This suggestion once again draws attention to the need for basic research that helps identify which couples are likely to struggle and which are likely to thrive.

As promising as it is, even this strategy may fail to deliver services to those couples who would benefit the most. To fill this gap, state and federal agencies now work with other stakeholders (e.g., religious and community organizations) to implement policies that will encourage or require couples to weigh their choices carefully before marrying, to prepare for marriage, and to seek professional counseling if problems arise. At first it might seem unusual that governments would adopt policies with the aim of influencing the private relationships of citizens. However, in the same way that policies are instituted and funds are allocated to reduce teenage pregnancy, the government is invested in strengthening marriage as a means of increasing the well-being of children and decreasing welfare payments needed to support one partner (typically the mother) as she and her ex-partner work to raise their children. (Recall from Chapter 1 that divorce is a leading cause of poverty in the United States. Although this effect can be temporary, women typically bear a greater financial burden after divorce than men; see Rank & Hirschl, 1999.)

Government programs designed to create change in intimate relationships raise a host of fascinating and controversial issues. For example, implementing policies is often motivated more by a need to take action in the face of some social problem than by accumulated research evidence identifying how

FIGURE 12.11 Divorce rates and policies. Cultures vary widely in how much they condone divorce. The Muslim couples on the left, married in a group ceremony, are from Amman, Jordan, where the divorce rate in 2002 was 1.22 per thousand people, about one-third the divorce rate in the United States (4.1 per thousand). The couple on the right is marrying in Nevada, the state with the highest divorce rate (7.1 per thousand in 2002). Laws and policies regarding divorce are controversial, in part because more-restrictive divorce laws can leave adults and children trapped in abusive situations, whereas less-restrictive laws can be viewed as encouraging people to abandon marriages too easily.

that problem can be addressed most effectively. As we've seen in this chapter, interventions for adverse marital outcomes, whether preventive or therapeutic in nature, come with no guarantee that they will yield lasting changes, and very little is known about how these programs work with low-income populations (Blanchard et al., 2009). Yet, social needs are pressing, and much might be learned by implementing policies and studying their effects on a large scale.

We need policies that maximize the chances that children will be raised by committed partners in a healthy environment, but how can this be done when many marriages are fraught with conflict, aggression, and infidelity? Making divorce more difficult to obtain can stabilize some family situations, while making painful traps out of others (FIGURE 12.11). Intervening to influence the decisions that individuals and couples make about marriage and divorce implies that the fate of marriages rests primarily in their hands. This may prove to be the most expeditious route for strengthening relationships, but left unexplored are systematic attempts to improve the contexts in which marriages and families reside, which can play a crucial role in determining the challenges couples face and the resources they have for overcoming them (see Chapter 11).

Particularly when compared to the clinical model for addressing relationship problems, which encourages careful consideration of each couple's unique assets and liabilities, the public health model encourages looking for common factors across all couples that might contribute to their destabilization. Low-wage jobs that demand long hours away from the family, inadequate health insurance, poor or inconsistent childcare, and unsafe neighborhoods are all likely to detract from the quality of interpersonal bonds, and all might serve as plausible targets for improving intimate relationships in future government initiatives.

MAIN POINTS

>> Therapeutic approaches provide resources for distressed couples, while public health approaches aim to enrich healthy relationships and prevent distress. Preventive approaches include counseling, questionnaire assessments, and training in communication skills.

>> Enrichment and prevention programs improve relationships in the short term, but their longer-term effects on distress and divorce rates have not been established.

>> The intensity and focus of public health programs must match the resources and skills of the couples in order to be successful.

>> Disseminating effective prevention programs to the couples who would benefit the most is important, but those who have a high risk of relationship distress are the least likely to make use of these programs.

>> Emerging strategies for preventing relationship distress focus on improving couple communication skills and the circumstances that make it difficult for couples to use those skills to keep their relationship healthy.

Seriously, What Should I Do?

Over the past two decades we have had the privilege of teaching thousands of undergraduates about intimate relationships, using a course we developed that essentially follows the outline of this book. We strive to give our students the most current information possible, and we hope we deliver that information in a compelling and memorable manner, emphasizing what we know and respecting the limitations of that knowledge. It can be easy to get caught up in a seemingly endless cycle of reading research, conducting research, and teaching about that research, and to lose sight of the fact that the conclusions emerging from the research are useful and can have real, practical benefits. Every time we teach the course, at least one courageous student comes up to us and says: "I took your course and I think I understood most of it . . . but, seriously, if you had to boil it all down to what matters most for someone wanting to have a good relationship, what should that person do?" Here are some answers:

■ Relationships can provide us with tremendous benefits, including better mental and physical health. If you want to reap these benefits, you have to make your relationship a priority in your life. Few of us are lucky enough to have great relationships without putting forth some real effort, over a sustained period of time. (See Chapter 1.)

- Making your relationship a priority means doing things to make your partner's life better and happier on a regular basis. Find ways to do this. Making your relationship a priority also means taking active steps to create new experiences and to reflect on the positive experiences that you or your partner has had recently. (See Chapter 7.)

- Western models of love and intimacy emphasize intense passion, which often fades as time passes. This is natural, but you need to create experiences in your relationship to replace it. If you really care about your partner, work on building a better relationship for the future instead of lamenting what you no longer have. Good relationships are less like surfing, in which the wave crashes and the ride is over, and more like mountain climbing. Keep moving forward and try to appreciate the new experiences you are creating. (See Chapter 7.)

- Never forget that a relationship thrives when the partners create security for each other and eliminate any sense of threat between them. We are driven by our biology to be in relationships, and we are inclined to stay in relationships when we feel understood, validated, and cared for. Expressions of gratitude, kindness, affection, and humor go far in keeping relationships strong. Being hostile, aggressive, selfish, and insensitive are the best ways to convince your partner that he or she is not understood, validated, or cared for. (See Chapter 8.)

- You cannot understand, validate, or care for your partner very well if you do not spend much time together, in person or otherwise. Intimate partners benefit from knowing what is going on in one another's lives. Some of this will involve knowing simply how your partner spent his or her day, and some of this will involve trying to figure out who your partner really is. Even your partner may not know this about himself or herself. (See Chapter 7.)

- Whether we realize it or not, we are constantly making choices about what to say and how to behave toward our partner. We alone are responsible for the words that come out of our mouth, and for the tone we use. Make good choices. Find ways to open rather than close the lines of communication. Be polite. Apologize when you make a mistake. (See Chapter 8.)

- One of the reasons to invest in your relationship is to keep it healthy and strong in case bad things happen. You don't have complete control over the forces that affect your relationship, and neither does your partner. One of you will get very sick. Somebody you know will die or have a chronic illness. Maybe you will lose your job or your house, through no fault of your own. Join with your partner to negotiate these challenges. Later challenges will be easier. Turn to others outside your relationship for support when you need it, and provide it to them when they need it— and even when they don't. (See Chapter 11.)

- Practice good mental hygiene. Think well of your partner. Give your partner the benefit of the doubt. When you are having a problem in your relationship, focus specifically on that problem and not on all the other grievances you might have. (See Chapter 9.)

- Learn how to talk effectively about difficult issues that arise between you. In the course of any long-term relationship, real problems and challenges will arise. You and your partner will disagree about something really important. You will experience sexual frustrations. You or your partner will feel inadequate as a person and maybe even get depressed. One of you will do or say something that is incredibly insensitive. You might give serious consideration to ending your relationship, and in fact you might actually end it. Successful couples are imperfect in many ways, but most of them figure out a way to talk about important and difficult issues. (See Chapter 8.)

- Disclosures are gifts that you and your partner give to each other. Learn to listen for these disclosures from your partner, however trivial they seem, and respond to them with interest in a kind and sensitive way. If you want your relationship to be more than just a friendship, you will also need to disclose your thoughts and feelings to your partner. (See Chapter 7.)

- Recognize that your partner is a unique and distinct person, trying to make a go of life just like you are. He or she has goals and quirks, and struggles and uncertainties, joys and sorrows, just as you do. Help him or her deal with these challenges in a way that you think he or she would want to be helped. Chances are you won't be able to change your partner in any fundamental way. You'll be much better off embracing and accepting your partner as a complete package and trying to understand what makes him or her tick. (See Chapter 6.)

- Look out for yourself. Find a partner you think is mature and healthy, someone whom you will want to care about and who you believe genuinely wants to care about you and your welfare. Don't be naïve. Some people have accumulated enormous debts, abuse drugs, break the law, or treat their partner badly, and you may not know these things early in your relationship. You will either want to avoid these kinds of problems or be prepared to respond when they arise. (See Chapter 6.)

- Recognize that not all relationships are destined to work out. Yet a relationship that is going to end can be ended constructively and with both partners showing mutual respect. If your relationship is not going well, take active steps to make it better or to end it well. You will be a better person for having done so. When the going gets rough, have the courage to talk to a therapist, either on your own or with your partner. (See Chapter 12.)

Nothing in this list will surprise you, and we doubt that research will prove us wrong on these points. But not every suggestion will work for you in every relationship. Good relationships are not easy to achieve. The very task of communicating well with our partner demands a lot from us: listening, empathizing, putting aside our own needs and desires—all of which can be hard to do. Communicating with an intimate partner is harder for some people than others, and it is easy to do in some situations and difficult in others. The best way to take care of yourself, paradoxically, is to take care of someone else, with the hope and belief that your kindness and generosity will be reciprocated. Most of the time it will be, so look for ways to confirm this. When you feel your generosity is not being reciprocated, maybe you are not giving enough of it or are not giving it in quite the right way. If it's obvious that you are being generous and kind, and you still are not getting what you need in return, share your concerns in an honest and open way.

CONCLUSION —

What might the new Secretary of Health and Human Services learn from reading this chapter? What steps are needed to improve relationships, build strong families, have healthy children, and maintain a prosperous nation? Our analysis provides only an introduction to this topic, but some lessons stand out clearly. First, interventions for relationships can have diverse goals (e.g., prevention, treatment), target populations (e.g., adolescents, younger couples, established couples), and settings (e.g., religious organizations, at work). Adopting a strategy that encompasses all of these opportunities for growth and improvement in relationships seems most promising. Second, notable progress has been made in developing models that capture key phenomena in relationships. In this chapter and elsewhere we have learned about the rich descriptive research base that has accumulated about relationships. This knowledge is valuable in its own right, and it provides a foundation for developing and refining the next generation of interventions. Third, the existing research does not provide answers to our most pressing questions about strengthening couples and families. In part this is due to the subtle and complex processes that must be understood before enduring changes can occur in relationships. Yet we must also acknowledge that our most potent tools, randomly controlled experiments with long-term follow-up data, have not been used to their fullest extent in this field. Investing heavily in experimental treatment research would be a wise decision. Fourth, it seems that the prevailing view about strengthening relationships necessarily involves interacting in some way with couples. This approach probably has real benefits, but it might also limit our vision of how we can intervene. Many other invisible or indirect ways of helping couples and families should be explored, such as reforming the workplace, improving wages and neighborhoods, and providing low-cost health care to families and creating Internet resources that enable couples to get credible and engaging information whenever they need it.

In a real sense, intimate relationships are a force of nature, and the purpose of therapeutic interventions is to harness their power and remove the obstacles that stand in their way. Progress in promoting human intimacy emerges from a combination of basic research on the principles of how relationships work naturally and applied research on how to make relationships work better. As we learn more and more about how (and how not) to improve relationships, we go back to the drawing board, ask new questions, and devise new intervention strategies.

13

Relationships Across the Lifespan

The Leap

As much as a successful intimate relationship can be a source of profound joy, the end of one can be the source of darkest despair. For some people, the prospect of life without love is simply intolerable, and at first glance the passage below appears to describe one of these people. It is easy to imagine it as the sad end to the story of a heartbroken man, devoid of hope, lacking the network of support most of us take for granted.

Standing on the Belle Isle Bridge, he gazed at the current of the river twenty-five feet below him. He had stripped down to his trousers, and with the raw wind factored in, the temperature was around twenty-five degrees Fahrenheit, but even though he was shivering, he seemed impervious to it. His mind was elsewhere, focusing on the water, going over what it would feel like when he sliced into it from that height. Right before he approached the railing, he hastily scribbled a makeshift will on an envelope. He wrote: "I leave all to Bess." Then, suddenly, he was ready. It's now or never, he thought. He tensed his muscles. "Good-bye," he impulsively shouted and jumped off the bridge. (Kalush & Sloman, 2006, pp. 185–186)

This man, a Hungarian immigrant named Ehrich Weiss, had arrived in the United States in 1878 at age 4. He was raised desperately poor, left home when he was 12, and was living on his own by the time he was 17, working in a necktie manufacturing company. From these beginnings, it is not hard to imagine why, at the age of 33, Weiss jumped off of the bridge into the Detroit River on November 26, 1907. Many immigrants who came to the U.S. before 1900 faced severe financial hardships, had trouble forming relationships, and eventually found themselves alone and desperate.

453

But Ehrich Weiss was not one of them. For one thing, he did not jump in solitude. On the contrary, thousands of people stood with him, watching expectantly and craning their necks to catch a glimpse of him as he fell. For another thing, most suicides do not have the foresight to bind their hands before they jump, but Weiss's wrists had been secured tightly by handcuffs before he jumped into the water. Finally, despite the freezing cold, the handcuffs, the great height, and the fact that not one of the thousand witnesses lifted a finger to help him, this jumper did not drown. After a few nerve-wracking seconds, he emerged, free from his shackles, to thunderous cheers from people who knew him by the name under which he had been performing, and would continue to perform, similar feats for years.

They knew him as Harry Houdini, and by 1914 he was the most famous man in the world. If his name is familiar to you a century later, you probably know him as a magician and escape artist. Houdini was the man no physical restraints could hold, as he proved repeatedly by slipping free from chains, handcuffs, straight jackets, and prison cells, all with apparent ease. To this day, his life and achievements continue to inspire fascination and awe.

Part of this fascination stems from the fact that, in all of Houdini's greatest accomplishments, he appears to have relied on no one but himself. Whereas solitude is a curse for many, Houdini's performances celebrated it. The classic images of Houdini reinforce this impression, picturing the magician by himself, often wrapped in chains, and frequently suspended by his feet (**FIGURE 13.1**). Before his audiences, Houdini must have appeared almost superhuman, and although he always carefully denied that he had any supernatural powers, he took pains to prove that he accomplished his amazing stunts without assistance. Indeed, Houdini's rise from penniless immigrant to celebrity was seen as a testament to the self-made man, and in the early 20th century, such a man represented the American ideal.

FIGURE 13.1 The handcuff king. To gain free publicity for his performances, Houdini regularly threw himself off bridges while bound in chains, thrilling the assembled crowds until he emerged again from the waters below. Houdini is credited with inventing the Chinese Water Torture Cell, in which he was lowered and locked upside down in a glass tank filled with water. How he regularly escaped from this trap remains a secret to this day.

Houdini was first and foremost a master of illusions. Thus we may ask: How self-sufficient was Houdini, really? In public, he celebrated the power of the solitary individual to transcend any barriers and escape from any bonds. In private, however, Houdini was anything but independent. Throughout Houdini's life and career he was bound by deep and lasting intimate relationships, relationships that extended across his life and from which he never freed himself—not even, as we shall see, in death.

QUESTIONS

Throughout this book, we have focused on intimate relationships between adults, particularly in the early and middle stages of life. In this final chapter, we expand the focus of previous chapters to include the full trajectory of an individual's life and ask: How does the capacity for intimacy develop across the life of an individual? How are our intimate relationships similar to or different from other close relationships we experience throughout our lives (e.g., relationships with siblings, friends, and family)?

Then we broaden our focus further, moving beyond the individual to ask: How have intimate relationships been changing over time and history? We conclude by speculating a bit about the future of intimate relationships. As a tool for illustrating many of these issues, throughout this chapter we refer to Harry Houdini's extraordinary life through the intimate relationships that shaped it.

Born into Intimacy:
The Effects of Adult Relationships on Children

Compared to many other creatures, even other primates, humans are extremely dependent at birth. The human infant cannot walk, cannot yet focus its eyes, and can barely lift its own head. Accordingly, the infant's capacity for intimacy is pretty limited. Yet, although infants themselves have little opportunity to express intimacy, most of them are born into a sea of intimate relationships from their earliest moments. The most significant of these is the relationship between the infant's primary caregivers, usually the parents. For most human beings, the relationship between the parents is the first model of adult intimacy to which we are exposed, and thus it forms the soil in which the seeds of our own capacity for intimacy are sown. This premise is the foundation of attachment theory, as we have described it throughout this book (see Chapters 3 and 6).

The man who grew up to become Harry Houdini was lucky in this regard, for he was born to parents who were devoted to each other. When they met in Budapest, Hungary, Harry's father, Mayer Samuel Weisz, was a widower whose first wife had died after giving birth to a son. A graduate of law school, Mayer lived in a Jewish community where arranged marriages were common, so Houdini's parents might have shared no emotional bond with each other at all. Mayer, however, escaped this fate when a close friend made an unusual request. That friend, a shy type, asked the more eloquent Mayer if he would deliver a message of love to a young woman named Cecilia Steiner, whose

FIGURE 13.2 Houdini's earliest social ties. In this photo, Houdini is in the middle, surrounded by four brothers, all of whom interacted regularly throughout their lives. How do you think the constant tumult of a busy household during his earliest years affected his capacity to socialize and interact effectively with others?

family was known to Mayer. In delivering the message, Mayer realized he had fallen in love with the girl himself, and when he discovered that his feelings were returned, Mayer and Cecilia were married.

The marriage lasted 28 years, until Mayer's death in 1891. Their lives together were not easy. In addition to Mayer's son from his first marriage, Mayer and Cecilia eventually had six children (**FIGURE 13.2**). Seeking opportunity in America, Mayer left Cecilia and the children alone in Hungary for nearly 2 years until he could bring them to join him in Appleton, Wisconsin, where he had established himself as a rabbi. When Mayer was fired by his congregation, the family was reduced to near poverty, relocating to urban Milwaukee and moving frequently to avoid bill collectors. The whole family had to work to survive, but throughout this time, Houdini's parents remained committed to each other and to their children. In later years, Houdini would tell of his 12th birthday, when his ailing father pulled him aside and made him vow that, after he died, Harry would ensure that his mother was well cared for. Mayer's concern for his wife's well-being set an example that Houdini would never forget.

Children as Observers of Adult Relationships

How might the strong relationship between his parents have affected the course of Houdini's life? As recently as the 1970s, this question sparked controversy among scholars. On one hand, therapists who worked with families were convinced that behavior problems in children have their roots in the relationship between their parents (e.g., Framo, 1975). On the other hand, some researchers suggested that the emotions expressed between adults were simply too complex for young children to understand (e.g., Herzog & Sudia, 1968).

In recent decades, this controversy has been resolved. Numerous studies have confirmed that even young children are exquisitely sensitive to the quality of the interactions of the adults around them. It probably will not surprise you to learn that children exposed to discord between their parents are more likely than children whose parents have a more harmonious relationship to experience depression, behavior problems in school, and difficulties in their own relationships with peers (Emery, 1982; Grych & Fincham, 1990). Moreover, these effects have been demonstrated across cultures and around the world (Cummings, Wilson, & Shamir, 2005; Shamir et al., 2005). It is not only overt hostility that affects children, but signs that parents are disengaged or withdrawn from each other that also predict distress in 6-year-olds, even after controlling for hostility (Davies et al., 2006). Importantly, the effects of the relationship between the parents continue to be influential, regardless of the warmth between each parent and the child.

How sophisticated an observer of adult interactions can a child be? It is one thing to feel distress when two adults are shouting at each other or withdrawn from each other. It is quite another to recognize the subtleties of a real adult conflict, where the simple phrase "I'm fine" can be loaded with multiple meanings, depending on how it is expressed. In an extensive program of research that has explored this question, developmental psychologist Mark Cummings and his colleagues asked children as young as 4 years old to watch videotapes of adults discussing typical marital problems. The adults in these tapes were not the children's parents; they were actors performing scripts developed by the researchers. Controlling exactly what the children observed, the researchers manipulated aspects of the adult interactions to identify the subtle shades of meaning young children can distinguish. In one study, the researchers showed children of various ages videotapes of adult couples having an argument, and then manipulated whether the conflict was resolved successfully or whether it ended without a resolution (Cummings et al., 1989). Regardless of their age, children were sensitive not only to the presence of conflict but also to how the conflict ended: A pleasant resolution mitigated the distress of being exposed to the conflict itself, whereas an angry or withdrawn ending made the effects of negativity during the conflict even worse.

In a separate study, developmental psychologists Kelly Shifflett-Simpson and Mark Cummings (1996) took this approach even further, examining whether children ages 5–7 and 9–12 could distinguish between the verbal content of a discussion (i.e., what the adults in the videotapes said to each other) and the underlying emotional content (i.e., how they said it). Of particular interest to these researchers was how the youngest children would respond to mixed messages, that is, communication in which the verbal and emotional content disagree. Adult conflicts, especially between parents, may contain lots of mixed messages, as parents attempt to shield their children from the presence of conflict. A negative message can be expressed with feigned cheerfulness—putting on a bright smile while saying "That's a terrible idea"—and a positive message can be expressed with biting sarcasm—the bitter tone of voice that might accompany "I'm so sorry you feel that way." Are these attempts at shielding children from negativity likely to work? Are young children insensitive to conflict when it is expressed in a positive way? To address these questions, children in this study were asked to watch ten conflict discussions, all of which were moderately negative. Then the researchers randomly attached one of twelve possible endings to each discussion, manipulating whether the conflict was resolved successfully, and, if the conflict was not resolved, whether the adults expressed themselves with a positive or negative emotional tone.

Even the youngest children in this study proved remarkably sophisticated at recognizing the difference between the verbal and emotional content of the adult interactions. When the children were asked whether the adults in the videos had resolved their problems, the young children rated the tapes with negative emotions as less resolved than the tapes with positive emotions. However, the adults' attempts at masking their conflicts made no difference to the children's levels of distress. Regardless of whether the continued conflict was expressed positively or negatively, the children were equally distressed by the adults' failure to resolve their conflicts.

The Importance of Adult Relationships to Children

To the extent that parents dominate a young child's social world, it makes sense that sensitivity to the emotional environment between parents develops from a very early age. For a creature utterly dependent on adults, knowing when those adults are likely to be in a good mood and willing to provide care, or a bad mood that might distract them from providing care, is an important survival mechanism. But there are also less obvious ways that relationships among adults affect children.

Imagine you're a small child, listening to a heated conversation between your parents. The two adults are arguing with each other, not with you, and may even be in another room, unaware that you can hear them. But you do hear them. What does it mean for you? How do you react? Clinical psychologists John Grych and Frank Fincham (1990) have proposed that the way adult conflicts affect children ultimately depends on how children answer these questions for themselves. Because children are so dependent on their parents, discord between parents demands attention and leads children to try to make sense of what is happening. The process of making sense of a potentially distressing event typically proceeds in two steps. When first aware of a conflict, a child engages in **primary appraisal**, which involves noticing the conflict and evaluating whether it represents a threat. Perhaps your parents are arguing about something trivial, soon to be forgotten. Perhaps your parents are highly expressive people, quick to anger but equally quick to forgive and exchange affection again. In these cases, the conflict may represent no threat at all; it can be ignored and your attention can turn to other things. But you might decide that the conflict is a serious one—something that raises fear about the stability of your parents' relationship or fear about their ability to care for you. According to this perspective, the more that conflict between parents is perceived as personally threatening, the more it will lead to emotional distress in the child. Repeated experiences of emotional distress, by interfering with the development of emotional security, can hurt a child's ability to regulate negative emotions in other relationships (Davies & Cummings, 1994).

When an adult conflict is perceived as personally threatening, the child usually makes a **secondary appraisal**, which involves trying to understand why the conflict is happening and what the child should do about it. In reaction to adult conflict, children often have a tendency to engage in **self-blame**, seeing themselves as causing or somehow being responsible for tension they are witnessing. Among children exposed to comparable levels of parental conflict, those who view themselves as the cause of those conflicts experience more guilt, shame, and depressive symptoms than those who can identify other causes for their parents' behavior (Fosco & Grych, 2007; Stocker et al., 2003).

Primary and secondary appraisals are both ways that children develop their own models of intimacy through their observations of the adults around them. This is an important extension of attachment theory, as psychiatrist John Bowlby (1969, 1973, 1980) originally described it. Whereas the early statements of attachment theory emphasized how children learn about intimacy from their direct relationships with their caregivers, this perspective suggests that children also learn from observing the relationships between their caregivers. Primary and secondary appraisals of adult conflict are therefore important for child development because they help shape children's attachment models, setting in place enduring patterns of behavior. Suppose, listening to that argument between your parents, you decide that in fact you are the source of their unhappiness. For some children, that conclusion will lead to a desire to intervene (Grych & Fincham, 1993). But how? You might run into your parents' room and demand that they stop fighting. You might run into a different room and loudly break something. You might decide that nothing you could do will make any difference, and hide your head in a pillow. Developmental psychologists Patrick Davies and Mark Cummings (1994) suggest that, if any of these behaviors is reinforced (e.g., if intervening *does* end the argument, distracting *does* get attention, or withdrawing *does* ease the child's distress), then the behavior is likely to be repeated and likely to affect subsequent relationships in the child's life (Shelton & Harold, 2007).

Indeed, children do seem to model their behaviors in their own relationships on their observations of adult relationships. One study, for example, videotaped husbands and wives discussing areas of conflict in their marriage, and then 3 years later asked the adolescent children of these couples to rate the level of hostility and aggressive behavior in their own romantic relationships (Stocker & Richmond, 2007). The more their parents expressed hostility in their videotaped discussions, the more the adolescents described their own relationships as being hostile and aggressive, as well.

In a rare experimental study demonstrating these effects (Cummings, Iannotti, & Zahn-Waxler, 1985), researchers invited groups of 2-year-old children to play in a room that had been furnished to look like a living room, complete with kitchenette. While the children were playing, a pair of research assistants entered the room three times to distribute juice and clean up. In one experimental condition, the two assistants were cordial to each other when they first visited the room, but on their second visit they engaged in an angry (and thoroughly scripted) argument over whose turn it was to do the dishes. On their third visit, they appeared to reconcile and were cordial again. In a separate experimental condition, one group of children returned to the research rooms a second time, where pretty much the same events occurred with a different pair of research assistants. In a final control condition, the two assistants were cordial with each other whenever they entered the room.

All three groups of children were videotaped, and researchers examined these videotapes closely to address two questions. First, how did exposure to adult conflict affect the way these toddlers behaved? It is not surprising that the children who witnessed the two adults fighting were more likely than children in the control condition to display obvious signs of distress, like covering their ears with their hands or verbally scolding the arguing adults ("Bad ladies!"). More significant, the children exposed to the angry adults behaved more aggressively toward other children after the adults had left the room. Although the adult conversation was in the background and not directed toward the children in any way, the exposed children were nevertheless more likely than the children in the control condition to express anger, grab toys from other children, and even physically attack another child after the adults had left the room. These behaviors declined dramatically after the adults returned for their final friendly interaction.

The second question for the researchers was whether the effects of adult conflict on children's behaviors changed with repeated exposures. Do children exhibit **desensitization**, becoming accustomed to the sound of adults arguing in the background? Or do they demonstrate **sensitization**, becoming increasingly reactive the more they are exposed? As FIGURE 13.3 shows, this study found strong evidence for sensitization. Although exposure to adult conflict predicted more aggressive behavior in all the experimental groups, children exposed twice to the angry interaction were far more aggressive than children in any other group.

If these researchers were able to observe such dramatic effects in their research rooms, there are several reasons to expect that the effects of adult conflict are far greater in real life. In this study, the adults were strangers to the children, but in real life, the arguing adults are often parents and others on whom the child depends. In this study, the argument was emotional but not violent, and the topic was of no direct relevance to the children. Imagine how much more distressing a physical confrontation must be or an argument about issues that relate to the child (such as parenting). Finally, in this study, children were much more sensitive to the adult conflict after being exposed only twice. Over time, repeated exposures to adult conflict appear to have long-term effects on children's emotional security and adjustment (Davies & Cummings, 1998).

(a)

(b)

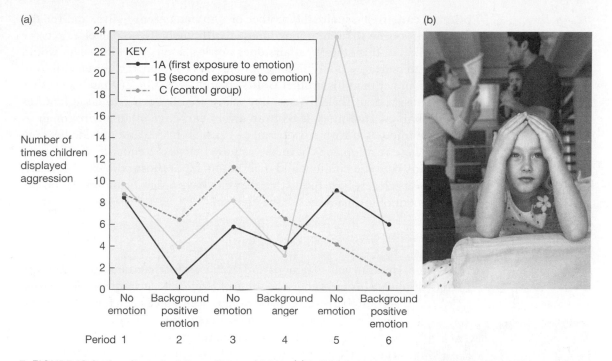

FIGURE 13.3 **The effect of adult conflict on children.** (a) In this study, children who were exposed to adults arguing were more aggressive themselves immediately afterward, compared to a control group who were not exposed. But children exposed a second time were even more aggressive, demonstrating sensitization. (Source: Cummings, Iannotti, & Zahn-Waxler, 1985.) (b) Even very young children are acutely sensitive to the quality of the relationships between adults around them.

MAIN POINTS

›› Although it was once thought that children could not appreciate the complexity of adult interactions, even young children are acutely sensitive to the quality of the interactions of the adults around them.

›› To the extent that children blame themselves for adult conflicts, observing conflict between adults can harm their developing self-image.

›› Children develop their own models of intimacy in part through observing adult relationships, and then generalizing to their own relationships.

›› Repeated exposures to negative adult interactions tend to predict increasingly negative reactions in children.

The Expanding Social World of Childhood

As Bowlby observed in his initial statements on attachment theory (see Chapter 3 and Chapter 6), the infant's first relationship is likely to be with a primary caregiver, usually the mother or another parent figure, and for the first weeks of life the infant may interact with virtually no one else. Yet, for most children, this state of affairs does not last long. The child who would grow up to be Harry Houdini, for example, was the fourth of seven children, 2 years younger than his brother Gottfried and 2 years older than his brother Theo. Thus, young Ehrich Weiss, like many people born into large families or tight-knit communities, lived from a very early age in an environment in which he interacted with a wide range of people inside and outside his own family. These relationships have been studied far less frequently than the relationships between children and their parents, but those who examine such attachments closely have found that they can have a significant impact on the development of intimacy across the lifespan.

Sibling Relationships and the Development of Intimacy

In his time, Houdini was so famous and so successful that numerous imitators tried to duplicate his feats and steal some of Houdini's acclaim for themselves. Although these competitors have long since been forgotten, while Houdini lived, one of his most persistent rivals was a fellow magician and escape artist named Hardeen. Wherever Houdini toured, Hardeen followed, and when Houdini was booked into the largest performance hall in a town, Hardeen was often booked into the second largest. The rivalry between the two men was very public, with each man proclaiming himself the master of the other, and the press reporting with gusto each snub and insult. What made the competition between Houdini and Hardeen especially delicious was the fact that Hardeen was actually Houdini's brother, Theo Weiss (**FIGURE 13.4**). Growing up, Harry had been closer to Theo than to any of his other siblings. Although Theo was 2 years younger, he was also bigger than Harry from an early age, protecting him, fighting for him, and even teaching him his first magic trick when they both were children. When Houdini first started out as an amateur magician, he briefly brought Theo in as a partner. This history between Hardeen and Houdini was no secret, and the fact that their public rivalry was also a sibling rivalry gave their conflict a mythic stature that audiences adored.

FIGURE 13.4 Houdini and Hardeen: brothers, partners, and rivals. Houdini's greatest competition for the title of Master Escape Artist was his brother Theo Weiss (in the foreground above), who performed under the stage name Hardeen. Their public rivalry was bitter, but it was also an act to drum up business and scare off real competition. In fact, the brothers were quite close.

Yet, away from the glare of the spotlight, the relationship between the brothers was far more complex than anyone knew. Their public feud was an act, staged as a way to drum up business for both men and drive other competitors out of town. In fact, the two brothers were quite close—Houdini himself chose Theo's stage name, designed his props and escapes, and helped book him into theaters. If a third competitor had the nerve to come to town, it was Theo who delivered the message that no other escape artists were welcome. At the same time, the private relationship between the two men was not entirely free of the rivalry they expressed so extravagantly in public. For example, Hardeen once commented to a reporter that Houdini would make him an excellent assistant. This Houdini judged to be going too far, and there was some real tension between the two men until Hardeen acknowledged, at least in private, which brother was really calling the shots.

Consider the complex blend of rivalry and affection, support and competition, that characterized the relationship between these two brothers. Although the details may differ, the tensions and contradictions in the relationship between Houdini and Hardeen are probably familiar to anyone raised with a sibling—nearly 90 percent of the population of the United States (Hernandez, 1997). Why should this relationship be so fraught with ambivalence? After all, siblings generally share a common background. They are likely to be more similar to each other than they are to unrelated individuals. They are likely to be pretty familiar to each other as well, as the relationship with a sibling is the single longest relationship most people will experience in their lifetimes. Everything we know about the effects of similarity and familiarity on attraction and liking (see Chapter 4) suggests that the relationship between siblings should be especially close and affectionate. Why is it that, in a study of elementary school children asked to describe the different relationships in their lives, conflict was described as more frequent between siblings than within any other relationship (Furman & Buhrmester, 1985)? Is it merely a coincidence that the first act of violence in the Bible occurs between the brothers Cain and Abel?

Evolutionary biologists suggest that competition between siblings is no coincidence at all, but rather the logical product of natural selection. As evidence, they point to the fact that competition between siblings is found everywhere in the animal kingdom. Birds, mammals, fish, and insects all contain species that regularly kill their siblings when food is scarce (Sulloway, 2001). The African black eagle lays two eggs at a time; the one that hatches first generally pecks its younger sibling to death, whether food is scarce or not (Mock, Drummond, & Stinson, 1990). Anthropologist William Hamilton (1964) explained all of this intrafamilial violence by noting that, although siblings are related, they share only half of their genes. Thus, their interests are not identical, and when the benefits of competition are particularly large (i.e., when competition promotes survival), then natural selection should favor sibling rivalry over cooperation.

In humans, the resource that siblings compete for most ferociously is attention from parents. Parents, being equally related to all of their biological children, ought to be equally invested in helping each of their children survive. Each child, reasonably, prefers the distribution of resources to be biased in his or her direction and stands to benefit when this happens. Deep in our ancestral past, natural selection should therefore have favored those who were sensitive to **differential parental treatment**, and those who were competitive enough to bend parental treatment in their own direction. Research on infants suggests that humans have indeed developed mechanisms for monitoring differential parental treatment. One study observed how 1-year-old infants responded when their mothers were asked to be unresponsive to them for a few moments (Hart et al., 1998). In some conditions, the mothers were asked to direct obvious attention toward a picture book while they ignored their child. In other conditions, the mothers were asked to direct their attention toward a life-size baby doll. As you might expect, the infants displayed obvious signs of distress whenever their mothers were unresponsive, but they were significantly more distressed when their mothers were attending to a doll than when their mothers were reading a book. In other words, although no baby likes to be ignored, babies seem especially sensitive to being ignored in favor of another baby.

Some have argued that the perception of differential parental treatment, and the competition for parental attention that this implies, lies at the heart of sibling rivalry and conflict (e.g., Brody, 1998; Dunn, 1983). In fact, numerous studies show that siblings who perceive that they are treated differently by their parents report more conflict and more rivalry in their relationships with each other (McHale et al., 2000; Richmond, Stocker, & Rienks, 2005). It is not just a matter of perceptions, either. In one study, researchers spent time in the homes of 96 families, observing how parents treated each sibling and rating the quality of the siblings' relationships (Stocker, Dunn, & Plomin, 1989). The more that mothers were observed treating siblings differently, the more competitive and controlling the siblings were observed to be in their interactions with each other. The problem with differential treatment is not the inequality itself; after all, different children have different needs. It might even be argued that parents' ability to tailor their treatment to the unique needs of each child is a mark of skillful parenting. Rather, differential parental treatment is associated with problems between siblings only when the treatment is perceived as unfair (Kowal et al., 2002). When siblings are wide apart in age or are different genders, differential treatment is viewed as more reasonable and therefore has fewer implications for sibling rivalry and competition (McHale et al., 2000).

What are the implications of sibling relationships for the development of a capacity for intimacy? We have already discussed how witnessing conflict between parents can inhibit the emotional growth of children. If merely watching conflict is bad, actually participating in conflict with a sibling should be even more harmful, with children experiencing more sibling conflict likely to have more problems developing successful intimate relationships later in life. The truth is not that simple. No matter how complicated and difficult sibling relationships may be, research suggests that interacting with siblings actually contributes to the development of intimate relationships later in life.

The earliest research to examine the implications of sibling relationships for social development was motivated by an interest in how children develop a **theory of mind**, or the recognition that other people have beliefs, knowledge, and desires that are different from one's own. Understanding what other people believe and feel about the world is a prerequisite for empathizing, deceiving, explaining, or communicating with other people, and some have argued that this recognition is the cornerstone of successful social interaction (e.g., Dunn, 1996). One tool for measuring the development of theories of mind is the **false belief test**, also called the Sally-Anne test (FIGURE 13.5). Young children are exposed to two characters: Sally, who has a basket, and Anne, who has a box. A marble is given to Sally; she puts it in her basket and leaves the room. While she is gone, Anne takes the marble from Sally's basket and puts it into her box. When Sally returns to the room, where will she look for the marble? Children observing this story know that the marble has switched places, but Sally, who was absent when the switch occurred, does not know this. Children younger than 3 years old generally cannot distinguish between

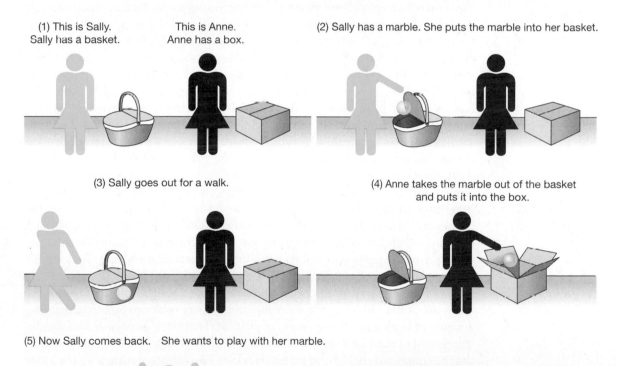

(1) This is Sally. Sally has a basket.   This is Anne. Anne has a box.

(2) Sally has a marble. She puts the marble into her basket.

(3) Sally goes out for a walk.

(4) Anne takes the marble out of the basket and puts it into the box.

(5) Now Sally comes back.   She wants to play with her marble.

(6) Where will Sally look for her marble?

FIGURE 13.5 Measuring a child's theory of mind. The false belief test is a simple way to measure whether children recognize that other people have beliefs, knowledge, and desires that are different from their own. Children who understand that Sally still thinks her marble is in the basket are said to have developed a theory of mind, and children with siblings tend to develop a theory of mind earlier than children without siblings.

their own knowledge and the character's knowledge, and they mistakenly guess that Sally will look in Anne's box for the marble. By about age 5, however, most children correctly understand that Sally has different information than they do, and guess that Sally will look in her own basket (Miller & Aloise, 1989; Wimmer & Perner, 1983).

What do siblings have to do with the development of theories of mind? In observational studies of young children interacting with family members in their homes, developmental psychiatrist Judy Dunn and her colleagues noted that younger children spent more time talking about emotions and mental states with their older siblings than they did with their parents (Brown & Dunn, 1992). This makes sense. Young children usually do not have to care for their parents; they don't have to understand much beyond their own needs, especially when interacting with their mother and father. The presence of a sibling, however, changes things. Siblings cannot be counted on to provide care. They need to be reasoned with and understood. Interactions with siblings therefore provide an opportunity for younger children to develop their theories of mind. Indeed, they must develop this kind of understanding if they are to interact with their older siblings successfully. It follows that young children with siblings should develop theories of mind more quickly than young children without siblings, and this is exactly what research on the subject has found. In a study of 80 children between ages 3 and 4, those who had one sibling did better on false belief tests than those with no siblings, and those with multiple siblings did better still (Perner, Ruffman, & Leekam, 1994). You may recall that Houdini, whose success as a magician depended on his ability to create false beliefs in his audience, was one of seven siblings.

To the extent that it benefits young children to confront opinions and desires other than their own, a bit of conflict between siblings might not be a bad thing. In fact, some conflict may be essential to developing strategies for managing differences of opinion successfully (Grotevant & Cooper, 1986). Of course, nobody benefits from a sibling relationship that is totally hostile. Serious physical aggression between siblings predicts aggressive behavior with peers in later life (Bank, Patterson, & Reid, 1996), and hostile relationships with an older sibling predict delinquency in the younger sibling (Slomkowski et al., 2001). But in a generally positive sibling relationship, experiencing a range of interactions, including conflict and support, may promote the development of social competence. Evidence for this idea comes from research that has observed children in generally happy homes interacting with their siblings. Across several of these studies, young children's ability to adopt another person's perspective was positively associated with the number of friendly interactions with siblings *and* with the number of sibling conflicts (e.g., Howe & Ross, 1990; Stormshak, Bellanti, & Bierman, 1996; Youngblade & Dunn, 1995). These studies are far from definitive, but they offer some support for the idea that the contradictions within sibling relationships—that unique combination of rivalry and support—may help prepare young people for the complexities of intimate relationships throughout life.

Childhood Friendships

During a 2-month engagement in Boston in 1906, Houdini faced one of his greatest challenges. Before a full audience and a judging committee of 300 men, he was bound with three pairs of handcuffs, and then sealed within a giant wicker basket fastened with iron bands and locked with three heavy padlocks. The locks on those padlocks were sealed with wax, the locked basket was further wrapped with ropes and chains, and finally a curtain was drawn around the whole thing. Could Houdini escape from such a cage? After 62 minutes, Houdini emerged from behind the curtain—exhausted, sweating, disheveled, and triumphant. The next morning's *Boston Globe* quoted the head of the judging committee, Dr. Joseph F. Waitt, saying to Houdini: "I surrender to you. For years I have been planning this test for you and I admit my defeat. I am satisfied that, unaided, except by your own strength and ingenuity, you have succeeded in accomplishing what myself and my associates believed absolutely impossible" (Kalush & Sloman, 2006, p. 184).

What the papers did not report, but what would have cast quite a different light on the proceedings if it had been known, was the fact that Waitt and Houdini had already been close personal friends for several years on the night of the great challenge. Waitt was a magic enthusiast (as well as a dentist). On a prior tour through Boston, he had met the great magician and they got along so well that Waitt volunteered to help him design some stunts and challenges. Houdini was a loyal friend and reliable correspondent, exchanging letters with Waitt throughout his life and relying on him frequently whenever an "impartial" judge was called for.

This was not the first time that Houdini's personal life and his professional life supported each other. When he was 9 years old, it was his friend Jack Hoeffler who gave him his first chance to perform in public when he invited Harry to do an acrobatics act in a five-cent circus he was organizing. A decade later, his friend and fellow magician Jacob Hyman suggested that they name their new magic act after their idol, the French magician Robert-Houdin. Together they performed as the Brothers Houdini, and though the two "brothers" soon went their separate ways, Hyman later helped in Houdini's many projects.

For Houdini, the ability to form and maintain relationships with people outside his own family proved time and again to be an important element of his success. For many children, developing this same ability marks a crucial step on the path to adult intimate relationships. A friendship is often the developing child's first relationship with someone who is not a relative or caretaker. As such, friendships can be seen as a bridge between the family unit and the broader social world (Dunn, 2004).

One defining feature of friendship, and the element that distinguishes it most clearly from familial relationships, is that friendships are *voluntary*. As the saying goes, you can't choose your family, but you can choose your friends. We can choose to end a friendship too, which means that an enduring friendship reflects an active decision to keep it going. Our relationships with family members, in contrast, are defined not by behavior but by biology and social structure, and they persist whether we maintain them or not. A second defining feature of friendship is *reciprocity* (Hartup & Stevens, 1997). One person cannot choose to be a friend alone; a friendship exists only when two individuals acknowledge and affirm their relationship to each other. This mutuality distinguishes being a friend from simply being popular; popularity describes affection traveling in a single direction.

A third defining feature is *equal status*. Because humans usually give birth to one child at a time, even sibling relationships usually involve differences in power arising from differences in age and birth order. In contrast, children tend to form their first friendships with other children their own age, and consequently friends are more likely to interact as equals (Volling, Young-blade, & Belsky, 1997). Observational research confirms that children ages 8–10 adopt different roles with their best friends than with their younger siblings (Stoneman, Brody, & MacKinnon, 1984). With a younger sibling, an older child is more likely to play the manager to the younger sibling's employee, with interactions marked by coercion and compliance (e.g., "You better do as I say"). Friends are more likely to work and play jointly, with all of the compromise and negotiation that implies.

A friendship, in other words, is a child's first real peer relationship. As such, friendships play a role in the life of the developing child that no family relationship can match. For example, several studies of children's relationships have examined whether having a good-quality relationship in one context (e.g., a strong bond with a sibling) can compensate for having a poor relationship in another context (e.g., few or negative peer relationships). Across studies, the results have been consistent: A strong bond with a friend can make up for a weak sibling relationship, but the best sibling relationships cannot make up for the lack of a good friend (Sherman, Lansford, & Volling, 2006; van Aken & Asendorpf, 1997).

The relative flexibility of children's friendships makes them an ideal laboratory in which to experiment with, and eventually learn, the foundations of intimacy. As Dunn (2004) observed through extensive observational studies of families in their homes, interacting with friends helps children develop a capacity for empathy. Dunn points out that the mutual affection between friends provides a motivation for empathy that is absent from most other relationships children experience. Because they have chosen and care about each other, friends are especially motivated to acknowledge each other's desires, resolve conflict effectively, and recognize the impact of their own behaviors on each other's feelings. One way this understanding emerges is through **shared imaginative play**. When children create and inhabit a fantasy world together—the living room pillows are turned into a fort, a bath towel into a superhero's cape, or a stuffed bear into a companion— the rules of their new world can become pretty elaborate pretty fast. Yet kids can still reach a quick consensus on who gets to fly and when, which characters live or die, what the secret mission is, and how to accomplish it. Part of the pleasure of playing pretend comes from sharing a mental world with someone else, from understanding and being understood by a peer. In adults, establishing shared assumptions about the world has been identified as a central task of a successful relationship (Berger & Kellner, 1964). By developing and sharing assumptions about their pretend worlds, children begin to develop the capacity to understand their peers' assumptions about the real world (Lillard et al., 2013). Of course, siblings also engage in shared imaginative play. However, perhaps because we are pretty much stuck with our siblings, there is less reason for siblings to try to compromise or adopt the other person's perspective when differences of opinion arise. As a consequence, conflicts between siblings are generally more heated, and more likely to involve physical aggression, than conflicts between friends (Furman & Buhrmester, 1985).

Just as friendships offer new ways to understand others, friendships also provide children with new sources of information about themselves. As we discussed in reference to attachment theory, infants learn from their first interactions with their primary caregivers whether to expect support and comfort from other people (Bowlby, 1969). When young children enter the social world outside the family, they have a chance to learn all over again whether to expect rejection or acceptance from others. To measure the extent to which children are accepted or rejected by their peers, researchers have used **sociometric testing**, a method of quantifying the social standing of individuals within a group (Hayvren & Hymel, 1984). The technique is very straightforward: Children in a defined group (often a classroom) are interviewed individually and asked to name who they like and who they dislike within the group. Then the researchers add up the number of positive and negative mentions that each child earns from the rest of the group.

This relatively simple process enables researchers to identify four distinct categories of social standing. Two of the categories are fairly intuitive. Those who are liked by many peers and disliked by few are classified as "popular." It is not hard to predict that children in this group should excel in a variety of different social situations, and in study after study, they do (Newcomb, Bukowski, & Pattee, 1993). One notable study examined the skills that predict popularity in young children by observing the behavior of 22 boys during the summer before they all entered first grade (Putallaz, 1983). Each boy was invited to interact with two other boys who knew each other (and who were actually confederates of the researcher). How did each new boy try to fit into the group formed by the other two boys? Some boys talked a lot, some talked a little. Some were argumentative ("You're doing that all wrong!") and some were conciliatory ("Hey, that's a great idea!"). Four months later, when the boys had all begun first grade, the researchers did sociometric testing to determine the social standing of each child. The most popular boys were the ones who, 4 months earlier, were the most agreeable and who had spoken the least. In other words, those who would turn out to be popular knew how to ease themselves into a new situation, a skill that comes in handy when a new school year begins, and at many other stages of life as well.

Those who are liked by few of their peers and disliked by many are classified as "rejected." What kinds of behaviors are associated with being rejected as a child? In the study above, the boys who would later be rejected by their first-grade peers were the opposite of the popular boys. They were the most talkative but also the most disagreeable—an extremely unpopular combination. Perhaps we have all met people who, trying desperately to join a group, are nevertheless unable to figure out the norms of the group. As a result, they behave inappropriately and end up being shunned instead (Newcomb et al., 1993). These patterns appear to be hard to break. In one study that followed 112 fifth-grade children for 7 years, those who had been rejected by their peers as children were significantly more likely to experience a range of negative outcomes as young adults, including poor performance in school, delinquency, and criminal behavior (Kupersmidt & Coie, 1990).

The two remaining categories in sociometric testing are less obvious. Those who are liked and disliked by many peers at the same time are classified as "controversial." How can someone be liked and disliked at the same time? Look at presidential candidates, who are passionately admired by their supporters and just as passionately disparaged by their detractors. Politicians tend to be noticed for attention-grabbing behaviors that some respond to and others reject. Controversial children are the same way: They are as aggressive as those in the rejected group, but they compensate with relatively high social skills like those in the popular group. Their outcomes tend to be much more positive than the outcomes of the rejected, another illustration of the benefits of even a small group of friends.

Those who are rarely mentioned as being liked or disliked are classified as "neglected," or socially isolated. Children in this group score low on measures of social skills and on measures of aggression; they are more shy and withdrawn. Although the children in this group are likely to have as few friends as children in the rejected group, their outcomes are quite different. Research that followed children from second through fifth grade found that, whereas children classified as neglected and rejected in second grade were all at higher risk for negative outcomes by fifth grade, rejected children were more likely to display externalizing behaviors (e.g., fighting with other children, vandalism, disobedience), whereas neglected children were more likely to display internalizing behaviors (e.g., withdrawal, depression) (Hymel et al., 1990).

What makes sociometric testing so powerful is that it neatly summarizes how children are likely to be treated by their peers, and this treatment has long-term implications. In Chapter 6, we discussed ways an individual's personality gets reinforced throughout life by interactions with others and the accumulated consequences of those interactions (Caspi, 1987; Caspi, Bem, & Elder, 1989). A child's social standing early in life is a significant factor in setting these patterns into motion. Children with more effective social skills are accepted by their peers, and from this they learn to trust that they will be accepted by others in the future. Children with weaker social skills may be rejected by their peers and may learn to be wary of rejection in the future (Boivin & Hymel, 1997). Thus, a child's early friendships reflect and reinforce behavior patterns that may extend across the lifespan.

To the extent that friendships in childhood help establish and reinforce general social skills, they should be especially relevant to the development of future intimate relationships. When researchers have examined this possibility directly, they have generally addressed the implications of three specific questions about children's friendships (Hartup & Stevens, 1997). Does the child have friends, and if so how many? Who are the child's friends? What kind of relationship does the child have with his or her friends? The answers have been shown to be related to the kinds of intimate relationships the child will have later.

With respect to the size of a child's friendship network, you might expect that children with more friends are set to have more successful relationships in adolescence. Indeed, there is evidence to support this view. Longitudinal studies show that children who have larger groups of friends of the opposite sex during childhood and early adolescence have longer and more involved intimate relationships in later adolescence (Feiring, 1999b). Those children who were classified as popular in sociometric testing during childhood do in fact date more in high school (Franzoi, Davis, & Vasquez-Suson, 1994). But the news is not all good for the popular kids. Those who are more accepted by their peers in early adolescence tend to start romantic relationships earlier than their less popular peers (Zimmer-Gembeck, Siebenbruner, & Collins, 2004), and this can have negative consequences (as we will discuss shortly). Although the benefits of being popular may be mixed, the implications of being rejected are quite clear. In a 12-year longitudinal study that compared the development of children who had a stable best friend with the development of children who lacked friends, those with no friends in childhood reported significantly lower self-worth and higher levels of depression and anxiety (Bagwell, Newcomb, & Bukowski, 1998). In other words, popularity may be a mixed blessing, but overall it is still a blessing, whereas being shunned has some real costs.

With respect to the composition of a child's friendship network, it appears that who you know makes a big difference to the development of intimacy. Peers are a powerful source of norms about intimate behavior: They teach us what sorts of behaviors are appropriate and when they are acceptable (Connolly & Goldberg, 1999). This process of peer education begins at a very early age (Connolly et al., 1999). It follows that a child's beliefs about intimacy and starting an intimate relationship will be shaped by who the child's peers turn out to be. Thus, 11-year-old children whose friends are mostly the same sex and mostly the same age are significantly less likely than children with older, opposite-sex friends to be dating by the time they are 15 (Cooksey, Mott, & Neubauer, 2002). Having friends who are sexually active is a strong predictor of early sexual experience as well (Sieving et al., 2006). In general, having friends who are experimenting with intimate relationships makes doing so seem appropriate and worthwhile and provides opportunities to follow suit.

With respect to the quality of a child's friendships, most research has emphasized continuity. In other words, children who can maintain supportive, close peer relationships in childhood are likely to grow up to have supportive, close intimate relationships in adulthood. A number of longitudinal studies that have followed children into early adulthood have supported this idea (e.g., Collins et al., 1997; Connolly, Furman, & Konarski, 2000; Seiffge-Krenke, Shulman, & Klessinger, 2001). The reverse also seems to be true: Hostility between friends in childhood predicts hostile romantic relationships in young adulthood, even after controlling for hostility between children and their parents (Stocker & Richmond, 2007). Yet, even though it is generally better to have good-quality friendships, the implications of friendship quality differ, depending on the characteristics of the friend. A strong relationship with an agreeable, supportive person is a fine thing, bringing out and reinforcing the best in a child. A strong relationship with a problematic person, however, seems to have the opposite effect. In research that followed seventh- and eighth-graders over the course of a school year, children whose friends were more disruptive at the beginning of the year became more disruptive themselves by the end of it, but only if they reported high-quality relationships with those disruptive friends (Berndt & Keefe, 1995).

GENDER DIFFERENCES IN CHILDREN'S FRIENDSHIPS. Many observers have described gender as a central organizing principle in children's friendships, and it is not hard to see why (FIGURE 13.6). For one thing, gender plays a major role in how young children choose their friends. As child psychologist Willard Hartup (1989) observed, children's friendships are same-sex friendships, and fewer than 5 percent of friendships among children cross gender lines (Maccoby & Jacklin, 1987). Observational studies of friendship behaviors in classroom settings and small groups further suggest that the friendships of boys and the friendships of girls take place in entirely separate cultures (e.g., Maccoby, 1998). The culture of girls' friendships is described as more intimate, whereas that of boys is described as more hierarchical.

Yet recent reviews of research on boys' and girls' friendships have suggested that the differences between them may be overstated (Underwood, 2004). The biggest differences between male and female friendships in childhood are found in studies that ask children to describe their behavior on self-report instruments, or that observe children in mixed-group settings. Behavioral differences between boys and girls are strongest when boys and girls are in each other's presence and diminish considerably when boys and girls are observed alone (Maccoby & Jacklin, 1987). However, even in mixed-group settings, there is considerable overlap between the types of friendship behaviors reported by each gender. In a survey that asked children ages 10–12 about the kinds of things they do with their best friends, girls did report

FIGURE 13.6 Boys at play, girls at play. Gender is a major organizing principle in children's friendships. But recent evidence suggests substantial overlap in boys' and girls' peer behaviors.

more socializing (e.g., going to restaurants, telling secrets) and boys did report more competitive play (e.g., team sports), but the overall differences were not large (Zarbatany, McDougall, & Hymel, 2000).

When researchers have examined the specific contexts in which boys and girls display different types of social behaviors, the gender differences become even less clear. For example, clinical psychologist Audrey Zakriski and her colleagues observed children's social behavior at a summer camp, taking note of not only each child's rates of aggressive behavior (e.g., hitting or teasing) and nurturing behavior (e.g., listening to others, showing positive emotion) but also the immediate social environments in which those behaviors took place (Zakriski, Wright, & Underwood, 2005). When they calculated overall rates of each kind of behavior, they found the expected differences: Girls were more nurturing and boys were more aggressive. But when they examined circumstances in which those behaviors occurred, they found that boys and girls encountered different kinds of social situations as well. Boys were more likely to be teased and provoked than girls, for instance. In other words, if boys were reacting more aggressively, part of the reason is that boys were more likely to be provoked, a situation that tends to elicit aggressive behavior. Within a specific situation, gender differences in social behavior were greatly reduced, especially in younger children. When teased by a peer, boys who were 11 years old and older were far more likely to respond with verbal aggression than girls of the same age, but boys and girls younger than 11 responded with verbal aggression at the same rate.

It's clear that different methods tell different stories about the role of gender in childhood friendships. The bottom line is that, even though the specific behaviors that characterize male and female friendships may differ somewhat, the implications of their friendships for the development of intimacy throughout life may not.

MAIN POINTS

>> Although siblings are familiar to each other and have much in common, children describe their relationships with siblings as containing more conflict than any other relationships in their lives, often as a result of competition for parental attention.

>> Conflict with siblings may help emotional development. Children with siblings are quicker to understand that other people have beliefs, knowledge, and desires that are different from their own, and they have greater social competence.

>> In contrast to relationships within the family, relationships with friends in childhood are voluntary, reciprocal, and of equal status, and thus teach children whether to expect acceptance or rejection from others.

>> Through sociometric testing, researchers have documented the benefits of popularity, the significant costs of being rejected, and the fact that children's friendship networks predict the quality and timing of their first intimate relationships.

Adolescence and Initial Steps into Intimacy

It is hard to find anyone with anything nice to say about adolescence. The pop singer Tori Amos calls it "the cruelest place on earth." The actress and comedienne Carol Burnett called it "one big walking pimple." Sounds pretty grim. Part of the problem, as developmental psychologist Erik Erikson explained in his classic text *Identity: Youth and Crisis* (1968), is that for adolescents the roles of childhood no longer fit, yet the roles of adulthood remain just out of reach. Defined by the World Health Organization as the period between the ages of 10 and 19 (Goodburn & Ross, 1995), adolescence amounts to several years in transition between one stage of life and another, and making it through can be awkward at best and terrifying at worst.

> " Adolescence is a border between childhood and adulthood. Like all borders, it's teeming with energy and fraught with danger."
>
> —Mary Pipher, psychotherapist, *Reviving Ophelia* (1994, p. 292)

What makes the transition especially poignant is that most of it takes place in public. Until adolescence, a child's main sources of support, security, and comfort lie within the family. Relationships with peers expand children's social world slightly, but even these relationships usually take place under the watchful eyes of parents, guardians, and teachers. During adolescence, however, young people begin to spend significant time together outside of adult supervision. This growing separation offers adolescents their first chance to find support, security, and comfort from the broader social world. Part of establishing an identity as an independent person, according to Erikson and others, involves developing sources of intimacy outside the family unit, shifting one's primary attachment relationship from a parent figure to a romantic partner (Hazan & Zeifman, 1994). Think of how risky that is! Adolescents are like trapeze artists, stepping away from a secure platform, swinging wildly into the air, and letting go. Why make that leap? The hope is that someone will be there to catch them and swing them over to a new platform—in other words, a new, reliable source of intimacy and protection. The danger, of course, lies in the real possibility of falling without a net.

FIGURE 13.7 Harry and Bess Houdini. The couple met when she was 18 and he was 20. They married within 2 weeks of their first meeting.

Houdini, the consummate showman, made this transition remarkably easily. History records little of his early romantic life, but we do know that Houdini was active in show business from an early age and spent most of his adolescence among show people. One of them was an adolescent when they met: Wilhelmina Beatrice Rahner, known to her friends as Bess. Like Houdini, Bess had also lost her father, a strict Roman Catholic, when she was relatively young, and Bess had to work in her brother's tailor shop from an early age. Yet Bess was, for the times, a free spirit with dreams of seeing the world. When she was 16, she took a job as a seamstress with a traveling circus. Two years later, she had joined a musical trio called the Floral Sisters, performing in the same circuits as the young Houdini.

Bess (then 18) and Houdini (then 20) were set up on a blind date by Harry's brother Theo, who was his performing partner at the time. The chemistry was immediate. In Bess, Houdini saw two things: a beautiful young girl with a passionate character to match his own, and someone small enough to fit into the trunk he and Theo were using for a new escape trick. Harry and Bess were married right away, and Bess quickly replaced Theo as Harry's partner in the act (**FIGURE 13.7**). In this way, Houdini completed a transition in his professional and personal lives at the same time, shifting his primary dependence from a family member (his brother) to someone outside the family (Bess, his new wife). Most adolescents make the same transition that Houdini did when he met Bess, although they usually take a bit more time getting through it.

How Adolescents Think About Intimate Relationships

In early childhood, as we noted earlier, the majority of children's friendships are same-sex friendships (Hartup, 1989). Still, even during a period when members of the opposite sex are widely regarded as having cooties, children absorb messages about intimate relationships from the world around them. Thus, they generally understand some of the core features from an early age. For example, surveys of boys and girls in the first years of adolescence find that even the youngest children surveyed (around age 9) clearly distinguish between intimate relationships and opposite-sex friendships, describing the former, but not the latter, in terms of longing, physical attraction, a high level of personal disclosure, and commitment (Connolly et al., 1999; Lempers & Clark-Lempers, 1993). It is important to note that young adolescents' ability to recognize different types of close relationships does not vary much by age (i.e., the descriptions of 9-year-olds are very similar to those of 16-year-olds) or by their own experience (i.e., it's not necessary to have a romantic relationship to know that romantic relationships are different from friendships). General ideas about intimate relationships thus seem to be embedded in a shared culture (Simon, Eder, & Evans, 1992).

At the same time, adolescents' understanding of intimacy does grow more sophisticated as they get older. In sixth grade, for example, adolescents may still wonder what counts as a date, or as a girlfriend or boyfriend (Darling et al., 1999). They know there is a difference, but they are a little vague on the details. By eighth grade, teenagers understand questions about romantic relationships immediately, but adolescents in middle school tend to emphasize the more superficial aspects (Roscoe, Diana, & Brooks, 1987). When asked about the qualities they value in a potential partner, younger adolescents are somewhat self-centered, focusing on the rewards they stand to receive from potential partners, like social approval and support (Feiring, 1996, 1999a). Older teens also want these things, of course, but they are equally likely to mention qualities that reflect an awareness of the other person, such as companionship and self-disclosure (Connolly & Johnson, 1996; Furman & Buhrmester, 1992; Furman & Wehner, 1994). College students (still considered adolescents at 18 and 19) begin to consider issues related to commitment, like mutual affection and plans for the future (Galotti, Kozberg, & Appleman, 1990; Roscoe et al., 1987), and they are more likely to acknowledge negative aspects of relationships as well, like jealousy and infidelity (Feiring, 1999b). Taking a broad view, psychiatrist Robert Waldinger and his colleagues (2002) have suggested that the same basic themes appear in the narratives of youths ages 14–16 as at age 25, but the young adults' narratives are more complex than the adolescents' narratives. This may reflect our greater experience with relationships as we grow older, and our greater awareness that intimate relationships can have significant implications, both positive and negative, for the rest of our lives (Connolly & Goldberg, 1999).

What about beliefs about sexuality in relationships? On average, adolescents have relatively conservative views on sex, at least as reported on surveys. For example, a national survey of 12- to 19-year-olds found that the majority of adolescents endorse the view that intercourse is not appropriate for high school teens at all, with rates of disapproval at 63 percent among boys, and 76 percent among girls (Albert, 2004). In the same survey, about 66 percent indicated that they "strongly agree" that sex should only occur within a serious romantic relationship (Albert, 2004). The message from these teens seems to be: Try to postpone having sex, but if you cannot wait, share it with someone you love.

> "If falling in love is anything like learning to spell, I don't want to do it. It takes too long."
>
> —Leo, age 7

Adolescents' shared culture communicates not only what intimate relationships are like, but also that intimate relationships are highly desirable and that everyone should have one. Barbie has Ken, Superman has Lois Lane, and even Mickey Mouse is not quite complete without Minnie. It's not surprising that, as early as sixth grade, adolescents are frequently preoccupied with developing intimate relationships themselves (Darling et al., 1999). There appears to be more variability in their desires for relationships than in their ideas about them. For instance, although boys generally express the same desires for relationships as girls do, those from European backgrounds express a greater interest than youths from Asian backgrounds, again highlighting the powerful role of culture in shaping early experiences with relationships (Connolly et al., 2004). Puberty also plays an important role. Although children of all ages can characterize intimate relationships accurately, they become more interested in experimenting themselves once their hormones kick in, and this occurs at different times for different children (Bearman, Jones, & Udry, 1997; Miller & Benson, 1999). Still, you might expect that on average the desire for a boyfriend or a girlfriend increases throughout adolescence, and a large study of adolescents between the fifth and eighth grades confirms that this is the case (Connolly et al., 2004).

Adolescent Experiences of Intimacy

Adolescents do more than think about relationships. By the time they reach age 18, nearly 80 percent of teenagers in the United States will have experienced their own romantic relationships for the first time (Carver, Joyner, & Udry, 2003). These initial relationships emerge gradually. Whereas childhood is characterized mostly by same-sex friendships, young adolescents begin to cross the invisible boundaries between boys and girls, socializing more frequently in mixed-sex groups. These groups then set the stage for couples to notice each other, develop mutual attraction, and eventually pair off (Feiring, 1999b). Adolescents grow more open to this sort of thing as they get older. One national study, for example, found that, at ages 11–12, only 8 percent of early adolescents report having dated (Cooksey et al., 2002). By ages 13–14, this number rises to 29 percent, and by ages 15–16, it reaches 54 percent.

Is this puppy love, something cute but easily dismissed? Hardly. It is worth remembering that Shakespeare made Romeo and Juliet adolescents, so clearly the Elizabethans had no trouble imagining that the 13-year-old Juliet could experience a depth of passion worth dying for. When modern adolescents fall in love, they too tend to fall hard (Larson, Clore, & Wood, 1999).

> " Each night I ask the stars up above, Why must I be a teenager in love? "
> —Doc Pomus and Mort Shuman (1959)

Most adolescents describe the degree of commitment and involvement in their relationships in terms that would be familiar to any adult. For example, in one survey of over 10,000 adolescents, 81 percent of those in romantic relationships described themselves as a couple, 67 percent went out together with no one else present, 68 percent told their partners that they loved them, 62 percent gave each other gifts, and 49 percent spent less time with their friends in order to spend more time with their partner (Carver et al., 2003). Given this level of involvement, it makes sense that adolescent relationships last a while. Caucasian adolescents report that the average length of their last romantic relationship was 12 months, Hispanic adolescents report an average of 15 months, and African American adolescents report an average of 24 months (Giordano, Manning, & Longmore, 2005). What are these couples up to when they are together? They are sharing typical activities that young people like to do: going out to eat and hanging out at school, the mall, or each other's homes (Feiring et al., 2002).

Also, they are having sex. As noted earlier, adolescents generally believe that sex is most appropriate within the context of a romantic relationship. It is not surprising, then, that sexual behavior among adolescents most often occurs between partners who are in a romantic relationship (Collins & Sroufe, 1999; Sprecher, Barbee, & Schwartz, 1995), and those who enter relationships earlier also tend to engage in sexual activities earlier (Thornton, 1990). When adolescents have sex for the first time, 50 percent report that they had been dating their partner first (Cooksey et al., 2002). And not merely dating: The majority of adolescents have their first sexual experience with someone they are going steady with or know well and like a lot (Abma et al., 2004; Martinez et al., 2006). Thus, for most adolescents, experimenting with sexual intimacy is part of experimenting with emotional intimacy. Indeed, when asked about their reasons for having sex, the most frequent answer is to have their partners love them more (Rodgers, 1996). This was almost certainly true for Bess Houdini. When she met the young magician, they had little else to offer each other but their love and commitment. She later commented that she had "sold her virginity to Houdini for an orange" (Kalush & Sloman, 2006, p. 30).

Although the romantic relationships of adolescents may be as emotionally intense as those of adults, it is worth noting the important ways that they differ. For example, even when teenagers are deeply in love with each other, they tend not to be very dependent on each other. These couples are probably not living together, sharing property or possessions, or raising children together. In some ways, the absence of these kinds of ties makes adolescent relationships relatively simple. They are almost exclusively about emotional connection. Adolescents rarely have to negotiate chores, or discuss how to pay the bills. When partners see each other, their only goal can be each other; in contrast, an adult partnership can be pursued for many reasons aside from intimacy. In other ways, however, their lack of interdependence makes adolescent relationships more fragile, because there are fewer barriers that prevent them from dissolving. Without concrete markers, a couple must define for themselves when and how their relationship begins and ends, and for young people still developing their definitions of relationships, this can be confusing. As an illustration of this confusion, researchers asked school-age adolescents to list the people with whom they had been in romantic relationships over the past year (Carver & Udry, 1997; Kennedy, 2006). Many of the students named had also been asked to provide their own lists, so the researchers were able to evaluate the agreement across students. They were surprised to find that, over 50 percent of the time, pairs of students disagreed about whether or not they had even been in a relationship!

A Preview of Coming Attractions

We have highlighted the continuity in the relationships a person experiences across the lifespan, describing how intimacy in adulthood has roots in relationships with caregivers in infancy, and with siblings and friends in early childhood. To a significant degree, romantic relationships in adolescence tend to repeat the patterns established in these earlier relationships. The best evidence for this continuity comes from studies that have measured the same individuals multiple times over the course of their lives. The Minnesota Longitudinal Study of Parents and Children, for example, followed 267 first-time mothers and their babies from 1975 to the present (e.g., Sroufe et al., 2005). Early on, the researchers videotaped the mothers as they interacted with their infants. Years later, those same infants were observed interacting with their friends as children, and later still with their boyfriends and girlfriends during adolescence. Analyses across these multiple waves of data reveal significant continuity in the kinds of relationships these children experienced at different stages of development (Carlson, Sroufe, & Egeland, 2004). Children whose interactions with their mothers were more positive during infancy grew up to have more satisfying and supportive peer and romantic relationships during adolescence, and those who were neglected or ignored during infancy had more difficulty establishing friendships and intimate relationships during adolescence.

In an independent 8-year longitudinal study that also drew on observational data, sociologist Rand Conger and his colleagues showed that when early adolescents' interactions with their parents were more involved and supportive, their interactions with romantic partners during later adolescence were more supportive and less hostile (Couger et al., 2000). Both of these studies highlight behaviors and beliefs as the mechanisms through which early relationships affect later ones. Consistent with the tenets of attachment theory, we appear to develop habits and expectations in childhood that affect the way we approach new relationships in adolescence and beyond.

Yet despite the wealth of important experiences we accumulate before adolescence, our first romantic relationships during adolescence are also new and strange. With romance come other elements mostly absent from an adolescent's prior relationships: the possibility of heartbreak, the euphoria of mutual attraction, and a chance to live out a new identity (Collins, 1997; Erikson, 1968). Even attachment theory recognizes that our ideas about relationships respond to experience and therefore are susceptible to change (Waters et al., 2000). Thus, adolescence may represent a unique period when ideas about relationships are especially flexible, when existing models of relationships can be reshaped by new experiences into the models the individual will carry through adulthood (Collins & Van Dulmen, 2006; Furman & Simon, 1999; Tallman, Burke, & Gecas, 1998). Indeed, data from the Minnesota study identified both continuity and change in the way young people approach their closest relationships through adolescence (Carlson et al., 2004). Although adolescent relationships are grounded in earlier experience, stumbling upon the right partner can provide a boost to someone with an otherwise problematic history, and tangling with the wrong partner can derail someone who might otherwise have flourished.

Romantic relationships during adolescence are consequential; they have the potential to affect the trajectory of a lifetime (Raley, Crissey, & Muller, 2007). Experiencing a breakup is no picnic for anyone, but for vulnerable adolescents, it can be the trigger for the first onset of major depression (Joyner & Udry, 2000; Monroe et al., 1999). Those who suffer from depression in adolescence are at significantly higher risk for marital distress and divorce as adults (Gotlib, Lewinsohn, & Seeley, 1998). In addition, adolescents report relatively high rates of aggression in their relationships. In one national study, nearly one-third of adolescents who had been in a romantic relationship over the past 18 months described themselves as having been victimized in some way, and 12 percent reported physical violence (Halpern et al., 2001). Those who come to accept violence during adolescence are later more likely to experience violent relationships as young adults (Capaldi et al., 2001).

MAIN POINTS

>> Adolescence usually involves shifting one's primary dependent relationship from a parent figure to a romantic partner.

>> Most adolescents agree that romantic relationships are highly desirable, and by the time they reach 18, nearly 80 percent will have experienced their own romantic relationships for the first time.

>> Most adolescents describe the degree of commitment and involvement in their relationships in terms that would be familiar to any adult; they consider themselves a couple, they go out on dates, they remain committed for months and years at a time.

>> Although intimate relationships during adolescence tend to repeat the patterns established in earlier relationships with friends and family members, specific experiences (such as a breakup or abuse) can affect the trajectory of the rest of their lives.

Major Transitions in Intimate Relationships During Adulthood

In 1901, Houdini was 27 years old and performing around the world. He was a success, well on his way to becoming a legend, filling theaters with audiences eager to see him slip free from the tightest bonds. Yet through it all, he remained bound by his lifelong relationships with two women. The first of these was his mother, Cecilia Weiss, to whom Houdini was devoted throughout his life. Recalling the childhood oath he'd made to his father, Houdini used his newly acquired wealth to make sure his mother was looked after, even though he continued to live modestly himself. Earlier that year, while performing in London, he passed by a shop window where a beautiful dress was on display. It had been custom-made for Queen Victoria, he was told, but the queen, alas, had died before she could wear it. Houdini purchased the dress for his mother, and arranged for her to meet him in Budapest so she could wear the dress at a reception he held for her in the town where she was born. A decade later, when Houdini was at the peak of his fame, he asked for and received an entire week's salary in gold pieces, and then went to his mother's side and literally poured the gold into her apron. Caring for his mother was one of the great joys of Houdini's life.

And yet, despite the closeness and significance of his relationship with his mother, from the time he was 20 years old, the primary relationship in Houdini's life was with his wife, Bess. He loved his mother, but, as he wrote to his wife, "the two loves do not conflict. . . . I love you as I shall never again love any woman" (Kalush & Sloman, 2006, p. 298). At the start of their relationship, Bess and Houdini were interdependent onstage and offstage, as performing partners and as husband and wife. In later years, when health problems prevented Bess from performing, she remained his traveling companion through years of touring the world. He called her his lucky charm, but as devoted as Harry claimed to be, theirs was far from an easy relationship. Houdini, the great romantic, was also a great philanderer, and his affairs were known to Bess and caused regular jealous rages. Perhaps to ease her sadness, Bess tended to drink too much and had flirtations of her own. Despite these significant difficulties, however, they stayed married for the rest of

Houdini's life, and even renewed their vows in a great ceremony and party in honor of their 25th wedding anniversary.

As difficult as it was to remain faithful, Houdini would return to Bess for comfort again and again. Thus, like most of us, Houdini crossed the threshold into adulthood by making a crucial transition—he had shifted his primary source of emotional security from someone within his family to a new individual outside his family. By the time that young people reach adulthood, most are engaged in or have completed the same transition (Fraley & Davis, 1997). But this is not the last transition that marks adult relationships.

Cohabitation

As recently as the 1970s, schoolyard rhymes were accurate in suggesting that, for most couples in the United States and Europe, first comes love, then comes marriage. Since then, however, deviations from this orderly progression have become increasingly common and accepted parts of adult intimacy. One of the most significant changes has been the rise of **cohabitation**, the sharing of a residence by unmarried partners. Between 1977 and 1997, the number of cohabiting couples in the United States more than quadrupled, going from less than 1 million in 1977 to more than 4 million in 1997 (Casper & Cohen, 2000). As of 2010, that number had risen to over 7.5 million (U.S. Census Bureau, 2010).

Do graphs such as the one shown in FIGURE 13.8 indicate a new stage of adult intimacy? Maybe the conventional wisdom should be revised: First comes love, then cohabitation, and then quickly on to marriage. Not so fast. In fact, most couples who cohabit do *not* go on to marry. On the contrary, the majority of cohabiting relationships end within a year, and 90 percent end within 5 years (Lichter, Qian, & Mellott, 2006).

Part of the reason cohabitation has been misunderstood is that cohabitors are often described as a homogeneous group, as if all couples who live together have the same goals. Closer examination of cohabiting couples reveals this assumption to be false. Sociologists Lynne Casper and Liana Sayer (2000) drew from nationally representative surveys that asked couples not only whether they were living together but also why. These data revealed four distinct groups of cohabiting couples:

1. *Precursor to marriage*, 46 percent. The largest group, these couples were engaged or about to become engaged, and they were living together as a step toward getting married.

2. *Coresidential daters*, 29 percent. These couples were romantically involved but had no plans to marry, and weren't even sure their relationship was permanent. They had moved in together for various reasons (including financial convenience) that had little to do with a serious investment in the relationship.

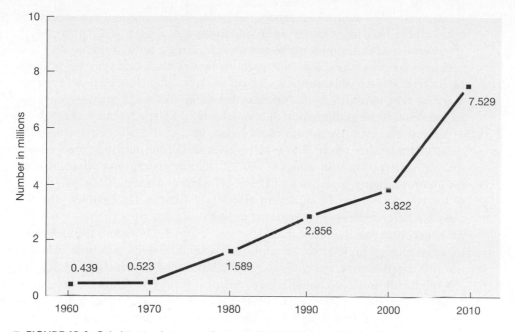

FIGURE 13.8 **Cohabitation becomes the norm.** The U.S. Census Bureau defines cohabitation as Persons of the Opposite Sex Sharing Living Quarters (POSSLQs). Data from the *Current Population Reports* were used to estimate trends in rates of POSSLQs, revealing a steady and steep increase over the past 50 years. (Source: U.S. Census Bureau, 2010.)

3. *Trial marriage*, 15 percent. These couples were not engaged and had no specific plans to get engaged, but they were open to the idea and hoped living together would help them evaluate whether marriage would be worth pursuing.

4. *Substitute marriage*, 10 percent. The smallest group, these couples had no intention of getting engaged or married, but nevertheless believed their relationship was permanent.

It is not surprising that the relative degree of closeness varies across the four groups. Those in the largest group, precursor to marriage, reported significantly greater closeness in their relationships than the coresidential daters (Pollard & Harris, 2007).

Although this variability means that cohabitation is far more than simply a stop on the way to marriage, it still indicates that a substantial proportion of couples who marry have lived together first. These rates are also increasing. Between 1965 and 1974, for example, about 10 percent of all married couples lived together before they got married. Between 1990 and 1994, in contrast, over 50 percent of all married couples had first lived together (Bumpass & Lu, 2000). This is a drastic shift, and it has led many scholars to ask: What is the effect of having lived together on the subsequent marriage? In surveys, couples themselves report the belief that living together promotes more stable marriages down the road (Bumpass, Sweet, & Cherlin, 1991). There is a lot of common sense to this idea. Sharing a household requires that couples make decisions together, spend time together, and thus learn about each other. Presumably, couples who do not like what they learn will not get married, which in turn means one less divorce in the world, thereby leaving a happier and more stable group of couples who do go on to marriage.

Despite the intuitive appeal of this idea, in fact the exact opposite is the case. In study after study, couples who cohabit before marriage report *lower* marital satisfaction and a *higher* risk of divorce than those who get married without living together first (Jose, O'Leary, & Moyer, 2010). Why? Part of the reason is due to a **selection effect** (see Chapter 1). Couples who live together before getting married tend to be those who are less traditional and more accepting of divorce in the first place (Axinn & Thornton, 1992). Even if these couples go on to have the same quality relationships as couples who did not live together first, the cohabitors may have a lower threshold for leaving the relationship when challenges arise. But selection is not the whole story. Analyses that have attempted to control for selection effects in various ways continue to show that married couples who lived together beforehand have more problems communicating and resolving problems than couples who did not first live together (Cohan & Kleinbaum, 2002). Cohabiting couples have higher rates of domestic violence than married couples as well (Kenney & McLanahan, 2006).

Some have suggested that couples who live together first have simply been together longer before marriage, so their relationships are older and less satisfying at any specific point in the marital timeline (Teachman & Polonko, 1990). However, studies that have controlled for the length of the relationship before marriage still find that couples who cohabited do worse (DeMaris & Rao, 1992). Others suggest that cohabiting creates its own momentum (i.e., a shared household becomes a barrier to ending the relationship), leading some couples to marry who otherwise would have (and maybe should have) broken up (Stanley, Rhoades, & Markman, 2006). There may also be something about the lack of social and legal support for cohabiting couples that interferes with the development of commitment and intimacy, even for those who go on to marry. So far, these issues have not yet been settled.

Marriage and the Transition to Parenthood

Regardless of whether or not they have cohabited first, over 90 percent of young people plan to get married (**FIGURE 13.9**). This expectation has not changed much over the last several decades (Thornton & Young-DeMarco, 2001). Currently, 91 percent of women and 89 percent of men do get married, but the age at the time of marriage has been increasing (Arnett, 2000). While it was not unusual in 1894 for Bess and Harry Houdini to marry at ages 18 and 20, in 2010 the median age of first marriage for Americans was 26.1 for women and 28.2 for men (U.S. Census Bureau, 2010).

What happens next? According to the schoolyard rhyme, then comes the baby in a baby carriage. This is a common sequence; however, over the past few decades, increasing numbers of couples have become parents before getting married, or without getting married at all (Carlson, McLanahan, & England, 2004). Among married couples who follow the traditional path, it is the happiest couples who become parents the earliest (Shapiro, Gottman, & Carrère, 2000). They might be motivated to begin raising children early because of their confidence in the relationship. Young married couples who are less satisfied are more likely to delay becoming parents or to avoid parenthood altogether. Houdini and Bess fell into this latter group. Houdini loved children and performed for them often, but he and Bess never had children of their own.

FIGURE 13.9 One story ends, another begins. Most people in the United States will get married at some point in their life. Romance novels and romantic comedies describe marriage as the culmination of a journey, the goal and the end of a love story. In contrast, this cartoon (and indeed this entire book) suggests that, for most couples, marriage is simply the beginning of a new and complicated journey.

It is hard to imagine a more dramatic transition than having a child (**FIGURE 13.10**). Pregnancy may last 9 months, but the arrival of a new baby itself, with its considerable demands and transcendent joys, is nevertheless sudden, leading to an abrupt shift in the way couples spend time together. Leisure time drops significantly after the birth of a first child, and returns gradually over the first year of the baby's life (Claxton & Perry-Jenkins, 2008). Egalitarian lifestyles, for couples who value them, tend also to be sacrificed for the sake of a new child. After they become parents, married couples generally adopt a more traditional division of labor, with wives taking on a disproportionate share of child care and housework, even if they also work outside the home (Cowan & Cowan, 1992; Nomaguchi & Milkie, 2003).

With the added stress of caring for a new life, it would make sense that the transition to parenthood would affect how spouses feel about their marriage overall. Yet the effects of parenthood on marital satisfaction have been surprisingly hard to pin down. Numerous studies have shown that satisfaction declines after the birth of a first child (Belsky & Pensky, 1988), but marital satisfaction tends to decline over time anyway (VanLaningham, Johnson, & Amato, 2001). The question is whether the declines experienced by new parents are steeper than the declines experienced by similar couples who have been married the same length of time but who have chosen not to have children. In a study that addressed this question directly, clinical psychologist Erika Lawrence and her colleagues examined marital satisfaction in newlyweds, none of whom yet had children, and then continued to assess these

"Please, don't hurt me—I have a wife, and I'm gradually becoming O.K. with the possibility of having children!"

FIGURE 13.10   A dramatic transition. Being mugged may be stressful in the moment, but having a child represents a drastic and lasting change in lifestyle for most couples, greatly increasing the demands on their time and reducing their flexibility. As a result, relationship satisfaction often declines after the transition to parenthood, but so does the likelihood of breaking up.

couples over time as some of them made the transition to parenthood and some did not (Lawrence et al., 2008). Comparing the two groups confirmed that the couples who became parents experienced steeper declines in satisfaction than those who did not, but the declines were especially steep for couples who had not planned to become parents. Planning, in parenthood as in contraception, offers some protection.

Most experiences that contribute to declines in marital satisfaction also raise the risk of divorce, but here parenthood is an exception. Married couples who have children together are significantly less likely to divorce than couples without children (White & Booth, 1985). Although children obviously make demands on couples that take time away from activities to enhance intimacy, children also provide powerful reasons to maintain the relationship, regardless of the level of intimacy. So what happens 18–20 years later, when the child leaves home and the parents face an empty nest? Do weary parents get a second honeymoon and maybe a boost in intimacy from all their new free time to spend together? Or do long-suffering parents finally call it quits? There is some evidence for both of these effects. On one hand, couples who have successfully navigated the challenges of parenting do experience an improvement in marital satisfaction immediately after their children leave home (White & Edwards, 1990). On the other hand, for the least satisfied parents, the departure of the last child removes a barrier to ending the relationship, and divorce rates go up slightly as well (Heidemann, Suhomlinova, & O'Rand, 1998).

Change and Novelty in Long-Term Relationships

In June 1908, Bess peeked out a third-story window and was shocked to find her husband climbing slowly up the outside of the building. Houdini had meant to surprise her, and so he did, but it was not a pleasant surprise. On the contrary, Bess was sick with fright until he made it safely through the window into their hotel room and presented her with the bouquet of red roses he had been holding in his teeth. This was how they celebrated their 14th wedding anniversary, and it perfectly encapsulates what the middle years of the Houdini marriage were like. One night, Houdini wrote in his diary: "Bess has been very sweet lately; hope she keeps it up." Two weeks later, his entry

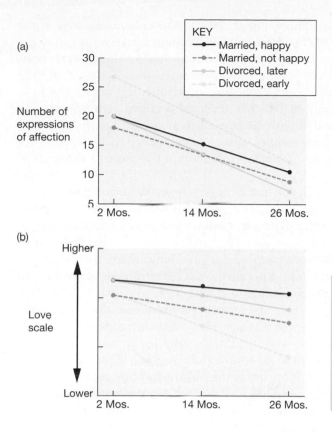

FIGURE 13.11 Declining positivity in the early married years. Newlyweds reported several times during the first years of marriage on the frequency of (a) their expressions of affection and (b) their feelings of love for each other. Both indicators declined, whether or not the couples went on to be relatively happy, relatively unhappy, or divorced. The happiness of newlyweds appears to be a peak that is hard to sustain. (Source: Adapted from Huston et al., 2001.)

is bleak: "When I get home, she is sore, and is sore for the night" (Kalush & Sloman, 2006, p. 162). From the romantic peaks of their early years, the relationship between Houdini and Bess had devolved into a cycle of fighting and reconciling, punctuated by extravagant public displays of commitment.

Their relationship illustrates one of the recurring themes of this book: Intimate relationships change, and on average they get worse rather than better. When couples remark on this change, they tend to comment, as Houdini did, on the negativity in the relationship, the increasing frequency of fighting and bitterness. Indeed, studies that have followed couples over many years suggest that the negativity in a relationship does tend to increase over time. The Denver Family Development Project, for example, began with a group of engaged couples and then observed them discussing their problems every year for the first 10 years of their marriages (Lindahl, Clements, & Markman, 1998). For the couples who stayed married throughout that time, these interactions grew more negative as the years passed.

Perhaps more striking is the drastic *decline in positivity* that other long-term studies have shown (**FIGURE 13.11**). In Chapter 7, in the context of behaviors that promote intimacy in relationships, we described research by social psychologist Ted Huston and his colleagues that followed newlyweds for the first 13 years of marriage (Huston et al., 2001). Reports of negativity in the marriage were fairly stable for these couples, perhaps because they were describing the relationship themselves, rather than having their interactions observed, as in the Denver Family Development Project. Yet even as their reports of negativity stayed about the same over time, the amount of love, affection, and responsiveness that they reported declined significantly, and these changes corresponded with changes in their overall satisfaction with the relationship. Thus, even couples who manage to keep their negativity in check may get discouraged if they fail to maintain the positive elements of their relationship.

A crucial positive element for many couples is sexual satisfaction, but on average the frequency of sex in relationships also declines over time. When premarital sex was less common than it is today, newlyweds were often advised to deposit a penny in a jar every time they had sex during their first year of marriage and then to remove a penny every time they had sex thereafter. The joke was that couples who follow this advice will never run out of change. No one we know has put this proposition to a direct test, but surveys do confirm that couples have sex less frequently as they get older, and the declines are steepest during the early years of marriage (Call, Sprecher, & Schwartz, 1995; Udry, 1980).

Why does this happen? How do couples lose sight of the love, affection, and sexual excitement that many list as the most rewarding aspects of adult intimacy? Part of the answer surely lies in the fact that the demands of adulthood and parenthood leave less time for intimacy-promoting behaviors as couples get older. But psychologists Arthur Aron and Elaine Aron (1986, 1996) have also suggested that, all else being equal, our brain is simply wired to take good things for granted. This is unquestionably true for many physical sensations. Walk into a home where chocolate chip cookies have just been baked, and your nose is delighted. But 20 minutes later, you cannot smell the cookies any more; your senses have become used to the aroma. A new romantic relationship is like walking into that house. Each new activity shared with a partner is a chance for discovery, and it makes sense that, in a dangerous world, we would have evolved an acute sensitivity to things that are new and unknown. According to the Arons, the novelty of another person is what makes the initial stages of intimacy so thrilling. Over time, however, the same shared activities simply become less novel. As couples develop routines, their brains habituate, and so the fortieth date does not carry the same charge of discovery as the first one.

This might seem a pessimistic model of love because it suggests that couples have no alternative but to become bored with each other. However, as we discussed in Chapter 7, it is possible for couples to reverse these trends and boost their satisfaction by finding new and exciting activities to engage in together (Aron et al., 2000). Reportedly, Houdini knew something about the value of novel activities. Bess would recall evenings late in their marriage when she and Houdini would pretend to be lovers meeting in secret.

This role-play turned a simple evening out into an adventure, a strategy for keeping their faltering romance alive. There is a lesson here for couples who worry about losing the spark.

Divorce and Remarriage

Through fights, reconciliations, and infidelities, Houdini and Bess never considered ending their marriage. Today, many couples make a different choice, electing to dissolve their marriages while both partners are still living. Considering only couples getting married for the first time, approximately 50 percent now entering marriage are expected to end their marriages through divorce or permanent separation (i.e., the couple lives apart and has divided their possessions, but has not filed for a legal divorce) (Bramlett & Mosher, 2002). Half of those divorces take place in the first 8 years of the marriage; the other half are spread out across the rest of the lifespan (Kreider & Fields, 2001).

All those divorces are associated with a lot of pain and suffering. As we discussed in Chapter 12, most couples wait until they are truly distressed before even considering getting help for their relationship, such as couples therapy. By the time they make the far more drastic decision to divorce, many couples have probably endured a lot of unhappiness. Sociologists Paul Amato and Denise Previti (2003) confirmed this assumption when they asked 208 divorced individuals to describe the reasons their marriages ended. Their answers speak to the ways that two people can make each other miserable: infidelity (the number one answer), incompatibility, drinking and drug use, growing apart, lack of communication, and abuse. To the extent that a spouse can be dangerous or abusive, divorce surely comes as a relief to some. Yet, in part as a consequence of how much they endure before ending the relationship, couples who divorce are at higher risk for a wide range of negative outcomes after ending the relationship, including physical and mental health problems (Kiecolt-Glaser & Newton, 2001), financial problems (Smock, Manning, & Gupta, 1999), and early death (Rogers, 1995; Waite & Gallagher, 2000).

People lose faith in their marriages, but they do not appear to lose faith in marriage as an institution. In an example of the power of optimism, nearly 80 percent of people who have been divorced remarry (Cherlin, 1992). And they remarry fairly quickly; the average time between a divorce and a remarriage is less than 4 years (Wilson & Clarke, 1992). One source of the widespread enthusiasm for leaping back into the marital saddle may be that most people do not see themselves as having much to do with their first marriages ending. On the contrary, people who have divorced generally blame their former partner for the end of the marriage (Amato & Previti, 2003). It makes sense, therefore, that divorced people—older, wiser, and with new partners—should reasonably hope to find more happiness in their second marriage than they found in their first.

The truth, however, is that remarriages are significantly more likely to dissolve than first marriages (Bumpass, Sweet, & Martin, 1990; Clarke & Wilson,

1994). What makes second marriages more vulnerable? Research results provide several answers. First, people who have divorced bring to their new marriages the same vulnerabilities that contributed to the problems in their first marriages. People who marry and divorce multiple times, for example, have been shown to score relatively high on measures of impulsivity and neuroticism (Brody, Neubaum, & Forehand, 1988). To the extent that these are traits that do not change much over time, people who possess them are likely to find all of their relationships more challenging.

A second reason for the vulnerability of remarriage is that people who have already been divorced may be more willing to consider ending the relationship when problems arise. The experience of divorce seems to change people's attitudes, and those who end their marriages typically become more accepting of divorce than those who stay married (Amato & Booth, 1991). Faced with the same sorts of challenges, first-married couples may therefore be less willing to consider ending the relationship compared to remarried couples, who have already faced this trauma and survived.

Finally, remarriages may simply be harder to maintain than first marriages, especially when they involve stepchildren. The presence of children from prior relationships raises difficult issues about how to allocate time and resources. As we described earlier, siblings from the same biological parents tend to compete for attention; these rivalries may be more severe in stepfamilies where both parents are not equally invested in all children. It is not surprising then that, even among remarriages, those involving stepchildren have higher divorce rates than those that do not (Booth & Edwards, 1992).

MAIN POINTS

>> Although rates of cohabition have increased rapidly, most cohabiting relationships end within 5 years. Couples who live together before marriage tend to have lower satisfaction and a higher risk of divorce, compared to couples who do not live together first.

>> The transition to parenthood is associated with lower relationship satisfaction, because a child changes the way couples spend time and allocate household responsibilities. Parenthood is also associated with a reduced risk of divorce, as having children makes ending the relationship more costly.

>> Over time, intimate relationships generally become less satisfying, with evidence of increases in negativity and striking declines in positivity.

>> Despite the fact that about half the couples who marry will divorce or permanently separate, most people who have been divorced remarry, suggesting some enduring optimism about the possibility of a satisfying marriage.

>> Remarriages are vulnerable, partly because those who have already divorced are more likely to choose this option again if their second marriage becomes distressed.

Intimate Relationships in Later Life

Having survived being chained underwater, buried alive, and hung by his heels while wearing a straightjacket, Harry Houdini considered himself virtually indestructible. Accordingly, he made plans for a long life. When he bought a townhouse in New York to serve as his main residence, he made sure it had extra rooms to store all the books he had not yet collected. As he explained to his mother: "Someday when I'm too old to perform, I'll spend my time writing about magic. And I won't have to search for source material. It will be here" (Kalush & Sloman, 2006, p. 163).

Houdini never grew too old to perform. In the autumn of 1926, he was still developing spectacular new stunts when he let a visitor to his dressing room deliver a blow to his abdomen, as a demonstration of Houdini's superior stomach muscles. Although he wasn't aware of it, the blow aggravated a developing case of acute appendicitis. Two days later, Houdini completed a Sunday night performance, walked off stage, and collapsed with a fever of 104°F. Surgeons at Grace Hospital in Detroit removed a ruptured and infected appendix, but the damage was done. On October 31, 1926—Halloween, of course—Harry Houdini died at the age of 52.

Even at the time, Houdini would not have been considered an old man. In the 1920s, the average person who had survived until the age of 50 could expect to live another 22 years. Nearly a century later, advances in public health and medical science have increased the average life expectancy in the United States by nearly 50 percent (Treas, 1995). A 50-year-old man can now expect to live another 28 years, and a 50-year-old woman can expect to live another 32 years (Arias, 2006). As the lifespan has been getting longer, what it means to be old has been changing as well. The United Nations currently considers 60 the threshold of old age (Gorman, 1999). Most researchers, in contrast, acknowledge that old age has little to do with chronological age, preferring definitions that focus on activity, wisdom, or role in society (Vaillant & Koury, 1993), all of which can extend well beyond age 60.

Although the category of old age remains fuzzy, the implications of an aging population are clear: Adults now spend more of their lives in intimate relationships than they did a century ago (Schoen & Weinick, 1993). Long-term couples today can expect to live together in relatively good health for decades after they have retired from work and parenting (FIGURE 13.12). Because later-life relationships did not exist

"Well, now that the kids have grown up and left I guess I'll be shoving along, too."

FIGURE 13.12 Pros and cons of the empty nest. Just as having a child brings both joy and stress, so does the departure of adult children from the home. The end of full-time parenting gives a couple more time together, but it can also remove barriers to ending the relationship.

before modern times, for many years they were virtually ignored by scientific research. As the proportion of older adults has risen, however, scholars have begun to investigate the implications of intimate relationships in the later stages of life.

Varieties of Intimacy for Older Adults

One way to describe the relationships of older adults is in terms of marital status. **FIGURE 13.13** draws on census data to compare the marital status of adults over 65 to that of the U.S. population as a whole (U.S. Census Bureau, 2006). As the pie charts show, 53 percent are married and 9 percent are divorced, similar to the 51 percent that are married and 10 percent that are divorced in the general population. In contrast to the general population, however, older adults are far less likely never to have married (5 percent vs. 31 percent), a reflection of the fact that most people eventually do get married in their lifetime. Older adults are also far more likely to be widowed (32 percent vs. 6 percent), and perhaps as a consequence they are more likely to live alone as well (45 percent vs. 27 percent; not shown in the figure).

Focusing on current marital status, however, masks several important sources of variability in the intimate relationships of older adults. First, in older populations, rates of marriage differ substantially between men and women (U.S. Census Bureau, 2006). Throughout their lives, men are more likely than women to remarry after losing a spouse through death or divorce. Men also generally die younger than women. As of 2003, for example, the average age of death for men in the United States was 74.8, while the average for women was 80.1 (National Center for Health Statistics, 2005). As a consequence, among adults older than 65, men are almost twice as likely to be married as women (72 percent vs. 40 percent). Women, in contrast, are nearly three times as likely as men to be living as a widow (44 percent vs. 14 percent). It follows that differences between men's and women's marital status get larger as people get older.

Second, current marital status ignores the rich and often complex relationship histories that lead to marital status in later

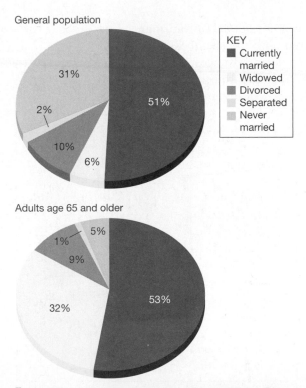

FIGURE 13.13 Marital status in older adulthood. Older adults are a little more likely to be married, far less likely never to have married, and far more likely to be widowed, relative to the population as a whole. (Source: U.S. Census Bureau, 2006.)

life. On average, men spend 45 percent of their lives married, and women spend 41 percent (Schoen & Weinick, 1993). However, people vary a great deal around these averages, and some remain married to one person whereas others marry, divorce, and remarry multiple times. To examine the implications of relationship histories for later life, sociologists Janet Wilmoth and Gregor Koso (2002) analyzed data from 9,824 adults over age 60, all of whom reported on their current marital status and also described their lifetime relationship histories. Among those who were currently married, 22 percent had remarried after having been divorced earlier in life. Others had divorced multiple times or remarried after being widowed. Controlling for whether they were currently married, these older adults were still feeling the impact of their prior experiences in relationships. Specifically, the researchers found that relationship disruptions interfere with the accumulation of wealth. In other words, the more disruptions people experience, the less financially secure they are likely to be in later life, independent of whether they remarry. This is especially true for women, whose financial situation in later life depends more on whether they marry and whom they marry (Holden & Smock, 1991).

Research on the implications of relationship histories for the health of older adults paints a similar picture. By the time they reach later life, people who have spent more of their lifetime married tend to be healthier, controlling for the number of times they have married (Dupre & Meadows, 2007). There are gender differences here too. Older men who have divorced and remarried have the same risk of heart disease as men who have been continuously married. In other words, remarriage allows divorced men to recover from the health risks associated with ending a marriage. Not so for divorced women, who are at increased risk for heart disease even if they remarry (Zhang & Hayward, 2006). All these analyses support the same general point: The accumulation of experiences in marriage and other intimate relationships throughout the lifespan makes a big difference in the quality of older adult lives, even if these experiences are not reflected in current marital status.

Third, as is true in younger people, being unmarried in older adulthood does not mean being without an intimate relationship. Older adults, even after long marriages that ended in divorce or the death of a partner, continue to seek intimacy. They date, they enter new relationships, and increasingly they are cohabiting, too. In one study, the researchers asked about the relationships of the unmarried older adults in their sample, and found that hundreds of them were cohabiting with romantic partners (Wilmoth & Koso, 2002). A study of 4,494 older adults in the Netherlands documented a similar trend, showing that nearly half of those who form new relationships after experiencing the loss of a spouse decide to live together rather than get married (de Jong Gierveld, 2004). It is worth recognizing that the older adults in these studies were born in the 1930s and 1940s and therefore lived through a period when divorce and cohabitation were far less accepted than they are today. We might expect that future generations will experience an even greater variety of intimate relationships in older adulthood.

The Quality of Intimacy in Later Life

The earliest research on the nature and quality of intimate experiences among older adults suggested that advancing age might flatten out, or modify, the emotional extremes of relationships. These studies found, for example, that older couples described fewer sources of disagreement with each other (Levenson, Carstensen, & Gottman, 1993), but expressed less love and passion as well (Swensen, Eskew, & Kohlhepp, 1984). Does this mean that older adults grow numb, becoming less sensitive to the highs and lows in their relationships? Not at all. When asked to recall emotionally charged times in their lives, older adults reported having physiological reactions that are just as intense as those of younger people (Levenson et al., 1991). Developmental psychologist Laura Carstensen draws from these sorts of results to argue that older adults actually become *more* sensitive to their emotional experiences over time. Her **socioemotional selectivity theory** proposes that, as people age, they become increasingly aware of their mortality. Knowing they have no time to waste, they pay close attention to the emotional aspects of their lives, seeking out circumstances and relationships that promote positive emotions, and actively avoiding those that lead to negative emotions (Carstensen, Fung, & Charles, 2003). Younger people, in contrast, should be more open to new experiences, even if they risk being negative or unpleasant.

Socioemotional selectivity theory has been supported by several lines of research on intimate relationship in older adults (Carstensen, Isaacowitz, & Charles, 1999). First, most older adults do describe themselves as happy with their relationships on average, and the oldest among them rate themselves happier with their relationships than the younger respondents (Chalmers & Milan, 2005). In part this seems to be the result of people in less satisfying relationships breaking up and leaving the survey population (Hatch & Bulcroft, 2004). As adults get older, they seem less likely to stick around in unsatisfying relationships, leaving the ones remaining in their relationships reporting higher satisfaction on average.

Second, older couples manage conflict differently, and apparently better, than younger couples. In a study that examined videotapes of 82 middle-aged and 74 older couples discussing problems in their relationships, Carstensen and her colleagues (Carstensen, Gottman, & Levenson, 1995) found that, even after controlling for marital satisfaction and the severity of the problems they were discussing, older couples still approached their problems expressing more affection and less hostility than younger couples. Moreover, even the unhappiest of the older couples were significantly less likely to initiate negative behaviors than the unhappiest younger couples. Far from being emotionally numb, the older couples showed signs of being emotional experts, choosing strategies that promoted positive feelings in the relationship, even when they were talking about difficult problems. Finally, as they get older, couples spend more time with each other and with close family members and less time with friends and acquaintances (Carstensen, 1992). In the interest of promoting positive experiences, older adults appear to gradually restrict their socializing to those people whose company they find most rewarding.

One of these rewards appears to be having sex. Until recently, stereotypes about older adults suggested that sexual desire fades to insignificance in the later years of life (Kellett, 2000). Surveys that directly ask older adults about their sexual behavior strongly reject this view. For example, a nationally representative study of adults ages 57–85 asked 1,550 women and 1,455 men living in the United States about their sexual activities (Lindau et al., 2007). As the results described in FIGURE 13.14a indicate, the proportion of sexually active adults declines with age. At all ages, women are less likely to be sexually active than men. But these trends may offer a misleading view of how sexuality changes in older adults, because they fail to account for the fact that as adults grow older they are increasingly likely to be without partners, and this is especially true for women. FIGURE 13.14b, in contrast, describes the frequency of sex only among respondents who indicated that they had been sexually active in the last year—that is, those most likely to have an intimate partner. These results paint a very different picture: Among those who remained sexually active, there is barely any drop-off in

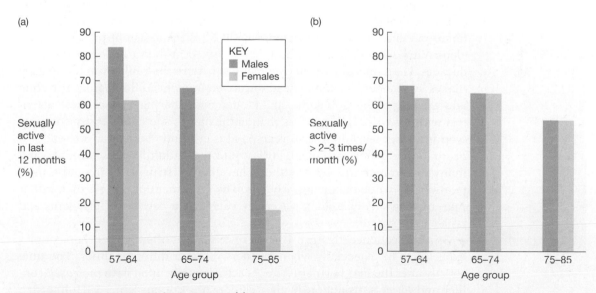

FIGURE 13.14 **Sexual activity in later life.** (a) The percentage of older adults who are sexually active declines with age, and men remain more active than women. Women are less likely than men to be living with an intimate partner. (b) Among those who are sexually active, there are no substantial differences based on either age or gender. (Source: Adapted from Lindau et al., 2007.)

sexual frequency by age, and gender differences virtually disappear. Even among the oldest age group studied, over half of men and women who were sexually active reported having sex more than two or three times a month. Far from withering with age, sexuality appears to be an important element of intimacy throughout the lifespan (Gott & Hinchliff, 2003).

The Mixed Blessing of Retirement

After years of working to support oneself and one's family, later life promises a substantial reward: retirement. The dream of eventually leaving work behind is enough to motivate young people to start up 401K savings accounts and return day after day to jobs that may or may not bring them fulfillment. For couples, the dream of retirement may be especially enticing. In younger couples, the demands of work can take time away from the activities that maintain and strengthen intimate relationships (see Chapter 11). After retirement, those external demands fall away, leaving couples who have made it that far free to enjoy each other's company, explore new activities together, and appreciate the strengths of the relationship.

> " O, blest retirement! friend to life's decline—
>
> How blest is he who crowns, in shades like these,
>
> A youth of labor with an age of ease!"
>
> —Oliver Goldsmith, "The Deserted Village" (1770)

The reality of retirement is more complicated, of course, for at least two reasons. First, because modern couples are increasingly composed of partners who are both employed outside the home, retirement does not necessarily happen for both at the same time. Consider, for example, the marriage of Bill, who at 64 is a year away from retiring from his job as the manager of an automobile factory, and Helen, who at 59 is the assistant principal at an elementary school. Although both have worked in the same jobs for several decades, Helen has always enjoyed her work more than Bill, even though she makes less money. Looking ahead toward retirement, Bill imagines traveling and working on his golf game, and he imagines sharing both of these activities with his wife. Helen is less than enthusiastic; she could easily continue working for at least another 6 years, and is currently being considered for a promotion to school principal. For most of their adult lives, this couple, and many dual-career couples like them, have had to struggle to maintain their relationship while balancing two jobs. The retirement of one partner, rather than making this balancing act easier, can raise a new set of problems and issues to negotiate.

As a consequence, the transition to retirement is often harder than couples expect it to be, especially when partners retire at different times. The time shortly after the first partner retires is actually associated with *increased* conflict and *lower* satisfaction in the relationship (Moen, Kim, & Hofmeister, 2001). If the husband is the first to retire, a couple who values traditional roles have a particularly hard time, as the continued employment of the wife explicitly reverses those gender roles (Szinovacz, 1996). Traditional husbands are often resistant to changes in their status in the home, even when their status as workers outside the home has ended. For example, after a husband retires, the division of labor within the household generally stays the same, and this can be a source of frustration for the working wife who expects a little extra help (Lee & Sheehan, 1989). Despite increased conflicts about the transition into retirement, couples that make it through the transition appear to adjust to the new status quo, and those who have been retired together for more than 2 years report relatively high satisfaction with their relationships (Moen et al., 2001).

A second complicating factor is the fact that retirement affects intimate relationships differently, depending on conditions before retirement. For example, the chance to spend more time with your partner is a wonderful dream, as long as you are fond of your partner. For happy couples, retirement offers a chance to experience more of that happiness. For distant or distressed couples, however, retirement leaves them with more time to irritate and interfere with each other. Indeed, the effects of retirement do appear to vary depending on the preretirement quality of the relationship, with the "intimacy rich" getting richer and the "intimacy poor" getting poorer (Kupperbusch, Levenson, & Ebling, 2003). Similarly, the opportunity to give up working is a blessing for people with stressful, hazardous, or tedious jobs. They will probably be relieved when they retire, and their intimate relationships will likely improve. However, people who love their jobs and those whose identities are deeply invested in their careers and their professional connections may find retirement dull or lonely, and their marriages tend to suffer after retirement (Myers & Booth, 1996).

> " When a man retires, his wife gets twice the husband but only half the income."
>
> —Chi Chi Rodriguez, golfer

All of this assumes that couples are in reasonable health. When couples who have been together for a long time face chronic illness or dementia, their challenges are even more complicated, as **BOX 13.1** describes.

Retirement can be a mixed blessing. On one hand, it offers couples more time to spend as they wish, and freedom from demands outside the home. On the other hand, it requires adjustments to long-standing habits, and some couples are better equipped to make those adjustments than others.

Widowhood

Bess Houdini never expected to outlive her husband. From early in their lives together, she had been the sickly one, traveling between doctors, eager to sample the latest tonics and treatments. As tempestuous as her relationship with Harry was, he nevertheless was the center of her emotional life and the foundation of her world, providing for her financially and sharing with her his status as a celebrity. After Harry died, a friend of the couple expressed some doubt about whether Bess would recover from the loss, noting that "He was more to her than the average husband" (Kalush & Sloman, 2006, p. 531).

BOX 13.1 SPOTLIGHT ON . . .

Romance Among Alzheimer's Patients

Without the ability to recognize a partner and recall past experiences together, there can be no relationship, only isolated interactions. Memory is thus the connective tissue that makes intimate relationships possible. What happens when this tissue dissolves? This is the unfortunate question the families of the 5.2 million Americans suffering from Alzheimer's disease face (Alzheimer's Association, 2008). Among those 71 and older, 16 percent of women and 11 percent of men have the disease (Plassman et al., 2007). They have memory loss, a decline in cognitive abilities, dementia, and complications that eventually lead to death. As the disease progresses, those afflicted gradually forget events from their own past, and in the late stages they have trouble recognizing even their own spouses and family members. The world of the Alzheimer's patient therefore grows more and more unfamiliar, as those they have loved most become strangers.

And yet, as the capacity to sustain a relationship diminishes, the need for companionship and intimacy persists, and even thrives (FIGURE 13.15). People who work closely with Alzheimer's patients report that new romances are common in institutional settings. Even as many cognitive abilities are failing, the capacity for love and intimacy can thrive.

In the fall of 2007, Sandra Day O'Connor, the former U.S. Supreme Court Justice, revealed to the public that John O'Connor, her husband of 54 years, had fallen in love with another woman at the age of 77 (Biskupic, 2007). John had been suffering from Alzheimer's for nearly two decades, but that year his family had finally decided he would receive better care in a facility catering to people with the disease. At first, the transition was difficult, and he was depressed and confused by his new surroundings. His mood brightened only when he got to know another woman at the facility. Suddenly, he was "a teenager in love," holding hands and sharing a porch swing with the new object of his affection. Did his wife, who had retired from the Supreme Court to care for him, feel betrayed when she arrived for a visit and her husband eagerly introduced his new girlfriend? She was relieved. With a new and constant companion, her husband was happier and more comfortable, and that was what she wanted for him. Her husband could not betray the memory of the decades they had spent together, because he had no memories of those decades to betray.

FIGURE 13.15 Love at sunset. In later life, even as many faculties begin to fail, the need for love and intimacy persists.

After couples have spent years adjusting and accommodating to each other, the death of a romantic partner is a deeply traumatic event (Holmes & Rahe, 1967). Whereas couples who divorce end their relationships voluntarily, a widowed husband or wife often faces independence unwillingly and sometimes unexpectedly. It is not surprising, then, that the death of a romantic partner has serious negative consequences for the well-being of the surviving partner. Older adults who have lost a spouse tend to report significant declines in their life satisfaction (Chipperfield & Havens, 2001), and they are at elevated risk for depression (Lee, Willetts, & Seccombe, 1998).

Women and men suffer from the loss of a spouse, but husbands experience problems that are different from those of wives. Because women are more likely to take responsibility for managing a family's relationships and social life, men who have lost their wives generally experience the social costs, such as loneliness and diminished contacts with friends (Hatch & Bulcroft, 1992). Perhaps as a result, they are at higher risk for depression than women who lose their husbands (Lee & DeMaris, 2007). In contrast, because men are still more likely to be the primary breadwinner in a household, women who have lost their husbands tend to experience a substantial drop in income and are at increased risk for falling into poverty (Burkhauser, Butler, & Holden, 1991). We might predict that those who have time to anticipate widowhood (e.g., when a partner dies after a long illness) might adjust more successfully than those who lose their partners without warning. In fact, research finds no differences between these groups (Hill, Thompson, & Gallagher, 1988). The depression, shock, and grief that follows the death of a partner is just as great when the death is sudden as when the death is expected (Carr et al., 2001).

One thing that does make a difference in adjusting to widowhood, however, is the prior relationship between the partners. Is a surviving partner happier when he or she can look back on a close, intimate relationship with the departed spouse, or does that closeness make the loss of a beloved partner harder to bear? Are the survivors of unhappy relationships relieved by the loss of a partner who caused them pain, or do they suffer even more from their unresolved, and now unresolvable, conflicts? The best evidence supports the idea that a good marriage continues to have benefits and a difficult marriage continues to have costs, even after one partner has died. A survey that followed 1,532 older adults over a period of time found that, among those who lost a spouse during the course of the study, those who reported more positive feelings toward their spouse were less likely to be depressed after 4 years, whereas those with more negative views were more likely to be depressed (Rhee & Antonucci, 2004). Although being satisfied with the marriage provides protection during widowhood, being dependent on the marriage carries risks. In the same sample, those spouses who had been more dependent on their spouses before their deaths reported more anxiety 6 months later (Carr et al., 2000). In addition, they tended to have symptoms of chronic depression 18 months afterward (Bonanno et al., 2002).

Bess Houdini, who might have reported low satisfaction with her marriage but high emotional dependence, would have fallen into the highest risk group after Harry's death, and indeed her life as a widow proved difficult. Unlike many widows, finances were not a problem for Bess. Between the money Harry had left her and his generous life insurance policy, she could live comfortably for the rest of her life. But emotionally she was a wreck. She was proud of her late husband, but at the same time she could not let go of the anger she had accumulated during their years of marriage. These ambivalent feelings expressed themselves in complicated and often contradictory ways. For example, in the first months after Houdini's death, Bess disposed of his precious collections, allegedly calling in a junk wagon to carry away the thousands of keys, lock-picks, manacles, and handcuffs the magician had accumulated over the years. Houdini would have been horrified by this disregard for his legacy. However, Bess kept, and proudly displayed, his trophies and awards. These tokens could not ward off depression, though, and Bess's losing battles with alcohol addiction hastened her decline.

Bess had hit bottom, but she was still luckier than many widows in that she lived many years after the death of her husband. There is some truth to the idea that, in some couples who have spent most of their lives together, the death of one partner predicts the death of the other shortly thereafter. For example, in one study of older adults receiving Medicare, 21 percent of men and 17 percent of women died within 6 months of the death of their spouse (Christakis & Allison, 2006). The good news is that, after 6 months, the risk of death for the recently widowed tapered off, returning to the rates observed in those who have not lost a spouse. In other words, although the period shortly after becoming a widow is hard, most people are resilient, adjusting to their new status (Bonanno et al., 2002).

Indeed, the death of an intimate partner, even late in life, does not mean the death of intimacy. Within 6 months of the death of a spouse, many older adults express a willingness to date again or remarry (Carr, 2004). One study of 548 older men and women who had lost their partners within the past 10 years found that 28 percent of them had formed new relationships (Lamme, Dykstra, & Broese Van Groenou, 1996). Bess Houdini did this when she met a man named Edward Saint, a former carnival performer. With a stage name of the International Smileless Man, his act was to offer audience members a prize if they could get him to crack a smile. This was a safe bet because, unbeknownst to his audiences, his facial muscles were paralyzed, rendering him incapable of smiling whether he wanted to or not. Her relationship with the straight-faced Saint provided Bess with the structure she had lacked since Houdini's death. For the 12 years they were together, he managed her public appearances, helped her control her alcoholism, and kept her first husband's legend alive by developing a sideline in Houdini souvenirs and memorabilia. Just as Bess benefited enormously from her relationship with Ed Saint, older adults who have lost their partners generally do better if they are able to form new relationships (Burks et al., 1988). In terms of wealth, for example, older adults who remarry or cohabit with a partner after widowhood look no different from those who have been continuously married, and all these groups are better off than those who remain alone (Wilmoth & Koso, 2002).

Bess did not remarry, but she remained devoted to Saint, and he to her, until he also died young at the age of 51. This time, as Bess wrote in a letter to Houdini's brother, "I just collapsed" (Kalush & Sloman, 2006, p. 557). She had lost a second man on whom she had become totally dependent, and this was too much for the fragile Bess to take. By the end of that year, she was in a nursing home in California, but her health was failing fast. A few months later, on February 11, 1943, she took a train to the East Coast, hoping to see her family one last time. She died soon after the train left the station. Bess was 67 years old, and she had outlived Houdini by 17 years.

>> Among adults older than 65, men are almost twice as likely to be married as women and women are nearly three times as likely to be living as widows.

>> Because the least satisfying relationships have already broken up, older adults in relationships tend to be relatively satisfied; they also have rewarding sex lives.

>> Retirement has complicated effects on relationships in older adulthood, such that happy couples generally benefit from more time to enjoy each other, whereas less happy couples can suffer because being at home together provides more opportunities for conflict.

>> In the short term, the death of a spouse has serious negative consequences for the well-being of the surviving partner, including increased risk of depression and declines in life satisfaction.

Historical Perspectives

Throughout this chapter, we have traced how intimate relationships develop and change across a person's lifespan. It is worth appreciating that relationships also develop and change from one historical period to another. As cultures and social norms evolve over time, intimate relationships evolve with them. Houdini and Bess, for example, met in 1893 during the final years of the 19th century. Grover Cleveland was president. The automobile was 5 years old, the airplane was not yet invented, and women would not be granted the right to vote for another 25 years. Wireless Internet connections were far beyond imagining. In so many ways, Houdini and Bess lived in a different world from ours, yet their goals and the challenges they faced meeting those goals are familiar to us. They wanted their relationship to be passionate and romantic, but they also wanted it to be a refuge where they could be cared for and supported. They expected each other to be sexually faithful and were jealous and angry when loyalty was betrayed. They each wanted to be adored by the other, they each complained about the other, they went on dates to keep the spark alive, they fought, they made up, they fought again. We recognize these behaviors. They seem contemporary, even though they took place generations ago.

Comparing relationships across history thus raises important questions about intimate relationships in general. What aspects of intimacy are constant for human beings regardless of the historical era? What aspects have changed as societies have changed over time? How might intimate relationships continue to change in the future?

To address these sorts of questions, family historian Stephanie Coontz (2005) traced how the meaning and structure of intimate relationships has developed over the past 10,000 years. She observes that intimate relationships existed for all of that time—they are a central characteristic of the human species. Nevertheless, for most of human history, intimate relationships often served to organize property and allegiances, and the most important form of relationship for fulfilling this function was marriage. She notes that, before there were governments or stock markets, marriages defined how people inherited property, divided up labor in the household and the community, and associated with other communities. For thousands of years, what we recognize today as romantic attraction and intimacy existed, but their role in most people's experience of relationships was secondary—a luxury rather than a necessity, a lucky bonus rather than an entitlement.

The idea that a satisfying intimate bond is the primary purpose of a relationship in fact emerged right around the time that Houdini and Bess were getting together. By the late 1800s, the Industrial Revolution was complete. While previously men and women worked together on family farms, now male and female domains were separate. Men were generally engaged in paid work outside the home, and women were occupied with unpaid work at home. Coontz notes: "As housekeeping became 'homemaking,' it came to be seen as an act of love rather than a contribution to survival" (2005, p. 155). The nuclear family, and the marital relationship at the center of it, began to be elevated as something sacred, set apart from the baser concerns that characterized the marketplace and industry. In the prior century, husbands and wives were advised not to spend too much time thinking about their relationship, as an unhealthy interest in each other would distract each partner from his and her responsibilities. Social leaders of late 19th century still described the marital relationship as serving social functions, but they held that without romantic love between spouses, marriages would be unable to perform those functions. When Houdini and Bess were growing up, romantic feelings between husbands and wives were being praised in song and story, much as they are today.

Yet, despite the significant continuities in intimate relationships since Houdini and Bess were alive, their relationship was also a product of its time. The world of the early 21st century differs from the world of the late 19th century in at least three ways that have profound implications for intimate relationships. First, men and women today no longer operate in separate spheres economically and socially. As romantic love was being praised in the 19th century, women were still unable to participate in paid work outside the home, at least within the middle and upper classes. Financial stability could be achieved only through marriage, providing a powerful motivation that had nothing to do with intimacy. When women successfully fought for the right to vote in the 1920s, they also earned the right to work, and currently 75 percent of marriages consist of two people who each earn an income outside the home (Raley, Mattingly, & Bianchi, 2006). The relative financial independence of women removes one of the barriers that in the past kept couples from separating.

Second, the nuclear family of today has far fewer ties to extended family members and community organizations. Bess and Houdini, even though they had no children together, were deeply involved in each other's extended families throughout their lives. Houdini famously doted on his mother, but he was also close to his brothers and sisters and their families. His loyalty to his wife, as shaky as it was, competed with other loyalties that were regarded as equally valid, including loyalties to his friends and colleagues. The modern couple, at least in Western cultures, operates much more as an independent unit. You may recall in Chapter 11 we discussed the book *Bowling Alone: The Collapse and Revival of American Community* (2000), in which the social scientist Robert Putnam documented the decline in social connections among Americans over the last decades of the 20th century. Americans are connected to their own partners and children, but compared to the 1970s, they are 58 percent less likely to be members of clubs, 43 percent less likely to gather with their extended families, and 35 percent less likely even to have friends over for dinner. Whereas the relationship between two people was once supported by a network of connections, today's relationships must succeed or fail on their own.

Third, although marriage remains a dominant and highly valued structure for intimate relationships, contemporary society accepts a much wider range of relationship structures than were tolerated, or even publicly mentioned, in the 19th century. At ages 18 and 20, if Bess and Houdini wanted to have a sexual relationship, share a home, have children, or even appear together in public, they had to be married. Marriage was a starting point for young couples, one that allowed them to build a home and develop their intimacy further. In the last decades of the 20th century, there were few changes in people's attitudes toward marriage (Thornton & Young-DeMarco, 2001). What changed were attitudes toward alternative family forms, such that there is now a greater acceptance of unmarried parents, cohabiting couples, and same-sex relationships. Moreover, because men and women today both often work outside the home, marriage is viewed not as a starting point but as one of several possible end points, a goal to be achieved after couples have arranged their education, career, and finances (Edin & Reed, 2005).

Each of these three historical developments has removed economic and social constraints that once compelled couples to get married and stay together. The consequence has been an increasing focus on intimacy. When a relationship had to serve an economic or social purpose, and the structure of that relationship was well defined by existing institutions, the quality of the intimacy between partners could take a backseat. Not any more. Where relationships once served to organize property, labor, and political power, these functions are now the responsibility of governments and individuals. Where marriage was once the only acceptable way for adults to express intimacy, men and women now have greater freedom to define intimacy for themselves. Demographer Andrew Cherlin (2004) suggests that these changes reflect the deinstitutionalization of American marriage. In other words, relationships between adults have become increasingly disconnected from social institutions, leaving the success or failure of relationships to rest almost exclusively on the intimate bond between the partners.

The primacy of the intimate bond has two implications for intimate relationships. On one hand, without the need to pursue relationships for material reasons, couples are freer than at any time in history to pursue their own and each other's emotional fulfillment. More people expect to be appreciated and validated by their partners, and fewer are willing to accept abuse, or even indifference. On the other hand, as expectations for intimacy rise, intimate relationships have also become more fragile. If intimacy has become the primary justification for relationships, it follows that couples are justified in ending their relationships when intimacy fails.

MAIN POINTS

» For most of human history, one of the most important functions of intimate relationships was to organize property and allegiances, and the most important form of relationship for serving this purpose was marriage.

» Only in the 19th century, after the Industrial Revolution, did people begin to believe that romantic love was an element that allowed marriages to fulfill their broader social roles.

» By the early 21st century, many of the economic and social constraints that once compelled couples to marry have fallen away, leaving couples to focus more and more on the quality of their intimacy.

CONCLUSION

As Houdini understood better than most people, the future is hard to predict. Clearly, intimacy itself is not going anywhere. People have needed and sought closeness with others for all of human history and will continue to do so. People have always experienced romantic attraction, and that will never go away. What is unknown is how relationships will be affected by the continued weakening of the rules that define and constrain the expression of intimacy between two people. It may be that future couples will be increasingly challenged to define the terms of their relationships for themselves. They may have to negotiate roles and expectations that prior generations, and even modern couples, take for granted. For some couples, this may be a burden, and the need for each couple to define their own intimacy may make relationships harder. But rising to this challenge may also make relationships better.

Glossary

ABC-X model: One of the earliest social ecological models of intimate relationships, developed by sociologist Reuben Hill to explain how external stressors (A), a family's resources (B), and their interpretation of the event (C) all combine to affect the outcome of a crisis (X). Also known as crisis theory. *See also* Double ABC-X model.

accommodation: The process of changing existing beliefs to integrate new information.

accuracy motive: The desire to understand a partner and to be understood in turn.

acute event: An experience that has a relatively clear onset and the possibility of an end point, such as a car accident, an illness, or a period of unemployment.

advocacy perspective: An approach to understanding and helping women affected by domestic violence, particularly intimate terrorism.

affect: Feeling or emotional expression; the emotional tone of verbal communication.

alternatives: The consequences of ending a relationship, such as starting another one or staying alone.

androgynous: Possessing masculine and feminine traits.

anonymity: The principle of keeping identity unknown. In a research study, anonymity ensures that the identities of research participants cannot be linked to the data they have provided; usually a requirement in ethical research.

archival research: A research design in which the researcher examines existing data that have already been gathered by someone else, often for an unrelated purpose.

arranged marriage: A marriage in which spouses have been brought together by family members or other parties responsible for selecting and approving potential mates.

assimilation: The process of integrating new information with existing knowledge without substantially changing the existing beliefs.

attachment behavior system: A set of behaviors and reactions that helps ensure a developing child's survival by keeping the child in close physical contact with caregivers.

attachment figure: A person whom an individual depends on as a source of comfort and care.

attachment style: An individual's relatively stable beliefs about the likelihood of other people providing support and care when it is needed. The four basic attachment styles are secure, preoccupied, dismissing, and fearful.

attachment theory: An influential theory of intimate relationships proposing that the relationships formed in adulthood are shaped largely by the nature of the bonds formed with primary caregivers in infancy and early childhood.

attitude: A positive or negative evaluation of someone or something.

attraction: The experience of evaluating another person positively.

attribution: An explanation for a behavior; the explanation attributes a behavior to some more general cause.

attrition bias: In longitudinal research, a bias caused by participants dropping out, leading to a final sample that differs from the initial sample in important ways.

barrier: One of many forces external to a relationship that keep partners together.

bases of attraction: The aspects of a person that tend to make him or her appealing to others.

behavioral confirmation: The process through which beliefs and expectations lead to behavior that elicits responses that confirm the initial beliefs and expectations.

behavioral couples therapy: An intervention for unhappy couples in which the therapist defines the problem in terms of specific problem behaviors, and clarifies the rewards and punishments that maintain these behaviors, thus perpetuating the couple's difficulties.

behavioral models: An approach to couples therapy that emphasizes behaviors exchanged between partners and the perceptions and interpretations that give rise to these behaviors.

behavioral synchrony: The tendency for partners who are mutually involved and attracted to mimic each other's movements unconsciously.

behavior exchange: This initial stage of traditional behavioral couples therapy, giving the therapist diagnostic information about the extent to which partners can generate new, positive experiences in their relationship; conveys that improving their relationship can be enjoyable rather than painful.

belief: An idea or theory about what the world is like.

bias: A tendency to process information to protect a particular point of view.

bidirectionality: A quality of interdependence that exists when both members of a relationship have the capacity to affect each other's outcomes to a similar degree.

A1

Big Five: The five broad personality traits that capture most of the personality differences between individuals: neuroticism, extraversion, openness, agreeableness, and conscientiousness.

bilateral aggression: Violent behavior perpetrated by both partners in a relationship. *See also* unilateral aggression.

broaden and build theory: The idea that experiencing and expressing positive emotions serve two purposes: to expand and enhance how we attend to, think about, and respond to daily events; and to accumulate the resources—including physical health, intellectual and creative capacities, spiritual connections, and social relationships—for maintaining our well-being.

capitalization: Within an intimate relationship, using positive events in each partner's life as opportunities to nurture and promote closeness.

causation: The idea that one event or circumstance directly gives rise to, or produces a change in, another.

chronic conditions: Aspects of the environment that are relatively stable and enduring, such as the quality of one's neighborhood or one's socioeconomic status.

clinical model: An approach to therapeutic intervention that involves treating relationship distress only after it has developed into a significant problem. *See also* public health model.

close relationship: A relationship characterized by strong, frequent, and diverse interdependence that persists over a significant period of time.

coding system: In the context of social learning theory, any one of several schemes researchers use for classifying observed behaviors.

coercion theory: An offshoot of social learning theory that explains how partners may inadvertently reinforce each other's negative behaviors by giving in only when the partner's negative behavior has grown particularly intense.

cognitive-behavioral couples therapy: An approach focusing on how couples interact and respond to each other and how they interpret each other's behavior. The premise of this approach is that dysfunctional patterns of behavior and cognition can be identified and corrected with training.

cognitive complexity: The extent to which a person's thoughts about particular subjects are well integrated and take multiple dimensions into consideration.

cognitive editing: The tendency in happy couples to respond to a partner's negative behaviors with neutral or even positive behaviors.

cognitive restructuring: A process by which the implications of a partner's perceived faults are minimized by linking them to perceptions of the partner's strengths.

cohabitation: Sharing a residence with an intimate partner without being married to that partner.

commitment: The intention to remain in and feel connected to a relationship; a product of satisfaction with and dependence on the relationship.

commitment calibration hypothesis: The idea that threats to a relationship should motivate activities to protect the relationship only if the threat is calibrated to partners' levels of commitment. For them to take action, a threat must be big enough to notice but not so big as to overwhelm their desire to remain in the relationship.

communication training: A technique in behavioral couples therapy in which partners receive concrete advice on how to listen and talk to each other productively.

companionate love: Type of love characterized by warm feelings of attachment, an authentic and enduring bond, a sense of mutual commitment, and satisfaction with shared goals and perspectives.

comparison level (CL): The standard against which individuals compare their outcomes to decide whether they are satisfied with them.

comparison level for alternatives (CL$_{alt}$): Expectations of the likely outcomes available from the potential alternatives to a current relationship; individuals compare their relationship outcomes to the expected alternatives to determine their dependence on the relationship.

complementarity: The idea that people are attracted to those who possess traits that they themselves lack.

conditional probability: In the context of couple interactions, the likelihood of one partner engaging in a specific behavior in response to a specific behavior by the other partner. *See also* unconditional probability.

confidentiality: The principle of privacy, which ensures that information about research participants is not shared or discussed with anyone not directly associated with the research; usually a requirement in ethical research.

confirmation bias: A preference for information that supports one's established beliefs and expectations.

conflict: The interference of the goals of one person by another person.

construct validity: The extent to which an operationalization adequately represents a particular psychological construct.

containment: According to psychodynamic models of couples therapy, the process by which one partner adopts and identifies with the partner's view of himself or herself.

content analysis: The process of coding open-ended materials in a way that allows material from different sources to be quantified and compared.

context: Everything that affects a relationship outside of the couple and their interactions; includes physical, social, cultural, and historical elements.

control: In a true experiment, the holding constant of all aspects of the experimental situation that are not being manipulated.

convenience sample: A sample of research participants recruited solely because they are easy to find.

correlational research: A research design that examines the naturally occurring associations among variables; aimed primarily at answering descriptive questions.

cost: Any consequence of being in a relationship that prevents partners from fulfilling their needs or desires.

crisis: A couple's experience of and response to a stressful event, represented by X in the ABC-X model.

cross-cultural studies: Research designed to compare and contrast behaviors, beliefs, and values across populations that vary in their culture, ethnicity, or country of origin.

cross-sectional data: Data that have been collected from individuals at one assessment, the data describe a cross-section, or a snapshot, of a single moment.

cross-validation: A strategy in which a researcher takes a specific finding in one study and tries to replicate it precisely within a second sample of data.

culture: The shared attitudes, beliefs, norms, and values of people who speak the same language and share a geographic area, during a specific period of time.

cycle of violence: A pattern of physical abuse marked by a tension-building phase when the woman senses a man's growing edginess and frustration; an acute battering phase, when the man inflicts rage and aggression on the woman; and a contrition phase, when the man apologizes and expresses remorse, leading eventually to renewed tension and frustration.

daily diary approach: A longitudinal research design that asks participants to provide data every day at about the same time.

demand/withdraw pattern: A behavioral sequence common in distressed relationships in which one partner expresses a desire for change and the other partner resists change by disengaging from the interaction.

dependence: The degree to which an individual feels free to leave a relationship; a function of how the outcomes in the current relationship compare to potential outcomes available in the likely alternatives to that relationship.

dependency regulation model: A model addressing how individuals in intimate relationships balance their desires for closeness to their partners with the recognition that intimacy also leaves them vulnerable to being hurt or betrayed; applied specifically to explain how those with low self-esteem may sabotage their relationships by underestimating how favorably their partners view them.

dependent variable: In experimental research, the effect or outcome the researchers want to understand. *See also* independent variable.

derogating alternative partners: Protecting a current relationship by evaluating possible alternatives to the relationship negatively.

desensitization: The tendency to react less strongly to a particular stimulus the more one is exposed to it. *See also* sensitization.

diagnosticity bias: A preference for information that may indicate important qualities in a partner or a relationship; the tendency to perceive such information to be more revealing than it may actually be.

differential parental treatment: Treating the siblings within a family unequally; a strong predictor of sibling rivalry.

disclosure reciprocity: Responding to someone's personal disclosure by immediately revealing something equally personal.

dismissing attachment style: A style of attachment characterized by a positive view of the self but a negative view of others; dismissing people are satisfied with solitude and doubtful that an intimate partner would improve their life.

distal context: Elements in the environment that are removed from a couple and affect them indirectly; for example, the social and cultural contexts within which relationships form and develop. *See also* proximal context.

Double ABC-X model: A revision of Hill's original ABC-X model that recognizes how each element in the original model may change over time as a couple copes with a stressful event.

downward social comparison: A way of feeling better about oneself relative to others who are doing worse.

d statistic: A standardized way of quantifying differences between groups, useful for comparing research results across multiple studies.

dyad: A group consisting of two people; the smallest possible social group.

effectiveness studies: Research designed to determine whether a therapeutic intervention does produce desired results in the real world; differs from efficacy studies by occuring in more typical treatment contexts, thus being less scientifically rigorous.

efficacy studies: Research designed to determine whether a therapeutic intervention can produce desired results; involves randomly assigning participants to one or more forms of therapy and comparing their outcomes to those of participants who did not receive the treatment.

egalitarian relationship: A relationship in which both partners play equal roles in decision making and child rearing, rejecting traditional gender roles and divisions of labor.

emotionally focused couples therapy: An approach focusing on and drawing out the emotional moments in couples' conversations, to create bonds rather than the bargains that typify traditional behavioral approaches.

emotion models: An approach to couples therapy that emphasizes the expression of vulnerabilities and core emotions and, in turn, healthy responses to these expressions that bring partners closer together.

empathic accuracy: The capacity of one partner in a couple to correctly understand what the other partner is thinking or feeling.

empathic joining: A technique for promoting acceptance in integrative behavioral couples therapy, whereby the practitioner encourages a couple to see a broader theme for their destructive interterpersonal patterns; they join together to find a solution.

empathy: The capacity to understand and share another person's thoughts and feelings.

empathy accuracy model: A framework to explain when partners should be more or less motivated to attend to and understand what each other is thinking and feeling. The model proposes that our motivation to understand our partner accurately varies, depending on how threatening our partner's thoughts and feelings are likely to be.

enhancement bias: The tendency to process information that supports positive beliefs about a partner and a relationship, rather than negative ones.

enhancement motive: The desire to support and strengthen positive views of a partner and a relationship.

environment of evolutionary adaptedness: The period of evolutionary history tens of thousands of years ago during which the human species took its current form.

escape conditioning: An offshoot of social learning theory that explains how negative behaviors may be inadvertently reinforced to the extent that their occurrence is associated with the end of an aversive stimulus; for example, if breaking into tears predicts the end of an uncomfortable argument, then breaking into tears is reinforced.

evolutionary psychology: A broad field within psychology guided by the idea that the mind evolved in response to specific selection pressures that lead some preferences and capacities to be associated with more successful reproduction, and others to be associated with less successful reproduction; explains human thoughts and behaviors in terms of their adaptive functions.

expectation: A prediction about what is likely to happen in the future, often based on general beliefs about how relationships function.

experience sampling: An approach to conducting longitudinal research by gathering data from participants throughout the day, literally "sampling" from the totality of their daily experiences.

experimental research: A research design in which researchers manipulate one element of a phenomenon to determine its effects on the rest of the phenomenon; ideal for examining questions of explanation and causation.

external locus of control: The belief that one's success or failure is primarily the result of outside forces. *See also* internal locus of control.

external validity: The extent to which results obtained in an experimental setting are likely to generalize to different contexts.

false belief test: A tool to measure the development of theories of mind in children. Children observe two girls, one of whom moves an object while the other is absent. Children are said to possess a theory of mind when they recognize that someone else has access to less information than they do.

falsifiable: Referring to the ability of a theory to suggest testable predictions that can be confirmed or disconfirmed by making systematic observations; a quality of good theories.

family of origin: The family in which a person was raised through childhood.

family sociology perspective: An approach to studying aggression in couples and families using large-scale surveys; it underestimates the level of very severe aggression.

fatal attraction: A type of attraction in which qualities in a partner that are initially perceived as attractive grow to be sources of irritation later in the relationship.

fearful attachment style: A style of attachment characterized by negative views of the self and others; fearful people long for social contact but tend to withdraw to protect themselves from being hurt.

felt security: A child's experience of safety and protection from being aware of a caregiver's presence and attention; the lack of felt security activates the attachment behavior system to seek proximity to a caregiver to restore the sense of security.

fight-or-flight response: A physiological response to stress or threat that prepares the body to take action, either by confronting the threat (fight) or by escaping it (flight).

fitness: The qualities of an organism that improve its chances of producing surviving offspring.

fixed-response scale: A survey instrument that presents respondents with a predetermined set of questions, each with a predetermined set of answers from which to choose.

flexible standards: Standards that can be changed over time so that whatever is currently perceived to be positive about a relationship is considered important and whatever is currently perceived to be negative is dismissed as unimportant.

forgiveness: The process, after being hurt by a partner's behavior, of transforming anger and the desire to retaliate into an altruistic orientation toward the offender, with a desire for reconciliation.

gender: The nonbiological and nonphysiological attributes, characteristics, and behaviors that are viewed as masculine or feminine; for example, how individuals dress; their feelings and expressions; their attitudes, values, and interests.

general lay theories: The ideas and beliefs of people who are not researchers about how relationships function. *See also* specific lay theories.

global measure: An instrument for assessing relationship satisfaction that asks partners only about their evaluations of their relationship as a whole.

home-based observation: A method of conducting research on behavior that records observations within a couple's home, either by sending observers with recording equipment to the home or by sending the equipment to couples so they can record themselves.

hypothesis: A concrete prediction, arising from a theory, about how different variables are likely to be associated.

ideal: The highest outcomes to which a person ultimately aspires.

ideal standards model: The theory that the amount of discrepancy between values for relationships in general and perceptions of the current relationship in particular determines whether a person will be satisfied with a relationship. The greater the discrepancy between general ideals and specific perceptions, the lower the evaluation of the relationship.

impact stage: The stage in the forgiveness process when partners learn of the transgression and begin to recognize the effect it has on them and their relationship; a time of disorientation, confusion, and hurt feelings.

impersonal relationship: A relationship that is formal and task-oriented, shaped more by the social roles individuals are filling than by their personal qualities.

independent variable: The element of an experiment the researcher manipulates, changing it "independently" of any other aspect of the situation to see if changes in this variable are associated with changes in the dependent variable.

information processing: All the ways we organize our perceptions, thoughts, and beliefs about the world.

informed consent: A written form of agreement signed by participants in a study, indicating they understand the research procedures and know what to expect; a requirement of ethical research.

integrative behavioral couples therapy: An approach that combines behavioral interventions with techniques to help couples tolerate and even accept displeasing aspects of the partner and the relationship.

interactive network: The set of people with whom an individual interacts regularly.

interdependence: A state in which the actions of person P affect the outcomes of person O at the same time that the actions of person O affect the outcomes of person P; the defining feature of any relationship.

interdependence theory: A version of social exchange theory that focuses on the rules predicting how interdependent partners will behave toward each other, and how the partners evaluate the outcomes of their actions.

intergenerational transmission effects: The characteristics of one's family of origin that carry forward to affect intimate relationships in adolescence and adulthood.

internal locus of control: The belief that one can bring about desired outcomes through one's own actions. *See also* external locus of control.

interpersonal perspective on aggression: An approach to explaining violence in couples that emphasizes the private and passionate nature of intimate relationships, the high degree of partner interdependence, the presence of disagreements, and variations in the behavioral and cognitive capacities partners express in their interactions.

interpretation of the event: The way a couple or a family defines a stressful experience, as a challenge to be overcome or a catastrophe to be endured; represented by C in the ABC-X model.

interrater reliability: In content analysis and the coding of observational data, the extent to which multiple independent coders agree on how a specific piece of content should be categorized.

intimacy process model: A framework that defines intimacy as arising from interactions in which person A discloses or expresses self-relevant thoughts and feelings to person B and, based on person B's response, comes to feel understood, validated, and cared for.

intimate relationship: A relationship characterized by strong, sustained, mutual influence across a wide range of interactions, including at least the potential for sexual interaction.

intimate terrorism: A form of aggression by one partner to dominate the other.

intraindividual perspectives on aggression: An approach to explaining violence in couples that focuses on the enduring qualities and personal histories of each partner.

intrasexual competition: The ways men and women compete with other members of their own sex to gain advantage in the mating marketplace.

introjective identification: In psychodynamic models of couples therapy, the means by which one partner takes in a modified version of himself or herself, as expressed by the partner, and assimilates this into his or her identity.

investment: A resource tied to a relationship that would be lost if the relationship were to end.

invisible support: Efforts to promote the well-being of a partner that the recipient is not aware of receiving. *See also* visible support.

item-overlap problem: Two different self-report instruments addressing the same ideas, leading to inflated estimates of the correlations between the constructs.

justification motive: A preference for information that supports a positive view of oneself, even if it does not support a relationship.

laboratory-based observation: In observational research, observing participants in a controlled environment, such as a research room, as they engage in a behavior of interest; eliminates the influence of outside factors that may alter behavior in other settings, and removes the behavior from the environment where it usually occurs.

lay relationship theories: The accumulated knowledge that people who are not researchers have about intimate relationships.

lifespan study: A longitudinal research design that gathers data from individuals repeatedly over the course of their entire lives.

locus dimension: With reference to attributions, the location of the cause of a behavior, usually distinguishing between causes that are internal or external to the actor. *See also* stability dimension.

locus of control: A person's expectation about his or her ability to bring about desired changes in some aspect of life.

long-distance relationship: A relationship in which partners spend most of their time physically separated from each other, restricting regular face-to-face interaction.

longitudinal research: A research design that collects measurements from the same individuals at two or more occasions.

macrosystem: The broadest level in Bronfenbrenner's social ecological model of development, consisting of sources of influence that are far removed from the individual's or couple's direct experience but are still influential, such as national, historical, and cultural contexts. *See also* mesosystem, microsystem.

matching phenomenon: The tendency for partners in intimate relationships to be similar in physical attractiveness.

mate selection: The process through which a committed relationship is formed.

material reward: One of the concrete benefits provided by a relationship, such as money, housing, food, and protection.

meaning stage: The stage in the forgiveness process when the offended partner tries to make sense of why the transgression happened.

memory bias: The tendency for people's memories of the past to be distorted by their current feelings and desires.

mere exposure effect: A preference for a stimulus that is familiar and experienced often, over a stimulus that is unfamiliar.

mesosystem: A level in Bronfenbrenner's social ecological model of development, consisting of the broader social context, including the neighborhoods, social networks, and institutions in which relationships take place. *See also* macrosystem, microsystem.

meta-analysis: A set of statistical techniques designed to combine results across studies of common variables and reveal the overall effects observed in a body of scientific research.

microsystem: A level in Bronfenbrenner's social ecological model of development consisting of the immediate environment that directly impacts individuals and couples, including living situation, stressful life events, and the presence or absence of other people. *See also* macrosystem, mesosystem.

misattribution of arousal: The tendency to mistakenly believe that physical arousal stemming from one cause is actually the result of another cause; a source of situational effects on romantic and sexual attraction.

monogamy: The practice of sexual and emotional exclusivity in an intimate relationship.

motive: A drive to reach a specific goal.

motivated reasoning: All the ways that motives, desires, and preferences shape how we select, interpret, and organize information, guided by satisfying specific needs and achieving specific goals.

moving-on stage: The stage in the forgiveness process when the victim finds a way to adjust to and move beyond the incident.

multiple-method approach: Operationalizing the constructs of interest in different ways, so the limitations of each measurement strategy may eventually cancel each other out and the effects the researcher is focused on can emerge clearly.

natural selection: The process whereby an organism with a particular gene is better able to survive and reproduce in a specific environment, thereby passing that gene down to future generations.

nature: Evolved or inherited biological substrates for human adaptation and behavior, often contrasted with nurture, or changes that result from the environment and socialization. *See also* nurture.

negative affectivity: *See* neuroticism.

negative correlation: An association between two variables in which high levels of one variable tend to be associated with low levels of the other one.

negative reciprocity: The interpersonal pattern in couples in which one person responds to the other's negative behavior with a negative behavior of his or her own; a common experience in distressed relationships.

negative reinforcement: Increasing the likelihood of some behavior recurring in the future by responding to it with the removal of some aversive stimulus. *See also* positive reinforcement.

network density: The degree to which members of an individual's social network are themselves connected to other people within the network.

network overlap: The extent to which partners in a relationship consider the same individuals to be part of their personal networks.

neuroticism: A personality trait distinguished by the tendency to experience and express pessimism and negative emotions.

null hypothesis: The assumption made by researchers that two variables are not associated or two groups do not differ statistically. Research is designed to seek out evidence that disconfirms or refutes this hypothesis.

nurture: Effects on human adaptation and behavior that result from experiences with the environment, including socialization; typically contrasted with nature. *See also* nature.

object relations couples therapy: An approach to therapeutic intervention with couples that assumes intimate communication is motivated by unconscious feelings and beliefs and aims to neutralize them so partners can relate to each other authentically.

observational measure: An approach to data collection permitting direct access to relationship events, typically in the form of conversations between partners assessed via video or audio records.

omnibus measure: A measure of a psychological construct that includes questions capturing a wide range of phenomena, usually applied to self-report instruments and characteristic of some measures of relationship satisfaction.

open-ended question: A measurement approach in which respondents are asked questions but are not provided a specific set of response options, thereby allowing them to answer the questions in their own words.

operationalization: A key stage in the research process in which an abstract concept (a psychological construct) is translated into concrete terms so that predictions about that concept can be tested.

opportunity cost: In social exchange theory, the idea that pursuing one rewarding experience (e.g., a relationship with one person) supplants the ability to pursue other potential rewards (e.g., a particular career choice).

outcome research: Studies undertaken to determine the effect, or outcome, of a particular form of intervention or therapy.

pairbond: A relationship between two individuals who have some degree of emotional and/or practical investment in one another, often with the purpose of reproducing.

passionate love: An emotional experience marked by infatuation, intense preoccupation with the partner, sexual longing, and, upon being reunited with the partner, feelings of exhilaration and relief.

perceptual confirmation: The tendency to interpret new and/or ambiguous information and experiences in a manner consistent with existing ideas, beliefs, and expectations, thereby reinforcing them.

personality: The relatively stable and distinctive qualities that characterize an individual, that have some coherence or internal organization to them, and that influence how the person behaves in and adapts to the world.

personal relationship: An interdependent relationship between two people who consider each other to be special and unique.

phantom other technique: A research procedure in which participants are asked to make judgments about a person believed to be real but is in fact a fiction constructed by the researchers.

physiological response: The body's involuntary biological reaction to stimuli and experiences.

polarized: Referring to polar opposites; in a personal relationship, a couple is polarized when the two partners adopt opposing viewpoints in an argument.

positive correlation: An association between two variables in which high levels of one variable tend to correspond with high levels of the other one, and low levels of one variable tend to correspond with low levels of the other one.

positive reinforcement: Increasing the likelihood of some behavior recurring in the future by responding to it with a pleasurable or rewarding stimulus. *See also* negative reinforcement.

power: An individual's capacity to alter the behavior and experiences of others, while also resisting the influence of others.

pratfall effect: The tendency for a few endearing flaws to make an otherwise wonderful person even more attractive.

preoccupied attachment style: A style of attachment characterized by a positive view of others but a low sense of self-worth.

primary appraisal: One's initial and immediate reaction to some event or circumstance, as in a child's response to interparental conflict and the determination of how threatening it is. *See also* secondary appraisal.

primary emotions: Feelings such as abandonment, fear of rejection, shame, and helplessness that can be masked or hidden by self-protective secondary emotions, like anger.

primary prevention: An intervention undertaken to reduce or eliminate the likelihood that some adverse or costly event or outcome will occur.

primary sex characteristics: Chromosomes, hormones, internal structures, and external genitalia that distinguish females and males.

problem-solving training: A component of traditional behavioral couples therapy in which couples learn to apply new communication skills to problems in their relationship, following specified guidelines.

proceptivity: Receptiveness or a nonverbal signal shown by one person to another indicating that it would be acceptable to initiate a conversation.

projection: In psychodynamic models of couples therapy, an unconscious tendency for a person to deny his or her own flaws and negative emotions, locating them instead in the external world; a person is said to project negative experiences onto the partner.

projective identification: A concept from object relations couples therapy capturing the way one person identifies with and responds to how the partner describes or experiences him or her.

protection effect: An association between two phenomena whereby one causes improvement or benefits in the other; for example, marriage appears to afford protection through improved health.

proximal context: The immediate circumstances or environmental factors that affect a psychological phenomenon; for example, the kitchen can be the proximal context for couples' arguments. *See also* distal context.

proximity: Nearness or physical closeness, a factor that can promote interpersonal contact and relationship formation.

psychoanalysis: The theory that first distinguished between the conscious and unconscious mind.

psychodynamic models: An approach to couples therapy that emphasizes the unconscious forces that govern how two partners perceive one another and the emotional reactions that follow from these perceptions.

psychological construct: An abstract concept, such as love, support, or trust, that social scientists strive to define, measure, and study.

psychological mechanism: One of many evolved preferences, capacities, responses, and strategies characterizing the human species that enable the implementation of some function or adaptation; often associated with the evolutionary perspective.

psychological network: Those who play important roles in a person's life.

public health model: Compared to a clinical or therapeutic model, a perspective on intervention that aims to help prevent or alleviate problems on a larger and more cost-effective social scale.

qualitative research: An approach to data collection that relies primarily on open-ended questions and other loosely structured information, often contrasted with research that emphasizes explicit quantification of concepts.

radical behavioralism: The idea that behaviors are shaped (or "conditioned") by their consequences.

random assignment: The assurance that every research participant has an equal chance of being assigned to any condition or treatment in the experiment; an essential element of experimental research.

reactivity: The possibility that the very act of observing a behavior or phenomenon might change that behavior or phenomenon.

reactivity hypothesis: A phenomenon in which unhappy partners are more sensitive and responsive to immediate events in their relationship, regardless of whether they are positive or negative.

reframe: A technique in which a couples therapist offers a more benign interpretation for a specific behavior or event so partners can understand it in a more positive and productive light. *Also called* relabel.

refutation: A way that partners accomplish cognitive restructuring, by interpreting negative behaviors to minimize their impact on the relationship. *See also* reinterpretation.

reinterpretation: A way that partners accomplish cognitive restructuring, by connecting a partner's acknowledged faults to higher-level positive ideals. *See also* refutation.

relabel: *See* reframe.

relationship maintenance: The routine behaviors and strategies partners undertake to help ensure that their relationship will continue and/or improve.

relationship quality: How good or how bad an individual judges his or her relationship to be.

relationship science: Application of the tools of the scientific method to answer questions about interpersonal relationships.

relationship status: Independent of relationship quality, the type of relationship an individual is currently experiencing (e.g., dating, married, divorced, widowed, or no relationship).

reliability: The trustworthiness of a measurement, including interobserver reliability or the extent to which different observers agree that a specified behavior has or has not occurred.

replication: Independent confirmation of a research finding.

representative sample: A research sample consisting of people who are demonstrably similar to the population to which the researchers would like to generalize.

resource: An asset; a source of practical, social, or emotional support outside a couple that contributes to their ability to interact effectively or adapt to stresses and circumstances; represented by B in the ABC-X model.

reward: In social exchange theory, any of the ways the relationship may fulfill the needs and desires of each partner.

romantic attraction: The experience of finding someone desirable as a potential intimate partner. *Also called* sexual attraction.

sample: In research, the people or couples who provide data; a subset of a broader population that, theoretically, could have provided very similar data.

schema: A cognitive category that organizes ideas and beliefs about certain concepts.

scientific method: A rigorous and self-correcting set of procedures used for making predictions, gathering data, and comparing the validity of competing claims about the world.

secondary appraisal: Cognitive processing of an event judged to be personally threatening or significant; when a child perceives parental conflict as personally threatening, the child's secondary appraisal is an effort to understand why the conflict is happening and what should be done about it. *See also* primary appraisal.

secondary emotions: Self-protective emotions, such as anger, that deflect attention from primary emotions, such as abandonment, fear of rejection, shame, and helplessness.

secondary prevention: An intervention directed at individuals or couples who are at elevated risk or vulnerable in some way to subsequent difficulties.

secondary sex characteristics: Anatomical characteristics that distinguish males and females and that facilitate courtship and mate selection, including breasts, finer skin, and more subcutaneous fat for females, and facial hair, a deep voice, and greater musculature for males.

secure attachment style: A style of attachment characterized by positive views of the self and others, thus enabling effective interpersonal relationships.

selection effect: An outcome when groups of people differ because of differences in the people who choose to enter those groups. Cohabitation predicts later relationship distress in some studies, for example, not because cohabitation is necessarily harmful for relationships but because people who choose to cohabit have a higher risk of later relationship distress than people who choose not to cohabit.

selective attention: Noticing and focusing on some information or stimuli in the environment and not others.

self-blame: A tendency to find fault in oneself for adverse events, often displayed by children in response to parental conflict.

self-expansion model: A perspective based on two assumptions: people want to increase their capacity and efficacy as individuals to achieve their goals and strive to acquire resources of various kinds, enrich their identities, and elaborate on what they know and what they can do; intimate relationships are a common way people attempt to accomplish self-expansion.

self-fulfilling prophesy: Behavior that leads to an expected experience or outcome.

self-report: A research participant's own descriptions and evaluations of his or her experiences.

self-serving bias: The tendency to take credit for our successes and to blame others or circumstances for our failures.

sensitization: The tendency to become increasingly reactive to a stimulus after repeated presentations of it; for example, children become sensitized to conflicts between their parents. *See also* desensitization.

sentiment override: The tendency for partners' global feelings about their relationship to color their perceptions of specific behaviors and experiences in the relationship.

sex: A categorical designation indicating whether an individual is male or female, biologically speaking.

sex role identity: The way people view themselves along dimensions of masculinity and femininity.

sex role traditionalism: The tendency to value a clear and conventional separation of the roles and responsibilities for men and women.

sexual attraction: The experience of finding someone desirable as a potential intimate partner. *Also called* romantic attraction.

sexual minorities: Individuals who do not identify themselves as primarily and exclusively straight in their sexual orientation; gay men and lesbians.

sexual selection: An aspect of natural selection whereby a feature of an organism proves adaptive and therefore is passed on to future generations, not because it increases the organism's chance of survival but because it helps the organism compete for or attract mates.

sexual strategies theory: An evolutionary perspective on attraction and mate selection that tries to explain the qualities men and women look for when they pursue long-term versus short-term relationships.

shared imaginative play: The creation and inhabiting of fantasy world by children together.

situational couple violence: A form of physical aggression between intimate partners that is usually mutual, widespread, and the result of emotional escalation.

social capital: The tangible and intangible benefits individuals derive from their relationships with others.

social comparison: An individual's use of information about others to evaluate his or her own attitudes and abilities.

social control theory: The view that interpersonal relationships organize and regulate how individuals behave, such that fewer, weaker, or poorer relationships increase the occurrence of deviant behavior.

social desirability effect: A tendency for research participants to provide answers that they think will make them look good to the researchers.

social ecological model: A theoretical framework designed to explain how stresses, supports, and constraints in the environment may affect the way partners think, feel, and act in a relationship.

social exchange theory: A perspective on interdependence in relationships that describes personal interactions in economic terms, with particular reference to the rewards and costs partners perceive in their relationship.

social integration: Involvement with, or connection to, people around us.

social learning theory: A theoretical perspective outlining how rewarding and costly interpersonal experiences influence how people evaluate themselves and their relationships.

social network: The families, friendships, neighborhoods, clubs, and institutions through which individuals are connected.

social penetration theory: A framework outlining how the breadth and depth of personal disclosures exchanged by two people affect the development of the relationship between them.

social reward: One of the benefits people derive from relationships, including companionship, validation, and security.

social structural theory: An explanation for psychological and behavioral differences between women and men based on physical specialization of the sexes, division of labor, social construction of gender, and local economies.

social support: Responsiveness to the needs of others.

sociocultural perspective on aggression: An approach to explaining violence in couples by recognizing how aggressive behavior may be promoted or inhibited by various social and cultural institutions.

socioeconomic status (SES): All the ways individuals differ in their ranking within a social structure, including income, education, and occupation.

socioemotional selectivity theory: The idea that because aging makes people aware of their mortality, they seek situations that promote positive emotions and avoid those that lead to negative emotions. Younger people are more open to new experiences, even if they risk being negative or unpleasant.

sociometric testing: A research technique in which children in a classroom are interviewed individually and asked to name who they like and who they dislike within the group, as a way to measure social standing among peers.

sociometry: A method of measuring and displaying the strength and number of relationships within a collection of individuals, achieved by asking all members of the group about the quality and quantity of their interactions with every other member of the group.

sociosexuality: The propensity to contemplate sex outside the context of a committed intimate relationship.

specific lay theories: Beliefs and values people hold about specific ongoing or prior relationships. *See also* general lay theories.

speed dating: An arranged social event where unacquainted people talk briefly with every potential romantic partner; each person identifies which others he or she wishes to see again; if that wish is reciprocated, a date can be scheduled.

stability dimension: With reference to attributions, the duration of the cause of a behavior, usually distinguishing between causes that are temporary or continuous. *See also* locus dimension.

stage theory: Any theory of relationship formation that describes relationships as developing through a specific sequence of steps.

stalking: Unwanted and disturbing attention from someone seeking to start or resume a romantic relationship.

standard: A yardstick for evaluating something; the minimum set of qualities and attributes partners require to be satisfied with their relationship.

statistical analysis: A set of tools and procedures for examing data collected in a research study, often to evaluate whether a particular hypothesis is or is not disconfirmed by those data.

statistically significant effect: An effect that is large enough to occur less than 5 percent of the time if the null hypothesis were true, thereby increasing confidence that the effect is not the product of random error.

stereotype accuracy effect: The fact that two partners may share beliefs and values and still be no more similar to each other than to any other member of their population, simply because most people share the same beliefs and values.

strategic pluralism: The idea that humans have developed the capacity to pursue long-term relationships or short-term relationships as their circumstances warrant.

stress crossover: The transmission of the effects of stress from one person to another.

stressor: An event or circumstance that makes demands on a person and requires some kind of adjustment, response, or adaptation; represented by A in the ABC-X model.

stress pile-up: The accumulation of stress, when one adverse event leads to other adverse events.

stress spillover: The transmission of the effects of stress from one domain in a person's life to other

domains, such as from outside a relationship to inside.

structural model of marital interaction: The idea that three dimensions of behavior distinguish happy and unhappy couples when they are trying to resolve a relationship problem: the positive and negative degrees of their behavior, the degree of predictability of behaviors between them, and their ability to exit cycles of reciprocal negative behavior.

subjective probability: A person's prediction of the likelihood that a particular reward or cost will occur.

subjective well-being: A person's experience of how happy he or she is generally in life.

substitutability: The degree to which different members of a social network may fulfill the same needs for an individual.

systems models: An approach to couples therapy that emphasizes the repetitive patterns of interaction that create tension between partners, and the unspoken rules and beliefs that govern those interactions.

talk table: A procedure for studying couple interactions during a problem-solving discussion in which they judge how positive and negative they intend their own messages to be and how positive and negative they experience the impact of their partners' messages, thus enabling researchers to specify sources of miscommunication.

tertiary prevention: Also known as therapy, an intervention undertaken to prevent further deterioration for an individual or couple who is already struggling.

tertiary sex characteristics: Behaviors learned from historical, social, and cultural circumstances.

theory: A proposed explanation for some phenomenon.

theory of mind: The recognition that other people have beliefs, knowledge, and desires that are different from one's own.

theory of parental investment: Trivers's observation that sexual selection pressures will vary according to the amount of energy and resources that each sex must invest to raise surviving offspring.

tolerance building: A technique used in integrative behavioral couples therapy designed to help individuals accept rather than change undesirable aspects of the partner or the relationship.

trait approach: The study of personality based on the adjectives that people use to describe themselves and others.

unconditional probability: In the context of couple interactions, the likelihood that a specific behavior will occur regardless of any other behaviors. *See also* conditional probability.

unified detachment: A technique used in integrative behavioral couples therapy to encourage the two partners to view their problems with less charged emotion and to talk about them in more neutral, descriptive terms.

unilateral aggression: Violence inflicted solely by one partner in a relationship. *See also* bilateral aggression.

unrequited love: Romantic attraction that is not reciprocated by the object of the attraction.

upward social comparison: Evaluating oneself in relation to others who are doing better in that domain.

value: An idea about what a person desires, aspires to, or believes should be true.

variable: An aspect of nature that can fluctuate and change over time, in regard to the situation or between people, that scientists aim to explain.

violent resistance: An unusual form of aggression in which the victim of severe abuse fights back, even to the point at which the perpetrator is killed.

visible support: Efforts to promote the well-being of a partner that the recipient is aware of receiving, potentially undermining its value. *See also* invisible support.

working model: One of many psychological structures that represent the conscious and unconscious beliefs, expectations, and feelings people have about themselves, others, and relationships; formed in infancy and childhood through experiences with caregivers, a central idea in attachment theory. *Also called* internal working model.

Yerkes-Dodson law: The idea that performance on a simple task improves as arousal increases but that performance then decreases as arousal continues to rise.

References

Abbey, A., & Melby, C. (1986). The effects of nonverbal cues on gender differences in perceptions of sexual intent. *Sex Roles, 15,* 283–298.

Abele, A. E. (2003). The dynamics of masculine-agentic and feminine-communal traits: Findings from a prospective study. *Journal of Personality and Social Psychology, 85,* 768–776.

Abma, J. C., Martinez, G. M., Mosner, W. D., & Dawson, B. S. (2004). Teenagers in the United States: Sexual activity, contraceptive use and childbearing, 2002. *Vital Health Statistics, 23,* 58.

Acitelli, L. K. (1992). Gender differences in relationship awareness and marital satisfaction among young married couples. *Personality & Social Psychology Bulletin, 18,* 102–110.

Acitelli, L. K., Kenny, D. A., & Gladstone, D. (1996). Do relationship partners embrace the same ideals for marriage? (Yes, but their images of each other don't agree.) Paper presented at the International Network on Personal Relationships, Seattle, WA.

Ackerman, C. (1963). Affiliations: Structural determination of differential divorce. *American Journal of Sociology, 69,* 13–20.

Adair, W. L., Weingart, L., & Brett, J. (2007). The timing and function of offers in U.S. and Japanese negotiations. *Journal of Applied Psychology, 92,* 1056–1068.

Adam, B. D. (2006). Relationship innovation in male couples. *Sexualities, 9,* 5–26.

Adam, J. J., Teeken, J. C., Ypelaar, P. J. C., Verstappen, F. T. J., & Pass, F. G. W. (1997). Exercise-induced arousal and information processing. *International Journal of Sport Psychology, 28,* 217–226.

Ahearn, L. M. (2001). *Invitations to love: Literacy, love letters, and social change in Nepal.* University of Michigan Press, Ann Arbor.

Ainsworth, M. D. S., Blehar, M. C., Waters, E., & Wall, S. (1978). *Patterns of attachment: A psychological study of the Strange Situation.* Hillsdale, NJ: Lawrence Erlbaum.

Albert, B. (2004) *With one voice: America's adults and teens sound off about teen pregnancy.* Washington, DC: National Campaign to Prevent Teen Pregnancy.

Albrecht, S. L. (1980). Reactions and adjustments to divorce: Differences in the experiences of males and females. *Family Relations, 29,* 59–68.

Alexandrov, E. O., Cowan, P. A., & Cowan, C. P. (2005). Couple attachment and the quality of marital relationships: Method and concept in the validation of the new couple attachment interview and coding system. *Attachment and Human Development, 7,* 123–152.

Allen, M., D'Alessio, D., & Brezgel, K. (1995). A meta-analysis summarizing the effects of pornography II: Aggression after exposure. *Human Communication Research, 22,* 258–283.

Altman, I., & Taylor, D. A. (1973). *Social penetration: The development of interpersonal relationships.* New York: Holt, Rinehart, and Winston.

Alzheimer's Association. (2008). *Alzheimer's disease facts and figures.* Chicago.

Amato, P. R. (2000). The consequences of divorce for adults and children. *Journal of Marriage and Family, 62,* 1269–1287.

Amato, P. R. (2003). Reconciling divergent perspectives: Judith Wallerstein, quantitative family research, and children of divorce. *Family Relations, 52,* 332–339.

Amato, P. R. (2004). Tension between institutional and individual views of marriage. *Journal of Marriage and Family, 66,* 959–965.

Amato, P. R., & Booth, A. (1991). The consequences of divorce for attitudes towards divorce and gender roles. *Journal of Family Issues, 12,* 306–322.

Amato, P. R., & Booth, A. (1997). *A generation at risk: Growing up in an era of family upheaval.* Cambridge, MA: Harvard University Press.

Amato, P. R., & Booth, A. (2001). The legacy of parents' marital discord: Consequence for children's marital quality. *Journal of Personality and Social Psychology, 81,* 627–638.

Amato, P. R., & Cheadle, J. (2005). The long reach of divorce: Divorce and child well-being across three generations. *Journal of Marriage and Family, 67,* 191–206.

Amato, P. R., & DeBoer, D. D. (2001). The transmission of marital instability across generations: Relationship skills or commitment to marriage? *Journal of Marriage and Family, 63,* 1038–1051.

Amato, P. R., & Keith, B. (1991). Consequences of parental divorce for children's well-being: A meta-analysis. *Psychological Bulletin, 110,* 26–46.

Amato, P. R., & Previti, D. (2003). People's reasons for divorcing: Gender, social class, the life course, and adjustment. *Journal of Family Issues, 24,* 602–626.

Amato, P. R., Booth, A., Johnson, D. R., & Rogers, S. J. (2007). *Alone together: How marriage in America is changing.* Cambridge MA: Harvard University Press.

Amato, P. R., Johnson, D. R., Booth, A., & Rogers, S. J. (2003). Continuity and change in marital quality between 1980 and 2000. *Journal of Marriage and Family, 65*, 1–22.

Amato, P. R., Loomis, L. S., & Booth, A. (1995). Parental divorce, marital conflict, and offspring well-being during early adulthood. *Social Forces, 73*, 895–915.

Andersen, S. M., & Bem, S. L. (1981). Sex typing and androgyny in dyadic interaction: Individual differences in responsiveness to physical attractiveness. *Journal of Personality and Social Psychology, 41*, 74–86.

Anderson, C., John, O. P., Keltner, D., & Kring, A. (2001). Who attains social status? Effects of personality and physical attractiveness in social groups. *Journal of Personality and Social Psychology, 81*, 116–132.

Anderson, E. (1999). *Code of the streets*. New York: W. W. Norton.

Anderson, K. J., & Leaper, C. (1998). Meta-analyses of gender effects on conversational interruption: Who, what, when, where, and how. *Sex Roles, 39*, 225–252.

Anderson, N. H. (1968). Likableness ratings of 555 personality-trait words. *Journal of Personality and Social Psychology, 9*, 272–279.

Andersson, G., Noack, T., Seierstad, A., & Weedon-Fekjaer, H. (2006). The demographics of same-sex marriages in Norway and Sweden. *Demography, 43*, 79–98.

Andreb, H.-J., & Brockel, M. (2007). Income and life satisfaction after marital disruption in Germany. *Journal of Marriage and Family, 69*, 500–512.

Andrews, J. A., Foster, S. L., Capaldi, D., & Hops, H. (2000). Adolescent and family predictors of physical aggression, communication, and satisfaction in young adult couples: A prospective analysis. *Journal of Consulting and Clinical Psychology, 68*, 195–208.

Archer, J. (2000). Sex differences in aggression between heterosexual partners: A meta-analytic review. *Psychological Bulletin, 126*, 651–680.

Archer, J. (2004). Sex differences in aggression in real-world settings: A meta-analytic review. *Review of General Psychology, 8*, 291–322.

Arias, E. (2006). United States Life Tables, 2003, National Vital Statistics Reports (Vol. 54). Hyattsville, MD: National Center for Health Statistics.

Aries, E. (1996). *Men and women in interaction: Reconsidering the differences*. New York: Oxford.

Aristotle. (350 BCE/1985). Nicomachean Ethics (T. Irwin, Trans.). Indianapolis: Hackett Publishing.

Arnett, J. J. (2000). Emerging adulthood: A theory of development from the late teens through the twenties. *American Psychologist, 55*, 469–480.

Aron, A. P., & Aron, E. N. (1996). Self and self-expansion in relationships. In G. J. O. Fletcher & J. Fitness (Eds.), *Knowledge structures in close relationships: A social psychological approach* (pp. 325–344). Mahwah, NJ: Erlbaum.

Aron, A. P., Aron, E. N., & Norman, C. (2001). Self-expansion model of motivation and cognition in close relationships and beyond. In M. Clark & G. Fletcher (Eds.), *Blackwell's handbook of social psychology, Volume 2: Interpersonal processes* (pp. 478–501). Oxford, England: Blackwell.

Aron, A. P., Mashek, D. J., & Aron, E. N. (2004). Closeness as including other in the self. In D. J. Mashek & A. Aron (Eds.), *Handbook of closeness and intimacy* (pp. 27–41). Mahwah, NJ: Erlbaum.

Aron, A. P., Norman, C. C., Aron, E. N., McKenna, C., & Heyman, R. E. (2000). Couples' shared participation in novel and arousing activities and experienced relationship quality. *Journal of Personality and Social Psychology, 78*, 273–284.

Aron, A. P., Norman, C. C., Aron, E. N., McKenna, C., & Lewandowski, G. (2002). Shared participation in self-expanding activities: Positive effects on experienced marital quality. In P. Noller & J. A. Feeney (Eds.), *Understanding marriage: Developments in the study of couple interaction* (pp. 177–200). Cambridge, England: Cambridge University Press.

Aron, A. P., Paris, M., & Aron, E. N. (1995). Falling in love: Prospective studies of self-concept change. *Journal of Personality and Social Psychology, 69*, 1102–1112.

Aron, A., & Aron, E. N. (1986). *Love and the expansion of self: Understanding attraction and satisfaction*. New York: Hemisphere.

Aron, A., Aron, E. N., & Allen, J. (1998). Motivations for unreciprocated love. *Personality and Social Psychology Bulletin, 24*, 787–796.

Aron, A., Dutton, D. G., Aron, E. N., & Iverson, A. (1989). Experiences of falling in love. *Journal of Social and Personal Relationships, 6*, 243–257.

Aron, A., Fisher, H., Mashek, D., Strong, G., Li, H., & Brown, L. K. (2005). Reward, motivation and emotion systems associated with early-stage intense romantic love. *Journal of Neurophysiology, 93*, 327–337.

Aron, E. N., & Aron, A. (1996). Love and expansion of the self: The state of the model. *Personal Relationships, 3*, 45–58.

Aronson, E., & Linder, D. (1965). Gain and loss of esteem as determinants of interpersonal attractiveness. *Journal of Experimental Social Psychology, 1*, 156–171.

Aronson, E., Willerman, B., & Floyd, J. (1966). The effect of a pratfall on increasing interpersonal attractiveness. *Psychonomic Science, 4*, 227–228.

Asendorpf, J. B., & Wilpers, S. (1998). Personality effects on social relationships. *Journal of Personality and Social Psychology, 74*, 1531–1544.

Atkins, D. C., Baucom, D. H., & Jacobson, N. S. (2001). Understanding infidelity: Correlates in a national random sample. *Journal of Family Psychology, 15*, 735–749.

Atkins, D. C., Yi, J., Baucom, D. H., & Christensen, A. (2005). Infidelity in couples seeking therapy. *Journal of Family Psychology, 19*, 470–473.

Avellar, S., & Smock, P. J. (2005). The economic consequences of the dissolution of cohabiting unions. *Journal of Marriage and Family, 67*, 315–327.

Axinn, W. G., & Thornton, A. (1992). The relationship between cohabitation and divorce: Selectivity or causal influence? *Demography, 29*, 357–374.

Bachman, J. G., Wadsworth, K. N., O'Malley, P. M., Johnston, L. D., & Schulenberg, J. E. (1997). *Smoking, drinking, and drug use in young adulthood: The impacts of new freedoms and new responsibilities*. Mahwah, NJ: Erlbaum.

Bachman, R., & Carmody, D. C. (1994). Fighting fire with fire: The effects of victim resistance in intimate versus stranger perpetrated assaults against females. *Journal of Family Violence, 9*, 317–331.

Backman, C. W., & Secord, P. F. (1959). The effect of perceived liking on interpersonal attraction. *Human Relations, 12*, 379–384.

Bagwell, C. L., Newcomb, A. F., & Bukowski, W. M. (1998). Preadolescent friendship and peer rejection as predictors of adult adjustment. *Child Development, 69*, 140–153.

Bailey, B. (1988). *From front porch to back seat: Courtship in twentieth-century America*. Baltimore: Johns Hopkins University Press.

Bailey, J. M., & Zucker, K. J. (1995). Childhood sex-typed behavior and sexual orientation: A conceptual analysis and quantitative review. *Developmental Psychology, 31*, 43–55.

Bakeman, R., & Gottman, J. M. (1997). *Observing interaction: An introduction to sequential analysis* (2nd ed.). New York: Cambridge University Press.

Bakeman, R., Quera, V., McArthur, D., & Robinson, B. F. (1997). Detecting sequential patterns and determining their reliability with fallible observers. *Psychological Methods, 2*, 357–370.

Baker, L. A., & Emery, R. E. (1993). When every relationship is above average: Perceptions and expectations of divorce at the time of marriage. *Law and Human Behavior, 17*, 439–448.

Baldwin, M. W. (1992). Relational schemas and the processing of social information. *Psychological Bulletin, 112*, 461–484.

Baldwin, M. W., & Fehr, B. (1995). On the instability of attachment style ratings. *Personal Relationships, 2*, 247–261.

Baldwin, M. W., Keelan, J. P. R., Fehr, B., Enns, V., & Koh-Rangarajoo, E. (1996). Social-cognitive conceptualization of attachment working models: Availability and accessibility effects. *Journal of Personality and Social Psychology, 71*, 94–109.

Ballard-Reisch, D. S., & Weigel, D. J. (1999). Communication processes in marital commitment: An integrative approach. In J. M. Adams & W. H. Jones (Eds.), *Handbook of interpersonal commitment and relationship stability* (pp. 407–424). New York: Plenum.

Balsam, K. F., Beauchaine, T. P., Mickey, R. M., & Rothblum, E. D. (2005). Mental health of lesbian, gay, bisexual, and heterosexual siblings: Effects of gender, sexual orientation, and family. *Journal of Abnormal Psychology, 114*, 471–476.

Bandura, A. (1977). Self-efficacy: Toward a unifying theory of behavioral change. *Psychological Review, 84*, 191–215.

Bank, L., Patterson, G. R., & Reid, J. B. (1996). Negative sibling interaction patterns as predictors of later adjustment problems in adolescent and young adult males. *Advances in Applied Developmental Psychology, 10*, 197–229.

Bard, K. A. (1992). Intentional behavior and intentional communication in young free-ranging orangutans. *Child Development, 63*, 1186–1197.

Barnes, J. (1991). *Talking it over*. New York: Knopf.

Barnett, O. W., Martinez, T. E., & Keyson, M. (1996). The relationship between violence, social support, and self-blame in battered women. *Journal of Interpersonal Violence, 11*, 221–233.

Barnett, R., & Rivers, C. (2004). *Same difference: How gender myths are hurting our relationships, our children, and our jobs*. New York: Basic Books.

Barron, K. E., & Harackiewicz, J. M. (2001). Achievement goals and optimal motivation: Testing multiple goal models. *Journal of Personality and Social Psychology, 80*, 706–722.

Bartels, A., & Zeki, S. (2000). The neural basis of romantic love. *NeuroReport, 11*, 3829–3834.

Bartels, A., & Zeki, S. (2004). The neural correlates of maternal and romantic love. *NeuroImage, 21*, 1155–1166.

Bartholomew, K. (1990). Avoidance of intimacy: An attachment perspective. *Journal of Social and Personal Relationships, 7*, 147–178.

Bartholomew, K., & Horowitz, L. M. (1991). Attachment styles among young adults: A test of a four-category model. *Journal of Personality and Social Psychology, 61*, 226–244.

Bartlett, F. C. (1932). *Remembering: A study in experimental and social psychology*. London: Cambridge University Press.

Baucom, D. H., & Epstein, N. (1989). The role of cognitive variables in the assessment and treatment of marital discord. In M. Hersen, R. M. Eisler, & P. M. Miller (Eds.), *Progress in behavior modification* (Vol. 24, pp. 223–248). Newbury Park: Sage.

Baucom, D. H., & Epstein, N. (1990). *Cognitive behavioral marital therapy*. New York: Brunner/Mazel.

Baucom, D. H., & Epstein, N. (2002). *Enhanced cognitive behavior therapy for couples: A contextual perspective*. Washington, DC: American Psychological Association.

Baucom, D. H., Epstein, N., Rankin, L. A., & Burnett, C. K. (1996). Assessing relationship standards: The Inventory of Specific Relationship Standards. *Journal of Family Psychology, 10*, 72–88.

Baumeister, R. F., & Leary, M. R. (1995). The need to belong: Desire for interpersonal attachments as a fundamental human motivation. *Psychological Bulletin, 117*, 497–529.

Baumeister, R. F., & Sommer, K. L. (1997). What do men want? Gender differences and two spheres of belongingness: Comment on Cross and Madson (1997). *Psychological Bulletin, 122*, 38–44.

Baumeister, R. F., Exline, J. J., & Sommer, K. L. (1998). The victim role, grudge theory, and two dimensions of forgiveness. In E. L. Worthington, Jr. (Ed.), *Dimensions of forgiveness: Psychological research and theological perspectives* (pp. 79–104). Philadelphia: John Templeton Press.

Baumeister, R. F., Wotman, S. R., & Stillwell, A. M. (1993). Unrequited love: On heartbreak, anger, guilt, scriptlessness, and humiliation. *Journal of Personality and Social Psychology, 64*, 377–394.

Baumeister, R. F. (2000). Gender differences in erotic plasticity: The female sex drive as socially flexible and responsive. *Psychological Bulletin, 126*, 347–374.

Bavelas, J. B., & Coates, L. (1992). How do we account for the mindfulness of face-to-face dialogue? *Communication Monographs, 59*, 301–305.

Baxter, L. A., & Bullis, C. (1986). Turning points in developing romantic relationships. *Human Communication Research, 12*, 469–493.

Baxter, L. A., & Wilmot, W. (1985). Taboo topics in close relationships. *Journal of Social and Personal Relationships, 2*, 253–269.

Bearman, P., Jones, J., & Udry, J. R. (1997). *The National Longitudinal Study on Adolescent Health: Research Design*. Chapel Hill, NC: Carolina Population Center.

Becker, G. S., Landes, E. M., & Michael, R. T. (1977). An economic analysis of marital instability. *Journal of Political Economy, 85*, 1141–1187.

Bellavia, G., & Murray, S. (2003). Did I do that? Self esteem-related differences in reactions to romantic partner's mood. *Personal Relationships, 10*, 77–95.

Belsky, J., & Hsieh, K.-H. (1998). Patterns of marital change during the early childhood years: Parent personality, co-parenting, and division-of-labor correlates. *Journal of Family Psychology, 12*, 511–528.

Belsky, J., & Pensky, E. (1988). Marital change across the transition to parenthood. *Marriage and Family Review, 12*, 133–156.

Belsky, J., Steinberg, L., Houts, R. M., Friedman, S. L., DeHart, G., Cauffman, E., et al., & the NICHD Early Child Care Research Network. (2007). Family rearing antecedents of pubertal timing. *Child Development, 78*, 1302–1321.

Bem, S. L. (1974). The measurement of psychological androgyny. *Journal of Consulting and Clinical Psychology, 42*, 155–162.

Bem, S. L. (1981). Gender schema theory: A cognitive account of sex typing. *Psychological Review, 88*, 354–364.

Bengston, V. L., Biblarz, T. J., & Roberts, R. E. L. (2002). *How families still matter: A longitudinal study of youth in two generations*. Cambridge, England: Cambridge University Press.

Bennett, W. J. (2001). *The broken hearth: Reversing the moral collapse of the American family*. New York: Doubleday.

Berenbaum, S. A., & Snyder, E. (1995). Early hormonal influences on childhood sex-typed activity and playmate preference: Implications for the development of sexual orientation. *Developmental Psychology, 31*, 31–42.

Berg, J. H. (1987). Responsiveness and self-disclosure. In V. J. Derlega & J. H. Berg (Eds.), *Self-disclosure: Theory, research and therapy* (pp. 101–130). New York: Plenum.

Berger, P. L., & Kellner, H. (1964). Marriage and the construction of reality: An exercise in the microsociology of knowledge. *Diogenes, 46*, 1–24.

Berger, R., & Hannah, M. (1999). *Preventive approaches in couples therapy*. New York: Routledge.

Berkman, L. F. (1985). The relationship of social networks and social support to morbidity and mortality. In S. Cohen & S. L. Syme (Eds.), *Social support and health* (pp. 243–161). Orlando, FL: Academic Press.

Berndt, T. J., & Keefe, K. (1995). Friends' influence on adolescents' adjustment to school. *Child Development, 66*, 1312–1329.

Bernstein, W. M., Stephenson, B. O., Snyder, M. L., & Wicklund, R. A. (1983). Causal ambiguity and heterosexual affiliation. *Journal of Experimental Social Psychology, 19*, 78–92.

Berscheid, E. (1983). Emotion. In H. H. Kelley, E. Berscheid, A. Christensen, J. H. Harvey, T. L. Huston, G. Levinger, E. McClintock, L. A. Peplau & D. R. Peterson (Eds.), *Close relationships* (pp. 110–168). New York: Freeman.

Berscheid, E. (1988). Some comments on love's anatomy: Or, whatever happened to good old-fashioned lust? In R. J. Sternberg & M. L. Barnes (Eds.), *The Psychology of Love* (pp. 359–374). New Haven, CT: Yale University Press.

Berscheid, E. (1998). A social psychological view of marital dysfunction and stability. In T. N. Bradbury (Ed.), *The developmental course of marital dysfunction* (pp. 441–459). New York: Cambridge University Press.

Berscheid, E. (1999). The greening of relationship science. *American Psychologist, 54*, 260–266.

Berscheid, E. (2006). Searching for the meaning of 'love.' In R. Sternberg & K. Weis (Eds.), *The new psychology of love* (pp. 171–183). New Haven: Yale University Press.

Berscheid, E., & Reis, H. T. (1998). Attraction and close relationships. In D. T. Gilbert & S. T. Fiske (Eds.), *The handbook of social psychology* (Vol. 2, pp. 193–281). New York: McGraw-Hill.

Berscheid, E., Dion, K., Walster, E., & Walster, G. W. (1971). Physical attractiveness and dating choice: A test of the matching hypothesis. *Journal of Experimental Social Psychology, 7*, 173–189.

Berscheid, E., Graziano, W., Monson, T., & Dermer, M. (1976). Outcome dependency: Attention, attribution, and attraction. *Journal of Personality and Social Psychology, 34*, 978–989.

Berscheid, E., Lopes, J., Ammazzalorso, H., & Langenfeld, N. (2001). Causal attributions of relationship quality. In V. Manusov & J. H. Harvey (Eds.), *Attribution, communication behavior, and close relationships* (pp. 115–133). New York: Cambridge.

Bettencourt, B. A., & Miller, N. (1996). Gender differences in aggression as a function of provocation: A meta-analysis. *Psychological Bulletin, 119*, 422–447.

Betzig, L. (1989). Causes of conjugal dissolution: A cross-cultural study. *Current Anthropology, 30*, 654–676.

Birchler, G., Weiss, R. L., & Vincent, J. P. (1975). Multimethod analysis of social reinforcement exchange between maritally distressed and nondistressed spouse and stranger dyads. *Journal of Personality and Social Psychology, 31*, 349–360.

Birdwhistell, R. L. (1970). *Kinesics and context*. Philadelphia: University of Pennsylvania Press.

Diskupic, J. (2007, November 13). A new page in O'Connors' love story. *USA Today*.

Black, D., Gates, G., Sanders, S., & Taylor, L. (2000). Demographics of the gay and lesbian population in the United States: Evidence from available systematic data sources. *Demography, 37*, 139–154.

Blanchard, V. L., Hawkins, A. J., Baldwin, S. A., & Fawcett, E .B. (2009). Investigating the effects of marriage and relationship education on couples' communication skills: A meta-analytic study. *Journal of Family Psychology, 23*, 203–214.

Blau, P. M. (1954). Patterns of interaction among a group of officials in a government agency. *Human Relations, 7*, 337–348.

Blee, K. M., & Tickamyer, A. R. (1995). Racial differences in men's attitudes about women's gender roles. *Journal of Marriage and Family, 57*, 21–30.

Blood, R. O. J. (1969). Kinship interaction and marital solidarity. *Merrill-Palmer Quarterly, 15*, 171–184.

Blum, D. (2002). *Love at Goon Park: Harry Harlow and the science of affection*. Cambridge, MA: Perseus.

Blumstein, P., & Kollock, P. (1988). Personal relationships. *Annual Review of Sociology, 14*, 467–490.

Blumstein, P., & Schwartz, P. (1983). *American couples: Money, work, and sex*. New York: Morrow.

Bodenhausen, G. V. (1993). Emotions, arousal, and stereotypic judgments: A heuristic model of affect and stereotyping. In D. M. Mackie & D. L. Hamilton (Eds.), *Affect, cognition, and stereotyping: Interactive processes in group perception* (pp. 13–37). San Diego, CA: Academic Press.

Bodenmann, G. (1995). A systemic-transactional conceptualization of stress and coping in couples. *Schweizerische Zeitschrift fuer Psychologie, 54*, 34–49.

Bodenmann, G. (1997). Dyadic coping: A systemic-transactional view of stress and coping among couples: Theory and empirical findings. *European Review of Applied Psychology/Revue Européenne de Psychologie Appliquée, 47*, 137–141.

Bodenmann, G., & Randall, A. K. (2009). The role of stress on close relationships and marital satisfaction. *Clinical Psychology Review, 29*, 105–115.

Bodenmann, G., & Shantinath, S. D. (2004). The Couples Coping Enhancement Training (CCET): A new approach to prevention of marital distress based upon stress and coping. *Family Relations, 53*, 477–484.

Boesch, R. P., Cerqueira, R., Safer, M. A., & Wright, T.L. (2007). Relationship satisfaction and commitment in long-term male couples. Individual and dyadic effects. *Journal of Social and Personal Relationships, 24*, 837–853.

Bogle, K. (2008). *Hooking up: Sex, dating, and relationships on campus*. New York: New York University Press.

Boivin, M., & Hymel, S. (1997). Peer experiences and social self-perceptions: A sequential model. *Developmental Psychology, 33*, 135–145.

Bolger, N., DeLongis, A., Kessler, R. C., & Wethington, E. (1989). The contagion of stress across multiple roles. *Journal of Marriage and Family, 51*, 175–183.

Bolger, N., Foster, M., Vinokur, A. D., & Ng, R. (1996). Close relationships and adjustment to life crisis: The case of breast cancer. *Journal of Personality and Social Psychology, 70*, 283–294.

Bolger, N., Zuckerman, A., & Kessler, R. C. (2000). Invisible support and adjustment to stress. *Journal of Personality and Social Psychology, 79*, 953–961.

Bonanno, G. A., Wortman, C. B., Lehman, D. R., Tweed, R. G., Haring, M., Sonnega, J., et al. (2002). Resilience to loss and chronic grief: A prospective study from preloss to 18–months postloss. *Journal of Personality and Social Psychology, 83*, 1150–1164.

Boo, K. (2003, August 18). The marriage cure: Is wedlock really a way out of poverty? *The New Yorker*.

Booth, A., & Edwards, J. N. (1992). Starting over: Why remarriages are more unstable. *Journal of Family Issues, 13*, 179–194.

Booth, A., Johnson, D. R., Granger, D. A., Crouter, A. C., & McHale, S. (2003). Testosterone and child and adolescent adjustment: The moderating role of parent-child relationships. *Developmental Psychology, 39*, 85–98.

Bornstein, R. F. (1989). Exposure and affect: Overview and meta-analysis of research, 1968–1987. *Psychological Bulletin, 106*, 265–289.

Botwin, M. D., Buss, D. M., & Shackelford, T. K. (1997). Personality and mate preferences: Five factors in mate selection and marital satisfaction. *Journal of Personality, 65*, 107–136.

Bowlby, J. (1969). *Attachment and loss* (Vol. I, *Attachment*). New York: Basic Books.

Bowlby, J. (1973). Attachment and loss (Vol. II, *Separation: Anxiety and anger*). New York: Basic Books.

Bowlby, J. (1979). *The making and breaking of affectional bonds*. London: Tavistock.

Bowlby, J. (1980). Attachment and loss (Vol. III, *Loss: Sadness and depression*). New York: Basic Books.

Bradbury, T. N. (1994). Unintended effects of marital research on marital relationships. *Journal of Family Psychology, 8*, 187–201.

Bradbury, T. N., & Fincham, F. D. (1990). Attributions in marriage: Review and critique. *Psychological Bulletin, 107*, 3–33.

Bradbury, T. N., & Lavner, J. A. (2012). How can we improve preventive and educational interventions for intimate relationships? *Behavior Therapy, 43*, 113-122.

Bramlett, M. D., & Mosher, W. D. (2002). Cohabitation, marriage, divorce, and remarriage in the United States (Vital and Health Statistics Series 23, No. 22). Hyattsville, Maryland: National Center for Health Statistics.

Braver, S. L., Shapiro, J. R., & Goodman, M. R. (2006). Consequences of divorce for parents. In M. A. Fine & J. H. Harvey (Eds.), *Handbook of divorce and relationship dissolution* (pp. 313–337). Mahwah, NJ: Erlbaum.

Braver, S. L., Whitley, M., & Ng, C. (1993). Who divorces whom? Methodological and theoretical issues. *Journal of Divorce & Remarriage, 20*, 1–19.

Brennan, K. A., & Shaver, P. R. (1995). Dimensions of adult attachment, affect regulation, and romantic relationship functioning. *Personality and Social Psychology Bulletin, 21*, 267–283.

Brennan, K. A., Clark, C. L., & Shaver, P. R. (1998). Self-report measurement of adult attachment: An integrative overview. In J. A. Simpson & W. S. Rholes (Eds.), *Attachment theory and close relationships* (pp. 46–76). New York: Guilford.

Bringle, R. G. (1995). Sexual jealousy in the relationships of homosexual and heterosexual men: 1980 and 1982. *Personal Relationships, 2*, 313–325.

Brinig, M., & Allen, D. W. (2000). These boots are made for walking: Why most divorce filers are women. *American Law and Economics Review, 2*, 126–129.

Brody, G. H. (1998). Sibling relationship quality: Its causes and consequences. *Annual Review of Psychology, 49*, 1–24.

Brody, G. H., Neubaum, E., & Forehand, R. (1988). Serial marriage: A heuristic analysis of an emerging family form. *Psychological Bulletin, 103*, 211–222.

Brody, L. (1999). *Gender, emotion, and the family*. Cambridge, MA: Harvard University Press.

Bronfenbrenner, U. (1977). Toward an experimental ecology of human development. *American Psychologist, 32*, 513–531.

Bronfenbrenner, U. (1977). 'Who needs parent education?' Position paper for the Working Conference on Parent Education, Charles Stewart Mott Foundation, Flint, Michigan.

Bronfenbrenner, U. (1979). *The ecology of human development*. Cambridge, MA: Harvard University Press.

Bronfenbrenner, U. (1986). Ecology of the family as a context for human development: Research perspectives. *Developmental Psychology, 22*, 723–742.

Brown, J. M. (2003). Eyewitness memory for arousing events: Putting things into context. *Applied Cognitive Psychology, 17*, 93–106.

Brown, J. R., & Dunn, J. (1992). Talk with your mother or your sibling? Developmental changes in early family conversations about feelings. *Child Development, 63*, 336–349.

Brown, J. R., Donelan-McCall, N., & Dunn, J. (1996). Why talk about mental states? The significance of children's conversations with friends, siblings, and mothers. *Child Development, 67,* 836–849.

Brown, R. P. (2003). Measuring individual differences in the tendency to forgive: Construct validity and links with depression. *Personality and Social Psychology Bulletin, 29,* 759–771.

Brown, S. L. (2000). The effect of union type on psychological well-being: Depression among cohabitors versus marrieds. *Journal of Health and Social Behavior, 41,* 241–255.

Brown, S. L. (2004). Family structure and child well-being: The significance of parental cohabitation. *Journal of Marriage and Family, 66,* 351–367.

Brown, S. L., Sanchez, L. A., Nock, S. L., & Wright, J. D. (2006). Links between premarital cohabitation and subsequent marital quality, stability, and divorce: A comparison of covenant versus standard marriages. *Social Science Research, 35,* 454–470.

Brunstein, J. C., Dangelmayer, G., & Schultheiss, O. C. (1996). Personal goals and social support in relationships: Effects on relationship mood and marital satisfaction. *Journal of Personality and Social Psychology, 71,* 1006–1019.

Bryant, C. M., & Conger, R. D. (1999). Marital success and domains of social support in long-term relationships: Does the influence of network members ever end? *Journal of Marriage and Family, 61,* 437–450.

Bryant, S., & Demian (1994). Relationship characteristics of American gay and lesbian couples: Findings from a national survey. *Journal of Gay and Lesbian Social Services, 1,* 101–117.

Buchanan, C. M., Maccoby, E. E., & Dornbush, S. M. (1996). *Adolescents after divorce.* Cambridge, MA: Harvard University Press.

Buehlman, K. T., Gottman, J. M., & Katz, L. F. (1992). How a couple views their past predicts their future: Predicting divorce from an oral history interview. *Journal of Family Psychology, 5,* 295–318.

Bui, K. T., Peplau, L. A., & Hill, C. T. (1996). Testing the Rusbult model of relationship commitment and stability in a 15-year study of heterosexual couples. *Personality and Social Psychology Bulletin, 22,* 1244–1257.

Bullis, C., Clark, C., & Sline, R. (1993). From passion to commitment: Turning points in romantic relationships. In P. J. Kalbfleisch (Ed.), *Interpersonal communication: Evolving interpersonal relationships* (pp. 213–236). Hillsdale, NJ: Erlbaum.

Bumpass, L. L. (1990). What's happening to the family? Interactions between demographic and institutional change. *Demography, 27,* 483–498.

Bumpass, L. L., Sweet, J. A., & Cherlin, A. (1991). The role of cohabitation in declining rates of marriage. *Journal of Marriage and Family, 53,* 913–927.

Bumpass, L. L., Sweet, J., & Martin, T. C. (1990). Changing patterns of remarriage. *Journal of Marriage and Family, 52,* 747–756.

Bumpass, L., & Lu, H. H. (2000). Trends in cohabitation and implications for children's family contexts in the United States. *Population Studies, 54,* 29–41.

Burgess, E. W., & Cottrell, L. S. (1939). *Predicting success or failure in marriage.* New York: Prentice-Hall.

Burgess, E. W., & Locke, H. J. (1945). *The family: From institution to companionship.* Oxford, England: American Book Company.

Burgess, E. W., Wallin, P., & Shultz, G. D. (1954). *Courtship, engagement, and marriage.* New York: Lippincott.

Burggraf, C. S., & Sillars, A. L. (1987). A critical examination of sex differences in marital communication. *Communication Monographs, 54,* 276–294.

Burkhauser, R. V., Butler, J. S., & Holden, K. C. (1991). How the death of a spouse affects economic well-being after retirement: A hazard model approach. *Social Science Quarterly, 72,* 504–519.

Burks, V. K., Lund, D. A., Gregg, C. H., & Bluhm, H. P. (1988). Bereavement and remarriage for older adults. *Death Studies, 12,* 51–60.

Burleson, B. R. (1994). Comforting messages: Significance, approaches, and effects. In B. R. Burleson, T. L. Albrecht, & I. G. Sarason (Eds.), *Communication of social support* (pp. 3–28). Thousand Oaks, CA: Sage.

Burleson, B. R., Kunkel, A. W., Samter, W., & Werking, K. J. (1996). Men's and women's evaluations of communication skills in personal relationships: When sex differences make a difference— and when they don't. *Journal of Social and Personal Relationships, 13,* 201–224.

Burman, B., John, R. S., & Margolin, G. (1992). Observed patterns of conflict in violent, nonviolent, and nondistressed couples. *Behavioral Assessment, 14,* 15–37.

Burns, G. L., & Farina, A. (1992). The role of physical attractiveness in adjustment. *Genetic, Social, and General Psychology Monographs, 118,* 157–194.

Burr, W. R. (1970). Satisfaction with various aspects of marriage over the life cycle: A random middle class sample. *Journal of Marriage and Family, 32,* 29–37.

Buss, D. M. (1985). Human mate selection. *American Scientist, 73,* 47–51.

Buss, D. M. (1989). Sex differences in human mate preferences: Evolutionary hypotheses tested in 37 cultures. *Behavioral and Brain Sciences, 12,* 1–14.

Buss, D. M. (1991). Conflict in married couples: Personality predictors of anger and upset. *Journal of Personality, 59,* 663–688.

Buss, D. M. (1994). *The evolution of desire: Strategies of human mating.* New York: Basic Books.

Buss, D. M. (1995). Evolutionary psychology: A new paradigm for psychological science. *Psychological Inquiry, 6,* 1–30.

Buss, D. M. (1998). Sexual strategies theory: Historical origins and current status. *Journal of Sex Research, 35,* 19–31.

Buss, D. M., & Barnes, M. (1986). Preferences in human mate selection. *Journal of Personality and Social Psychology, 50,* 559–570.

Buss, D. M., & Dedden, L. A. (1990). Derogation of competitors. *Journal of Social and Personal Relationships, 7,* 395–422.

Buss, D. M., & Kenrick, D. T. (1998). Evolutionary social psychology. In D. T. Gilbert, S. T. Fiske, & G. Lindzey (Eds.), *The handbook of social psychology* (4th ed., vol. 2, pp. 982–1026). Boston: McGraw-Hill.

Buss, D. M., & Shackelford, T. K. (1997). From vigilance to violence: Mate retention tactics in married couples. *Journal of Personality and Social Psychology, 72,* 346–361.

Buss, D. M., Abbott, M., Angleitner, A., Asherian, A., Biaggio, A., Blanco-Villasenor, A., et al. (1990). International preferences in selecting mates: A study of 37 cultures. *Journal of Cross-Cultural Psychology, 21,* 5–47.

Buss, D., & Schmidt, D. P. (1993). Sexual strategies theory: An evolutionary perspective on human mating. *Psychological Review, 100,* 204–232.

Butler, M. H., & Wampler, K. S. (1999). A meta-analytic update of research on the Couple Communication program. *American Journal of Family Therapy, 27,* 223–237.

Buunk, B. P., Angleitner, A., Oubaid, V., & Buss, D. M. (1996). Sex differences in jealousy in evolutionary and cultural perspective: Tests from Netherlands, Germany, and the United States. *Psychological Science, 7,* 359–363.

Byers, E. S. (2005). Relationship satisfaction and sexual satisfaction: A longitudinal study of individuals in long-term relationships. *Journal of Sex Research, 42,* 113–118.

Byers, E. S., & Heinlein, L. (1989). Predicting initiations and refusals of sexual activities in married and cohabiting heterosexual couples. *Journal of Sex Research, 26,* 210–231.

Byers, E. S., & Lewis, K. (1988). Dating couples' disagreements over the desired level of sexual intimacy. *Journal of Sex Research, 24,* 15–29.

Byrne, D. (1961). Interpersonal attraction and attitude similarity. *Journal of Abnormal and Social Psychology, 62,* 713–715.

Byrne, D., & Clore, G. L. (1970). A reinforcement model of evaluative processes. *Personality: An International Journal, 1,* 103–128.

Byrne, D., & Nelson, D. (1965). Attraction as a linear function of proportion of positive reinforcements. *Journal of Personality and Social Psychology, 1,* 659–663.

Byrne, D., Ervin, C. R., & Lamberth, J. (1970). Continuity between the experimental study of attraction and real-life computer dating. *Journal of Personality and Social Psychology, 16,* 157–165.

Call, V. R. A., & Heaton, T. B. (1997). Religious influence on marital stability. *Journal for the Scientific Study of Religion, 36,* 382–392.

Call, V., Sprecher, S., & Schwartz, P. (1995). The incidence and frequency of marital sex in a national sample. *Journal of Marriage and Family, 57,* 639–652

Cameron, J. J., Holmes, J. G., & Vorauer, J. D. (2009). When self-disclosure goes awry: Negative consequences of revealing personal failures for lower self-esteem individuals. *Journal of Experimental Social Psychology, 45,* 217–222.

Campbell, J. C. (2002). Health consequences of intimate partner violence. *The Lancet, 359,* 1331–1336.

Campbell, L., Simpson, J. A., Boldry, J., & Kashy, D. A. (2005). Perceptions of conflict and support in romantic relationships: The role of attachment anxiety. *Journal of Personality and Social Psychology, 88,* 510–531.

Cantos, A. L., Neidig, P. H., O'Leary, K. D. (1994). Injuries of women and men in a treatment program for domestic violence. *Journal of Family Violence, 9,* 113–124.

Capaldi, D. M., & Clark, S. (1998). Prospective family predictors of aggression toward female partners for at-risk young men. *Developmental Psychology, 34,* 1175–1188.

Capaldi, D. M., Dishion, T. J., Stoolmiller, M., & Yoerger, K. (2001). Aggression toward female partners by at-risk young men: The contribution of male adolescent friendships. *Developmental Psychology, 37,* 61–73.

Capaldi, D. M., Shortt, J. W., & Crosby, L. (2003). Physical and psychological aggression in at-risk young couples: Stability and change in young adulthood. *Merrill-Palmer Quarterly, 49,* 1–27.

Carlson, E. A., Sroufe, L. A., & Egeland, B. (2004). The construction of experience: A longitudinal study of representation and behavior. *Child Development, 75,* 66–83.

Carlson, M., McLanahan, S., & England, P. (2004). Union formation in fragile families. *Demography, 41,* 237–261.

Carmichael, M. S., Humbert, R., Dixen, J., Palmisano, G., Greenleaf, W., & Davidson, J. M. (1987). Plasma oxytocin increases in the human sexual response. *Journal of Clinical Endocrinology and Metabolism, 64,* 27–31.

Carpenter, C. (2008, February 7). Self-help books get the "tough love" treatment. *Christian Science Monitor.*

Carr, D. (2004). The desire to date and remarry among older widows and widowers. *Journal of Marriage and Family, 66,* 1051–1068.

Carr, D., House, J. S., Kessler, R. C., Nesse, R. M., Sonnega, J., & Wortman, C. (2000). Marital quality and psychological adjustment to widowhood among older adults: A longitudinal analysis: Erratum. *Journals of Gerontology: Series B: Psychological Sciences and Social Sciences, 55,* S374.

Carr, D., House, J. S., Wortman, C., Neese, R., & Kessler, R. C. (2001). Psychological adjustment to sudden and anticipated spousal loss among older widowed persons. *Journals of Gerontology: Series B: Psychological Sciences and Social Sciences, 56,* S237–S248.

Carroll, A. (Ed.). (2001). *War letters: Extraordinary correspondence from American wars.* New York: Scribner.

Carroll, A. (Ed.). (2005). *Behind the lines: Powerful and revealing American and foreign war letters— and one man's search to find them.* New York: Scribner.

Carstensen, L. L. (1992). Social and emotional patterns in adulthood: Support for socioemotional selectivity theory. *Psychology and Aging, 7,* 331–338.

Carstensen, L. L., Fung, H. H., & Charles, S. T. (2003). Socioemotional selectivity theory and the regulation of emotion in the second half of life. *Motivation and Emotion, 27,* 103–123.

Carstensen, L. L., Gottman, J. M., & Levenson, R. W. (1995). Emotional behavior in long-term marriage. *Psychology and Aging, 10,* 140–149.

Carstensen, L. L., Isaacowitz, D. M., & Charles, S. T. (1999). Taking time seriously: A theory of socioemotional selectivity. *American Psychologist, 54,* 165–181.

Carter, C. S. (1998). Neuroendocrine perspectives on social attachment and love. *Psychoneuroendocrinology, 23,* 779–818.

Carver, C. S., & Scheier, M. F. (1990). Origins and functions of positive and negative affect: A control-process view. *Psychological Review, 97,* 19–35.

Carver, K. P., & Udry, J. R. (1997). Reciprocity in the identification of adolescent romantic partners. Paper presented to the Population Association of America, Washington, DC.

Carver, K. P., Joyner, K., & Udry, J. R. (2003). National estimates of adolescent romantic relation-ships. In P. Florsheim (Ed.), *Adolescent romantic relations and sexual behavior: Theory, research, and practical implications* (pp. 23–56). Mahwah, NJ: Erlbaum.

Cascardi, M., & Vivian, D. (1995). Context for specific episodes of marital violence: Gender and severity of violence differences. *Journal of Family Violence, 10,* 265–293.

Cascardi, M., O'Leary, K. D., Lawrence, E., & Schlee, K. A. (1995). Characteristics of women physically abused by their spouses and who seek treatment regarding marital conflict. *Journal of Consulting and Clinical Psychology, 63,* 616–623.

Casper, L. M., & Sayer, L. C. (2000). Cohabitation transitions: Different attitudes and purposes, different paths. Paper presented at the Annual Meeting of the Population Association of America, Los Angeles, CA.

Casper, L. M., & Cohen, P. N. (2000). How Does POSSLQ measure up? Historical estimates of cohabitation. *Demography, 37,* 237–245.

Caspi, A. (1987). Personality in the life course. *Journal of Personality and Social Psychology, 53,* 1203–1213.

Caspi, A., & Herbener, E. (1990). Continuity and change: Assortative marriage and the consistency of personality in adulthood. *Journal of Personality and Social Psychology, 58,* 250–258.

Caspi, A., & Roberts, B. W. (1999). Personality continuity and change across the life course. In L. A. Pervin & O. P. John (Eds.), *Handbook of personality psychology: Theory and research* (2nd ed., pp. 300–326). New York: Guilford.

Caspi, A., Bem, D. J., & Elder, G. H. (1989). Continuities and consequences of interactional styles across the life course. *Journal of Personality, 57,* 375–406.

Caspi, A., Elder, G. H., Jr., & Bem, D. J. (1987). Moving against the world: Life-course patterns of explosive children. *Developmental Psychology, 23,* 308–313.

Caspi, A., Herbener, E. S., & Ozer, D. J. (1992). Shared experiences and the similarity of personalities: A longitudinal study of married couples. *Journal of Personality and Social Psychology, 62,* 281–291.

Cassiday, J. (1999). The nature of the child's ties. In J. Cassidy & P. R. Shaver (Eds.), *Handbook of attachment: Theory, research, and clinical applications* (pp. 3–20). New York: Guilford.

Cate, R. M., Koval, J., Lloyd, S. A., & Wilson, G. (1995). Assessment of relationship thinking in dating relationships. *Personal Relationships, 2,* 77–95.

Cattell, V. (2001). Poor people, poor places, and poor health: The mediating role of social networks and social capital. *Social Science & Medicine, 52,* 1501–1516.

Caughlin, J. P., Huston, T. L., & Houts, R. M. (2000). How does personality matter in marriage? An examination of trait anxiety, interpersonal negativity, and marital satisfaction. *Journal of Personality and Social Psychology, 78,* 326–336.

Caverlee, J., & Webb, S. (2008). A large-scale study of MySpace: Observations and implications for online social networks. Association for the Advancement of Artificial Intelligence. http://faculty.cs.tam.edu/caverlee/pubs/caverlee08alarge.pdf.

Centers for Disease Control. (October 19, 2005). Divorce rates by State: 1990, 1995, and 1999–2004. Retrieved July 21, 2008, from http://www.cdc.gov/nchs/data/nvss/divorce90_04.pdf

Chalmers, L., & Milan, A. (2005). Marital satisfaction during the retirement years. *Canadian Social Trends, 76,* 14–17.

Chang, S.-C., & Chan, C.-N. (2007). Perceptions of commitment change during mate selection: The case of Taiwanese newlyweds. *Journal of Social and Personal Relationships, 24,* 55–68.

Chartrand, T. L., & Bargh, J. A. (1999). The chameleon effect: The perception-behavior link and social interaction. *Journal of Personality and Social Psychology, 76,* 893–910.

Chase, K. A., O'Leary, K. D., & Heyman, R. E. (2001). Categorizing partner–violent men within the reactive-proactive typology model. *Journal of Consulting and Clinical Psychology, 69,* 567–572.

Check, J., & Malamuth, N. (1984). Can there be positive effects of participation in pornography experiments? *Journal of Sex Research, 20,* 14–31.

Cheng, C. (2005). Processes underlying gender-role flexibility: Do androgynous individuals know more or know how to cope? *Journal of Personality, 73,* 645–673.

Cherlin, A. J. (1992). *Marriage, divorce, remarriage* (2nd ed.). Cambridge, MA: Harvard University Press.

Cherlin, A. J. (1996). *Public and private families: An introduction.* New York: McGraw-Hill.

Cherlin, A. J. (2004). The deinstitutionalization of American marriage. *Journal of Marriage and Family, 66,* 848–861.

Cherlin, A. J., Burton, L. M., Hurt, T. R., & Purvin, D. M. (2004). The influence of physical and sexual abuse on marriage and cohabitation. *American Sociological Review, 69,* 768–789.

Cherlin, A. J., Furstenberg, F. F. Jr., Chase-Lansdale, P. L., Kiernan, K. E., Robins, P. K., Morrison, D. R., & Teitler, J. O. (1991). Longitudinal studies of effects of divorce on children in Great Britain and the United States. *Science, 252,* 1386–1389.

Chipperfield, J. G., & Havens, B. (2001). Gender differences in the relationship between marital status transitions and life satisfaction in later life. *Journals of Gerontology: Series B: Psychological Sciences and Social Sciences, 56,* P176–P186.

Chivers, M. L., Rieger, G., Latty, E., & Bailey, J. M. (2004). A sex difference in the specificity of sexual arousal. *Psychological Science, 15,* 736–744.

Christakis, N. A., & Allison, P. D. (2006). Mortality after the hospitalization of a spouse. *New England Journal of Medicine, 354,* 719–730.

Christensen, A., Atkins, D. C, Baucom, B., & Yi, J. (2010). Marital status and satisfaction five years following a randomized clinical trial comparing traditional versus integrative behavioral couple therapy. *Journal of Consulting and Clinical Psychology, 78,* 225–235.

Christensen, A., Atkins, D. C., Baucom, D. H., Yi, J., & George, W. H. (2006). Couple and individual adjustment for 2 years following a randomized clinical trial comparing traditional versus integrative behavioral couple therapy. *Journal of Consulting and Clinical Psychology, 74,* 1180–1191.

Christensen, A., Eldridge, K., Catta-Preta, A. B., Lim, V. R., & Santagata, R. (2006). Cross-cultural consistency of the demand/withdraw interaction pattern in couples. *Journal of Marriage and Family, 68,* 1029–1044.

Christensen, A., & Heavey, C. L. (1990). Gender and social structure in the demand/withdraw pattern and marital conflict. *Journal of Personality and Social Psychology, 59,* 73–81.

Christensen, A., & Heavey, C. L. (1999). Interventions for couples. *Annual Review of Psychology, 50,* 165–190.

Christensen, A., & Jacobson, N. S. (2000). *Reconcilable differences.* New York: Guilford.

Christensen, A., & Nies, D. C. (1980). The Spouse Observation Checklist: Empirical analysis and critique. *American Journal of Family Therapy, 8,* 69–79.

Christensen, A., & Shenk, J. L. (1991). Communication, conflict, and psychological distance in nondistressed, clinic, and divorcing couples. *Journal of Consulting and Clinical Psychology, 59,* 458–463.

Christensen, A., & Sullaway, M. (1984). Communication Patterns Questionnaire. Unpublished manuscript: University of California, Los Angeles.

Christensen, A., Sulloway, M., & King, C. E. (1983). Systematic error in behavioral reports of dyadic interaction: Egocentric bias and content effects. *Behavioral Assessment, 5,* 129–140.

Christianson, S., & Loftus, E. F. (1991). Remembering emotional events: The fate of detailed information. *Cognition and Memory, 5,* 81–108.

Christopher, F. S., & Sprecher, S. (2000). Sexuality in marriage, dating, and other relationships: A decade review. *Journal of Marriage and Family, 62,* 999–1017.

Clark, M. S., Fitness, J., & Brissette, I. (2001). Understanding people's perceptions of relationships is crucial to understanding their emotional lives. In G. J. Fletcher & M. S. Clark (Eds.), *Blackwell handbook of social psychology: Interpersonal processes* (pp. 253–278). Oxford, England: Blackwell.

Clark, M. S., Mills, J., & Powell, M. C. (1986). Keeping track of needs in communal and exchange relationships. *Journal of Personality and Social Psychology, 51,* 333–338.

Clark, R. D., & Hatfield, E. (1989). Gender differences in receptivity to sexual offers. *Journal of Psychology & Human Sexuality, 2,* 39–55.

Clarke, S. C., & Wilson, B. F. (1994). The relative stability of remarriages: A cohort approach using vital statistics. *Family Relations, 43,* 305–310.

Clark-Ibáñez, M., & Felmlee, D. (2004). Interethnic relationships: The role of social network diversity. *Journal of Marriage and Family, 66,* 293–305.

Claxton, A., & Perry-Jenkins, M. (2008). No fun anymore: Leisure and marital quality across the transition to parenthood. *Journal of Marriage and Family, 70,* 28–43.

Clore, G. L. (1992). Cognitive phenomenology: Feelings and the construction of judgment. In L. L. Martin & A. Tesser (Eds.), *The construction of social judgments* (pp. 133–163). Hillsdale, NJ: Erlbaum.

Cloutier, P. F., Manion, I. G., Walker, J. G., & Johnson, S. M. (2002). Emotionally focused interventions for couples with chronically ill children: A 2-year follow-up. *Journal of Marital and Family Therapy, 28,* 391–398.

Coan, J. A., Schaefer, H. S., & Davidson, R. J. (2006). Lending a hand: Social regulation of the neural response to threat. *Psychological Science, 17,* 1032–1039.

Cochran, S. D., Sullivan, J. G., & Mays, V. M. (2003). Prevalence of mental disorders, psychological distress, and mental health services use among lesbian, gay, and bisexual adults in the United States. *Journal of Consulting and Clinical Psychology, 71,* 53–61.

Cohan, C. L., & Bradbury, T. N. (1997). Negative life events, marital interaction, and the longitudinal course of newlywed marriage. *Journal of Personality and Social Psychology, 73,* 114–128.

Cohan, C. L., & Cole, S. W. (2002). Life course transitions and natural disaster: Marriage, birth, and divorce following Hurricane Hugo. *Journal of Family Psychology, 16,* 14–25.

Cohan, C. L., & Kleinbaum, S. (2002). Toward a greater understanding of the cohabitation effect: Premarital cohabitation and marital communication. *Journal of Marriage and Family, 64,* 180–192.

Cohen, A. (1949). *Everyman's Talmud: The major teachings of the rabbinic sages.* New York: Schocken Books.

Cohen, J. (1983). *Applied multiple regression: Correlational analysis for the behavioral sciences* (2nd ed.). Hillsdale, NJ: Erlbaum.

Cohen, S., & Wills, T. A. (1985). Stress, support, and the buffering hypothesis. *Psychological Bulletin, 98,* 310–357.

Cohen, S., Frank, E., Doyle, W. J., Skoner, D. P., Rabin, B. S., & Gwaltney, J. M., Jr. (1998). Types of stressors that increase susceptibility to the common cold in adults. *Health Psychology, 17,* 214–223.

Collins, N. L. (1996). Working models of attachment: Implications for explanation, emotion, and behavior. *Journal of Personality and Social Psychology, 71,* 810–832.

Collins, N. L., & Feeney, B. C. (2000). A safe haven: An attachment theory perspective on support-seeking and caregiving in adult romantic relationships. *Journal of Personality and Social Psychology, 78,* 1053–1073.

Collins, N. L., & Feeney, B. C. (2004). An attachment theory perspective on closeness and intimacy. In D. J. Mashek, & A. Aron (Eds.), *Handbook of closeness and intimacy* (pp. 163–187). Mahwah, NJ: Erlbaum.

Collins, N. L., & Miller, L. C. (1994). Self-disclosure and liking: A meta-analytic review. *Psychological Bulletin, 116,* 457–475.

Collins, N. L., & Read, S. J. (1990). Adult attachment, working models, and relationship quality in dating couples. *Journal of Personality and Social Psychology, 58,* 644–663.

Collins, R. L., Elliott, M. N., Gerry, S. H., Kanouse, D. E., Kunkel, D., Hunter, S. B., & Miu, A. (2004). Watching sex on television predicts adolescent initiation of sexual behavior. *Pediatrics, 114,* e280–e289.

Collins, W. A. (1997). Relationships and development during adolescence: Interpersonal adaptation to individual change. *Personal Relationships, 4,* 1–14.

Collins, W. A. (2003). More than myth: The developmental significance of romantic relationships during adolescence. *Journal of Research on Adolescence, 13,* 1–24.

Collins, W. A., & Sroufe, L. A. (1999). Capacity for intimate relationships: A developmental construction. In W. Furman, B. B. Brown & C. Feiring (Eds.), *The development of romantic relationships in adolescence* (pp. 125–147). New York: Cambridge University Press.

Collins, W. A., & Van Dulmen, M. (2006). "The Course of True Love(s) . . .": Origins and pathways in the development of romantic relationships. In A. C. Crouter & A. Booth (Eds.), *Romance and sex in adolescence and emerging adulthood: Risks and opportunities* (pp. 63–86). Mahwah, NJ: Erlbaum.

Collins, W. A., Hennighausen, K. C., Schmit, D. T., & Sroufe, L. A. (1997). Developmental precursors of romantic relationships: A longitudinal analysis. In S. Shulman & W. A. Collins (Eds.), *Romantic relationships in adolescence: Developmental perspectives* (pp. 69–84). San Francisco, CA: Jossey-Bass.

Condon, J. W., & Crano, W. D. (1988). Inferred evaluation and the relation between attitude similarity and interpersonal attraction. *Journal of Personality and Social Psychology, 54,* 789–797.

Conger, R. D., Cui, M., Bryant, C. M., & Elder, G. H. (2000). Competence in early adult romantic relationships: A developmental perspective on family influences. *Journal of Personality and Social Psychology, 79,* 224–237.

Conger, R. D., Elder, G. H., Lorenz, F. O., Conger, K. J., Simons, R. L., Whitbeck, L. B., et al. (1990). Linking economic hardship to marital quality and instability. *Journal of Marriage and Family, 52,* 643–656.

Conger, R. D., Rueter, M. A., & Elder, G. H. (1999). Couple resilience to economic pressure. *Journal of Personality and Social Psychology, 76,* 54–71.

Connolly, J. A., & Goldberg, A. (1999). Romantic relationships in adolescence: The role of friends and peers in their emergence and development. In W. Furman, B. B. Brown & C. Feiring (Eds.), *The development of romantic relationships in adolescence* (pp. 266–290). New York: Cambridge University Press.

Connolly, J. A., & Johnson, A. (1996). Adolescents' romantic relationships and the structure and quality of their close interpersonal ties. *Personal Relationships, 2,* 185–195.

Connolly, J. A., Craig, W., Goldberg, A., & Pepler, D. (1999). Conceptions of cross-sex friendships and romantic relationships in early adolescence. *Journal of Youth and Adolescence, 28,* 481–494.

Connolly, J. A., Craig, W., Goldberg, A., & Pepler, D. (2004). Mixed-gender groups, dating, and romantic relationships in early adolescence. *Journal of Research on Adolescence, 14,* 185–207.

Connolly, J., Furman, W., & Konarski, R. (2000). The role of peers in the emergence of heterosexual romantic relationships in adolescence. *Child Development, 71,* 1395–1408.

Constantine, J. A., & Bahr, S. J. (1980). Locus of control and marital stability: A longitudinal study. *Journal of Divorce, 4,* 11–22.

Cook, W., & Kenny, D. (2005). The Actor-Partner Interdependence Model: A model of bidirectional effects in developmental studies. *International Journal of Behavioral Development, 29,* 101–109.

Cooksey, E. C., Mott, F. L., & Neubauer, S. A. (2002). Friendships and early relationships: Links to sexual initiation among American adolescents born to young mothers. *Perspectives on Sexual and Reproductive Health, 34,* 118–126.

Coontz, S. (1992). *The way we never were: American families and the nostalgia trap.* New York: Basic Books.

Coontz, S. (2005). *Marriage, a history: From obedience to intimacy or how love conquered marriage.* New York: Viking.

Costa, P. T., Jr., & McCrae, R. R. (1985). *The NEO Personality Inventory manual.* Odessa, FL: Psychological Assessment Resources.

Costa, P. T., Jr., & McCrae, R. R. (1994). Set like plaster? Evidence for the stability of adult personality. In T. F. Heatherton & J. L. Weinberger (Eds.), *Can personality change?* (pp. 21–40). Washington, DC: American Psychological Association.

Costello, E. J., Compton, S. N., Keeler, G., & Angold, A. (2003). Relationships between poverty and psychopathology: A natural experiment. *Journal of the American Medical Association, 290,* 2023–2029.

Cowan, C. P., & Cowan, P. A. (1992). *When partners become parents: The big life change for couples.* New York: Basic Books.

Cox, M. J., Paley, B., Burchinal, M., & Payne, C. C. (1999). Marital perceptions and interactions across the transition to parenthood. *Journal of Marriage and Family, 61,* 611–625.

Coyne, C., Rohrbaugh, M. J., Shoham, V., Sonnega, S., Nicklas, M., & Cranford, A. (2001). Prognostic importance of marital quality for survival of congestive heart failure. *American Journal of Cardiology, 88,* 526–529.

Coyne, J. C., & DeLongis, A. (1986). Going beyond social support: The role of social relationships in adaptation. *Journal of Consulting and Clinical Psychology, 54,* 454–460.

Coyne, J. C., & Smith, D. A. (1991). Couples coping with a myocardial infarction: A contextual perspective on wives' distress. *Journal of Personality and Social Psychology, 61,* 404–412.

Coyne, J. C., Wortman, C. B., & Lehman, D. R. (1988). The other side of support: Emotional overinvolvement and miscarried helping. In B. H. Gottlieb (Ed.), *Marshaling social support* (pp. 305–330). Thousand Oaks, CA: Sage.

Craddock, A. E. (1980). The effect of incongruent marital role expectations upon couples' degree of goal-value consensus in the first year of marriage. *Australian Journal of Psychology, 32,* 117–125.

Craddock, A. E. (1983). Correlations between marital role expectations and relationship satisfaction among engaged couples. *Australian Journal of Sex, Marriage and Family, 4,* 33–46.

Cramer, R. B. (2000). *Joe DiMaggio: The hero's life*. New York: Simon & Schuster.

Creasey, G., & Ladd, A. (2005). Generalized and specific attachment representations: Unique and interactive roles in predicting conflict behaviors in close relationships. *Personality and Social Psychological Bulletin, 31*, 1026–1038.

Crouse, B., Karlins, M., & Schroder, H. (1968). Conceptual complexity and marital happiness. *Journal of Marriage and Family, 30*, 643–646.

Crouter, A. C., & Bumpus, M. F. (2001). Linking parents' work stress to children's and adolescents' psychological adjustment. *Current Directions in Psychological Science, 10*, 156–159.

Crowell, J. A., Treboux, D., & Waters, E. (2002). Stability of attachment representations: The transition to marriage. *Developmental Psychology, 38*, 467–479.

Crowell, J. A., Treboux, D., Gao, Y., Fyffe, C., Pan, H., & Waters, E. (2002). Assessing secure base behavior in adulthood: Development of a measure, links to adult attachment representations, and relations to couples' communication and reports of relationships. *Developmental Psychology, 38*, 679–693.

Crown, C. L. (1991). Coordinated interpersonal timing of vision and voice as a function of interpersonal attraction. *Journal of Language and Social Psychology, 10*, 29–46.

Cruz, J. M., & Firestone, J. M. (1998). Exploring violence and abuse in gay male relationships. *Violence and Victims, 13*, 159–173.

Cummings, E. M., Goeke-Morey, M., & Papp, L. M. (2003). Children's responses to everyday marital conflict tactics in the home. *Child Development, 74*, 1918–1929.

Cummings, E. M., Iannotti, R. J., & Zahn-Waxler, C. (1985). Influence of conflict between adults on the emotions and aggression of young children. *Developmental Psychology, 21*, 495–507.

Cummings, E. M., Vogel, D., Cummings, J. S., & El-Sheikh, M. (1989). Children's responses to different forms of expression of anger between adults. *Child Development, 60*, 1392–1404.

Cummings, E. M., Wilson, J., & Shamir, H. (2005). Reactions of Chilean and U.S. children to marital discord. *International Journal of Behavioral Development, 29*, 437–444.

Cummings, E. M., & Davies, P. T. (1994). *Children and marital conflict: The impact of family dispute and resolution*. New York: Guilford.

Cummings, E. M., & Davies, P. T. (2010). *Marital conflict and children: An emotional security perspective*. New York: Guilford.

Cunningham, M. R., Barbee, A. P., & Pike, C. L. (1990). What do women want? Facialmetric assessment of multiple motives in the perception of male facial physical attractiveness. *Journal of Personality and Social Psychology, 59*, 61–72.

Cunningham, M. R., Roberts, A. R., Barbee, A. P., Druen, P. B., & Wu, C. (1995). "Their ideas of beauty are, on the whole, the same as ours": Consistency and variability in the cross-cultural perception of female physical attractiveness. *Journal of Personality and Social Psychology, 68*, 261–279.

Cuperman, R., & Ickes, W. (2009). Big Five predictors of behavior and perceptions in initial dyadic interactions: Personality similarity helps extraverts and introverts, but hurts "disagreeables." *Journal of Personality and Social Psychology, 97*(4), 667–684.

Curtis, R. C., & Miller, K. (1986). Believing another likes or dislikes you: Behaviors making the beliefs come true. *Journal of Personality and Social Psychology, 51*, 284–290.

Cutrona, C. E. (1996). *Social support in marriage*. Thousand Oaks, CA: Sage.

Cutrona, C. E., & Suhr, J. A. (1994). Social support communication in the context of marriage: An analysis of couples' supportive interactions. In B. R. Burleson, T. L. Albrecht, & I. G. Sarason (Eds.), *Communication of social support: Messages, interactions, relationships, and community* (pp. 113–135). Thousand Oaks, CA: Sage.

Cutrona, C. E., Russell, D. W., Abraham, W. T., Gardner, K. A., Melby, J. M., Bryant, C., et al. (2003). Neighborhood context and financial strain as predictors of marital interaction and marital quality in African American couples. *Personal Relationships, 10*, 389–409.

Cutrona, C. E., Russell, D. W., Brown, P. A., Clark, L. A., Hessling, R. M., & Gardner, K. A. (2005). Neighborhood context, personality, and stressful life events as predictors of depression among African American women. *Journal of Abnormal Psychology, 114*, 3–15.

D'Onofrio, B. M., Turkheimer, E., Emery, R. E., Harden, K. P., Slutske, W. S., Heath, A. C., Madden, P. A., et al. (2007). A genetically informed study of the intergenerational transmission of marital instability. *Journal of Marriage and Family, 69*, 793–809.

D'Onofrio, B. M., Turkheimer, E., Emery, R. E., Slutske, W. S., Heath, A. C., Madden, P. A., et al. (2006). A genetically informed study of the processes underlying the association between parental marital instability and offspring adjustment. *Developmental Psychology, 42*, 486–499.

Dahlquist, L. M., Czyzewski, D. I., Copeland, K. G., Jones, C. L., Taub, E., & Vaughan, J. K. (1993). Parents of children newly diagnosed with cancer:

Anxiety, coping, and marital distress. *Journal of Pediatric Psychology, 18,* 365–376.

Darley, J. M., & Fazio, R. H. (1980). Expectancy confirmation processes arising in the social interaction sequence. *American Psychologist, 35,* 867–881.

Darling, N., Dowdy, B. B., Van Horn, M. L., & Caldwell, L. L. (1999). Mixed-sex settings and the perception of competence. *Journal of Youth and Adolescence, 28,* 461–480.

Darwin, C. (1859/2006). *On the origin of species by means of natural selection, or the preservation of favoured races in the struggle for life.* Mineola, NY: Dover Thrift Editions.

Dash, L. (2003). *When children want children: The urban crisis of teenage childbearing.* Champaign: University of Illinois Press.

Davies, P. T., & Cummings, E. M. (1994). Marital conflict and child adjustment: An emotional security hypothesis. *Psychological Bulletin, 116,* 387–411.

Davies, P. T., & Cummings, E. M. (1998). Exploring children's emotional security as a mediator of the link between marital relations and child adjustment. *Child Development, 69,* 124–139.

Davies, P. T., Sturge-Apple, M. L., Winter, M. A., Cummings, E. M., & Farrell, D. (2006). Child adaptational development in contexts of interparental conflict over time. *Child Development, 77,* 218–233.

Davila, J., & Cobb, R. J. (2003). Predicting change in self-reported and interviewer-assessed attachment security: Tests of the individual and life-stress model. *Personality and Social Psychology Bulletin, 29,* 859–870.

Davis, D. (1981). Implications for interaction versus effectance as mediators of the similarity-attraction relationship. *Journal of Experimental Social Psychology, 17,* 96–117.

Davis, D. (1982). Determinants of responsiveness in dyadic interaction. In W. Ickes & E. S. Knowles (Eds.), *Personality, roles, and social behaviors* (pp. 85–139). New York: Springer-Verlag.

Davis, F. Hadland. (1932). *Myths and legends of Japan.* (Illustrations by Evelyn Paul.) New York: Farrar & Rinehart.

de Jong Gierveld, J. (1995). Research into relationship research designs: Personal relationships under the microscope. *Journal of Social and Personal Relationships, 12,* 583–588.

de Jong Gierveld, J. (2004). Remarriage, unmarried cohabitation, living apart together: Partner relationships following bereavement or divorce. *Journal of Marriage and Family, 66,* 236–243.

De La Ronde, C., & Swann, W. B. Jr. (1998). Partner verification: Restoring shattered images of our intimates. *Journal of Personality and Social Psychology, 75,* 374–382.

De Munck, V. C. (1996). Love and marriage in a Sri Lankan Muslim community: Toward an evaluation of Dravidian marriage practices. *American Ethnologist, 23,* 698–716.

De Munck, V. C. (1998). Lust, love, and arranged marriages in Sri Lanka. In V. C. De Munck (Ed.), *Romantic love and sexual behavior: Perspectives from the social sciences* (pp. 285–300). Westport, CT: Praeger/Greenwood.

Deaux, K., & Major, B. (1987). Putting gender into context: An interactive model of gender-related behavior. *Psychological Review, 94,* 369–389.

DeMaris, A., & Rao, K. V. (1992). Premarital cohabitation and subsequent marital stability in the United States: A reassessment. *Journal of Marriage and Family, 54,* 178–190.

Demir, A., & Fisiloglu, H. (1999). Loneliness and marital adjustment of Turkish couples. *Journal of Psychology, 133,* 230–240.

Denton, W. H., Burleson, B. R., & Sprenkle, D. H. (1995). Association of interpersonal cognitive complexity with communication skill in marriage: Moderating effects of marital distress. *Family Process, 34,* 101–111.

Derlega, V. J., Metts, S., Petronio, S., & Margulis, S. T. (1993). *Self-disclosure.* Newbury Park, CA: Sage.

Derlega, V. J., Wilson, M., & Chaikin, A. L. (1976). Friendship and disclosure reciprocity. *Journal of Personality and Social Psychology, 34,* 578–582.

Dermer, M., & Thiel, D. L. (1975). When beauty may fail. *Journal of Personality and Social Psychology, 31,* 1168–1176.

Diamond, L. M. (2000). Sexual identity, attractions, and behavior among young sexual-minority women over a two-year period. *Developmental Psychology, 36,* 241–250.

Diamond, L. M. (2003). What does sexual orientation orient? A biobehavioral model distinguishing romantic love and sexual desire. *Psychological Review, 110,* 173–192.

Diamond, L. M. (2004). Emerging perspectives on distinctions between romantic love and sexual desire. *Current Directions in Psychological Science, 13,* 116–119.

Diamond, L. M. (2006). The intimate same-sex relationships of sexual minorities. In A. L. Vangelisti & D. Perlman (Eds.), *The Cambridge Handbook of Personal Relationships* (pp. 293–312). New York: Cambridge University Press.

Diamond, L. M. (2008). Female bisexuality from adolescence to adulthood: Results from a 10-year longitudinal study. *Developmental Psychology, 44,* 5–14.

Dicks, H. V. (1967). *Marital tensions.* New York: Basic Books.

Diener, E., Gohm, C. L., Suh, E., & Oishi, S. (2000). Similarity of the relations between marital status and subjective well-being across cultures. *Journal of Cross-Cultural Psychology, 31*, 419–436.

Diener, E., Suh, E. M., Lucas, R. E., & Smith, H. L. (1999). Subjective well-being: Three decades of progress. *Psychological Bulletin, 125*, 276–302.

Diener, E., Wolsic, B., & Fujita, F. (1995). Physical attractiveness and subjective well-being. *Journal of Personality and Social Psychology, 69*, 120–129.

Dimidjian, S., Martell, C. R., & Christensen, A. (2008). Integrative behavioral couple therapy. In A. S. Gurman (Ed.), *Clinical handbook of couple therapy* (4th ed., pp. 73–103). New York: Guilford.

Dindia, K., & Allen, M. (1992). Sex differences in self-disclosure. A meta-analysis. *Psychological Bulletin, 112*, 106–124.

Dindia, K., & Baxter, L. A. (1987). Strategies for maintaining and repairing marital relationships. *Journal of Social and Personal Relationships, 4*, 143–158.

Dion, K., Berscheid, E., & Walster, E. (1972). What is beautiful is good. *Journal of Personality and Social Psychology, 24*, 285–290.

Dobash, R. E., & Dobash, R. P. (1979). *Violence against wives: A case against patriarchy*. New York: Free Press.

Dobash, R. E., & Dobash, R. P. (1990). How theoretical definitions affect research and policy. In D. J. Besharov (Ed.), *Family violence: Research and public policy issues* (pp. 108–129). Washington, DC: AEI Press.

Doherty, W. J. (1981). Locus of control differences and marital dissatisfaction. *Journal of Marriage and Family, 43*, 369–377.

Doherty, W. J., & Ryder, R. G. (1979). Locus of control, interpersonal trust, and assertive behavior among newlyweds. *Journal of Personality and Social Psychology, 37*, 2212–2220.

Doi, T. (1971/2002). *The anatomy of dependence*. Tokyo: Kodansha.

Dominus, S. (2004, May 23). One very tangled post-9/11 affair. *New York Times Magazine*, pp. 36–41.

Donellan, M. B., Conger, R. D., & Bryant, C. M. (2004). The Big Five and enduring marriages. *Journal of Research in Personality, 38*, 481–504.

Doss, B. D., Atkins, D. C., & Christensen, A. (2003). Who's dragging their feet? Husbands and wives seeking marital therapy. *Journal of Marital and Family Therapy, 29*, 165–177.

Doss, B. D., Simpson, L. E., & Christensen, A. (2004). Why do couples seek marital therapy? *Professional Psychology: Research & Practice, 35*, 608–614.

Doumas, D. M., Margolin, G., & John, R. S. (2003). The relationship between daily marital interaction, work, and health-promoting behaviors in dual-earner couples: An extension of the work-family spillover model. *Journal of Family Issues, 24*, 3–20.

Downey, G., & Feldman, S. (1996). Implications of rejection sensitivity for intimate relationships. *Journal of Personality and Social Psychology, 70*, 1327–1343.

Downey, G., Freitas, A. L., Michaelis, B., & Khouri, H. (1998). The self-fulfilling prophecy in close relationships: Rejection sensitivity and rejection by romantic partners. *Journal of Personality and Social Psychology, 75*, 545–560.

Drigotas, S. M., & Rusbult, C. E. (1992). Should I stay or should I go? A dependence model of breakups. *Journal of Personality and Social Psychology, 62*, 62–87.

Dryer, D. C., & Horowitz, L. M. (1997). When do opposites attract? Interpersonal complementarity versus similarity. *Journal of Personality and Social Psychology, 72*, 592–603.

Dube, R. (2007, November 15). Nursing home infidelity bittersweet but common. *Globe and Mail*.

Dunn, J. (1983). Sibling relationships in early childhood. *Child Development, 54*, 787–811.

Dunn, J. (1996). The Emanuel Miller Memorial Lecture 1995: Children's relationships: Bridging the divide between cognitive and social development. *Journal of Child Psychology and Psychiatry, 37*, 507–518.

Dunn, J. (2004). *Children's friendships: The beginnings of intimacy*. Malden, MA: Blackwell.

Dunn, R. L., & Schwebel, A. L. (1995). Meta-analytic review of marital therapy outcome research. *Journal of Family Psychology, 9*, 58–68.

Dupre, M. E., & Meadows, S. O. (2007). Disaggregating the effects of marital trajectories on health. *Journal of Family Issues, 28*, 623–652.

Dush, C. M. K., Cohan, C. L., & Amato, P. R. (2003). The relationship between cohabitation and marital quality and stability: Change across cohorts? *Journal of Marriage and Family, 65*, 539–549.

Dutton, D. G. (1995). *The batterer*. New York: Basic Books.

Dutton, D. G., & Aron, A. P. (1974). Some evidence for heightened sexual attraction under conditions of high anxiety. *Journal of Personality and Social Psychology, 30*, 510–517.

Dweck, C. S. (1986). Motivational processes affecting learning. *American Psychologist, 41*, 1040–1048.

Eagly, A. H., & Wood, W. (1991). Explaining sex differences in social behavior: A meta-analytic perspective. *Personality & Social Psychology Bulletin, 17*, 306–315.

Eagly, A. H., & Wood, W. (1999). The origins of sex differences in human behavior: Evolved dispositions versus social roles. *American Psychologist, 54,* 408–423.

Eagly, A. H., Makhijani, M. G., & Klonsky, B. G. (1992). Gender and the evaluation of leaders: A meta-analysis. *Psychological Bulletin, 111,* 3–22.

Eagly, A. H., Wood, W., & Johannesen-Schmidt, M. C. (2004). Social role theory of sex differences and similarities: Implications for the partner preferences of women and men. In A. H. Eagly, A. E. Beall, & R. J. Sternberg (Eds.), *The psychology of gender* (2nd ed., pp. 269–295). New York: Guilford.

Eastwick, P. W., & Finkel, E. J. (2008). Sex differences in mate preferences revisited: Do people know what they initially desire in a romantic partner? *Journal of Personality and Social Psychology, 94,* 245–264.

Eastwick, P. W., Finkel, E. J., Mochon, D., & Ariely, D. (2007). Selective versus unselective romantic desire: Not all reciprocity is created equal. *Psychological Science, 18,* 317–319.

Ebbesen, E. B., Kjos, G. L., & Konecni, V. J. (1976). Spatial ecology: Its effects on the choice of friends and enemies. *Journal of Experimental Social Psychology, 12,* 505–518.

Eccles, J., & Gootman, J. A. (Eds.). (2002). *Community programs to promote youth development.* Washington, DC: National Academy of Sciences.

Edin, K. (2000). What do low-income single mothers say about marriage? *Social Problems, 47,* 112–133.

Edin, K., & Kefalas, M. (2005). *Promises I can keep: Why poor women put motherhood before marriage.* Berkeley: University of California Press.

Edin, K., & Reed, J. M. (2005). Why don't they just get married? Barriers to marriage among the disadvantaged. *The Future of Children, 15,* 117–138.

Edin, K., Kefalas, M. J., & Reed, J. M. (2004). A peek inside the black box: What marriage means for poor unmarried parents. *Journal of Marriage and Family, 66,* 1007–1014.

Edlund, J. E., Heider, J. D., Scherer, C. R., Farc, M., & Sagarin, B. J. (2006). Sex differences in jealousy in response to actual infidelity. *Evolutionary Psychology, 4,* 462–470.

Edwards, J. N., & Booth, A. (1994). Sexuality, marriage, and well-being: The middle years. In A. S. Rossi (Ed.), *Sexuality across the life course* (pp. 233–259). Chicago: University of Chicago Press.

Egan, P. J., & Sherrill, K. (2005). Marriage and the shifting priorities of a new generation of lesbians and gays. *Political Science and Politics 38,* 229–232.

Ehrensaft, M. K., & Vivian, D. (1996). Spouses' reasons for not reporting existing marital aggression as a marital problem. *Journal of Family Psychology, 10,* 443–453.

Ehrensaft, M. K., Cohen, P., Brown, J. Smailes, E., Chen, H., & Johnson, J. G. (2003). Intergenerational transmission of partner violence: A 20-year prospective study. *Journal of Consulting and Clinical Psychology, 71,* 741–753.

Eibl-Eibesfeldt, I. (1979). Human ethology: Concepts and implications for the sciences of man. *Behavioral and Brain Sciences, 2,* 1–57.

Eidelson, R. J., & Epstein, N. (1982). Cognition and relationship maladjustment: Development of a measure of dysfunctional relationship beliefs. *Journal of Consulting and Clinical Psychology, 50,* 715–720.

Eisenberg, N., & Lennon, R. (1983). Sex differences in empathy and related abilities. *Psychological Bulletin, 94,* 100–131.

Eisenstein, V. W. (1956). *Neurotic interaction in marriage.* New York: Basic Books.

Elder, G. H., & Clipp, E. C. (1989). Combat experience and emotional health: Impairment and resilience in later life. *Journal of Personality, 57,* 313–341.

Eldridge, K. A., Sevier, M., Jones, J., Atkins, D. C., & Christensen, A. (2007). Demand-withdraw communication in severely distressed, moderately distressed, and nondistressed couples: Rigidity and polarity during relationship and personal problem discussions. *Journal of Family Psychology, 21,* 218–226.

Elliott, E. S., & Dweck, C. S. (1988). Goals: An approach to motivation and achievement. *Journal of Personality and Social Psychology, 54,* 5–12.

Ellis, B. J. (1992). The evolution of sexual attraction: Evaluative mechanisms in women. In J. Barkow, L. Cosmides, & J. Tooby (Eds.), *The adapted mind: Evolutionary psychology and the generation of culture* (pp. 267–288). New York: Oxford University Press.

Ellis, B. J., McFadyen-Ketchum, S., Dodge, K. A., Pettit, G. S., & Bates, J. E. (1999). Quality of early family relationships and individual differences in the timing of pubertal maturation in girls: A longitudinal test of an evolutionary model. *Journal of Personality and Social Psychology, 77,* 387–401.

Ellis, L., Robb, B., & Burke, D. (2005). Sexual orientation in United States and Canadian students. *Archives of Sexual Behavior, 34,* 569–581.

El-Sheikh, M., Buckhalt, J. A., Mize, J., & Acebo, C. (2006). Marital conflict and disruption of children's sleep. *Child Development, 77,* 31–43.

Elwood, D. T., & Jencks, C. (2004). The uneven spread of single-parent families: What do we know? What do we need to know? Where do we look for answers? In K. M. Neckerman (Ed.), *Social inequality* (pp. 3–118). New York: Russell Sage Foundation.

Emery, R. (1982). Interparental conflict and the children of discord and divorce. *Psychological Bulletin, 92*, 310–330.

Emery, R. E. (1999). *Marriage, divorce, and children's adjustment* (2nd ed.). Thousand Oaks, CA: |Sage.

Epictetus. (1888). *The Discourses of Epictetus; with the Encheiridion and fragments* (George Long, Trans.). London: George Bell & Sons.

Epstein, N., & Eidelson, R. J. (1981). Unrealistic beliefs of clinical couples: Their relationship to expectations, goals, and satisfaction. *American Journal of Family Therapy, 9*, 13–22.

Erikson, E. H. (1968). *Identity, youth, and crisis*. New York: Norton.

Evans, G. W. (2004). The environment of childhood poverty. *American Psychologist, 59*, 77–92.

Evans-Pritchard, E. E. (1951). *Kinship and marriage among the Nuer*. Oxford: Clarendon Press.

Ewart, C. K. (1993). Marital interaction: The context for psychosomatic research. *Psychosomatic Medicine, 55*, 410–412.

Feeney, B. C. (2004). A secure base: Responsive support of goal strivings and exploration in adult intimate relationships. *Journal of Personality and Social Psychology, 87*, 631–648.

Feeney, B. C., & Collins, N. L. (2001). Predictors of caregiving in adult intimate relationships: An attachment theoretical perspective. *Journal of Personality and Social Psychology, 80*, 972–994.

Fehr, B. (1988). Prototype analysis of love and commitment. *Journal of Personality and Social Psychology, 55*, 557–579.

Fein, D. J. (2004). Married and poor: Basic characteristics of economically disadvantaged married couples in the U.S. (Supporting Healthy Marriage Evaluation, Working Paper SHM-01).

Fein, E., & Schneider, S. (1995). *The rules*. New York: Grand Central Publishing.

Feingold, A. (1988). Matching for attractiveness in romantic partners and same-sex friends: A meta-analysis and theoretical critique. *Psychological Bulletin, 104*, 226–235.

Feingold, A. (1990). Gender differences in effects of physical attractiveness on romantic attraction: A comparison across five research paradigms. *Journal of Personality and Social Psychology, 59*, 981–993.

Feingold, A. (1992). Gender differences in mate selection preferences: A test of the parental investment model. *Psychological Bulletin, 112*, 125–139.

Feingold, A. (1994). Gender differences in personality: A meta-analysis. *Psychological Bulletin, 116*, 429–456.

Feinstein, B.A., Goldfried, M.R., & Davila, J. (2012). The relationship between experiences of discrimination and mental health among lesbians and gay men: An examination of internalized homonegativity and rejection sensitivity as potential mechanisms. *Journal of Consulting and Clinical Psychology, 80*, 917–927.

Feiring, C. (1996). Concept of romance in 15-year-old adolescents. *Journal of Research on Adolescence, 6*, 181–200.

Feiring, C. (1999a). Gender identity and the development of romantic relationships in adolescence. In W. Furman, B. B. Brown & C. Feiring (Eds.), *The development of romantic relationships in adolescence* (pp. 211–232). New York: Cambridge University Press.

Feiring, C. (1999b). Other-sex friendship networks and the development of romantic relationships in adolescence. *Journal of Youth and Adolescence, 28*, 495–512.

Feiring, C., Deblinger, E., Hoch-Espada, A., & Haworth, T. (2002). Romantic relationship aggression and attitudes in high school students: The role of gender, grade, and attachment and emotional styles. *Journal of Youth and Adolescence, 31*, 373–385.

Felmlee, D. H. (1995). Fatal attractions: Affection and disaffection in intimate relationships. *Journal of Social and Personal Relationships, 12*, 295–311.

Felmlee, D. H. (1998). "Be careful what you wish for . . .": A quantitative and qualitative investigation of "fatal attractions." *Personal Relationships, 5*, 235–253.

Felmlee, D. H. (2001). From appealing to appalling: Disenchantment with a romantic partner. *Sociological Perspectives, 44*, 263–280.

Felmlee, D. H. (2001). No couple is an island: A social network perspective on dyadic stability. *Social Forces, 79*, 1259–1287.

Felmlee, D., Sprecher, S., & Bassin, E. (1990). The dissolution of intimate relationships: A hazard model. *Social Psychology Quarterly, 53*, 13–30.

Feng, D., Giarusso, R., Bengston, V., & Frye, N. (1999). Intergenerational transmission of marital quality and marital instability. *Journal of Marriage and Family, 61*, 451–463.

Festinger, L. (1954). A theory of social comparison processes. *Human Relations, 7*, 117–140.

Festinger, L. (1957). *A theory of cognitive dissonance*. Evanston, IL: Row, Peterson.

Festinger, L., & Carlsmith, J. M. (1959). Cognitive consequences of forced compliance. *Journal of Abnormal and Social Psychology, 58*, 203–210.

Festinger, L., Schacter, S., & Back, K. (1950). *Social pressures in informal groups*. New York: Harper.

Filsinger, E. E., & Thoma, S. J. (1988). Behavioral antecedents of relationship stability and adjustment: A five-year longitudinal study. *Journal of Marriage and Family, 50*, 785–795.

Fincham, F. D. (2000). The kiss of the porcupines: From attributing responsibility to forgiving. *Personal Relationships, 7*, 1–23.

Fincham, F. D., & Bradbury, T. N. (1987). The impact of attributions in marriage: A longitudinal analysis. *Journal of Personality and Social Psychology, 53*, 510–517.

Fincham, F. D., & O'Leary, K. D. (1983). Causal inferences for spouse behavior in maritally distressed and nondistressed couples. *Journal of Social and Clinical Psychology, 1*, 42–57.

Fincham, F. D., Beach, S. R. H., & Davila, J. (2004). Forgiveness and conflict resolution in marriage. *Journal of Family Psychology, 18*, 72–81.

Fincham, F. D., Bradbury, T. N., & Grych, J. H. (1990). Conflict in close relationships: The role of intrapersonal phenomena. In S. Graham & V. S. Folkes (Eds.), *Attribution theory: Applications to achievement, mental health, and interpersonal conflict* (pp. 161–184). Hillsdale, NJ: Erlbaum.

Fincham, F. D., Paleari, G., & Regalia, C. (2002). Forgiveness in marriage: The role of relationship quality, attributions, and empathy. *Personal Relationships, 9*, 27–37.

Finkel, E. J., Eastwick, P. W., & Matthews, J. (2007). Speed dating as an invaluable tool for studying romantic attraction: A methodological primer. *Personal Relationships, 14*, 149–166.

Finkel, E. J., Rusbult, C. E., Kumashiro, M., & Hannon, P. A. (2002). Dealing with betrayal in close relationships: Does commitment promote forgiveness? *Journal of Personality and Social Psychology, 82*, 956–974.

Fischer, H. E. (1989). Evolution of human serial pairbonding. *American Journal of Physical Anthropology, 78*, 331–354.

Fisher, J. D., Nadler, A., & Whitcher-Alagna, S. (1982). Recipient reactions to aid. *Psychological Bulletin, 91*, 27–54.

Flaherty, J. F., & Dusek, J. B. (1980). An investigation of the relationship between psychological androgyny and components of self-concept. *Journal of Personality and Social Psychology, 38*, 984–992.

Fleming, C. B., White, H. R., & Catalano, R. F. (2010). Romantic relationships and substance use in early adulthood: An examination of the influences of relationship type, partner substance use, and relationship quality. *Journal of Health and Social Behavior, 51*, 153–167.

Fletcher, G. J. O. (2002). *The new science of intimate relationships*. Oxford, England: Blackwell.

Fletcher, G. J. O., & Fincham, F. D. (1991). Attribution processes in close relationships. In G. J. O. Fletcher & F. D. Fincham (Eds.), *Cognition in close relationships* (pp. 7–36). Hillsdale, NJ: Erlbaum.

Fletcher, G. J. O., & Kininmonth, L. (1992). Measuring relationship beliefs: An individual differences scale. *Journal of Research in Personality, 26*, 371–397.

Fletcher, G. J. O., & Simpson, J. A. (2000). Ideal standards in close relationships: Their structure and functions. *Current Directions in Psychological Science, 9*, 102–105.

Fletcher, G. J. O., & Thomas, G. (1996). Close relationship lay theories: Their structure and function. In G. J. O. Fletcher & J. Fitness (Eds.), *Knowledge structures in close relationships: A social psychological perspective* (pp. 3–24). Mahwah, NJ: Erlbaum.

Fletcher, G. J. O., Simpson, J. A., & Thomas, G. (2000). Ideals, perceptions, and evaluations in early relationship development. *Journal of Personality and Social Psychology, 79*, 933–940.

Fletcher, G. J. O., Simpson, J. A., Thomas, G., & Giles, L. (1999). Ideals in intimate relationships. *Journal of Personality and Social Psychology, 76*, 72–89.

Flouri, E., & Buchanan, A. (2002). What predicts good relationships with parents in adolescence and partners in adult life: Findings from the 1958 British birth cohort. *Journal of Family Psychology, 16*, 186–198.

Floyd, F. J., & Markman, H. J. (1983). Observational biases in spouse observation: Toward a cognitive/behavioral model of marriage. *Journal of Consulting and Clinical Psychology, 51*, 450–457.

Folkes, V. S. (1982). Communicating the reasons for social rejection. *Journal of Experimental Social Psychology, 18*, 235–252.

Fomby, P., & Cherlin, A. J. (2007). Family instability and child well-being. *American Sociological Review, 72*, 181–204.

Foran, H. M., Slep, A. M., & Heyman, R. E. (2011). Prevalences of intimate partner violence in a representative U.S. Air Force sample. *Journal of Consulting and Clinical Psychology, 79*, 391–397.

Ford, K., Sohn, W., & Lepkowski, J. (2001). Characteristics of adolescents' sexual partners and their association with use of condoms and other contraceptive methods. *Family Planning Perspectives, 33*, 100–105, 132.

Fosco, G. M., & Grych, J. H. (2007). Emotional expression in the family as a context for children's appraisals of interparental conflict. *Journal of Family Psychology, 21*, 248–258.

Fraenkel, P. (1997). Systems approaches to couple therapy. In W. K. Halford & H. J. Markman (Eds.), *Clinical handbook of marriage and couples interventions* (pp. 379–413). Hoboken, NJ: Wiley.

Fraley, R. C. (2002). Attachment stability from infancy to adulthood: Meta-analysis and dynamic modeling of developmental mechanisms. *Personality and Social Psychology Review, 6*, 123–151.

Fraley, R. C., & Davis, K. E. (1997). Attachment formation and transfer in young adults' close friendships and romantic relationships. *Personal Relationships, 4*, 131–144.

Fraley, R. C., & Shaver, P. R. (1998). Airport separations: A naturalistic study of adult attachment dynamics in separating couples. *Journal of Personality and Social Psychology, 75*, 1198–1212.

Fraley, R. C., & Waller, N. G. (1998). Adult attachment patterns: A test of the typological model. In J. A. Simpson & W. S. Rholes (Eds.), *Attachment theory and close relationships* (pp. 77–114). New York: Guilford.

Framo, J. L. (1975). Personal reflections of a family therapist. *Journal of Marital and Family Therapy, 1*, 15–28.

Franklin, K. M., Janoff-Bulman, R., & Roberts, J. E. (1990). Long-term impact of parental divorce on optimism and trust: Changes in general assumptions or narrow beliefs? *Journal of Personality and Social Psychology, 59*, 743–755.

Franzoi, S. L., Davis, M. H., & Vasquez–Suson, K. A. (1994). Two social worlds: Social correlates and stability of adolescent status groups. *Journal of Personality and Social Psychology, 67*, 462–473.

Frazier, P. A., Byer, A. L., Fischer, A. R., Wright, D. M., & DeBord, K. A. (1996). Adult attachment style and partner choice: Correlational and experimental findings. *Personal Relationships, 3*, 117–136.

Frederickson, B. (2001). The role of positive emotions in positive psychology: The broaden-and-build theory of positive emotions. *American Psychologist, 56*, 218–226.

Fremouw, W. J., Westrup, D., & Pennypacker, J. (1997). Stalking on campus: The prevalence and strategies for coping with stalking. *Journal of Forensic Sciences, 42*, 666–669.

Frieze, I. H., Olson, J. E., & Russell, J. (1991). Attractiveness and income for men and women in management. *Journal of Applied Social Psychology, 21*, 1039–1057.

Fritz, H. L., & Helgeson, V. S. (1998). Distinctions of unmitigated communion from communion: Self-neglect and overinvolvement with others. *Journal of Personality and Social Psychology, 75*, 121–140.

Funk, J. L., & Rogge, R. D. (2007). Testing the ruler with item response theory: Increasing precision of measurement for relationship satisfaction with the Couples Satisfaction Index. *Journal of Family Psychology, 21*, 572–583.

Furman, W. (1984). Some observations on the study of personal relationships. In J. C. Masters & K. Yarkin-Levin (Eds.). *Boundary areas in social and developmental psychology* (pp. 15–42). Orlando: Academic Press.

Furman, W., & Buhrmester, D. (1985). Children's perceptions of the personal relationships in their social networks. *Developmental Psychology, 21*, 1016–1024.

Furman, W., & Buhrmester, D. (1992). Age and sex differences in perceptions of networks of personal relationships. *Child Development, 63*, 103–115.

Furman, W., & Flanagan, A. (1997). The influence of earlier relationships on marriage: An attachment perspective. In W. K. Halford & H. J. Markman (Eds.), *Clinical handbook of marriage and couples interventions* (pp. 179–202). New York: Wiley.

Furman, W., & Simon, V. A. (1999). Cognitive representations of adolescent romantic relationships. In W. Furman, B. B. Brown & C. Feiring (Eds.), *The development of romantic relationships in adolescence* (pp. 75–98). New York: Cambridge University Press.

Furman, W., & Wehner, E. A. (1994). Romantic views: Toward a theory of adolescent romantic relationships. In R. Montemayor, G. R. Adams & T. P. Gullotta (Eds.), *Personal relationships during adolescence* (pp. 168–195). Thousand Oaks, CA: Sage.

Furstenberg, F. F., Brooks-Gunn, J., & Chase-Lansdale, L. (1989). Teenaged pregnancy and childbearing. *American Psychologist, 44*, 313–320.

Gable, S. L., Gonzaga, G. C., & Strachman, A. (2006). Will you be there for me when things go right? Supportive responses to positive event disclosures. *Journal of Personality and Social Psychology, 91*, 904–917.

Gable, S. L., Reis, H. T., Impett, E., & Asher, E. R. (2004). What do you do when things go right? The intrapersonal and interpersonal benefits of sharing positive events. *Journal of Personality and Social Psychology, 87*, 228–245.

Gabriel, S., & Gardner, W. L. (1999). Are there "his" and "hers" types of interdependence? The implications of gender differences in collective versus relational interdependence for affect, behavior, and cognition. *Journal of Personality and Social Psychology, 77*, 642–655.

Gagne, F. M., & Lydon, J. E. (2004). Bias and accuracy in close relationships: An integrative review. *Personality and Social Psychology Review, 8*, 322–338.

Gahler, M., Hong, Y., & Bernhardt, E. (2009). Parental divorce and union disruption among young adults in Sweden. *Journal of Family Issues, 30*, 668–713.

Gaines, S. O. Jr. (1995). Relationships between members of cultural minorities. In J. T. Wood & S. Duck (Eds.), *Under-studied relationships: Off the beaten track* (pp. 51–88). Thousand Oaks, CA: Sage.

Gaines, S. O. Jr., & Agnew, C. R. (2003). Relationship maintenance in intercultural couples: An interdependence analysis. In D. J. Canary & M. Dainton (Eds.), *Maintaining relationships through communication: Relational, contextual, and cultural variations* (pp. 231–253). Mahwah, NJ: Erlbaum.

Gallo, L. C., & Matthews, K. A. (2003). Understanding the association between socioeconomic status and physical health: Do negative emotions play a role? *Psychological Bulletin, 129*, 10–51.

Gallo, L. C., Troxel, W. M., Matthews, K. A., & Kuller, L. H. (2003). Marital status and quality in middle-aged women: Associations with levels and trajectories of cardiovascular risk factors. *Health Psychology, 22*, 453–463.

Gallup Values and Beliefs Survey. (2008, June). Americans evenly divided on morality of homosexuality. Retrieved March 31, 2008, from http://www.gallup.com/poll/108115/Americans-Evenly-Divided-Morality-Homosexuality.aspx

Galotti, K. M., Kozberg, S. F., & Appleman, D. (1990). Younger and older adolescents' thinking about commitments. *Journal of Experimental Child Psychology, 50*, 324–339.

Gangestad, S. W., & Simpson, J. A. (1990). Toward an evolutionary history of female sociosexual variation. *Journal of Personality, 58*, 69–96.

Gangestad, S. W., & Simpson, J. A. (2000). The evolution of human mating: Trade-offs and strategic pluralism. *Behavioral and Brain Sciences, 23*, 573–644.

Garcia, S., Stinson, L., Ickes, W., & Bissonnette, V. (1991). Shyness and physical attractiveness in mixed-sex dyads. *Journal of Personality and Social Psychology, 61*, 35–49.

Geen, R. G., & Donnerstein, E. (Eds.). (1998). *Human aggression: Theories, research, and implications for social policy*. San Diego: Academic Press.

Geis, S., & O'Leary, K. D. (1981). Therapist ratings of frequency and severity of marital problems: Implications for research. *Journal of Marital and Family Therapy, 7*, 515–520.

Gesell, A., & Thompson, H. (1934). *Infant behavior: Its Genesis and Growth*. New York: McGraw-Hill.

Giese-Davis, J., Hermanson, K., Koopman, C., Weibel, D., & Spiegel, D. (2000). Quality of couples' relationship and adjustment to metastatic breast cancer. *Journal of Family Psychology, 14*, 251–266.

Gill, M. J., & Swann, W. B. (2004). On what it means to know someone: A matter of pragmatics. *Journal of Personality and Social Psychology, 86*, 405–418.

Gillath, O., Mikulincer, M., Fitzsimons, G. M., Shaver, P. R., Schachner, D. A., & Bargh, J. A. (2006). Automatic activation of attachment-related goals. *Personality and Social Psychology Bulletin, 32*, 1375–1388.

Gimbel, C., & Booth, A. (1994). Why does military combat experience adversely affect marital relations? *Journal of Marriage and Family, 56*, 691–703.

Giordano, P. C., Manning, W. D., & Longmore, M. A. (2005). The romantic relationships of African-American and white adolescents. *Sociological Quarterly, 46*, 545–568.

Giordano, P. C., Manning, W. D., & Longmore, M. A. (2006). Adolescent romantic relationships: An emerging portrait of their nature and developmental significance. In A. C. Crouter & A. Booth (Eds.), *Romance and sex in adolescence and emerging adulthood: Risks and opportunities* (pp. 127–150). Mahwah, NJ: Erlbaum.

Givens, D. B. (1978). The nonverbal basis of attraction: Flirtation, courtship, and seduction. *Psychiatry: Journal for the Study of Interpersonal Processes, 41*, 346–359.

Givens, D. B. (1983). *Love signals: How to attract a mate*. New York: Crown.

Gladue, B. A., & Delaney, H. J. (1990). Gender differences in perception of attractiveness of men and women in bars. *Personality and Social Psychology Bulletin, 16*, 378–391.

Glass, S. P., & Wright, T. L. (1985). Sex differences in type of extramarital involvement and marital dissatisfaction. *Sex Roles, 12*, 1101–1120.

Glass, S. P., & Wright, T. L. (1992). Justifications for extramarital relationships: The association between attitudes, behaviors, and gender. *Journal of Sex Research, 29*, 361–387.

Glenn, N. D., & Kramer, K. B. (1987). The marriages and divorces of children of divorce. *Journal of Marriage and Family, 49*, 811–825.

Glenn, N. D., & Weaver, C. N. (1981). The contribution of marital happiness to global happiness. *Journal of Marriage and Family, 43*, 161–168.

Glenn, N., & Marquardt, E. (2001). *Hooking up, hanging out, and hoping for Mr. Right: College women on dating and mating today*. An Institute for American Values Report to the Independent Women's Forum. Web. 27 August 2009.

Golden, A. (1998). *Memoirs of a geisha*. New York: Knopf.

Golding, J. M. (1999). Intimate partner violence as a risk factor for mental disorders: A meta-analysis. *Journal of Family Violence, 14*, 99–132.

Goodburn, E. A., & Ross, D. A. (1995). *A picture of health: A review and annotated bibliography of the health of young people in developing countries*. Geneva: World Health Organization and UNICEF.

Goode, E. (1996). Gender and courtship entitlement: Responses to personal ads. *Sex Roles, 34*, 141–169.

Gordon, K. C., & Baucom, D. H. (1998). Understanding betrayals in marriage: A synthesized model of forgiveness. *Family Process, 37*, 425–449.

Gorman, M. (1999). Development and the rights of older people. In J. Randel et al. (Eds.), *The ageing and development report: Poverty, independence and the world's older people* (pp. 3–21). London: Earthscan.

Gortner, E., Berns, S. B., Jacobson, N. S., & Gottman, J. M. (1997). When women leave violent relationships: Dispelling clinical myths. *Psychotherapy, 34*, 343–353.

Gotlib, I. H., Lewinsohn, P. M., & Seeley, J. R. (1998). Consequences of depression during adolescence: Marital status and marital functioning in early adulthood. *Journal of Abnormal Psychology, 107*, 686–690.

Gott, M., & Hinchliff, S. (2003). How important is sex in later life? The views of older people. *Social Science and Medicine, 56*, 1617–1628.

Gottman, J. M. (1979). *Marital interaction: Experimental investigations*. New York: Academic Press.

Gottman, J. M. (1982). Temporal form: Toward a new language for describing relationships. *Journal of Marriage and Family, 44*, 943–962.

Gottman, J. M. (1993). The roles of conflict engagement, escalation, and avoidance in marital interaction: A longitudinal view of five types of couples. *Journal of Consulting and Clinical Psychology, 61*, 6–15.

Gottman, J. M. (1994). *What predicts divorce? The relationship between marital processes and marital outcomes*. Hillsdale, NJ: Erlbaum.

Gottman, J. M., & Krokoff, L. J. (1989). Marital interaction and satisfaction: A longitudinal view. *Journal of Consulting and Clinical Psychology, 57*, 47–52.

Gottman, J. M., & Levenson, R. W. (1986). Assessing the role of emotion in marriage. *Behavioral Assessment, 8*, 31–48.

Gottman, J. M., & Levenson, R. W. (1992). Marital processes predictive of later dissolution: Behavior, physiology, and health. *Journal of Personality and Social Psychology, 63*, 221–233.

Gottman, J. M., & Levenson, R. W. (1999a). How stable is marital interaction over time? *Family Process, 38*, 159–165.

Gottman, J. M., & Levenson, R. W. (1999b). Rebound from marital conflict and divorce prediction. *Family Process, 38*, 287–292.

Gottman, J. M., & Levenson, R. W. (1999c). What predicts change in marital interaction over time? A study of alternative models. *Family Process, 38*, 143–158.

Gottman, J. M., & Levenson, R. W. (2000). The timing of divorce: Predicting when a couple divorce over a 14-year period. *Journal of Marriage and Family, 62*, 737–745.

Gottman, J. M., Coan, J., Carrere, S., & Swanson, C. (1998). Predicting marital happiness and stability from newlywed interactions. *Journal of Marriage and Family, 60*, 5–22.

Gottman, J. M., Levenson, R. W., Gross, J., Fredrickson, B. L., McCoy, K., Rosenthal, L., Ruef, A., & Yoshimoto, D. (2003). Correlates of gay and lesbian couples' relationship satisfaction and relationship dissolution. *Journal of Homosexuality, 45*, 23–43.

Gottman, J., Notarius, C., Markman, H. J., Bank, S., Yoppi, B., & Rubin, M. E. (1976). Behavior exchange theory and marital decision making. *Journal of Personality and Social Psychology, 34*, 14–23.

Gottschall, J., & Nordlund, M. (2006). Romantic love: A literary universal? *Philosophy and Literature, 30*, 450–470.

Gracia, E., & Herrero, J. (2004). Personal and situational determinants of relationship-specific perceptions of social support. *Social Behavior and Personality, 32*, 459–476.

Grammer, K. (1990). Strangers meet: Laughter and nonverbal signs of interest in opposite-sex encounters. *Journal of Nonverbal Behavior, 14*, 209–236.

Grammer, K., & Thornhill, R. (1994). Human facial attractiveness and sexual selection: The role of averageness and symmetry. *Journal of Comparative Psychology, 108*, 233–242.

Green, B. L., & Kenrick, D. T. (1994). The attractiveness of gender-typed traits at different relationship levels: Androgynous characteristics may be desirable after all. *Personality and Social Psychological Bulletin, 20*, 244–253.

Greenberg, L. S., & Johnson, S. M. (1988). *Emotionally focused therapy for couples*. New York: Guilford.

Gregor, T. (1985). *Anxious pleasures: The sexual lives of an Amazonian people*. Chicago: University of Chicago Press.

Grello, C. M., Welsh, D. P., & Harper, M. S. (2006). No strings attached: The nature of casual sex in college students. *Journal of Sex Research, 43*, 255–267.

Griffin, D., & Bartholomew, K. (1994). Models of the self and other: Fundamental dimensions underlying measures of adult attachment. *Journal of Personality and Social Psychology, 67*, 430–445.

Grotevant, H. D., & Cooper, C. R. (1986). Individuation in family relationships: A perspective on individual differences in the development of identity and role-taking skill in adolescence. *Human Development, 29*, 82–100.

Grych, J. H., & Fincham, F. D. (1990). Marital conflict and children's adjustment: A cognitive-contextual framework. *Psychological Bulletin, 108,* 267–290.

Grych, J. H., & Fincham, F. D. (1993). Children's appraisals of marital conflict: Initial investigations of the cognitive-contextual framework. *Child Development, 64,* 215–230.

Grych, J. H., & Fincham, F. D. (2001). *Interparental conflict and child development: Theory, research, and application.* Cambridge, England: Cambridge University Press.

Guastello, D. D., & Guastello, S. J. (2003). Androgyny, gender role behavior, and emotional intelligence among college students and their parents. *Sex Roles, 49,* 663–673.

Guerney, B. (1987). Relationship enhancement. State College, PA: IDEALS.

Guldner, G. T. (1996). Long-distance romantic relationships: Prevalence and separation-related symptoms in college students. *Journal of College Student Development, 37,* 289–296.

Gump, B. B., & Matthews, K. A. (1999). Do background stressors influence reactivity to and recovery from acute stressors? *Journal of Applied Social Psychology, 29,* 469–494.

Gupta, M., Coyne, J. C., & Beach, S. R. H. (2003). Couples treatment for major depression: Critique of the literature and suggestions for some different directions. *Journal of Family Therapy, 25,* 317–46.

Gupta, U., & Singh, P. (1982). An exploratory study of love and liking and type of marriages. *Indian Journal of Applied Psychology, 19,* 92–97.

Gurman, Alan S., & Jacobson, Neil S. (eds.) (2002). *Clinical handbook of couple therapy* (3rd ed., pp. 420–435). New York: Guilford Press.

Haas, S. M., & Stafford, L. (1998). An initial examination of maintenance behaviors in gay and lesbian relationships. *Journal of Social and Personal Relationships, 15,* 846–855.

Hagedoorn, M., Kuijer, R. G., Buunk, B. P., DeJong, G. M., Wobbes, T., & Sanderman, R. (2000). Marital satisfaction in patients with cancer: Does support from intimate partners benefit those who need it most? *Health Psychology, 19,* 274–282.

Hahlweg, K., & Klann, N. (1997). The effectiveness of marital counseling in Germany: A contribution to health services research. *Journal of Family Psychology, 11,* 410–421.

Hahlweg, K., Markman, H. J., Thurmaier, F., Engl, J., & Eckert, V. (1998). Prevention of marital distress: Results of a German prospective longitudinal study. *Journal of Family Psychology, 12,* 543–556.

Hahlweg, K., Reisner, L., Kohli, G., Vollmer, M., Schindler, L., & Revenstorf, D. (1984). Development and validity of a new system to analyze interpersonal communication: Kategoriensystem fur Partnerschaftliche Interaktion. In K. Hahlweg & N. S. Jacobson (Eds.), *Marital interaction: Analysis and modification* (pp. 182–198). New York: Guilford.

Hajratwala, M. (2009). *Leaving India: My family's journey from five villages to five continents.* New York: Houghton Mifflin Harcourt.

Haley, J. (1963). *Strategies of psychotherapy.* New York: Grune & Stratton.

Halford, W. K., & Moore, E. N. (2002). Relationship education and the prevention of couple relationship problems. In A. S. Gurman & N. S. Jacobson (Eds.), *Clinical handbook of couple therapy* (3rd ed., pp. 400–419). New York: Guilford.

Halford, W. K., Gravestock, F. M., Lowe, R., & Scheldt, S. (1992). Toward a behavioral ecology of stressful marital interactions. *Behavioral Assessment, 14,* 199–217.

Halford, W. K., Sanders, M. R., & Behrens, B. C. (2000). Repeating the errors of our parents? Family of origin spouse violence and observed conflict management in engaged couples. *Family Process, 39,* 219–235.

Halford, W. K., Sanders, M. R., & Behrens, B. C. (2001). Can skills training prevent relationship problems in at-risk couples? Four-year effects of a behavioral relationship education program. *Journal of Family Psychology, 15,* 750–768.

Halford, W. K., Scott, J. L., & Smythe, J. (2000). Couples and coping with cancer: Helping each other through the night. In K. B. Schmaling & T. G. Sher (Eds.), *The psychology of couples and illness: Theory, research, & practice* (pp. 135–170). Washington, DC: American Psychological Association.

Halford, W. K. (2001). *Brief therapy for couples: Helping partners help themselves.* New York: Guilford.

Halford, W. K., Hahlweg, K., & Dunne, M. (1990). The cross-cultural consistency of marital communication associated with marital distress. *Journal of Marriage and Family, 52,* 487–500.

Halford, W. K., Markman, H. J., Kline, G. H., & Stanley, S. M. (2003). Best practices in couple relationship education. *Journal of Marital and Family Therapy, 29,* 385–406.

Hall, J. A. (1984). *Nonverbal sex differences: Communication accuracy and expressive style.* Baltimore: Johns Hopkins University Press.

Halpern, C. T., Oslak, S. G., Young, M. L., Martin, S. L., & Kupper, L. L. (2001). Partner violence among adolescents in opposite-sex romantic relationships: Findings from the National Longitudinal Study of Adolescent Health. *American Journal of Public Health, 91,* 1679–1685.

Hamermesh, D. S., & Biddle, J. E. (1994). Beauty and the labor market. *American Economic Review, 84,* 1174–1195.

Hamilton, W. D. (1964). The genetical evolution of social behavior, I and II. *Journal of Theoretical Biology, 7,* 1–16, 17–52.

Hampson, S. E., Goldberg, L. R., & John, O. P. (1987). Category-breadth and social-desirability values for 573 personality terms. *European Journal of Personality, 1,* 241–258.

Hampson, S. E., John, O. P., & Goldberg, L. R. (1986). Category breadth and hierarchical structure in personality: Studies of asymmetries in judgments of trait implications. *Journal of Personality and Social Psychology, 51,* 37–54.

Hanson, T. L., McLanahan, S. S., & Thomson, E. (1998). Windows on divorce: Before and after. *Social Science Research, 27,* 329–349.

Hardoy, I., & Schøne, P. (2008). Subsidizing "stayers"? Effects of a Norwegian child care reform on marital stability. *Journal of Marriage and Family, 70,* 571–584.

Harker, L., & Keltner, D. (2001). Expressions of positive emotion in women's college yearbook pictures and their relationship to personality and life outcomes across adulthood. *Journal of Personality and Social Psychology, 80,* 112–124.

Harkless, L. E., & Fowers, B. J. (2005). Similarities and differences in relational boundaries among heterosexuals, gay men, and lesbians. *Psychology of Women Quarterly, 29,* 167–176.

Harper, J. M., Schaalje, B. G., & Sandberg, J. G. (2000). Daily hassles, intimacy, and marital quality in later life marriages. *American Journal of Family Therapy, 28,* 1–18.

Harris, J. R. (1995). Where is the child's environment? A group socialization theory of development. *Psychological Review, 102,* 458–489.

Harris, H. (1995). Rethinking Polynesian heterosexual relationships: A case study on Mangaia, Cook Islands. In W. Jankowiak (Ed.), *Romantic passion: A universal experience?* New York: Columbia University Press.

Harris, P. L. (2000). *The work of the imagination.* Malden, MA: Blackwell.

Hart, S., Field, T., Del Valle, C., & Letourneau, M. (1998). Infants protest their mothers' attending to an infant-size doll. *Social Development, 7,* 54–61.

Hartup, W. W. (1989). Social relationships and their developmental significance. *American Psychologist, 44,* 120–126.

Hartup, W. W., & Stevens, N. (1997). Friendships and adaptation in the life course. *Psychological Bulletin, 121,* 355–370.

Hassebrauck, M. (1997). Cognitions of relationship quality: A prototype analysis of their structure and consequences. *Personal Relationships, 4,* 163–185.

Hatch, L. R., & Bulcroft, K. (1992). Contact with friends in later life: Disentangling the effects of gender and marital status. *Journal of Marriage and Family, 54,* 222–232.

Hatch, L. R., & Bulcroft, K. (2004). Does long–term marriage bring less frequent disagreements? Five explanatory frameworks. *Journal of Family Issues, 25,* 465–495.

Hatfield, E. (1988). Passionate and companionate love. In R. J. Sternberg & M. L. Barnes (Eds.), *The psychology of love* (pp. 191–217). New Haven, CT: Yale University Press.

Hatfield, E., & Rapson, R. L. (1993). Historical and cross-cultural perspectives on passionate love and sexual desire. *Annual Review of Sex Research, 4,* 67–97.

Hatfield, E., & Rapson, R. L. (1996). *Love and sex: Cross-cultural perspectives.* Boston: Allyn & Bacon.

Hatfield, E., & Walster, G. W. (1978). *A new look at love.* Chicago: Addison-Wesley.

Hatfield, E., Walster, G. W., Piliavin, J., & Schmidt, L. (1973). "Playing hard to get": Understanding an elusive phenomenon. *Journal of Personality and Social Psychology, 26,* 113–121.

Hawkins, A. J., Blanchard, V. L., Baldwin, S. A., & Fawcett, E. B. (2008). Does marriage and relationship education work? A meta-analytic study. *Journal of Consulting and Clinical Psychology, 76,* 723–734.

Hawkins, M. W., Carrère, S., & Gottman, J. M. (2002). Marital sentiment override: Does it influence couples' perceptions? *Journal of Marriage and Family, 64,* 193–201.

Hayvren, M., & Hymel, S. (1984). Ethical issues in sociometric testing: Impact of sociometric measures on interaction behavior. *Developmental Psychology, 20,* 844–849.

Hazan, C., & Shaver, P. R. (1987). Romantic love conceptualized as an attachment process. *Journal of Personality and Social Psychology, 52,* 511–524.

Hazan, C., & Zeifman, D. (1994). Sex and the psychological tether. In K. Bartholomew & D. Perlman (Eds.), *Attachment processes in adulthood* (Vol. 5, pp. 17–52). London: Jessica Kingsley.

Headey, B., Veenhoven, R., & Wearing, A. (1991). Top-down versus bottom-up theories of subjective well-being. *Social Indicators Research, 24,* 81–100.

Heaton, T. B., & Blake, A. M. (1999). Gender differences in determinants of marital disruption. *Journal of Family Issues, 20,* 25–45.

Heavey, C. L., Christensen, A., & Malamuth, N. M. (1995). The longitudinal impact of demand and withdrawal during marital conflict. *Journal of Consulting and Clinical Psychology, 63*, 797–801.

Heavey, C. L., Lane, C., & Christensen, A. (1993). Gender and conflict structure in marital interaction: A replication and extension. *Journal of Consulting and Clinical Psychology, 61*, 16–27.

Heidemann, B., Suhomlinova, O., & O'Rand, A. M. (1998). Economic independence, economic status, and empty nest in midlife marital disruption. *Journal of Marriage and Family, 60*, 219–231.

Helgeson, V. S. (1993). Two important distinctions in social support: Kind of support and perceived versus received. *Journal of Applied Social Psychology, 23*, 825–845.

Helgeson, V. S. (1994). Relation of agency and communion to well-being: Evidence and potential explanations. *Psychological Bulletin, 116*, 412–428.

Helgeson, V. S., Shaver, P., & Dyer, M. (1987). Prototypes of intimacy and distance in same-sex and opposite-sex relationships. *Journal of Social and Personal Relationships, 4*, 195–233.

Heller, D., Watson, D., & Ilies, R. (2004). The role of person vs. situation in life satisfaction: A critical examination. *Psychological Bulletin, 130*, 574–600.

Helweg-Larsen, M., & Shepperd, J. A. (2001). The optimistic bias: Moderators and measurement concerns. *Personality and Social Psychology Review, 5*, 74–95.

Henderson-King, D. H., & Veroff, J. (1994). Sexual satisfaction and marital well-being in the first years of marriage. *Journal of Social and Personal Relationships, 11*, 509–534.

Hendrick, C., & Brown, S. R. (1971). Introversion, extraversion, and interpersonal attraction. *Journal of Personality and Social Psychology, 20*, 31–36.

Henly, J. R., Danziger, S. K., & Offer, S. (2005). The contribution of social support to the material well-being of low-income families. *Journal of Marriage and Family, 67*, 122–140.

Herdt, A. M., Cohler, B. J., Boxer, G., & Floyd, I. (1993). Gay and lesbian youth. In P. H. Tolan & B. J. Cohler (Eds.), *Handbook of clinical research and practice with adolescents* (pp. 249–280). Oxford: John Wiley and Sons.

Herek, G. M., Gillis, J. R., & Cogan, J. C. (1999). Psychological sequelae of hate-crime victimization among lesbian, gay, and bisexual adults. *Journal of Consulting and Clinical Psychology, 67*, 945–951.

Herek, G. M., & Garnets, L. D. (2007). Sexual orientation and mental health. *Annual Review of Clinical Psychology, 3*, 353–375.

Hernandez, D. J. (1997). Child development and the social demography of childhood. *Child Development, 68*, 149–169.

Herz, R. S., & Cahill, E. D. (1997). Differential use of sensory information in sexual behavior as a function of gender. *Human Nature, 8*, 275–286.

Herzog, E., & Sudia, C. E. (1968). Fatherless homes: A review of research. *Children, 15*, 177–182.

Hetherington, E. M., & Clingempeel, W. G. (1992). Coping with marital transitions. *Monographs of the Society for Research in Child Development, 57*, 2–3. Chicago: University of Chicago Press.

Hetherington, E. M., & Kelly, J. (2002). *For better or for worse: Divorce reconsidered*. New York: W. W. Norton.

Hewitt, B., Western, M., & Baxter, J. (2006). Who decides? The social characteristics of who initiates marital separation. *Journal of Marriage and Family, 68*, 1165–1177.

Heyman, R. E. (2001). Observation of couple conflicts: Clinical assessment applications, stubborn truths, and shaky foundations. *Psychological Assessment, 13*, 5–35.

Heyman, R. E., & Slep, A. M. S. (2001). The hazards of predicting divorce without cross-validation. *Journal of Marriage and Family, 63*, 473–479.

Heyman, R. E., O'Leary, K. D., & Jouriles, E. (1995). Alcohol and aggressive personality styles: Potentiators of serious physical aggression against wives? *Journal of Family Psychology, 9*, 44–57.

Heymann, S. J. (2000). *The widening gap: Why America's working families are in jeopardy—and what can be done about it*. New York: Basic Books.

Heymann, S. J., & Earle, A. (1999). The impact of welfare reform on parents' ability to care for their children's health. *American Journal of Public Health, 89*, 502–505.

Heymann, S. J., Boynton-Jarrett, R., Carter, P., Bond, J., & Galinsky, E. (2002). Work-family issues and low-income families. Retrieved June 1, 2003, from http://www.economythatworks.net/reports/ford _analysisfinal.pdf.

Hicks, A. M., & Diamond, L. M. (2008). How was your day? Couples' affect when telling and hearing daily events. *Personal Relationships, 15*, 205–228.

Hill, C. D., Thompson, L. W., & Gallagher, D. (1988). The role of anticipatory bereavement in older women's adjustment to widowhood. *The Gerontologist, 28*, 792–796.

Hill, C. T., & Peplau, L. A. (1998). Premarital predictors of relationship outcomes: A 15-year follow-up of the Boston Couples Study. In T. N. Bradbury (Ed.), *The developmental course of marital dysfunction* (pp. 237–278). New York: Cambridge University Press.

Hill, M. (2004, January 12). Post-trauma marital strains expected. Spurned, wives blame 9/11 firemen's widows. *Philadelphia Inquirer*, p. A01.

Hill, M. A. (1988). Marital stability and spouses' shared time. *Journal of Family Issues, 9*, 427–451.

Hill, R. (1949). *Families under stress*. New York: Harper & Row.

Hinde, R. A. (1979). *Towards understanding relationships*. London: Academic Press.

Hirschi, T. (1969). *The causes of delinquency*. Berkeley: University of California Press.

Hirschl, T. A., Altobelli, J., & Rank, M. R. (2003). Does marriage increase the odds of affluence? Exploring the life course probabilities. *Journal of Marriage and Family, 65*, 927–938.

Hoffman, C., Wilcox, L., Gomez, E., & Hollander, C. (1992). Sociometric applications in a corporate environment. *Journal of Group Psychotherapy, Psychodrama and Sociometry, 45*, 3–16.

Holden, K. C., & Smock, P. J. (1991). The economic costs of marital dissolution: Why do women bear a disproportionate cost? *Annual Review of Sociology, 17*, 51–78.

Holmberg, D., & Holmes, J. G. (1994). Reconstruction of relationship memories: A mental models approach. In N. Schwarz & S. Sudman (Eds.), *Autobiographical memory and the validity of retrospective reports* (pp. 267–288). New York: Springer Verlag.

Holmberg, D., Orbuch, T. L., & Veroff, J. (2004). *Thrice told tales: Married couples tell their stories*. Mahwah, NJ: Erlbaum.

Holmes, T. H., & Rahe, R. H. (1967). The Social Readjustment Rating Scale. *Journal of Psychosomatic Research, 11*, 213–218.

Holtzworth-Munroe & Hutchinson (1993). Attributing negative intent to wife behavior: The attributions of maritally violent versus nonviolent men. *Journal of Abnormal Psychology, 102*, 206–211.

Holtzworth-Munroe, A., & Jacobson, N. S. (1985). Causal attributions of married couples: When do they search for causes? What do they conclude when they do? *Journal of Personality and Social Psychology, 48*, 1398–1412.

Holtzworth-Munroe, A., Smutzler, N., & Stuart, G. L. (1998). Demand and withdraw communication among couples experiencing husband violence. *Journal of Consulting and Clinical Psychology, 66*, 731–743.

Homans, G. C. (1958). Social behavior as exchange. *American Journal of Sociology, 63*, 597–606.

Homans, G. C. (1961). *Social behavior: Its elementary forms*. New York: Harcourt, Brace & World.

Hooley, J., & Hahlweg, K. (1989). Marital satisfaction and marital communication in German and English couples. *Behavioral Assessment, 11*, 119–133.

Hornstein, G. A., & Truesdell, S. E. (1988). Development of intimate conversation in close relationships. *Journal of Social and Clinical Psychology, 7*, 49–64.

Hortaçsu, N. (1999). The first year of family- and couple-initiated marriages of a Turkish sample: A longitudinal investigation. *International Journal of Psychology, 34*, 29–41.

Horwitz, A. V., White, H. R., & Howell-White, S. (1996). Becoming married and mental health: A longitudinal study of a cohort of young adults. *Journal of Marriage and Family, 58*, 895–907.

Howe, N., & Ross, H. S. (1990). Socialization, perspective-taking, and the sibling relationship. *Developmental Psychology, 26*, 160–165.

Hsueh, J., Alderson, D. P., Lundquist, E., Michalopoulos, C., Gubits, D., Fein, D., & Knox, V. (2012). The supporting healthy marriage evaluation: Early impacts on low-income families. *OPRE Report 2012-11*. Washington, DC: Office of Planning, Research and Evaluation, Administration for Children and Families, U.S. Department of Health and Human Services.

Hughes, D. K., & Surra, C. A. (2000). The reported influence of research participation on premarital relationships. *Journal of Marriage and Family, 62*, 822–832.

Huston, T. L., & Burgess, R. L. (1979). Social exchange in developing relationships: An overview. In R. L. Burgess & T. L. Huston (Eds.), *Social exchange in developing relationships* (pp. 3–28). New York: Academic Press.

Huston, T. L., & Vangelisti, A. L. (1991). Socioemotional behavior and satisfaction in marital relationships: A longitudinal study. *Journal of Personality and Social Psychology, 61*, 721–733.

Huston, T. L., & Vangelisti, A. L. (1994). Behavioral buffers on the effect of negativity on marital satisfaction: A longitudinal study. *Personal Relationships, 1*, 223–239.

Huston, T. L., Caughlin, J. P., Houts, R. M., Smith, S. E., & George, L. J. (2001). The connubial crucible: Newlywed years as predictors of marital delight, distress, and divorce. *Journal of Personality and Social Psychology, 80*, 237–252.

Huston, T. L., Surra, C. A., Fitzgerald, N. M., & Cate, R. M. (1981). From courtship to marriage: Mate selection as an interpersonal process. In S. Duck & R. Gilmore (Eds.), *Personal relationships 2: Developing personal relationships* (Vol. 2, pp. 53–88). New York: Academic Press.

Hyde, J. S. (2005). The gender similarities hypothesis. *American Psychologist, 60*, 581–592.

Hymel, S., Rubin, K. H., Rowden, L., & LeMare, L. (1990). Children's peer relationships: Longitudinal prediction of internalizing and externalizing problems from middle to late childhood. *Child Development, 61*, 2004–2021.

Ickes, W. (1993). Empathic accuracy. *Journal of Personality, 61*, 587–610.

Ickes, W., & Simpson, J. A. (1997). Managing empathic accuracy in close relationships. In W. J. Ickes (Ed.), *Empathic accuracy* (pp. 218–250). New York: Guilford Press.

Ickes, W., Gesn, P. R., & Graham, T. (2000). Gender differences in empathic accuracy: Differential ability or differential motivation? *Personal Relationships, 7*, 95–109.

Impett, E. A., Peplau, L. A., & Gable, S. L. (2005). Approach and avoidance sexual motives: Implications for personal and interpersonal well-being. *Personal Relationships, 12*, 465–482.

Inoff-Germain, G., Arnold, G., Nottelmann, E. D., Susman, E. J., Cutler, G. B., & Chrousos, G. P. (1988). Relations between hormone levels and observational measures of aggressive behavior of young adolescents in family interactions. *Developmental Psychology, 24*, 129–139.

Irving, L. M., & Berel, S. R. (2001). Comparison of media-literacy programs to strengthen college women's resistance to media images. *Psychology of Women Quarterly, 25*, 103–111.

Isaacson, W. (2007). *Einstein: His life and universe.* New York: Simon & Schuster.

Jacobson, N. S. (1989). The politics of intimacy. *Behavior Therapist, 12*, 29–32.

Jacobson, N. S. (1990). Contributions from psychology to an understanding of marriage. In F. D. Fincham & T. N. Bradbury (Eds.), *The psychology of marriage* (pp. 258–275). New York: Guilford.

Jacobson, N. S. (1994). Rewards and dangers in researching domestic violence. *Family Process, 33*, 81–85.

Jacobson, N. S., & Addis, M. E. (1993). Research on couples and couple therapy: What do we know? Where are we going? *Journal of Consulting and Clinical Psychology, 61*, 85–93.

Jacobson, N. S., & Christensen, A. (1996). *Acceptance and change in couple therapy: A therapist's guide to transforming relationships.* New York: W. W. Norton.

Jacobson, N. S., & Gottman, J. M. (1998). *When men batter women: New insights into ending abusive relationships.* New York: Simon & Schuster.

Jacobson, N. S., & Margolin, G. (1979). *Marital therapy: Strategies based on social learning and behavior exchange principles.* New York: Brunner/Mazel.

Jacobson, N. S., & Moore, D. (1981). Spouses as observers of the events in their relationship. *Journal of Consulting and Clinical Psychology, 49*, 269–277.

Jacobson, N. S., Follette, W. C., & McDonald, D. W. (1982). Reactivity to positive and negative behavior in distressed and nondistressed married couples. *Journal of Consulting and Clinical Psychology, 50*, 706–714.

Jacobson, N. S., Follette, W. C., & Pagel, M. (1986). Predicting who will benefit from behavioral marital therapy. *Journal of Consulting and Clinical Psychology, 54*, 518–522.

Jacobson, N. S., Follette, W. C., Revenstorf, D., Baucom, D. H., Hahlweg, K., & Margolin, G. (1994). Variability in outcome and clinical significance of behavioral marital therapy: A reanalysis of outcome data. *Journal of Consulting and Clinical Psychology, 52*, 497–504.

Jacobson, N. S., McDonald, D. W., Follette, W. C., & Berley, R. A. (1985). Attributional processes in distressed and nondistressed married couples. *Cognitive Therapy and Research, 9*, 35–50.

Jacobson, N. S., Schmaling, K. B., & Holtzworth-Munroe, A. (1987). Component analysis of behavioral marital therapy: 2-year follow-up and prediction of relapse. *Journal of Marital and Family Therapy, 13*, 187–195.

Jaffee, S., & Hyde, J. S. (2000). Gender differences in moral orientation: A meta-analysis. *Psychological Bulletin, 126*, 703–726.

Jankowiak, W. R., & Fischer, E. F. (1992). A cross-cultural perspective on romantic love. *Ethnology, 31*, 149–155.

Jekeilek, S. M. (1998). Parental conflict, marital disruption and children's emotional well-being. *Social Forces, 76*, 905–935.

Jin, G. Z., & Xu, L. C. (2006). Matchmaking means and marriage quality: Evidence from China. Retrieved December 26, 2008 from www.glue.umd.edu/~ginger/research/jin-xu-0906.pdf

John, O. P., Hampson, S. E., & Goldberg, L. R. (1991). The basic level in personality-trait hierarchies: Studies of trait use and accessibility in different contexts. *Journal of Personality and Social Psychology, 60*, 348–361.

Johnson, D. J., & Rusbult, C. E. (1989). Resisting temptation: Devaluation of alternative partners as a means of maintaining commitment in close relationships. *Journal of Personality and Social Psychology, 57*, 967–980.

Johnson, D. R., & Booth, A. (1998). Marital quality: A product of the dyadic environment or individual factors? *Social Forces, 76*, 883–904.

Johnson, D. R., Amoloza, T. O., & Booth, A. (1992). Stability and developmental change in marital quality: A three-wave panel analysis. *Journal of Marriage and Family, 54*, 582–594.

Johnson, M. D. (2012). Healthy marriage initiatives: On the need for empiricism in policy implementation. *American Psychologist, 67*, 296–308.

Johnson, M. D., Cohan, C. L., Davila, J., Lawrence, E., Rogge, R. D., Karney, B. R., Sullivan, K. T., & Bradbury, T. N. (2005). Problem-solving skills and affective expressions as predictors of change in marital satisfaction. *Journal of Consulting and Clinical Psychology, 73*, 15–27.

Johnson, M. P. (1973). Commitment: A conceptual structure and empirical application. *Sociological Quarterly, 14*, 395–406.

Johnson, M. P. (2011). Gender and types of intimate partner violence: A response to an anti-feminist literature review. *Aggression and Violent Behavior, 16,* 289–296.

Johnson, M. P. (1995). Patriarchal terrorism and common couple violence: Two forms of violence against women. *Journal of Marriage and Family, 57,* 283–294.

Johnson, M. P. (2006). Violence and abuse in personal relationships: Conflict, terror, and resistance in intimate partnerships. In A. L. Vangelisti & D. Perlman (Eds.), *The Cambridge handbook of personal relationships* (pp. 557–576). New York: Cambridge University Press.

Johnson, M. P. (2008). *A typology of domestic violence.* Lebanon, NH: Northeastern University Press.

Johnson, M. P., & Ferraro, K. J. (2000). Research on domestic violence in the 1990s: Making distinctions. *Journal of Marriage and Family, 62,* 948–963.

Johnson, S. M. (2004). *The practice of emotionally focused couple therapy: Creating connection* (2nd ed.). New York: Brunner-Routledge.

Johnson, S. M., & Denton, W. (2002). Emotionally focused couple therapy: Creating secure connections. In A. S. Gurman & N. S. Jacobson (Eds.), *Clinical handbook of couple therapy* (3rd ed., pp. 221–250). New York: Guilford.

Johnson, S. M., & Greenman, P. S. (2006). The path to a secure bond: Emotionally focused couple therapy. *Journal of Clinical Psychology: In Session, 62,* 597–609.

Johnson, S. M. (1986) Bonds or bargains: Relationship paradigms and their significance for marital therapy. *Journal of Marital and Family Therapy, 12,* 259–267.

Joiner, T. E., & Metalsky, G. I. (1995). A prospective test of an integrative interpersonal theory of depression: A naturalistic study of college roommates. *Journal of Personality and Social Psychology, 69,* 778–788.

Jones, D. (1995). Sexual selection, physical attractiveness, and facial neoteny: Cross-cultural evidence and implications. *Current Anthropology, 36,* 723–748.

Jones, E. E., & Archer, R. L. (1976). Are there special effects of personalistic self-disclosure? *Journal of Experimental Social Psychology, 12,* 180–193.

Jose, A., Daniel O'Leary, K., & Moyer, A. (2010). Does premarital cohabitation predict subsequent marital stability and marital quality? A meta-analysis. *Journal of Marriage and Family, 72,* 105–116.

Jourard, S. (1959). Self-disclosure and other-cathexis. *Journal of Abnormal & Social Psychology, 59,* 428–431.

Jourard, S. (1964). *The transparent self: Self-disclosure and well-being.* Princeton, NJ: Van Nostrand.

Jourard, S. (1971). *Self-disclosure: An experimental analysis of the transparent self.* New York: Wiley.

Joyner, K., & Udry, J. R. (2000). You don't bring me anything but down: Adolescent romance and depression. *Journal of Health and Social Behavior, 41,* 369–391.

Julien, D., & Markman, H. J. (1991). Social support and social networks as determinants of individual and marital outcomes. *Journal of Social and Personal Relationships, 8,* 549–568.

Julien, D., Arellano, C., & Turgeon, L. (1997). Gender issues in heterosexual, gay, and lesbian couples. In W. K. Halford & H. J. Markman (Eds.), *Clinical handbook of marriage and couples interventions* (pp. 108–127). New York: Wiley.

Julien, D., Markman, H. J., Léveillé, S., Chartrand, E., & Begin, J. (1994). Networks' support and interference with regard to marriage: Disclosures of marital problems to confidants. *Journal of Family Psychology, 8,* 16–31.

Kahn, M. (1970). Nonverbal communication and marital satisfaction. *Family Process, 9,* 449–456.

Kaiser Family Foundation (2001, November). Inside-OUT: A report on the experiences of lesbians, gays, and bisexuals in America and the public's views on issues and policies related to sexual orientation. Retrieved May 20, 2009, from http://www.kff.org

Kalick, S. M., & Hamilton, T. E. (1986). The matching hypothesis reexamined. *Journal of Personality and Social Psychology, 51,* 673–682.

Kalick, S. M., Zebrowitz, L. A., Langlois, J. H., & Johnson, R. M. (1998). Does human facial attractiveness honestly advertise health? Longitudinal data on an evolutionary question. *Psychological Science, 9,* 8–13.

Kalush, W., & Sloman, L. (2006). *The secret life of Houdini: The making of America's first superhero.* New York: Atria Books.

Kaplan, R. M., & Kronick, R. G. (2006). Marital status and longevity in the United States population. *Journal of Epidemiology and Community Health, 60,* 760–765.

Karney, B. R., & Bradbury, T. N. (1995). The longitudinal course of marital quality and stability: A review of theory, methods, and research. *Psychological Bulletin, 118,* 3–34.

Karney, B. R., & Bradbury, T. N. (2000). Attributions in marriage: State or trait? A growth curve analysis. *Journal of Personality and Social Psychology, 78,* 295–309.

Karney, B. R., & Coombs, R. H. (2000). Memory bias in long-term close relationships: Consistency or improvement? *Personality and Social Psychology Bulletin, 26,* 959–970.

Karney, B. R., Bradbury, T. N., Fincham, F. D., & Sullivan, K. T. (1994). The role of negative affectivity in the association between attributions and marital satisfaction. *Journal of Personality and Social Psychology, 66*, 413–424.

Karney, B. R., Davila, J., Cohan, C. L., Sullivan, K. T., Johnson, M. D., & Bradbury, T. N. (1995). An empirical investigation of sampling strategies in marital research. *Journal of Marriage and Family, 57*, 909–920.

Kasen, S., Chen, H., Sneed, J., Crawford, T., & Cohen, P. (2006). Social role and birth cohort influences on gender-linked personality traits in women: A 20-year longitudinal analysis. *Journal of Personality and Social Psychology, 91*, 944–958.

Kaysen, S. (1993). *Girl, interrupted*. New York: Random House.

Kayser, K. (1993). *When love dies: The process of marital disaffection*. New York: Guilford.

Kearns, J. N., & Leonard, K. E. (2004). Social networks, structural interdependence, and marital quality over the transition to marriage: A prospective analysis. *Journal of Family Psychology, 18*, 383–395.

Keim, J., & Lappin, J. (2002). Structural-strategic marital therapy. In A. S. Gurman & N. S. Jacobson (Eds.), *Clinical handbook of couple therapy* (3rd ed., pp. 86–117). New York: Guilford.

Kellett, J. M. (2000). Older adult sexuality. In L. T. Szuchman & F. Muscarella (Eds.), *Psychological perspectives on human sexuality* (pp. 355–382). Hoboken, NJ: Wiley.

Kelley, D. L., & Burgoon, J. K. (1991). Understanding marital satisfaction and couple type as functions of relational expectations. *Human Communication Research, 18*, 40–69.

Kelley, H. H. (1967). Attribution theory in social psychology. In D. Levine (Ed.), *Nebraska symposium on motivation* (Vol. 15, pp. 192–238). Lincoln: University of Nebraska Press.

Kelley, H. H. (1979). *Personal Relationships: Their Structures and Processes*. Hillsdale, NJ: Erlbaum.

Kelley, H. H., Berscheid, E., Christensen, A., Harvey, J. H., Huston, T. L., Levinger, G., et al. (1983). Analyzing close relationships. In H. H. Kelley, E. Berscheid, A. Christensen, J. H. Harvey, T. L. Huston, G. Levinger, E. McClintock, L. A. Peplau & D. R. Peterson (Eds.), *Close relationships* (pp. 20–67). New York: Freeman.

Kelley, H. H., Berscheid, E., Christensen, A., Harvey, J. H., Huston, T. L., Levinger, G., McClintock, E., Peplau, L. A., & Peterson, D. R. (1983). *Close relationships*. New York: Freeman.

Kelly, E. L., & Conley, J. J. (1987). Personality and compatibility: A prospective analysis of marital stability and marital satisfaction. *Journal of Personality and Social Psychology, 52*, 27–40.

Keltner, D., Gruenfeld, D. H., & Anderson, C. (2003). Power, approach, and inhibition. *Psychological Review*, 110, 265–284.

Kennedy, D. P. (2006, July 17). *Reciprocation of adolescent romantic partner nominations and the implications for depression etiology in adolescents*. Paper presented at the Add Health Users Conference, Bethesda, MD, July 17, 2006.

Kenney, C. T., & McLanahan, S. S. (2006). Why are cohabiting relationships more violent than marriages? *Demography, 43*, 127–140.

Kenny, D. A., & Acitelli, L. K. (1994). Measuring similarity in couples. *Journal of Family Psychology, 8*, 417–431.

Kenny, D. A., & LaVoie, L. (1982). Reciprocity of interpersonal attraction: A confirmed hypothesis. *Social Psychology Quarterly, 45*, 54–58.

Kenrick, D. T., & Keefe, R. C. (1992). Age preferences in mates reflect sex differences in human reproductive strategies. *Behavioral and Brain Sciences, 15*, 75–133.

Kenrick, D. T., Gutierres, S. E., & Goldberg, L. L. (1989). Influence of popular erotica on judgments of strangers and mates. *Journal of Experimental Social Psychology, 25*, 159–167.

Kenrick, D. T., Keefe, R. C., Bryan, A., Barr, A., & Brown, S. (1995). Age preference and mate choice among homosexuals and heterosexuals: A case for modular psychological mechanisms. *Journal of Personality and Social Psychology, 69*, 1166–1172.

Kenrick, D. T., Sadalla, E. K., Groth, G., & Trost, M. R. (1990). Evolution, traits, and the stages of human courtship: Qualifying the parental investment model. *Journal of Personality, 58*, 97–116.

Kenrick, D. T., Groth, G. E., Trost, M. R., & Sadalla, E.K. (1993). Integrating evolutionary and social exchange perspectives on relationships: Effects of gender, self-appraisal, and involvement level on mate selection criteria. *Journal of Personality and Social Psychology, 64*, 951–969.

Kephart, W. M. (1967). Some correlates of romantic love. *Journal of Marriage and Family*, 29, 470–474.

Kern, H. L. (2010). The political consequences out of marriage in Great Britain. *Electoral Studies, 29*, 249–258.

Kiecolt-Glaser, J. K., & Newton, T. L. (2001). Marriage and health: His and hers. *Psychological Bulletin, 127*, 472–503.

Kiecolt-Glaser, J. K., Bane, C., Glaser, R., & Malarkey, W. B. (2003). Love, marriage, and divorce: Newlyweds' stress hormones foreshadow relationship changes. *Journal of Consulting and Clinical Psychology, 71*, 176–188.

Kiecolt-Glaser, J. K., Loving, T. J., Stowell, J. R., Malarkey, W. B., Lemeshow, S., Dickinson, S. L.,

& Glaser, R. (2005). Hostile marital interactions, proinflammatory cytokine production, and wound healing. *Archives of General Psychiatry, 62*, 1377–1384.

Kiecolt-Glaser, J. K., Malarkey, W. B., Chee, M., Newton, T., Caccioppo, J. T., Mao, H.-Y., & Glaser, R. (1993). Negative behavior during marital conflict is associated with immunological down-regulation. *Psychosomatic Medicine, 55*, 395–409.

Kiecolt-Glaser, J. K., Newton, T., Caccioppo, J. T., MacCallum, R. C. Glaser, R. & Malarkey, W. B. (1996). Marital conflict and endocrine function: Are men really more physiologically affected than women? *Journal of Consulting and Clinical Psychology, 64*, 324–332.

Kim, H. J., & Stiff, J. B. (1991). Social networks and the development of close relationships. *Human Communication Research, 18*, 70–91.

Kim, H. S., Sherman, D. K., & Taylor, S. E. (2008). Culture and social support. *American Psychologist, 63*, 518–526.

Kim, H. K., Capaldi, D. M., & Crosby, L. (2007). Generalizability of Gottman and colleagues' affective process models of couples' relationship outcomes. *Journal of Marriage and Family, 69*, 55–72.

Kim, H. K., Laurent, H. K., Capaldi, D. M., & Feingold, A. (2008). Men's aggression toward women: A 10-year panel study. *Journal of Marriage and Family, 70*, 1169–1187.

King, K. B., Reis, H. T., Porter, L. A., & Norsen, L. H. (1993). Social support and long-term recovery from coronary artery surgery: Effects on patients and spouses. *Health Psychology, 12*, 56–63.

King, V. (2002). Parental divorce and interpersonal trust in adult offspring. *Journal of Marriage and Family, 64*, 642–656.

Kinnunen, U., & Pulkkinen, L. (2003). Childhood socio-emotional characteristics as antecedents of marital stability and quality. *European Psychologist, 8*, 223–237.

Kirkpatrick, L. A., & Hazan, C. (1994). Attachment styles and close relationships: A four-year prospective study. *Personal Relationships, 1*, 123–142.

Kirkwood, C. (1993). *Leaving abusive partners: From the scars of survival to the wisdom for change.* Newbury Park, CA: Sage.

Kitson, G. C. (1992). *Portrait of divorce: Adjustment to marital breakdown.* New York: Guilford.

Kitson, G. C., Holmes, W. M., & Sussman, M. B. (1983). Withdrawing divorce petitions: A predictive test of the exchange model of divorce. *Journal of Divorce, 7*, 51–66.

Klein, K. J. K., & Hodges, S. D. (2001). Gender differences, motivation, and empathic accuracy: When it pays to understand. *Personality and Social Psychology Bulletin, 27*, 720–730.

Klinetob, N. A., & Smith, D. A. (1996). Demand-withdraw communication in marital interaction: Tests of interspousal contingency and gender role hypotheses. *Journal of Marriage and Family, 58*, 945–957.

Kling, C. C. (2000, October 29). Follow these simple instructions. *New York Times*.

Klohnen, E. C., & Bera, S. (1998). Behavioral and experiential patterns of avoidantly and securely attached women across adulthood: A 31-year longitudinal perspective. *Journal of Personality and Social Psychology, 74*, 211–223.

Klohnen, E. C., & Mendelsohn, G. A. (1998). Partner selection for personality characteristics: A couple-centered approach. *Personality and Social Psychology Bulletin, 24*, 268–278.

Klusmann, D. (2002). Sexual motivation and the duration of partnership. *Archives of Sexual Behavior, 31*, 275–287.

Knapp, M. L., & Vangelisti, A. L. (1991). *Interpersonal communication and human relationships (2nd ed.).* Boston: Allyn & Bacon.

Knee, C. R. (1998). Implicit theories of relationships: Assessment and prediction of romantic relationship initiation, coping and longevity. *Journal of Personality and Social Psychology, 74*, 360–370.

Knobloch, L. K., & Carpenter-Theune, K. E. (2004). Topic avoidance in developing romantic relationships: Associations with intimacy and relational uncertainty. *Communication Research, 31*, 173–205.

Kobak, R. R., & Hazan, C. (1991). Attachment in marriage: Effects of security and accuracy of working models. *Journal of Personality and Social Psychology, 60*, 861–869.

Koerner, K., & Jacobson, N. S. (1994). Emotion and behavioral couple therapy. In S. M. Johnson & L. S. Greenberg (Eds.), *The heart of the matter: Perspectives on emotion in marital therapy* (pp. 207–226). New York: Brunner/Mazel.

Kollock, P., Blumstein, P., & Schwartz, P. (1985). Sex and power in interaction: Conversational privileges and duties. *American Sociological Review, 50*, 34–60.

Kosfeld, M., Heinrichs, M., Zak, P. J., Fischbacher, U., & Fehr, E. (2005). Oxytocin increases trust in humans. *Nature, 435*, 673–676.

Kowal, A., Kramer, L., Krull, J. L., & Crick, N. R. (2002). Children's perceptions of the fairness of parental preferential treatment and their socio-emotional well-being. *Journal of Family Psychology, 16*, 297–306.

Kreider, R. M., & Fields, J. M. (2001). Number, timing, and duration of marriages and divorces: Fall 1996. In *Current Population Reports* (pp. 70–80). Washington, DC: U.S. Census Bureau.

Kring, A. M., & Gordon, A. H. (1998). Sex differences in emotion: Expression, experience, and physiology. *Journal of Personality and Social Psychology, 74*, 686–703.

Krokoff, L. J., Gottman, J. M., & Roy, A. K. (1988). Blue-collar and white-collar marital interaction and communication orientation. *Journal of Social and Personal Relationships, 5*, 201–221.

Ku, L., Sonenstein, F. L., & Pleck, J. H. (1994). The dynamics of young men's condom use during and across relationships. *Family Planning Perspectives, 26*, 246–251.

Kumar, P., & Dhyani, J. (1996). Marital adjustment: A study of some related factors. *Indian Journal of Clinical Psychology, 23*, 112–116.

Kunda, Z. (1990). The case for motivated reasoning. *Psychological Bulletin, 108*, 480–498.

Kupersmidt, J. B., & Coie, J. D. (1990). Preadolescent peer status, aggression, and school adjustment as predictors of externalizing problems in adolescence. *Child Development, 61*, 1350–1362.

Kupersmidt, J. B., DeRosier, M. E., & Patterson, C. P. (1995). Similarity as the basis for children's friendships: The roles of sociometric status, aggressive and withdrawn behavior, academic achievement and demographic characteristics. *Journal of Social and Personal Relationships, 12*, 439–452.

Kupperbusch, C., Levenson, R. W., & Ebling, R. (2003). Predicting husbands' and wives' retirement satisfaction from the emotional qualities of marital interaction. *Journal of Social and Personal Relationships, 20*, 335–354.

Kurdek, L. A. (1991). Correlates of relationship satisfaction in cohabiting gay and lesbian couples. *Journal of Personality and Social Psychology, 61*, 910–922.

Kurdek, L. A. (1992). Assumptions versus standards: The validity of two relationship cognitions in heterosexual and homosexual couples. *Journal of Family Psychology, 6*, 164–170.

Kurdek, L. A. (1993). The allocation of household labor in gay, lesbian, and heterosexual married couples. *Journal of Social Issues, 49*, 127–139.

Kurdek, L. A. (1998). Relationship outcomes and their predictors: Longitudinal evidence from heterosexual married, gay cohabiting, and lesbian cohabiting couples. *Journal of Marriage and Family, 60*, 553–568.

Kurdek, L. A. (1999). The nature and predictors of the trajectory of change in marital quality for husbands and wives over the first 10 years of marriage. *Developmental Psychology, 35*, 1283–1296.

Kurdek, L. A. (2001). Differences between heterosexual-nonparent couples, and gay, lesbian and heterosexual parent couples. *Journal of Family Issues, 22*, 727–754.

Kurdek, L. A. (2002). On being insecure about the assessment of attachment styles. *Journal of Social and Personal Relationships, 19*, 811–834.

Kurdek, L. A. (2004). Are gay and lesbian cohabiting couples *really* different from heterosexual married couples? *Journal of Marriage and the Family, 66*, 880–900.

Kurdek, L. A. (2005). What do we know about gay and lesbian couples? *Current Directions in Psychological Science, 14*, 251–254.

Kurz, D. (1993). Physical assaults by husbands: A major social problem. In R. Gelles & D. R. Loseke (Eds.), *Current controversies on family violence* (pp. 88–103). Newbury Park, CA: Sage.

L'Abate, L. (1990). *Building family competence: Primary and secondary prevention strategies*. Beverly Hills, CA: Sage.

La Guardia, J. G., Ryan, R. M., Couchman, C. E., & Deci, E. L. (2000). Within-person variation in security of attachment: A self-determination theory perspective on attachment, need fulfillment, and well-being. *Journal of Personality and Social Psychology, 79*, 367–384.

Lackey, C., & Williams, K. R. (1995). Social bonding and the cessation of partner violence across generations. *Journal of Marriage and Family, 57*, 295–305.

Lackenbauer, S. D., & Campbell, L. (2012). Measuring up: The unique emotional and regulatory outcomes of different perceived partner-ideal discrepancies in romantic relationships. *Journal of Personality and Social Psychology, 103*, 427–488.

LaFrance, M., Hecht, M. A., & Paluck, E. L. (2003). The contingent smile: A meta-analysis of sex differences in smiling. *Psychological Bulletin, 129*, 305–334.

Lamb, M. E. (1997). The development of father-infant relationships. In M. E. Lamb (Ed.), *The role of the father in child development* (3rd ed., pp. 104–120). Hoboken, NJ: Wiley.

Lambert, T. A., Kahn, A. S., & Apple, K. J. (2003). Pluralistic ignorance and hooking up. *Journal of Sex Research, 40*, 129–133.

Lamm, H., Wiesmann, U., & Keller, K. (1998). Subjective determinants of attraction: Self-perceived causes of the rise and decline of liking, love, and being in love. *Personal Relationships, 5*, 91–104.

Lamme, S., Dykstra, P. A., & Broese Van Groenou, M. I. (1996). Rebuilding the network: New relationships in widowhood. *Personal Relationships, 3*, 337–349.

Langlois, J. H., Kalakanis, L., Rubenstein, A. J., Larson, A., Hallam, M., & Smoot, M. (2000). Maxims or myths of beauty? A meta-analytic and theoretical review. *Psychological Bulletin, 126,* 390–423.

Langlois, J. H., Ritter, J. M., Roggman, L. A., & Vaughn, L. S. (1991). Facial diversity and infant preferences for attractive faces. *Developmental Psychology, 27,* 79–84.

Langlois, J. H., Roggman, L. A., & Musselman, L. (1994). What is average and what is not average about attractive faces? *Psychological Science, 5,* 214–220.

Langston, C. A. (1994). Capitalizing on and coping with daily-life events: Expressive responses to positive events. *Journal of Personality and Social Psychology, 67,* 1112–1125.

Larson, J. H., Anderson, S. M., Holman, T. B., & Niemann, B. K. (1998). A longitudinal study of the effects of premarital communication, relationship stability, and self-esteem on sexual satisfaction in the first year of marriage. *Journal of Sex and Marital Therapy, 24,* 193–206.

Larson, J. H., Wilson, S. M., & Beley, R. (1994). The impact of job insecurity on marital and family relationships. *Family Relations, 43,* 138–143.

Larson, R. W., & Almeida, D. M. (1999). Emotional transmission in the daily lives of families: A new paradigm for studying family process. *Journal of Marriage and Family, 61,* 5–20.

Larson, R. W., Clore, G. L., & Wood, G. A. (1999). The emotions of romantic relationships: Do they wreak havoc on adolescents? In W. Furman, B. B. Brown & C. Feiring (Eds.), *The development of romantic relationships in adolescence* (pp. 19–49). New York: Cambridge University Press.

Larson, R., & Richards, M. H. (1994). *Divergent realities: The emotional lives of mothers, fathers, and adolescents.* New York: Basic Books.

LaSala, M. C. (2004). Monogamy of the heart: Extra-dyadic sex and gay male couples. *Journal of Gay and Lesbian Social Services, 17,* 1–24.

Latty-Mann, H., & Davis, K. E. (1996). Attachment theory and partner choice: Preference and actuality. *Journal of Social and Personal Relationships, 13,* 5–23.

Laub, J. H., Nagin, D. S., & Sampson, R. J. (1998). Trajectories of change in criminal offending: Good marriages and the desistance process. *American Sociological Review, 63,* 225–238.

Laurenceau, J.-P., Barrett, L. F., & Pietromonaco, P. R. (1998). Intimacy as an interpersonal process: The importance of self-disclosure and perceived partner responsiveness in interpersonal exchanges. *Journal of Personality and Social Psychology, 74,* 1238–1251.

Laurenceau, J.-P., Barrett, L. F., & Rovine, M. J. (2005). The interpersonal process model of intimacy in marriage: A daily-diary and multilevel modeling approach. *Journal of Family Psychology, 19,* 314–323.

Lauster, N. (2008). Better homes and families: Housing markets and young couple stability in Sweden. *Journal of Marriage and Family, 70,* 891–903.

Lavee, Y., McCubbin, H. I., & Olson, D. H. (1987). The effect of stressful life events and transitions on family functioning and well-being. *Journal of Marriage and Family, 49,* 857–873.

Lavee, Y., McCubbin, H. I., & Patterson, J. M. (1985). The Double ABCX Model of Family Stress and Adaptation: An empirical test by analysis of structural equations with latent variables. *Journal of Marriage and Family, 47,* 811–825.

Lawrence, E., & Bradbury, T. N. (2007). Trajectories of change in physical aggression and marital satisfaction. *Journal of Family Psychology, 21,* 236–247.

Lawrence, E., Pederson, A., Bunde, M., Barry, R. A., Brock, R. L., Fazio, E., Mulryan, L., Hunt, S., Madsen, L., & Dzankovic, S. (2008). Objective ratings of relationship skills across multiple domains as predictors of marital satisfaction trajectories. *Journal of Social and Personal Relationships, 25,* 445–466.

Lawrence, E., Rothman, A. D., Cobb, R. J., Rothman, M. T., & Bradbury, T. N. (2008). Marital satisfaction across the transition to parenthood. *Journal of Family Psychology, 22,* 41–50.

Leary, M. R., Tambor, E. S., Terdal, S. K., & Downs, D. L. (1995). Self-esteem as an interpersonal monitor: The sociometer hypothesis. *Journal of Personality and Social Psychology, 68,* 518–530.

Lebow, J. L., Chambers, A. L., Christensen, A., & Johnson, S. M. (2012). Research on the treatment of couple distress. *Journal of Marital and Family Therapy, 38,* 145–168.

Lederer, W. J., & Jackson, D. D. (1968). *The mirages of marriage.* New York: W. W. Norton.

Lee, G. R. (1979). Effects of social networks on the family. In W. R. Burr, R. Hill, F. I. Nye & I. L. Reiss (Eds.), *Contemporary theories about the family: Research-based theories* (Vol. 1, pp. 27–56). New York: Free Press.

Lee, G. R., & DeMaris, A. (2007). Widowhood, gender, and depression: A longitudinal analysis. *Research on Aging, 29,* 56–72.

Lee, G. R., & Sheehan, C. L. (1989). Retirement and marital satisfaction. *Journal of Gerontology: Social Sciences, 44,* s226–s230.

Lee, G. R., Willetts, M. C., & Seccombe, K. (1998). Widowhood and depression: Gender differences. *Research on Aging, 20,* 611–630.

Lee, L., Loewenstein, G. F., Ariely, D., Hong, J., & Young, J. (2008). If I'm not hot, are you hot or not? Physical-attractiveness evaluations and dating preferences as a function of one's own attractiveness. *Psychological Science, 19,* 669–677.

Legler, G. (2005). *On the ice: An intimate portrait of life at McMurdo Station, Antarctica.* Minneapolis: Milkweed Editions.

Lehmiller, J. J., & Agnew, C. R. (2006). Marginalized relationships: The impact of social disapproval on romantic relationship commitment. *Personality and Social Psychology Bulletin, 32,* 40–51.

Lehmiller, J. J., & Agnew, C. R. (2007). Perceived marginalization and the prediction of romantic relationship stability. *Journal of Marriage and Family, 69,* 1036–1049.

Lemay, E. P., Jr., & Dudley, K. L. (2011). Caution: Fragile! Regulating the interpersonal security of chronically secure partners. *Journal of Personality and Social Psychology, 100,* 681–702.

Lempers, J. D., & Clark-Lempers, D. S. (1993). A functional comparison of same-sex and opposite sex friendships during adolescence. *Journal of Adolescent Research, 81,* 89–108.

Leon, G. R. (2005). Men and women in space. *Aviation, Space, and Environmental Medicine, 76,* Section II, B84–B88.

Leonard, K. E., & Quigley, B. (1999). Drinking and marital aggression in newlyweds: An event-based analysis of drinking and the occurrence of husband marital aggression. *Journal of Studies on Alcohol, 60,* 537–545.

Leonard, K. E., & Roberts, L. (1998). The effects of alcohol on the marital interactions of aggressive and nonaggressive husbands and their wives. *Journal of Abnormal Psychology, 107,* 602–615.

Lerman, R. I. (2002). *Married and unmarried parenthood and economic well-being: A dynamic analysis of a recent cohort.* Washington, DC: Urban Institute. Retrieved October 23, 2008 from http://www.urban.org/publications/410540.html

Leslie, L. A., Huston, T. L., & Johnson, M. P. (1986). Parental reactions to dating relationships: Do they make a difference? *Journal of Marriage and Family, 48,* 57–66.

LeVay, S., & Valente, S. M. (2006). *Human sexuality* (2nd ed.). Sunderland MA: Sinauer Associates.

Levenson, R. W., & Gottman, J. M. (1983). Marital interaction: Physiological linkage and affective exchange. *Journal of Personality and Social Psychology, 45,* 587–597.

Levenson, R. W., & Gottman, J. M. (1985). Physiological and affective predictors of change in relationship satisfaction. *Journal of Personality and Social Psychology, 49,* 85–94.

Levenson, R. W., Carstensen, L. L., & Gottman, J. M. (1993). Long-term marriage: Age, gender, and satisfaction. *Psychology and Aging, 8,* 301–313.

Levenson, R. W., Carstensen, L. L., Friesen, W. V., & Ekman, P. (1991). Emotion, physiology, and expression in old age. *Psychology and Aging, 6,* 28–35.

Lever, J. (1994, August 23). Sexual revelations. *The Advocate,* 17–24.

Leverentz, A. M. (2006). The love of a good man? Romantic relationships as a source of support or hindrance for female ex-offenders. *Journal of Research in Crime and Delinquency, 43,* 459–488.

Levine, R., Sato, S., Hashimoto, T., & Verma, J. (1995). Love and marriage in eleven cultures. *Journal of Cross-Cultural Psychology, 26,* 554–571.

Levinger, G. (1986). Compatibility in relationships. *Social Science, 71,* 173–177.

Levinger, G. (1976). A social psychological perspective on marital dissolution. *Journal of Social Issues, 32,* 21–47.

Levinger, G. (1966). Sources of marital dissatisfaction among applicants for divorce. *American Journal of Orthopsychiatry, 36,* 803–807.

Levy, S. Y., Wamboldt, F. S., & Fiese, B. H. (1997). Family-of-origin experiences and conflict resolution behaviors of young adult dating couples. *Family Process, 36,* 297–310.

Lewin, K. (1948). The background of conflict in marriage. *Resolving social conflicts: Selected papers on group dynamics.* New York: Harper & Row.

Lewis, R. A. (1973). A longitudinal test of a developmental framework for premarital dyadic formation. *Journal of Marriage and Family, 35,* 16–25.

Lewis, R. A., & Spanier, G. B. (1979). Theorizing about the quality and stability of marriage. In W. R. Burr, R. Hill, F. I. Nye, & I. L. Reiss (Eds.), *Contemporary theories about the family: Research-based theories* (pp. 268–294). New York: Free Press.

Lewis, R. A., & Spanier, G. B. (1982). Marital quality, marital stability, and social exchange. In F. I. Nye (Ed.), *Family relationships: Rewards and costs* (pp. 49–65). Beverly Hills, CA: Sage.

Liberman, R. P. (1970). Behavioral approaches to family and couple therapy. *American Journal of Orthopsychiatry, 40,* 106–118.

Lichter, D. T., Qian, Z. C., & Mellott, L. M. (2006). Marriage or dissolution? Union transitions among poor cohabiting women *Demography, 43,* 223–240.

Lie, G., Schilit, R., Bush, J., Montague, M., & Reyes, L. (1991). Lesbians in currently aggressive relationships: How frequently do they report aggressive past relationships? *Violence and Victims, 6,* 121–135.

Lillard, A. S., Lerner, M. D., Hopkins, E. J., Dore, R. A., Smith, E. D., & Palmquist, C. M. (2013). The impact of pretend play on children's development:

A review of the evidence. *Psychological Bulletin, 139*, 1–34.

Lindahl, K., Clements, M., & Markman, H. (1998). The development of marriage: A 9-year perspective. In T. N. Bradbury (Ed.), *The developmental course of marital dysfunction* (pp. 205–236). Cambridge: Cambridge University Press.

Lindau, S. T., Schumm, L. P., Laumann, E. O., Levinson, W., O'Muircheartaigh, C. A., & Waite, L. J. (2007). A study of sexuality and health among older adults in the United States. *New England Journal of Medicine, 357*, 762–774.

Lippa, R. A. (1991). Some psychometric characteristics of gender diagnosticity measures: Reliability, validity, consistency across domains and relationship to the Big Five. *Journal of Personality and Social Psychology, 61*, 1000–1011.

Lippa, R. A. (2005). *Gender, nature, and nurture* (2nd ed.). Mahwah, NJ: Erlbaum.

Lippa, R. A. (2007). The relation between sex drive and sexual attraction to men and women: A cross-national study of heterosexual, bisexual, and homosexual men and women. *Archives of Sexual Behavior, 36*, 209–222.

Lippa, R. A. (2008). Sex differences and sexual orientation differences in personality: Findings from the BBC Internet survey. *Archives of Sexual Behavior, 37*, 173–187.

Lippert, T., & Prager, K. J. (2001). Daily experiences in intimacy: A study of couples. *Personal Relationships, 8*, 283–298.

Litzinger, S., & Gordon, K. C. (2005). Exploring relationships among communication, sexual satisfaction, and marital satisfaction. *Journal of Sex and Marital Therapy, 31*, 409–424.

Lloyd, S. A., & Emery, B. C. (1994). Physically aggressive conflict in romantic relationships. In D. Cahn (Ed.), *Conflict in personal relationships* (pp. 27–46). Mahwah, NJ: Erlbaum.

Lloyd, S. A., & Emery, B. C. (2000). *The dark side of courtship: Physical and sexual aggression*. Thousand Oaks, CA: Sage.

Locke, H. J., & Wallace, K. M. (1959). Short marital adjustment prediction tests: Their reliability and validity. *Marriage and Family Living, 21*, 251–255.

Lockwood, R. L., Kitzmann, K. M., & Cohen, R. (2001). The impact of sibling warmth and conflict on children's social competence with peers. *Child Study Journal, 31*, 47–69.

Loftus, E. F. (1979). The malleability of human memory. *American Scientist, 67*, 312–320.

Long, E. C. J., Cate, R. M., Fehsenfeld, D. A., & Williams, K. M. (1996). A longitudinal assessment of a measure of premarital sexual conflict. *Family Relations, 45*, 302–308.

Lorber, M. F., & O'Leary, K. D. (2004). Predictors of the persistence of male aggression in early marriage. *Journal of Family Violence, 19*, 329–338.

Lucas, R. E. (2005). Time does not heal all wounds: A longitudinal study of reaction and adaptation to divorce. *Psychological Science, 16*, 945–950.

Lucas, R. E., Clark, A. E., Georgellis, Y., & Diener, E. (2003). Reexamining adaptation and the set point model of happiness: Reactions to changes in marital status. *Journal of Personality and Social Psychology, 84*, 527–539.

Lundy, D. E., Tan, J., & Cunningham, M. R. (1998). Heterosexual romantic preferences: The importance of humor and physical attractiveness for different types of relationships. *Personal Relationships, 5*, 311–325.

Luo, S., & Klohnen, E. C. (2005). Assortative mating and marital quality in newlyweds: A couple-centered approach. *Journal of Personality and Social Psychology, 88*, 304–326.

Lydon, J. E., Fitzsimons, G. M., & Naidoo, L. (2003). Devaluation versus enhancement of attractive alternatives: A critical test using the calibration paradigm. *Personality and Social Psychology Bulletin, 29*, 349–359.

Lydon, J. E., Meana, M., Sepinwall, D., Richards, N., & Mayman, S. (1999). The commitment calibration hypothesis: When do people devalue attractive alternatives? *Personality and Social Psychology Bulletin, 25*, 152–161.

Lydon, J. E., Menzies-Toman, D., Burton, K., & Bell, C. (2008). If-then contingencies and the differential effects of the availability of an attractive alternative on relationship maintenance for men and women. *Journal of Personality and Social Psychology, 95*, 50–65.

Lykins, A. D., Meana, M., & Strauss, G. P. (2008). Sex differences in visual attention to erotic and non-erotic stimuli. *Archives of Sex Research, 37*, 219–228.

Lykken, D. T., & Tellegen, A. (1993). Is human mating adventitious or the result of lawful choice? A twin study of mate selection. *Journal of Personality and Social Psychology, 65*, 56–68.

Maccoby, E. E. (1998). *The two sexes: Growing up apart, coming together*. Cambridge, MA: Belknap Press/Harvard University Press.

Maccoby, E. E., & Jacklin, C. N. (1987). Gender segregation in childhood. In H. W. Reese (Ed.), *Advances in child development and behavior* (Vol. 20). San Diego, CA: Academic Press.

MacDonald, T. K., & Ross, M. (1999). Assessing the accuracy of predictions about dating relationships: How and why do lovers' predictions differ from those made by observers? *Personality and Social Psychology Bulletin, 25*, 1417–1429.

Mace, D., & Mace, V. (1980). *Marriage east and west.* New York: Dolphin Books.

Madanes, C. (1983). *Strategic family therapy.* San Francisco: Jossey-Bass.

Madden, M., & Lenhard, A. (2006). Online dating [Electronic Version]. *Pew Internet & American Life Project.* Web. 8 June 2009.

Maddux, W. W., & Brewer, M. B. (2005). Gender differences in the relational and collective bases for trust. *Group Processes and Intergroup Relations, 8*, 159–171.

Magdol, L., Moffitt, T. E., Caspi, A., & Silva, P. A. (1998). Developmental antecedents of partner abuse: A prospective-longitudinal study. *Journal of Abnormal Psychology, 107*, 375–389.

Major, B., Barr, L., Zubek, J., & Babey, S. H. (1999). Gender and self-esteem: A meta-analysis. In W. B. Swann, J. H. Langlois, & L. A. Gilbert (Eds.), *Sexism and stereotypes in modern society: The gender science of Janet Taylor Spence* (pp. 223–253). Washington, DC: American Psychological Association.

Major, B., Carnevale, P. J., & Deaux, K. (1981). A different perspective on androgyny: Evaluations of masculine and feminine personality characteristics. *Journal of Personality and Social Psychology, 41*, 988–1001.

Major, B., Carrington, P. I., & Carnevale, P. J. (1984). Physical attractiveness and self-esteem: Attributions for praise from an other-sex evaluator. *Personality and Social Psychology Bulletin, 10*, 43–50.

Malamuth, N., & Check, J. (1981). The effects of mass media exposure on acceptance of violence against women: A field experiment. *Journal of Research in Personality, 15*, 436–446.

Manlove, J., Ryan, S., & Franzetta, K. (2007). Contraceptive use patterns across teens' sexual relationships: The role of relationships, partners, and sexual histories. *Demography 44*, 603–621.

Manne, S., Ostroff, J., Rini, C., Fox, K., Goldstein, L., & Grana, G. (2004). The interpersonal process model of intimacy: The role of self-disclosure, partner disclosure, and partner responsiveness in interactions between breast cancer patients and their partners. *Journal of Family Psychology, 18*, 589–599.

Manning, W., Longmore, M., & Giordano, P. (2000). The relationship context of contraceptive use at first intercourse. *Family Planning Perspectives, 32*, 104–110.

Marcus, R. F. (2012). Patterns of partner violence in young adult couples: Nonviolent, unilaterally violent, and mutually violent couples. *Violence and Victims, 27*, 299–314.

Margolin, G. (1981). Behavior exchange in happy and unhappy marriages: A family cycle perspective. *Behavior Therapy, 12*, 329–343.

Margolin, G., & Wampold, B. E. (1981). Sequential analysis of conflict and accord in distressed and nondistressed marital partners. *Journal of Consulting and Clinical Psychology, 49*, 554–567.

Margolin, G., John, R. S., & Gleberman, L. (1988). Affective responses to conflictual discussions in violent and nonviolent couples. *Journal of Consulting and Clinical Psychology, 56*, 24–33.

Margolin, G., Talovic, S. & Weinstein, C. D. (1983). Areas of Change Questionnaire: A practical approach to marital assessment. *Journal of Consulting and Clinical Psychology, 51*, 944–955.

Markey, P. M., Lowmaster, S., & Eichler, W. (2010). A real time assessment of interpersonal complementarity. *Personal Relationships, 17(1)*, 13–25.

Markman, H. J. (1981). Prediction of marital distress: A 5-year follow-up. *Journal of Consulting and Clinical Psychology, 49*, 760–762.

Markman, H. J., & Floyd, F. (1980). Possibilities for the prevention of marital discord: A behavioral perspective. *American Journal of Family Therapy, 8*, 29–48.

Markman, H. J., Renick, M. J., Floyd, F. J., Stanley, S. M., & Clements, M. (1993). Preventing marital distress through communication and conflict management training: A 4- and 5-year follow-up. *Journal of Consulting and Clinical Psychology, 61*, 70–77.

Markman, H., Stanley, S., & Blumberg, S. L. (1994). *Fighting for your marriage.* San Francisco: Jossey-Bass.

Marks, G. N., & Fleming, N. (1999). Influences and consequences of well-being among Australian young people: 1980–1995. *Social Indicators Research, 46*, 301–323.

Marquart, B. S., Nannini, D. K., Edwards, R. W., Stanley, L. R., & Wayman, J. C. (2007). Prevalence of dating violence and victimization: Regional and gender differences. *Adolescence, 42*, 645–657.

Marsiglio, W., & Scanzoni, J. (1995). *Families and friendships.* New York: HarperCollins.

Martin, L. L., Seta, J. J., & Crelia, R. A. (1990). Assimilation and contrast as a function of people's willingness and ability to expend effort in forming an impression. *Journal of Personality and Social Psychology, 59*, 27–37.

Martin, R. W. (1991). Examining personal relationship thinking: The relational cognition complexity instrument. *Journal of Social and Personal Relationships, 8*, 467–480.

Martin, R. (1992). Relational cognition complexity and relational communication in personal relationships. *Communication Monographs, 59*, 150–163.

Martinez, G. M., Chandra, A., Abma, J. C., Jones, J., & Mosher, W. (2006). Fertility, contraception, and fatherhood: Data from the 2002 National Survey of Family Growth. *Vital Health Statistics, 23*, 246.

Matthews, G., Davies, D. R., Westerman, S. J., & Stammers, R. B. (2000). *Human performance: Cognition, stress, and individual differences*. Philadelphia: Psychology Press.

Mauldon, J. G., London, R. A., Fein, D. J., & Bliss, S. J. (2002). *What do they think? Welfare recipients' attitudes toward marriage and childbearing* (Research Brief from the Welfare Reform and Family Formation Project). Bethesda, MD: Abt Associates.

Maume, M. O., Ousey, G. C., & Beaver, K. (2005). Cutting the grass: A reexamination of the link between marital attachment, delinquent peers and desistance from marijuana use. *Journal of Quantitative Criminology, 21*, 27–53.

Mazzella, R., & Feingold, A. (1994). The effects of physical attractiveness, race, socioeconomic status, and gender of defendants and victims on judgments of mock jurors: A meta-analysis. *Journal of Applied Social Psychology, 24*, 1315–1344.

McCrae, R. R., & Costa, P. T., Jr. (1990). *Personality in adulthood*. New York: Guilford.

McCubbin, H. I., & Patterson, J. M. (1982). Family adaptation to crises. In H. I. McCubbin, A. E. Cauble, & J. M. Patterson (Eds.), *Family stress, coping, and social support* (pp. 26–47). Springfield, IL: Thomas.

McCubbin, H. I., & Patterson, J. M. (1983). The family stress process: The double ABCX model of adjustment and adaptation. *Marriage and Family Review, 6*, 7–37.

McCullough, M. E., & Hoyt, W. T. (2002). Transgression-related motivational dispositions: Personality substrates of forgiveness and their links to the Big Five. *Personality and Social Psychology Bulletin, 28*, 1556–1573.

McCullough, M. E., Rachal, K. C., Sandage, S. J., Worthington, E. L., Jr., Brown, S. W., & Hight, T. L. (1998). Interpersonal forgiving in close relationships: II. Theoretical elaboration and measurement. *Journal of Personality and Social Psychology, 75*, 1586–1603.

McCullough, M. E., Worthington, E. L., Jr., & Rachal, K. C. (1997). Interpersonal forgiving in close relationships. *Journal of Personality and Social Psychology, 73*, 321–336.

McEwen, B. S. (1998). Protective and damaging effects of stress mediators. *New England Journal of Medicine, 338*, 171–179.

McFarland, C., & Ross, M. (1987). The relation between current impressions and memories of self and dating partners. *Personality and Social Psychology Bulletin, 13*, 228–238.

McHale, S. M., Updegraff, K. A., Jackson-Newsom, J., Tucker, C. J., & Crouter, A. C. (2000). When does parents' differential treatment have negative implications for siblings? *Social Development, 9*, 149–172.

McKenna, K. Y. A., & Bargh, J. A. (1999). Causes and consequences of social interaction on the Internet: A conceptual framework. *Media Psychology, 1*, 249–269.

McLanahan, S. (2004). Diverging destinies: How children are faring under the second demographic transition. *Demography, 41*, 607–627.

McLanahan, S., & Sandefur, G. (1994). *Growing up with a single parent: What hurts, what helps?* Cambridge, MA: Harvard University Press.

McLaughlin, I. G., Leonard, K. E., & Senchak, M. (1992). Prevalence and distribution of premarital aggression among couples applying for a marriage license. *Journal of Family Violence, 7*, 309–319.

McLeod, J. (1991). Childhood parental loss and adult depression. *Journal of Health and Social Behavior, 32*, 205–220.

McNulty, J. K. (2008). Neuroticism and interpersonal negativity: The independent contributions of perceptions and behaviors. *Personality and Social Psychology Bulletin, 34*, 1439–1450.

McNulty, J. K. & Fisher, T. D. (2008). Gender differences in response to sexual expectancies and changes in sexual frequency: A short-term longitudinal study of sexual satisfaction in newly married couples. *Archives of Sexual Behavior, 37*, 229–240.

Medora, N. P., Larson, J. H., Hortaçsu, N., & Dave, P. (2002). Perceived attitudes towards romanticism: A cross-cultural study of American, Asian-Indian, and Turkish young adults. *Journal of Comparative Family Studies, 33*, 155–178.

Menaghan, E. (1983). Marital stress and family transitions: A panel analysis. *Journal of Marriage and Family, 45*, 371–386.

Meston, C. M., & Buss, D. M. (2007). Why humans have sex. *Archives of Sexual Behavior, 36*, 477–507.

Mettee, D., Taylor, S. E., & Friedman, H. (1973). Affect conversion and the gain-loss like effect. *Sociometry, 36*, 505–519.

Metts, S. (1989). An exploratory investigation of deception in close relationships. *Journal of Social and Personal Relationships, 6*, 159–179.

Meyer, I. H. (1995). Minority stress and mental health in gay men. *Journal of Health and Social Behavior, 36*, 38–56.

Meyer, I. H. (2003). Prejudice, social stress, and mental health in lesbian, gay, and bisexual populations: Conceptual issues and research evidence. *Psychological Bulletin, 129,* 674–697.

Michael, R. T., Gagnon, J. H., Laumann, E. O., & Kolata, G. (1994). *Sex in America: A definitive survey.* Boston: Little, Brown.

Mickelson, K. D., Kessler, R. C., & Shaver, P. R. (1997). Adult attachment in a nationally representative sample. *Journal of Personality and Social Psychology, 73,* 1092–1106.

Mikulincer, M. (1998). Adult attachment style and individual differences in functional versus dysfunctional experiences of anger. *Journal of Personality and Social Psychology, 74,* 513–524.

Mikulincer, M., & Nachson, O. (1991). Attachment styles and patterns of self-disclosure. *Journal of Personality and Social Psychology, 61,* 321–331.

Mikulincer, M., & Shaver, P. R. (2007). *Attachment in adulthood: Structure, dynamics, and change.* New York: Guilford.

Mikulincer, M., Florian, V., & Weller, A. (1993). Attachment styles, coping strategies, and post-traumatic psychological distress: The impact of the Gulf War in Israel. *Journal of Personality and Social Psychology, 64,* 817–826.

Mikulincer, M., Shaver, P. R., & Slav, K. (2006). Attachment, mental representations of others, and gratitude and forgiveness in romantic relationships. In M. Mikulincer & G. Goodman (Eds.), *Dynamics of romantic love: Attachment, caregiving, and sex* (pp. 190–215). New York, NY: Guilford Press.

Milardo, R. M., & Allan, G. (1997). Social networks and marital relationships. In S. Duck (Ed.), *Handbook of personal relationships: Theory, research and interventions* (2nd ed., pp. 506–522). New York: Wiley.

Miller, B. C., & Benson, B. (1999). Romantic and sexual relationship development during adolescence. In W. Furman, B. B. Brown & C. Feiring (Eds.), *The development of romantic relationships in adolescence* (pp. 99–121). New York: Cambridge University Press.

Miller, D. T., & Ross, M. (1975). Self-serving biases in attribution of causality: Fact or fiction? *Psychological Bulletin, 82,* 213–225.

Miller, P. C., Lefcourt, H. M., & Ware, E. E. (1983). The construction and development of the Miller Marital Locus of Control scale. *Canadian Journal of Behavioral Science, 15,* 266–279.

Miller, P. C., Lefcourt, H. M., Holmes, J. G., Ware, E. E., & Saleh, W. E. (1986). Marital locus of control and marital problem solving. *Journal of Personality and Social Psychology, 51,* 161–169.

Miller, P. H., & Aloise, P. A. (1989). Young children's understanding of the psychological causes of behavior: A review. *Child Development, 60,* 257–285.

Miller, R. B., & Wright, D. W. (1995). Detecting and correcting attrition bias in longitudinal family research. *Journal of Marriage and Family, 57,* 921–929.

Miller, R. S. (1997a). Inattentive and contented: Relationship commitment and attention to alternatives. *Journal of Personality and Social Psychology, 73,* 758–766.

Miller, R. S. (1997b). We always hurt the ones we love: Aversive interactions in close relationships. In R. M. Kowalski (Ed.), *Aversive interpersonal interactions* (pp. 13–30). New York: Plenum.

Miller, S. A., & Byers, E. S. (2004). Actual and desired duration of foreplay and intercourse: Discordance and misperceptions within heterosexual couples. *Journal of Sex Research, 41,* 301–309.

Miller, S. L., Miller, P. A., Nunnally, E. W., & Wackman, D. B. (1991). *Talking and listening together: Couple Communication.* Littleton, CO: Interpersonal Communication Programs.

Mintz, S., & Kellogg, S. (1988). *Domestic revolutions: A social history of American family life.* New York: Free Press.

Minuchin, S. (1974). *Families and family therapy.* Cambridge, MA: Harvard University Press.

Mita, T. H., Dermer, M., & Knight, J. (1977). Reversed facial images and the mere-exposure hypothesis. *Journal of Personality and Social Psychology, 35,* 597–601.

Mitchell, A. E., Castellani, A. M., Herrington, R. L., Joseph, J. I., Doss, B. D., & Snyder, D. K. (2008). Predictors of intimacy in couples' discussions of relationship injuries: An observational study. *Journal of Family Psychology, 22,* 21–29.

Mock, D. W., Drummond, H., & Stinson, C. H. (1990). Avian siblicide. *American Scientist 78,* 438–449.

Moen, P., Kim, J. E., & Hofmeister, H. (2001). Couples' work/retirement transitions, gender, and marital quality. *Social Psychology Quarterly, 64,* 55–71.

Monroe, S. M., Rohde, P., Seeley, J. R., & Lewinsohn, P. M. (1999). Life events and depression in adolescence: Relationship loss as a prospective risk factor for first onset of major depressive disorder. *Journal of Abnormal Psychology, 108,* 606–614.

Montesi, J. L., Fauber, R. L., Gordon, E. A., & Heimberg, R. G. (2010). The specific importance of communicating about sex to couples' sexual and overall relationship satisfaction. *Journal of Social and Personal Relationships, 28,* 591–609.

Montoya, R. M. (2005). The environment's influence on mate preferences. *Sexualities, Evolution, and Gender, 7,* 115–134.

Montoya, R. M. (2008). I'm hot, so I'd say you're not: The influence of objective physical attractiveness on mate selection. *Personality and Social Psychology Bulletin, 34*, 1315–1331.

Montoya, R. M., Horton, R. S., & Kirchner, J. (2008). Is actual similarity necessary for attraction? A meta-analysis of actual and perceived similarity. *Journal of Social and Personal Relationships, 25(6)*, 889–922.

Moore, M. R. (2003). Socially isolated? How parents and neighbourhood adults influence youth behaviour in disadvantaged communities. *Ethnic and Racial Studies, 26*, 988–1005.

Moore, T. M., Stuart, G. L., Meehan, J. C., Rhatigan, D. L., Hellmuth, J. C., & Keen, S. M. (2008). Drug abuse and aggression between intimate partners: A meta-analytic review. *Clinical Psychology Review, 28*, 247–274.

Moreno, J. L. (1951). *Sociometry, experimental method and the science of society: An approach to a new political orientation*. Beacon, NY: Beacon House.

Morton, T. L. (1978). Intimacy and reciprocity of exchange: A comparison of spouses and strangers. *Journal of Personality and Social Psychology, 36*, 72–81.

Muehlenhard, C. L., Koralewski, M. A., Andrews, S. L., & Burdick, C. A. (1986). Verbal and nonverbal cues that convey interest in dating: Two studies. *Behavior Therapy, 17*, 404–419.

Munson, M. L., & Sutton, P. D. (2006). Births, marriages, divorces, and deaths: Provisional data for 2005. *National vital statistics reports, 54*. Hyattsville, MD: National Center for Health Statistics.

Murray, S. L., & Holmes, J. G. (1994). Storytelling in close relationships: The construction of confidence. *Personality and Social Psychology Bulletin, 20*, 650–663.

Murray, S. L., & Holmes, J. G. (1997). A leap of faith? Positive illusions in romantic relationships. *Personality and Social Psychology Bulletin, 23*, 586–604.

Murray, S. L., & Holmes, J. G. (1999). The (mental) ties that bind: Cognitive structures that predict relationship resilience. *Journal of Personality and Social Psychology, 77*, 1228–1244.

Murray, S. L., Bellavia, G. M., Rose, P., & Griffin, D. W. (2003). Once hurt, twice hurtful: How perceived regard regulates daily marital interactions. *Journal of Personality and Social Psychology, 84*, 126–147.

Murray, S. L., Holmes, J. G., & Griffin, D. (2000). Self-esteem and the quest for felt security: How perceived regard regulates attachment processes. *Journal of Personality and Social Psychology, 78*, 478–498.

Murray, S. L., Holmes, J. G., & Griffin, D. W. (1996). The benefits of positive illusions: Idealization and the construction of satisfaction in close relationships. *Journal of Personality and Social Psychology, 70*, 79–98.

Murray, S. L., Holmes, J. G., & Griffin, D. W. (1996). The self-fulfilling nature of positive illusions in romantic relationships: Love is not blind, but prescient. *Journal of Personality and Social Psychology, 71*, 1155–1180.

Murray, S. L., Holmes, J. G., Dolderman, D., & Griffin, D. W. (2000). What the motivated mind sees: Comparing friends' perspectives to married partners' views of each other. *Journal of Experimental Social Psychology, 36*, 600–620.

Murray, S. L., Holmes, J. G., Griffin, D. W., Bellavia, G., & Rose, P. (2001). The mismeasure of love: How self-doubt contaminates relationship beliefs. *Personality and Social Psychology Bulletin, 27*, 423–436.

Murray, S. L., Rose, P., Bellavia, G., Holmes, J., & Kusche, A. G. (2002). When rejection stings: How self-esteem constrains relationship-enhancement processes. *Journal of Personality and Social Psychology, 83*, 556–573.

Myers, S. M., & Booth, A. (1996). Men's retirement and marital quality. *Journal of Family Issues, 17*, 336–357.

Myers, S. M., & Booth, A. (1999). Marital strains and marital quality: The role of high and low locus of control. *Journal of Marriage and Family, 61*, 423–436.

Napier, A. Y. (1978). The rejection-intrusion pattern: A central family dynamic. *Journal of Marriage and Family Counseling, 4*, 5–12.

National Center for Health Statistics (2005). *Health, United States, 2005: With chartbook on trends in the health of Americans (Table 27)*. Hyattsville, Maryland: National Center for Health Statistics. (2003, July 14). Retrieved July 16, 2003, from http://www.cdc.gov/nchs/.

Neff, L. A., & Karney, B. R. (2002). Judgments of a relationship partner: Specific accuracy but global enhancement. *Journal of Personality, 70*, 1079–1112.

Neff, L. A., & Karney, B. R. (2003). The dynamic structure of relationship perceptions: Differential importance as a strategy of relationship maintenance. *Personality and Social Psychology Bulletin, 29*, 1433–1446.

Neff, L. A., & Karney, B. R. (2004). How does context affect intimate relationships? Linking external stress and cognitive processes within marriage. *Personality and Social Psychology Bulletin, 30*, 134–148.

Neff, L. A., & Karney, B. R. (2005). Gender differences in social support: A question of skill or responsiveness? *Journal of Personality and Social Psychology, 88*, 79–90.

Neff, L. A., & Karney, B. R. (2005). To know you is to love you: The implications of global adoration and specific accuracy for marital relationships. *Journal of Personality and Social Psychology, 88*, 480–497.

Neimeyer, G. J. (1984). Cognitive complexity and marital satisfaction. *Journal of Social and Clinical Psychology, 2*, 258–263.

Neruda, P. (1996). *100 love sonnets* (Trans. Stephen Tapscott). Austin: University of Texas Press.

Newcomb, A. F., Bukowski, W. M., & Pattee, L. (1993). Children's peer relations: A meta-analytic review of popular, rejected, neglected, controversial, and average sociometric status. *Psychological Bulletin, 113*, 99–128.

Newcomb, M. D., & Bentler, P. M. (1981). Marital breakdown. In S. Duck & R. Gilmour (Eds.), *Personal relationships: Personal relationships in disorder* (Vol. 3, pp. 57–94). New York: Academic Press.

Newcomb, T. M. (1961). *The acquaintance process.* New York: Holt, Rinehart & Winston.

Newman, D. L., Caspi, A., Moffitt, T. E., & Silva, P. A. (1997). Antecedents of adult interpersonal functioning: Effects of individual differences in age 3 temperament. *Developmental Psychology, 33*, 206–217.

Neyer, F. J., & Asendorpf, J. B. (2001). Personality-relationship transaction in young adulthood. *Journal of Personality and Social Psychology, 81*, 1190–1204.

Nisbett, R. E., Caputo, C., Legant, P., & Marecek, J. (1973). Behavior as seen by the actor and as seen by the observer. *Journal of Personality and Social Psychology, 27*, 154–164.

Noller, P. (1980). Misunderstandings in marital communication: A study of couples' nonverbal communication. *Journal of Personality and Social Psychology, 39*, 1135–1148.

Noller, P. (1981). Gender and marital adjustment level differences in decoding messages from spouses and strangers. *Journal of Personality and Social Psychology, 41*, 272–278.

Noller, P., & Gallois, C. (1988). Understanding and misunderstanding in marriage: Sex and marital adjustment differences in structured and free interaction. In P. Noller & M. A. Fitzpatrick (Eds.), *Perspectives on marital interaction* (pp. 53–77). Philadelphia: Multilingual Matters.

Noller, P., Feeney, J. A., Bonnell, D., & Callan, V. J. (1994). Longitudinal study of conflict in early marriage. *Journal of Social and Personal Relationships, 11*, 233–252.

Nomaguchi, K. M., & Milkie, M. A. (2003). Costs and rewards of children: The effects of becoming a parent on adults' lives. *Journal of Marriage and Family, 65*, 356–374.

Norton, R. (1983). Measuring marital quality: A critical look at the dependent variable. *Journal of Marriage and Family, 45*, 141–151.

Novak, D. W., & Lerner, M. J. (1968). Rejection as a consequence of perceived similarity. *Journal of Personality and Social Psychology, 9*, 147–152.

O'Leary, K. D. (1988). Physical aggression between spouses: A social learning theory perspective. In V. B. Van Hasselt, R. L. Morrison, A. S. Bellack, & M. Hersen (Eds.), *Handbook of family violence* (pp. 11–55). New York: Plenum.

O'Leary, K. D., & Arias, I. (1983). The influence of marital therapy on sexual satisfaction. *Journal of Sex and Marital Therapy, 9*, 171–181.

O'Leary, K. D., Barling, J., Arias, I., Rosenbaum, A., Malone, J., & Tyree, A. (1989). Prevalence and stability of physical aggression between spouses: A longitudinal analysis. *Journal of Consulting and Clinical Psychology, 57*, 263–268.

O'Leary, K. D., Vivian, D., & Malone, J. (1992). Assessment of physical aggression against women in marriage: The need for multimodal assessment. *Behavioral Assessment, 14*, 5–14.

O'Leary, K.D. (1999). Developmental and affective issues in assessing and treating partner aggression. *Clinical Psychology: Science and Practice, 6*, 400–414.

O'Leary, D. (1988). Physical aggression between spouses: A social learning theory perspective. In Vincent B. Van Hasselt & Randall L. Morrison (Eds.), *Handbook of family violence* (pp. 31–55). New York: Plenum.

Ohbuchi, K., Kameda, M., & Agarie, N. (1989). Apology as aggression control: Its role in mediating appraisal of and response to harm. *Journal of Personality and Social Psychology, 56*, 219–227.

Oliver, M. B., & Hyde, J. S. (1993). Gender differences in sexuality: A meta-analysis. *Psychological Bulletin, 114*, 29–51.

Olson, D. H., & Olson, A. K. (1999). PREPARE/ENRICH Program: Version 2000. In R. Berger & M. Hannah (Eds.), *Preventive approaches in couples therapy* (pp. 196–216). Philadelphia: Brunner/Mazel.

Ooms, T. (2005). *The new kid on the block: What is marriage education and does it work?* (Couples and Marriage Series Brief No. 7). Washington, DC: Center for Law and Social Policy.

Orbuch, T. L., Veroff, J., Hassan, H., & Horrocks, J. (2002). Who will divorce: A 14-year longitudinal study of black couples and white couples. *Jour-*

nal of Social and Personal Relationships, 19, 179–202.

Organization for Economic Cooperation and Development. (2008). SF8. Marriage and Divorce Rates (Retrieved July 24, 2009, from Organization for Economic Cooperation and Development, Directorate for Employment, Labour and Social Affairs: www.oecd.org/els/social/family/database).

Orth, U., Robins, R.W., & Widaman, K.F. (2012). Life-span development of self-esteem and its effects on important life outcomes. Journal of Personality and Social Psychology, 102, 1271–1288.

Otis, M. D., Rostosky, S. S., Riggle, E. D. B., & Hamlin, R. (2006). Stress and relationship quality in same-sex couples. Journal of Social and Personal Relationships, 23, 81–99.

Overall, N., Fletcher, G. J. O., Simpson, J. A., & Sibley, C. G. (2009). Regulating partners in intimate relationships: The costs and benefits of different communication strategies. Journal of Personality and Social Psychology, 96, 620–639.

Overbeek, G., Vollebergh, W., de Graff, R., Scholte, R., de Kemp, R., & Engels, R. (2006). Longitudinal associations of marital quality and marital dissolution with the incidence of DSM-III-R disorders. Journal of Family Psychology, 20, 284–291.

Overbye, D. (2000). Einstein in love: A scientific romance. New York: Viking.

Owen, W. F. (1987). The verbal expression of love by women and men as a critical communication event in personal relationships. Women's Studies in Communication, 10, 15–24.

Paleari, F. G., Regalia, C., & Fincham, F. D. (2005). Marital quality, forgiveness, empathy, and rumination: A longitudinal analysis. Personality and Social Psychology Bulletin, 31, 368–378.

Paley, B., Cox, M. J., Burchinal, M. R., & Payne, C. C. (1999). Attachment and marital functioning: Comparison of spouses with continuous-secure, earned-secure, dismissing, and preoccupied attachment stances. Journal of Family Psychology, 13, 580–597.

Papp, L. M., Cummings, E. M., & Goeke-Morey, M. C. (2009). For richer, for poorer: Money as a topic of marital conflict in the home. Family Relations, 58, 91–103.

Parke, R. D. (1998). A developmentalist's perspective on marital change. In T. N. Bradbury (Ed.), The developmental course of marital dysfunction (pp. 393–409). New York: Cambridge University Press.

Parks, M. R., & Eggert, L. L. (1991). The role of social context in the dynamics of personal relationships. In W. H. Jones & D. Perlman (Eds.), Advances in

personal relationships: A research annual (Vol. 2, pp. 1–34). Oxford, UK: Kingsley Publishers.

Parks, M. R., Stan, C. M., & Eggert, L. L. (1983). Romantic involvement and social network involvement. Social Psychology Quarterly, 46, 116–131.

Pasch, L. A., & Bradbury, T. N. (1998). Social support, conflict, and the development of marital dysfunction. Journal of Consulting and Clinical Psychology, 66, 219–230.

Patterson, G. R. (1982). Coercive family process. Eugene, OR: Castalia.

Patterson, G. R., & Hops, H. (1972). Coercion, a game for two: Intervention techniques for marital conflict. In R. E. Ulrich & P. Mountjoy (Eds.), The experimental analysis of social behavior (pp. 424–440). New York: Appleton Century-Crofts.

Patterson, G. R., & Reid, J. (1970). Reciprocity and coercion: Two facets of social systems. In J. Michaels & C. Neuringer (Eds.), Behavior modification for psychologists (133–177). New York: Appleton-Century-Crofts.

Paul, E. L., & Hayes, K. A. (2002). The causalities of "casual" sex: A qualitative exploration of the phenomenology of college students' hookups. Journal of Social and Personal Relationships, 19, 639–661.

Paul, E. L., McManus, B., & Hayes, A. (2000). "Hookups": Characteristics and correlates of college students' spontaneous and anonymous sexual experiences. Journal of Sex Research, 37, 76–88.

Pavalko, E. K., & Elder, G. H. (1990). World War II and divorce: A life-course perspective. American Journal of Sociology, 95, 1213–1234.

Pearce, J. W., LeBow, M. D., & Orchard, J. (1981). Role of spouse involvement on weight loss in a behavioral treatment program: A retrospective investigation. Journal of Consulting and Clinical Psychology, 49, 236–244.

Pence, E., & Paymar, M. (1993). Education groups for men who batter: The Duluth model. New York: Springer.

Peplau, L. A., & Fingerhut, A. W. (2007). The close relationships of lesbians and gay men. Annual Review of Psychology, 58, 405–424.

Peplau, L. A., Fingerhut, A. W., & Beals, K. P. (2004). Sexuality in the relationships of lesbians and gay men. In J. Harvey, A. Wenzel, & S. Sprecher (Eds.), Handbook of sexuality in close relationships (pp. 350–369). Mahwah, NJ: Erlbaum.

Peplau, L. A., Hill, C. T., & Rubin, Z. (1993). Sex role attitudes in dating and marriage: A 15-year follow-up of the Boston Couples Study. Journal of Social Issues, 49, 31–52.

Peplau, L. A., Veniegas, R. C., & Campbell, S. M. (1996). Gay and lesbian relationships. In R. C. Savin-Williams (Ed.), The lives of lesbians, gays, *and bisexuals: Children to adults*. New York: Wadsworth.

Perlman, D., & Oskamp, S. (1971). The effects of picture content and exposure frequency on evaluations of Negroes and whites. *Journal of Experimental Social Psychology, 7*, 503–514.

Perner, J., Ruffman, T., & Leekam, S. R. (1994). Theory of mind is contagious: You catch it from your sibs. *Child Development, 65*, 1228–1238.

Perper, T. (1989). Theories and observations on sexual selection and female choice in human beings. *Medical Anthropology, 11*, 409–454.

Perper, T., & Weis, D. L. (1987). Proceptive and rejective strategies of U.S. and Canadian college women. *Journal of Sex Research, 23*, 455–480.

Perrett, D. I., May, K. A., & Yoshikawa, S. (1994). Facial shape and judgements of female attractiveness. *Nature, 368*, 239–242.

Peterson, C. D., Baucom, D. H., Elliott, M. J., & Farr, P. A. (1989). The relationship between sex role identity and marital adjustment. *Sex Roles, 21*, 775–787.

Peterson, D. R. (1979). Assessing interpersonal relationships by means of interaction records. *Behavioral Assessment, 1*, 221–236.

Piaget, J. (1929). *The child's conception of the world*. New York: Harcourt Brace Jovanovich.

Pittman, J. F., Solheim, C. A., & Blanchard, D. (1996). Stress as a driver of the allocation of housework. *Journal of Marriage and Family, 58*, 456–468.

Plassman, B. L., Langa, K. M., Fisher, G. G., Heeringa, S. G., Weir, D. R., Ofstedal, M. B., et al. (2007). Prevalence of dementia in the United States: The Aging, Demographics, and Memory Study. *Neuroepidemiology 29*, 125–132.

Pollard, M. S., & Harris, K. M. (2007). Measuring cohabitation in add health. In S. Hofferth & L. Casper (Eds.), *Handbook of measurement issues in family research* (pp. 35–51). Mahwah, NJ: Erlbaum.

Pollet, T. V., Roberts, S. G. B., & Dunbar, R. I. M. (2011). Use of social network sites and instant messaging does not lead to increased offline social network size, or to emotionally closer relationships with offline network members. *Cyberpsychology, Behavior, and Social Networking, 14*, 253–258.

Popenoe, D. (2001). Marriage decline in America (Testimony before the Committee on Ways and Means, Subcommittee on Human Resources, House of Representatives). Washington, DC.

Popper, K. R. (1959). *The logic of scientific discovery*. New York: Basic Books.

Prager, K. J. (1995). *The psychology of intimacy*. New York: Guilford.

Prager, K. J., & Roberts, L. J. (2004). Deep intimate connection: Self and intimacy in couple relationships. In D. J. Mashek & A. Aron (Eds.), *Handbook of closeness and intimacy* (pp. 43–60). Mahwah, NJ: Erlbaum.

Presser, H. B. (1995). Job, family, and gender: Determinants of nonstandard work schedules among employed Americans in 1991. *Demography, 32*, 577–598.

Presser, H. B. (2000). Nonstandard work schedules and marital instability. *Journal of Marriage and Family, 62*, 93–110.

Presser, H. B., & Cain, V. S. (1983). Shift work among dual-earner couples with children. *Science, 219*, 876–879.

Priluck, J. (2002). Miniskirt forays. In A. Chin (Ed.), *Split: Stories from a generation raised on divorce* (pp. 53–67). New York: Contemporary Books.

Proulx, C. M. Helms, H. M., & Buehler, C. (2007). Marital quality and personal well-being: A meta-analysis. *Journal of Marriage and Family, 69*, 576–593.

Purnine, D. M., & Carey, M. P. (1997). Interpersonal communication and sexual adjustment: The roles of understanding and agreement. *Journal of Consulting and Clinical Psychology, 65*, 1017–1025.

Putallaz, M. (1983). Predicting children's sociometric status from their behavior. *Child Development, 54*, 1417–1426.

Putnam, R. D. (2000). *Bowling alone: The collapse and revival of American community*. New York: Simon & Schuster.

Quigley, B. M., & Leonard, K. E. (1996). Desistance of husband aggression in the early years of marriage. *Violence and Victims, 11*, 355–370.

Rafaeli, E., & Gleason, M. E. J. (2009). Skilled support within intimate relationships. *Journal of Family Theory and Review, 1*, 20–37.

Raley, K., & Bumpass, L. (2003). The topography of the divorce plateau: Levels and trends in union stability in the United States after 1980. *Demographic Research, 8*, 245–259.

Raley, R. K., Crissey, S., & Muller, C. (2007). Of sex and romance: Late adolescent relationships and young adult union formation. *Journal of Marriage and Family, 69*, 1210–1226.

Raley, S. B., Mattingly, M. J., & Bianchi, S. M. (2006). How dual are dual-income couples? Documenting change from 1970 to 2001. *Journal of Marriage and Family, 68*, 11–28.

Ramsey, J. L., Langlois, J. H., Hoss, R. A., Rubenstein, A. J., & Griffin, A. M. (2004). Origins of a stereotype: Categorization of facial attractiveness by 6-month-old infants. *Developmental Science, 7*, 201–211.

Rank, M. R., & Hirschl, T. A. (1999). The economic risk of childhood in America: Estimating the probability of poverty across the formative years. *Journal of Marriage and Family, 61*, 1058–1067.

Rauer, A. J., & Volling, B. L. (2007). Differential parenting and sibling jealousy: Developmental correlates of young adults' romantic relationships. *Personal Relationships, 14*, 495–511.

Raush, H. L., Barry, W. A., Hertel, R. K., & Swain, M. A. (1974). *Communication, conflict, and marriage.* San Francisco: Jossey-Bass.

Reeve, C. (1998). *Still me.* New York: Ballantine.

Regan, P. C., & Berscheid, E. (1997). Gender differences in characteristics desired in a potential sexual and marriage partner. *Journal of Psychology and Human Sexuality, 9*, 25–37.

Rehman, U. S., & Holtzworth-Munroe, A. (2006). A cross-cultural analysis of the demand-withdraw marital interaction: Observing couples from a developing country. *Journal of Consulting and Clinical Psychology, 74*, 755–766.

Reis, H. T. (1998). Gender differences in intimacy and related behaviors: Context and process. In D. J. Canary & K. Dindia (Eds.), *Sex differences and similarities in communication: Critical essays and empirical investigations of sex and gender in interaction* (pp. 203–231). Mahwah, NJ: Erlbaum.

Reis, H. T. (2002). Action matters, but relationship science is basic. *Journal of Social and Personal Relationships, 19*, 601–611.

Reis, H. T., & Patrick, B. C. (1996). Attachment and intimacy: Component processes. In E. T. Higgins & A. W. Kruglanski (Eds.), *Social psychology: Handbook of basic principles* (pp. 523–563). New York: Guilford.

Reis, H. T., & Shaver, P. (1988). Intimacy as an interpersonal process. In S. Duck (Ed.), *Handbook of personal relationships* (pp. 367–389). Chichester, England: Wiley.

Reis, H. T., & Wheeler, L. (1991). Studying social interaction with the Rochester Interaction Record. In M. P. Zanna (Ed.), *Advances in experimental social psychology* (Vol. 24). San Diego: Academic Press.

Reis, H. T., Capobianco, A., & Tsai, F.-T. (2002). Finding the person in personal relationships. *Journal of Personality, 70*, 813–850.

Reis, H. T., Collins, W. A., & Berscheid, E. (2000). The relationship context of human behavior and development. *Psychological Bulletin, 126*, 844–872.

Reis, H. T., Nezlek, J., & Wheeler, L. (1980). Physical attractiveness in social interaction. *Journal of Personality and Social Psychology, 38*, 604–617.

Reis, H. T., Senchak, M., & Solomon, B. (1985). Sex differences in the intimacy of social interaction:

Further examination of potential explanations. *Journal of Personality and Social Psychology, 48*, 1204–1217.

Reissman, C., Aron, A., & Bergen, M. R. (1993). Shared activities and marital satisfaction: Causal direction and self-expansion versus boredom. *Journal of Social and Personal Relationships, 10*, 243–254.

Repetti, R. L. (1989). Effects of daily workload on subsequent behavior during marital interaction: The roles of social withdrawal and spouse support. *Journal of Personality and Social Psychology, 57*, 651–659.

Repetti, R. L., Taylor, S. E., & Seeman, T. E. (2002). Risky families: Family social environments and the mental and physical health of offspring. *Psychological Bulletin, 128*, 330–366.

Revelle, W. (1995). Personality processes. *Annual Review of Psychology, 46*, 295–328.

Revenson, T. A. (1994). Social support and marital coping with chronic illness. *Annals of Behavioral Medicine, 16*, 122–130.

Rhee, N., & Antonucci, T. (2004). *Adjustment to widowhood: A dynamic process.* Paper presented at the Annual Meeting of the Gerontological Society of America, Washington DC.

Rhodes, G., Yoshikawa, S., Clark, A., Lee, K., McKay, R., & Akamatsu, S. (2001). Attractiveness of facial averageness and symmetry in non-Western cultures: In search of biologically based standards of beauty. *Perception, 30*, 611–625.

Richmond, M. K., Stocker, C. M., & Rienks, S. L. (2005). Longitudinal associations between sibling relationship quality, parental differential treatment, and children's adjustment. *Journal of Family Psychology, 19*, 550–559.

Rieger, G., Linsenmeier, J. A. W., Gygax, L., & Bailey, J. M. (2008). Sexual orientation and childhood gender nonconformity: Evidence from home videos. *Developmental Psychology, 44*, 46–58.

Rindfuss, R. R., & Stephen, E. H. (1990). Marital cohabitation: Separation does not make the heart grow fonder. *Journal of Marriage and Family, 52*, 259–270.

Robbins, M. M. (1999). Male mating patterns in wild multimale mountain gorilla groups. *Animal Behaviour, 57*, 1013–1020.

Roberts, L. J. (2000). Fire and ice in marital communication: Hostile and distancing behaviors as predictors of relationship distress. *Journal of Marriage and Family, 62*, 693–707.

Roberts, L. J., & Greenberg, D. R. (2002). Observational "windows" to intimacy processes in marriage. In P. Noller & J. A. Feeney (Eds.), *Understanding marriage: Developments in the study of couple interaction* (pp. 118–149). Cambridge, England: Cambridge University Press.

Robins, R. W., Caspi, A., & Moffitt, T. E. (2000). Two personalities, one relationship: Both partners' personality traits shape the quality of their relationship. *Journal of Personality and Social Psychology, 79*, 251–259.

Robins, R. W., Caspi, A., & Moffitt, T. E. (2002). It's not just who you're with, it's who you are: Personality and relationship experiences across multiple relationships. *Journal of Personality, 70*, 925–964.

Robins, R. W., Fraley, R., Roberts, B. W., & Trzesniewski, K. J. (2001). A longitudinal study of personality change in young adulthood. *Journal of Personality, 69*, 617–640.

Robles, T. F., & Kiecolt-Glaser, J. K. (2003). The physiology of marriage: Pathways to health. *Physiology and Behavior, 79*, 409–416.

Rodgers, J. (1996). Sexual transitions in adolescence. In J. Graber, J. Brooks-Gunn & A. Peterson (Eds.), *Transitions through adolescence: Interpersonal domains and context* (pp. 85–110). Mahwah, NJ: Erlbaum.

Rogers, R. G. (1995). Marriage, sex, and mortality. *Journal of Marriage and Family, 57*, 515–526.

Rogge, R. D., Johnson, M. D., Lawrence, E., Cobb, R., & Bradbury, T. N. (2002). The CARE program: A preventive approach to marital intervention (pp. 420–435). In N. S. Jacobson & A. S. Gurman (Eds.), Clinical handbook of couple therapy (3rd edition). New York: Guilford.

Rogge, R. D., & Bradbury, T. N. (1999). Till violence does us part: The differing roles of communication and aggression in predicting adverse marital outcomes. *Journal of Consulting and Clinical Psychology, 67*, 340–351.

Rogge, R. D., Bradbury, T. N., Hahlweg, K., Engl, J., & Thurmaier, F. (2006). Predicting marital distress and dissolution: Refining the two-factor hypothesis. *Journal of Family Psychology, 20*, 156–159.

Roisman, G. I., Clausell, E., Holland, A., Fortuna, K., & Elieff, C. (2008). Adult romantic relationships as contexts of human development: A multimethod comparison of same-sex couples with opposite-sex dating, engaged, and married dyads. *Developmental Psychology, 44*, 91–101.

Rollins, B. C., & Cannon, K. L. (1974). Marital satisfaction over the family life cycle: A reevaluation. *Journal of Marriage and Family, 36*, 271–282.

Rollins, B. C., & Feldman, H. (1970). Marital satisfaction over the family life cycle. *Journal of Marriage and Family, 32*, 20–28.

Rook, K. S. (1998). Investigating the positive and negative sides of personal relationships: Through a lens darkly? In B. H. Spitzberg & W. R. Cupach (Eds.), *The dark side of close relationships* (pp. 369–393). Mahwah, NJ: Erlbaum.

Rook, K., Dooley, D., & Catalano, R. (1991). Stress transmission: The effects of husbands' job stressors on the emotional health of their wives. *Journal of Marriage and Family, 53*, 165–177.

Roscoe, B., Diana, M. S., & Brooks, R. H. (1987). Early, middle, and late adolescents' views on dating and factors influencing partner selection. *Adolescence, 22*, 59–68.

Rosenberg, M. (1979). *Conceiving the self*. New York: Basic Books.

Rosenfeld, M. J., & Thomas, R. J. (2012). Searching for a mate: The rise of the Internet as a social intermediary. *American Sociological Review, 77*, 523–547.

Rosenfeld, H. M. (1964). Social choice conceived as a level of aspiration. *Journal of Abnormal and Social Psychology, 68*, 491–499.

Rosenthal, R. (1991). *Meta-analytic procedures for social research* (rev. ed.) Newbury Park, CA: Sage.

Rosenthal, R. (1994). Science and ethics in conducting, analyzing, and reporting psychological research. *Psychological Science, 5*, 127–134.

Ross, M., & Buehler, R. (1994). Creative remembering. In U. Neisser & U. Fivush (Eds.), *The remembering self: Construction and accuracy in the self-narrative* (pp. 205–235). New York: Cambridge University Press.

Ross, M., & Holmberg, D. (1992). Are wives' memories for events in relationships more vivid than their husbands' memories? *Journal of Social and Personal Relationships, 9*, 585–604.

Rothbaum, F., & Tsang, B. Y. (1998). Lovesongs in the United States and China: On the nature of romantic love. *Journal of Cross-Cultural Psychology, 29*, 306–319.

Rotter, J. B. (1975). Some problems and misconceptions related to the construct of internal versus external control of reinforcement. *Journal of Consulting and Clinical Psychology, 43*, 56–67.

Rowatt, W. C., Cunningham, M. R., & Druen, P. B. (1999). Lying to get a date: The effect of facial physical attractiveness on the willingness to deceive prospective dating partners. *Journal of Social and Personal Relationships, 16*, 209–223.

Rubin, Z. (1970). Measurement of romantic love. *Journal of Personality and Social Psychology, 16*, 265–273.

Rubin, Z., & Mitchell, C. (1976). Couples research as couples counseling: Some unintended effects of studying close relationships. *American Psychologist, 31*, 17–25.

Rubin, Z., Hill, C. T., Peplau, L. A., & Dunkel-Schetter, C. (1980). Self-disclosure in dating couples: Sex roles and the ethic of openness. *Journal of Marriage and Family, 42*, 305–317.

Rusbult, C. E. (1980). Commitment and satisfaction in romantic associations: A test of the investment model. *Journal of Experimental Social Psychology, 16*, 172–186.

Rusbult, C. E. (1983). A longitudinal test of the investment model: The development (and deterioration) of satisfaction and commitment in heterosexual involvements. *Journal of Personality and Social Psychology, 45,* 101–117.

Rusbult, C. E., & Martz, J. M. (1995). Remaining in an abusive relationship: An investment model analysis of nonvoluntary dependence. *Personality and Social Psychology Bulletin, 21,* 558–571.

Rusbult, C. E., Onizuka, R. K., & Lipkus, I. (1993). What do we really want? Mental models of ideal romantic involvement explored through multidimensional scaling. *Journal of Experimental Social Psychology, 29,* 493–527.

Rusbult, C. E., Van Lange, P. A. M., Wildschut, T., Yovetich, N. A., & Verette, J. (2000). Perceived superiority in close relationships: Why it exists and persists. *Journal of Personality and Social Psychology, 79,* 521–545.

Rusbult, C. E., Verette, J., Whitney, G. A., Slovik, L. F., & Lipkus, I. (1991). Accommodation processes in close relationships: Theory and preliminary empirical evidence. *Journal of Personality and Social Psychology, 60,* 53–78.

Ruvolo, A. P., & Rotondo, J. L. (1998). Diamonds in the rough: Implicit personality theories and views of partner and self. *Personality and Social Psychology Bulletin, 24,* 750–758.

Ruvolo, A. P., Fabin, L. A., & Ruvolo, C. M. (2001). Relationship experiences and change in attachment characteristics of young adults: The role of relationship breakups and conflict avoidance. *Personal Relationships, 8,* 265–281.

Sager, C. J. (1976). *Marriage contracts and couple therapy: Hidden forces in intimate relationships.* New York: Brunner/Mazel.

Sanchez, L., Nock, S. L., Wright, J. D., & Gager, C. T. (2002). Setting the clock forward or back? Covenant marriage and the "divorce revolution." *Journal of Family Issues, 23,* 91–120.

Sander, F. M. (1998). Psychoanalytic couples therapy. In F. M. Dattilio (Ed.), *Case studies in couple and family therapy: Systemic and cognitive perspectives* (pp. 427–449). New York: Guilford.

Sanders, M. R., Halford, W. K., & Behrens, B. C. (1999). Parental divorce and premarital couple communication. *Journal of Family Psychology, 13,* 60–74.

Sanders, S. A., & Reinisch, J. M. (1999). Would you say you "had sex" if . . .? *Journal of the American Medical Association, 281,* 275–277.

Sanderson, C. A., & Evans, S. M. (2001). Seeing one's partner through intimacy-colored glasses: An examination of the processes underlying the intimacy goals relationship satisfaction link. *Personality and Social Psychology Bulletin, 27,* 463–473.

Savin-Williams, R. C. (1996). Dating and romantic relationships among gay, lesbian, and bisexual youths. In R. C. Savin-Williams (Ed.), *The lives of lesbians, gays, and bisexuals: Children to adults.* New York: Wadsworth.

Sayegh, M. A., Fortenberry, J. D., Shew, M., & Orr, D. P. (2006). The developmental association of relationship quality, hormonal contraceptive choice and condom non-use among adolescent women. *Journal of Adolescent Health, 39,* 388–395.

Sayer, L., Wright, N., & Edin, K. (2003). *Class differences in family values: A 30-year exploration of Americans' attitudes toward the family* (Paper presented at the annual meeting of the Population Association of America). Minneapolis.

Scanzoni, J. H. (1970). *Opportunity and the family.* New York: Free Press.

Schaap, C. (1982). *Communication and adjustment in marriage.* Lisse: Swets & Zeitlinger.

Schafer, J., Caetano, R., & Clark, C. L. (1998). Rates of intimate partner violence among U.S. couples. *American Journal of Public Health, 88,* 1702–1704.

Scharfe, E., & Bartholomew, K. (1994). Reliability and stability of adult attachment patterns. *Personal Relationships, 1,* 23–43.

Scharfe, E., & Bartholomew, K. (1995). Accommodation and attachment representations in young couples. *Journal of Social and Personal Relationships, 12,* 389–401.

Scharff, J. S., & Bagnini, C. 2002. Object relations couple therapy. In A. S. Gurman & N. S. Jacobson (Eds.), *Clinical handbook of couple therapy* (3rd ed., pp. 59–85). New York: Guilford Press.

Schmaling, K. B., & Sher, T. G. (Eds.). (2000). *The psychology of couples and illness: Theory, research, and practice.* Washington, DC: American Psychological Association.

Schmitt, D. P. (2005). Sociosexuality from Argentina to Zimbabwe: A 48-nation study of sex, culture, and strategies of human mating *Behavioral and Brain Sciences, 28,* 247–311.

Schmitt, D. P., and 118 members of the International Sexuality Description Project. (2003). Universal sex differences in the desire for sexual variety: Tests from 52 nations, 6 continents, and 13 islands. *Journal of Personality and Social Psychology, 85,* 85–104.

Schoen, R., & Weinick, R. M. (1993). The slowing metabolism of marriage: Figures from 1988 U.S. Marital Status Life Tables. *Demography, 30,* 737–746.

Schopenhauer, A. (1851). *Parerga and Paralipomena* (vol. 2). Oxford: Oxford University Press.

Schramm, D. G. (2006). Individual and social costs of divorce in Utah. *Journal of Family and Economic Issues, 27,* 133–151.

Schramm, D. G., Marshall, J. P., Harris, V. W., & Lee, T. R. (2005). After "I do": The newlywed transition. *Marriage and Family Review, 38*, 45–67.

Schroder, H. M. (1971). Conceptual complexity and personality organization. In H. M. Schroder & P. Suedfeld (Eds.), *Personality theory and information processing* (pp. 240–273). New York: Ronald Press.

Schumacher, J. A., & Leonard, K. E. (2005). Husbands' and wives' marital adjustment, verbal aggression, and physical aggression as longitudinal predictors of physical aggression in early marriage. *Journal of Consulting and Clinical Psychology, 73*, 28–37.

Schwartz, M. D. (2000). Methodological issues in the use of survey data for measuring and characterizing violence against women. *Violence Against Women, 6*, 815–838.

Schwarz, N. (1999). Self-reports: How the questions shape the answers. *American Psychologist, 54*, 93–105.

Schwarz, N., & Clore, G. L. (1983). Mood, misattribution, and judgments of well-being: Informative and directive functions of affective states. *Journal of Personality and Social Psychology, 45*, 513–523.

Schwarz, N., & Clore, G. L. (2003). Mood as information: 20 years later. *Psychological Inquiry, 14*, 296–303.

Scott, M. E., Schelar, E., Manlove, J., & Cui, C. (2009). *Young adult attitudes about relationships and marriage: Times may have changed but expectations remain high* (Research Brief No. 2009–30). Washington, DC: Child Trends.

Sears, D. O. (1986). College sophomores in the laboratory: Influences of a narrow data base on psychology's view of human nature. *Journal of Personality and Social Psychology, 51*, 515–530.

Sedikides, C., & Green, J. D. (2000). On the self-protective nature of inconsistency-negativity management: Using the person memory paradigm to examine self-referent memory. *Journal of Personality and Social Psychology, 79*, 906–922.

Sedikides, C., & Strube, M. J. (1995). The multiply motivated self. *Personality and Social Psychology Bulletin, 21*, 1330–1335.

Seiffge-Krenke, I. J., Shulman, S., & Klessinger, N. (2001). Adolescent precursors of romantic relationships in young adulthood. *Journal of Social and Personal Relationships, 18*, 327–346.

Seligman, M. E. P. (1995). The effectiveness of psychotherapy: The *Consumer Reports* study. *American Psychologist, 50*, 965–974.

Shadish, W. R., & Baldwin, S. A. (2003). Meta-analysis of MFT interventions. *Journal of Marital and Family Therapy, 29*, 547–570.

Shadish, W. R., & Baldwin, S. A. (2005). Effects of behavioral marital therapy: A meta-analysis of randomized controlled trials. *Journal of Consulting and Clinical Psychology, 73*, 6–14.

Shadish, W. R., Montgomery, L. M., Wilson, P., Bright, I., & Okwumabua, T. (1993). Effects of family and marital psychotherapies: A meta-analysis. *Journal of Consulting and Clinical Psychology, 61*, 992–1002.

Shainess, N. (1979). Vulnerability to violence: Masochism as process. *American Journal of Psychotherapy, 33*, 174–189.

Shakespeare, W. (1917). *The tragedy of Hamlet, Prince of Denmark* (J.R. Crawford, Ed.). New Haven: Yale University Press.

Shamir, H., Cummings, E. M., Davies, P. T., & Goeke-Morey, M. C. (2005). Children's reactions to marital conflict in Israel and in the United States. *Parenting: Science and Practice, 5*, 371–386.

Shapiro, A. F., Gottman, J. M., & Carrère, S. (2000). The baby and the marriage: Identifying factors that buffer against decline in marital satisfaction after the first baby arrives. *Journal of Family Psychology, 14*, 59–70.

Shaver, P. R., Papalia, D., Clark, C. L., Koski, L. R., Tidwell, M. C., & Nalbone, D. (1996). Androgyny and attachment security: Two related models of optimal personality. *Personality and Social Psychological Bulletin, 22*, 582–597.

Shaver, P., Hazan, C., & Bradshaw, D. (1988). Love as attachment: The integration of three behavioral systems. In R. J. Sternberg & M. L. Barnes (Eds.), *The psychology of love* (pp. 68–99). New Haven: Yale University Press.

Shaver, P., Wu, S., & Schwartz, J. C. (1991). Cross-cultural similarities and differences in emotion and its representation. *Review of Personality and Social Psychology, 13*, 175–212.

Shelton, K. H., & Harold, G. T. (2007). Marital conflict and children's adjustment: The mediating and moderating role of children's coping strategies. *Social Development, 16*, 497–512.

Shepperd, J. A. (1993). Student derogation of the Scholastic Aptitude Test: Biases in perceptions ans presentations of college board scores. *Basic and Applied Social Psychology, 14*, 455–473.

Sherman, A. M., Lansford, J. E., & Volling, B. L. (2006). Sibling relationships and best friendships in young adulthood: Warmth, conflict, and well-being. *Personal Relationships, 13*, 151–165.

Shifflett-Simpson, K., & Cummings, E. M. (1996). Mixed message resolution and children's responses to interadult conflict. *Child Development, 67*, 437–448.

Shotland, R. L., & Craig, J. M. (1988). Can men and women differentiate between friendly and sexually interested behavior? *Social Psychology Quarterly, 51*, 66–73.

Showers, C. J., & Kevlyn, S. B. (1999). Organization of knowledge about a relationship partner: Implications for liking and loving. *Journal of Personality and Social Psychology, 76*, 958–971.

Showers, C. J., & Zeigler-Hill, V. (2004). Organization of partner knowledge: Relationship outcomes and longitudinal change. *Personality and Social Psychology Bulletin, 30*, 1198–1210.

Sieving, R. E., Eisenberg, M. E., Pettingell, S., & Skay, C. (2006). Friends' influence on adolescents' first sexual intercourse. *Perspectives on Sexual Reproductive Health, 38*, 13–19.

Sillars, A., Roberts, L. J., Leonard, K. E., & Dun, T. (2000). Cognition during marital conflict: The relationship of thought and talk. *Journal of Social and Personal Relationships, 17*, 479–502.

Simon, R. W., Eder, D., & Evans, C. (1992). The development of feeling norms underlying romantic love among adolescent females. *Social Psychology Quarterly, 55*, 29–46.

Simons, R. L. (1996). *Understanding differences between divorced and intact families*. Thousand Oaks, CA: Sage.

Simpson, J. A. (1990). Influence of attachment styles on romantic relationships. *Journal of Personality and Social Psychology, 59*, 971–980.

Simpson, J. A., & Gangestad, S. W. (1991). Individual differences in sociosexuality: Evidence for convergent and discriminant validity. *Journal of Personality and Social Psychology, 60*, 870–883.

Simpson, J. A., & Gangestad, S. W. (1992). Sociosexuality and romantic partner choice. *Journal of Personality, 60*, 31–51.

Simpson, J. A., & Gangestad, S. W. (2001). Evolution and relationships: A call for integration. *Personal Relationships, 8*, 341–355.

Simpson, J. A., & Harris, B. A. (1994). Interpersonal attraction. In A. L. Weber & J. H. Harvey (Eds.), *Perspectives on close relationships* (pp. 45–66). Needham Heights, MA: Allyn & Bacon.

Simpson, J. A., Campbell, B., & Berscheid, E. (1986). The association between romantic love and marriage: Kephart (1967) twice revisited. *Personality & Social Psychology Bulletin, 12*, 363–372.

Simpson, J. A., Collins, W. A., Tran, S., & Haydon, K. C. (2007). Attachment and the experience and expression of emotions in romantic relationships: A developmental perspective. *Journal of Personality and Social Psychology, 92*, 355–367.

Simpson, J. A., Fletcher, G. J. O., & Campbell, L. (2001). The structure and function of ideal standards in close relationships. In G. J. O. Fletcher & M. S. Clark (Eds.), *Blackwell handbook of social psychology: Interpersonal processes* (pp. 86–106). Oxford: Blackwell.

Simpson, J. A., Oriña, M. M., & Ickes, W. (2003). When accuracy hurts, and when it helps: A test of the empathic accuracy model in marital interactions. *Journal of Personality and Social Psychology, 85*, 881–893.

Simpson, J. A., Rholes, W. S., & Nelligan, J. S. (1992). Support seeking and support giving within couples in an anxiety-provoking situation: The role of attachment styles. *Journal of Personality and Social Psychology, 62*, 434–446.

Simpson, L. E., & Christensen, A. (2005). Spousal agreement regarding relationship aggression on the Conflict Tactics Scale-2. *Psychological Assessment, 17*, 423–432.

Sinclair, H. C., & Frieze, I. H. (2000). Initial courtship behavior and stalking: How should we draw the line? *Violence and Victims, 15*, 23–40.

Skrypnek, B. J., & Snyder, M. (1982). On the self-perpetuating nature of stereotypes about men and women. *Journal of Experimental Social Psychology, 18*, 277–291.

Skynner, A. C. R. (1976). *One flesh—separate persons: Principles of family and marital psychotherapy*. London: Constable and Company.

Skynner, A. C. R. (1976). *Systems of family and marital psychotherapy*. New York: Brunner/Mazel.

Slatcher, R. B., & Pennebaker, J. W. (2006). How do I love thee? Let me count the words: The social effects of expressive writing. *Psychological Science, 17*, 660–664.

Slomkowski, C., Rende, R., Conger, K. J., Simons, R. L., & Conger, R. D. (2001). Sisters, brothers, and delinquency: Evaluating social influence during early and middle adolescence. *Child Development, 72*, 271–283.

Small, L. L., & Dworkin, N. (2003). *You know he's a keeper/you know he's a loser: Happy endings and horror stories from real-life relationships*. New York: Perigee.

Smith, C. T., Ratliff, K. A., & Nosek, B. A. (2012). Rapid assimilation: Automatically integrating new information with existing beliefs. *Social Cognition, 30*, 199–219.

Smith, D. A., Vivian, D., & O'Leary, K. D. (1990). Longitudinal prediction of marital discord from premarital expressions of affect. *Journal of Consulting and Clinical Psychology, 58*, 790–798.

Smith, E. R. (1996). What do connectionism and social psychology offer each other? *Journal of Personality and Social Psychology, 70*, 893–912.

Smith, T. W., Gallo, L. C., Goble, L., Ngu, L. Q., & Stark, K. A. (1998). Agency, communion, and cardiovascular reactivity during marital interaction. *Health Psychology, 17*, 537–545.

Smock, P. J., & Gupta, S. (2002). Cohabitation in contemporary North America. In A. Booth & A. C. Crouter (Eds.), *Just living together: Implications of cohabitation on families, children, and social policy* (pp. 53–84). Mahwah, NJ: Lawrence Erlbaum Associates.

Smock, P. J., Manning, W. D., & Gupta, S. (1999). The effect of marriage and divorce on women's economic well-being. *American Sociological Review, 64,* 794–812.

Snyder, D. K., & Fruchtman, L. A. (1981). Differential patterns of wife abuse: A data-based typology. *Journal of Consulting and Clinical Psychology, 49,* 878–885.

Snyder, D. K., Castellani, A. M., & Whisman, M. A. (2006). Current status and future directions in couple therapy. *Annual Review of Psychology, 57,* 317–344.

Snyder, D. K., Wills, R. M., & Grady-Fletcher, A. (1991). Long-term effectiveness of behavioral versus insight-oriented marital therapy: A 4-year follow-up study. *Journal of Consulting and Clinical Psychology, 59,* 138–141.

Snyder, M., Tanke, E. D., & Berscheid, E. (1977). Social perception and interpersonal behavior: On the self-fulfilling nature of social stereotypes. *Journal of Personality and Social Psychology, 35,* 656–666.

Solomon, S. E., Rothblum, E. D., & Balsam, K. F. (2005). Money, housework, sex, and conflict: Same-sex couples in civil unions, those not in civil unions, and heterosexual married siblings. *Sex Roles, 9/10,* 561–575.

Sorce, J. F., Emde, R. N., Campos, J. J., & Klinnert, M. D. (1985). Maternal emotional signaling: Its effect on the visual cliff behavior of 1-year-olds. *Developmental Psychology, 21,* 195–200.

Soskin, W. F., & John, V. P. (1963). The study of spontaneous talk. In R. G. Barker (Ed.), *The stream of behavior: Exploration of its structure and content* (pp. 228–281). New York: Appleton-Century-Crofts.

South, S. J. (2001). The geographic context of divorce: Do neighborhoods matter? *Journal of Marriage and Family, 63,* 755–766.

South, S. J., & Lloyd, K. M. (1992). Marriage opportunities and family formation: Further implications of imbalanced sex ratios. *Journal of Marriage and Family, 54,* 440–451.

South, S. J., & Lloyd, K. M. (1995). Spousal alternatives and marital dissolution. *American Sociological Review, 60,* 21–35.

South, S. J., & Spitze, G. (1994). Housework in marital and nonmarital households. *American Sociological Review, 59,* 327–347.

South, S. J., Bose, S., & Trent, K. (2004). Anticipating divorce: Spousal agreement, predictive accuracy, and effects on labor supply and fertility. *Journal of Divorce and Remarriage, 40,* 1–22.

South, S. J., Trent, K., & Shen, Y. (2001). Changing partners: Toward a macrostructural-opportunity theory of marital dissolution. *Journal of Marriage and Family, 63,* 743–754.

Spaht, K. S. (1998). Louisiana's covenant marriage: Social analysis and legal implications. *Louisiana Law Review, 59,* 63–130.

Spanier, G. B., Lewis, R. A., & Cole, C. L. (1975). Marital adjustment over the family life cycle: The issue of curvilinearity. *Journal of Marriage and Family, 37,* 263–275.

Sprague, H. E., & Kinney, J. M. (1997). The effects of interparental divorce and conflict on college students' romantic relationships. *Journal of Divorce and Remarriage, 27,* 85–104.

Sprecher, S. (1989). The importance to males and females of physical attractiveness, earning potential, and expressiveness in initial attraction. *Sex Roles, 21,* 591–607.

Sprecher, S. (1999). "I love you more today than yesterday": Romantic partners' perceptions of changes in love and related affect over time. *Journal of Personality and Social Psychology, 76,* 46–53.

Sprecher, S. (2002). Sexual satisfaction in premarital relationships: Associations with satisfaction, love, commitment, and stability. *Journal of Sex Research, 39,* 190–196.

Sprecher, S., & Cate, R. M. (2004). Sexual satisfaction and sexual expression as predictors of relationship satisfaction and stability. In J. H. Harvey, A. Wenzel, & S. Sprecher (Eds.), *The handbook of sexuality in close relationships* (pp. 235–256). Mahwah, NJ: Erlbaum.

Sprecher, S., & Felmlee, D. (1992). The influence of parents and friends on the quality and stability of romantic relationships: A three-wave longitudinal investigation. *Journal of Marriage and Family, 54,* 888–900.

Sprecher, S., & Metts, S. (1989). Development of the "Romantic Beliefs Scale" and examination of the effects of gender and gender-role orientation. *Journal of Social and Personal Relationships, 6,* 387–411.

Sprecher, S., & Regan, P. C. (2002). Liking some things (in some people) more than others: Partner preferences in romantic relationships and friendships. *Journal of Social and Personal Relationships, 19,* 463–481.

Sprecher, S., Aron, A., Hatfield, E., Cortese, A., Potapova, E., & Levitskaya, A. (1994). Love: American style, Russian style and Japanese style. *Personal Relationships, 1,* 349–369.

Sprecher, S., Barbee, A., & Schwartz, P. (1995). "Was it good for you too?" Gender differences in first sexual intercourse experience. *Journal of Sex Research, 32,* 3–15.

Sprecher, S., Felmlee, D., Orbuch, T. L., & Willetts, M. C. (2002). Social networks and change in personal relationships. In A. L. Vangelisti & H. T. Reis (Eds.), *Stability and change in relationships* (pp. 257–284). New York: Cambridge University Press.

Sprecher, S., Sullivan, Q., & Hatfield, E. (1994). Mate selection preferences: Gender differences examined in a national sample. *Journal of Personality and Social Psychology, 66,* 1074–1080.

Sroufe, L. A., Egeland, B., Carlson, E., & Collins, W. A. (2005). Placing early attachment experiences in developmental context: The Minnesota Longitudinal Study. In K. E. Grossmann, K. Grossmann & E. Waters (Eds.), *Attachment from infancy to adulthood: The major longitudinal studies* (pp. 48–70). New York: Guilford.

Srull, T. K., & Wyer, R. S., Jr. (1986). The role of chronic and temporary goals in social information processing. In R. M. Sorrentino & E. T. Higgins (Eds.), *Handbook of motivation and cognition: Foundations of social behavior* (pp. 503–549). New York: Guilford Press.

Stack, S., & Eshleman, J. R. (1998). Marital status and happiness: A 17-nation study. *Journal of Marriage and Family, 60,* 527–536.

Stander, V. A., Hilton, S. M., Kennedy, K. R., & Robbins, D. L. (2004). Surveillance of completed suicide in the Department of Navy. *Military Medicine, 169,* 301–306.

Stanley, S. M., Amato, P. R., Johnson, C. A., & Markman, H. J. (2006). Premarital education, marital quality, and marital stability: Findings from a large, random household survey. *Journal of Family Psychology, 20,* 117–126.

Stanley, S. M., Rhoades, G. K., & Markman, H. J. (2006). Sliding versus deciding: Inertia and the premarital cohabitation effect. *Family Relations, 55,* 499–509.

Steinglass, P. (1978). The conceptualization of marriage from a systems theory perspective. In T. J. Paolino & B. S. McCrady (Eds.), *Marriage and marital therapy: Psychoanalytic, behavioral and systems theory perspectives* (pp. 298–394). New York: Brunner/Mazel.

Steinmetz, S. K. (1978). Wife-beating: A critique and reformulation of existing theory. *Bulletin of the American Academy of Psychiatry and the Law, 6,* 322–334.

Sternberg, R. J., & Grajek, S. (1984). The nature of love. *Journal of Personality and Social Psychology, 47,* 312–329.

Stets, J. (1992). Interactive processes in dating aggression: A national study. *Journal of Marriage and Family, 54,* 165–177.

Stets, J., & Straus, M. A. (1990). Gender differences in reporting of marital violence and its medical and psychological consequences. In M. A. Straus & R. J. Gelles (Eds.), *Physical violence in American families: Risk factors and adaptations to violence in 8,145 families* (pp. 151–165). New Brunswick, NJ: Transaction.

Stith, S. M., Rosen, K. H., Middleton, K. A., Busch, A. L., Lundberg, K., & Carlton, R. P. (2000). The intergenerational transmission of spouse abuse: A meta-analysis. *Journal of Marriage and Family, 62,* 640–654.

Stocker, C. M., & Richmond, M. K. (2007). Longitudinal associations between hostility in adolescents' family relationships and friendships and hostility in their romantic relationships. *Journal of Family Psychology, 21,* 490–497.

Stocker, C. M., Dunn, J., & Plomin, R. (1989). Sibling relationships: Links with child temperament, maternal behavior, and family structure. *Child Development, 60,* 715–727.

Stocker, C. M., Richmond, M. K., Low, S. M., Alexander, E. K., & Elias, N. M. (2003). Marital conflict and children's adjustment: Parental hostility and children's interpretations as mediators. *Social Development, 12,* 149–161.

Stoneman, Z., Brody, G. H., & MacKinnon, C. (1984). Naturalistic observations of children's activities and roles while playing with their siblings and friends. *Child Development, 55,* 617–627.

Stoolmiller, M., Eddy, J. M., & Reid, J. B. (2000). Detecting and describing preventive intervention effects in a universal school-based randomized trial targeting delinquent and violent behavior. *Journal of Consulting and Clinical Psychology, 68,* 296–306.

Storaasli, R. D., & Markman, H. J. (1990). Relationship problems in the early stages of marriage: A longitudinal investigation. *Journal of Family Psychology, 4,* 80–98.

Storms, M. D. (1973). Videotape and the attribution process: Reversing actors' and observers' points of view. *Journal of Personality and Social Psychology, 27,* 165–175.

Stormshak, E. A., Bellanti, C. J., & Bierman, K. L. (1996). The quality of sibling relationships and the development of social competence and behavioral control in aggressive children. *Developmental Psychology, 32,* 79–89.

Straus, M. A. (1979). Measuring intrafamily conflict and violence: The Conflict Tactics (CT) Scales. *Journal of Marriage and Family, 41,* 75–88.

Straus, M. A. (1999). The controversy over domestic violence by women: A methodological, theoretical, and sociology of science analysis. In X. B. Arriaga & S. Oskamp (Eds.), *Violence in intimate relationships* (pp. 17–44). Thousand Oaks, CA: Sage.

Straus, M. A., & Gelles, R. J. (1986). Societal change in family violence from 1975 to 1985 as revealed by two national surveys. *Journal of Marriage and Family, 48,* 465–479.

Straus, M. A., & Gelles, R. J. (Eds.). (1990). *Physical violence in American families: Risk factors and adaptations to violence in 8,145 families.* New Brunswick, NJ: Transaction.

Straus, M. A., Hamby, S. L., Boney-McCoy, S., & Sugarman, D. B. (1996). The Revised Conflict Tactics Scales (CTS2): Development and preliminary psychometric data. *Journal of Family Issues, 17,* 283–316.

Streufert, S., & Fromkin, H. L. (1972). Complexity and social influence. In J. Tedeschi (Ed.), *Social influence processes* (pp. 220–255). Chicago: Aldine.

Stroebe, W., & Stroebe, M. (1996). The social psychology of social support. In E. T. Higgins & A. W. Kruglanski (Eds.), *Social psychology: Handbook of basic principles* (pp. 597–621). New York: Guilford.

Strube, M. J. (1988). The decision to leave an abusive relationship: Empirical evidence and theoretical issues. *Psychological Bulletin, 104,* 236–250.

Strube, M. J., & Barbour, L. S. (1983). The decision to leave an abusive relationship: Economic dependence and psychological commitment. *Journal of Marriage and Family, 45,* 785–793.

Stuart, R. B. (1969). Operant-interpersonal treatment of marital discord. *Journal of Consulting and Clinical Psychology, 33,* 675–682.

Sturge-Apple, M. L., Davies, P. T., & Cummings, E. M. (2006). Impact of hostility and withdrawal in interparental conflict on parental emotional unavailability and children's adjustment difficulties. *Child Development, 77,* 1623–1641.

Stutzer, A., & Frey, B. S. (2006). Does marriage make people happy, or do happy people get married? *Journal of Socio-Economics, 35,* 326–347.

Suitor, J. J., Pillemer, K., Straus, M. A. (1990). Marital violence in a life course perspective. In M. A. Straus & R. J. Gelles (Eds.), *Physical violence in American families: Risk factors and adaptations to violence in 8,145 families* (pp. 305–313). New Brunswick, NJ: Transaction.

Sullivan, K. T., & Bradbury, T. N. (1997). Are premarital prevention programs reaching couples at risk for marital dysfunction? *Journal of Consulting and Clinical Psychology, 65,* 24–30.

Sulloway, F. J. (2001). Birth order, sibling competition, and human behavior. In P. S. Davies & H. R. Holcomb (Eds.), *Conceptual challenges in evolutionary psychology: Innovative research strategies* (pp. 39–83). Dordrecht: Kluwer Academic.

Sun, Y. (2001). Family environment and adolescents' well-being before and after parents' marital disruption: A longitudinal analysis. *Journal of Marriage and Family, 63,* 697–713.

Surra, C. A. (1988). The influence of the interactive network on developing relationships. In R. M. Milardo (Ed.), *Families and social networks* (pp. 48–82). Thousand Oaks, CA: Sage.

Swan, S., & Snow, D. L. (2002). A typology of women's use of violence in intimate relationships. *Violence Against Women, 8,* 286–319.

Swann, W. B. (1984). Quest for accuracy in person perception: A matter of pragmatics. *Psychological Review, 91,* 457–477.

Swann, W. B. Jr. (1990). To be adored or to be known? The interplay of self-enhancement and self-verification. In E. T. Higgins & R. M. Sorrentino (Eds.), *Handbook of motivation and cognition: Foundations of social behavior* (pp. 408–448). New York: Guilford.

Swann, W. B., & Schroeder, D. G. (1995). The search for beauty and truth: A framework for understanding reactions to evaluations. *Personality and Social Psychology Bulletin, 21,* 1307–1318.

Swann, W. B., De La Ronde, C., & Hixon, J. G. (1994). Authenticity and positivity strivings in marriage and courtship. *Journal of Personality and Social Psychology, 66,* 857–869.

Swann, W. B., Jr., Rentfrow, P. J., & Guinn, J. S. (2003). Self-verification: The search for coherence. In M. R. Leary & J. P. Tangney (Eds.), *Handbook of self and identity* (pp. 367–383). New York: Guilford.

Sweeney, M. M. (2002). Remarriage and the nature of divorce: Does it matter which spouse chose to leave? *Journal of Family Issues, 23,* 410–440.

Swensen, C. H., Eskew, R. W., & Kohlhepp, K. A. (1984). Five factors in long-term marriages. *Journal of Family and Economic Issues, 7,* 94–106.

Swindle, R., Jr., Heller, K., Pescosolido, B., & Kikuzawa, S. (2000). Responses to nervous breakdowns in America over a 40-year period: Mental health policy implications. *American Psychologist, 55,* 740–749.

Symons, D. (1979). *The evolution of human sexuality.* New York: Oxford University Press.

Szinovacz, M. (1996). Couples' employment/retirement patterns and perceptions of marital quality. *Research on Aging, 18,* 243–268.

Tafarodi, R. W., Bonn, G., Liang, H., Takai, J., Moriizumi, S., Belhekar, V., & Padhye, A. (2012). What makes for a good life? A four-nation study. *Journal of Happiness Studies, 13,* 783–800

Tallman, I., Burke, P. J., & Gecas, V. (1998). Socialization into marital roles: Testing a contextual, developmental model of marital functioning. In T. N. Bradbury (Ed.), *The developmental course of marital dysfunction* (pp. 312–342). New York: Cambridge University Press.

Tamres, L. K., Janicki, D., & Helgeson, V. S. (2002). Sex differences in coping behavior: A meta-analytic review and an examination of relative coping. *Personality and Social Psychology Review, 6*, 2–30.

Tasker, F., & Richards, M. P. M. (1994). Adolescent attitudes toward marriage and marital prospects after parental divorce: A review. *Journal of Adolescent Research, 9*, 340–362.

Taylor, J. (1999). *Falling: The story of one marriage*. New York: Ballantine Books.

Taylor, S. E. (2002). *The tending instinct: How nurturing is essential to who we are and how we live*. New York: Holt.

Taylor, S. E., Repetti, R. L., & Seeman, T. (1997). Health psychology: What is an unhealthy environment and how does it get under the skin? *Annual Review of Psychology, 48*, 411–447.

Teachman, J. D., & Polonko, K. A. (1990). Cohabitation and marital stability in the United States. *Social Forces, 69*, 207–220.

Tennov, D. (1979). *Love and limerance*. New York: Stein and Day.

Terman, L. M., Buttenwieser, P., Ferguson, L. W., Johnson, W. B., & Wilson, D. P. (1938). *Psychological factors in marital happiness*. New York: McGraw-Hill.

Tesser, A. (2000). On the confluence of self-esteem maintenance mechanisms. *Personality and Social Psychology Review, 4*, 290–299.

Tesser, A., & Beach, S. R. H. (1998). Life events, relationship quality, and depression: An investigation of judgment discontinuity in vivo. *Journal of Personality and Social Psychology, 74*, 36–52.

Testa, M., & Leonard, K. E. (2001). The impact of marital aggression on women's psychological and marital functioning in a newlywed sample. *Journal of Family Violence, 16*, 115–130.

Thibaut, J. W., & Kelley, H. H. (1959). *The social psychology of groups*. New York: Wiley.

Thomas, G. L. (2002). *Sacred marriage*. Grand Rapids, MI: Zondervan.

Thomas, G., & Maio, G. R. (2008). Man, I feel like a woman: When and how gender-role motivation helps mind-reading. *Journal of Personality and Social Psychology, 95*, 1165–1179.

Thomas, G., Fletcher, G. J. O., & Lange, C. (1997). On-line empathic accuracy in marital interaction. *Journal of Personality and Social Psychology, 72*, 839–850.

Thomas, J. R., & French, K. E. (1985). Gender differences across age in motor performance: A meta-analysis. *Psychological Bulletin, 98*, 260–282.

Thomas, K. W. (2004). *Calling in "the one": 7 weeks to attract the love of your life*. New York: Three Rivers Press.

Thompson, A., & Bolger, N. (1999). Emotional transmission in couples under stress. *Journal of Marriage and Family, 61*, 38–48.

Thompson, L., & Walker, A. J. (1989). Gender in families: Women and men in marriage, work, and parenthood. *Journal of Marriage and Family, 51*, 845–871.

Thornhill, R., & Gangestad, S. W. (1999). The scent of symmetry: A human sex pheromone that signals fitness? *Evolution and Human Behavior, 20*, 175–201.

Thornhill, R., & Moller, A. P. (1997). The relative importance of size and asymmetry in sexual selection. *Behavioral Ecology, 9*, 546–551.

Thornton, A. (1990). The courtship process and adolescent sexuality. *Journal of Family Issues, 11*, 239–273.

Thornton, A. (2009). Framework for interpreting long-term trends in values and beliefs concerning single-parent families. *Journal of Marriage and Family, 71*, 230–234.

Thornton, A., & Young-DeMarco, L. (2001). Four decades of trends in attitudes toward family issues in the United States: The 1960s through the 1990s. *Journal of Marriage and Family, 63*, 1009–1037.

Till, A., & Freedman, E. M. (1978). Complementarity versus similarity of traits operating in the choice of marriage and dating partners. *Journal of Social Psychology, 105*, 147–148.

Timmer, S. G., & Veroff, J. (2000). Family ties and the discontinuity of divorce in black and white newlywed couples. *Journal of Marriage and Family, 62*, 349–361.

Timmer, S. G., Veroff, J., & Hatchett, S. (1996). Family ties and marital happiness: The different marital experiences of black and white newlywed couples. *Journal of Social and Personal Relationships, 13*, 335–359.

Tishkoff, S. A., Reed, F. A., Ranciaro, A., Voight, B. F., Babbitt, C. C., Silverman, J. S. et al. (2007). Convergent adaptation of human lactase persistence in Africa and Europe. *Nature Genetics, 39*, 31–40.

Tjaden, P. & Thoennes, N. (2000). Extent, nature, and consequences of intimate partner violence: Findings from the National Violence Against Women Survey. Washington, DC: U.S. Department of Justice. Publication NCJ 181867.

Todd, T. C. (1986). Structural-strategic marital therapy. In N. S. Jacobson & A. S. Gurman (Eds.), *Clinical handbook of marital therapy* (pp. 71–105) New York: Guilford.

Todosijevic, J., Rothblum, E. D., & Solomon, S. E. (2005). Relationship satisfaction, affectivity, and gay-specific stressors in same-sex couples joined in civil unions. *Psychology of Women Quarterly, 29,* 158–166.

Trail, T. E., & Karney, B. R. (2012). What's (not) wrong with low-income marriages? *Journal of Marriage and Family, 74,* 413–427.

Treas, J. (1995). Older Americans in the 1990s and beyond. *Population Bulletin, 50,* 1–47.

Triandis, H. C. (1999). Odysseus wandered for 10, I wondered for 50 years. In W. J. Lonner & D. L. Dinnel (Eds.), *Merging past, present, and future in cross-cultural psychology: Selected papers from the Fourteenth International Congress of the International Association for Cross-Cultural Psychology* (pp. 46–50). Lisse, Netherlands: Swets & Zeitlinger.

Triandis, H. C. (1996). The psychological measurement of cultural syndromes. *American Psychologist, 51,* 407–415.

Trivers, R. (1972). Parental investment and sexual selection. In B. Campbell (Ed.), *Sexual selection and the descent of man, 1871–1971* (pp. 136–179). Chicago: Aldine.

Troxel, W. M., & Matthews, K. A. (2004). What are the costs of marital conflict and dissolution to children's physical health? *Clinical Child and Family Psychology Review, 7,* 29–57.

Trzesniewski, K. H., Donnellan, M. B., & Robins, R. W. (2003). Stability of self-esteem across the lifespan. *Journal of Personality and Social Psychology, 84,* 205–220.

Turell, S. C. (2000). A descriptive analysis of same-sex relationship violence for a diverse sample. *Journal of Interpersonal Violence, 15,* 281–293.

Tweed, R., & Dutton, D. G. (1998). A comparison of impulsive and instrumental subgroups of batters. *Violence and Victims, 13,* 217–230.

Tyndall, L. W., & Lichtenberg, J. W. (1985). Spouses' cognitive styles and marital interaction patterns. *Journal of Marital and Family Therapy, 11,* 193–202.

U.S. Census Bureau. (2006). American Community Survey: 2006 (No. S1201): Marital Status.

U.S. Census Bureau. (2007). American Community Survey 2007 Release: Table S1101. Households and Families (Publication. Retrieved July 13, 2009, from American FactFinder: http://factfinder.census.gov.).

U.S. Census Bureau. (2008). Current Population Survey: Table MS-2. Estimated Median Age at First Marriage, by Sex: 1890 to the Present (Publication. Retrieved July 13, 2009: www.census.gov/population/socdemo/hh-fam/ms2.xls).

U.S. Census Bureau. (2010). Current Population Survey, "America's Families and Living Arrangements" for 2010 (Table UC3). www.census.gov/population/www/socdemo/hh-fam/cps2010.html.

U.S. Census Bureau (1998). Statistical abstract of the United States (118th ed.) Washington, DC: U.S. Government Printing Office.

U.S. Census Bureau. (2000). Statistical Abstract of the United States: 2000. Retrieved April 23, 2009 from http://www.census.gov/prod/2001pubs/statab/sec01.pdf

U.S. National Center for Health Statistics. (2003). Births: Preliminary data for 2002. Retrieved March 11, 2009, from http://www.cdc.gov/nchs/data/nvsr/nvsr51/nvsr51_11.pdf

Udry, J. R. (1980). Changes in the frequency of marital intercourse from panel data. *Archives of Sexual Behavior, 9,* 319–325.

Underwood, M. K. (2004). Gender and peer relations: Are the two gender cultures really all that different? In J. B. Kupersmidt & K. A. Dodge (Eds.), *Children's peer relations: From development to intervention* (pp. 21–36). Washington, DC: American Psychological Association.

Uvänas-Moberg, K., Arn, I., & Magnusson, D. (2005). The psychobiology of emotion: The role of the oxytocinergic system. *International Journal of Behavioral Medicine, 12,* 59–65.

Vaillant, C. O., & Vaillant, G. E. (1993). Is the U-curve of marital satisfaction an illusion? A 40-year study of marriage. *Journal of Marriage and Family, 55,* 230–239.

Vaillant, G. E., & Koury, S. H. (1993). Late mid-life development. In G. H. Pollock & S. I. Greenspan (Eds.), *Late adulthood* (Vol. 6. Rev. ed., pp. 1–22). Madison, CT: International Universities Press.

Van Aken, M. A. G., & Asendorpf, J. B. (1997). Support by parents, classmates, friends and siblings in preadolescence: Covariation and compensation across relationships. *Journal of Social and Personal Relationships, 14,* 79–93.

Van Horn, K. R., Arnone, A., Nesbitt, K., Desilets, L., Sears, T., Giffin, M., et al. (1997). Physical distance and interpersonal characteristics in college students' romantic relationships. *Personal Relationships, 4,* 25–34.

Van Lange, P. A. M., & Rusbult, C. E. (1995). My relationship is better than—and not as bad as—yours is: The perception of superiority in close relationships. *Personality and Social Psychology Bulletin, 21,* 32–44.

Van Lange, P. A. M., Rusbult, C. E., Drigotas, S. M., Arriaga, X. B., Witcher, B. S., & Cox, C. L. (1997). Willingness to sacrifice in close relationships. *Journal of Personality and Social Psychology, 72,* 1373–1395.

VanLange,P.A.M.,Rusbult,C.E.,Semin-Goossens,A., Görts, C. A., & Stalpers, M. (1999). Being better than others but otherwise perfectly normal: Perceptions of uniqueness and similarity in close relationships. *Personal Relationships, 6,* 269–289.

van Schaick, K., & Stolberg, A. L. (2001). The impact of paternal involvement and parental divorce on young adults' intimate relationships. *Journal of Divorce and Remarriage, 36,* 99–122.

Vangelisti, A. L. (2001). Making sense of hurtful interactions in close relationships. In V. Manusov & J. H. Harvey (Eds.), *Attribution, communication behavior, and close relationships* (pp. 38–58). New York: Cambridge University Press.

Vangelisti, A. L., & Daly, J. A. (1997). Gender differences in standards for romantic relationships. *Personal Relationships, 4,* 203–220.

VanLaningham, J., Johnson, D. R., & Amato, P. (2001). Marital happiness, marital duration, and the U-shaped curve: Evidence from a five-wave panel study. *Social Forces, 78,* 1313–1341.

Veroff, J., Douvan, E., & Hatchett, S. J. (1995). *Marital instability: A social and behavioral study of the early years.* Greenwich, CT: Greenwood.

Veroff, J., Kulka, R. A., & Douvan, E. (1981). *Mental health in America: Patterns of help-seeking from 1957 to 1976.* New York: Basic Books.

Vincent, C. E. (1973). *Sexual and marital health.* New York: McGraw-Hill.

Vincent, J., Weiss, R. L., & Birchler, G. R. (1975). A behavioral analysis of problem-solving in distressed and nondistressed married and stranger dyads. *Behavior Therapy, 6,* 475–487.

Vincent, N. (2006). *Self-made man: One woman's journey into manhood and back again.* New York: Viking.

Vohs, K. D., & Baumeister, R. F. (2004). Sexual passion, intimacy, and gender. In D. Mashek & A. Aron (Eds.), *Handbook of closeness and intimacy* (pp. 189–199). Mahwah, NJ: Erlbaum.

Vohs, K. D., Catanese, K. R., & Baumeister, R. F. (2004). Sex in "his" versus "her" relationship. In J. H. Harvey, A. Wenzel, & S. Sprecher (Eds.), *The handbook of sexuality in close relationships* (pp. 455–474). Mahwah, NJ: Erlbaum.

Volling, B. L., Youngblade, L. M., & Belsky, J. (1997). Young children's social relationships with siblings and friends. *American Journal of Orthopsychiatry, 67,* 102–111.

Vorauer, J. D., & Ross, M. (1996). The pursuit of knowledge in close relationships: An informational goals analysis. In G. J. O. Fletcher & J. Fitness (Eds.), *Knowledge structures in close relationships: A social psychological perspective* (pp. 369–396). Mahwah, NJ: Erlbaum.

Waite, L. J., & Gallagher, M. (2000). *The case for marriage: Why married people are happier, healthier, and better off financially.* New York: Doubleday.

Waldinger, R. J., Diguer, L., Guastella, F., Lefebvre, R., Allen, J. P., Luborsky, L., et al. (2002). The same old song?—Stability and change in relationship schemas from adolescence to young adulthood. *Journal of Youth and Adolescence, 31,* 17–29.

Walker, L. E. (1979). *The battered woman.* New York: Harper & Row.

Wallerstein, J. S., Lewis, J. M., & Blakeslee, S. (2000). *The unexpected legacy of divorce: A 25-year landmark study.* New York: Hyperion.

Walster, E., Aronson, V., Abrahams, D., & Rottmann, L. (1966). Importance of physical attractiveness in dating behavior. *Journal of Personality and Social Psychology, 4,* 508–516.

Warren, B. L. (1966). A multiple variable approach to the assortive mating phenomenon. *Eugenics Quarterly, 13,* 285–290.

Waters, E., Merrick, S., Treboux, D., Crowell, J., & Albersheim, L. (2000). Attachment security in infancy and early adulthood: A twenty-year longitudinal study. *Child Development, 71*(3), 684–689.

Watson, D., & Clark, L. A. (1984). Negative affectivity: The disposition to experience aversive emotional states. *Psychological Bulletin, 96,* 465–490.

Watson, D., Klohnen, E. C., Casillas, A., Simms, E. N., Haig, J., & Berry, D. S. (2004). Match makers and deal breakers: Analyses of assortative mating in newlywed couples. *Journal of Personality, 72,* 1029–1068.

Watzlawick, P., Weakland, J. H., & Fisch, R. (1974). *Change: Principles of problem formation and problem resolution.* New York: W. W. Norton.

Weiner, B. (1972). *Theories of motivation: From mechanism to cognition.* Chicago: Rand McNally.

Weiner, B., Graham, S., Peter, O., & Zmuidinas, M. (1991). Public confession and forgiveness. *Journal of Personality, 59,* 281–312.

Weinfield, N. S., Sroufe, L. A., & Egeland, B. (2000). Attachment from infancy to early adulthood in a high-risk sample: Continuity, discontinuity, and their correlates. *Child Development, 71,* 695–702.

Weiss, R. L. (1978). The conceptualization of marriage from a behavioral perspective. In T. J. Paolino & B. S. McCrady (Eds.), *Marriage and marital therapy: Psychoanalytic, behavioral and systems theory perspectives* (pp. 165–239). New York: Brunner /Mazel.

Weiss, R. L. (1980). Strategic behavioral marital therapy: Toward a model for assessment and intervention. In J. P. Vincent (Ed.), *Advances in fam-*

ily intervention, assessment, and theory (Vol. 1, pp. 229–271). Greenwich, CT: JAI Press.

Weiss, R. L. (1984). Cognitive and behavioral measures of marital interaction. In K. Hahlweg & N. S. Jacobson (Eds.), *Marital interaction: Analysis and modification* (pp. 232–252). New York: Guilford.

Weiss, R. L., & Perry, B. A. (1983). The Spouse Observation Checklist: Development and clinical applications. In E. E. Filsinger (Ed.), *Marriage and family assessment: A sourcebook for family therapy* (pp. 65–84). Beverly Hills, CA: Sage.

Weiss, R. L., Hops, H., & Patterson, G. R. (1973). A framework for conceptualizing marital conflict: A technology for altering it, some data for evaluating it. In L. D. Handy & E. L. Mash (Eds.), *Behavior change: Methodology, concepts, and practice* (pp. 309–342). Champaign, IL: Research Press.

Weiss, R. S. (1973). *Loneliness: The experience of emotional and social isolation*. Cambridge, MA: MIT Press.

Weiss, R. S. (1975). *Marital separation*. New York: Basic Books.

Weiss, R. S. (1986). Continuities and transformations in the social provisions of relationships from childhood to adulthood. In W. Hartup & Z. Rubin (Eds.), *Relationships and development*. Hillsdale, NJ: Lawrence Erlbaum Associates.

Wells, B. E., & Twenge, J. M. (2005). Changes in young people's sexual behavior and attitudes, 1943–1999: A cross-temporal meta-analysis. *Review of General Psychology, 9*, 249–261.

Westen, D. (1998). The scientific legacy of Sigmund Freud: Toward a psychodynamically informed psychological science. *Psychological Bulletin, 124*, 333–371.

Wethington, E., & Kessler, R. C. (1986). Perceived support, received support, and adjustment to stressful life events. *Journal of Health and Social Behavior, 27*, 78–89.

Wheeler, L., & Kim, Y. (1997). What is beautiful is culturally good: The physical attractiveness stereotype has different content in collectivistic cultures. *Personality and Social Psychology Bulletin, 23*, 795–800.

Whisman, M. A. (2001). The association between depression and marital dissatisfaction. In S. R. H. Beach (Ed.), *Marital and family processes in depression: A scientific foundation for clinical practice* (pp. 3–24). Washington, DC: APA.

Whisman, M. A., & Bruce, M. L. (1999). Marital dissatisfaction and incidence of major depressive episode in a community sample. *Journal of Abnormal Psychology, 108*, 674–678.

Whisman, M. A., & Snyder, D. K. (2007). Sexual infidelity in a national survey of American women: Differences in prevalence and correlates as a function of method of assessment. *Journal of Family Psychology, 21*, 147–154.

Whisman, M. A., Dixon, A. E., & Johnson, B. (1997). Therapists' perspectives of couple problems and treatment issues in couple therapy. *Journal of Family Psychology, 11*, 361–366.

Whitaker, D. J., Haileyesus, T., Swahn, M., & Saltzman, L. S. (2007). Differences in frequency of violence and reported injury between relationships with reciprocal and nonreciprocal intimate partner violence. *American Journal of Public Health, 97*, 941–947.

White, G. L. (1980). Physical attractiveness and courtship progress. *Journal of Personality and Social Psychology, 39*, 660–668.

White, H. R., & Chen, P.-H. (2002). Problem drinking and intimate partner violence. *Journal of Studies on Alcohol, 63*, 205–214.

White, L. K., & Booth, A. (1985). The transition to parenthood and marital quality. *Journal of Family Issues, 6*, 435–449

White, L., & Edwards, J. N. (1990). Emptying the nest and parental well-being: An analysis of national panel data. *American Sociological Review, 55*, 235–242.

Whyte, M. (1978). *The status of women in preindustrial societies*. Princeton, NJ: Princeton University Press.

Wickrama, K. A. S., Lorenz, F. O., Conger, R. D., Elder, G. H., Jr., Abraham, W. T., & Fang, S.-A. (2006). Changes in family financial circumstances and the physical health of married and recently divorced mothers. *Social Science and Medicine, 63*, 123–136.

Widmer, E. D., & LaFarga, L. (2000). Family networks: A sociometric method to study relationships in families. *Field Methods, 12*, 108–128.

Widmer, E. D., Kellerhals, J., & Levy, R. (2004). Types of conjugal networks, conjugal conflict and conjugal quality. *European Sociological Review 20*, 63–77.

Wiederman, M. W. (1993). Evolved gender differences in mate preferences: Evidence from personal advertisements. *Ethology and Sociobiology, 14*, 331–351.

Wile, D. (1981). *After the honeymoon: How conflict can improve your relationship*. New York: Wiley.

Wilkins, R., & Gareis, E. (2006). Emotional expression and the locution "I love you": A cross-cultural study. *International Journal of Intercultural Relations, 30*, 51–75.

Williams, D. E., & D'Alessandro, J. D. (1994). A comparison of three measures of androgyny and their relationship to psychological adjustment. *Journal of Social Behavior & Personality, 9*, 469–480.

Williams, K., & Umberson, D. (2004). Marital status, marital transitions, and health: A gendered life course perspective. *Journal of Health and Social Behavior, 45*, 81–98.

Williams, R. B., Barefoot, J. C., Califf, R. M., Haney, T. L., Saunder, W. B., Pryor, D. B., et al. (1992). Prognostic importance of social and economic resources among medically treated patients with angiographically documented coronary artery disease. *Journal of the American Medical Association, 267*, 520–524.

Williams, S. L., & Frieze, I. H. (2005). Patterns of violent relationships, psychological distress, and marital satisfaction in a national sample of men and women. *Sex Roles, 52*, 771–784.

Wills, T. A., Weiss, R. L., & Patterson, G. R. (1974). A behavioral analysis of the determinants of marital satisfaction. *Journal of Consulting and Clinical Psychology, 42*, 802–811.

Wilmoth, J., & Koso, G. (2002). Does marital history matter? Marital status and wealth outcomes among preretirement adults. *Journal of Marriage and Family, 64*, 254–268.

Wilson, B., & Clarke, S. (1992). Remarriages: A demographic profile. *Journal of Family Issues, 13*, 123–141.

Wilson, J. Q. (2002). *The marriage problem: How our culture has weakened families*. New York: Harper Collins.

Wilson, W. J. (1987). *The truly disadvantaged: The inner city, the underclass, and public policy*. Chicago: University of Chicago Press.

Wimmer, H., & Perner, J. (1983). Beliefs about beliefs: Representation and constraining function of wrong beliefs in young children's understanding of deception. *Cognition, 13*, 103–128.

Winch, R. F. (1958). *Mate selection: A theory of complementary needs*. New York: Harper & Brothers.

Wolfinger, N. H. (2005). *Understanding the divorce cycle: The children of divorce in their own marriages*. New York: Cambridge University Press. Conference on Parent Education. Charles Stewart Mott Foundation, Flint, MI.

Wong, S., & Goodwin, R. (2009). Experiencing marital satisfaction across three cultures: A qualitative study. *Journal of Social and Personal Relationships, 26*, 1011–1028.

Wood, W., & Eagly, A. H. (2002). A cross-cultural analysis of the behavior of women and men: Implications for the origins of sex differences. *Psychological Bulletin, 128*, 699–727.

Wood, R. G., McConnell, S., Moore, Q., Clarkwest, A., & Hsueh, J. (2012). The effects of building strong families: A healthy marriage and relationship skills education program for unmarried parents. *Journal of Policy Analysis and Management, 31*, 228–252.

Wood, W., Rhodes, N., & Whelan, M. (1989). Sex differences in positive well-being: A consideration of emotional style and marital status. *Psychological Bulletin, 106*, 249–264.

Woodin, E. M., & O'Leary, K. D. (2006). Partner aggression severity as a risk marker for male and female violence recidivism. *Journal of Marital and Family Therapy, 32*, 283–296.

Wortman, C. B., Adesman, P., Herman, E., & Greenberg, R. (1976). Self-disclosure: An attributional perspective. *Journal of Personality and Social Psychology, 33*, 184–191.

Xiaohe, X., & Whyte, M. K. (1990). Love matches and arranged marriages: A Chinese replication. *Journal of Marriage and Family, 115*, 217–228.

Yang, H.-C, & Schuler, T. A. (2009). Marital quality and survivorship: Slowed recovery for breast cancer patients in distressed relationships. *Cancer, 115*, 217–228.

Yeh, H.-C., & Lempers, J. D. (2004). Perceived sibling relationships and adolescent development. *Journal of Youth and Adolescence, 33*, 133–147.

Yelsma, P., & Athappilly, K. (1988). Marital satisfaction and communication practices: Comparisons among Indian and American couples. *Journal of Comparative Family Studies, 19*, 37–54.

Yerkes, R. M., & Dodson, J. D. (1908). The relation of strength of stimulus to rapidity of habit formation. *Journal of Comparative Neurology and Psychology, 18*, 459–482.

Youngblade, L. M., & Dunn, J. (1995). Individual differences in young children's pretend play with mother and sibling: Links to relationships and understanding of other people's feelings and beliefs. *Child Development, 66*, 1472–1492.

Zajonc, R. B. (1968). Attitudinal effects of mere exposure. *Journal of Personality and Social Psychology, 9* (Monograph Supplement No. 2, Part 2), 1–27.

Zakriski, A. L., Wright, J. C., & Underwood, M. K. (2005). Gender Similarities and Differences in children's social behavior: Finding personality in contextualized patterns of adaptation. *Journal of Personality and Social Psychology, 88*, 844–855.

Zarbatany, L., McDougall, P., & Hymel, S. (2000). Gender-differentiated experience in the peer culture: Links to intimacy in preadolescence. *Social Development, 9*, 62–79.

Zautra, A. J., Hoffman, J. M., Matt, K. S., Yocum, D., Potter, P. T., Castro, W. L., & Roth, S. (1998). An examination of individual differences in the relationship between interpersonal stress and disease activity among women with rheumatoid arthritis. *Arthritis Care and Research, 11*, 271–279.

Zentner, M., & Mitura, K. (2012). Stepping out of the caveman's shadow: Nations' gender gap predicts degree of sex differentiation in mate preferences. *Psychological Science, 23,* 1176–1185.

Zhang, Z., & Hayward, M. D. (2006). Gender, the marital life course, and cardiovascular disease in late midlife. *Journal of Marriage and Family, 68,* 639–657.

Zill, N., Morrison, D. R., & Coiro, M. J. (1993). Long-term effects of parental divorce on parent-child relationships, adjustment, and achievement in young adulthood. *Journal of Family Psychology, 7,* 91–103.

Zimmer-Gembeck, M. J., Siebenbruner, J., & Collins, W. A. (2004). A prospective study of intraindividual and peer influences on adolescents' heterosexual romantic and sexual behavior. *Archives of Sexual Behavior, 33,* 381–394.

Credits

Name Index

Subject Index